This remarkable book is the most comprehensive study ever written of the history of moral philosophy in the seventeenth and eighteenth centuries. Its aim is to set Kant's still influential ethics in its historical context by showing in detail what the central questions in moral philosophy were for him and how he arrived at his own distinctive ethical views.

The book is organized into four main sections. In the first J. B. Schneewind discusses the dominant seventeenth-century view of morality, the natural law view. After sketching its earlier versions and some questions about them raised by Montaigne and Machiavelli, he presents the theories of Suarez, Grotius, Hobbes, Cumberland, Pufendorf, Locke, and Thomasius. The second section examines perfectionist ethics in the work of Lord Herbert of Cherbury and his Stoic predecessors, Descartes, the Cambridge Platonists, Spinoza, Malebranche, and Leibniz. In the third section, Schneewind discusses thinkers who explored the extent to which morality might keep its force without reliance on God. The philosophers considered include Gassendi, Bayle, the British moralists through Reid and Bentham, and de Sade. The fourth section considers Kant's more immediate predecessors, particularly the major German figures, Wolff and Crusius, and Rousseau. Schneewind then follows the development of Kant's own views up to the point at which he was first able to formulate the central position of his mature ethics: the claim that we are autonomous agents who impose morality on ourselves by legislating a formal practical principle. In an epilogue the author discusses Kant's view of his own historicity and of the aims of moral philosophy.

In its range, its analyses of many philosophers not usually considered in histories of ethics, and its discussions of the interweaving of religious and political concerns with moral philosophy, this is an unprecedented account of the developments that led up to Kant's ethics. Extensive quotations allow the reader to understand the philosophy through the vocabularies that the philosophers themselves used.

J. B. Schneewind has written a history of modern ethics that will be essential reading not only for students of moral philosophy and religious thought but also for all those interested in the history of philosophy, the history of political theory, and European intellectual history.

The invention of autonomy

The invention of autonomy

A history of modern moral philosophy

J. B. SCHNEEWIND

Johns Hopkins University

PUBLISHED BY THE PRESS SYNDICATE OF THE UNIVERSITY OF CAMBRIDGE
The Pitt Building, Trumpington Street, Cambridge CB2 1RP, United Kingdom

CAMBRIDGE UNIVERSITY PRESS
The Edinburgh Building, Cambridge CB2 2RU, United Kingdom
40 West 20th Street, New York, NY 10011-4211, USA
10 Stamford Road, Oakleigh, Melbourne 3166, Australia

First published 1998

Printed in the United States of America

Typeset in Palatino

Library of Congress Cataloging-in-Publication Data
Schneewind, J. B. (Jerome B.), 1930 –
The invention of autonomy : a history of modern moral philosophy /
J. B. Schneewind.
p.   cm.
Includes bibliographical references and indexes.
ISBN 0-521-47399-3. – ISBN 0-521-47938-X (pbk.)
1. Ethics, Modern – 17th century. 2. Autonomy (Philosophy) –
History – 17th century. 3. Ethics, Modern – 18th century.
4. Autonomy (Philosophy) – History – 18th century. 5. Kant, Immanuel,
1724–1804 – Ethics. I. Title.
BJ301.S35   1997
170′.9′032 – DC21   97-7570
                                                             CIP

A catalog record for this book is available from
the British Library

ISBN 0 521 47399 3 hardback
ISBN 0 521 47938 X paperback

For
Sarah   Rachel   Hannah

Contents

Preface

I started on the work that led to this book because there were many aspects of Kant's moral philosophy that I could not understand. I thought that I would have a better chance of understanding them if I knew what questions Kant believed he had to answer when he began considering the subject. In earlier work on Sidgwick, I had found some help in history. I came to think that the history of moral philosophy is not a seamless carpet stretching uninterruptedly from Socrates to us. I thought I could locate a point in that history of which it made sense to say: here is a largely new set of issues from which there developed the specific problems that Sidgwick addressed. Sidgwick seemed more comprehensible to me when I knew what he was trying to do in his philosophizing. I thought there must be counterparts for Kant. This book comes from my attempt to find them.

In 1976 I read Josef Schmucker's *Die Ursprünge der Ethik Kants.* Although published in 1961 it had not then – it has not yet – been reviewed in English. Schmucker supersedes almost all previous work on the origins of Kant's ethics. I found his studies of the ethics of Wolff and Crusius a revelation, and I remain greatly indebted to his book. But even he did not answer all my questions. He deliberately said little or nothing about what led up to the work of the moral philosophers whose influence Kant acknowledged. He also left me unclear about the rationales for the basic differences among these philosophers. Much as I learned from him, I wanted more than he provided.

When in 1981 I was able to begin work on this project, I had no idea of how far back I would have to go or how widely I would have to range in order to think that I had found accounts of Kant's questions that illuminated his answers. It was clear from the start that I would have to study a large number of philosophers about whom many commentators had already written. I might not have undertaken the project if I had immediately realized how many philosophers I would need to discuss. But by the time I had developed an outline for the book, and had recognized the rashness of the plan, it seemed too late to stop. I have tried to learn enough from the work of experts to keep serious errors out of my own remarks on their subjects; but I am sure that there are many points at which they will see that I have failed.

Hobbes says that it is often with fraudulent design that men "stick their corrupt Doctrine with the Cloves of other men's wit." There are a great many quotations in what follows, but not, I hope, for the reason Hobbes gives. They are meant to provide evidence for my accounts of the philosophers I discuss and also to give the reader some sense of the language in which they expressed themselves. We need to avoid describing past thought exclusively in our own terms. We should try not only to situate it in the intellectual, social, political, and religious contexts of which its creators were aware, but also to understand it through the vocabularies that they themselves used or could have used. Both efforts are needed if we are to see past thought as its creators and readers would have seen it. I would like to have done more than I have to locate the moral philosophies of Kant and his predecessors in the practical problems that gave them their urgency. To have said more, however, would have lengthened an already long volume and exposed even more of my ignorance.

The reasons for trying to see the past in its distinctive specificity are philosophical as well as historiographical. Great moral philosophy does not come primarily from concerns arising within philosophy itself. It comes from engagement with serious problems about personal, social, political, and religious life. Since these problems change, we need to see the contexts of the moral philosophy of the past as well as its arguments in order to understand fully why it developed as it did. Once we see how such changes have affected our predecessors, we may hope to become clear about similar considerations affecting ourselves. Awareness of the historicity of what we take to be our own central issues gives us a critical hold on them that we cannot get in any other way.

I planned from the beginning to make Kant the focal point of this study because I thought, as I still do, that his conception of morality as autonomy provides a better place to start working out a contemporary philosophical understanding of morality than anything we can get from other past philosophers. Kant has some particular moral convictions that I find repugnant, but I think that they do not pose difficulties of principle for using his insights as a starting point. Some of his theoretical views about morality are much more problematic. These, it now seems to me, are often part of his response to inherited issues that need not concern us. Historical study thus helps us to disentangle from his overall position what we can use to move forward.

Leibniz somewhere says that we might compare a perfect being to "a learned author who includes the greatest number of truths in the smallest possible volume." Readers of this volume will rightly think me far from being such an exemplary author. I have tried to be accurate and concise; but I am painfully aware of how far short I come of anything like the Leibnizian ideal. Writing the book has given me, I think, a better understanding of Kant's theory and of what we might make of it today. I hope that readers, too, will find the history illuminating. Perhaps some of them will even be tempted into joining the now happily growing number of those who have tried to increase our knowledge of the past of moral philosophy. The most any one author can do is to make some small improvements in our grasp of the thought of single thinkers and of the broader scenes in which they worked. The task is large, and more help would be welcome.

Acknowledgments

One of the pleasures of studying the history of thought is the sense one has of taking part in a long cooperative endeavor. To the textual editors, commentators, and previous historians without whose work I could not even have begun, I can offer only the thanks of footnote and bibliography. To the institutions, friends, and colleagues who have helped me over the years I can, happily, make more personal acknowledgment.

The first seventeen chapters were drafted in 1992–3, at the Center for Advanced Study in the Behavioral Sciences in Stanford. The Center, its expert staff, and the other fellows, provided an ideal environment for such work. My stay there was made possible by financial assistance from the Andrew W. Mellon Foundation and by a sabbatical leave from Johns Hopkins University. I am most grateful for their generosity. I should also like to thank the Stanford University Library for its courtesy to a visitor, and the staff of its Rare Book Room for its skillful assistance.

The remaining chapters were drafted in 1994 during time made available by Johns Hopkins. Deans Matthew Crenson and Stephen Knapp were generous with their support, as Deans Lloyd Armstrong and George Fisher had been earlier. I am grateful to them for continuing the Hopkins tradition of encouraging research. The Hopkins Library has been a great help throughout my work.

I began trying out some ideas about Kant's development in 1983 at a Summer Institute sponsored by the National Endowment for the Humanities. Since then I have lectured on the history of ethics at many colleges, universities, and conferences. Of particular importance for me were series of talks I was asked to give at Notre Dame University, the University of Virginia, the University of Pittsburgh, San Diego University, and Princeton University. Daniel Garber's NEH Summer Institute in 1988 and Wade Robison's in 1990 made me think in more synoptic ways than I had previously done about the history I was studying. The 1987 Kant Conference in Sigriswill, organized by Ottfried Höffe, and the Pufendorf Conference in Göttingen in 1989, directed by Istvan Hont and Hans-Erich Bödecker, enabled me to discuss common interests with scholars I would otherwise never have met. From them and from audiences and friends on all of these occasions I learned a great deal; their help in shaping both my ideas and the presentation of them was invaluable. Many of my recent publications resulted from the lectures given for these meetings; and I have shamelessly plundered these writings for the present work, using, without specific acknowledgment, ideas, phrasing, and whole pages from various essays, which I list in the bibliography.

As always I have learned much from students. Undergraduates and graduates at Johns Hopkins have listened to and discussed endless versions of much of what I present here. Whether they knew it or not, they were forcing me to be clearer and more precise than I would have been without them. To three Hopkins students I owe particular thanks. Chris Grau commented insightfully on a number of the chapters and helped with bibliographical matters. Carolyn McConnell worked on the bibliography of primary sources. I am especially grateful to Natalie Brender, whose discussions of many of my chapters have been unfailingly helpful, and whose expert work over the past few years on bibliography and other research matters has been of immeasurable assistance.

Students elsewhere have also been most helpful. My thanks go to Jeffrey Stout for enabling me to teach a seminar on the history of ethics in the Department of Religions at Princeton in 1985, and to John Cooper for inviting me to give another seminar on the subject for the Princeton Philosophy Department in 1992. Members of both seminars provided useful criticism. The participants in a 1992 Summer Seminar funded by the National Endowment for the Humanities worked with me in assessing what became the basic plan of the book, and their criticisms and suggestions helped to shape its content.

So many colleagues and friends have discussed issues in the history of ethics with me, over so long a period, that I cannot hope to list them all. David Sachs died before he could see most of this work, but his comments on some of my earlier papers were always acute and – even when devastating – constructive and encouraging. John Cooper listened patiently, during our year together at the Center, to my worries about what I was writing; he spent much time then and has spent more since then giving me the benefit of his unparalleled knowledge of ancient thought and his great philosophical acumen. Discussions with Richard Rorty of his forceful challenges to Kantianism and to systematic moral philosophy generally have long helped me in rethinking my approach to their history. John Rawls's work, and his encouragement, have been an inspiration to me for many years. Robert Adams, Karl Ameriks, Rüdiger Bittner, Charlotte Brown, Edwin Curley, Stephen

Darwall, Jeffrey Edwards, Richard Flathman, Paul Guyer, Knud Haakonssen, Jennifer Herdt, Barbara Herman, T. E. Hill Jr., Ian Hunter, Christine Korsgaard, Larry Krasnoff, Mark Larrimore, Alasdair MacIntyre, Elijah Millgram, Onora O'Neill, John Pocock, Thomas Pogge, Andrews Reath, Michael Seidler, Ludwig Siep, Quentin Skinner, Mack Walker, and Susan Wolf are among those whose conversation and encouragement over the years has been most beneficial to me. Robert Shaver sent me helpful comments on a number of chapters. Jay Hullett graciously responded to some practical questions with important advice based on his long experience in publishing. To Chris Grau, again, and to Dan Callcut, many thanks for their hard work on proofs and indexes. Brian MacDonald edited the manuscript with skill and meticulous care. Terence Moore, of the Cambridge University Press, provided invaluable guidance concerning the book and has been patient in awaiting its completion. I wish that I could have made the final result show more fully how much I have gained from the help I have been given.

I can find no words adequate to thank Elizabeth Schneewind for her support while I worked on the book, and for all else.

J. B. Schneewind

A note on references and abbreviations

The first bibliography, Sources, lists material published prior to 1800. It includes a number of early histories of moral philosophy as well as the works of the authors who are my main concern. When I cite any of these works, I use the author's name if there is only one work listed, a short title of the work, or one of the abbreviations listed here. Quotations from anthologies, which are also gathered under Sources, following the primary authors, are similarly identified by indicating the editor's name and the page number.

Citations from later commentators and historians are identified in all cases by author and date. The works I refer to are listed in the second bibliography, Commentary. Occasionally I refer to a modern work just once and incidentally; in these cases bibliographical details are given only in the citation.

DJBP	Hugo Grotius, *On the Law of War and Peace* (*De Jure Belli ac Pacis Libri Tres*). Trans. Francis W. Kelsey. Oxford, 1925.
DJN	Samuel Pufendorf, *On the Law of Nature and Nations* (1672). Trans. C. H. Oldfather and W. A. Oldfather. Oxford, 1934.
DJP	Hugo Grotius, *Commentary on the Law of Prize and Booty* (*De Jure Praedae Commentarius*) (1604). Trans. Gwladys L. Williams and Walter H. Zeydel. Oxford, 1950.
ECHU	John Locke, *An Essay concerning Human Understanding* (1689). Ed. Peter Nidditch. Oxford, 1979.
LCCorr	Samuel Clarke and G. W. F. Leibniz, *The Leibniz-Clarke Correspondence*. Ed. H. G. Alexander. Manchester, 1944.
LE	Immanuel Kant, *Lectures on Ethics*. Ed. Peter Heath and J. B. Schneewind. Trans. Peter Heath. Cambridge, 1997.
MM	Immanuel Kant, *The Metaphysics of Morals*. Trans. Mary Gregor. Cambridge, 1991.

ST   St. Thomas Aquinas, *Summa Theologica.* Trans. Fathers of
         the English Dominican Province. New York, 1947.

TP   Immanuel Kant, *Theoretical Philosophy, 1755–1770.* Trans.
         and ed. David Walford and Ralf Meerbote. Cam-
         bridge, 1992.

Introduction

1

Themes in the history of modern moral philosophy

Kant invented the conception of morality as autonomy. I use the notion of invention as Kant himself did in an early remark. "Leibniz thought up a simple substance," he said, "which had nothing but obscure representations, and called it a *slumbering monad*. This monad he had not explained, but merely invented; for the concept of it was not given to him but was rather created by him."[1] Autonomy, as Kant saw it, requires contracausal freedom; and he believed that in the unique experience of the moral ought we are "given" a "fact of reason" that unquestionably shows us that we possess such freedom as members of a noumenal realm. Readers who hold, as I do, that our experience of the moral ought shows us no such thing will think of his version of autonomy as an invention rather than an explanation.[2] Those with different views on freedom and morality may wish that I had called this book *The Discovery of Autonomy*. We can probably agree that Kant's moral thought is as hard to understand as it is original and profound. Systematic studies from Paton and Beck to the present have greatly improved our critical grasp of his position. In this book I try to broaden our historical comprehension of Kant's moral philosophy by relating it to the earlier work to which it was a response.

---

1 "Leibniz dachte sich eine einfache Substanz, die nichts als dunkle Vorstellungen hätte, und nannte sie eine *schlummernde Monade*. Hier hatte er night diese Monade erklärt, sondern erdacht; denn der Begriff derselbe war ihm nicht gegeben, sondern von ihm erschaffen worden." *Gesammelte Schriften* 2.277; *TP*, 249 where the translation is somewhat different. See also *Critique of Pure Reason* A729 = B757.

2 For a compact and learned review of the history of the term, see Pohlmann 1971. Initially standing for a political conception in Greek thought, the term came to be used in religious controversies during the Reformation; but its main use in early modern times was in political discussions. Kant seems to have been the first to assign broader significance to it, using it in his theoretical as well as his practical philosophy.

i. *Moral philosophy and social change*

There are reasons beyond the particular importance of Kant's own views for studying the history of the moral thought out of which they emerged.

During the seventeenth and eighteenth centuries established conceptions of morality as obedience came increasingly to be contested by emerging conceptions of morality as self-governance. On the older conception, morality is to be understood most deeply as one aspect of the obedience we owe to God. In addition, most of us are in a moral position in which we must obey other human beings. God's authority over all of us is made known to us by reason as well as by revelation and the clergy. But we are not all equally able to see for ourselves what morality requires. Even if everyone has the most fundamental laws of morality written in their hearts or consciences, most people need to be instructed by some appropriate authority about what is morally required in particular cases. And because most people usually do not understand the reasons for doing what morality directs, threats of punishment as well as offers of reward are necessary in order to assure sufficient compliance to bring about moral order.

The new outlook that emerged by the end of the eighteenth century centered on the belief that all normal individuals are equally able to live together in a morality of self-governance. All of us, on this view, have an equal ability to see for ourselves what morality calls for and are in principle equally able to move ourselves to act accordingly, regardless of threats or rewards from others.[3] These two points have come to be widely accepted – so widely that most moral philosophy now starts by assuming them. In daily life they give us the working assumption that the people we live with are capable of understanding and acknowledging in practice the reasons for the moral constraints we all mutually expect ourselves and others to respect. We assume, in short, that people are equally competent as moral agents unless shown to be otherwise. There are many substantive points on which modern moral views differ from what was widely accepted at the beginning of the seventeenth century, but our assumption of prima facie equal moral competence is the deepest and most pervasive difference.

The conception of morality as self-governance provides a conceptual framework for a social space in which we may each rightly claim to direct our own actions without interference from the state, the church, the neighbors, or those claiming to be better or wiser than we. The older conception of morality as obedience did not have these implications.

---

3   Darwall 1995, p. 8 and n. 18, uses a narrower notion of self-governance than I do.

The early modern moral philosophy in which the conception of morality as self-governance emerged thus made a vital contribution to the rise of the Western liberal vision of the proper relations between individual and society. That form of life could not have developed without the work of moral philosophers.

My attribution to moral philosophy of this essential role in aiding basic social change may seem surprising, but it should not be. Humanly meaningful differences among individuals and societies are in large part not biological. They are cultural and therefore impossible without shared vocabularies and concepts. This is certainly true of the moral, political, and religious aspects of life. In these matters we can only be what we can think and say we are. Philosophical debate in the seventeenth and eighteenth centuries was a major source of new ways of conceptualizing our humanity and of discussing it with one another. Our own moral philosophy carries on from the point to which those earlier discussions took us. Seeing how we got to that point is not just seeing how we came to ask some of the philosophical questions we are still asking. It is also seeing how we came to a distinctively modern way of understanding ourselves as moral agents.

ii. *Morality and self-governance*

My main theme in what follows is the emergence of various conceptions of morality as self-governance. As early as Machiavelli and Montaigne there were thinkers who set aside the conception of morality as obedience in order to work out an alternative. But most of the philosophers who rethought morality in the seventeenth and early eighteenth centuries did not intend to replace the older conception with a conception of morality as self-governance. They were for the most part trying to solve problems arising within the older view. Most of them were hoping to show how Christian morality could continue to offer helpful guidance in the face of difficulties that no one had previously faced. To solve the problems that new social and political circumstances posed for their moral and religious commitments, some of them developed new ways of thinking about morality and politics. They could not have foreseen the uses to which later thinkers eventually put their ideas.

It was only from about the early eighteenth century that the effort to create a theory of morality as self-governance became self-conscious. Moral and political concerns led increasing numbers of philosophers to think that the inherited conceptions of morality did not allow for a proper appreciation of human dignity, and therefore did not properly allow even for the moral teachings of the Christianity that many of them still accepted. Such concerns had already been strongly voiced during the seventeenth century. Eighteenth-century philosophers could therefore draw on the work of predecessors as they sought ways to develop new understandings of morality. The moral philosophies of Reid, Bentham, and Kant are the final eighteenth-century efforts to articulate the normative belief about the dignity and worth of the individual that led to conceptions of morality as self-governance.[4]

Kant's explanation of this belief was fuller and more radical than any other. He alone was proposing a truly revolutionary rethinking of morality. He held that we are self-governing because we are autonomous. By this he meant that we ourselves legislate the moral law. It is only because of the legislative action of our own will that we are under moral law; and the same action is what always enables everyone to be law-abiding. Kant was the first to argue for autonomy in this strong sense. His theory is, of course, of more than historical interest. It is more fully involved in current philosophical ethics than is the work of any other early modern thinker, with the possible exception of Hobbes. In the narrative that follows, therefore, I have kept Kant in mind. Naturally enough this skews my selection of philosophers and topics for presentation. But I have tried to give a fair presentation of the complex debates out of which there emerged the questions Kant tried to answer.

Bentham, Reid, and Kant came to questions in moral philosophy with different concerns about politics and religion. If they all read some of the same earlier philosophers, continental as well as British, Kant knew the work of others who were not on the British horizon at all. Much of what he made of moral philosophy was shaped by his German predecessors. Unless we know something about them as well as about the more familiar thinkers from whom he learned, we will not see how profoundly different the sources were that contributed to his invention of autonomy.

iii. *Morality and religion*

Conceptions of morality as self-governance reject the inequality of moral capacity among humans that was a standard part of conceptions of morality as obedience. What is the role of God in these two families of conceptions? What is the moral bearing of inequality between God and human beings? If God's superiority is not acceptable, must all ties between morality and religion be severed? The debates about these issues form another major theme in what follows.

Events outside of philosophy itself were largely responsible for stimulating the rethinking of morality that occurred in the seventeenth and eighteenth centuries. The Reformation and the Counter-Reformation

---

4 Reid's theory allows for self-governance but, as I point out in Chapter 20.v, it is not clear that Bentham's position does.

made anything tied to religion a matter of controversy – and everything was tied to religion.[5] The warfare that racked Europe almost continuously from the sixteenth century until the middle of the seventeenth century, and the civil conflicts in Britain that lasted almost until the century's end, were understood in terms of issues about religion. If God's rule of the world as transmitted by the clergy was the only hope for order, it could well seem that peace was not to be obtained. Morality as interpreted by churches that were themselves rent by sectarian disagreements could not provide either an inner sense of community or external constraints sufficient to make civilized life possible.

Could politics by itself provide those constraints? Repressive force could indeed keep the peace for a while. But who was to control such force, and to what ends? The questions were pressing. Those who asked them increasingly wanted to be given reasons for submitting to authorities whose traditional standing was no longer enough. Religious controversy affected internal state authority as much as it did international affairs. New groups within each polity began to demand access to power, justifying their claims with theories about how government should be handled and limited, and who should be involved in it. Religious strife undermined the claims of clergy to be the sole authorities in morals; political strife led ever more people to demand recognition as fully competent to take an active part in affairs. A morality of self-governance was a better view with which to defend such claims than previously available theories. The need for new generally acceptable justifications of authority and the distribution of power made a rethinking of morality inescapable. Philosophy, appealing to reason and not to any authority, seemed an appropriate source of help.

It is often supposed that the amazing sixteenth- and seventeenth-century developments in science provided the impetus for new efforts in philosophy generally, and as part of that, in philosophical ethics. There is no reason to doubt that the development of science from Copernicus and Galileo through Newton and on into the eighteenth century was profoundly important in shaping the course of philosophy. But morality would have required reexamination and reshaping even if there had been no new science. Without the science, the course that moral philosophy took would no doubt have been quite different. But the problems arising from religious dissension and from calls for wider participation in politics were not themselves due to advances in scientific knowledge. And it was the former, not the latter, that primarily gave rise to modern moral philosophy.

5 See Febvre 1982, chs. 9 and 10, for a brilliant discussion of how religious belief so saturated sixteenth-century French vocabulary that it was nearly impossible to think beyond religion, or even to notice that one could not do so.

What I have called conceptions of morality as self-governance are often thought to result from a major effort by Enlightenment thinkers to bring about a secularized society. It is assumed that there was an "Enlightenment project" to show that morality had no need of religion because it had its own, wholly rational, foundations. Modern views of morality are then assumed to have been thought out as part of this effort. I find the assumptions questionable in several respects.

There were, of course, some atheists who published their views during the seventeenth and eighteenth centuries. Bentham, after all, was not the first to crusade for a fully secular morality. But there were many more people who, without being atheists or even doubters, were taken to be antireligious only because they held that institutional religion was doing great harm. They certainly hoped to see the churches or the clergy reformed, but they sought no secular ethic. Anticlericalism is not atheism.

A wide variety of writers in the latter part of the period I shall be considering called themselves "enlightened" and wanted others to think them so. If some were atheists, the majority were not; and they differed in many other respects as well. Like many other scholars I consequently do not find it helpful to think in terms of a single movement of Enlightenment or *Aufklärung* or *Lumières*, still less of anything that might be called a single project involving all those who claimed to be enlightened.[6] The error about moral philosophy and secularizing enlightenment is particularly egregious.

Briefly, the claim that the main effort of the moral philosophy of the eighteenth century was to secularize morality simply does not stand up to even the most cursory inspection. Indeed, if I were forced to identify something or other as "the Enlightenment project" for morality, I should say that it was the effort to limit God's control over earthly life while keeping him essential to morality. Naturally this effort took different forms, depending on how the relations between God and morality were conceived.

As I shall be reiterating, there are two basic approaches to keeping God essential to morality. One is now usually called "voluntarism."[7] Voluntarists hold that God created morality and imposed it upon us by an arbitrary fiat of his will. He is essential to morality, therefore, because he created it and can always, in principle, alter it – as he seems to do on those rare occasions, such as his commanding Abraham to sacrifice Isaac, when he intervenes in it. On the other approach, often called "intellectualism," God did not create morality. When he gives us moral

6 See Porter and Teich 1981, and for an overview, Outram 1995, ch. 1.

7 According to the *Oxford English Dictionary* the term is a nineteenth-century coinage.

commandments, his will is guided by his intellect's knowledge of eternal standards. He is nonetheless essential to morality because his providential supervision ensures that we live in a morally ordered world.

For both the intellectualist and the voluntarist, morality in practice is a matter of compliance with rules or laws, not of direct pursuit of the common good. But all agree that morality is meant to serve the common good. Hence it may well seem to us that individual obedience to moral directives is futile. Many people disobey, and chance seems to have a large hand in determining the actual results of what we do. God, for the intellectualist, is the divine supervisor, coordinating the actual results of individual actions so that all will be for the best on the whole. Morality is not, despite the voluntarists, God's creation; but we must be certain of God's existence to be sure that moral action is neither pointless nor self-defeating.

Voluntarists can accept the part of intellectualism that sees God as actively superintending the universe he created. But they need not do so. They do not have to hold that the universe is morally intelligible to us. Intellectualists cannot accept the most basic claim of the voluntarists. But they can agree that without God's command the truths at the basis of morality would not have the status of laws imposing obligations on us. Other mediating positions are also possible; but many seventeenth- and eighteenth-century religious believers vehemently rejected voluntarism in any form, and devoted much effort to making a thorough intellectualism acceptable. A concern with voluntarism was unavoidable in discussions of religion and morality during the period I shall be considering.

Among antireligious thinkers there were many who talked as if the only interpretation of religion on which God is essential to morality is that of the strong voluntarists. They presented the issue as if a religious believer who rejected voluntarism would have to hold that morality is wholly independent of religion. They could thus argue as if they had already won their point about morals; but we should not be taken in by their error, or, more likely, their pretenses. For everyone except the atheists, morality and religion remained tightly linked in early modern moral philosophy. The ethics of self-governance was created by both religious and antireligious philosophers.

iv. *Morality, epistemology, and moral psychology*

Proponents of conceptions of morality as self-governance all take it that moral agents must possess certain specfic psychological capacities. Normal adults are able to be aware of or to know, with no external help, what morality directs or approves, and to bring themselves to live accordingly regardless of threats and rewards. In the discussions out of which these conceptions emerged, questions about the epistemology of moral belief and of moral psychology played a central role. The topic of our awareness of morality and its relation to our motives forms a third recurrent theme in what follows.

Some fairly standard assumptions may get in the way of understanding this issue. Books going under the title of "History of Philosophy" ordinarily concentrate on the development of theories of knowledge and metaphysics, treating ethics, if at all, as a sort of appendix. The assumption seems to be that once the philosopher's epistemology and ontology are settled, the theory of morality is derivable as a consequence. The conceptual assumption is then treated as yielding a genuine grasp of the historical development of theories about morality. They are to be explained as results of the desire to make morality fit into a previously established epistemology or metaphysics. Starting with an interest in the history of thought about morality, however, I have not found this approach helpful.

I will point in due course to several cases of a different relation between theories of knowledge and theories of morality, but I will indicate here what is perhaps the most important instance. The conventional division of seventeenth- and eighteenth-century theories of knowledge into empiricist, rationalist, and (eventually) Kantian seems to me essentially sound, despite objections that have been made to it. Empiricism from Bacon through Locke had a strong affinity with voluntarism in ethics. Voluntarism in ethics tended to be associated with extreme conceptions of morality as obedience to God. Objections to the latter, based as much on moral as on purely theological grounds, were therefore taken as objections both to voluntarism and to empiricism, particularly to empiricist views of meaning and the limitations they imposed on our concepts. Rationalists argued against empiricism as much because of what they believed to be the grave moral defects it entailed as because of the errors they saw in it about concepts and a priori knowledge.

Rationalism itself was not exempt from moral criticism. Critics thought that some of its versions were unavoidably tied to a conception of morality as obedience to a social elite. The critics thought that in those versions it could not explain how the knowledge its theorists held to be at the basis of morality could be equally available to everyone alike. For those moved by normative considerations to defend a morality of self-governance, this kind of rationalism was therefore unacceptable. And if for moral reasons they found empiricism equally unacceptable, they were forced to work out new forms of ethical rationalism.

Kant himself was moved by considerations of this kind. Like some of his predecessors, he sought a rational principle simple enough to be known and used by everyone, and carrying its motivational force with it. It seems to me not unreasonable to suppose that his normative commitment to a strong conception of morality as self-governance was at least a large part of what motivated him to develop his remarkable constructivist theory of knowledge as well as his motivational psychology. His is not the only case where the conventional portrayal of the historical relations between epistemology and moral philosophy is worse than useless.

v. *A map of the book*

All of the theorists I discuss were engaged in one way or another in controversies about morality and self-governance, the relations of morality and religion, and the epistemological and psychological needs of different moral outlooks. I have not tried to gather the arguments about these topics into separate chapters. I have, however, organized what follows in a way that is topical as well as roughly chronological. There seem to me to be four main phases of the development of modern moral philosophy, and I have grouped the philosophers I study accordingly. The lives of some of the philosophers whom I treat in one section overlapped the lives of some discussed in other sections, but within the sections I proceed chronologically.

In the first section I present what I take to be the dominant seventeenth-century view of morality, the natural law view. To bring out the novelty of the work of Grotius and his successors, I begin with brief sketches of Thomas Aquinas's classical natural law doctrine, and of some of the medieval alternatives to the view; and I consider the ways in which Luther and Calvin used these other positions in shaping their own views of the place of law in the moral life. Well before the atheists of the eighteenth century, there were those who asked what we could make of our lives together if we did not bring Christianity into our views. To illustrate the options open to later thinkers, I consider Machiavelli's radical secular politics and the skepticism that Montaigne made memorable. I then proceed to Suarez and Grotius, both of whom tried to restate natural law theory in response to the difficulties they saw facing it and their world. Suarez is a great traditionalist; Grotius is often – and, I argue, rightly – taken as initiating a new view. I discuss the major proponents of "modern" natural law thought, and end the section with a discussion of Locke and Thomasius, the last of the major advocates of the Grotian view. From their work it became evident why natural law theory seemed unable to meet the moral demands placed on it. Although Locke did not think it a failure, Thomasius did. There were no major natural law thinkers after these two, and I try to indicate why.

The main seventeenth-century alternative to natural law thought is my topic in the second section. Where the natural lawyers saw the maintenance of social order as the crucial issue, others took individual self-perfection as the central theme for moral reflection. Influenced by Stoicism, rationalist thinkers from Lord Herbert of Cherbury and Descartes through Leibniz offered various versions of perfectionist ethics. Some thought we should focus on perfecting our knowledge, others, especially the Cambridge Platonists, emphasized perfecting our wills. Leibniz combined perfectionism with a radical rejection of almost every interpretation of morality that the seventeenth century had produced. His critique of Pufendorf, the most widely read Grotian natural lawyer, and the response to Leibniz's criticisms by Barbeyrac, an assiduous disseminator of Grotian thought, show natural law theory and its most fully developed alternative exposing each other's weaknesses without achieving a new understanding of morality.

For perfectionists and natural lawyers alike, despite their many differences, God remains essential to morality. In the third section I trace some efforts to show that morality can make do without God, or at least without his active presence, and some of the responses they occasioned. Deism, the view that although God created the world he does not interfere with its operation, emerged at the end of the seventeenth century, and atheism came to be mentionable, if not respectable, in the eighteenth. But even religious believers of orthodox persuasions aimed to show that morality requires much less of God's direct operation than their predecessors had thought. This line of thinking began in the seventeenth century, with Gassendi's revival of Epicureanism. Other French thinkers, who believed that God hides himself from us, developed a new idea about how society can operate as if by design but without any observable divine guidance. Some of the philosophers and reformers of the French enlightenment, and some of their British contemporaries, continued the effort to see how well morality would fare in a world on its own. In doing so they were inevitably led to develop theories of morality as self-governance, and their religious opponents did not always reject their views.

The natural lawyers held that readiness to obey was the proper human attitude toward God and the laws he lays down for us. The perfectionists did not hold this view. Believing that our minds have access to God's and that our wills can be controlled by our knowledge, they saw us as capable of moving toward ever increasing self-governance. Through increase of knowledge we could become God-like if not actually divine. Among those who saw little or no presence of God in the world the question was not whether humanity could and should be self-directing. After all, for them there was no alternative. The question was only whether the capacity for self-governance belongs to all normal people, or only to some.

These were the main divisions in theorizing about morality during the century and a half prior to Kant. German thinkers generally knew of the work being done in the rest of Europe and took leads from it as well as from their own Leibniz. In the fourth section I begin with consideration of Wolff and Crusius, the two most original German philosophers between Leibniz and Kant. Known little or not at all in France and England, they were major figures in the German philosophical literature on morality during the first half of the eighteenth century. I then look at the French thought that overlapped theirs. Much of it was unoriginal; but Rousseau, briefly a friend and then a vehement critic of the reformist and radical thinkers who took themselves to be creating a French enlightenment, was a true innovator. His admiration for classical republicanism and his remarkable ideas on community and freedom suggested a deep departure from previous ways of understanding morality.

All these currents of thought helped shape the issues of moral philosophy as Kant faced them. I begin to discuss his relations to his predecessors by looking at his early thought. I trace the development of his views about morality up to the point at which he was ready to work out the central position of his mature moral philosophy, the claim that we are autonomous agents who impose morality on ourselves by legislating a formal practical principle. I then go on to discuss the relations between Kant's mature views and the earlier controversies that I have been following. In doing so I give what is in effect an overview of much of the historical material discussed in earlier sections. The reader who simply wants to know how it all turned out will find many of the answers here; others may find that going through this chapter first helps to focus the earlier chapters.

In the final chapter I discuss Kant's view of his own historicity, and of the point or aim of moral philosophy. This involves me in a brief discussion of Kant's idea of the highest good. But most of the chapter is a more general discussion of alternative ways of thinking about the history of moral philosophy, among others the one I have tried to exemplify in this book.

PART I

The rise and fall of modern natural law

2

Natural law: From intellectualism to voluntarism

The belief that human action should be guided by natural laws that apply to all people, no matter what their race, sex, location, or religion, originated outside of Judaism and Christianity. Once accepted into Christian thought, the idea of natural law became central to the European way of understanding morality. In this chapter I indicate briefly the origins of natural law theory and review its classical exposition in the work of St. Thomas. Then, after presenting some of the major points on which critics disagreed with St. Thomas, I go on to discuss the outlook on morality of the two main founders of the Protestant Reformation, Luther and Calvin, for whom voluntarism was of central importance. These different Christian interpretations of natural law were far more significant for the development of modern moral philosophy than the ethical writings of Plato or Aristotle.

i. *Origins of natural law theory*

The concept of natural law is at least as old as the Stoics. It was developed as the city-state was ceasing to be the dominant political form of Mediterranean life and was transmitted by the Stoic school to the Romans. In Rome the idea came into fruitful contact with actual legal practice. Roman law covered all the dealings of Roman citizens in great detail. As Rome expanded, its citizens increased the amount of business they did with foreigners. Legal problems inevitably arose during these transactions, yet non-Romans could not be expected to be familiar with, or to care about, all the technicalities of Roman law. To cope with these issues lawyers developed a set of rules and procedures less complex than those of the Roman law. The law of peoples (*jus gentium*), as it was called, was meant to incorporate commonly accepted ideas of honesty and fair dealing that might be accepted by civilized people everywhere. It was to be simple enough so that everyone could understand it and use it. It thus came close to exemplifying what the Stoics thought of as the supreme principles for all people. The term

"natural law" (*jus naturale*) was the Latin equivalent of the Greek philosophical term the Stoics used for this law.

The most widely read transmitter of the idea of natural law was
Cicero.[1] His writings, though far from original, made Stoic doctrine
(and indeed much of the Greek philosophical heritage) known throughout the civilized West. In accordance with Stoic teaching Cicero identified natural law with the dictates of right reason.[2] Reason speaks with
the voice of nature, showing us eternal and unchangeable laws applicable to all. It is the legislation of the gods, not alterable by human rulers.
The ideas of *jus gentium* and *jus naturale* coalesced, one providing specificity and content to philosophical abstractions, the other increasing the
equity and universality of existing practice.

Ideas of natural law found a vital place in the development of
Christian thought about the guidance of action. St. Paul provided the
ground for incorporating them, in one of the most influential and frequently cited passages of the New Testament, Romans 2.14–15:

> For when the Gentiles, which have not the law, do by nature the things
> contained in the law, these, having not the law, are a law unto themselves
>   Which show the work of the law written in their hearts, their con-
> science also bearing witness, and their thoughts the meanwhile accusing
> or else excusing one another.

As the church, after early centuries of persecution and hiding, became a far-flung organization of great wealth, power, complexity, and
responsibility, it was forced to expand its internal regulations. Church
lawyers drew upon the precedents and practices of Roman civil lawyers, and like them found it necessary, after some centuries, to codify
rulings and procedures that had grown without much direct or coherent supervision. Several attempts were made to codify canon law. The
decisive work, the *Decretals*, was put together by a monk of Bologna,
Gratian, in about 1140. It remained authoritative for centuries (Dante
gave Gratian a place in Paradise). In it the crucial step was taken of
identifying the natural law both with the directives contained in the

---

1   See *De Re Publica* III.xxii.33; and *De Legibus* I.vi.18–19. See Watson, in Long
1971, for an excellent overview.

2   Cicero, *De Re Publica* III.xxi.33: "True law is right reason in agreement with
nature; it is of universal application, unchanging and everlasting." *De Legibus*
I.vii.23: "Those who have reason in common must also have right reason in common.
And since right reason is law, we must believe that men have law also in common
with the gods." For brief studies of right reason, see Frankena 1983 and Bärthlein
1965, who is more detailed.

Bible and with the law common to all people, the law they are led to acknowledge by a natural instinct.[3]

ii. *St. Thomas's natural law morality*

Aquinas put this tangled heritage into clear philosophical and Christian order. In his *Summa Theologica* he sets his account of law within a vision of a hierarchical universe filled with many different kinds of created being. God created all things to work harmoniously together, and he governs the creation by his eternal law to make sure that it fulfills its purpose. Consequently nothing can happen outside or against his will (*ST* I.22.2, 3; I.103.3, 4, 7, 8). God, St. Thomas says, is the chief governor of his universe, giving orders to subordinate governors, whose plans must all be derived from his (Ia.IIae.93.3 A). Because God is the greatest good himself, he made all things to be good and seek the good, each in its own way. What defines the proper mode of operation of each kind of thing is the law directing things with that nature to the attainment of their divinely ordained end or goal.

Thomas defines law as "an ordinance of reason for the common good, promulgated by him who has the care of the community" (Ia.IIae.90.4 R). Like all created beings, we humans are moved to pursue whatever we think is good. But we, like the angels and unlike lower beings, can know our end and the laws that show us what we are to do to attain it. Our laws are the effect in us of God's eternal law, and our end is union with God through contemplation (Ia.IIae.3.7, 8).[4] Only this achievement of the theoretical intellect can give us the happiness we necessarily seek, since only this fully realizes the highest potential of our nature and thus satisfies our desires. We need God's freely given grace in order to attain complete happiness, and we may hope for it only in another life. But we can now try to achieve rectitude of will, which is also necessary for the attainment of earthly happiness (Ia.IIae.4.4). If salvation is not to be attained through moral behavior alone, morality nonetheless has an essential role in attaining it (Ia.IIae.100.12, 106.2).

The moral virtues, Aquinas holds, are habits enabling us to control the passions and desires that tend to lead us away from our true good. As habits concerned with practice these virtues must be guided by the principles of practical reason; and the principles of reason concerning the good are the laws of nature. We may indeed say, with Aristotle, that

3   For some of the complexities of interpreting Paul's text, see Martens 1994. For Gratian, see Welzel 1962; Berman 1983, pp. 143–51; Haggenmacher 1983, pp. 324–5, 470–5; Kelley 1990, pp.118–20.
4   See Kirk 1932 for a magisterial study of this topic.

virtue involves a mean, because when we deviate by defect or by excess from what reason requires, we fall into vice (Ia.IIae.61.4, 63.2, 64.1). But Thomas departs from Aristotle in holding that the laws of the virtues can be formulated and used in practical reasoning. There are laws containing precepts for all the virtues and thus providing rational guidance whenever we need it (Ia.IIae.65.3; cf. Ia.IIae.94.3). Thomas does not invoke the Aristotelian insight of the virtuous agent as our final guide. For him, the virtues are basically habits of obedience to laws.

For Thomas, because "the will can tend to nothing except under the aspect of good," the will is necessarily guided by what the intellect shows it as good (I.82.2R1; Ia.IIae.8.1). In practice as in theory, the first principles of knowledge must be self-evident. The basic self-evident principle governing practical reason is that "good is to be done and promoted, and evil is to be avoided." This shows the nature of the good and the evil quite generally, and is not restricted to moral good and evil. And it reveals a natural tendency within all things, not merely an imperative wholly external to actual behavior. Hence for beings with complex natures like ours, there is more than one law. We see what the laws for us are by applying the basic precept to the several features of our nature. We naturally tend to try to preserve ourselves and to propagate our kind, to seek knowledge of God, and to live in society. We can choose how to respond to our natural tendencies, and the precept tells us to turn them toward good (Ia.IIae.94.2). Thus it tells us to try to preserve ourselves, to worship God, and to behave in a sociable manner. By nature we are always moved, at least to some degree, to act as the law of nature directs, although we are also moved by other motives. When Christ summarized the laws, he told us to love God above all else and our neighbor as ourself (Matthew 22.37–39). Not surprisingly, Thomas thinks that the laws of nature turn out to say the same thing. They teach us how to love rightly.[5]

We can know the laws because seeds of them are naturally implanted in the part of the conscience that Thomas calls the synteresis (Ia.IIae.94.1R2; I.79.12).[6] But although everyone has some grasp of the most basic law, not everyone has the same ability to become fully aware, without assistance, of what follows from it. "The truth," as Thomas says, "is the same for all, but it is not equally known to all" (Ia.IIae.94.4, 93.5). There are two reasons for this inequality. One is the

---

5   For valuable discussion of the basic law and its application, see the essays by Donagan and Grisez in Kenny 1969. See also the later elaboration of Grisez's view in Grisez, Boyle, and Finnis 1987.

6   The technical term "synteresis" is also spelled "synderesis." For a review of the history of this term and the earlier term "syneidesis," see d'Arcy 1961, pp. 1–100. See also Greene 1991.

sinful nature we inherited from Adam. Human reason, "habituated to sin," may know the principles and still fail to judge properly in particular cases (Ia.IIae.99.2; cf. 94.6). Another is that some of the conclusions to be drawn from the laws of nature require so much consideration of circumstances that "not all are able to do this carefully, but only those who are wise" (Ia.IIae.100.1).

Men can make laws for themselves, though no human edict that contravenes the laws of nature can count as a real law (Ia.IIae.95.2). But we must not extend our idea of law making too far. In particular we must not misunderstand St. Paul's dictum in Romans 2.14–15. It does not say that we rule ourselves. "[P]roperly speaking," Thomas says, "none imposes a law on his own actions" (Ia.IIae.93.5). Through our awareness of the laws of nature, however imperfect, we participate in God's eternal law. But St. Paul means that the law is within us not only "as in one who rules, but also . . . as in one that is ruled" (Ia.IIae.90.3). Our participation in the eternal law shows that we are not self-governed. We are governed by another.

The substantive morality that Thomas connects with the law of nature is the law of the Decalog supplemented by the love commandment. Since this part of his view was scriptural it could not be contested. All the rest could be, and much of it was. Although his medieval critics agreed that there are laws of nature structuring a harmonious universe directed to the good of each and all its members, their views of the will and its relation to good differed profoundly from Aquinas's.

iii. *Will and the good in voluntarism*

The opposition I noted in Chapter 1.iii between the theological positions that scholars now call intellectualism and voluntarism originated in medieval disagreement with St. Thomas's view.[7] One of the points of difference concerns the psychology of individual choice. Thomas's critics think he has a problem about explaining responsibility for sin. The intellectualist view seems to imply that we can act wrongly only if we fail to know what is good. But is our ignorance blameworthy? Before Thomas the issue had been discussed by Anselm (1033–1109), who saw it arising out of the case of the fall of the devil. How could God escape responsibility for the devil's sin? Suppose the devil's will is moved only by his perception of the greatest good. Then if he had

---

7   On voluntarism see de Muralt 1978; Foster 1935–6; Oakley 1984; Ilting 1983, pp. 62–5; Haggenmacher 1983, pp. 475–82. Kent 1995 gives an important treatment of the background of Duns Scotus's moral psychology and of the post-Thomistic debates surrounding his work. Her chapter on voluntarism focuses on topics other than the one that is central for my purposes.

known that obedience was the greatest good, he would not have fallen. And if he did not know it, who is to blame? He could not have chosen ignorance if he had known that ignorance was a lesser good than knowledge. Does this not leave God responsible for the fall?[8] Anselm thought that it did not; and his views were the starting point from which John Duns Scotus (1266–1308) worked out his own discussion of Lucifer's sin.

Lucifer's fall, Duns Scotus thinks, was due to an inordinate desire for his own happiness. Lucifer improperly or inordinately desired good for someone he loved or to whom he wished well.[9] It could not have been God for whose good he had an inordinate desire, since God is himself so lovable that it is impossible to love him excessively. It is unlikely that Lucifer sought good for anyone else; so it must have been himself whom he loved to excess. Now how is this possible? The will naturally seeks the advantageous and, if only this aspect of the will is involved, seeks as much as possible. This is very like the Thomistic view that we desire and will only what we take to be good, and that we desire it in proportion to its goodness. But Duns Scotus thinks there is another aspect to the will. The will can seek what is just, not merely what is useful or pleasant. And justice puts a check on the extent to which one may properly seek the useful or the agreeable. The latter are always good, but it may not be good that one have something good at precisely this time or obtain it in exactly this way. For instance, one should not pursue what one does not yet deserve to have. Lucifer's sin, then, was not due to ignorance. It was a deliberate pursuit of a good he knew he ought not to pursue, and which he did not have to pursue. He was free to pursue a justly obtainable good instead (pp. 463–5).

Imagine that there were an angel, Duns Scotus says, "with an affection for the beneficial, but without an affection for justice." This angel would not be free; it would be unable not to covet the beneficial above all else. "But this would not be imputed to it as sin, because the appetite would be related to intellect . . . necessarily following what is shown to it by that cognitive power" (p. 469). Only if there is angelic affection for justice as well as for the beneficial can we think that there is angelic freedom of will and understand how the appetite for the beneficial can be checked; and only then can sin be imputed. Scotus draws the moral with exemplary clarity:

---

8   Anselm, *De Casu Diaboli,* in Hopkins and Richard 1976, 2. 139ff. For discussion, see Normore 1994, and Boler 1993.

9   Duns Scotus associates this with St. Augustine's view that two loves create two different cities, an ordinate love creating the city of God and an inordinate love creating the earthly city. Page references to Duns Scotus are from the edition of Wolter.

if some power were exclusively appetitive . . . [it] could not sin. . . . for it would be powerless to seek anything other than what the intellect would show it. . . . But this same power, having been made free . . . could moderate itself in willing. . . . from the fact that it could moderate this, it is bound to do so according to the rule of justice it has received from a higher will. . . . a free will is not bound in every way to seek happiness. (p. 471)

Duns Scotus thus attributes two powers to the will, "the affection for justice and the affection for the advantageous," where Aquinas attributes only the latter. Duns Scotus's other main departure from St. Thomas's position also involves a way in which will is not tied to the pursuit of good. Here the question concerns the divine will.

Aquinas, as I noted, held that the first principles of natural law are rational, and agreed with Cicero's view that right reason, in showing them to us, shows us principles that properly govern God's will as well as ours.[10] Hence for Thomas, Duns Scotus says, "what is commanded [in the Decalog] is not good merely because it is commanded, but commanded because it is good in itself" (p. 273). But for Duns Scotus the will is nobler than the intellect and is not tied by what the intellect can show it. He can appeal to the divine word for this view: Christ said that "With God all things are possible" (Mark 10.27). Hence it seems that God can will anything. Duns Scotus sees only one limit to God's will. God cannot will anything that goes against his own nature. Laws of nature, therefore, can require only what God could not reject without the self-contradiction involved in denying his own nature.

It follows, Duns Scotus thinks, that only the first two commandments are genuine laws. They follow strictly from the necessary truth that if God exists, he alone is to be loved as God. Hence God could not will their opposite (p. 277).[11] But the commandments of the second table – those concerning relations among humans – do not follow in this way from any necessary truth. Duns Scotus allows that they are "exceedingly in harmony" with the strict laws of nature, and that in this derivative way they can be considered laws of nature themselves (p. 279). The harmony of the precepts of the second table with the natural laws of the

10 See, e.g., *ST* Ia.IIae.93.1. I ignore here the complexities of the idea of this separation of the two faculties in Thomas's theory.

11 The command concerning the sabbath perplexes Duns Scotus. That we should express our love of God through worship seems to him to follow strictly from the first two laws, but that the worship should be on a specified day of the week does not. How can we be required to do something that must take place at some definite time, without being required to do it at some definite time? Yet if the third commandment does not follow strictly from God's nature then – contrary to the accepted division – it must belong to the second table (p. 279).

first arises because a perfect love of God would be orderly, and therefore not jealous. It would lead us to wish well to others, that is, to wish others to love God as we do. The second table then dictates the ways in which we are to express that love. But Duns Scotus insists that the first two commandments do not impose the positive requirement of loving God. They require us only not to hate him. And we can refrain from such hatred without going on to love our neighbor. Moreover, even if I love my neighbors in the sense that I want them to love God, it does not strictly follow that I must will to preserve their lives or their bodily integrity. Hence God need not have willed that we are not to kill and not to commit adultery, as in fact he has (pp. 283–5).

Could God, then, have willed otherwise? Could he have made murder and adultery right? Duns Scotus answers with a distinction between absolute power and ordered or ordained power. The latter is the power to comply with a just law. The former is the power to act contrary to such a law. If finite beings exercise their absolute power and violate a law, they act in a disorderly way. Thus if we violate God's laws we are always disorderly.

> But whenever the law and its rectitude are in the power of the agent, so that the law is right only because it has been established, then the agent can freely order things otherwise than this right law dictates and still can act orderly, because he can establish another right or just law according to which he may act orderly. (p. 257)

When God acts according to laws he has instituted, he uses his ordered power. But he can use his absolute power "to do anything that is not self-contradictory or act in any way that does not include a contradiction (and there are many such ways he could act)" (p. 257). So God's absolute power would enable him to lay down other laws for the second table than he did; but, as long as he confines himself to his ordered power, he will not do so.

Duns Scotus agrees that there are laws of nature that are fundamental to human morality. Moreover he thinks God wills them for the benefit of a community that is to live under them (p. 253).[12] Most so-called laws, however, are on his view included under that name only by courtesy. Only those concerning the worship of God command something because it is good; the others make something good because they command it. They do not have any basis in prior goodness arising from the nature of what they command or the results of those actions. Consequently we could not infer anything about how we are to behave from

---

12 According to Duns Scotus (pp. 291–3), God could command bigamy in circumstances where it would be of greater benefit than monogamy.

any knowledge we might have about the nature of specific actions. William of Ockham (c. 1285–1349) took this view to a radical conclusion.[13] God, he suggests, could even command that he not be loved. If he commanded that he be hated, he would not contradict himself, and hatred of God would be a virtue.[14] The content of any divine law does not explain or justify its being a law. God in exercising his absolute power is indifferent to what he commands; only his ordered power is checked by preestablished laws.

Duns Scotus and Ockham held that only their view could properly explain some of God's particular acts. God did indeed command all the precepts of the Decalog, and he added many other laws for the Jews. But he also commanded Abraham to kill his son, the Jews to steal goods from the Egyptians, and Hosea to marry a prostitute. How could God go against his own laws? How are we to explain God's power to give dispensation for transgression? Since the biblical texts had to be accommodated, the issue was inescapable. The voluntarists resolved it by saying that God's absolute power enables him to alter the nature of the particular acts that would otherwise have contravened his laws. Aquinas's intellectualism, not allowing this, makes it difficult to give any account of God's dispensing power.

The most basic consideration leading Duns Scotus to the voluntarist position was the desire to maintain God's omnipotence. If all the precepts of the Decalog were genuine laws of nature, "true by reason of their terms," they would have to be true "even if, to assume the impossible, no act of willing existed." Then God's will would have to agree with them or be wrong, a limitation on God that Duns Scotus rejects. Moreover the intellectualist view requires us to say that God's will "is necessarily determined in an unqualified sense in regard to willing things other than himself." But Duns Scotus believes he has shown that God's will "tends to nothing other than himself except contingently" (p. 275). Omnipotence is secured, at the cost of making God's commands concerning the moral relations of human beings to one another an outcome of his arbitrary will. Luther and Calvin did not mind the cost. Voluntarism became an inescapable issue for later thinkers because of the decisive place they gave it in their moral theologies.

13   See M. Adams 1987, 2, ch. 28, for a careful analysis of Ockham on divine omnipotence, with some references to earlier medievals.

14   The question had a long life. Burman asked Descartes if God "could have commanded a creature to hate him, and thereby made this a good thing to do," and Descartes replied that although God could not do it now, we cannot see why he could not have done so, presumably prior to his willing that he be loved (*Writings* III.343).

iv. *Luther's two kingdoms*

Martin Luther (1483–1546) broke the Roman Catholic church's monopolistic control over Christian life and worship. His interpretation of Christian doctrine was also deeply anti-Catholic. He said that he was simply removing errors and returning to the teaching of the Bible and the early fathers of the church, St. Augustine in particular. He was not the only radical to claim the sanction of ancient tradition for his views.

The difference between law and Gospel, and their relation to one another, are crucial to Luther's doctrine. The category of law is broad. It includes the ruler's positive law, the Mosaic law given to the Jews, and the natural law. Of these only the natural law holds for all human beings. Some sort of knowledge of it exists even in impious men; the wiser heathens possessed it; and we can learn about it by studying Aristotle and Cicero.[15] Although Luther grants that reason gives us knowledge of the law, he stresses, more emphatically than St. Thomas, the effects of sin in weakening our powers of reasoning, and the consequent importance of God's repromulgation of the laws through the Mosaic Decalog and Christ's teaching.[16] These points do not show any marked departure from the classical theory of natural law. Luther's innovations come rather in the roles he assigns the law in our lives, or, as he puts it, in the uses of the law. From these we can also see the role of the Gospel.

The first use of law, for Luther, is simply "to bridle the wicked." In our fallen state, most people are in the grip of lusts that would lead them to the worst sorts of sin unless they were controlled by fear of "the prison, the sword, and the hangman" (p. 139). Man in his fallen state is, like the devil, "wholly turned to self and to his own." He seeks worldly wealth and power without limit; to anyone who stands in his way his response is uncontrollable rage and fury (p. 192). Without strongly enforced laws, therefore, we simply could not live together. But God intended us to live together, and gave us, in the law of nature, guidance as to how we are to do so.

The second use, and the main point, of the law is to convince us all that we are sinners, "to reveal unto a man his sin, his blindness, his misery, his impiety, ignorance, hatred and contempt of God, death, hell, the judgment and deserved wrath of God." As long as we remain unaware of our actual condition we will be full of pride and presumption (pp. 139–41). But the natural laws, as repeated in the Decalog,

15 Cranz 1959, pp. 104–11.
16 *Commentary on Galatians,* in *Works,* ed. Pelikan and Lehman, 26.117, on Gal. 2.14. Unless otherwise noted, references to Luther are from the *Selections* edited by Dillenberger.

"show us what we ought to do but do not give us the power to do it. They are intended to teach man to know himself, that through them he may recognize his inability to do good and may despair of his own ability" (p. 57).[17]

In this powerful statement, Luther is not saying that we cannot behave externally as the laws require. We can indeed control our actions; but we cannot control the motives that lead us to do what the laws require. "God does not just want such works by themselves," Luther says, "He wants them to be performed gladly and willingly. And when there is no joy in doing them and the right will and motive are absent, then they are dead in God's eyes."[18] Works alone do not save. Only a right will does; and only those who are given grace can act from the right will. The Gospel brings the good news that we may hope for the grace that will turn our souls toward love.

Those who have been given grace are in one important sense beyond the law. "Christians," Luther says, "have in their hearts the Holy Spirit, who instructs them and causes them to wrong no one." For them good action does not come from reasoning but from the love that faith makes possible for them.[19] It is Christ within who guides recipients of grace in their relations to God and neighbor alike. Luther cites St. Paul (I Timothy 1.9) in support of his view: "The law is not given for the righteous, but for the unrighteous" (pp. 368–9). Those who are given grace enjoy the freedom of a Christian, "that Christian liberty . . . which . . . makes the law and works unnecessary for any man's righteousness" (pp. 58–9).[20]

---

17 Aquinas also attributes this function to the old, or Mosaic, law. The new law, he says, is the law of grace. It could only function after man had been "left to himself under the state of the Old Law," because he was thus taught to "realize his weakness and acknowledge his need of grace" (*ST* Ia.IIae.106.3).

18 "Sermon on the Three Kinds of Good Life," in *Works* 44.240.

19 Cited in Rupp 1953, p. 227.

20 I Timothy 1.9 is cited again here. The same view is held by Zwingli. "Laws have been given for the sake of wicked people, as Paul says in I Tim. 1.9–11 . . . . [God] gives ordinances which are useful to us and serve well to enable us to live happily and well with one another. And he says, 'You shall not steal; you shall not commit adultery. . . . ' All of these commandments we should not need at all if we would only keep that other commandment, 'You shall love your neighbor as yourself.' But since we do not keep that, God had to issue all these other commandments." Zwingli, vol. 2: Sermon, "Divine and Human Righteousness" (1523).

The reading of I Timothy 1.9 as Luther read it, and the appeal to it, are common among Reformed writers. Thus Johannes Althusius, explaining why "proper law" enacted by magistrates, is needed in addition to natural law, says: "The second reason is that natural law is not so completely written on the hearts of men that it is sufficiently efficacious in restraining men from evil and impelling them to good. . . .

St. Augustine taught that there are two cities, the earthly and the
heavenly city, one constituted by those in the grip of wrongful love who
value earthly goods disproportionately, the other by those who through
grace have a right love, valuing earthly goods only at their true worth.[21]
Luther adopts the Augustinian view in one of his most important
doctrines, the doctrine of the two realms or kingdoms. The two govern-
ments under which God has put us are

> the spiritual, which by the Holy Spirit under Christ makes Christians and
> pious people, and the secular, which restrains the unchristian and wicked
> so that they must needs keep the peace outwardly, even against their
> will. . . . these two kingdoms must be sharply distinguished, and both be
> permitted to remain; the one to produce piety, the other to bring about
> external peace and prevent evil deeds; neither is sufficient in the world
> without the other. (pp. 370–1)

For Luther the spiritual realm is not to be found only in an afterlife. It
is constituted by those who have been given grace, even while they live
with those who have not. When God saves us, he does not alter our
sinful nature; he merely counts us as righteous, for the sake of Christ,
who carries the burden of our sins for us. We continue to be sinners
even when we are saved. We still have the same lawless desires and
spiteful hates we had before, but we are better able to control them and
we know we are saved despite them. "Thus a Christian man is both
righteous and a sinner, holy and profane, an enemy of God and yet a
child of God" (p. 130). Even the saved are not perfect. If "both the
wicked and the pious man have the Law," they expect different things
from it. The pious man knows better than to hope for salvation from
external compliance. The righteous man "has what the Law demands
and he has been established without it."[22] But because he remains a
sinner even while being accounted justified before God, he continues to
need the law. Faith saves but does not eliminate the need for works.
    Works, in Luther's theory, have two important functions. They show,
first, that faith has indeed been given to someone. "For if good works
and love do not blossom forth," Luther says, "it is not genuine faith" (p.
18). Second, because they are needed for our life on earth, we must
attend to them carefully. All the different kinds of work needed to

It is therefore necessary that there be a proper law by which men who are led neither
by the love of virtue nor by the hatred of vice may be restrained by the fear of
punishment. . . . In this sense, it is said that 'law is set forth not for the just, but the
unjust'" (pp. 139–40). Althusius was a Calvinist political theorist who published his
major work in 1603.
    21 *City of God* XI.34; XIV.13, 28.
    22 *Lectures on I Timothy,* in *Works* 28.231–3.

sustain life are equally valuable in God's eye. We should not disdain any calling, however humble. We can and indeed ought to make our contribution to earthly life in a special role or station, and – if we work in the right spirit – we are serving God as much by being a hangman or soldier or wife as we are by being a priest or king.[23]

Luther distinguishes in several ways between the two kingdoms.[24] At times he thinks of the kingdom of God as comprising only those who have been given grace, and of all the rest as belonging to the kingdom of the devil. But along with this dichotomy there is another, between two aspects of all human beings. All are subjects of God. Even those who are not saved have a place, if only a wretched one, in the spiritual world. And all of us, saved or not, are always, in this life, in need of the law to control our external behavior. Taken in this way, Luther's two realms are not constituted by different inhabitants. They are constituted by the different kinds of governance set over us. All live under the Law, only some under the Gospel.[25] The crucial question, then, is, What must we do to be saved?

v. *Luther's voluntarism*

In the spiritual realm each person must be saved as an individual. No merely human mediation can be a substitute for God's direct acceptance. Luther is blunt: "this truth is irrefragable," he says, "each one stands for himself where the divine promise is concerned. His own faith is required. Each must respond for himself, and bear his own burden" (p. 283). The Roman church, claiming that its mediation was essential to salvation, had gotten matters seriously wrong. Consequently it could not relieve the anguished sense of sin overwhelming anyone who realizes the individual's total inability to achieve the right relation to God. It had simply institutionalized our tendency toward pride and self-reliance, encouraging the delusion that we can become acceptable to God through our own works. Luther accuses the church of following the erring steps of Pelagius, the fifth-century British monk who taught that we can freely decide to act rightly, and that if we do we will deserve

23 See, e.g., Luther at pp. 373–5, 378–9. Cf. Taylor 1989, part III, for valuable discussion of the significance of "the affirmation of ordinary life" in later moral thought.

24 See Thompson 1984, ch. III.

25 "The secular rule can also be called the kingdom of God. For he intends it to stand, and us to be obedient in it. But it is only the kingdom of his left hand. The kingdom of his right hand, which he rules himself . . . is that in which the gospel is preached to the poor." Cited in Ebeling 1970, p. 189; and see his discussion in ch. 11.

salvation, which a just God cannot then refuse us.[26] The church must be
drastically altered, Luther held, to make its structure as well as its
teaching show that faith alone justifies, and that faith comes only as
God's gift of grace.

Aquinas thought of himself as opposed to Pelagianism. He held that
nature and grace cooperate, grace enabling us to use our natural abilities to the full rather than replacing them, so that our free will and
God's freely given help together may bring us to salvation. For Luther
even the thought that we might cooperate in bringing about our own
salvation is a sign of the pride that is the source of all sin. Far from
trying to reconcile reason and faith, as Aquinas did, Luther accepted the
Augustinian view that mystery is unavoidable in Christianity. Reason
has a role in secular affairs, but in sacred matters it is a source of
corruption.

The central mystery is that a just and loving God made us with a
nature that would inevitably lead us to sin and so to deserve eternal
punishment. Some are saved by divine grace; but Luther accepts the
Augustinian doctrine that grace is prevenient. It comes before we can
do anything to deserve it; and since without it we cannot love rightly or
be saved, the responsibility for our sin seems to revert back to God.
When Luther deals with the problem he has no qualms in declaring that
we simply cannot understand it all. God hardened Pharaoh's heart, so
that he refused even to seek salvation. Why? "This question," Luther
replies,

> touches on the secrets of His Majesty. . . . it is not for us to inquire into
> these mysteries, but to adore them. . . . The same reply should be given to
> those who ask: Why did God let Adam fall, and why did He create us all

---

26   On Pelagius, see Brown 1983, chs. 29–31. A brief excerpt from a letter Pelagius wrote in 413 contains the essentials of his teaching: "Instead of regarding the
commands of our illustrious King as a privilege, . . . we cry out at God, in the
scornful sloth of our hearts, and say, 'This is too hard and difficult. We cannot do it.
We are only human, and hindered by the weakness of the flesh.' Blind folly and
presumptuous blasphemy! We ascribe to the God of knowledge the guilt of twofold
ignorance; ignorance of his own creation and of his own commands. As if, forgetting
the weakness of men, his own creation, he had laid upon men commands which they
were unable to bear. . . . we ascribe to the Just One unrighteousness and cruelty to
the Holy One; the first, by complaining that he has commanded the impossible, the
second, by imagining that a man will be condemned by him for what he could not
help; so that . . . God is thought of as seeking our punishment rather than our
salvation. . . . No one knows the extent of our strength better than he who gave us
that strength. . . . He has not willed to command anything impossible, for he is
righteous; and he will not condemn a man for what he could not help, for he is holy"
(Bettenson, p. 74).

tainted with the same sin, when he might have kept Adam safe, and might have created us of other material? . . . God is he for whose will no cause or ground may be laid down as its rule and standard; for nothing is on a level with it or above it, but it is itself the rule for all things. . . . What God wills is not right because he ought or was bound so to will; on the contrary, what takes place must be right, because he so wills. (pp. 195–6)

Luther thus accepts a voluntarist position about God's commands, and accepts with it the conclusion that we can neither understand God nor judge his decisions.[27]

If His justice were such as could be adjudged just by human reckoning, it clearly would not be Divine; it would in no way differ from human justice. But inasmuch as He is the one true God, wholly incomprehensible and inaccessible to man's understanding, it is reasonable, indeed inevitable, that His justice also should be incomprehensible. (p. 200)

There is no law for God, who has no need to control sinful passions; and the law he gives us has no comprehensible ground. God is outside and infinitely distant from any human community formed by morality.

Without grace we are totally self-centered; and if our salvation were up to us, we could never be sure we would obtain it. "If I lived and worked to all eternity, my conscience would never reach comfortable certainty as to how much it must do to satisfy God" (p. 199). Luther goes so far as to say that God would be a tyrant because he demands of us something we are not able to give – but grace prevents the reproach.[28] Once God chooses to save us, no one can take us away from him. The very arbitrariness of God's judgment is a comfort, and the doctrine of salvation by faith the only teaching that can assuage our fear of God. Our free will extends only to secular matters. We cannot by ourselves do anything about spiritual goods (pp. 181–2, 189–90). It is only after God's will makes us righteous in his eyes by accepting us that our will enables us to act rightly, from love.[29]

---

27 See the discussion of Gabriel Biel in Oberman 1963.

28 *Commentary on Galatians* 2.16, in *Works* 26.128, where Luther is commenting on Duns Scotus's view.

29 In the early *Lectures on Romans* (*Works* 25.19, n. 13) Luther gives a voluntarist account of human righteousness: "a man is not considered righteous by God because he is righteous; but because he is considered righteous by God, therefore he is righteous." See Ebeling 1970, ch. 9, who at p. 150 cites Luther as saying that the righteous man's righteousness "does not spring from works, but his works from righteousness. . . . This is contrary to Aristotle, who says 'by doing right one becomes righteous.'"

vi. *Calvin's humanistic voluntarism*

In many respects the views of John Calvin (1509–64) agree with those of Luther. Most importantly, both accept the need for justification by faith and for prevenient grace, mediated by Christ. There are also important differences between the two reformers. Calvin's views on church governance and on politics were not those of Luther. And where Luther had been educated as a monk by the Catholic Church, Calvin was formed by a humanistic and legal education. When the philosophers of antiquity spoke of the inner life, they aroused Luther's hatred. The worst of all was Aristotle, whose works were taught at every university. "This pagan has attained supremacy," Luther cried in outrage,

> impeded and almost suppressed the Scriptures of the living God. . . . I cannot avoid believing that the Evil one introduced the study of Aristotle. . . . his book on Ethics is worse than any other book, being the direct opposite of God's grace and the Christian virtues. . . . Oh! away with such books from any Christian hands. (pp. 470–1)

Calvin had no such attitude. In his early years he wrote a humanistic commentary on Seneca's treatise on clemency, and all his life he tried to find ways to accommodate the insights of philosophers to Christianity. Admitting that the fall had weakened our faculties and clouded our reason, he thought the damage less than Luther thought it. Yet he was as determined as Luther to teach the total inadequacy of works to procure salvation.

Like Luther, Calvin is a voluntarist. God, the creator and director of the cosmos, is far beyond human understanding. That it was predestined from eternity that Adam would sin, that in his sin all mankind would be ruined, that out of the mass of totally undeserving beings some would mercifully be chosen for salvation, that those not chosen would be left to suffer the anguish of permanent separation from God (*Institutes* II.v.12) – all this is God's justice and is incomprehensible to us (III.xi.7). How, then, can we be sure that it is just?

> God's will is so much the highest rule of righteousness that whatever he wills, by the very fact that he wills it, must be considered righteous. When, therefore, one asks why God has so done, we must reply: because he has willed it. But if you proceed further to ask why he has so willed, you are seeking something greater and higher than God's will, which cannot be found. (*Institutes* III.xxiii.2)[30]

30   Calvin also says in the same section that "we do not advocate the fiction of 'absolute might'; because this is profane, it ought rightfully to be hateful to us." I follow Wendel 1963, pp. 127ff., in not taking this to be a repudiation of voluntarism

Calvin also follows Luther in holding that humans are to be governed by two kinds of ruler, divine and earthly. There is, he says,

> a twofold government in man: one aspect is spiritual, whereby the conscience is instructed in piety and in reverencing God; the second is political, whereby man is educated for the duties of humanity and citizenship that must be maintained among men. . . . the former sort of government pertains to the life of the soul, while the latter has to do with the concerns of the present life – not only with food and clothing but with laying down laws whereby a man may live his life among other men holily, honorably, and temperately. For the former resides in the inner mind, while the latter regulates only outward behavior. (III.xix.15)

God's most basic dictates form what Calvin calls "the moral law." It is indeed, as Paul declared in Romans 2.14, written in our hearts, but "man is so shrouded in the darkness of errors" that he can hardly understand it from that source. Hence in the Decalog God "has provided us with a written law to give us a clearer witness of what was too obscure in the natural law" (II.viii.1). This was absolutely necessary if we were to know how to worship God, because the fall wholly destroyed the original human awareness of the need for piety. But Calvin holds that there are still some sparks within us of the initial divine light as regards the political or earthly kingdom. "Since man is by nature a social animal," Calvin says, and naturally seeks society,

> we observe that there exist in all men's minds universal impressions of a certain civic fair dealing and order. Hence no man is to be found who does not understand that every sort of human organization must be regulated by laws, and who does not comprehend the principles of those laws. Hence arises that unvarying consent of all nations and of individual mortals with regard to laws. (II.ii.13)

The first table of the Decalog shows us our duties toward God; the principles of the laws that structure civic fair dealing are in the second table (II.ii.24). Calvin sums up both as requiring us to love God and our neighbor, thus agreeing with Aquinas that Christ's formulation of the law, though not expressly stated in the Decalog, is its principle (IV.xx.15). But Calvin's view of the uses of the moral law makes clear that he is much closer to Luther than to Thomas in his understanding of the laws of nature.

but a repudiation of some extreme interpretations of that position. See Steinmetz 1988 for discussion of Calvin's rejection of the distinction between absolute and ordained power. On other points (e.g., the ability of the devil to resist temptation) Calvin does not follow Duns Scotus. Like Luther he also tries to defend his view against the charge that it makes God into a tyrant. *Institutes* III.xxiii.2.

Calvin assigns three uses to the law in place of Luther's two. The first function is to increase transgression and to convince us of our sinfulness: the law shows us what we ought to do and thereby forces us to learn that we cannot do it. The second function is to restrain the wicked, by threats of punishment. Calvin cites I Timothy 1.9, and interprets it as Luther does. That the law is not for the just but for the unjust simply means that the law is intended to check those whose outer behavior displays the "raging lusts of the flesh" (II.vii.10). It does not mean that Christians have no need of law at all (II.vii.13; cf. II.xix.15). It is in accordance with this that the principal function of the law is for Calvin the third: to teach those who are of the elect to know their duty more clearly. "The Lord," he explains, "instructs by their reading of [the law] those whom he inwardly instills with a readiness to obey" (II.vii.3–12).

The precepts of the second table are thus meant to provide the structure for all worldly societies. Paul's dictum in Romans 2.14–15 shows us that we are sometimes better at "knowing the rule for the right conduct of life" than we are at knowing higher precepts (II.ii.22). Even the pagans, Calvin allows, had some knowledge of this part of the law of nature. But he insists that the law requires more than outer conformity. The point is obvious as regards the first table, which dictates that we love God with all our hearts. It is also true for the second. The sixth commandment, for example, does not simply prohibit killing. It is meant, Calvin says, to shape our souls as well. "For it would be ridiculous that he who looks upon the thoughts of the heart . . . should instruct only the body in true righteousness. Therefore this law also forbids murder of the heart and enjoins the inner intent to save a brother's life" (II.viii.39). Even when we can control our inordinate passions so that our outer actions are correct, the attainment of the requisite inner state remains beyond our power. This is why the law teaches us that we need grace. We cannot even seek our own chief good, eternal blessedness, without it (II.ii.26–7).

There is an additional purpose served by the law. When we know what it requires, we are accountable – and since we cannot comply with it, we are inexcusable. Calvin even suggests that one might define natural law as "that apprehension of the conscience which distinguishes sufficiently between just and unjust, and which deprives men of the excuse of ignorance, while it proves them guilty by their own testimony" (II.ii.22). We know what we ought to do but we do not do it. The will therefore does not always follow the intellect's prompting. The deviation is not to be explained by appeal to any freedom of the will: like Luther Calvin thinks it would be almost blasphemous to think we can truly initiate any action, as God can (II.ii.4; II.iii.9). Those not predestined to salvation sin necessarily and willingly. Because they want to do what they see is sinful, they sin voluntarily, not because of compulsion; but the will is now so corrupted that no one can choose rightly without grace. Calvin is not asking whether we can carry out what we have willed, but whether the will itself is free (II.iv.8). His denial is emphatic. It is accompanied by equally strong denials "that sin ought less to be reckoned as sin merely because it is necessary" and that since sin is voluntary it is avoidable. The devil could not turn away from evil, nor can good angels turn away from good, yet their wills do not on that account cease to be wills (II.v.1). Our inability to comply with the law of nature is reckoned to our account, although without grace we could not do otherwise.

Once grace is given, the person is transformed. Calvin does not mean that the elect are perfect in this life. They still feel temptations and commit sins. But they are assured that they will be counted as righteous before God despite their failings. Election does not lead to sloth and self-satisfaction. Far from it: since the elect have been chosen to lead a blameless life, election ought to "goad us eagerly" to become ever better. The elect will obey the law not out of fear but out of love. They will endure the trials and sufferings of life like sentries at a post, serving God's will and not their own. They will become less selfish and more concerned to serve others (III.ix.4; III.vii.1–5). And each will labor industriously in the occupation to which God has called him, which is the best way, Calvin says, to follow God's direction rather than one's own will. "God has appointed duties for every man in his particular way of life," he remarks, adding that even if someone thinks up an apparently praiseworthy venture outside his calling, God will not find it acceptable (III.x.6). Just as we are to obey the laws even if we do not understand them, so we must continue in our posts regardless of what the outcome seems to be. Here the providentialist view that Calvin expounds in the first book of the *Institutes* finds one of its most important expressions. God made and watches over the whole world; there is no such thing as fortune or chance. God manages the particular course of events, bringing good out of men's evildoing and order out of human chaos: "he directs everything by his incomparable wisdom and disposes it to his own end" (I.xvi.4–5).

In portraying the selfishness of fallen humanity and the strife, miseries, and uncertainties of life, Calvin can be quite eloquent (I.xvii.10; III.ix.1). Yet he allows the possibility of creating at least a similacrum of justice in the world. God directly bridles the passions of some, and makes some more virtuous than others even without grace. Among the pagans, Caligula and Nero were monsters but Titus and Trajan were just, moderate, and equitable. Even if the difference between them is only the difference between unrighteousness and a "dead image" of righteousness, it is still important. God rewards with worldly goods this "external and feigned righteousness" because the order it helps create is serviceable (III.xiv.2). Thus the law of nature can guide even the unregenerate to some extent. What it cannot do is substitute for the order arising from grace. "As for the virtues that deceive us with their vain show, they shall have their praise in the political assembly and in common renown among men; but before the heavenly judgment they shall be of no value to acquire merit" (II.iii.4).

For both Luther and Calvin, then, morality as such concerns human life on earth. It extends no further. It has no bearing on the life of the soul after death. And it can have no hold on God. Since he has no unruly passions he needs no law, and in any case there is no one who could impose a law on him. We must obey God in the community he rules, and we must be always aware of the need for obedience. He can touch our lives by his mysterious grace, for which we may hope. But because we cannot by ourselves do anything to bring him to give us grace, he is in an important sense above the human community and not part of it.

3

Setting religion aside: Republicanism and skepticism

In the fifteenth and sixteenth centuries an open avowal of atheism was very likely to get one burned at the stake. But it was not necessary to deny Christian teaching in order to explore how life might look if one more or less set it aside. In this chapter I present the work of three writers who engaged in this kind of venture. Neither Machiavelli nor Montaigne had any wish to write systematic philosophy; Charron tried, but it was the temerity of his conclusions rather than the power of his arguments that gave his main work its great popularity. Each investigated, in different ways, how people might be ruled or guided without calling upon any truths of Christianity. Machiavelli thought he could draw lessons about political self-rule from the history of pagan antiquity. Montaigne and Charron, skeptics both, were concerned about personal life as well as politics. They were led, consequently, to make the first modern efforts to articulate a morality of self-governance.

i. Virtú *and the manipulative prince*

No thinker of the sixteenth century more visibly shocked Christian sensibilities than Niccolo Machiavelli (1469–1527).[1] His vehement rejection of Christian doctrine as a guide in matters of politics, and the strikingly immoral advice he deliberately offered to princes, made his first name into a synonym for the devil in Elizabethan England, and he is still remembered mainly for advising unscrupulous manipulation in politics. He did much more than that, however, so much more that there is considerable controversy over what he really meant and intended. Without entering into the disputes we can perhaps see enough in what he certainly said to understand why he was so upsetting – and how his understanding of political community also provided an important point of departure for later thinkers.

---

1 For references to page numbers of the works of Machiavelli discussed here, *The Prince* and the *Discourses*, I use the translations by Gilbert.

Machiavelli did not reject Christianity because he thought it unimportant. He believed religion to be of the greatest importance in holding a community together. Who mattered more to Rome, he asks, its political founder, Regulus, or the bringer of its religion, Numa? He unhesitatingly chooses the latter. Once a religion is established you can set up armed forces; it is much harder to create these institutions in the other order. Religion is particularly necessary for anyone wishing to introduce basic new laws. "Because many good things are known to a prudent man that are not in themselves so plainly rational that others can be persuaded of them. Therefore wise men, who wish to remove this difficulty, have recourse to God" (*Discourses* 1.11, pp. 224–5). The religion of Numa, Machiavelli holds, was the main source of Roman prosperity. "Because religion caused good laws; good laws make good fortune; and from good fortune came the happy results of the city's endeavors" (1.11, p. 225). Religion, then, is vital; and Machiavelli also holds that the Christian religion – "our religion" – is the true one. Why then does he not apply its teachings to politics?

The answer is simple. What makes a well-governed city successful is what Machiavelli called the *virtù* of the citizens. The term is not really translatable. It does not mean "virtue" in any Christian sense. It calls instead on pagan meanings. The man[2] of *virtù* is energetic, fit, filled with eagerness to fight for the common good, skilled in warfare, ready to seek glory either in warding off external threats to his city or in extending its power over others. But Christianity makes us esteem honor much less than pagan religion did; our religion does not call, as it did, for fierce and vigorous action. Rather "[o]ur religion has . . . set up as the greatest good humility, abjectness and contempt for human things; the other put it in grandeur of mind, in strength of body" and in whatever makes for boundless energy. Little wonder then that the world has become prey to the wicked. A religion that teaches men to endure insults in the hope of heaven rather than to avenge them for the sake of honor, destroys *virtù* and makes men effeminate and worthless. Since a decent community can be preserved only by force, a religion like ours is a liability (*Discourses* 2.2, p. 331).[3]

There are accordingly no appeals to Christian virtues in Machiavelli's reflections on how to create and sustain a proper community, and no mention at all of divinely ordained or sanctioned laws of nature.

---

2   Women feature in Machiavelli's commentary only as a source of trouble. Conflict about them can cause the downfall of a state (*Discourses* 3.26, p. 488). The prince is warned not to meddle with his subjects' women, property, or honor, not much distinction being made among them (*Prince* 19, p. 67).

3   See also his complaints about "modern notions" that give rise to "feeble education," making men queasy about harsh punishments, *Discourses* 3.27, p. 490.

Limits to what citizens may do are imposed by the laws that are in force where they live; and there are no natural limits to the valid authority of the ruler. It was because Machiavelli advised princes to ignore morality when it was not useful for their political aims that his book was so shocking.

The Prince was not a new kind of book. Many books of advice to princes had been published before Machiavelli's. His turned them upside-down, teaching that the maintenance of power is the goal to keep in mind and urging rulers not to count the moral cost. Books have often told us, Machiavelli says, that the good prince is liberal, truthful, merciful, kindly, reliable; but although all these virtues may sometimes be useful, it is more important to know exactly when they are and when they are not – and to be ready to ignore them when doing so preserves one's power (*Prince* 15, pp. 58–9). Though a sensible prince wants to be thought merciful, he must often be cruel; his mind will not be troubled if he is so (17, p. 61). Being feared is better for keeping the people under control than being loved. The appearance of virtue matters, since the populace likes it, and the wise prince does what he can "to avoid everything that makes him hated and despised" (19, p. 67). Shrewdness and cunning are more valuable than strength; it is often necessary to deceive others; and the ruler must always be ready to break his word, murder his formerly trusted advisers, or send his people to war for his own glory if such deeds enable him to stay in power.

None of this was what the older advice books urged, nor was it taught by Seneca and Cicero, on whom many of the books drew.[4] Machiavelli rejects all these teachings because he has a deeply different idea of what it takes to have the best kind of civic life. The Roman Republic was his model, and a commentary on a book concerning its history the major exposition of his thought. His arguments are not drawn from abstract principles but from the facts of history. If Roman philosophers themselves misunderstood the sources of Rome's strength, so much the worse for them.

ii. *The self-governing republic*

Societies began as leagues for defense, Machiavelli holds, and at the beginning the accepted leader was simply the strongest man. The need for cooperation soon led members of the group to distinguish the strong from those who devotedly worked for the common good. The distinction between honorable or good, and pernicious or evil, arose at this

---

4 For a good brief survey of Machiavelli's rejection of the older tradition, see Skinner's introduction to Machiavelli's *The Prince* (1988).

point, men naturally condemning those who were ungrateful enough to harm anyone who was helpful and generous. To protect against such evil, laws were made and with them came the first idea of justice (*Discourses* 1.2, p. 197).

People find it difficult to live together even in a society that provides them with common benefits. This is because men are evil. They are disposed to go their own way, seeking only their own good. They are endlessly ambitious, their wants are insatiable, and discontent is common (*Discourses* 1.3, p. 201; 1.37, p. 272; 2 pref., p. 323). It takes laws and strong government to keep a community together. Even when both exist, the perpetual flux of human affairs leads to instability; and so the question arises of whether it is possible to find a form of government that will escape basic change. (2 pref., p. 322; 1.2, pp. 197ff.).

Only a republic has much chance of doing so. In a republic, there is a role for everyone in governing. Those who are most able to lead in war, to devise laws, and to cope with emergencies are rulers, but only for a time. They propose their policies to the public, which is to pass judgment. Machiavelli has a relatively low opinion of the masses on most matters – they will only work if hunger presses and will only be good if law makes it necessary – but he thinks they are generally apt to judge well at least on particular issues (*Discourses* 1.47, pp. 292–3). Inconstant though the multitude often is, "a people that commands and is well organized will be just as stable, prudent, and grateful as a prince, or will be more so" (1.58, p. 315). A pure democracy would be a milling mob, never presented with good advice about what to do; an hereditary aristocracy would make into leaders men less able than their forebears; a monarchy tends to tyranny. In a republic the best men take turns ruling and being ruled; new talent is sought, poverty is no bar, results are what matter, and, with the populace ever jealous of its freedom, not even a wealthy ruler can long get away with arrogating too much power (cf. 1.4, p. 203).

The subjects as well as the ruling group in a republic will be devoted to the common good. Citizens win glory and honor by working together for it. Good citizens forget private wrongs in order to benefit their city and do not seek great wealth (3.47, p. 526). They see their own glory not only in commanding but in serving honorably under those whom they have previously commanded, or in taking lower offices after holding higher ones (1.36, pp. 271–2). Inequality is therefore the curse of republics. The laws must strictly regulate wealth, and religion must reinforce the law.

What then is the common good? An independent republic always seeks two things: "the first, to make gains; the second, to keep herself free" (1.29, p. 258). Enemies from without are the first danger of all republics. Hence all of them must be organized for self-defense. But the

Roman Republic was in addition organized to expand, and its duration and the empire it acquired are the proofs of its success as well as its enduring claim to honor. Machiavelli does not see the republic as centrally concerned with wealth and comfort. He lays it down that "the most useful thing a free state can bring about is to keep its citizens poor" (3.25, p. 486). Money and commerce are sources of corruption, making men want more wealth than anyone needs. Machiavelli scornfully applies the term "gentlemen" to those who "without working live in luxury on the returns from their landed possessions," contributing nothing to the common good. Men of this kind are always a danger in a republic because they try to use politics simply to increase their own power, thereby threatening the liberty of all (1.55, p. 308). It is perhaps paradoxical that for Machiavelli freedom, which the populace always wants, is at the same time the condition under which cities can most prosper.

> The reason is easy to understand, because not individual good but common good is what makes cities great. Yet without doubt this common good is thought important only in republics, because everything that advances it they act upon, and however much harm results to this or that private citizen, those benefitted by the said common good are so many that they are able to press it on against the inclination of those few who are injured by its pursuit. (2.2, p. 329)

Machiavelli thus thinks that a communitarian view of the good is the sole hope for a stable and enduring city. Such a city will be forced into expansionist warfare, but conquest will give its subjects ever more chances for honor and glory, which in turn will keep them attached to the city. A communitarian psychology underpins this. If the people are well governed, they will find their own satisfaction in their city's flourishing; if not, they will become corrupt. "Because just as good morals, if they are to be maintained, have need of the laws, so the laws, if they are to be observed, have need of good morals" (1.18, p. 241). If the people fail to make good judgments on questions of public moment, it is the rulers' fault, not theirs; this is generally true of "the sins of the people" (3.29, pp. 493–4).

A single person must be the founder of an enduring republic, Machiavelli thinks, and even he must neither rule too long nor pass on his power to his family (1.9, p. 218). It is not clear where such a person will come from and how his psyche will be formed. It is, however, clear that Machiavelli does not think of him as divine, even if the founder invokes divinities to convince others to obey him. The classical republic is a human contrivance to defy change, fate, and fortune. Even the language of just and unjust, honorable and disgraceful, *virtù* and corruption, is part of our effort to create and sustain a livable city. To do so, in a

world of insatiable appetite and endless conflict, humans need no superiors but those they can choose and dismiss.

iii. *Pyrrhonism rediscovered*

Machiavelli was not worried about skepticism, despite his concerns
about how we are to know what is good for the republic. Luther and
Calvin held that most people cannot clearly grasp the laws of nature
and that without divine revelation we cannot acquire the most important truths of all. But despite the limits they put on natural knowledge
of how to live, they were no skeptics. They never questioned the certainty of revelation, and that was certainty enough for them.

For many it was not enough. In the seventeenth century doubts were
raised about the inerrancy of the Bible and about whether anyone had
the right to control anyone else's interpretation of it. Preceding these
doubts, and providing formulations and arguments to increase them,
was a sixteenth-century revival of ancient skepticism, made newly
available to cultured readers through editions and translations of the
classics, and especially of the work of Sextus Empiricus. Skepticism
thus came to be a major concern for philosophy in the seventeenth
century, not least for moral philosophy.[5]

The version of skepticism that most influenced the sixteenth century
was that attributed originally to Pyrrho, as reported by Sextus Empiricus. The Pyrrhonic skeptic, unlike the modern descendant of the
Cartesian skeptic, was not interested in problems of epistemology for
their own sake. Like the Stoic and the Epicurean, he was in quest of the
good life, and he found it only when his repeated failures to come to
know the highest good led him to abandon the search. Knowing nothing of what was good or bad, he was no longer agitated by changing
beliefs about what to pursue or avoid, and this absence of agitation
turned out to be the tranquillity he had vainly sought. As Sextus says,
"the man who determines nothing as to what is naturally good or bad
neither shuns nor pursues anything eagerly; and in consequence he is
unperturbed."[6]

If skepticism is taken to be a way of life, like Stoicism and Epicurea-

---

5   See Popkin 1979; Burnyeat 1983, especially the essays by Burnyeat and by
Schmitt; Annas and Barnes 1985, with a useful bibliography. In what follows I am
particularly indebted to Myles Burnyeat, "Can the Skeptic Live His Skepticism," in
Burnyeat 1983. See also Burnyeat 1984. Annas, "Doing without Objective Values," in
Schofield and Striker 1986, pp. 3–29, is also a valuable discussion.
   For skepticism as a concern of the natural law theorists, see Tuck 1983, 1987.
6   Sextus Empiricus, *Outlines* I.25–8. Cf. Burnyeat 1984, pp. 241–2.

nism, the question naturally arises, Can anyone live that way? Would not the skeptic fall over a cliff or burn himself in a fire if he had no convictions about the good and the bad?[7] To this commonly made objection, there is a reply. The skeptic allows himself to be moved by "the appearances." He does not doubt that the cliff looks dangerous, or that the fire feels hot; and these appearances lead him to stay away from both. The skeptic can live, because he lives by the appearances. How are we to understand this?

Appearances, for the Pyrrhonist, are to be contrasted with beliefs about the way things are. The master skeptic has no such beliefs. He comes to this condition by working through a wide variety of arguments. In all of them he contrasts one way in which things look with another, or one claim about moral good with another, or one claim about proper law with another; and he finds no way to decide which of these appearances is true. The skeptic does not deny that there is a truth about all these things, but he finds it inaccessible. He is left with nothing but the appearances – the way things seem to him.[8] When he says he has no beliefs, he means "beliefs about the truth of the matter." He does not say that assent is altogether impossible. He assents to appearances, but that kind of assent is not belief. Belief is assent making claims about how things really are; and belief is what the skeptic does not have. Because of "the state of mind produced in the inquirer after his search," Sextus Empiricus tells us, the Skeptic School is called "suspensive" (*Outlines* I.iii).[9]

What then is included under the term "appearances?" Not simply sense impressions, but everything the skeptic may be tempted to believe, can count as an appearance. That the fire is hot, that I would be hurt if I fell off the cliff, that bigamy is wicked, that there is nothing certain – all of these are appearances. Being an appearance is, as Burnyeat puts it, "entirely independent of subject matter." The contents of the mind are not divided into sensory appearances and propositional beliefs. They are divided rather into subjective states claiming to reach truth about the way things are, and subjective states not making any such claim. Consequently, "the skeptic who adheres strictly to appearance is withdrawing to the safety of a position not open to challenge or inquiry. He may talk about anything under the sun – but only to note

7   For sources of these objections, see Burnyeat 1984, p. 248 n. 44.

8   The skeptic does not, to the best of my knowledge, raise any doubts about his ability to formulate in language the way things appear to him, or to communicate to others the way things appear to him.

9   As a result of considering the opposing appearances, Sextus says, we are supposed to be brought "firstly to a state of mental suspense and next to a state of 'unperturbedness' or quietude." *Outlines* I.iv.

how it appears to him, not to say how it really is."[10] Nonetheless, so it appears to the skeptic, this suffices for the guidance of life, and even for the attainment of tranquillity or what appears to be the good.[11]

Stoicism and Epicureanism as well as skepticism came to be used as sources of guidance for life during the early modern period. If some who accepted their teachings were deliberately seeking alternatives to Christianity, others were not. Christianized forms of all three outlooks were propagated, some of them becoming widespread among the educated. To Christianize skepticism was easier than one might think. Treat Christian doctrine as above all a matter of faith, not of proof, and it is possible to deny that there can be any evidence or rational argument in support of it while nonetheless being a devout believer. Faith may be better than knowledge.

iv. *Montaigne: Skepticism and faith*

Classical skepticism was given its most lasting modern embodiment in the widely read *Essays* of Michel de Montaigne (1533–92). He has not always been admired. In our own century he has been accused of a most unadmirable conservatism.[12] In 1815 Dugald Stewart treated him as a low-minded and commonplace skeptic, scattering his writings with "indecent levities," the first propagator of "the rudiments of a great part of the licentious philosophy of the eighteenth century," the source of a philosophy on which the "excesses of the French Revolution have entailed such merited disgrace." But even Stewart had to admit that Montaigne was widely read. "He has done more, perhaps, than any other author," he allowed, "to introduce into men's houses (if I may borrow an expression of Cicero) what is now called the new philosophy. . . . In the fashionable world, he has, for more than two centuries, maintained his place as the first of moralists."[13] Montaigne was indeed a moralist, a rich source of memorable apothegms about the human condition and how to live. But he was much more than that. He was the first to explore fully the consequences for daily life of the loss of publicly acknowl-

---

10   Burnyeat, in Burnyeat 1983, p. 128.

11   Francisco Sanches published *That Nothing Is to Be Known* in 1581; it was reprinted several times. In it he argues strongly for skeptical views, without being particularly Pyrrhonic. He says little or nothing about morality, does not see tranquillity as an outcome of skepticism, and does not attack natural law. He does argue for the right to think for oneself. Who are you to think that truth waited for you to reveal it? Well, he replies, it wasn't waiting for others either. "Nothing is new then; but if so, why did Aristotle write? Or why are we to keep silence?" (p. 169).

12   Horkheimer 1988, pp. 243–4. Page references to the *Essays* are to pages in the Frame translation.

13   Stewart 1854, pp. 100–5, 111, 107.

edged moral authority in a religiously divided world. If he exposed the
inadequacies of the European inheritance of practical wisdom, he also
articulated the questions that the new European situation made unavoidable and began to explore possible answers. His moral skepticism
was the starting point of modern moral philosophy. We have been
concerned with Montaigne's questions ever since he asked them.

Montaigne does not offer us a system of thought about morality, or
about anything else. His essays even display a refusal to think systematically. Their topics are diverse; their tone is continually altering; they
return again and again to certain questions without seeming to come to
a single consistent answer to any of them; they digress from an announced subject and do not come back. Where does it all lead? There is
no easy way of saying. The complexity is deliberate, and to highlight is
unavoidably to distort. Yet there are definite themes running through
the *Essays,* and Montaigne meant to be taken seriously as a thinker, not
only as a writer. "[W]hen I hear someone dwell on the language of these
essays," he comments, "I would rather he said nothing. This is not so
much to extol the style as to deprecate the sense" (*Essays* I.40, pp. 184–
5).

The skeptical side of Montaigne's thought is most evident in the
longest of the essays, the "Apology for Raymond Sebond." He there
repeats a large array of Pyrrhonic arguments to lead us to acknowledge
the fallibility of our senses, and the weakness of our reason. Aware of
the traps into which the skeptic may fall, he tries to avoid asserting that
we know nothing, or that everything is doubtful: it is for this reason, he
tells us, that what he wants to say is best put in the form of the question
that he took as his motto: "What do I know?" (II.12, p. 393).

His skepticism extends to morality. Attacking one claim about natural law directly, he says he can find no doctrines about right and wrong,
or about how to live, which are universally accepted. Only universal
consent would show laws to be natural.[14] "For what nature had truly
ordered for us we would without doubt follow by common consent" –
but, he adds, "Let them show me just one law of that sort – I'd like to see
it." "What am I to make," he asks, "of a virtue that I saw in credit
yesterday, that will be discredited tomorrow, and that becomes a crime
on the other side of the river? What of a truth that is bounded by these
mountains and is falsehood to the world that lives beyond?" (II.12, p.
437). In other essays Montaigne reflects on reports of distant places with
quite un-French customs, on cannibals, and on the innumerable variations of sexual practices and religious belief. Where there are all these

14 See St. Augustine, *On Christian Doctrine* 3.14, for the claim that universal
agreement on the principle "Do unto others . . ." refutes the skepticism naturally
arising from the variability of customs.

opinions, and no certain criterion for choosing among them, suspension of belief is the outcome.

He supports his skepticism in other ways as well. He presses us to admit how many purely accidental factors have a role in determining our opinions; how many of our opinions seem due to our temperament, the country we happened to have been born in, or the education and social position luck has given us. How then can we attribute much weight to our convictions? "If nature enfolds within the bounds of her ordinary progress, like all other things, also the beliefs, judgments, and opinions of men . . . what magisterial and permanent authority are we attributing to them?" (II.12, p. 433). He compares our intelligence, our morals, even our religion, to those of animals – much to our detriment. He reports the endless variety of philosophical opinion about the divine, about the soul. and about the highest good (II.12, pp. 382–3, 405–8, 435–6). Nowhere does he find anything he can rely on.

We do not understand Montaigne's position if we think of it simply as making an epistemological claim, one that might be refuted by finding a foundation for knowledge, including moral knowledge, or by showing that the skeptical arguments are fallacious. Montaigne is a fideist, using skeptical commonplaces in the service of faith. He humbles human reason in order to exalt God and divine grace. It is because we are made of nothing that we have no communication with being, Montaigne says, and because we are nothing, we can do nothing without God's assistance (II.12, pp. 455–7). Some truths are revealed by divine grace and embodied in the teaching of the Roman Catholic Church. From this point of view our proper stance in relation to God is clear.

> The first law that God ever gave to man was a law of pure obedience; it was a naked and simple commandment about which man had nothing to know or discuss; since to obey is the principal function of a reasonable soul, recognizing a heavenly superior and benefactor. From obeying and yielding spring all other virtues, as from presumption all sin. . . . The plague of man is the opinion of knowledge. That is why ignorance is so recommended by our religion as a quality suitable to belief and obedience. (II.12, pp. 359–60)

Montaigne, in short, accepts, as a matter of faith, something like a voluntarist view of the content of morality, and an Augustinian attitude toward it. But his essays are not theology. They are his own private ruminations. And because, in most un-Christian fashion, he doubts that we can have any natural knowledge of natural law, he treats morality simply as something practiced, or ignored, by most men, most of the time – not as divine legislation, but as human creation. "The laws of conscience, which we say are born of nature," he remarks, "are borne of custom. Each man, holding in inward veneration the opinions and the behavior approved and accepted around him, cannot break loose from them without remorse, or apply himself to them without self-satisfaction" (I.23, p. 83). Given the variety of customs, a Pyrrhonic skepticism about morals is an obvious outcome. But Montaigne is not satisfied with this skeptical result. He finds no tranquillity in the suspension of opinion. He is therefore driven to ask repeatedly what he can learn about how to live, when this question must be answered without supernatural aid.

v. *Montaigne's test*

Because Montaigne's interest in theories of how to live is a practical interest, he has a way of assessing the advice that European thought has so far offered. His question is always, Can I really live that way? Suppose I cannot tell whether the theories wise men have proposed are true or false. I can still ask whether their views of the good life engage me personally strongly enough to motivate me in a stable and enduring way. That is what I need to still my disquiet. Montaigne does not think he is the first to apply this test. "Pyrrho . . . tried, like all the others who were truly philosophers, to make his life correspond to his doctrine" (*Essays* II.29, p. 533).[15] But Montaigne's way of understanding the test involves novel elements, not present in the classical doctrines he considers and not of major concern to those who strove to embody them.

The ancient philosophers never thought that many people had in fact attained the wisdom required to live virtuously, nor were they concerned about the matter. But to pass Montaigne's test, a doctrine or a model must be useful for more than the rare sage. It must be able to guide ordinary people. Montaigne speaks only for himself, but he takes himself to be undistinguished either for wisdom or for virtue; and he is not interested in a doctrine that can only guide the great. "Since there are deaths good for fools, deaths good for wise men, let us find some that are good for people in between" (III.9, pp. 752–3). The great heroic acts of an Alexander are not, in this light, as useful to us as the humdrum activities of a Socrates. Alexander knows how to subdue the world. Socrates knows how to "lead the life of man in conformity with its natural condition," which is "much more general, more weighty, and more legitimate" (III.2, pp. 614, 787).[16] The frenzies and heroic ecstasies of some of the great men of the past may have enabled them to perform deeds of virtue that are beyond us. But their very achievements put

---

15   Aristotle, *Nicomachean Ethics* 1172b1–4 and 1179a19–20, makes a similar point.

16   At times even Socrates seems to set too high a standard: *Essays* III.4, p. 632.

those heroes beyond us as models. They may represent perfection of some sort; but we cannot reach so high, Montaigne says, and to try to do so would be madness, not wisdom (II.2, p. 251).[17]

Montaigne's test includes another condition that marks an even greater departure from the ancient understanding of doctrines of the good life. Aristotle thought his views should be acceptable to the wise and should agree with widely accepted views. Montaigne does not think he is wise, nor does he think there is any respectable public consensus. But for him an acceptable doctrine must be able to accommodate his own already existing convictions about what is right and what wrong, what good and what bad – not all of them, perhaps, but at least those so deeply rooted that he finds he cannot live without trying to adhere to them. To engage and move him is to engage, not just his desires and needs, but these convictions as well.

He finds out what his deepest convictions are by trying simply to portray himself honestly over a whole lifetime.[18] With Socrates he seeks to know himself: he himself must be the source of acceptable guidance. In this mood he is far from the skeptical attitude in which he feels that "humility and submissiveness alone can make a good man" and that no one should judge his duty for himself (II.12, p. 359). The more general point Montaigne is making must be kept in mind. "I set forth," he says, "a humble and inglorious life; that does not matter. You can tie up all moral philosophy with a common and private life just as well as with a life of richer stuff. Each man bears the entire form of man's estate" (III.2, p. 611).[19] In examining his life he is therefore not doing something others cannot do. The self he portrays is the self as it can be understood by experience and reflection, without the aid either of revelation or of tradition. It is the self without grace – the natural man, discovered by our natural abilities. It is therefore the self of each of us, if we choose to look.

The natural man has two aspects, which, not surprisingly, do not

---

17 "What is the use of . . . these rules that exceed our use and our strength? I often see people propose to us patterns of life which neither the proposer nor his hearers have any hope of following, or what is more, any desire to follow. . . . It would be desirable that there should be more proportion between the command and the obedience; and a goal that we cannot reach seems unjust" (*Essays* III.9, pp. 756–7).

18 This is why he did not delete or alter passages from earlier editions in later ones, but only added. The book becomes a record to be read over and over; the opinions of his old age are not to be taken as truer than those of his youth; they all help us to see him.

19 For an excellent discussion of the Aristotelian epistemology behind this statement, see Screech 1983, esp. chs. 11–15.

easily fit together. On one hand, Montaigne, like the moralists of antiquity, seeks the good in tranquillity. But if he aims at stable inner peace, he admits, with the skeptic, that we are inconstant beings. We change our opinions readily. We find it difficult to adhere to plans. Our desires shift with the wind (II.1, p. 240). Even my opinions are inconstant. Not only is there endless diversity of opinion among people, but I myself am inconstant. What I wholly believe today, I take for false tomorrow (II.12, p. 423).

Should we look outside ourselves for guidance? Customs differ from place to place and from time to time, and we are creatures of custom. Along with universal laws of nature, Montaigne dismisses the thought that we might find our good in an ideal society. It is pointless to pursue such an ideal. We can hope for civil peace only from adherence to the laws and customs of our own country. "It is the rule of rules," Montaigne says, "and the universal law of laws, that each man should observe those of the place he is in" (I.23, p. 86). This is not because its laws are good and just. "Now laws remain in credit not because they are just, but because they are laws. . . . There is nothing so grossly and widely and ordinarily faulty as the laws. Whoever obeys them because they are just, does not obey them for just the reason he should" (III.13, p. 821).

In any event, external constancy, even if we could get it, is not enough. We need some rule of life, or some advice concerning the good and how to attain it. "A man who has not directed his life as a whole toward a particular goal cannot possibly set his particular actions in order. A man who does not have a picture of the whole in his head cannot possible arrange the pieces" (II.1, p. 243). Has anyone managed to give us such a theory?

The answer, developing gradually as Montaigne tries out the different philosophies, is no. No one, not even the great wise men of the past, lived wholly in accordance with any theory. Socrates was not always wise, nor Alexander always temperate. Self-proclaimed religious believers fail to act as their doctrines direct. Their professions are one thing, their lives another, and, Montaigne says strongly, this condition is "more damnable than that of a man consistent with himself and dissolute throughout" (I.56, p. 230). A man with a truly viable theory would always show "an infallible relation between his principles and his practice" (II.1, p. 240). Montaigne consequently objects to "rules that exceed our use and our strength" and "patterns of life which neither the proposer nor his hearers have any hope of following" (III.9, p. 756).[20] Real belief shows itself in action. If we had a genuine belief in the Christian

20   Montaigne has Stoic ideals in mind, and possibly also the Lutheran interpretation of the laws of the Decalog.

God whom we profess to accept, he says, "it would appear all over: not merely our words, but also our works would bear its light and luster" (II.12, p. 322). Not only exalted doctrines must pass the test: it bears on all our lives. "If a man has any good in him, let him show it in his conduct, in his ordinary talk, in the way he loves or quarrels . . . in the conduct of his affairs and the management of his household" (II.37, p. 596).

vi. *A Montaignian ethic?*

Montaigne's test is thus exceptionally severe. It is perhaps no surprise that it seems as if the exploration of the natural man leaves us with little hope except supernatural assistance. Of course Montaigne believes such assistance is necessary; but that is not the whole story. There have been great humans, even in cases where we cannot suppose they had divine help. Socrates is one, Alexander and Cato are others. Montaigne insists that they are wholly human, and that their greatness is also wholly human. They themselves may have claimed divine inspiration or ecstatic raptures taking them out of the body and putting them into touch with divinity, but Montaigne dismisses these claims impatiently. They were on their own, neither guided nor aided by the gods. What it was in them to become is therefore also an option for us. Cato shows us "how high human virtue and constancy could go" (I.37, p. 171). Socrates, for Montaigne the most admirable of men, "did a great favor to human nature by showing how much it can do by itself" (III.12, p. 794).[21] And it is not only the great whom we can admire. "Let us look on the earth at the poor people we see scattered there, heads bowed over their toil, who know neither Aristotle nor Cato. . . . From them Nature every day draws deeds of constancy and endurance purer and harder than those that we study with such care in school" (III.12, p. 795).

Where, then, does this leave us? In the late essays Montaigne allows himself two main conclusions. First, by the end of his life he has reached some firm ideas about daily living. These apply only to himself, but Montaigne believes each of us can get as far as he has. Our own experience of ourselves, he says, is "certainly sufficient to inform us of what we need" (III.13, p. 821). This does not mean that there are plain general rules by which we can live. Montaigne has learned about human ignorance from himself, not only from Socrates, and he has not forgotten the lesson. If there are some similarities among any two things it is equally true that "every example is lame" (III.13, p. 819). We must not expect exact rules for guidance in life's difficulties. But, says Montaigne, "I have lived long enough to give an account of the practice that has

21   See Screech 1983, esp. p. 113.

guided me so far. For anyone who wants to try it I have tasted it like his cupbearer" (III.13, p. 827). What Montaigne then gives us is some casually stated indications of habits of living which he has formed. They concern sleeping and eating, enjoyment and work, what to do in illness and how to stay healthy. These are not trivial. They embody Montaigne's strongly antiascetic attitude about the pleasures of the body. We are not merely souls, he says, we are embodied souls, and to be human we must take care of both parts of ourselves. Marriage is not a second best: celibacy and the raptures of the Christian mystics are for the very few indeed.

In the second place Montaigne finds that he has some firm convictions about the rights and wrongs of action. Lying, for example, is an "accursed vice," the penalty for which can scarcely be too severe (I.9, p. 23). Torture is an abomination. So is the whole business of taking people to be witches and killing them in horrible ways. Perhaps most importantly, Montaigne insists on an acceptance of the natural self. He does not repent much. Repentance is "a disavowal of our will." Montaigne does what he does with his whole heart. He refuses, in other words, to think himself the sinful vacuity that, in his deepest despairing skepticism he held all humans to be (III.2, pp. 612, 617). Whatever any theory may or may not direct, whatever uncertainties the variability of customs from one side of the mountains to another may cause, these convictions finally escape skeptical doubt.

These then are beliefs Montaigne can be honest in professing because he can consistently keep his behavior in line with them. It may not seem like much, but Montaigne thinks it more important than anything else. "Have you been able to think out and manage your own life? You have done the greatest task of all. . . . Our great and glorious masterpiece is to live appropriately. All other things, ruling, hoarding, building, are only little appendages and props, at most" (III.13, pp. 850–1).

The account of how he has won through to a certain degree of stability in his life shows one kind of skeptical response to the appearances. After much reflection, Montaigne says, he has discovered within himself "a pattern all his own, a ruling pattern" (*une forme maistresse*), and anyone can make a similar discovery (III.2, p. 615). This is the pattern according to which he now lives. It provides all the guidance he needs. In finding the pattern Montaigne appeals only to his own experience. Within that experience he includes his reading of the classical writers. But what matters to him is his reactions to them, not any authority they have over him. "Men are diverse in inclination and strength," Montaigne says, "they must be led to their own good according to their nature and by diverse routes" (III.12, p. 805). We cannot gain much from "foreign examples." We must rather "profit from the experience we have of ourselves, which is more familiar to us, and certainly sufficient to inform us of what we need" (III.13, p. 821). Life presents him with appearances of good and ill, through books or through daily occurrences; and he accepts or rejects them according to some pattern of his own, which he is eventually able to articulate. The "forme mais-tresse" is Montaigne's own personal essence. It is not something mod-eled on an eternal or universal form.

Is it too much to call this a method of ethics? Montaigne does not claim that his particular ruling form holds for others, and it gives him no guidance for anything outside his private life. Nonetheless he thinks that the way he has found his pattern may provide his readers with a useful model. Things or ways of living present themselves, through experience or through books, as attractive or admirable; Montaigne asks if he can go along with the way the appearances draw him, if he can incorporate them in himself in a steady mode of life. His question is not whether the views of the Stoics or the Epicureans are true or false; his question is whether he finds, after reflection, that his own enduring response is acceptance or rejection.

Montaigne thus forms his pattern from his purely personal re-sponses to the way things appear to him. He uses no criterion, and thus avoids Pyrrhonic doubts about how to justify one. He simply responds, in a reasonably constant way. In his gloomier phase or mood he finds man a lowly and despicable being, dependent on God for anything he can do that is decent and upright. In the more affirmative mood that dominates the later essays, he finds himself emulating Socrates, who showed us how much human nature can do for itself. He particularly dismisses Socrates's claim to have been guided by the Delphic oracle or some mysterious inner voice. Socrates governed himself, Montaigne thinks, and he suggests that each of us can do what Socrates did. We can each have a skeptic's method of ethics.

vii. *Charron: Eclectic skepticism*

The tensions between Montaigne's attitudes often amount to con-tradictions. They are reconciled, if at all, by his treatment of them as simply parts of his life. He has lived with the feeling of abject depen-dence on God (*Essays* II.12, pp. 455–7) and with the belief that wisdom wastes her time meddling with heaven (III.12, p. 793), with the urgent need to learn how to die by studying philosophers (I.19, 20), and with the calmer belief that nature will teach him enough about dying on the spot when the time comes (III.12, p. 804). Presented as philosophical positions, the views are harder to fit together. The difficulty of doing so seems to have been no bar to the success of a book by Montaigne's disciple and adopted son, the French lawyer and priest Pierre Charron (1541–1603). His long tract *De la sagesse* (*On Wisdom*), published in 1601, reprinted many times, and translated several times into English, is an attempt to lay out in systematic form an essentially Montaignian message.[22]

Charron fails to convey important aspects of Montaigne: his questioning, seeking tone, his standing disbelief that people will ever agree about the good life, his persistent inability to find any useful and universally applicable rules for living. *On Wisdom* is blunter than the *Essays,* far more concentrated on the question of how to live, and far less charming. But Charron's very concentration and lack of subtlety enable him to bring to the fore more sharply than Montaigne's own essays do a central thought suggested by them: that a purely secular morality can be sufficient for our inner as well as our outer life.

Charron has long been said to have presented the first sketch of an ethic independent of religion.[23] The opposition his book aroused among the orthodox and his popularity with freethinking libertines of the period indicate that this is how he was read at the time. Yet the matter is perhaps not quite so simple. Charron's earlier book, *Les trois vérités* (1593) was a defense of religion, arguing that God exists, that the Christian religion is true, and that Catholicism is the best form of Christianity. There is no reason to suppose him insincere, even if his arguments were somewhat skeptical and even if the comments about religion in *On Wisdom* sound rather more so.[24] We may perhaps take him, as we may take Montaigne, as a fideist, truly accepting Catholic Christianity but doubting that any rational path to belief is available. That, at any rate, is how he presents matters in his later book.[25] There he also presents a sketch of a kind of wisdom about life that is independent of religion. His remarks about the relations between religion and the moral guidance of life given by wisdom strongly suggest that the more independent the guidance is, the better.

The frontispiece to the second edition shows wisdom as a naked woman looking in a mirror, standing on a pedestal beneath which are

---

22   I cite from the English translation, *Of Wisdom,* by Lennard, who translated the second edition. I have checked the passages I quote against the French, using the Duval edition. See Grendler 1963, p. 221, for some details on the popularity of the book.

23   See, e.g., Sabrié 1913, ch. XIII.

24   See Charron 1960 for a reading that stresses Charron's religious sincerity.

25   Thus in II.II, he extols awareness of our ignorance by claiming that "agitations and vices" spring from "that opinion of science which we thinke to have . . . from thence do spring pride, ambition, immoderate desires . . . troubles, sects, heresies." Getting rid of the belief that we know so much is the best preparation for receiving Christianity. Make men into academic and Pyrrhonian skeptics, and then show them the truth. God may then give them faith; if not, nothing will (pp. 254–5).

four chained and clothed female figures representing the passions, popular opinion, superstition, and a "pedantical science" of virtue, "with a
sullen visage, her eyelids elevated reading in a book, where was written
Yea, No."[26] Wisdom, then, is to come from self-knowledge, not from
opinions alone or from books, and not even from the Bible. The wisdom
Charron speaks of is not the mundane kind that enables shrewd people
to get on in the world, nor is it the metaphysical wisdom that the clergy
claims to give us. His wisdom comes from philosophers; it tries to
persuade, rather than to command. And we are to obtain it by looking
into ourselves in our natural condition (pref. and I.I, pp. 3–4).

The first book of *On Wisdom* is not an inquiry; it is rather an encyclopedia of what we already know about ourselves, our bodies as well as
our souls. Only after we know this much can we learn the general
principles of wisdom. Charron presents the principles in book II, and
then in book III, which is largely devoted to politics, he applies them,
organizing his views in terms of the virtues of prudence, justice, fortitude, and temperance.[27] Christian ideas have a positive role in the
discussion of justice. He takes that virtue as being concerned with giving each his due. The duties of justice are the Christian duties to God,
self, and neighbor and are summed up in the command to love our
neighbor as ourself (III.V, p. 446). Elsewhere Charron is far from drawing on religion. On the contrary: he does considerably more to display
the dangers of religion than its benefits.

In his early days Charron had been involved in the heated religious
warfare going on in France. He knew at first hand the risks a country
could run from fanatics. The piety he thinks wise consists first in acknowledging that God exists, is our creator, and exercises providential
care over his creation, and second in offering to this being a pure heart.
We should indeed engage in whatever ceremonies are standard where
we live – but we should not tie our beliefs and our feelings to them. We
must be aware that there is a difference between "pietie and probity,
religion and honesty, devotion and conscience." It is important to avoid
the view that "religion is the generality of all good" and that there is "no
other virtue or honesty but that which is opened with the key of religion." To hold that view is to be politically dangerous as well as vicious. It is to be ready for anything, even treachery, treason, and rebellion, if they can be given the color of religion. We know that there can
be religion without virtue, as the Pharisees showed us; we must affirm
also that there can be virtue without religion, "as in many philosophers
good and vertuous yet irreligious" (II.IIII [sic], pp. 299–302, 305).

26 Charron's own description, preface, sec. 6.
27 For Charron's politics see Grendler 1963; Keohane 1980, pp. 139–44; Tuck
1993, pp. 83–8.

Superstitious zealots and scholastic pedants guided by a book want us to be religious before we are honest. They think we can only be honest from fear of hell or hope of paradise. "O miserable honesty!" Charron exclaims, telling his reader to be honest because "thou canst not consent to be any other, except thou goe against thy self, thy essence, thy end" (II.IIII, pp. 303–4). And this is possible for us all because of what we are by nature, which Charron has taught us in book I.

We are, for one thing, plagued by all the weaknesses of intellect and temperament that the skeptics have described. Charron takes his language as well as his ideas from Montaigne in describing our inferiority to animals, our inconstancy and mutability, our general inability to agree with one another, the weakness of our reasoning powers, and our resulting ignorance. He adds to this, however, a more specific picture than Montaigne offered of the sources of belief, and he tries to account for the considerable differences of intellectual ability and tendency he finds among us.

Charron repeats the skeptical commonplaces about the deceptiveness of the senses while admitting that they are indispensable for knowledge. But he refuses to accept the Aristotelian and Thomistic view that nothing is in the intellect that was not first in the senses. The intellect is superior to the senses and should not "have to beg its knowledge" from such a low faculty. Moreover intellectual abilities vary far more greatly than sensory, so scientific knowledge cannot be derived solely from the senses. However much we learn from them, "the seeds of all sciences and vertues are naturally dispersed and insinuated into our spirits, so that they may be rich and merry with their own." It is these seeds that enable us to think rationally – however poorly we generally do it – and to find out what wisdom and virtue require simply by examining ourselves.[28]

Charron is quite happy to allow that the inner seeds of virtue come from God. The pattern of honesty is "this equitie and universal reason which shineth in every one of us." It is called a law of nature because God gave it to us as his first law. But the divine origin immediately sinks into unimportance. The Decalog, the Roman law, and the moral instructions the clergy offers us are all mere copies of the inner law. We need instruction as little as we need threats to lead us to act as we can see we ought. We are capable of an honesty that is "proper, inward, essential . . . not for any outward consideration or proceeding from without" (II.III, pp. 268–73). We can govern ourselves.

Can we then state the principles that we develop from the inner seeds of rationality in all of us? Here two things stand in Charron's way.

---

28 I.IX, X, pp. 39ff.; I.XIII, pp. 54–5. On Charron's theory of knowledge, see Horowitz 1971, arguing for Stoic influence.

The first is his belief that general agreement is the test of truth: "that which Nature shall have truly ordained for us, we with a common consent shall follow without doubting." If this links him with classical natural law theory, Charron promptly gives us the skeptical estimate of where the test leaves us. "Now there is not anything in the world which is not denied and contradicted, not by one nation but by divers" (I.XIV, p. 62; II.III, p. 275).[29] For this reason his only hope is that people will think for themselves, turn away from custom, convention, and popular opinion, and look within, something he repeatedly urges upon us.

Yet there is little reason to expect good results from this option. Charron believes there are deep differences in human abilities to acquire knowledge generally, and moral knowledge in particular. The difference in the amounts of heat in people's brains is a partial explanation (I.XIII, p. 55). In addition men are given different temperaments by the different places in which they are born and raised. The result is not only that some understand more, and some less. It is also that some are born to serve and obey, and others to lead. Some, like the dogmatist Aristotle, are born to accept the laws and opinions of their society without question, while others, of the school of Socrates, question, doubt, and inquire. Most people will not think for themselves, and their opinions are only those they hold due to all these natural factors. The best argument for the truth of an opinion is universal agreement on it, but "the number of fooles doth farre exceed the number of the wise." There is no rational way to get general consent, and therefore we have little hope of certain and assured truth (I.XIV, p. 62).

In short it seems that although a wisdom not dependent on religion is in principle available we will never have it in the form of statable and incontestable principles. Charron is in fact pleasantly tentative in recommending rules of wisdom. If he does not fall into the dogmatism he abhors, he remains within the commonplaces he urges us to avoid. He is not an original social or political thinker. His originality lies in his effort to work out a new view of how it might be possible to have what he called wisdom, and what we call morality.

viii. *War and morality*

Machiavelli worked out his politics to try to solve problems arising in the city-states of Italy. For Montaigne and Charron, local politics mattered less than the warfare involved in the Reformation breakup of Christendom. Despite this difference between Machiavelli and the two

---

29 Horowitz 1974 argues for the predominance of Stoic natural law theory in Charron. It is certainly there, along with many other things; but his attitude toward the availability of natural law for social purposes is far more Montaignian.

skeptics, their thought helps us to see quite clearly one of the major roots of modern moral philosophy. What frames their inquiries is an unquestioned agreement with one of the deepest assumptions of antiquity and of Christianity. All assume that the question of how we are to live must be answered in terms that show us how to attain the highest good that the individual can hope for.[30] Aquinas thinks that God has made a world in which the laws we must obey direct us to the individual as well as to the common good. Machiavelli, Montaigne, and Charron ask what guidance there can be for life without divine assurance that the same actions forward both the good of each and the good of all. The question of the highest individual good continues nonetheless to be central for them.

In Machiavelli's world politics provides the only possible answer. We must make our city into one in which each of us can find his good in being a participating citizen. If that entails warfare against other cities, so be it. For Montaigne and Charron war had become intolerable. They had no sanguine hopes that citizenship in the kind of state they lived in could provide them with the good life. And in the end, even Charron could not offer much more than Montaigne in the way of grounding political advice on norms that everyone would accept. If war makes public life hopeless, perhaps the search for one's own private good is all that makes sense.

The revived skepticism of the sixteenth and seventeenth centuries stayed within the bounds of this inherited question. But Montaigne pushed the inquiry in a new direction. He thought that there was not much point in arguing about the highest good, since we could not reasonably expect agreement about it. We must each answer the question about the highest good for ourselves. But then in a warring world a new question seems unavoidable: can we find laws that bind us all alike even if we do not agree on the good?

30 See Annas 1993 for an excellent study of ancient thought on this topic.

4

Natural law restated: Suarez and Grotius

In rejecting natural law theory, Montaigne was rejecting the dominant European understanding of universal morality. During the fifteenth and sixteenth centuries all the universities taught their students the basic points of the theory; and it was important outside the academy as well. In 1594 the Protestant Richard Hooker produced a magnificent restatement of Thomistic natural law doctrine in order to justify, against Catholics and Calvinists, his claim that the English government could rightly determine what its churches taught and how they were to be organized. Sixteenth-century Spanish Catholic theologians were prolific sources of commentary on both intellectualist and voluntarist theories of natural law. Their greatest successor was Francisco Suarez, whose early seventeenth-century synthesis was designed to support his efforts to justify papal supremacy over all baptized Christians, including such heretics as King James I, and to defend tyrannicide.[1] Hooker addressed a local issue and was influential only in England. Suarez spoke to problems of international order, and was read everywhere.[2]

Hooker restated the Thomistic belief that under a divine supervisor all things follow laws directing them to act for the common good of the universe as well as their own, and that natural law directs us in particular to both ends equally. Quietly incorporating some elements of voluntarism, he tried to make his position acceptable to Calvinists as well as to members of his own church. His presentation is accordingly eloquent rather than meticulously detailed.[3] Suarez, who reveled in technicalities, accepted some fundamental voluntarist views while claiming

---

1 He thinks tyrannicide permissible only under narrowly defined conditions. Suarez, *Selections*, pp. 697–700, 709–10. See Skinner 1978, II.176–8.

2 Nathanael Culverwell was an English disciple. He is often considered one of the Cambridge Platonists, but he held a voluntaristic view of morality, unlike the others in the group. See the introduction to Culverwell, and Darwall 1995, pp. 23–33.

3 For Hooker see McGrade's introduction to Hooker (1989), and Tuck 1993, pp. 146–53.

that he agreed in the main with St. Thomas. Like Hooker he saw himself as carrying forward an old tradition; and he felt no need to address the issues Montaigne raised. Hugo Grotius took up those issues quite directly. He created a new conception of natural law not only to serve political purposes different from those of Suarez but also to reply to contemporary skeptical worries about the very existence of laws binding all alike. Suarez was the last great exponent of the Catholic theory of natural law. Grotius was the first Protestant to claim the same conceptual space.

i. *Suarez: Will and intellect in law*

In the preface to *On Law and on God the Lawgiver* (1612), Suarez explains why the theologian must be the authority on the laws of nature.[4] The vision of God is our last end and ultimate goal, he says, and moral rectitude [*morum rectitudo*], derived in large part from obedience to the laws of nature, helps us to that goal.[5] Since salvation is at issue, natural law belongs within the domain of theology.

Suarez lays more stress than Thomas or Hooker on the difference between the laws of nature that govern us and the ways in which God governs the rest of his creation. It is only metaphorically, Suarez holds, that we speak of "laws" for inanimate things and brutes. Law properly speaking pertains only to rational beings with free wills (*De Legibus* I.III.8, I.IV.2). God is providential, governing lower things through eternal law, but in a different way. Man and nature do not form a single community of law (II.III.7).

There is no absolute necessity that law should exist. God is the only necessarily existing being. But once God created free rational beings, law is necessary because "an intellectual creature, by virtue of the very fact that he is a created being, has a superior to whose providence and control he is subject," and that control is exercised by law. In addition to being appropriate, law is useful. Created beings can turn to evil as well as to good, and laws are necessary to improve what they do to attain their divinely assigned end (I.III.2–3). Law, unlike advice or counsel, must involve the command of a superior (I.I.7, I.III.3).

---

4   Permission to publish the work was given in 1610 and 1611, and some copies are dated 1611. Copies for general distribution and sale are dated 1612. See Suarez, ed. Perena, 1971, I.xvii–xxi. Quotations in the text are from *Selections*, trans. Williams, Brown, and Waldron.

5   Suarez is always aware of "the mists exhaled from the fetid pools of the Reformers," which had infected King James of England. Suarez, *Selections*, p. 649. In counting the rectitude acquired through obeying natural law as part of the way to salvation, he is opposing the Reformation stress on faith alone.

To be a law such a command must be "a common precept," not an order to a particular individual. Law must function to direct a community, and when we are considering natural law, we have in mind simply the community of rational agents (I.VI.8, 18). All authorities agree that law aims at the good of this community (I.VII.1). Divinely given laws necessarily aim at such good, and human laws ought to aim at it (I.VII.3–4, 9). Directives that fail to meet these standards are not really laws, Suarez says, no matter what people call them (I.I.6, I.IX.4). Suarez moves beyond these Thomistic commonplaces in clarifying the nature of law.

His central concern is the relations of intellect and will in constituting law. Law is made to direct action, so it must have a "demonstrative" function, showing us what is good and what bad for a rational nature (II.VI.3). But it must also have a "preceptive" function. For "law does not merely enlighten, but also provides motive force and impels; and, in intellectual processes, the primary faculty for moving to action is the will" (I.IV.6–7). Thus any legislator, human or divine, must use both intellect and will in making law (II.V.1, II.VI.1). The question of the relation between them in divine legislation leads Suarez to the debate between intellectualists and voluntarists.

He offers Gregory of Rimini as an example of the former, taking Gregory to hold

> that even if God did not exist, or if He did not make use of reason, or if He did not judge of things correctly, nevertheless, if the same dictates of right reason dwelt within man, constantly assuring him, for example, that lying is evil, those dictates would still have the same legal character which they actually possess because they would constitute a law pointing out that evil exists intrinsically in the object. (II.VI.3)

Against this Suarez argues that we do not convict a man of a crime by showing only that he knew his act was evil. His knowledge alone is not a law. It is merely awareness of some quality in the act; and, analogously for natural law, the knowledge that an act is good or bad for a rational nature does not by itself constitute a law. Further, since God's knowledge of essences is eternal, if knowledge alone sufficed to impose a natural law, God himself would be subordinated to law; but as he has no superior, this is not possible. Finally, someone who points out the nature of something need not be a superior; he might only be a teacher. When such a person tells us that a certain act is good, he does not thereby make a law. Only someone with authority can obligate in the way that law does (II.VI.6).

On the other side, Suarez lists several philosophers who agree with Ockham "that no act is wicked save in so far as it is forbidden by God, and that there is no act incapable of becoming a good act if commanded by God." They hold also that good or evil in relation to the law of nature has its basis "in God's will, and not in a judgment of reason, even on the part of God Himself, nor in the very things which are prescribed or forbidden" (II.VI.4; cf. I.V.8). Suarez argues that this position is also wrong. It is an axiom among theologians, he says, "that certain evils are prohibited because they are evil" (II.VI.11). But then they do not become evil because they are prohibited. Those who deny this are committed to denying the eternity of essences, and this is not a tenable position. St. Augustine said that "certain acts cannot be committed with a righteous intention." He has the support of "the metaphysical principle that the nature of things is immutable in so far as their essence is concerned, and hence also, in so far as concerns the consistency or inconsistency of natural properties." Something may lose a natural property, or even gain an opposite character, but it cannot be "connatural" or normal that it should have an opposite property. Thus it cannot be normal for adultery to be righteous, because part of its essence is to be unrighteous. Even God could not make adultery normally righteous by fiat of will (II.VI.11).

Suarez's own view is a mediating position that he attributes to Thomas: "Not only does the natural law indicate what is good or evil, but furthermore, it contains its own prohibition of evil and command of good" (II.VI.5). Some things are naturally good for beings with a rational nature. But it is fitting that God, as "supreme Governor," should add his own command that we pursue them. Willing this as our governor, he creates an obligation to act, while leaving us free not to do so (II.VI.8–9). Natural law is thus preceptive because it includes God's command that we do good. Natural goodness provides the material for God's command and justifies it; the formality of command alone makes obligation supervene upon natural goodness.

Why does God command that we do what is good for us? Is he not free to give other commands? Suarez has a complex discussion of this issue, mediating once again between extreme voluntarism and pure intellectualism (II.II–IV). God can have no superior; no law imposes legal necessity of any kind on God; God may use his absolute power to disregard any law he has made for his creation. But God cannot act in opposition to his own decrees, not because of what is in the decree but because of his own nature. "[I]f he should move in opposition to an absolute decree, there would be in existence . . . contrary decrees . . . he would have willed absolutely two contradictories, a conception which is repugnant to reason" (II.II.6–7; cf. I.IX.3). Once God created humans susceptible to definite goods and ills, and capable of knowing and choosing them, he "could not have refrained from willing to forbid that [we] should commit acts intrinsically evil, nor could He have willed not to prescribe the necessary righteous acts" (II.VI.23). To do so would have defeated his own purpose in creating us.

ii. *Suarez: The law and its promulgation*

Explicitly rejecting the views of "the heretics," Suarez says that God "does not command that which is impossible." Law is essentially "practicable" (I.IX.17–18).[6] We must thus be able to know what it commands as well as to obey. But in discussing the content of the natural law Suarez does not try to show how to apply the basic principle to cases. He asks rather whether all moral directives belong to natural law as such, or only some of them; and he asks whether the law is one or many.

The subject matter of natural law, he holds, is not all the good that might be desired by humans, but only "the good which is essentially righteous [*honestum*], or necessary to righteousness" (II.VII.1). Righteousness is the condition we can strive for as our part of earning salvation; the natural law, of course, does not tell us about the supernatural grace that is also needed (II.VIII.1).[7] Suarez argues that everything concerned with moral goodness falls within the domain of natural law, not just (as some have held) the first principles. All the precepts of the Decalog, for instance, are laws of nature (II.VII.4–6). There are also natural laws concerning the virtues, imposing obligations of differing strictness for different kinds of virtue (II.VII.11–12). The ceremonial and sacramental precepts of the Bible are not, however – despite the authority of Gratian – part of the natural law. But Gratian would have been right had he said that "the natural law is the rule whereby each of us is commanded to do to another, what he would wish done to himself" (II.VII.8–9).

How, then, if at all, do these many precepts form one law? For the individual they make up a unified set because they all come together in one basic principle, or because some take precedence of others, or because they have one end as well as one lawgiver. Suarez makes no choice among these options (II.VIII.2). Considering whether there is one law for all men, however, he holds the definite view "that the natural

---

6   He also rejects the view, held by some Protestants, that the law of nature was ordained for man in his unfallen condition, and that it must now be replaced by other laws. For Suarez, "true natural precepts . . . are commonly applicable to both the incorrupted and the corrupted states" (*De Legibus* II.VIII.9).

7   Suarez argues at length that natural law "is binding in conscience" and therefore has a bearing on reward and punishment after death (*De Legibus* II.IX). Catholic theologians held that there are "purely penal" laws that do not bind in conscience. They do not impose a moral obligation to the acts they require but only to acceptance of the penalty for disobedience. Thus a monk might break a rule of his order if he were willing to pay the penalty; such disobedience is not a violation of conscience.

law in so far as it relates to its substance is one and the same among all men, but that, in so far as it concerns the knowledge of it, the law is not complete . . . among all" (II.VIII.5). Suarez here touches on the important matter of promulgation.

Promulgation of the law, he says, is "essential to a fitting and prudent providence and government over mankind" (II.VI.24; cf. II.I.1). God could not achieve his end without making his law known, but no special revelation of it is required. The natural light, through the faculty of judgment – a part of right reason – teaches us what we are to do. It also tells us that punishment will follow disobedience or sin. Reason thus shows us the law in its demonstrative and in its preceptive character; and, as such, it gives the law sufficient promulgation.

At least reason promulgates it to some people. Following Thomas (see Chapter 2.ii), Suarez distinguishes among the most general principles of the law of nature, promulgated to everyone alike; principles that he describes as "more definite and specific, which, nevertheless, are also self-evident," such as that justice must be observed and that God must be worshiped; and a third class containing inferences from principles of the first two kinds. Some moral conclusions are fairly easily grasped and are available to a large number of people, for example, that adultery and theft are wrong. But "other conclusions require more reflection, of a sort not easily within the capacity of all, as is the case with the inferences that fornication is intrinsically evil, that usury is unjust, that lying can never be justified, and the like" (II.VII.5; cf. II.VIII.3).

The law works more, Suarez adds, through these hard-to-infer proximate principles than it does through the self-evident general ones (II.VII.7). And although ignorance of the latter is not possible, ignorance of the former is. Moreover ignorance respecting the precepts that require greater reflection can be invincible, "especially," Suarez says, "on the part of the multitude." This ignorance, we are told, cannot occur or at least cannot persist "without guilt" (II.VIII.7), but we do not get from Suarez any more explicit connection between the sinfulness of our fallen nature and our ignorance of what morality requires.[8]

---

8 Culverwell makes a little more than Suarez does of the role of sin in preventing us from having full knowledge of the laws of nature. See Culverwell, p. 54, and p. 61: "those Lawes which *Nature* had engraven . . . upon the tables of their hearts, sin like a moth had eaten and defaced (as in all other men it had done)." The English Puritans had no hesitation in declaring ignorance of the law to be an effect of sin. Thus William Ames asks why we need a written promulgation of the moral law, which must surely be inscribed on our hearts, and answers that in "the state of innocency" we did not: "But ever since the corruption of our nature, such is the blindness of our understanding and perverseness of our will and disorder of our affections, that there are only some relics of that law remaining in our hearts . . . and

Suarez offers no methodical way of coming to know the laws of
nature. He does not suggest that we should use the "Do unto others"
principle to test our proposed actions. He notes without endorsing
Thomas's suggestion that the natural law must enable us to perfect all
the parts of our nature (II.VIII.4). His own view is that the law is one for
all humans because it is tied to the rational nature common to all. Thus
"the synteresis is one and the same in all men" (II.VIII.5). Conscience, as
the natural light concerned with principles, supplies such knowledge of
the laws of nature as we have. Conscience also applies the laws (cf.
II.V.14−15). If our conscience is defective, we should presumably defer
to those better equipped.

iii. *Suarez: Motives for obedience*

Suarez works with a threefold division of ways in which one person
can try to move another to action: "precept [or law], counsel and petition." A petition is usually from an inferior to a superior; counsel
"passes essentially between equals"; but precept or law "essentially
proceeds from a superior with respect to an inferior" (I.XII.4). Law,
unlike counsel, "binds and (as it were) coerces" the will (II.V.12). Binding force is "the chief, or very nearly the sole effect" of law (II.IX.1).
What then is the binding force? And how is it related to our motive or
motives for obeying?

The binding force of law is its power of justifiably imposing a requirement or obligation to act in a certain way. Different kinds of laws
have binding force over different groups of people, and require
different kinds of things. Civil law has binding force for the subjects of a
magistrate but not for citizens of other regimes. It requires external
compliance but not specific motivation. The Mosaic law has binding
force for the Jews but none for Christians. Divine positive law, stipulat-
ing ceremonies and church governance (as Suarez holds in opposition
to Hooker) binds all Christians but not infidels. The natural law has
binding force for all people. And because it carries over into the next
world, setting, in part, the terms for salvation, it requires not merely
outer obedience but also proper motivation. Suarez discusses inner
compliance when he considers what "manner of performance" of action is required by natural law.

We can conform to the natural law unwittingly and thus involuntarily, Suarez notes, but that is not enough. Natural law requires voluntary compliance. This does not mean that we are to act with pleasure

therefore by the voice and power of God it ought to be renewed as with a fresh
pencil. Therefore is there nowhere found any true right practical reason, pure and
complete in all parts, but in the written law of God" (Ames, *Conscience*, bk. v, ch. 1).

and from a firm habit, as Aristotle thinks. Some kinds of reluctance to comply are compatible with acting voluntarily; the only kind excluded is that which shows that one obeys only because forced to do so (II.X.3–4; 7). But we must think of our action in specific ways if it is to be voluntary (II.X.2). We must believe that there is a precept governing this specific act, and we must act with the thought that in doing the act we are obeying the precept. This form of willing, Suarez says, is necessary "in order that the observance of the precept may be moral, that it may be the effect of the law or precept, and that this fact may be attributed to the man himself" (II.X.5).

When we do what is prescribed, are we to will the act "because it is prescribed and with that fact as the motive for one's action?" Suarez thinks most people do not act from such a formal motive. Most act, rather, "with attention fixed upon the righteous character pertaining to the individual precepts themselves [*ad proprias honestates singulorum praeceptorum*]" (II.X.6). When we act in this manner we comply with natural law. Suarez sums up the requirement by saying that "one must act for righteousness' sake [*propter honestatem*]" (II.X.11). He does not say anything about the Thomistic view that in all voluntary action we are moved only by what we take to be the good. In speaking of concern for *honestas* rather than for *utilitas* or *bonitas,* he implies that he rejects Thomas's view. He does not, of course, deny that we are often moved by beliefs about good; but here he holds that we can be moved by the thought that a given act would be righteous because required by a specific natural law. There are further complexities about charitable action, but these, he says, can be included under the general rubric of acting for righteousness's sake (II.XI.2–3). Hence if conscience informs us adequately of the relevant precept and shows us that the case at hand falls under it, and we act with those considerations in mind, we do all that the law requires, inwardly as well as outwardly.

Suarez must have been familiar with the discussions of Lucifer's responsibility for his fall. He here takes up the dualistic position concerning motivation that Anselm and Scotus adopted in order to explain it (see Chapter 2.iii). In moral action we have a genuine option. We can pursue what we desire because we think it good, or we can act for righteousness's sake, refusing a good which it would be unjust for us to have. The natural law does not coerce us by making choice impossible. Suarez carefully distinguishes between the efficaciousness of God's will in bringing about the performance of what his law requires, and its efficaciousness in constituting obligations. God does not efficaciously will the performance of all that he requires. If he did, "all these precepts would be executed." But he does efficaciously will that there be binding force, and hence obligation, to what the natural law requires (I.IV.7–8). Natural law "as it were coerces" the will by showing those who can grasp it that they have no justifiable alternative to doing what it requires.

iv. *Grotius and religious belief*

In 1705 Christian Thomasius published a short book on the foundations of natural law. In it he paid tribute to Hugo Grotius as the founder of the discipline: "Grotius was the first to try to resuscitate and purify this most useful science, which had become completely dirtied and corrupted by scholastic filthiness, and was at its last gasp."[9] A year later, in the *Historical and Critical Account of the Science of Morality* that he prefixed to his widely read translation of Pufendorf, Jean Barbeyrac likewise gave Grotius this honor. Stimulated by Sir Francis Bacon, Grotius was "the first who broke the ice" of frozen scholastic doctrine and started a line of thought about natural law that went on, by way of Pufendorf, to a culmination in the work of John Locke (XXIX, p. 79). In 1739 Grotius was again singled out as an initiator in Friedrich Glafey's exhaustive history of natural law doctrine. With Grotius's work, he remarks, there began "a new period, in which students of natural law did nothing more than dispute about his *Law of War and Peace*, comment on it, turn it into compendia and diagrams, and finally translate it into other languages."[10]

Hugo Grotius (1583–1645) is now studied mainly by scholars of international law, who debate both his long-standing reputation as "father" of the subject and the present vitality of his teaching.[11] Historians of religious and political thought have also concerned themselves with his work.[12] Historians of moral philosophy tend to give him at most a respectful nod. But I think we must treat him instead as the earlier historians of natural law did. We should see him as making the first modern effort to rethink morality in response to the kinds of questions that Montaigne raised.

Of course Grotius himself did not understand his work in those terms. The title of his major work, *On the Law of War and Peace* (1625)

---

9   Thomasius, *Fundamenta*, pref. 1.

10   Glafey III.27, p. 111. In 1815 Dugald Stewart, who did not admire natural law theory, allowed that Grotius "gave a new direction to the studies of the learned." His work alone in the period was comparable with that of Bacon and Descartes in determining new directions of thought. Stewart 1854, pp. 170–1.

11   C. G. Roelofsen, "Grotius and the International Politics of the Seventeenth Century," in Bull, Kingsbury, and Roberts 1992, provides an excellent brief biography. See also the other essays in Bull et al. 1992.

12   For the political thought, see Tuck 1979; 1993, ch. 5.

shows quite plainly what his subject was.[13] Though Grotius did lay down principles for some areas of domestic law, contract, and other matters not directly concerned with the causes, conduct, and conclusion of war, he concentrated on the latter.[14] In spelling out the ways of discussing war, he was led to positions that we take to be of importance for moral philosophy as we now understand it, as a subject distinct from political and legal theory. Grotius was not particularly systematic in dealing with such matters, and even his admirers perceived omissions as well as errors in his work that left them much to do. "Grotius pretended not to give a complete system," Barbeyrac notes, "'Tis only occasionally that he touches upon the greatest Part of the principal points of natural Right." Barbeyrac goes on to list the topics that should be handled by anyone writing on the subject, and he suggests that later writers in the tradition, particularly Pufendorf, provided much fuller treatments of them.[15] His claim is in effect that the Grotian program for the reconstruction of natural law provided the first major positive impetus that led beyond ancient thought, beyond medieval natural law, beyond restatements of natural law theory tied to specific religious confessions, and beyond skepticism. Barbeyrac's claim is sound.

The question of exactly how, and indeed even whether, Grotius was original in his treatment of natural law has long been debated.[16] For some time he was thought, largely on the basis of a comment in the prolegomena to the *Law of War and Peace*, to have been the first writer to attempt to set forth a wholly secular theory of natural law. Having argued that there is a law of nature, he remarks that "What we have been saying would have a certain degree of validity even if we should

13   In citing *DJBP* I give first the book, chapter, section, and paragraph numbers and then the page number of the translation. The reader will note that Grotius subdivides his text one time more than was standard. I use the paragraph numbers now standard for the prolegomena, although they were not in Grotius's own text and were only introduced by his son in the edition of 1667; see Haggenmacher in Bull et al. 1992, p. 153 n. 76. I give references to *DJP* and to *The Truth of the Christian Religion* by chapter and page number.

14   Haggenmacher 1983 stresses Grotius's intention to present a systematic treatment of the law of war and peace and again in Bull et al. 1992.

15   *Historical Account* XXXI, p. 84. The topics he lists include the status of moral attributes, the characteristics of human action, the basis for attribution of responsibility, and the nature of law and its different kinds. "It would have been impossible for Grotius to have so completely restored everything that had been corrupted in this discipline," Thomasius comments, "that Pufendorf would have had no occasion to present many things more fully and thoroughly." Thomasius, *Fundamenta*, pref.

16   See Haggenmacher, in Bull et al. 1992, for a discussion of Grotius's originality on matters dealing specifically with the law of war and peace. My claim concerns his general approach to natural law.

concede that which cannot be conceded without the utmost wickedness, that there is no God, or that the affairs of men are of no concern to
him" (*DJBP*, prol. 11, p. 13). This sentence is often referred to by using
the Latin phrase for "even if we should concede," *etiamsi daremus*. It was
taken to show that Grotius was working out a system of natural law
that made no appeal to religion. But even if it had been wholly novel to
attempt such a thing, the sentence is weak evidence for the claim.
Grotius did not accept the infamous hypothesis. And the very issue
addressed by the sentence had already been debated – as we have
seen – among scholastics, including Suarez.[17] Grotius would have to
have said more than that to entitle his admirers to claim him as the first
secular natural law theorist.

   In fact if Grotius was original it is not because he was trying to show
how there could a wholly secular law of nature. There is no doubt that
he was himself a sincere Christian, despite accusations, in his lifetime
and afterward, that he deviated from Protestant orthodoxy.[18] His
discussions of natural law, in both the mature *Law of War and Peace*
(1625) and the early *Commentary on the Law of Prize and Booty* (1604),
make untroubled use of the thesis that God's creation gives us pointers
to his will. He wrote a Christian tract, *The Truth of the Christian Religion*,
(1627) designed to help mariners to sustain their own faith and to
convert infidels. Perhaps more importantly, he was working on practical issues involving relations between states, all of which officially professed to be Christian. A nonreligious treatise on law would have had
no hope of influencing any of the parties to the fierce controversies that
concerned him.[19]

   17   Villey 1968, pp. 612–13, arguing for the Stoic origins of Grotius's view, notes
a similar passage in Marcus Aurelius, *Meditations* VI.44, p. 101: "If [the gods] took no
thought for anything at all – an impious thing to believe – . . . even if it is true that
they care nothing for our mortal concerns, I am still able to take care of myself."

   18   Glafey reports that Grotius was accused of being a libertine or free thinker in
religious matters, that he was certainly an Arminian, and – still worse – that he
showed himself "not disinclined" to Roman Catholicism. Glafey III.32, p. 115. In fact
Grotius rejected the strong Calvinist doctrines of prevenient grace and predestination. He was a member of a Dutch group, the Remonstrants, who believed that the
human will had some part in gaining salvation; and it was membership in this
group, along with his political allegiances, that caused him to be sentenced to life in
prison. (He escaped, through his wife's daring maneuvers, after about two years.)
He was also active in the cause of reconciling the different religious confessions,
including the Roman, with one another – yet another reason for suspicion in an era
when strong sectarian allegiance was thought to be indispensable for a loyal subject.
See Tuck 1993, pp. 179–85.

   19   Haggenmacher, in Bull et al. 1992, p. 171 n. 129, treats the issue as anachronistic. Given that Charron was notorious for having tried to produce an ethic

There is however a striking difference between the essentials of religion as outlined in *The Truth of the Christian Religion* and the essentials as they appear in the *Law of War and Peace*. What Grotius presents in his brief religious tract is a minimal version of Christianity. All reasonable people believe that there is a God or first cause, unless their own lives are so disreputable that they fear the truth (I.2, pp. 20–1). The one God is infinite, eternal, all-perfect, and the maker of all things. Each thing tries to preserve itself and serves "also for the good and benefit of the whole [universe]" (I.3–7, pp. 21–5).[20] Evil comes from human actions, not from God. God is providential, and looks after his creation, as miracles show. And the sufferings of good men prove that there must be an afterlife in which they can receive compensation (I.21–4, pp. 87–93).

Thus much about religion in general: when, in the second book of *The Truth of the Christian Religion,* Grotius comes to Christianity he is content to say that history shows that Jesus actually lived, performed miracles, was worshiped, and was resurrected. He promised more than the Jews were promised and taught us about immortality, of which the world previously had had, at best, faint glimmerings. His moral teaching was superior to that of the pagans and the "Mahumetans." And the teachings of the pagans, Jews, and Mahumetans are faulty in various other ways. Thus Christianity is the best faith.

In the handbook Grotius makes no mention of the Trinity, the fall, sin, the need for redemption, or Christ as savior. In *On the Law of War and Peace* he holds that natural law requires even fewer articles of faith. The subject arises because, especially in dealing with non-Christian peoples, there is a question as to whether it is just to wage war in order to avenge crimes against God. God can of course take care of himself (*DJBP* II.XX.xliv.1, p. 508). But religion is so important to separate human societies and to the greater society that includes us all that the corruption of religion harms everyone (II.XX.xliv.6, p. 510). What then are the essentials that must be protected, by force if need be?

Grotius thinks that there are four points that must be avowed by all: that God is, and is one; that he is not a visible being, but a higher one; that he is providential, caring for human affairs and judging all humans; and that he created everything beside himself. These points are taught by the first table of the Decalog. They can be proved, and they can be learned even by those who cannot grasp proofs. Refusing to keep the Sabbath is tantamount to denying that God is the creator, and denying providence is equivalent to denying that God exists (*DJBP*

without religion, this is not quite right. The option was available, but Grotius did not even discuss it.

20 "Neque vero singula tantum ad peculiarem suum finem ordinantur, sed et ad communem Universi."

II.XX.xlv–xliv, pp. 510–13). Those who deny these things may be punished, but it is not just to wage war against people simply because they do not accept Christianity (II.XX.xlviii, pp. 516–17).[21]

What we need to know about God for purposes of understanding and complying with natural law excludes all sectarian doctrine. Each person can know, as an individual, what it is necessary to know about religion. Lawyers and philosophers can think through the whole theory of natural law, so there is no need for the moral theologian. It is additionally noteworthy that among the doctrines that Grotius thinks not needed to sustain society or moral order is the belief expressed in his religious tract that all things work both for their own good and for the good of the whole. There is no mention of this in *On the Law of War and Peace,* and the omission is significant. Its bearing on the question of Grotius's originality emerges from a look at the issue that moved him to write his first extended treatment of natural law.

v. *The Grotian problematic*

In 1603 a Dutch sea captain seized a Portuguese carrack as a prize. A Dutch court held a hearing on whether the ship was taken justifiably. The court decided that it was and that the East India Company, then responsible for the captain's venture, was entitled to most of the profits. Some Mennonite shareholders disputed the decision on religious grounds, and Grotius was asked to write a defense. The result was a lengthy manuscript on the law of prize and booty, most of which remained unpublished until 1864. The twelfth chapter, on the freedom of the seas, was published in 1609; but the point of interest here is made at the very beginning. It is a simple point. "It would be a waste of effort," Grotius says, "to pass judgement regarding acts whose scope is international rather than domestic – acts committed, moreover, under conditions not of peace but of war – solely on the basis of written laws" (*DJP* I, p. 6). We must find another basis. As Cicero and other ancients have said, we must appeal to a law that springs not from human edicts but from nature; not from the twelve tables of the Roman law, but "from the inmost heart of philosophy" (I. p. 7). The problem is to find a position from which to work out a reasonable settlement of a dispute over rights between warring parties of different religions. Grotius's problem forces him to a consideration of two major issues.

---

21   In *DJBP* II.XX.xlviii.3, p. 517, Grotius argues that the phrase "compel them to come in" (Luke 14.23) is not to be read in a way that licenses intolerance or efforts to coerce belief. Suarez also held that a nation's failure to accept Christianity does not warrant going to war against it.

First there are the skeptic's claims about politics. If all one can say about law and justice is that one should obey the laws of one's own country, then there can be no way of settling international disputes other than force. To show that questions of justice between nations are discussable, and to establish principled limits to the justifiability of war and prize taking, it is necessary to go beyond Montaigne and Charron.

Second, if the nations in a dispute are as widely divided on the particulars of religion as the Protestant Dutch and the Catholic Portuguese and Spanish, then no appeal to the Bible or to specific Christian doctrines will help. Each side interprets the Bible in its own way, and each has its own understanding of the details of Christian doctrine. As I noted in Chapter 3.iii, the impossibility of finding a criterion to settle such disputes was one of the sources of the strength of Pyrrhonic skepticism in the seventeenth century. An overtly atheistic morality could not possibly have the standing to serve in settling a public issue; but neither Calvin nor the Thomists could provide the kind of doctrine Grotius needed.

Skepticism was simply not an issue for the classical natural law theorists.[22] Grotius makes confrontation with it a priority. In his early work on prizes he refers briefly to a representative of ancient academic skepticism, Carneades, without seriously trying to counter his view. He attributes to him the view that justice is based only on local laws – precisely the Pyrrhonic position (*DJP* VII, pp. 76–7). In the prolegomena to *On the Law of War and Peace* he makes Carneades stand for those holding that law is never more than a matter of expediency and custom, changing with the times and reflecting the fact that men, like animals, are moved only toward what benefits themselves. Such skeptics conclude "that, consequently, there is no justice, or, if such there be, it is supreme folly" (*DJBP*, prol. 5, pp. 10–11). The skepticism here resembles Montaigne's in reducing justice to conformity to local norms.[23] But what lies behind the refutation that Grotius offers amounts to a central reformulation of natural law theory.

Grotius does not deny that humans seek their own benefit. He adds, however, that we all have "an impelling desire for society . . . not of any and every sort, but peaceful, and organized according to the measure of [our] intelligence" (*DJBP*, prol. 6, p. 11). He is not asserting the Aristotelian view that social life is an essential goal, an end that we must attain

---

22 See Tuck 1983, p. 51.

23 Carneades was not a Pyrrhonic but an academic skeptic. Grotius does no more than hint at the kind of argument he takes "Carneades" to have in mind. In common with most people during the seventeenth century, he was not careful about distinguishing kinds of skepticism.

to realize our nature.[24] We can be completely human even outside
society. Social life is something we all just want; and we would want it
even if we did not need one another's help in getting the material
necessities of life (prol. 16, p. 15). We are indeed self-seeking, but we are
sociable as well. And since we use language, and have the ability to
know and act according to general principles, we want a kind of society
different in kind from any available to animals. "The maintenance of the
social order . . . consonant with human intelligence," Grotius asserts,
"is the source of law properly so called" (prol. 7–8, pp. 11–12).

Grotius thinks no skeptic will deny either that we are prone to controversy or that we all want to live together. Nor can anyone deny that it
is possible to discover some ways of doing this that are better than
others. Hence he thinks he has based natural law on principles as clear
and evident as what the senses show when they are used under normal
conditions. Law rests on conceptions so fundamental that no one can
deny them "without doing violence to himself" (prol. 39, p. 23).
Whether or not he has refuted the skepticism he attributes to Carneades, his understanding of the depth and importance of the problem
involved in maintaining the social order leads him to a new way of
understanding natural law.

The first word in the text of *On the Law of War and Peace* itself is
"controversies" (*controversiae*), and Grotius tells us that he proposes to
discuss "such controversies, of any and every kind, as are likely to
arise" (*DJBP* I.I.i, p. 33). It is plain that he thinks humans peculiarly
prone to strife. He does not attribute this propensity to sin – as I noted,
he does not discuss sin even in his account of Christianity – and while
he deplores the present "lack of restraint" in war and the haste with
which men engage in it, he nowhere condemns it as such. Controversy,
with war as the most extreme form, is one of the facts of life. We are self-
preserving and quarrelsome beings; but we are also sociable. These two
aspects of human nature make the problem of maintaining the social
order quite definite: how are quarrelsome but socially minded beings
like ourselves to live together? What limits must we place on our tendency to controversy in order to satisfy our sociable desires? Grotius's
central thought is that the laws of nature are empirically discoverable
directives that show us how to solve this problem.[25]

24   Cf. Aristotle, *Politics* I.2, 1253a1 ff.; III.6, 1278b20–23.
25   Haggenmacher 1983, p. 618, sees the concept of controversy as the germ of
Grotius's thought and as discreetly dominating the discussion at least in book I, but
does not take it to be as central as I do in explaining Grotius's originality. See also his
essay in Bull et al. 1992, p. 169: for Grotius war stands for "a wide, philosophical
notion of human conflict." Villey 1968, p.620, stresses Grotius's belief that the function of law and of the jurist is the maintenance of order. The jurist does not try to

Grotius does not appeal to a divine manager of the universe whose governance assures us that obedience to natural law will contribute to the cosmic good while bringing us our own as well. He does not tell us that natural law points us toward perfecting our nature, or toward living as God's eternal law requires. He considers only the empirical data about human conflict and its resolution. We all want sociable living, yet a concern for our own benefit works against getting it. Natural law shows us how to manage.

Is the sociable living that we all want the good, or the highest good? Grotius does not ask. He is content to appeal only to what we can see that people pursue. In one of the most astonishing passages in the whole of *On the Law of War and Peace*, Grotius dismisses in one sentence the core questions of ancient political and moral thought:

> Just as, in fact, there are many ways of living, one being better than another, and out of so many ways of living each is free to select that which he prefers, so also a people can select the form of government it wishes; and the extent of its legal right in the matter is not to be measured by the superior excellence of this or that form of government, in regard to which different men hold different views, but by its free choice. (*DJBP* I.III.viii.2, p. 104)[26]

If nothing else is original in Grotius, his way of construing the problem that gives natural law its point is. What made Grotius's successors into a distinctively modern school of natural law was their acceptance of the Grotian problematic.

vi. *"Even if we should concede . . ."*

The famous *etiamsi daremus* sentence says that even if God did not exist we would be under binding obligations to do whatever makes social life possible. In a footnote to this passage in his translation of *On the Law of War and Peace*, Barbeyrac objects. No, he says, "to speak exactly, the *duty* and obligation, or the indispensable necessity of conforming to these ideas and maxims [about social life] necessarily supposes a superior power, a supreme master of mankind."[27] Suarez accepted a view like this, which stems, as I have indicated, from the

distribute just shares of goods to everyone. His task is negative. "It is most significant that Grotius envisages law from the point of view of war, of the violence (public or private) which it is necessary to limit or to suppress before its birth. . . . Morality is the instrument of order and of social peace." This, says Villey, is what the new ruling class wanted: peace as a condition of security for their possessions.

26 See Tuck 1993, pp. 193–4, for the political issues behind this statement.
27 Grotius 1738, p. xix n.

voluntarist position. Barbeyrac's objection thus raises two related questions about Grotius's view. To what extent, if at all, is he a voluntarist? And what is his theory of obligation?[28]

Grotius follows the scholastic tradition in distinguishing counsel or advice from obligation (*DJBP* I.I.ix.1, p. 38). He follows it as well in ascribing an important role to right reason. And what he says about reason and obligation seems to make it clear that he does not accept an extreme voluntarist position. The law of nature is "a dictate of right reason," which shows us "that an act, according as it is or is not in conformity with rational nature, has in it a quality of moral baseness or moral necessity; and that, in consequence, such an act is either forbidden or enjoined by the author of nature, God." This sounds like Suarez; but in the next sentence Grotius specifically asserts that such acts are "in themselves either obligatory or not permissible" and that God necessarily directs us according to these qualities (I.I.x.1–2, pp. 38–9).

If the remark that acts can be inherently obligatory is opposed to voluntarism, other comments are not. Thus Grotius holds that "the free will of God" is a source of law beyond nature, since God willed us to exist with our special traits (prol. 12, p. 14). This sounds like the voluntarist view that God was free to create beings with any nature but once having created beings with our nature could not on pain of contradiction will any other laws for us than those which conform to it. Grotius seems more decisive in a passage in which he declares that the law of nature cannot be changed, even by God. "Just as even God, then, cannot cause that two and two should not make four, so He cannot cause that which is intrinsically evil to be not evil" (I.I.x.5, p. 40). But this is not decisive unless being good is equivalent to, or entails, being obligatory; and that is exactly what is at issue.

What then are we to conclude? The general tenor of his remarks is opposed to voluntarism, and Grotius's readers all took him to be opposed to it.[29] By the time of *On the Law of War and Peace,* he knew Suarez's compromise position and could have accepted it. The fact that he did not even discuss the matter may indicate that he did not intend to go as far as Suarez went in accepting voluntarism. It may also show that he thought that discussion of such theological issues would not help in working out laws of war and peace acceptable to all parties.[30]

---

28   See Tuck 1993, ch. 5, for Grotius's changes of mind on this issue, and note 30 for further discussion.

29   So Pufendorf, as we shall see in Chapter 7; and so Stewart 1854, pp. 173–4.

30   Haggenmacher 1983 thinks Grotius more voluntaristic than I here allow. Like Tuck 1993, he appeals to *DJP*, where matters seem at first to be somewhat different. Grotius opens his formal derivation of laws of nature by declaring that first place belongs to the rule "What God has shown to be His Will, that is law" (*DJP* II, p. 8).

He is therefore left with the problem of explaining exactly how acknowledging an obligation differs from noting goods and ills. But he
says nothing about the matter. Barbeyrac, writing a century later, offers
an excuse for him. Even today, he says, famous writers suppose that
rules of morality impose obligation all by themselves. It is not surprising, therefore, that the notions of a pioneer like Grotius "are not entirely
just." And Barbeyrac points out what is at stake here. If rules impose
obligation independently of the will of God, then it is not clear why
God's will must be invoked at all. "The will and authority of God would
. . . be no more than a sort of accessory, which, at most, would only
make the obligation stronger."[31] Barbeyrac fears that God would then
be irrelevant to morality. Grotius's refusal to call openly either on the
voluntarist God who creates morality by fiat, or on the intellectualist
God who keeps the universe in moral order, gives point to the fear. The
nature of obligation and of God's involvement in morality posed unavoidable questions for later Grotians.

vii. *The insufficiency of virtue*

Grotius presents himself as trying, for the first time, to produce a
systematic understanding of the laws governing the relations of states
(*DJBP*, prol. 1, p. 9). There are two ways to ground a theory. One is to
give a priori proofs starting from self-evident truths, thereby showing
what is in necessary agreement with "a rational and social nature." The
self-evident or a priori truths Grotius has in mind are, however, learned
from experience, of the kind all people have.[32] He thinks them comparable in certainty, as I have noted, with what the senses show us under

---

The divine will is revealed preeminently in the world itself, understood as designed
by its creator. We might take this to indicate that for Grotius God is untrammeled in
creating the world with the nature that it has, but once having created it as it is, he
must on pain of contradiction lay down for us the laws that fit the nature he gave us.
This would indeed show Grotius to be closer to voluntarism than he seems to be in
DJBP. But what Grotius cites as authority for his statement that God's will is law is St.
Thomas's claim that there are in God's mind exemplars serving as eternal patterns of
everything he creates, and that the exemplar of his wisdom is law. Will is not
mentioned (*ST* Ia.IIa.93.1).

    In his essay in Bull et al. 1992, Haggenmacher makes less of the role of voluntar-
ism in *DJBP*, in which, he says, "Grotius's obvious implication was to play the
volitional element down . . . and he was usually understood in that way by his
successors" (p. 171 n. 129).

    31   Grotius 1738, note to I.I.x.2, pp. 10–11.
    32   Grotius cites Romans 2.14–15 only once in *DJBP*, at I.I.xvi.6, p. 47, as part of
an argument to show that Christians are not now bound by the Jewish law. He makes
no use of it to show that knowledge of natural law is self-evident because innate.

proper conditions; but his model of proof is mathematical. And in fact Grotius likens himself, somewhat disingenuously, to a mathematician, ignoring particular issues and controversies and dealing impartially with abstract theory (prol. 58, pp. 29–30).[33] The second way is to give a posteriori proof, drawn from the general agreement of the learned and the civilized of all times. Grotius does this by profuse quotation of authorities. General consent is available once we clearly distinguish laws of nature from municipal laws and the law of nations, which spring from human will (I.I.xii.1–2, pp. 42–3; prol. 39–41, pp. 23–4). It is significant that he feels that he must clear away the views of one dissenting authority before he can proceed: the position of Aristotle on the virtue of justice.

In his early work on prize and booty, Grotius accepts the idea that virtue is a mean and cites Aristotle as his authority for saying that "Justice consists in taking a middle course." He takes this to mean that "it is wrong to inflict injury, but it is also wrong to endure injury" (DJP I, pp. 23). If this is not exactly pure Aristotle, it does point in the direction of Grotius's later position. In the prolegomena to On the Law of War and Peace he devotes three paragraphs to a criticism of Aristotle's doctrine that virtue consists in a mean in passion and action. The theory of the mean is one way of bringing out an important point of difference between understanding morality as centering on virtue and taking it as essentially centered on law. It articulates the virtue theorist's belief that no antecedently statable set of rules or laws can substitute for the moral knowledge the virtuous agent possesses. Grotius plainly wants nothing to do with it.

His criticisms are brief. The doctrine of the mean is implausible for virtues such as truthfulness (supposedly a mean between boastfulness and dissimulation) (DJBP, prol. 43, p. 25). It cannot even be made to work when it tries to account for justice. Aristotle himself, says Grotius, could not point to a mean in any appropriate passion, or any action coming from the passions, that could plausibly be said to constitute justice. So he resorted to making claims about the things justice is concerned with – possessions, honors, security – because only about these would it be reasonable to say that there could be a too much or a too little. Even here, Grotius continues, the doctrine of the mean fails. A single example shows this. It may be a fault not to take what is my own property; but it is surely not doing an injustice to another to claim less than is mine.[34]

---

33 On the significance of using a mathematical model, see Tuck 1993, pp. 171–2.
34 The fault Grotius had in mind, as DJP shows (IV, p. 49), is that of harming one's country by refusing to take a prize that is justly yours, and that would help

Justice consists wholly in "abstaining from that which is another's." Grotius adds that "it does not matter whether injustice arises from avarice, from lust, from anger, or from ill-advised compassion." What matters is only whether one is taking what another has a right to. He concedes that some virtues do keep passions under control, but this is not due to the nature of virtue. It is due, rather, to the fact that "right reason, which virtue everywhere follows," sometimes prescribes moderation. At other times, as in worshiping God, or in hoping for eternal bliss, it does not. These cannot be excessive, any more than hatred of sin can be too great (*DJBP,* prol. 44–5, pp. 25–6).[35]

The immediate target of the attack, the doctrine of the mean, need not form part of a virtue-centered theory, but Grotius is rejecting more than that doctrine. He is saying that a central feature of theories centering on virtue is wrong. The point of justice has nothing to do with the agent's motives. To be just is simply to have the habit of following right reason with respect to the rights of others. Since right reason shows us the laws of nature, Grotius is assimilating virtue to obedience to law, as we have seen St. Thomas do. But more emphatically than his predecessors, he says that it does not matter why the agent has and sustains the habit. And rights, as we shall see, are not, for Grotius, the kind of good that virtuous dispositions regard. Rights are or spring from – Grotius is not entirely clear – a special moral attribute attaching to human nature, which even God must respect. They make acts required or forbidden regardless of the good brought about by respecting them.

Grotius later rejects another aspect of the Aristotelian ethics of virtue, its attribution of special moral insight to the virtuous agent. He does not think the laws of nature determine what we are to do down to the last detail. Where the law is indeterminate, however, what operates is not insight but discretion.[36] In such cases we make nonmoral choices among permissible acts. Grotius brings this out in direct confrontation with Aristotelianism. Because so many complexities enter into morals,

defray war costs. See Hardie 1968, pp. 182–4, 186, for some pertinent comments on this kind of criticism.

35   St. Thomas, *ST* IIa.IIae.27.6, argues that the theological virtues, faith, hope, and charity, cannot be excessive. In *On Charity* he says that the theological virtues are not means between extremes, and that only the moral virtues are: article II, reply 10 and 13, p. 31. That God cannot be loved inordinately is also a point of Scotus's, as I noted in Chapter 2.iii.

36   Aristotle, *Nicomachean Ethics* 1106b29–33, says: "there are many ways to be in error . . . but there is only one way to be correct . . . that is why it is easy to miss the target and hard to hit it." The earlier natural lawyers discuss the possibility of interpreting law to fit hard cases under the heading of *epieikeia,* but it is not clear that this is the same as Grotius's notion of discretion. See Suarez, *De Legibus* II.XVI.

he says, and circumstances always alter cases, it comes about "that between what should be done and what it is wrong to do there is a mean, that which is permissible; and this is now closer to the former, now to the latter. . . . This is what Aristotle means when he says: 'Oftentimes it is hard to decide what choice one should make'" (*DJBP* II.XX-III.i, p. 557). The virtuous are simply those who obey the law where it is specific, and stay within the bounds of the permissible where it leaves room for discretion. In the Grotian morality of rule and act there is no room for any special cognitive ability arising from virtue.

viii. *Rights and community*

St. Thomas treated the virtues of prudence, temperance, and courage as having to do with the inner condition of the agent, and justice as covering the whole of our relations to other persons (*ST* Ia.IIae.66.4). Even our relations to God fall under this heading (IIa.IIae.80.1).[37] Luther held that rational natural law could direct only our outer behavior and had nothing valid to say about that inner life which religion alone can enable us to understand. Grotius rejects both these views.

Dugald Stewart notes that while justice can easily be treated as a matter of explicit rules, the modern natural lawyers aimed to treat all the virtues in this way, as definable in terms of rights and duties. Pufendorf, he says, was the main proponent of this view but Grotius was the first. One of the tools was his distinction between perfect and imperfect rights.[38] In the form in which he introduces this distinction, Grotius was indeed original.[39] Stewart's comment indicates the significance of some of the technicalities involved in it.

A right, Grotius says, is "a moral quality of a person, making it possible to have or do something lawfully" (*DJBP* I.I.iv, p. 35). Laws, we know, tell us what is or is not in accordance with the kind of society of

37 I am indebted to Mahoney 1987, pp. 247–53, for drawing my attention to the importance of this point.

38 Stewart 1854, pp. 175–7. He points out also that Grotius did not do a very thorough job in working out the theory.

39 St. Thomas distinguishes between perfect and imperfect virtues, but he is not making the same kind of point that Grotius makes (*ST*. I.65.1). An approach to Grotius's concern is suggested in Seneca's discussion, in *On Benefits,* III.5–14, of whether ingratitude should be punished. Suarez, *De Legibus* II.viii.11–12, makes a distinction somewhat close to Grotius's; he comes even closer in his brief treatment of negative and positive precepts at II.IX.9. The structure of the problem handled by Grotius's distinction is clear in Duns Scotus's treatment of the obligation to keep the Sabbath, noted in Chapter 2.iii n. 11, which Suarez follows in discussing the third commandment (II.XV.23). I cannot trace discussion of duties with this structure any further back.

rational beings that we all want. They do so in the first instance in a negative way. That is lawful which is not unjust; and to be unjust is simply to violate rights (I.I.iii.1, p. 34). Taking someone's property, not returning someone's property, not keeping one's word, not punishing a violator of rights – these are the fundamental injustices (prol. 8, p. 12). It is easy to see that among needy beings prone to conflict such unjust acts would be sufficiently disruptive to make community impossible, and so would be out of harmony with human nature. Thus, for Grotius, law points to good but is defined, not in terms of good, but in terms of injustice.

There are for Grotius two kinds of rights, perfect and imperfect. When the moral quality of having a right is complete, the agent has a perfect right, also called a legal right or a right strictly speaking. A perfect right gives rise to the kind of law under which people have strict obligations. As we would expect, justice is concerned with perfect rights and the obligations arising from them. The violation of perfect rights gives just cause for war, and also for the use of lesser degrees of force (*DJBP* II.I.i–vii, pp. 169–75; cf. I.II.i.4–6, pp. 52–4).[40] The possessor of such a right may therefore protect it through law courts if available, by other means if necessary. An imperfect right, by contrast, is an agent's "aptitude" or worthiness to possess or control something. This kind of right is associated, not with strict obligation, but with "those virtues which have as their purpose to do good to others," for example, generosity and compassion (I.I.iii–x.4, pp. 34–9). Grotius does not treat these rights as enforceable, but he does suggest, in scattered passages, that there is a law associated with them.

He calls it the law of love, or a rule of love. It is in accordance with "the law of a well-ordered love" that innocent persons should receive goods before guilty ones (*DJBP* I.II.viii.10, p. 75). If you are selling grain, and you know a large shipment is about to arrive, you do not have a strict obligation to tell the news to a prospective purchaser; but to do so would be praiseworthy, and failure to do so would be against "the rule

---

40   I do not think Grotius intends to make it true by definition that a perfect right is one that may be secured by the use of force. (Grotius is indifferent to questions of this kind, though his successors were not.) It is a fact, if a deeply rooted one, that people tend to violate such rights, which can often only give security if forceful protection is available.

The right to kill in defense of chastity is not open to doubt, Grotius says (*DJBP* II.I.vii, p. 175); but he does not definitely say that rape is contrary to a strict law of nature. Discussing the law of nations (which is not part of the law of nature), he seems to side with those who condemn rape not because of the injury to the victim but because of "the unrestrained lust of the act" (*DJBP* III.IV.xix.1–2, pp. 656–7). But he adds nothing about what the law of nature says concerning it.

of love" (II.XII.ix.2, p. 347). The law of love is not a law properly so
called. A citizen of a besieged city, who by giving himself up to the
enemy would cause the siege to be lifted, is not strictly obligated to the
sacrifice, but "it does not follow also that love permits him to do otherwise." If the heroic deed is not required by strict justice, it is praiseworthy, and perhaps its omission is even blameworthy (II.XXV.iii.3, p. 579).

There are a few other places where Grotius distinguishes between
the obligatory and the praiseworthy (*DJBP* I.II.i.3, p. 52), although he
does not elaborate either this distinction or that between laws of justice
and a law of love. But it is significant that he treats the law of love as on
an equal footing with the law of justice. Everyone may be expected to
observe both. There is no claim that any special grace is required for
compliance with the latter, as there is, for instance, in Calvin. The laws
of love and justice mark off realms of enforceable and unenforceable
obligations within one community; they do not separate two
kingdoms.[41]

Grotius's view of society is deeply shaped by his theory of rights.
They are the part of our rational and sociable nature which God respects in enjoining or forbidding certain kinds of conduct. They belong
to us, therefore, regardless of the good or ill that their possession entails.
This sets the Grotian theory apart from earlier views of rights that
explained them as created by laws. On this view laws assign people
various tasks or positions, which carry with them specific duties and
therefore the right to do or have whatever is required for carrying out
those duties. If the laws involved are classical laws of nature, they will
assign those duties with an eye to a common good as well as to the good
of each performer. Rights, in such a case, would be moral qualities
assigned to individuals because of the usefulness of that assignment.
But Grotius does not treat them this way. He treats them as qualities
grounding law, not as derived from law. They are personal possessions,
belonging to each of us prior to and independently of our belonging to
any community.

Because our rights are our property, they can be given up or traded
away. However this alienability is to be explained, it makes rights at
best an ambivalent blessing.[42] They provide no guarantee against per-

41 Calvin discusses the "precepts of love" in connection with property in *Institutes* III.X.5. Grace is requisite for compliance with them, because "he who merely
performs all the duties of love does not fulfill them, even though he overlooks none;
but he, rather, fulfills them who does this from a sincere feeling of love" (*Institutes*
III.VII.7), which, of course, the unredeemed cannot have.

Suarez allows that there is some natural love of God, discussing actions springing
from it briefly in *De Legibus* II.XI.1–5.

42 On this last point see esp. Tuck 1979, pp. 77–81.

sonal slavery or governmental authority. Just as "every man is permitted to enslave himself to anyone he pleases," so also a community may do so. A community, like an individual, might prefer slavery to death (*DJBP* I.III.viii.1–3, pp. 103–4). Thus political authority need not arise from consent. It can equally well arise from conquest,or from a community's justifiable doubts about whether it is capable of governing itself, or from transfer from one ruler to another. Moreover, not all rule is for the benefit of the governed. A good deal of it is for the good of the ruler. And there is really nothing for the people to do but endure it. The people must obey whether the king governs well or not (I.III.viii.8–15, ix.1–2, pp. 106–11). Grotius's suggestion is that having a society is what matters, and that to have it one must be prepared to pay a high price.

It is common to say that Grotius is one of the founders of individualism. His view of rights may or may not be an entirely innovative one.[43] But it is through him that the idea of rights as natural attributes of individuals came to occupy a commanding place in modern European thought. Grotius also makes the individual's right to pursue his own good one central pillar of society. Life in a community is, however, equally important. We may start each with our own rights and a self-preservative desire to see them observed.[44] But we want to end by living with one another. Laws reflect our rights in order to enable us to form communities. And we want society for its own sake. The laws of nature include the law of love. They are not based simply on expediency, though they have its backing (*DJBP*, prol. 16, p. 15). They are so deeply rooted in our nature as sociable rational beings, created as such by God, that it is self-defeating to flout them. Despite Carneades, it is not those who obey nature's laws who are foolish, but those who ignore them to pursue private interests. Grotius is far from ignoring the importance to us of living in community. What is at the center of his concerns, however, is the difficulty of doing so. The history of the world since 1914 suggests that we have not yet found how to make it easier.

43   See Tuck 1979. Villey 1957 argues that nominalist thinkers, denying that anything but particulars exist, treated individual rights as inhering in individuals, with laws being no more than summary statements of what rights there are. His position is criticized in Tierney 1988, which gives numerous references; see also Tierney's discussion of Tuck, Tierney 1983, 1989. Kobusch 1993, pp. 31–7, gives a brief review.

44   Like so many others, Grotius ignores the fact that we start as newborn babies.

5

Grotianism at the limit: Hobbes

Grotius removed natural law from the jurisdiction of the moral theologian, to whom Suarez assigned it, and made its theory the responsibility of lawyers and philosophers. Numerous Protestant writers on ethics and the foundations of politics followed him in using the language of natural law while detaching it from the specific doctrines of any particular religious confession, whether Protestant or Catholic. If in a broad sense they are all Grotians, some of them accepted more from the master than others. There were, of course, commentators and interpreters who confined themselves to explaining and defending Grotius's view. The Grotians who made a difference, however, did more than that.

In this chapter and the next I consider two Protestant natural law theorists who took Grotianism to its limits, or beyond: Thomas Hobbes and his critic, Richard Cumberland. Both of them were widely read, but neither founded a school. Insofar as there was a Grotian orthodoxy beyond the writings of the commentators, it derived from the position elaborated by Samuel Pufendorf, which I discuss in Chapter 7. Departing on some matters from Grotius, Pufendorf avoided the extreme positions of both Hobbes and Cumberland. He was accused of being a political trimmer in his life and an eclectic in his theory, but he became the most widely studied natural law theorist identified as a Grotian. Hobbes and Cumberland originated views whose descendants are still live options for us. Pufendorf's theory is dead. We need to know about all three in order to understand the varied seventeenth-century effects of the Grotian impetus.

i. *Desire and conflict*

In 1676 Samuel Rachel, a German jurisprudentialist, published a treatise on the law of nature and of nations in which he spent some seventeen pages answering Grotius's objections to Aristotle on virtue. Though highly critical of Grotius's theory, he plainly respected the man. But he could not limit his wrath when he came to consider his next opponent. "We will give the last place to Thomas Hobbes," Rachel said, "for filth falls on the hindmost. . . . Never . . . have I lighted on any writer who has put before the world views more foolish or more foul." The intemperance was not uncommon among Hobbes's critics, nor was Rachel's charge that Hobbes deliberately misused his talents in order to forward atheism, tyranny, and "every kind of wickedness."[1]

Hobbes's books were widely read and he had followers and admirers in his lifetime.[2] But some of those who, like Pufendorf, adopted elements of his theory still took pains to distance themselves from him; and his enemies were more numerous and far more vocal than his supporters. Hobbes's theories were not merely shocking to delicate sensibilities. They aroused lasting hatred and fear in some of the strongest thinkers of the time. Starting with a problem whose existence everyone admitted, he supported solutions few wanted to accept with arguments no one could easily refute. Many tried to find basic flaws in his theories; and the controversies continue. No other seventeenth-century moral philosopher has stimulated as large a body of current commentary, defense, attack, and creative reformulation.[3]

Like Grotius Hobbes wrote about war and peace; but his concern was civil rather than international strife. He lived through the horrendous English civil war and experienced many of its consequences himself. A late statement shows the central place it had in his thinking:

> the utility of moral and civil philosophy is to be estimated, not so much by the commodities we have by knowing these sciences, as by the calamities we receive from not knowing them. Now, all such calamities as may be avoided by human industry, arise from war, but chiefly from civil war. . . . The cause . . . of civil war is, that men know not the causes neither of war nor peace, there being but few in the world that have learned those duties which unite and keep men in peace, that is to say, that have learned the rules of civil life sufficiently. Now, the knowledge of these rules is moral philosophy. (*De Corpore* 1.7)

Philosophy, for Hobbes, is the rational discovery of connections of causes and effects "to the end to be able to produce . . . such Effects, as

1 Rachel, pp. 71–5.

2 See Bowle 1951 and Mintz 1969 for the negative reactions. See Skinner 1965–6, 1972, and Jacoby, in King 1993, vol. I, for positive responses. Hobbes acquired an early reputation as an important scientific writer; it was his work on morals, politics, and religion that caused him to be so vituperated. See Malcolm, "Hobbes and the Royal Society," in Rogers and Ryan 1988.

3 The interest in Hobbes as a source of positive ideas for moral philosophy is largely a twentieth-century development. See Sacksteder 1982, and Curley 1990 for bibliography, and King 1993 for reprints of a large selection of articles published between 1922 and 1988.

humane life requireth" (*Leviathan* XLVI.1).[4] What we chiefly require is peace. The point of moral philosophy is to enable us to keep our society from disintegrating under the stresses produced by human nature.[5]

Because he thinks that war is caused by ignorance, Hobbes says more about the causes of human conflict than Grotius does. At the center of his analysis is his view of the passions and desires. His psychology is intimately tied to his physics. The best way to think of the physical world is to conceive it as composed simply of indivisible atoms moving in space. Individual persons are to be understood as groups of atoms moving in persistent clusters. We are alive as long as certain motions, vital motions, continue within the cluster that is our body. Hobbes defines desire and aversion in terms of the smallest motions – the "endeavors" – of the atoms that constitute us. When we are moved toward some perceived or imagined object we say that we desire it, and conversely with aversion; of what moves us not at all we say that it is contemptible. When we are moved toward something, we call that toward which we are moved "good." Thus we do not desire something because we think it good. We think it good simply because the thought of it moves us to get it (*Leviathan* VI).

Desire and aversion are thus tied directly to the motion that constitutes life. Consequently Hobbes does not think of moral philosophy in terms of the search for the human highest good or final end. Going beyond Grotius, who simply sets the issue aside, Hobbes flatly asserts that "there is no such *Finis ultimis* (utmost ayme,) nor *Summum bonum,* (greatest Good,) as is spoken of in the Books of the old Moral Philosophers" (*Leviathan* XI.1).[6] Aquinas's description of the condition we would be in if we attained the highest good shows why Hobbes had no use for the concept. For Aquinas, as I have noted, we are made by God to find our good only in him. Ignorance makes us believe we want other, earthly, goods, but we remain dissatisfied when we get them.

---

4 To facilitate references to *Leviathan,* I use the paragraph numbers Curley inserts in each chapter, although they were not used by Hobbes.

5 I think that the problem, often discussed, of how on Hobbes's view we might get out of a state of nature is not a real problem for him. As the remark just cited shows, he thinks the point of moral philosophy is to help us to avoid falling into a state of nature. He addresses people who are already in a society, under a sovereign. Otherwise he could hardly be writing books, in language that is conventional and not given by nature, with the aim of teaching us the costs of the dissolution of society and the means to prevent it. Moral philosophy gives the individual rules for avoiding danger and death (*Leviathan* XXX.21). To society it gives rules for avoiding anarchy (*Leviathan* XXXI.1).

6 For this reason, among others, Hobbes is not an Epicurean, as some of his enemies tried to portray him, since Epicureanism is tied to the search for the highest good.

"Man is not perfectly happy," Aquinas says, "so long as something remains for him to desire and seek" (*ST* Ia.IIae.3.8). Once we know God, we will desire nothing more. But for Hobbes the absence of desire is the absence of motion, and that is, simply, death. Felicity lies rather in seeking and obtaining whatever we happen to want. "For there is no such thing as perpetual Tranquillity of mind, while we live here; because Life itself is but perpetual motion" (*Leviathan* VI.58).

Hobbesian desires prevent us not only from having a final end but also from having naturally common or harmonious ends. In advancing the psychology that yields this conclusion Hobbes is rejecting the Stoic theory of desire and passion. According to Plutarch, the Stoics say that "passion is no different from reason . . . For appetite and anger and fear and all such things are corrupt opinions and judgments" (Long/Sedley, p. 412). When we think of something as good, however confused or mistaken we may be, that thought is an impulse to try to obtain the thing. The Stoics, Stobaeus reports, say that "all impulses are acts of assent, and the practical impulses also contain motive power . . . propositions are the objects of acts of assent, but impulses are directed toward predicates which are contained in a sense in the propositions" (Long/Sedley, p. 197). Thinking that something has the predicate "good" constitutes having an impulse toward it. Hence for the Stoics we desire what we think good because we think it good.

Hobbesian desires, however, are not propositional in the Stoic way. They are compounds of movement toward or away from something – desire or aversion – with a thought that causes such movements. The endeavor that is the moving part of the desire or aversion is not the same as the thought of the object. Hobbes's definitions of desires and aversions show how our words assemble the ideas we get from experience of the usual causal connections between movements and the thoughts that cause them. Desire caused by the opinion that you will get what you want is called "hope"; aversion together with "opinion of *hurt* from the object" is fear; "covetousness" is "desire of riches" (*Leviathan* VI.14, 16, 23). A thought may arouse desire or aversion in some people but not others, or in one person at some times but not others. The propositionality that Hobbes incorporates in his definitions should not conceal the basic theoretical point, that desires are causal forces. They stem from the interaction between our bodies and causal chains originating outside them, and they determine literally our every move.

The Stoics thought the world was infused by rational deity and was consequently ordered toward harmony. If our desires represented the world and the goods in it accurately, we would live harmoniously, finding a highest good for ourselves which could be shared with all other like-minded people. Hobbes has no such view. Physical laws like those Galileo discovered hold no promise of humanly meaningful order. Since our desires are simply part of the physical world, there is no reason to suppose that any two people will naturally desire or be averse to the same things. There is no "common Rule of Good and Evill, to be taken from the nature of the objects themselves." Rules for avoiding civil war can come only from some other source (*Leviathan* VI.1–7).

In explaining what moves us to live with one another, Hobbes not only departs from Aristotle; he goes beyond the limits of Grotianism. He rejects the idea of natural sociability. We are not "by nature" political beings, we have no natural desire to come together, and we are not moved to society by love of other people. "We doe not therefore by nature seek Society for its own sake, but that we may receive some Honour or Profit from it; these we desire Primarily, that Secondarily" (*De Cive* I.2).[7] Although self-interest thus causes us to form societies, it also causes the immense difficulties we have in sustaining them. Selfishness seems, in fact, to be the main and perhaps sole operative human motive.

Hobbes's statements on the extent of human egoism vary, however, and so do interpretations of his theory. At times he asserts what seems to be straightforward egoism. Thus he says that "whatsoever is voluntarily done, is done for some good to him that wills it" and that "of the voluntary acts of every man, the aim is some *Good to himselfe*" (*De Cive* II.8; cf. VI.11; *Leviathan* XIV.8). Since for Hobbes to call something good is only to say one wants it, commentators rightly note that statements like this tell us nothing about what in particular the agent wants and therefore thinks good. They then point to Hobbesian remarks that seem to allow that we sometimes want to benefit others. In one of his most infamous analyses Hobbes says that we act charitably in order to show our own power (*Elements* I.9.17). This may be – what it was long taken to be – a cynical debunking of any claim that humans might be disinterested. But the passage can also be read as saying that we really care for those whose good we procure in displaying our power. True, in this passage Hobbes then seems to restrict that kind of concern to one's children and dependents.[8] But he elsewhere includes unselfish desires in our makeup, among them charity or benevolence defined as "desire

---

7   In a note Hobbes allows the fact of helpless infancy, not to recognize the importance of mothers and families but to show that "all men, because they are born in Infancy, are born unapt for Society." If we are fit for society, it because we become so through education. Our nature is – against Aristotle's view – what we have when we begin, not what we develop toward.

8   So also the famous remark on pity, *Elements* 9.10., which allows that we feel grief at another's calamity but explains it as arising from the fear that similar misfortunes might occur to us. For a kinder, gentler Hobbes, see Sorrell 1986, pp. 97–8; and for a survey of the discussion see Curley 1990, pp. 171–5.

of good to another," and kindness, or "love of persons for society" (*Leviathan* VI.22, 30).

The thesis of universal human selfishness may thus be less pervasive in Hobbes's theory than his critics took it to be. What may be more important for his explanation of our propensity to conflict are some of the substantive aversions and desires that he thinks we all share, despite the diversity of our bodily constitutions. We fear death and shun it above all else; and we seek glory, or the acknowledgment of our superiority over others. These aims, taken with certain of our circumstances, give us good reason to be deeply at odds with those others whom we nonetheless find useful.

Our situation is this: setting aside the kinds of power over others we have only in society, we are naturally all roughly equal to one another (*Leviathan* XIII.1–3). Anyone can kill anyone else, and everyone is vulnerable when asleep. Perhaps driven by an insatiable desire for security, we each want to be superior to everyone else. No abundance of material goods, therefore, would put a stop to our perpetual search for advantage over others. We see that some people rob and kill others, and we cannot tell who is likely to threaten us, and who not. We are therefore, with reason, constantly in fear of everyone else. Hence we try to protect ourselves by endlessly increasing our power, and we know that everyone else is in the same frame of mind. The outcome is the famous war of all against all. In the state of nature, the condition we are in without government, we each have conclusive reason to be constantly ready for hostilities. Even if we are not actually fighting, our fear of one another inhibits almost all cooperation; and it leaves us all much worse off than we would be if we could somehow trust one another.[9] But we seem unable to find any reason to do so.

The laws of nature, for Hobbes as for Grotius, point out the way to escape, or more accurately to avoid, this terrible condition. It is striking that although Hobbes's portrayal of our nature and its social effects rivals in its vivid pessimism the dismal pictures of St. Augustine, Luther, and Calvin, his point is not theirs.[10] For Hobbes ours is not a "fallen" world. He explicitly refuses to say that our nature is sinful (*Leviathan* XIII.10). He is simply giving a scientific account of the factors that cause the problem we must learn to solve. It is the Grotian problem, pushed to the limit of solubility.

9 The structure of Hobbes's argument to show the inevitability of a mutually destructive state of nature is now frequently explained in game-theoretical terms. Curley 1990, pp. 178–87, surveys and assesses these readings. See also Gauthier 1969, Kavka 1986, Hampton 1986.

10 See, e.g., Augustine, *City of God* XIX.4; Luther, in *Selections*, ed. Dillenberger, pp. 139–40; Calvin, *Institutes* III.IX.1.

ii. *From psychology to morality*

Words, for Hobbes, are mostly human inventions serving human purposes. The only exceptions are some animal names that God taught to Adam, thereby showing him how to make up more names as they were needed (*Leviathan* IV.1). We use words in order to create deductively certain scientific knowledge. Without them we would have at best belief resting solely on experience (V). And we need scientific knowledge to avoid the state of nature. Reason has no aims of its own. "The thoughts are to the desires as scouts and spies, to range abroad and find the way to the things desired." Thoughts unguided by desires would be random and incoherent. Pure contemplation has no role in the Hobbesian psychology. For him all reasoning is practical (VIII.16). Like Grotius, he is opposing skepticism, not because of detached interest in epistemology but because our lives depend on defeating it.[11] How then does Hobbes define the key terms involved in the laws of nature so that he can derive a science of practice?

I have already pointed out that "good" and "bad" are initially defined in terms of each individual's desires. There comes to be a shared content for these terms only under a government, when the sovereign's single set of desires replaces the divergent desires of the subjects as the standard for what is good or bad (*De Cive,* pref.; *Leviathan* VI.7). The other terms are explained most fully in chapter XIV of *Leviathan;* but to follow the account Hobbes gives we must return to his determinism, one of the doctrines that was most offensive to his readers.

Since minds, for Hobbes, are no more than tiny particles of matter, they are as fully determined as visible bodies. The effects of impacts of external atoms on our bodies differ in strength, and therefore so do passions; and, like other opposing tugs and pulls, they may alter or cancel one another's force. In a complex situation we will feel moved in various directions. The conflict of desires and aversions thus constituted is what we call "deliberation," and its outcome – the last appetite, the one that effectively causes one's body to behave in a definite way, or, as we say, moves one to act – is the act of will (*Leviathan* VI.49). If the will is caused by an apparent good, the act is spontaneous, and a spontaneous act following deliberation is voluntary. If the will is moved by fear we do not call the act spontaneous, but acts done from fear and those done from hope are both caused in the same general way (*Works*

11   On Hobbes and skepticism see Tuck 1988 and 1993, pp. 284–98. Skinner 1990 argues convincingly that Hobbes is defending the certainty of a science of morality not against Cartesian skepticism but against forms of argument taught and used by rhetoricians that seem to undercut the possibility of arriving at clear decisions about what counts as virtuous or vicious.

IV.242–3). Hobbes's account of human action is thus thoroughly naturalistic. We can explain the causes of our motions in terms of thoughts
and desires, without knowing their ultimate constitution. But these
"mental" causes are themselves motions, so that in the end psychology
needs no explanatory notions that would not be needed in physics.

Hobbes spells out the implications of his position quite baldly. What
necessitates and determines every action "is the sum of all things,
which being now existent, conduce and concur to the production of that
action hereafter, whereof if any one thing now were wanting, the effect
could not be produced"; and all of these determinants were equally
caused to be by previous states of the world (*Works* IV.246; italics omitted). We can sensibly talk of liberty of action, then, if we mean only the
absence of any bar, external to one's body, to doing what one wills
(*Leviathan* XIV.2). It makes no sense to speak of will itself as free. "I
acknowledge this *liberty*," Hobbes says pithily, "that I *can* do if I *will*; but
to say I can *will* if I *will*, I take to be an absurd speech" (*Works* IV.240).

From this deterministic apparatus Hobbes derives the rest of the
moral vocabulary. The key notion is necessity. In a particularly strong
statement of his view he says that we all flee what we take to be the
chief evil, death, "by a certain impulsion of nature, no less than that
whereby a stone moves downward" (*De Cive* 1.7). If he is to be taken
literally here – and at times he puts the matter differently – then acts
that prevent death are acts we simply have to will, and, if free, to do.
Each of us tries to think out how to avoid death. In the state of nature,
right reason is whatever reasoning the agent thinks right (*De Cive* I.10
and note).[12] Whatever my reason leads me to think I must have is
something to which I have a right. The "right of nature" is then, Hobbes
says, our liberty to act as we will, using our power for self-preservation
(*Leviathan* XIV.1).

In the state of nature each has a right to all things and so no one is
acting unjustly whatever ones does for self-preservation. The war in a
state of nature is hence not unjust. We can however see that in that
condition our lives are threatened; and we literally cannot will to sustain a clearly visible threat to our lives.[13] On Hobbes's view this is what

12   There is no such thing as "right reason," Hobbes holds, if that phrase means
an infallible faculty (*De Cive* II.1n; *Leviathan* V.3). Until there is a sovereign to set a
common standard we must each think for ourselves. See also *Works,* ed. Molesworth,
V.194.

13   This and the next two paragraphs are based on *Leviathan* XIV. My interpretation is contentious, as is every interpretation of Hobbes on these matters. I offer it as a
reading that incorporates the determinism and the strong naturalism of Hobbes's
position. I do not try to show that it is consistent with everything Hobbes wrote, or
that it can be worked out in a fully consistent and satisfactory manner.

it means to say that there is a law of nature that "forbids" doing what threatens our lives. Since we are determined to do whatever we must to preserve ourselves, we find ourselves necessitated to seek peace. That is, our recognition of the threat from others in the state of nature will cause us to desire peace; and if peace is not attainable, it will cause an endeavor to use all our strength to stay alive. "Seek peace" is accordingly the first law of nature; and the second is "if peace is not attainable, do what you must to stay alive." Normative laws reflect psychological necessities.

How is peace to be attained? By giving up our right to all things. And what can this mean? Only this: recognizing that I must have peace, I will cease to have an overpoweringly strong desire for unlimited power, glory, and anything else I have previously wanted. I will come to want only as much as allows me to coexist with others who have a similarly limited set of desires. But this desire will be my effective last appetite or will *only if* I am quite sure others have also come to want only this much. When this occurs, I am said to "lay down my right" to all things. This means that I cease to use my liberty to prevent others from getting what they want.

Hobbes thinks I can lay down my right either by simply ceasing to have unlimited desires or by adding to my self-limitation the desire that someone else should benefit from it. Once I actually limit my desires, then it may be said that I am bound or obliged not to interfere with the use made of the right I have given up; or that I ought not or have a duty not to interfere. There is thus, as Hobbes says, "no obligation on any man which ariseth not from some act of his own" (*Leviathan* XXI.10). Being obliged or duty-bound arises from the belief that I will benefit from the self-limitation that puts me under obligations to others (either definite others, or indefinite). And there are limits to what I can thus bind myself to do. I literally cannot, for example, give up my right to defend myself against a clear threat of death.[14] This is the only right that is not alienable, because I cannot desire to cease living. All my other rights can be given up.[15]

Suarez distinguished between the binding force of a law, as what justifies its claim to our obedience, and the motives that might lead us to

14 See Tuck 1979, pp. 119–25, concerning changes in Hobbes's views on this point.

15 Hobbes thinks that I can contract with someone to keep my life in exchange for giving him total control over my actions. Hobbes does not call this "slavery," which he restricts to servitude without agreement; but he essentially agrees with Grotius that yielding oneself into complete servitude is an acceptable option (*Leviathan* XX.10–12).

obey. Grotius referred to the moral necessity inherent in certain acts as what explains why God commands them, but said little about motivation. Hobbes's account of binding force or moral necessity eliminates any distinction between justification and motivation in obligation. Being under the necessity of obeying the laws of nature, like being obligated to obey the laws of a sovereign, involves the only kind of necessity there is. The necessity is the same as that in the determination of the motion of atoms.[16] The obligation of conscience is no different. It is simply the desire we inevitably have, once we understand why the laws of nature matter to us, that everyone, ourselves included, live by those laws (*Leviathan* XV.36–7).

Montaigne had asked what authority we could give to our opinions, including our opinions about what is good or bad, if they like all other things are simply part of the course of nature and are determined by natural causes (see Chapter 3.iv). Hobbes has an answer.[17] Their strength in moving us is all the authority they either need or can have. Hobbes gives a similarly naturalistic account of responsibility. The practices of praising, blaming, rewarding, and punishing are, he thinks, untouched by determinism. What makes an act unjust, and hence worthy of punishment, is only that it comes from a will to break the law, not from the necessity or lack of it leading to that will. The threat of punishment might deter a potential lawbreaker, and no more is needed to explain the usefulness of these concepts (*Works* IV.252, 255–6; *Leviathan* XXX.23–4).[18]

Morality begins, then, with our need for self-preservation, and the first two laws reflect this concern for self. The remaining laws rest on the fact that we are capable of using other people as indirect means to our own ends, the most pressing of which is self-preservation. Obligations and duties arise when we use other people by giving our rights to them either generally or through specific contracts. When we limit our desires in favor of allowing others to act freely, the others are said to

16   There are complexities here because of Hobbes's views about the proper method for attaining scientific knowledge. Experience alone does not yield knowledge strictly speaking. For that we must have deductive inference from explicitly stated and indubitable premises. Necessity comes in by means of words we make up. Only after we have words and see their connections can we understand anything as necessarily tied to anything else. Having made all necessity verbal in some sense, Hobbes treats all of science as working in the same way, and does not distinguish kinds of necessity (*Leviathan* V).

17   For Hobbes's knowledge of Montaigne, see Skinner 1990, p. 37.

18   These naturalistic explanations did not satisfy his chief opponent, Bishop Bramhall: see his *Defence of True Liberty*, in *Works*, pp. 88–99.

obligate us: it is necessary that we abstain from interfering with them. Moral obligation is thus explained as psychological necessity transmitted through the wills of other agents.[19]

When Hobbes comes to consider what reason can show us about the honor and worship we owe to God, he brings in the same kinds of considerations. We fear God's power over us because we believe that he can award eternal goods and ills. Believers thus consent to obey him. When they have a strong idea of what is proper in worshiping God, they will be moved just as they are by strong ideas about what is required for civil peace. When believers think that God wills them to worship him in a certain way, his will becomes a law that they are bound to obey (*Leviathan* XXXI. 5, 7).

iii. *Morality in practice*

Morality, says Hobbes, is outlined in his laws of nature. They have the attributes that have always been thought to characterize such laws. They are immutable and eternal, and they cover the same ground as the traditional virtues. Since no one denies that "the science of virtue and vice is moral philosophy," the truth about the laws of nature is the truth about moral philosophy (*Leviathan* XV.40). Hobbes is wholly traditional in thinking that in showing what leads to self-preservation he is working out a moral philosophy.[20]

Hobbes says also that he is not proposing new laws of nature. From the law requiring that we seek peace, he proceeds to demonstrate laws requiring us to be just, which for him means honoring contracts, to show gratitude, to do our best to get along with others, to judge fairly between disputing parties, to avoid arrogance and pride, and many others. These laws are contained in the Decalog. Its second table is summed up in the injunction to love one's neighbor as oneself, its first table in the requirement that one love God; and these together form a fine summary of the laws of nature, useful in public instruction (*Leviathan* XXX.13). What is new in his position, Hobbes thinks, is his explana-

19 In the period that concerns us the adjective "moral" almost always refers to whatever involves the will or choice or decision of conscious agents. Thus moral science is science about distinctively human actions, which come from the will.

20 The novelty of Hobbes's conception of the self and its interests is not the reason usually given for questioning whether Hobbes has a theory about morality. Curley 1990, pp. 187–94, reviews some discussions of the question, which seems to make sense only on the Kantian assumption that a morality cannot be a set of laws or imperatives whose justification is that they direct agents to their own good. It is, of course, anachronistic to use this conception of morality to discuss Hobbes, or indeed most of the moral philosophers who preceded him.

tion of these moral requirements. Older writers placed virtue in "a mediocrity of passions." Hobbes claims that he is the first to see that the real source of their praiseworthiness is that they are "meanes of peaceable, sociable, and comfortable living" (*Leviathan* XV.40).

Hobbes does not think that each individual is to be an interpreter of the laws of nature. In a statement that did as much as anything he said to outrage his contemporaries, he claims "that there are no authentical doctrines concerning right and wrong, good and evil, besides the constituted laws in each realm and government" (*De Cive*, pref.). The Pyrrhonists held that one is to obey local laws without any concern about their justice. A similar conclusion is the practical outcome of Hobbes's antiskeptical, mathematically certain demonstration of fundamental laws binding us all alike. We are each to obey the laws of nature as they are specified by the positive laws laid down by our own ruler, and there is no further law that we are to obey. Hobbes differs from Montaigne in thinking that we must each admit that our own sovereign's laws are just. His laws may not be good; they may fail to help preserve peace; but "no law can be unjust" because we have contracted to obey (*Leviathan* XXX.20). The contract gives us no standing to object to the ruler's declaration of what the laws require. In contracting to obey, we give up the right of private judgment.

In denying that we can appeal to natural law in order to criticize positive law, Hobbes is repudiating a major point in classical natural law theory. He is also attacking those who think that everyone has a private source of illumination about morals or religion, which would put each of us in a position to interpret the laws of nature for ourselves. The Calvinistic account of conscience given by the great puritan divine William Ames is representative of this position.[21] "The Conscience of man," so Ames begins his widely used casuistical treatise of 1630, "is a man's judgment of himself, according to the judgment of God of him" (*Conscience* I.i.1). It has the power of God's will, and "stands in the place of God himself" (I.iii.2, 6). No human command can override it; and even if erroneous it is to be followed. "The reason is, because he that doth against it, doth against Gods will; though not materially, and truly; yet formally . . .: because what the conscience doth declare, it declareth as Gods will" (I.iv. 6). The havoc that could be wreaked by such teaching in a time of deep division over religion does not need to be explained; the constant turmoil in England between 1640 and 1660 shows

---

21 Ames (1576–1633) was one of the most influential of Puritan writers. His casuistical treatise was translated into English in 1637, reprinted many times, and used in the American colonies as well as in England.

how the doctrine could work with economic and political strife to endanger civil society itself.

Hobbes's own account of conscience undercuts Ames's. Conscience for Hobbes is not itself a source of knowledge or even of revelation. It is simply the individual's judgment; and "as the Judgment, so also the Conscience may be erroneous" (*Leviathan* XXIX.6–7).[22] It cannot be our supreme ruler, because we give up our right to take our own opinion as the sole measure of reason when we give up our right to all things. Sovereigns have never given up that right, and in their consciences, therefore, God may be said to reign. But subjects are to take their morality from their rulers.

How then are the subjects to know what they ought to do? Hobbes allows that most people will not be able to follow his arguments. He has two remedies for this. One is regular teaching. An important responsibility of the sovereign is to see to it that the common people receive instruction in the basic natural laws and the ways in which they require complete obedience (*Leviathan* XXX.6, 10). Hobbes suggests that there is a second remedy. Everyone can use the simple formula, "do not that to another, which thou wouldest not have done to thyself" (*De Cive* III.26; cf. *Leviathan* XXVI.13).[23] Those who apply it will be led to do what the laws of nature require. They will not, however, understand why the laws direct what they do. They will have a method for making moral decisions that gives them the right answers; but they will not see what makes right acts right.

Hobbes thus agrees with Aquinas and Suarez that obedience to moral rules and positive laws is in most people the result of commands issued by an authority with power to penalize disobedience. The masses will understand the rules but not their rationale. Unlike Suarez, he does not say that obedience may come simply from a direct concern for righteousness, aroused by awareness of a law.[24] Hobbes's theory as a whole leaves little space outside the state of nature for anyone to exercise moral self-governance. Those who understand his theory may be self-governing in choosing to remain under their sovereign's rule.

22   In *Elements* I.6.8 conscience is defined as a man's own opinion that what he believes is true: this takes the etymology (*con* and *scio*, what I know with myself) to show that conscience essentially involves reflection on one's own beliefs.

23   Earlier Hobbes cites this commandment as the equivalent of the second law of nature requiring that each lay down the right to all things when others do so as well (*Leviathan* XIV.5).

24   Hobbes distinguishes between just acts and just people, and describes just people as those who take care that all their acts should be just; but he does not analyze their motivation for taking such care (*Leviathan* XV.12).

But beyond that, no one in a stable society is self-governing except where the ruler's laws are silent (*Leviathan* XXI.6, 18).[25]

iv. *Hobbesian voluntarism*

Hobbes frequently deprecated the work of his predecessors and claimed that he was the first to show the scientific basis of moral law (*De Corpore* I.1, I.7; *Leviathan* XXX.5, XXXI.41, XLVI). His innovations are largely theoretical, not substantive. As we have seen, he thinks that the laws he tries to prove concerning human interaction are commonplace. This is hardly surprising, since his theory implies that without obedience to such laws no societies could have existed. "The savages of America are not without some good moral sentences," Hobbes says, just as they can add and divide small numbers. What they lack is not morals but science (*Leviathan* XLVI.6).

Hobbes also goes out of his way to include another commonplace of the time. He ties morality to religion by claiming that dictates of reason about how to live, such as those he has established, are only theorems concerning self-preservation. They cannot be called laws unless we think that God commands us to obey them (*Leviathan* XV.41; cf. XXVI.8; *De Cive* III.33, IV.1). Hobbes uses here the familiar natural law distinction between advice or counsel and law or command. He seems to be taking a view similar to that of Suarez, and of Suarez's English follower Culverwell, whose *Discourse of the Light of Nature* was published in 1652, a year after *Leviathan*. Readers of the time would have recognized this as a familiar point about the nature of law. They would have coupled it with Hobbes's notorious remark that God's right to reign over men "is to be derived, not from his creating them (as if he required obedience, as of gratitude for his benefits), but from his *irresistible power*" (*Leviathan* XXXI.5). And they would have concluded that Hobbes was presenting a voluntarist view of morality.

The impression would have been reinforced by some of Hobbes's other statements. With Suarez, and departing from Aquinas, Hobbes holds that it is improper to speak of God having a kingdom that includes all of the creation, inanimate as well as animate. Only beings capable of being moved to obey by threats of punishment and offers of reward can be subjects in any but a metaphorical sense (*Leviathan*

---

25   In stressing the moral aspect of self-governance, I mean to avoid addressing the more general question of how much liberty Hobbes thinks is available to subjects within society. He himself defended religious toleration in strong terms. Flathman 1993 stresses ways in which a Hobbesian theory leaves much latitude for individual choice, and argues that a sovereign would do well to remain silent about most of life.

XXXI.2). God's law, the law of nature properly speaking, is meant for us, and has no counterpart in the rest of the universe. Another aspect of voluntarism, one made central by Luther and Calvin, is an offshoot of this point. We are not to expect to understand God, still less to see justice in his action.

> That which men make amongst themselves here by pacts and covenants, and call by the name of justice, and according whereunto men are accounted and termed rightly *just* or *unjust*, is not that by which God Almighty's actions are to be measured and called just. . . . That which he does, is made just by his doing it; just, I say, in him, though not always just in us. (*Works* IV.249)

In a comment about Job, Hobbes makes his position clear. God did not afflict Job because he had sinned. Punishment properly so called must be consequent on wrongdoing, but "the right of afflicting is not always derived from men's Sinne but from God's power" (*Leviathan* XXXI.6; *Works* V.17, 229). There is no solution to the problem of evil. We should not expect to see any moral point in the distribution of goods and ills in this world. However unjust it may seem in human terms, it comes from God's power and must therefore be accepted. The similarity of this Hobbesian comment to Protestant doctrines of prevenient grace and election to salvation could not have been missed.

It is not only in matters of justice that Hobbes thinks that God is incomprehensible to us. Almost no language applied to God can be literal. We can speak literally of God's power, but beyond that we are confined to metaphor and merely expressive language. To say that God has "will" is to say no more than that he has power; and the other terms we can apply to him are either negative, like "infinite," or honorific. When we call God "good," we are only expressing an indefinite admiration for him. Admiration is also expressed when we speak of God as existing, as not identical with the world, as having no shape or parts or location or passions. With such language we are not describing anything; we are honoring God by expressing our feelings of fear and hope (*Leviathan* XXXI.8–28). All of this is quite in line with the Lutheran and Calvinist view that God is beyond our intellectual grasp.

There are some differences between Hobbes's use of the idea that a command is necessary in order to make laws out of mere theorems of prudence and Suarez's use. Hobbes does not use God's command, as Suarez does, to explain how natural law obligates or creates "a moral impulse to action" (*De Legibus* II.VI.22). The Suarezian moral impulse may be the impulse to righteousness, or to compliance with law as such, but that, as I have noted, is absent from Hobbes's theory. Hobbes agrees instead with Grotius in thinking that reason teaches us directives whose obligatory force does not depend on God. If command is needed for law, it is unnecessary for obligation; Hobbes indeed insists that God commands only what reason shows to be obligatory for our preservation. It is not hard to see why Hobbes should invoke a command theory of positive law. The sovereign must be able to order his commonwealth simply by uttering commands, thereby transmitting the strength of each subject's general contractual obedience to the specific laws needed in daily life. It is not as clear what role there is for the lawfulness of natural laws.[26] It seems that Barbeyrac's objection to Grotius's view, that it makes God superfluous, might as well have been expressed in connection with Hobbes.

I do not think, however, that this would help us understand Hobbes's view of God's role in morality, still less his understanding of religion generally. We may never know whether or not he himself was an atheist.[27] Given some of the things he said about religion, it is understandable that he should so often have been, and still is, thought to be one. He offers naturalistic accounts of religious belief, tracing it to natural curiosity and to fear arising from our ignorance of the causes of things that affect our safety (*Leviathan* XI.25; XII). He holds that if God exists, he is material. So too is the soul, which Hobbes denies is naturally immortal (XLIV.14–15). These claims, and many others, gave his readers ample ground for thinking Hobbes insincere in his professions of belief. But there were Christians before him who had held similar views, and it may be that Hobbes himself was merely a very unorthodox believer.[28]

26 Curley points out that the Latin version of *Leviathan* does not contain Hobbes's remarks about God's command being needed to transform prudential theorems into law (*Leviathan* XV.41, n. 7).

One of the most contentious passages in Hobbes's writings is his discussion of the fool who denies the existence of God, thinking he can thereby evade the force of his promise to obey the sovereign. A notable point about Hobbes's solution to the problem the fool poses is the absence of any appeal to punishments after death. The aim is to show that considerations of a secular sort will adequately convince the fool to comply (XV.4). There is little agreement about the exact interpretation, still less about the success, of Hobbes's argument here.

27 Opinion on Hobbes's religious position is radically divided. See King 1993, vol. IV, for a range of articles on the subject, Martinich 1992 for a defense of the claim that Hobbes is a serious religious thinker, State 1991 for a careful discussion of natural law and religion in Hobbes, Curley's introduction to his edition of *Leviathan* and Curley 1992 for a carefully phrased and thoughtfully weighed "atheistic" reading taking into account the real dangers of open avowal of disbelief in Hobbes's lifetime, and Arrigo Pachi, "Hobbes and the Problem of God," in Rogers and Ryan 1988, for a balanced statement of a different view.

28 See Curley 1992. Martinich 1992 shows many ways in which Hobbes's views about religion have undeniably Christian exponents.

Discussions of religion in general and of Christianity in particular occupy an important place in many of his writings. Half of *Leviathan* is devoted to the subject. He says one cannot escape God's power; he frequently cites Scripture to support his views; he argues for his special interpretations of biblical passages; he tells us that belief in Christ is needful for salvation. Believer or unbeliever, he had strong views about what was at stake. In an important way, therefore, his private convictions do not matter. Readers who took him to be an atheist would still have to react seriously to his understanding of religion.

I have suggested that Hobbes is most naturally taken to be expounding a voluntarist position; and the question for us is about its significance in his theory. Hobbes studied religion out of a concern similar to Machiavelli's. Both think that civil religion is important because it affects the willingness of citizens to obey the sovereign. Hobbes's aim is consistently to present a theology that reinforces the need for obedience to the ruler. Unlike Machiavelli he makes a serious effort to show that Christianity can be the appropriate civil religion. It is no surprise that he rejects Roman Catholic Christianity, but given the profoundly disruptive effect of Puritanism and its struggles against the established church in Hobbes's lifetime, it is surprising that he finds even Protestantism acceptable.

What he is arguing for is in fact a minimalist Christianity not unlike the kind that Grotius expounded (see Chapter 4.iv). The two things needful for salvation are "faith in Christ and obedience to laws" (*Leviathan* XLIII.3). We are to believe that Jesus was the king promised by God to reign eternally; this is shown by the Bible, and no theological theses beyond it are necessary (XLIII.11–18). The obedience required is obedience to the laws of nature and then to the laws laid down by one's own sovereign, which, Hobbes says, "contain each other and are of equal extent" (XXVI.8). The most important conclusion from this is that no one can ever rightly think that God commands disobedience to the sovereign.

I have already noted that Hobbes's reductionist account of conscience rules out one way of claiming that directions from God justify rebellion or civil disobedience, and that another is excluded by his view that God's command presupposes the obligatoriness of certain kinds of action discovered by reason. A third is ruled out by his insistence that no alleged private communication between God and some specific person can rightly claim belief from anyone else. Hobbes does not so much deny personal revelation as bar it from any public use (XXXII.5–6). Access to God is shut off in yet another way by Hobbes's philosophical rejection of "separated essences" and "substantial forms." Such entities would not be tied to human sensory experience, and so might offer us a bridge to God's thoughts. But Hobbes thinks that his theory of language shows us that there is no more to entities of that kind than empty words that people make up to assist their own search for power (XLVI.16–30). The critique of this "vain philosophy" is thus another aspect of Hobbes's severe restrictions on meaningful language about God. The upshot is that we can neither know nor coherently think we know anything about God and his commands that would give us reason to reject the obligation to obey our sovereign's laws.

Hobbes thinks that the human tendency to fear unknown threats to life mobilizes so much energy that people will inevitably make up, believe, and act on religious stories. To control this dangerous tendency, the sovereign must be "the supreme ecclesiastical doctor," controlling public avowals of belief and the church governance that goes with them (*Works* V.269; *Leviathan* XXXI.37–8). Hobbes's account of religion shows us what doctrines he thinks the sovereign should have everyone taught. He apologizes if he proposes anything new that his sovereign excludes as doctrine, but he thinks his new doctrine may be what is now needed (*Leviathan*, A review and conclusion, 13). His theology reinforces the power of the "Mortal God" whom we make our sovereign (XVII.13). Our mortal god decides both what is good and bad and what is to be believed about the immortal god. He is a humanly created version of the voluntarist's deity.[29]

I do not think we should take Hobbes to be "secularizing" morality. He thinks that religious belief is the chief cause of anarchy. It is therefore vitally important to his political aims to make impossible any claims about the relation of religion and morality other than his. The God of voluntarism has a crucial role in Hobbes's preemptive strategy. If the God who is adumbrated in Hobbes's voluntarist terms is essential to morality, constituting it as such by his command, then Hobbes's theory implies that the management of our lives must be entirely up to us. Priests and churches and Scriptures have no authority; only our mortal deity does.

Luther and Calvin do not intend voluntarism to take God out of the human community. They use it to ensure that his inscrutable ways will always be in our thoughts, entrenched within our daily lives by showing us that morality has only a limited control over us. Their voluntarism gives the word of God, conveyed through conscience, the kind of independent standing Ames asserted for it. Hobbesian voluntarism has an entirely different function. Its point is to back up the thesis that the

---

29 Replying to Bishop Bramhall, Hobbes dismisses the charge that his deity is a tyrant. The term originally meant only "king" and a king the Hobbesian God certainly is. The term now means "a displeasing king," and Hobbes, who rejects the eternal punishment of the wicked, thinks the Calvinist deity who predestines millions to eternal torment is far more displeasing than his own (*Works* V.215–16).

content and maintenance of morality are our business. God gives our theorems their formal status as law, but we cannot think that he does anything more than that. He leaves us to our own devices.

We should not be misled by the fact that Hobbes claims to provide foundations for morality that defeat skepticism. When he says that the laws of nature are "immutable and eternal" we should keep in mind exactly what he means. He means only that the necessary means to ends that beings with our nature necessarily have can never cease to be such means. Necessity belongs to our propositions only when they are part of a science. And science, for him, rests on arbitrary verbal definitions. When God taught us a few names, we learned how to go on. Now we make up our own words, deduce consequences from them, and accept the whole structure if it serves our purposes.

Our words are not God's words; our purposes are also not his, because, Hobbes says, "God has no ends" (*Leviathan* XXXI.13). If the argument to a first cause shows that God exists, it shows no more about him (XII.6). The theorems God turns into laws are moral laws only for us. They cannot be laws for God because he has no ruler over him to command him (*Works* V.212). Moreover he does not have the nature from which our laws derive their obligatory force. If Hobbesian moral science defeats skepticism it does so only for us. And for Hobbes, God is not one of us.

6

A morality of love: Cumberland

Richard Cumberland (1631–1718), bishop of Peterborough, saw a profound threat to Christian morality and religion in what he called the "wicked doctrines" of Hobbes.[1] A number of pamphleteers before him had taken potshots at the outworks of the Hobbesian fortress. Cumberland's *De Legibus Naturae* (1672) was the first attempt to mount a full-scale philosophical assault on the whole massive structure of Leviathan.[2]

To counter Hobbes, Cumberland found it necessary to put forward a new theory of morality. Experience, he thought, teaches us that we are required to work together for the greatest possible happiness. Because he asserted this particular basic principle Cumberland has long been thought of as the first utilitarian.[3] If the characterization is overly simple, there is still a substantial amount of truth in it. But Cumberland's reasons for asserting the principle were very different from those that led the later writers who called themselves utilitarians to their version of it. They sought a publicly acceptable rationale for political and social reform. Cumberland saw his principle as the only one that could embody a morality common to God and human beings – and that, in so doing, could rebut Hobbes's denial of the possibility of such a morality. He was not a reformer. But he was the first philosopher who created an

---

1 *Treatise*, introd. xxx, p. 36. References to Cumberland throughout are to book, section, and page numbers of the Maxwell translation. I do not repeat the typographical idiosyncracies of the text.

2 Barbeyrac thought that Cumberland took up moral philosophy in order to refute Hobbes, whose terrible views he rightly feared might dazzle those already disposed to believe such things. Barbeyrac judged Cumberland's book probably the best philosophical response in English to Hobbes – and this seventy years after its publication (see his preface to his translation of Cumberland, pp. iii–iv). Cumberland was a careful critic; among other things he compared the English and Latin editions of *Leviathan*, noting discrepancies (see 3.ii, p. 169; 3.iv, p.173).

3 E.g., Albee 1901.

important new ethical theory because he thought it was morally required in order to defeat voluntarism.

i. *Love as law*

Hobbes accepted the Grotian problematic, increasing the social tensions at its basis by denying natural sociability and tying his theory to a more detailed psychology than Grotius had offered. He sought to give moral philosophy the certainty of mathematics while making sensory experience its ultimate basis. He never acknowledged a debt to Grotius, but the basic similarities between their views are undeniable. Cumberland expressed great admiration for Grotius.[4] He held, as Grotius and Hobbes did, that mathematics provides the standard to which the science of natural law should aspire (4.iv, pp. 185–7). He also derived the first principle of that science, from which all else follows, from experience; but he did not accept the Grotian problematic. He was consequently not a wholly modern natural law theorist. He was not simply a classical theorist either. His statement of the basic law of nature makes this clear.

There are two biblical citations on Cumberland's title page: the love commandment from Matthew 22.37–9 and St. Paul's succinct dictum in Romans 13.10 that love is the fulfilling of the law. Grotius made room for disinterested love, assigning it its own law of nature; Hobbes sometimes grudgingly allowed its existence; both of them saw morality as centered on law. Culverwell remarked, somewhat enigmatically, that "Laws should be cords of love" (p. 32). Cumberland, unlike these writers, aimed to show that love is the core of morality, and law only its instrument. He invoked nothing less than the universe to do so.

"The fundamental cornerstone of the Temple of Concord is laid by Nature" (2.viii, p. 107). Cumberland's dictum points to his central belief. God's creation must be harmonious. Concord must be natural in both the material and the moral world. It is the view held by Aquinas and Hooker. The material universe is a complex unity of great order and beauty. Its parts function to preserve not merely themselves but the corporeal whole as well. Cumberland aims to bring this view up to date and to give a new account of the concord that governs the moral world.

The Cartesian theory of vortices demonstrates, Cumberland thinks, that all the parts of the world collaborate to keep it going in an orderly fashion (1.xxv, p. 70).[5] Numerous studies of animal life show us how

---

4 Stewart 1854, pp. 76–7, claims that Grotius came to be studied in Britain due to Cumberland's influence.

5 It is worth reminding the reader, as Haakonssen 1996 does, that Cumberland

animals cooperate with one another (2.xv, pp. 119–20). They are not endlessly aggressive against those of their own kind; they show concern for others in trying to continue their species; they are generally benevolent toward one another (2.xvii–xxi, pp. 121–42). Looking at these truths and others of the same kind we must conclude that all things are ordered by a first cause, "God the Governor of the World," who knows what will happen when agents of different kinds interact and who directs them toward the common good of "the most enlarged society," a society in which human beings are "subordinate members" and God is the head (2.iii, p. 101; cf. 5.xlix, p. 280).

Cumberland sounds like an old-fashioned intellectualist natural law theorist, and so in part he is. But what he puts forward as the basic law of nature involves a major break with his predecessors. Cumberland states his law in various ways, not all of them perspicuous. One of the clearer statements reads as follows:

> The greatest benevolence of every rational agent towards all forms the happiest state of every, and of all the benevolent, as far as is in their power; and is necessarily requisite to the happiest state which they can attain, and therefore the common good is the supreme law. (1.iv, p. 41)[6]

Although stated in descriptive language, Cumberland takes this principle, for reasons I discuss in section iii, as giving guidance to our actions. It provides a law of love. He explains that he speaks of benevolence rather than love in stating it because love might be a mere wish for the good of others, but benevolence includes the idea of willing to bring it about (1.iv, p. 42). The subject of the proposition asserting the law, he says, is "the greatest benevolence toward all rationals, which . . . does consist in a constant volition of the greatest good towards all" (I.xiii, p. 53). The good of all rational beings is an aggregate greater than the combined goods of any lesser number and so is "truly the greatest good" (2.iii, p. 97). The common good includes "the greatest happiness of mankind" as well as honor to God, and is preferable to all other things (5.xxiv, p. 227). In this formulation Cumberland includes both motive and outcome in his law. We shall see that he is concerned with both, although in other statements he sometimes makes the effects of benevolence basic and says that the law directs us simply to bring about the greatest public good (5.iv, p. 196; 5.lvii, p. 296).

Aquinas and Hooker would have agreed with the affirmation of cosmic concord embodied in Cumberland's assumption that the private

preceded Newton, Malebranche, and Locke, and that he probably did not know Spinoza's writings or the early work of Pufendorf.

6   For other statements, more or less complete, see introd. xxiv, p. 30; 1.v, p. 43; 1.xiii, p. 53; 1.xv, p. 56; 2.iii, p. 97; 5.ix, p. 204; 5.lvii, p. 296; 6.v, p. 308; 8.xiii, p. 342.

good of individuals is best forwarded when each pursues the common good. But when they said that the first law of nature is that good is to be pursued and evil avoided, they were not thinking in terms of aggregates of goods of individuals, and they certainly did not have maximization of such an aggregate in mind. These ideas make their first appearance in Cumberland. He leaves us in no doubt that we are to understand the good in thoroughly quantitative terms. He repeatedly describes separate goods as being aggregated to make up the greatest good which is our proper end (e.g., 1.xxxiii, p. 87; 5.xix, p. 220; 5.xxxv, p. 246). The separate goods are the various amounts of happiness of individuals, families, and states; and Cumberland's empiricism leads him to stress that we know what these are (5.xvi, p. 216). He compares the common good with a mathematical whole, and says that the proposition that the whole is the sum of its parts is as true in the one case as in the other (1.xxxiii, p. 87; 4.iv, p. 184).

Cumberland thinks that we can appeal to the mathematical constitution of the good in making practical judgments. Like Grotius, he thinks this gives us something Aristotle never managed to produce – a "rule or measure" for the prudent man's judgment (introd. xxiv, p. 30). He does not suggest that a cardinal ordering of all individual good states of affairs is possible. But because the common good is "the Sum of all things naturally Good, and therefore, the greatest Good," comparison with it enables us to construct an ordinal ranking. Nothing can fail to be less good than the common good, and we can tell, roughly, how much less good anything else is. We can rank acts by making the comparison because "the Greatest [good] . . . is more obvious to our understandings than the rest." It gives us a "determinate Quantity," which is better known than the lesser amounts we rank by it (7.xiii, pp. 342–5).

Grotius did not think his law of love could be stated precisely, and he did not consider it to be the foundation of the laws of justice. When Cumberland spelled out precisely what the law of love is and claimed that it is the sole basis of all of morality, he was quite deliberately taking a radical new step in moral theory.

ii. *The status of the law of love*

Cumberland states his basic principle in descriptive terms because, like Grotius, he thinks he can base the law of nature on experience. This matters, because in his battle against Hobbes he proposes to fight with the enemy's own tools. He will not appeal to innate ideas, nor will he appeal to any metaphysics he thinks would be rejected by "the Epicureans, with whom is our chief controversy" (introd. v, p. 14).[7] Hobbes

---

7   He knew some of the work of the Cambridge revivers of Platonism (discussed

refused to allow that God could be bound by the same laws that bind us. Cumberland thinks that without appealing beyond experience he can show that Hobbes is wrong.

He begins mildly enough by allowing that all our ideas and beliefs come from experience, either introspective or sensory. The ideas involved in the moral law are no exception. We learn what benevolence is from noticing it in ourselves, and we easily observe the effects of benevolence on ourselves and others. Experience shows that maximal benevolence causes as much happiness as humans can create, given their situation in the world. We are said to be happy when we possess many good things (1.v, pp. 42–3). The idea of good applied here and in the law also comes from observation. We see natural bodies assisting one another; it is obvious that humans do so as well. Hence we form the idea of "that which preserves, or enlarges and perfects, the faculties of any one thing, or of several," and this gives us the meaning of the term "good." So used, the word refers to natural good, the good tied to the nature of each kind of thing. We have not yet seen what specifically moral good is; but even without that we can now understand the status of the basic law of nature (3.i, pp. 165–6). It is an empirically based truth, but it is more than that as well.

To explain this, Cumberland attacks Hobbes's view of the meaning of "good." He is mistaken in thinking that to call something good is to say that we desire it. After all, Cumberland points out, a madman may desire to stay mad, as a sick man may not want medicine, but that hardly makes the one good and the other bad. On the contrary: we come to desire something only because we first think it good. Hobbes has misunderstood our common language (3.ii, p. 168). More importantly, he has misunderstood the way language works. Cumberland rejects the Hobbesian view that our words and deductive systems are inventions we make to serve our desires. Ideas and the truths they form when brought together are, rather, impressed upon us by the world. Ideas are images of things, and positive truths are "joinings, by affirmation, of apprehensions impressed upon the mind by the same objects" (2.vii, pp. 105–6). Truth is thus the conformity of our ideas "with the things themselves" that they concern. Our words enable us to communicate with one another because they name experiences everyone has had and abstractions everyone makes. Without that shared common basis we could have no common language (2.ix–xi, pp. 108–11).

From this point Cumberland moves to what he takes to be a major

in Chapter 10), thought that their program was consonant with his, and did not want to criticize them, though he thought them ineffectual against the common enemy. He does not take note of Lord Herbert of Cherbury's innatist theory, though he could well have known it (see Chapter 9.ii).

departure from Hobbes. His aim is to show that the moral law is eternally true. To do so he must prove it necessarily true. And he thinks that
experience enables us to establish moral truths that have the same
necessity as those of mathematics (introd. xxviii, pp. 34–5). He wants to
go beyond what Hobbes would allow as the truth in this claim, but he is
unfortunately less than clear about how he thinks he can get there.
Experience, he says, gives us separate ideas and then it shows us that
they are ideas of states of affairs that are either identical or necessarily
connected. It thereby teaches us necessary truths. Just as the motion of a
point necessarily causes a line, so "greatest benevolence" as cause necessarily leads to "greatest happiness" as effect. Regardless of whether
anyone proposes the greatest happiness of all as his aim, the proposition that the greatest benevolence causes the greatest happiness may
"be proved necessarily true. For the whole truth . . . depends upon the
natural and necessary efficacy of such actions, as causes, to produce
such effects" (1.v–vii, pp. 42–5).[8]

Establishing a necessary and eternally true principle of morality is
for Cumberland the key to defeating Hobbes's voluntarist denial that
God and we form a single moral community. He thinks that it is imperative to win this point. Unless we do, we are left with Hobbes's conten-
tion that God rules solely because of his irresistible power (7.vi, p. 319;
vii, p. 321). Acceptance of that doctrine would tempt men to rely on
immoral force for their own ends. More basically, it would make impossible a community united in a law of love, and Cumberland thinks we
do form such a community, with God included (5.viii, p. 202). Unlike
Hobbes, Cumberland thinks that we can be sure that God possesses
perfect reason, prudence, and constancy. We ourselves have them to
some degree, and our creator could not have given them to us unless he
had them himself (5.xix, p. 220).

Cumberland also holds that we can learn more about God from
experience than merely that he exists and created the universe. We can
learn his morality. We do not need to appeal to innate ideas or to
metaphysics to see this. Modern science has established the necessary
geometrical laws of the physical universe (5.iv, p. 197). Cumberland
thinks that he himself has done the same for morality. If there is an
eternally and necessarily true moral law, then God must know it and be
guided by it (introd. xxviii, pp. 34–5). He and we must think of morality
in the same way.

---

8 Cumberland thinks there is a perfect analogy in mathematics. You may or
may not aim, for instance, to bisect an angle, but if you do, you have to follow the
laws of geometry to achieve it. The laws are necessary, regardless of your aim.

iii. *From self-love to benevolence*

When Aquinas asserted that the basic law of nature is that good is to be done and evil to be avoided, he meant to be both describing a fundamental tendency in the nature of all things, and showing us the law that we, as rational beings, ought to obey (Chapter 2.ii). Cumberland reasserts this position in language intended to make it more scientific. He presents the law of nature as a statement of necessary causal connections relating benevolence, individual happiness, and the greatest happiness of all rationals. He then says that the assertion that an action contributes to the common natural good can equally well be expressed as the command that we promote the common good, or "in the form of a gerund" by saying that we "ought" to promote the good. These verbally different forms "mean the same thing, whether the understanding judges this best to be done, or commands it, or tells me . . . that I am bound to do it" (4.i, pp. 180–1). Cumberland thus claims that his declarative formulation of a moral principle can serve as the basis for "practical propositions" telling us what we ought to do.[9]

The transition from the descriptive law to the moral prescription has two aspects. One is psychological. Cumberland tries to show that we naturally progress from desiring predominantly our own good to being primarily benevolent, and thus desiring the good of all. The other is conceptual. Acting as we desire is not yet acting in a *morally* good way, even if we are benevolent. Cumberland explains the relation of obligation to God's will in order to show how morality comes in. He needs both sides of his theory because he wants to show that we can behave outwardly in a loving way from inner love, and that we are morally good when we do so. I begin with his psychology of moral development.

Cumberland is Grotian in holding that people are strongly self-interested, conceding at times even that our concern for our own good is stronger than our affection for others (5.xxviii, pp. 234–5). But people also have desires for the good of others, and most of Hobbes's psychology is mistaken. His claims about our overwhelming tendency to ag-

---

9 A practical proposition relates means to ends proposed by a rational agent. Geometrical theorems become practical propositions for someone who wants to construct a specific figure. The law of nature becomes practical when rational agents try to attain either their own happiness or the common good (4.i–iv, pp. 179–84).

One further condition must be met by any proposition that can be a law. Cumberland is no Lutheran. He thinks that we cannot be obligated to do what is impossible (5.iii, p. 194; xviii, p. 219). Experience shows everyone that we can affect the well-being of others.

gression and to endless self-aggrandizement in the quest for glory are confuted by innumerable empirical observations. In fact, Cumberland concludes, people are naturally quite strongly inclined to be benevolent to others (2.xxii, pp. 136–43). He adds that it is no use arguing against this by noting that children are not yet so. We see real human nature in the mature adult who uses reason, not in the baby (3.iv, pp. 171–2; cf. 2.iii, p. 96).[10] Even Hobbes sometimes admits that humans act benevolently (3.ii, pp. 168–9). And unbiased observation shows that benevolence is not even rare (cf. (5.lv, p. 293).

It is clear, Cumberland thinks, that we need one another's help to secure the necessities as well as the pleasures of life (1.xxi, pp. 62–4; 2.xvii, pp. 122–3). But we do not help others only to receive help in return. The exercise of benevolence constitutes a central part of our happiness. In general we are happy when we use our abilities to the fullest. And the task of benefiting others as much as possible calls us, more than any other, to strenuous exertion. Because there can be no greater recipients of benefits than God, who can be honored, and humans, whose lot can be improved, nothing can make a greater demand on us, or, consequently, make possible a greater sense of achievement (5.xii–xvi, pp. 207–16). Doing good to others from benevolence brings happiness directly to the benevolent agent. Cumberland here makes an effort to call on Grotian sociability to fill the void left by the Grotian refusal to say anything about the content of the good life.

What enables and in the end compels us to move from narrow self-interest to benevolence is a basic fact about our motivation. Human beings are as naturally moved by reasons as physical objects are by pushes and pulls (5.lvii, p. 297). When we propose ends to ourselves, it is not simply because of blind desire. As the very meaning of the term "good" shows, we desire what we think good. Whenever we act for a reason, we are trying to avoid apparent evil or obtain apparent good, and we must will what we judge to be good (5.xi, p. 206; 3.ii, p. 168; 3.iv, p. 173).

Cumberland relies on this anti-Hobbesian proposition without arguing for it; and it is fundamental to his thought. From it he infers that "we must of necessity desire like things, to things which are necessarily judged alike." Cumberland puts this principle of generalization forward as a truth of psychology, not of practical logic, and uses it to ground his view of moral development. We know the feelings of others as well as we know our own (5.xvi, p. 216). So if I think something will be good for me, I can come to think it would be good for another in like circumstances; and since thinking it good is what leads me to desire it

10   He here attacks what Hobbes says in *De Cive* I.2n.

for myself, it will lead me to desire it for anyone. "Hence we desire to others . . . like advantages as to ourselves" (5.xiv, p. 211).

What matters to us is thus, despite Hobbes, solely the amount of good we can bring about, regardless of who will benefit from it (5.xii, p. 208; xxvii, p. 233). Reason can show us that the good of all is greater than our own good. Reason can be practical not only because it tells us means to ends we already have, but also because it can change our ends. It tells us "what is every man's best and most necessary end" (2.vii, p. 105). Hobbes is wrong in thinking that reason is only a scout for the desires. Knowledge of good brings us to desire new ends. Through reason we can be moved from desiring only our own good to desiring the good of everyone alike.

The original meaning of the now misunderstood slogan that charity begins at home underlies Cumberland's thought here. The love commandment tells us to love others as we love ourselves. A long tradition of thought took this dictum to mean that we learn about the good and its steady and prudent pursuit in the first instance from our own case, and that we are then able to generalize to others.[11] *Caritas incipit a se* because our own interests first show us that the goodness of what I can bring about gives me a reason to do it. From there it is only a step to the realization that what is good need not benefit me in order to provide me with a good reason to bring it about. When I learn that I can help another, I am moved to act by the thought of that good, just as I was previously moved to act only for my own good.[12] It is the perfection of our nature, not its initial condition, to be moved by reason. The law of nature requires us to love perfectly in order that we may do our part in bringing about the greatest good. In loving as perfectly as we can, moreover, we have the same desire that God has. Only thus do we fully obey the law (5.xlvii, p. 275). For Cumberland, motive matters as much as result.

iv. *God, law, and obligation*

Reasoning from our experience, we learn that Cumberland's basic principle is an eternally necessary truth. But more is needed, Cumberland thinks, to account for the claim that the principle we have found is

11   This tradition is richly explored in Schneiders 1971, to which I am much indebted here and elsewhere.

12   Charron puts the point concisely when he says that the love commandment "doth not only set down the duty of a man towards another . . . but it sheweth and ruleth it according to the patterne of that dutie and love he oweth towards himself: for as the Hebrews say, a man must beginne charity with himself" (*Wisdom* III.v, p. 446).

truly a law. Hobbes said that the dictates of reason about what we must do to preserve ourselves can be laws only if God commands us to comply with them. Cumberland thinks Hobbes was hypocritical in saying this (1.xi–xii, pp. 51–3; cf. 4.i, pp. 180–1). He himself, however, is quite in earnest in asserting that God's will must be introduced in order for "the conclusions of reason in moral matters" to count as laws. An inquiry into the causes of the truths that we learn from reason will lead us to their first cause, "from whose essential perfections, and internal sanction of them by rewards and punishments, . . . their authority arises." Only then will we have knowledge of "the will or laws of God" (introd. iv, p. 13).

Like the natural lawyers before him, Cumberland thinks that morality requires that there be laws directing our actions. We might pursue natural good out of desire, but, as I indicated earlier, even our pursuit of the greatest good of all rational beings would not count as moral without a law commanding it. Cumberland here introduces a distinction between natural and moral good.[13] The idea of the former, we have seen, comes from knowing what helps and harms things. No idea of a law is needed. The idea of moral good, by contrast, includes reference to law. Moral goodness is attributable only to acts and habits of rational agents. They are morally good insofar as they bring about natural good because doing so complies with laws, natural or civil (3.i, pp. 165–6). What, then, is law?

Cumberland gives a rather Thomistic definition. A law is "a practical proposition concerning the prosecution of the common good, guarded by the sanctions of rewards and punishments" (5.xxxv, p. 247). Earlier he speaks of the parts of a law as being the precept and the sanctions (5.i, p. 189). The precept in a law differs from a precept in counsel, since a law comes from one who commands or legislates (4.i, p. 181). Law thus supposes a superior (5.xix, p. 221). Its main effect is to put those subject to it under obligation to do what it directs. In putting subjects under an obligation, the legislator makes it necessary for the obligated

---

13   His distinction develops a point implicit in some earlier writers. Calvin, after noting that there is a natural well-being or good which we seek by "an inclination of nature," warns us that here "good" refers not to virtue or justice but to condition, as when things go well with man (*Institutes* II.II.26, p. 286). Suarez says that human acts are good or evil depending on whether or not they accord with right reason. And over and above this kind of goodness, "human actions possess a special good or wicked character in their relation to God, in cases which furthermore involve a divine law" (*De Legibus* II.VI.17, in *Selections*). Suarez's main concern is with obligation, but his language comes close to Cumberland's. "[T]he law of nature . . . may superimpose its own moral obligation . . . over and above what may be called the natural evil or virtue inherent in the subject-matter" of the law (II.VI.12).

person to do certain actions. What, then, are the relations of sanctions to obligation and to the necessity of doing what is obligatory?

To follow Cumberland's rather obscure account of his answer, we must recall the complexity of the law of nature itself. It tells us that each agent's own good is included in the common good of all rationals and that the best way to promote the former is to promote the latter. We must also keep in mind that Cumberland thinks that there is moral development from a desire for one's own good to the benevolent desire for the common good. These two points make intelligible his key statement:

> Obligation is that act of a legislator, by which he declares that actions conformable to his law are necessary to those for whom the law is made. An action is . . . necessary to a rational agent, when it is certainly one of the causes necessarily requir'd to that happiness, which he naturally, and consequently, necessarily, desires. (5.xxvii, p. 233)

God legislates by telling us that it is necessary for us to act to bring about the greatest good of all rationals. This is true because, no matter whether we pursue our own good or the good of others, we can reach our end fully only by acting in ways that forward the greatest good. The obligation of law comes, then, simply from God's telling us the truth about what it is necessary for us to do, given our ends. We can learn the truth from experience; and since we have the ends, the truth is a practical proposition for us; but what puts us under a moral obligation to live by it is the formal point that God declares it to us.

A law must, by definition, include sanctions. But their point is not to obligate us. Immediately following the definition of law, just quoted, Cumberland insists that he does not derive the obligation of law from the sanction (5.xxxv, p. 248). The sanctions have two functions (5.xlii, p. 266). First, they "persuade" us to do what God commands, because even if we do not see that our own good is best served by striving for the common good, we can surely understand threats of punishment and offers of reward. Sanctions thus make it necessary to do, as a means to our own good, what is obligatory because God has told us that it serves the common good (cf. 5.xxii, p. 225). The necessity within moral obligation is psychological. Second, sanctions show us that God has indeed commanded the law of nature. They do so because, on Cumberland's view, sanctions are present throughout our earthly life. We need not wait for them until after death. As ill health is a punishment for gluttony and drunkenness, so happiness is a reward for benevolently exercising our abilities to make others happy (5.xxii, p. 224; xxiii, p. 226). Cumberland's claim that empirical evidence shows the truth of the law of nature is thus a claim about natural sanctions. Selfishness is self-punishing, benevolence self-rewarding, and these facts are empirical ways in which the obligation to strive for the common good is "pub-lish'd" or promulgated (5.xxiv, p. 227).[14]

Cumberland points out that on his view "natural obligation is not discovered by man in the same order, in which it is founded and estab-lish'd in nature" by God. We respond first to natural sanctions that affect our own good. We only gradually come to see that these natural sanctions teach us God's will concerning the greatest good of all ra-tionals. We can explain what we first learn – the distribution of sanctions – by what is last discovered but first in the order of things, God's will for the greatest good. Our own moral development leads us from ignorant and narrow-minded selfishness to reasonable love of all good, wherever enjoyed. At the same time it teaches us the nature of obligation in God's harmonious cosmos (5.xlv, pp. 271–3). For Cumber-land nature enables us to move from what we do desire to what is truly desireable, and the law of nature is thus a schoolmaster to lead us to God (Galatians 3.24).[15]

The psychological necessity carried by moral obligation reflects the basic fact that "we are determined, by some sort of natural necessity, to pursue good foreseen, especially the greatest, and to avoid evils" (5.xxvii, p. 233; cf. 5.xi, p. 206). Cumberland sees no threat to liberty here. Although reluctant to engage in discussion of the subject, he is willing to say that liberty does not require the power to do better or worse, or an absence of determination by perceived good. It is the power to act for the best, according to one's own judgment (2.iv, p. 102; cf. 4.i, p. 180). To be acting freely in doing as we are obligated to do – to pursue the greatest good – we need no more.

Cumberland's views of obligation and freedom enable him to ex-plain how it is that God and human beings can both be directed by the

14 Cumberland must inevitably seem to us to be moving – he is not the last to do so – from a sow's ear of self-interest to a silk purse of benevolence. If his law is true, being fully benevolent will bring me my own greatest good as well as con-tribute maximally to the greatest good of all rationals. But even if I want my own greatest good and it is true that being fully benevolent would give me my greatest good, it does not follow that I want to be fully benevolent. Cumberland's account of the necessity in obligation seems to require that he glide over the conceptual differ-ence between desiring something as my own greatest good and desiring something that would in fact bring me my own greatest good. If the necessity of obligation lies in the rational connection between a means and a desired end, then God cannot show me the necessity of acting from benevolence unless I already desire the com-mon good of all under that description. If I do, then if acting from benevolence is the best way for me to contribute to my end, I will come to desire to be fully benevolent.

15 The Stoics also taught that what comes last in development is first in nature or significance; Grotius reasserts the point, *DJBP* I.II.I.2.

same moral law. It is true that we cannot say that God is literally obligated to command us to do only what is naturally good for us. Obligation arises only from law, law only from the command of a superior, and God, of course, has no superior. But Cumberland thinks he can get around the difficulty. Since the will must seek clearly perceived good, what God understands about good is "analogous to a natural law"; and since his understanding is infinite, the necessity with which he follows it is much greater than any that could be induced by sanctions. There is therefore an "intrinsic propension of the divine will" that makes it impossible for God to violate the dictate that the greatest good is to be pursued (7.vi, pp. 317–18).

This necessity is no more incompatible with divine freedom than it is with ours (7.vii, p. 320; cf. 5.xix, p. 221). But God in fact possesses an additional freedom. There are infinitely many different ways in which God might have constructed the world, and we cannot say that among these one must be best. If several possible worlds contain equal amounts of good, and in all of them rational beings enjoy more good than rational beings enjoy in any other world, God can choose freely which one to create. Complete liberty does not require that one be able to bring about more or less good. God is free to distribute good as he pleases, as long as the total amount is one of the maximal amounts (7.vii, p. 320).

v. *Rationality in morality*

Cumberland thus thinks that we need not fear Hobbesianism because he has shown that God thinks rationally, as we do. God and we must know and follow the same moral law. We can confidently apply our understanding of morality to God in order to conclude that God is just; and because God could not reveal anything "contradictory to the just conclusions of our reason," we are to believe the Scriptures (introd. vi, p. 15; xxvii, p. 34). Cumberland's antivoluntaristic stress on the rationality of morality leads him to several further points of importance.

It leads him, first, to approach a hedonistic interpretation of the good. Although Cumberland usually states his basic law in terms of maximizing the common good, he also puts it in terms of maximizing happiness or felicity (introd. xx, p. 26; 1.xv, p. 56; 6.x, p. 312). He is also concerned with maximizing perfection, both of mind and of body. These items are connected by Cumberland's account of natural good in terms of what "preserves or enlarges or perfects, the faculties" of what it benefits (3.i, p. 165). But this poses a problem. Since God is rational we are to strive for his good. How? The definition seems to entail that we cannot increase God's good, since we cannot affect the perfection of his faculties. That leaves open the possibility that God and we cannot share a common end, and that, in turn, opens the way for voluntarism.

Cumberland avoids the problem by saying that this definition of good applies only to creatures, and that there is an analogous sense in which we can think of good in relation to God. Whatever we see as preserving or perfecting us puts our minds into a state of tranquillity or joy. Admittedly God cannot be made more perfect, but "because Tranquillity, Joy, or Complacency, may be conceived separately from Imperfection, these may safely be ascribed to the Divine Majesty" (5.ix, p. 203). Thus a state of mind may be common, more or less, to God and us, and we can try to maximize it in all rationals.

Is it pleasure? We have seen that actions using our faculties fully bring us happiness, on Cumberland's view, and he thinks it does not matter whether happiness consists in the most vigorous action of our faculties or in "a most grateful sense of them, join'd with tranquillity and joy, which by some is called pleasure" (5.xiii, p. 209). God's actions can give him joy, and when we conform to God's will, we give him joy or complacency (introd. x, p. 17). The good to be maximized, then, is for Cumberland a subjective condition, caused one way in us and another in God. Its value is independent of how it is caused. If Cumberland is a hedonist, however, it is not because he thinks that enjoyable life is the point of morality. He is no Epicurean.[16] But in order to assure the rationality of morals, he must find something that both God and we can aim to maximize.[17]

The importance of securing the rationality of morals brings Cumberland to a second point. If the near-hedonism underpins the ability of his principle to serve as a clear guide to the prudent man's choice, deliberation is also helped by the fact that all specific moral laws are derived from a single universal basic law. Rights, for example, have no independent standing. As "subordinate members" of the Kingdom of God, we are each entitled to only as much personal good as is in proportion to our importance in that Kingdom – just as each limb gets only the nourishment it needs to help the whole body it belongs to (5.xlvii, p. 277). Our rights are therefore determined by the law of beneficence governing the whole (1.xxii, p. 64). Hobbes was wrong on this matter as on so

16   Sharp 1912 argues that Cumberland is a hedonist. In a way this is quite right, but it is too simple. Cumberland would rather be a perfectionist; his hedonism is part of the battle against voluntarism.

17   If we accept his principle, "moral and political questions are converted into terms in use among natural philosophers, whether these efficient causes can produce this effect, or no? And to questions thus express'd, an answer may be given, which is capable of demonstration" (5.iv, p. 196).

many others. It cannot be known that any individual has a right even to self-preservation unless it is first known "that this will contribute to the common good." We have individual rights, in short, only insofar as it serves the common good for us to have them. Even virtue itself for Cumberland is only good because it leads to acts that contribute to the public good. It is not, as the Stoics held, good in itself (5.v, pp. 199–200).

The perfection of practical reason, Cumberland thinks, requires that all who are guided by it share a common end. He has shown, or so he thinks, how this works out on his own view. He offers a brief anti-Hobbesian argument to support his claim. On Hobbes's view of the meaning of "good," different people mean different things when they apply the word. I mean what I desire and you mean what you desire. But then the language is "altogether equivocal" and in being so it undermines the whole point of speech, "the communication of knowledge." The only way to avoid this linguistic anarchy is Cumberland's. We must admit that "good" signifies what is of common benefit to all (5.xvi, pp. 214–15). Hobbes's view would make it impossible to reason together on good and ill.

If there is only a single aim and only a single principle, the rationality of morals seems assured. But Cumberland does, in fact, find an additional law of practical reason. No two true propositions can be inconsistent. So if any of us judges that our taking something we need to support our own life would be permissible, we must admit that a similar act by anyone else similarly situated would be so as well. "Whoever therefore judges truly, must judge the same things, which he thinks are truly lawful to himself, to be lawful to others in a like case" (2.vii, pp. 105–6). Whatever a truly rational being thinks ought to be done for him, he also wills for others (5.xxx, p. 237). It is interesting that Cumberland does not see this principle as in any way threatening his claim that we are to maximize the good in each of our acts. He sees it, rather, as bringing home to us the blessings of mutual dependence in a harmonious universe. Avoiding the inconsistency of judging like cases differently is a source of social harmony. It also brings inner peace, since holding contrary judgments about similar things is a "kind of madness" that "greatly hurts the soundness, peace, and contentment of the mind in its actions," while uniformity of judgment produces tranquillity (5.xvi, pp. 215–16). Universalizing our judgments is a means to happiness.[18]

---

18 Cumberland never considers how the application of his basic law of beneficence will be affected by the constraint coming from the rational requirement of universalizability.

vi. *Ignorance and obedience*

Benthamite utilitarianism treats the right and the obligatory as definable in terms of productiveness of good. Cumberland treats the obligatory and the good as separate categories. What makes an act obligatory is not the amount of good it produces but its being commanded by God.[19] Benthamite utilitarianism is a theoretical endeavor to get away from the need for any such authority. It is fairly obvious why a clergyman of the Church of England would wish to make room for God's authority in his moral system. But we may still ask exactly how it is that he can do so. After all, he has argued that without the action of a lawgiver God is necessitated to pursue the greatest good. His obligation is self-imposed. Why, then, must obligation for us depend on a superior and require obedience? God can be self-governed simply because he knows what is the greatest good: why not we as well, since we have minds like his? The answer is that we do not have God's knowledge. Cumberland suggests, without going into much detail, that our ignorance has two aspects.

We need God's direction to tell us what the greatest good is and that our own good is inseparable from it. The evil in the world might mislead us into thinking that God does not will that all rationals should be happy (introd. xvii, pp. 22–3). Even if we do not make this mistake, we do not have enough knowledge to understand God's plans. We need to obey laws given by God, not because he and they are in themselves inexplicable but because we have only a limited ability to understand what each of us contributes to the good of the whole. Individual workmen, Cumberland says, cannot be expected to understand an architect's design; they need a superior mind directing all the work. Similarly, the enterprise of bringing about a human society in which all are as happy as possible could not succeed unless "a subordination of rational beings be establish'd, and all obey God, as the supreme and most perfect rational agent, by observing those natural laws, common to all nations, which I have explained" (9.v, p. 348). Only a morality of obedience gives us the guidance we need to play our parts in the joint venture on which we and God are embarked (cf. 7.vi, p. 319).

More than simple lack of knowledge is involved, however. If we are naturally moved by reasons, why are so many of us not concerned about the greatest good of all rational beings? Why are we so stubbornly stuck in pursuit of our own good, at the expense of greater goods for others (and indeed for ourselves as well)? Cumberland does not appeal explicitly to original sin, but his answer does not take him far

19   On this point see Haakonssen 1996, and also Haakonssen 1990, to both of which I am much indebted.

from it. We remain ignorant of the law of nature and we fail to comply
with it because, he says, we are willful and thoughtless. We refuse to
turn our attention to the best way to attain our own ends. Haste and
turbulent passions distract us. If they did not, the rational arguments
Cumberland gives us would effectively lead everyone to morally good
actions out of concern for the best end (5.xxxv, p. 248; xxvii, p. 234; 3.iv,
p. 172).

These points suggest some problems for Cumberland's position. The
admission that we know of distressing amounts of evil in the world
suggests that the evidence that God wills everyone's happiness is not
uniform. Our willfulness suggests that the passions and desires are not
as open to alteration by knowledge as the scheme of moral development presupposes. If we do not see how the good is to be brought
about, it is not evident that Cumberland's principle gives us guidance
to action that is far superior to Aristotle's.[20]

We get no answer to these questions from Cumberland, but he himself draws a conclusion from our ignorance of purely human affairs that
shows an important aspect of his own moral stance. Human ignorance,
he argues, justifies our keeping the present system of private property
intact. Our dependence on one another makes the private use of things
serviceable in bringing about the common good. Right reason therefore
dictates that the goods God gave us in common should be divided and
assigned to specific owners and to their posterity (1.xxii–xxiii, pp. 64–8;
7.i–ii, pp. 313–15). Cumberland does not suppose that reason dictates
the exact division to be made. But justice consists in observing the rights
of possessors, and those rights must be treated as inviolable (7.iii–iv, pp.
315–16). Moreover we must acquiesce even in a division of property
that arose from chance, such as casting lots or first occupancy, because
the importance of having settled ownership is so great. He thinks,
moreover, that any change in the present distribution risks more than it
could gain. Wise redistribution requires more knowledge than any one
man or assembly could possess. Opinions would differ so radically that
only confusion would result. Hence "a desire of innovation in things
pertaining to property, is unjust" because necessarily inconsistent with
the fundamental law requiring pursuit of the greatest good (7.ix, p. 323).
Ignorance puts us into a condition where we must all be obedient to
God, and where most of us must be obedient as well to the wealthy and
the powerful in this world.

20 Conscience for Cumberland is not an independent source of moral knowledge – not a synteresis, or repository of principles. It is simply our own judgment of
our own actions, accompanied by joy or sorrow (2.xii, p. 112).

7

The central synthesis: Pufendorf

Samuel Pufendorf (1632–94) published his great work on natural jurisprudence in 1672, the year that Cumberland's treatise on the subject appeared. In the following year he brought out a compendium of it meant for students. Both the lengthy *De Jure Naturae et Gentium* and the short version, *De Officio Hominis et Civis juxta Legem Naturalem,* were translated into many of the European languages, reprinted innumerable times, and used as textbooks in Protestant universities on the continent and in Scotland and the American colonies.[1] Pufendorf was

---

1 Roman Catholic countries did not accept Pufendorf, and though he was known in England he did not have much influence there. Othmer 1970 presents a solid study of the spread of Pufendorf's work, centering on the importance of Barbeyrac's translations into French. There is a good brief summary of Pufendorf's influence in Krieger 1965, pp. 255–66 (see note 4). Wieacker 1967 gives an excellent account of the general influence of the writers of *Vernunftrecht,* pp. 272–80, with special reference to Pufendorf, and then discusses Pufendorf more particularly on pp. 305–12. For examples of discussion of Pufendorf in the Scottish enlightenment, see Duncan Forbes, "Natural Law and the Scottish Enlightenment," in Campbell and Skinner 1982, pp. 186–204; James Moore and Michael Silverthorne, "Gershom Carmichael and the Natural Jurisprudence Tradition in Eighteenth-Century Scotland," in Hont and Ignatieff 1983, pp. 73–88; and in the same volume, the essay by the editors, "Needs and Justice in the *Wealth of Nations:* An Introductory Essay," pp. 1–44.

For Pufendorf and Leibniz, see Schneider 1967. Rüping 1968 discusses Pufendorf's influence on Thomasius and his followers. Derathé 1950 is a pioneering discussion of Rousseau and Pufendorf; Wokler 1994 is an important advance on it.

On the subject of modern natural law, I am much indebted to the general discussion and the papers at the conference on the theme of Pufendorf and Unsocial Sociability organized by Istvan Hont and Hans-Erich Bödecker and held in Göttingen in June 1989. What I say in section vi is a development of a paper I presented there.

Page references to *De Jure Naturale* are from the translation of C. H. and W. A. Oldfather, those to *De Officio* from the translation of Silverthorne.

treated as a major figure in eighteenth-century histories of natural law, and as late as 1798 he was given a chapter in Christian Garve's German-language account of the main systems of moral philosophy, in which Hume is not even mentioned.[2] But in Carl Friedrich Stäudlin's pioneering *Geschichte der Moralphilosophie* of 1822, the first comprehensive modern treatment of the history of ethics, Pufendorf receives only a page or two, as a follower of Grotius; and that much, or less, is all that those interested in moral philosophy have gotten about him from their historians since then.[3] Yet his theory exercised such a lasting and extensive influence on European thought about natural law that we must take it as the paradigm of the modern version of that kind of doctrine.[4]

Pufendorf had views on a wide range of topics and spelled them out in great detail. He wrote on political theory, history, theology, and the relations of church and state, as well as on natural law. On all these matters he was attacked by numerous critics, with whom he did not hesitate to engage in sometimes furious controversies.[5] Setting much of this aside, I try to abstract the aspects of his thought that make up the core of what we would now think of as his moral philosophy.

i. *Moral entities*

The Grotian problematic, I said in Chapter 4.v, takes as central the existence of an enduring tension between our social and our antisocial

2 See Tuck 1979, pp. 175–6. Garve sees Grotius as the first modern moral philosopher, and Pufendorf as his follower, but treats Pufendorf at greater length. He discusses only Hutcheson, Ferguson, Adam Smith, Clarke, and Wollaston (in that order) among the "English" moralists. Most of the book is devoted to an account of Kant's ethics.

As late as 1808 Pufendorf was still widely enough known to allow Kleist to refer offhandedly to him in a comedy: "Die Welt, sagt unser Sprichwort, wird stets klüger, / Und alles liest, ich weiss, den Pufendorf . . ." (The world, our proverb says, grows always wiser; and I know we all read our Pufendorf). Kleist, *Der Zerbrochene Krug*, I.4.

3 Pufendorf is barely given passing notice in Sidgwick 1889, and not even that in MacIntyre 1966. Ignoring Pufendorf seems to be characteristic mainly of those writing on the history of moral philosophy. Historians of political thought usually take him into account. Leidhold 1985, who is an exception, is interested in Hutcheson's politics as well as his ethics.

4 The fullest study of Pufendorf is Denzer 1972, to which I am much indebted. It contains an excellent bibliography. See also Welzel 1986, Krieger 1965, Medick 1973, and Laurent 1982. Pufendorf figures in the important study by Schneiders 1971. See also Zerbrucken 1971 and Dufour, in Burns 1991.

5 See Döring 1992 for an extensive bibliography on all aspects of Pufendorf's work and influence, and ground-breaking essays on his life and his work as historian and theologian.

dispositions or needs, treats natural laws as empirically discoverable prescriptions for living together despite that tension, and refuses to use a substantive conception of the highest good to derive specific laws. In these terms Pufendorf is without doubt a Grotian. He accepts and elaborates many other elements of the Grotian position as well; but he begins with what he takes to be a marked departure from Grotius.

His theory of the ontological status of morality, presented in the opening chapter of *On the Law of Nature* (*DJN*), makes plain his view of their disagreement. At its core is a distinction between physical and moral entities.[6] Physical entities are those whose causal power or strength moves them to motion with no direction at all from perception or reflection, or with very little. Humans are not wholly physical entities in this sense, because we are open to guidance that comes through intelligence and will. Pufendorf leaves it to others to speak of what may be done with our purely cognitive abilities. His special task is to note

> how, chiefly for the direction of the acts of the will, a specific kind of attribute has been given to things and their natural motions, from which there has arisen a certain propriety in the actions of man. . . . Now these attributes are called Moral Entities, because by them the morals and actions of men are judged and tempered. (I.i.2, pp. 4–5)

The world considered simply as containing moving bodies that interact causally may be called "physical," and the things in it are properly said to have been "created" by God. Moral entities are better said to arise from "imposition." They are dependent on physical entities in the sense that they presuppose the existence of such things. But Pufendorf declares emphatically that "they do not arise out of the intrinsic nature of the physical properties of things, but they are superadded, at the will of intelligent entities, to things already existent and physically complete." Unlike physical beings, moral entities have no causal powers: "the active force which lies in them does not consist in their ability directly to produce any physical motion or change in any thing, but only in this, that it is made clear to men along what line they should govern their liberty of action" (I.i.3–4, pp. 5–6).

God imposes some moral entities on all human beings, and these may be called "natural." The moral entities that we impose are not natural in that sense, but otherwise the two are of the same kind (I.i.7, p. 7). Both serve to bring order into human life (I.i.5, p. 6). The natural duties and rights which are central to morality and law obviously have this function (I.i. 19–20, pp. 18–19). When we organize our affairs by

---

6 Pufendorf was taught the distinction by Erhard Weigl; see Denzer 1971, p. 69, and for a fuller study, Röd 1969. But Weigl is nearly unreadable, and it was through Pufendorf that the idea attained European importance.

giving individuals and groups socially defined roles such as husband, mayor, and town council, we are imposing moral entities upon their physical being (I.i.12, p. 11). The prices we set for things are moral entities. So also are the esteem we accord to people and all the culturally diverse distinctions constituting the offices, honors, and titles governing the right to esteem (I.i.12–13, pp. 11–13; I.i.17–18, pp. 17–18).[7] As physical and biological beings we are independent of moral entities; but those entities constitute all the other aspects of the human world.[8]

The theory of moral entities is not worked out in any great detail in *On the Law of Nature* and is omitted entirely from *On the Duty of Man and Citizen*. But Pufendorf takes it to separate his position on the status of morality quite sharply from that of Grotius. Grotius thinks that there is a "quality of moral baseness or necessity" intrinsic to certain acts, which guides God's legislation. Pufendorf maintains strongly that it is a mistake to say "that some things are noble or base of themselves, without any imposition, and that these form the object of natural and perpetual law, while those, the good repute or baseness of which depends upon the will of a legislator, fall under the head of positive laws" (I.ii.6, p. 27).[9]

He offers several reasons for his position. One rests on the claim that the nobility or baseness of action arises from the conformity of action to law, and since "law is the bidding of a superior" there cannot be nobility or baseness antecedent to law.[10] Another is that man's reason alone cannot account for the difference between bodily motions that are sinful and those that are not. Reason alone might enable us to do more cleverly or efficiently what animals do, and so to make a distinction be-

---

7   Pufendorf devotes a lengthy chapter (*DJN* VIII.iv, pp. 1229–73) to "the value of persons in common life, in accordance with which they can be equalled or compared with other persons, and ranked either before or after them." This kind of value is different from rights and obligations, though the amount of "simple esteem" one is entitled to is a function of the extent to which one performs one's duties reliably (VIII.iv.1–6, pp. 1229–33). Another kind of esteem, "intensive esteem," comes from the offices and honors that the sovereign may award, and this is the main topic of the chapter.

8   Pufendorf does not present a developed epistemology in his works on natural law. He operates as an empiricist, as I note later. It did not occur to him that if moral entities are constituted by volition, theoretical entities might be so also. Hence he does not discuss the issue of the social construction of theoretical or factual knowledge.

9   As I pointed out in Chapter 4.vi, it is not entirely clear that Grotius and Pufendorf are as sharply divided on this matter as Pufendorf makes out that they are.

10   Cf. also *DJN* II.iii.4, pp. 183–4. Grotius, as I noted, uses a different definition of "law."

tween what is expeditiously done and what is not. But without a law it would never enable us "to discover any morality in the actions of a man."

These rather specious arguments do not reveal Pufendorf's central concern. It is the voluntarist concern. To set up "an eternal rule for the morality of human actions beyond the imposition of God" is to admit some external principle coeternal with God, "which He Himself had to follow in the assignment of forms of things." Pufendorf finds this quite unacceptable. Any such principle would limit God's freedom of action in creating man. But everyone, he thinks, admits that God created man and all his attributes freely. So God must have been able to give man any nature he wished. Hence there cannot be any eternal and independent moral properties in things (I.ii.6, pp. 27–8; cf. II.i.3, p. 146). Morality first enters the universe from acts of God's will, not from anything else.

In expounding his theory of moral entities, Pufendorf does not use the technical voluntarist terminology in which a distinction is made between God's absolute power and his ordained power. He shows, however, that he has the distinction in mind when he considers the objection, often made to divine command theories of morality, that God might issue other commands than the ones he has issued, and then – unthinkably – such acts as rape and murder would have to be considered obligatory. Pufendorf replies that it seems "idle and childish to inquire what God *might* have done" when it is so clear what he did do. The question, moreover, is absurd. God does not contradict his own will. He did not have to create man, or to give him his actual nature. But once he had decided to make man a rational and social animal, then "it was impossible for the natural law not to agree with his constitution, and that not by an absolute, but by a hypothetical necessity. For if man had been bound to the opposite duties, no social animal but some kind of wild and bestial creature would have been produced." In short, if man is to have a social nature (and that was not necessary), then the present laws of nature must hold; God has created man with such a nature; so as long as God does not change human nature, the same laws will be in force; and we have no reason to suppose God will change human nature (II.iii.4, pp. 184–5).[11]

---

11   Barbeyrac argues that Pufendorf is holding this version of voluntarism, rather than a more extreme version, and therefore takes him to differ very little from Grotius. See Barbeyrac's note 7, p. 3, to *DJN* I.I.iv, note 2, p. 20, to I.II.vi, and note 5, p. 122, to *DJN* II.III.iv in Kennett's translation of Barbeyrac's French translation. See also Barbeyrac's *Jugement d'un anonyme* which I discuss in Chapter 12.iv. It is worth adding that Pufendorf holds that God's glory would not have been less had he

Pufendorf notes that some acts are named by words that imply wick-edness, for example, "adultery." But this does not show that morality is rooted in physical reality, and independent of law. Words of that kind do not refer only to a kind of physical motion. They also indicate that such motions are contrary to a law. Without the law, no act could count as adulterous (I.ii.6, pp. 29–30). It is as important for Pufendorf as it is for Hobbes that we not be deceived by language into giving morality a status it does not have.

ii. *Moral good and natural good*

For a fuller understanding of moral entities, we have to look at the relation between them and the good. Pufendorf works throughout with a sharp distinction between "moral good" and "natural good." Hobbes makes such a distinction without attributing much importance to it.[12] It is of considerable significance for Cumberland, as I noted in Chapter 6.ii and iv. If Pufendorf's way of drawing it sounds like Cumberland's, it rests on a quite different assumption.

The assumption emerges in the comment with which Pufendorf in-troduces his discussion of natural good: "Now good is considered in an absolute way by some philosophers, so that every entity, actually exist-ing, may be considered good; but we pay no attention to such a mean-ing" (I.iv.4, p. 55). With this apparently casual remark Pufendorf breaks with a long-standing tradition in which goodness and being are equa-ted.[13] Grotius would have been at least sympathetic to the tradition, and Cumberland takes it as obvious that "Good is as extensive as Being" (5.xiii, p. 210). Hobbes's definition of good in terms of desire indicates that he rejects the equation, but he does not think the meta-physical point worthy of note. Pufendorf elaborates on it in ways that separate him from Hobbes as well as from Cumberland.

He concentrates on what is good or bad in relation to persons. So understood, he says, "the nature of good seems to consist in an aptitude

created nothing at all. The existence of the world is as contingent as its constitutive laws (*DJN* II.iii.4, p. 184).

12   He makes such a distinction in his controversy with Bramhall, arguing in support of his own view that good is "relative to those that are pleased with it." Bramhall says that right reason shows us the moral good. Hobbes replies that a gentle, reliable horse is good, but not morally good, and that "[i]t is the law from whence proceeds the difference between the moral and the natural goodness." Law is all that Bramhall can mean by "right reason" as distinguishing the two kinds of good (*Works,* ed. Molesworth, V.192–3).

13   See MacDonald 1991 for articles discussing the history and systematic com-plexities of this point.

whereby one thing is fitted to help, preserve, or complete another."
Such aptitudes are part of the nature of things and do not depend on
what people want or what they think about them. With Cumberland
and against Hobbes, Pufendorf takes the relations which make one
thing good for another as purely objective. He goes out of his way to
indicate that although the good arouses desire whenever perceived, it
may be misperceived, or overlooked, and in that case desire would
mistakenly urge us to pursue an "imaginary" good (I.iv.4, p. 56). Moral
goodness is quite different from natural. Moral goodness belongs to
actions insofar as they agree with law. For complete moral goodness, an
act must accord materially with the law or moral rule, and must be done
because it does so accord (I.vii.3–4, pp. 114–16).[14]

In his definition of law Pufendorf breaks as radically with tradition
as he does in abandoning the equation of goodness and being – and he
does so just as casually. "Law" is defined simply as "a decree by which a
superior obligates a subject to adapt his actions to the former's command" (I.vi.4, p. 89).[15] Suarez and Cumberland, following Thomas,
held that law is necessarily ordered to the common good, and even
Hobbes defined law in terms of what on his view is the supreme good,
life.[16] Grotius apparently disagreed. Law has the backing of expediency, he held, but that does not make expediency part of its definition
(*DJBP*, prol. 16). Pufendorf's definition, severing all connection with
good, allows him to hold that a morally right or good act may not bring
about any natural good. The point is linked to his more general view
that moral entities are in principle independent of the natural properties of physical things.[17]

14   Pufendorf does not go on to discuss the goodness of moral agents in this
section. He discusses instead their justice. A person is just when "he delights in
acting justly, . . . applies himself to justice." So a just person can do some unjust acts
(*DJN* I.vii.6, p. 117). To explain goodness of persons Pufendorf needs his notion of
merit, which in turn requires the notion of imperfect duties. I discuss this in section v.

15   In section vi I discuss Pufendorf's views on obligation, and the problem he
has in relating the justification or validity of obligation to the motivating force that
comes with recognition of a valid obligation.

16   For St. Thomas, see *ST* Ia.IIae.90.2. In an early work Grotius follows Thomas:
see *Jurisprudence of Holland*, I.ii.i, p. 5: "Law is a product of reason ordaining for the
common good what is honorable, established and published by one who has authority over a community of men." The view drops out of the later work.

17   At *DJN* I.i.15, p. 15, Pufendorf remarks that moral entities should only be
imposed when some benefit will accrue to mankind, but that they are sometimes
constituted without regard for such benefits. He criticizes imposing entities in this
way but does not suggest that it is impossible.

The independence of moral and natural good has practical implications. Although some moral entities, for example, the role of husband, can be imposed only on physical entities with specific physical qualities, abilities that enable one to bring about natural good are not among them. Neither strength nor beauty nor wit necessarily entitles one to anything. Neither do facts about one's biological parentage. The logic of moral entities entails that nature cannot morally require us to accept hereditary rulers; and power alone entitles no one – not even God – to authority.

Pufendorf does not deprecate natural good. His point is only that as such it is not the determinant of moral entities. Natural good becomes morally significant when it is enjoined by law and brought about voluntarily because of law. But many things which naturally assist humans and so are naturally good need not be morally good, since they need not come from voluntary action; and there are helpful actions, such as those done by animals, which have no moral quality. Pufendorf holds, as we shall see, that the laws of nature always do have some relation to what helps or harms humans; but not everything naturally good is the object of natural law (I.i.6, pp. 28–9).

There is an important further connection between moral good and natural good. "The dignity of man's nature," Pufendorf says, does not allow our good to be confined to bodily goods. The soul is intended to do more than keep the body alive. That could be done by "a much less elaborate provision" (II.i.5, p. 148). "And surely it was not for nothing," he continues,

> that God gave man a mind which could recognize a seemly order, and the power to harmonize his actions therewith, but it was of a surety intended that man should use those God-given faculties, for the greater glory of God and his own richer felicity. (II.i.5, p. 149)

Pufendorf is here saying that the good God intended us to achieve with our special nature is not restricted to natural good. It must include a good indicated by the higher aspect of our nature – reason and will. These distinctively human faculties make us able to know and obey laws, and show that God meant us to live in accordance with laws (II.i.1–5, pp. 145–9). It follows that even from God's point of view the laws of nature are not simply instrumental for the achievement of a human good that could be specified without reference to them. Like Luther, Pufendorf holds that the law shows us what we must do to be pleasing to God. Unlike Luther, he does not add that we cannot do it. The moral good of obedience to the creator is as much a part of the end we are now to strive for as is the natural good of happiness.

iii. *Knowledge of natural law*

Pufendorf thinks that our natural understanding is flawed because of original sin, yet not so corrupted as to prevent us from knowing the laws of nature. On the contrary, the part of our understanding whose special function is to weigh the reasons for good and ill and pass judgment on what is to be done possesses a "natural rectitude, which does not allow us to be misled in moral questions," just as the part of understanding whose function is to know the physical world is naturally sound (I.iii.1–2, pp. 38–9). No mature person of ordinary capacity is "too dull to comprehend at least the more general precepts of natural law" (I.iii.3, p. 40). Like the natural lawyers before him, Pufendorf thinks that ordinary people are not capable of deriving the more detailed laws of nature by themselves. They must learn these from others, and receive them on authority (II.iii.13, p. 204). But some people can find out the law for themselves. If we allow that revelation teaches us the law, "it can still be investigated and definitely proved, even without such aid, by the power of reason" (II.iii.13, p. 201; cf. II.iii.20, p. 220). One central aim of the *Law of Nature* is to explain how we can obtain this natural knowledge.

As a preliminary, Pufendorf defends the possibility of achieving certainty in our knowledge of natural law. Some have denied this possibility because they have made a simple mistake. They think, correctly, that to have certainty we must deduce a conclusion from principles. The conclusion is then necessary. But it does not follow, as they mistakenly suppose, that the subject of the conclusion by itself is a necessarily existing entity. We can have certain knowledge of contingent things – a point that Pufendorf obviously needs in order to claim that we can have knowledge about moral entities (I.ii.2, p. 23).

Others object that moral guidance cannot involve knowledge because it lacks mathematical precision. Pufendorf agrees about the imprecision. Moral entities cannot be measured in the same way as physical entities; but that is because the end to be served by moral entities does not require quantitative exactness. "It was enough for the purpose of man's life," he says, "that persons, things, and actions be roughly rated and compared" (I.ii.10, p. 35). Practical knowledge – knowledge of moral entities – does not tell us anything about the physical world, but of course it is not meant to do so. It conforms to different standards because it has its own function.

Some doubters, including Carneades, have said that morality is nothing but a matter of personal utility, which varies so much from society to society, and from person to person, that we cannot obtain fixed and certain principles to direct our effort to attain it (II.iii.10, pp.

194–9). Pufendorf agrees that self-interest has this defect; but he holds that morality is not a matter of personal advantage. Its principles do not suffer from these uncertainties. They are utterly secure and leave no doubt about the conclusions deduced from them (I.ii.4, pp. 24–5). To make this out is the task of the entire book.

Pufendorf is firm in rejecting several views about the attainment of moral knowledge. He denies, for instance, that moral rules are so clearly imprinted in the mind at birth that we have but to look within ourselves to know them. He finds this objectionable first on epistemo-logical grounds. Pufendorf is an empiricist and thinks that we must be able to learn the laws of nature from evidence available in experience.[18] His treatment of St. Paul's claim in Romans 2.14–15, that the Gentiles have the law written in their hearts, emphasizes his empiricism. Paul's phrase, Pufendorf comments, "is a figure of speech," meaning only that the knowledge of the laws of nature is clear and is deeply fixed in us, due either to our own observation or to habit and training (II.iii.13, p. 202).[19] Although Pufendorf sets conditions for knowledge that sound Cartesian – deducibility of what is known from basic propositions that cannot be doubted (I.ii.2–3, pp. 22–3) – he insists that "the dictates of sound reason are true principles that are in accordance with the prop-erly observed and examined nature of things" (II.iii.13, p. 203). As his practice shows, this means that what he calls the axioms or basic princi-ples of natural law are to be gathered from experience. On these matters Pufendorf is at one with Grotius, Hobbes, and Cumberland.

Pufendorf's second objection to a method relying on innate princi-ples might be called moral or, more broadly, practical. It occurs in his discussion of conscience. For him conscience is simply the ability of men to judge actions in terms of laws. Hence, he says, "if one wishes to ascribe to the practical judgement or conscience some particular power to direct actions, which does not emanate or arise from law, he ascribes the power of laws to any fantastic idea of men, and introduces the utmost confusion into human affairs" (I.iii.4, p. 41). Grotius, Hobbes, and Cumberland would have been sympathetic to this way of defining conscience. All of them hoped, with Pufendorf, that insisting on observ-able evidence to support moral claims would offer a way to damp down some of the fiercest outbursts of human unsociability.

Despite his agreement with Hobbes and Cumberland about empiri-cism, Pufendorf disagrees with both of them in explaining how we are to obtain moral knowledge. He does not adopt Hobbes's method of

18   On this point see Denzer 1972, pp. 40–8.
19   See also Pufendorf's remark about how childhood training makes us think moral qualities are natural, *DJN* I.ii.6, pp. 29–30.

deriving the content of the laws of nature from considering the means
which will secure our private end. Pufendorf does not think men are
motivated solely by self-interest, which is what he takes Hobbes to
think.[20] But he does insist that we must admit self-interest to have the
first place in any estimate of human nature. It is not the sole measure of
what we are to do; it is just an important fact about us to be considered
in deriving natural law (II.iii.14, p. 207).

Pufendorf also rejects the claim that we can derive knowledge of the
laws of nature by discovering what serves God's ultimate end. His
rejection of this thesis arises first from his voluntarism. He questions
"whether it can be said in any useful sense that *God set before Himself and
man* a common *end,* or that the order constituted for man, that is, the
observance of the law of nature, produces the end of creation as set
down by God."[21] And even if one admitted the possibility, Pufendorf
adds, it would be "impossible to understand clearly and distinctly what
integral relation each of the precepts of the law of nature bears" to
God's purposes for the entire universe. We could not do the calculations
necessary to discover the details of the laws of nature (II.iii.12, p. 201).
Pufendorf is here attacking a continental theorist, not Cumberland; but
his response plainly entails a rejection of Cumberland's method for
obtaining moral guidance, which rests on the belief that God and we do
share a common end.

His rejection of these ways of deriving laws from consideration of
consequences does not rest on any thought that natural good and evil
are irrelevant to morality. On the contrary: Pufendorf is convinced that
"by the wisdom of the Creator the natural law has been so adapted to
the nature of man, that its observation is always connected with the
profit and advantage of men" (II.iii.18, p. 213). The question, then, is
how our knowledge of the natural goodness of consequences is involved in our discovery of the moral rightness or wrongness of actions.
Pufendorf's answer makes central to modern natural law theory some
ideas that had already been canvassed in traditional versions.[22]

His method has, like older views, a religious underpinning. One of
Pufendorf's avowed aims is to show that morality, or natural law, has a
firm basis which does not rely on controversial religious claims (pref., p.
ix). But this aim does not, on his view, require him to dismiss religion

20   There are occasional statements which are inconsistent with this general
stand. See, e.g., *DJN* VII.i.2, p. 951: "to what good is the love of individuals drawn
save to what each of them has judged to be good for himself?"
21   I return in the final section of this chapter to the significance of Pufendorf's
denial that God and we can have a common purpose.
22   At *De Legibus* II.viii.4 (*Selections*, p. 219), Suarez discusses without accepting
a method allied to the one Pufendorf uses. See also St. Thomas, *ST* Ia.IIae.94.2.

completely from natural law theory. There are religious convictions which all reasonable men share, and to which appeal can be made. Thus he assumes both that "it has long been established by men of discernment . . . that God is the maker and controller of this universe," and that this belief is a common possession of mankind (II.iii.20, p. 217; cf. III.iv.4, p. 383). It is only revealed religion that must be excluded from natural law theory. Natural religion is vital to it.[23]

If we can assume that at least as regards their main features things of each kind were created for some good purpose, then those features can be used to indicate how God meant things of that kind to behave or operate. We will need empirical observation to establish the main special or salient features of things of each kind. But in the case of humans, these features are so well known and so obvious that no complex or difficult inquiry will be needed to establish what they are. Assertions about them will be so plain and obvious that they will not be open to doubt. We can then argue from these factually indubitable premises to conclusions about how God intended us to act. And we should treat God's intentions, indicated by his creation, as being laws for us. Here, at least, Pufendorf agrees with Cumberland.

Because the special features of humans are clear signs of God's intentions for us, the best way to learn the laws of nature is to consider man's "nature, condition, and desires," paying attention to his circumstances and particularly to "such things as work for his advantage or disadvantage." Regardless of whether we think of the law as meant to help men to happiness or to restrain their evil inclinations, the law is best learned "by observing when man needs assistance and when he needs restraint" (II.iii.14, p. 205).

We can see the method at work by following the derivation of the first law of nature. Experience shows that humans can be helped or harmed, so that things can be good or bad for them. We know that humans are rational and free, and this indicates that they are intended to live under laws (II.i.1–5, pp. 145–9). To get a definite law, we move beyond these obvious points. The first salient feature of humans is their self-love. If concern for one's own benefit is not absolute and exceptionless – we love our children and our friends – it is nonetheless generally what is foremost in each person's mind. We always try first of all to protect ourselves, obtain what we need, and flee whatever threatens our lives. In addition, we are "at all times malicious, petulant,

23 Pufendorf does not always steer clear of revealed religion. He seems to appeal to revelation to counter Hobbes's claim that mankind was originally in a state of war: Scripture tells us otherwise (*DJN* II.ii.7, pp. 168–9). And as we shall see, he appeals to Scripture to show that there are divine punishments for those who break the laws of nature (II.iii.21, p. 224). But he is plainly unhappy about having to do so.

and easily irritated." Thus it is a striking feature of our nature that it cannot be easy for us to live with one another. Yet as a second salient feature makes evident, we must. We are much weaker than other animals. Without assistance we cannot secure even our own good effectively, much less that of those we care for (II.iii.14, pp. 205–7). More than any other animal we are made to need help and to be able to give it.

Now consider these features together, and ask how they can best work for the advantage of humans, which is how God must have meant them to work. The answer is that they can work for our advantage when we live socially, in mutually helpful groups. And from this Pufendorf derives the first fundamental law of nature: "Every man, so far as in him lies, should cultivate and preserve toward others a sociable attitude, which is peaceful and agreeable at all times to the nature and end of the human race" (II.iii.15, pp. 207–8).

The basic law of nature responds, in Grotian fashion, to our natural unsuitability for the sociable living we naturally need. The remaining laws are all treated as showing us means to cope with the many different facets of the problem posed by our contrariness. If we are obligated to an end we are obligated to the means to it. So "all things which necessarily work to that sociable attitude are understood to be commanded by natural law" (II.iii.15, p. 208). Finding out what things are conducive to the sociable attitude requires empirical investigation. It can be done in one area of life after another, looking simply to ordinary facts. For example, it helps sociability greatly if all of us treat one another as equals, unless we have agreed to consider some people as superiors (III.ii, pp. 330ff.). A habit of abstaining from harming others is obviously required for a sociable attitude. But this is not enough. The sociable attitude is strengthened if we confer positive benefits on one another as well, and therefore it is a law of nature that we should do so (III.iii.1, p. 346). This in turn requires us to cultivate our talents, so as to be generally ready to confer benefits; to grant to others things which we can give them at no cost to ourselves, such as water from our spring, or passage across our property; and to be hospitable (III.iii.2–9, pp. 347–63).

The patient elaboration of detailed and specific laws covering contract, marriage, commercial transactions, and international relations shows that Pufendorf's method does not require us to calculate the amounts of good and evil that would be generated by different possible laws. It does not involve balancing utilities or maximizing good results. Following the laws of nature is for our advantage, he says, for God sees to that; but in giving a reason for a law or for fostering the sociable attitude, "one does not refer to the advantage accruing therefrom, but to the common nature of all men" (II.iii.18, pp. 213–14).

Pufendorf's view of the distinctive human good is itself an application of the kind of teleological argument from which he derives the laws of nature. The most striking difference between us and other created beings is that we are able to know and obey laws. But then, plainly, doing so is something God requires of us. When we obey the fundamental law by increasing our own sociability, we are developing a certain character. It is a character that suits us for communal living, and so it is useful in satisfying human needs. And in developing such a character we are also realizing the complex good that God has let us know is his end for us. Through it we may hope to become pleasing to him.

iv. *Perfect and imperfect duty*

What is most immediately evident about Pufendorf's presentation of the laws of nature is his stress on requirements concerned with performing specific duties. Literally hundreds of pages of the *Law of Nature* are devoted to spelling out detailed rules governing myriad aspects of social life. Though Pufendorf is concerned about character and the inner life, the concern is not nearly so obvious.[24] He explicitly connects this emphasis on external action with the claim that natural law is limited to what can be known by reason. We cannot know about immortality or about what we have to hope or fear from it except from revelation; moral theology rather than natural jurisprudence is therefore the discipline that properly discusses the matter, and with it the inner conditions that make us worthy of salvation.

Suarez had claimed that the moral theologian is the proper authority to work out the laws of nature, on the grounds that they state, however incompletely, some of the conditions of salvation. In the preface to his *Duty of Man*, Pufendorf claims that natural law is a wholly secular discipline, with no room for the moral theologian (*De Officio*, pref. i, p. 7). He holds accordingly that "the decrees of natural law are fitted only to the human court," and concludes that

> as human jurisdiction is concerned only with a man's external actions and does not penetrate to what is hidden in the heart which gives no external effect or sign, and consequently takes no account of it, natural law too is largely concerned with forming men's external actions. (pref. vii, p. 9)

---

24 Pufendorf says that self-love will lead us to wish to have such a character that others will want to help us. Hence we will try to avoid being "malevolent, perfidious, ungrateful and inhuman" (*DJN* II.iii.16, p. 213). The deeper significance of character emerges in connection with imperfect duties, which I discuss next. See Döring 1992, pp. 79–80.

The qualification of the limitation to external actions implicit in the word "largely" is of considerable importance, as Pufendorf makes clear. The Savior, he says, reduced the whole law to two commands: love God, and love your neighbor. And these headings do indeed cover the whole of natural law in Pufendorf's version of it, "for sociality, which we have laid out as the foundation of natural law, can readily be resolved into love of one's neighbor" (pref. viii, p. 12). Despite first impressions, we must read Pufendorf as giving us as much an ethic of love as one of law, or rather as trying to spell out the proper relations of law and love in morality.

The relation is handled chiefly through a distinction Pufendorf makes in the *Law of Nature* between perfect and imperfect duties. His way of making the distinction is a development of one made by Grotius between perfect and imperfect rights. (See Chapter 4.viii, and note 39.) Pufendorf has a more theoretical cast of mind than Grotius, and pushes further in the direction of explicit clarification than his master. Thus he not only accepts the Grotian distinction between perfect and imperfect rights and duties, he tidies it up as well. Rights generally are moral powers obtained under law – the law of nature or enacted law – and, as there are two kinds of moral power, so there are two kinds of right. In the case of perfect right, I am by definition entitled to use force to protect my exercise of the power. Within a political society this means I can go to court; between nations, it allows the justification of war. Imperfect rights by definition do not permit their holder to exact compliance by force, though it is to be admitted that wrongly hindering their exercise is inhumane (*DJN* I.i.19–20, pp. 18–20).

The domain of imperfect duties is "universal justice," which covers all our obligations outside the domain of strict justice.[25] Pufendorf gives as examples coming to someone's aid "with counsel, goods, or personal assistance," or performing a service of "piety, respect, gratitude, or generosity" where one is indebted in some way to the person thus aided. In carrying out these imperfect duties, the point is only to give to the possessor of the imperfect right some good or other. This is to be done "without observing whether the service furnished is equal to, or less than, that which was the reason for the obligation" (I.vii.7–9, pp. 118–21). Perfect rights and duties, by contrast, require precisely specifiable behavior. We have perfect rights to our lives; everyone therefore has a duty not to kill us. We have similar rights to our bodies, so that no one has a right to use them without our consent. We can use force to

---

25 Pufendorf thinks there can be no obligation to oneself. One can have duties whose point is to do something about or for oneself, such as the duty, touched on earlier, to develop one's talents; but the obligation must be to someone else (*DJN* I.vi.7, p. 94).

protect these rights. Contracts also give rise to perfect rights and duties, and we can appeal to the lawcourt to compel everyone to comply with the requirements they entail. Thus precision as well as enforceability marks perfect rights and duties, imprecision and unenforceability mark the imperfect.

If Pufendorf is tidier than Grotius in distinguishing kinds of rights, he is also more interested in explaining the distinction functionally. He offers his explanation in two stages. The first explains why perfect rights are enforceable. Among the laws of nature some must be observed if society is to exist at all, whereas others conduce to "an improved existence." Perfect rights and duties take their character from the first kind of law, the imperfect from the second. The next stage of explanation spells out how imperfect and perfect rights and duties supplement one another. Men have many needs that can be satisfied only if others help; but

> not all men are so constituted that they are willing to do everything, with which they can help others, out of mere humanity and love . . . while it is often the case that the things which can come to us from others are of such a nature that we cannot have the boldness to ask that they be done for us gratis. . . . And so, if mutual offices, the real fruit of humanity, are to be practiced more frequently . . . it was necessary for men themselves to agree . . . on the mutual rendering of such services as a man could not also be certain of for himself on the mere law of humanity. (III.iv.1, p. 379)

If perfect rights represent necessities, and thus seem more important than imperfect rights, the latter have a different claim to our attention. It is they alone that can give rise to merit, "the efficacy of which, as some would claim," Pufendorf adds cautiously, "will be found to avail even against God," presumably as balance for our sins. The caution arises from Pufendorf's commitment to keeping God untrammeled. God cannot be a debtor to humans because of our merit, "except through a free promise which his goodness would not allow him to break" – a promise given, though it would be inappropriate for Pufendorf to mention it in this work, through Christ. We acquire merit only when we do something not strictly owed to another (I.ix.5, pp. 138–40). Hence what Pufendorf calls the works of love must be done from the appropriate loving motive. They cannot spring from recognition of a perfect duty, for in that case I would not be giving anything that is really mine to give; nor can they come from private interest, "for as soon as a kindness is done for private advantage, it loses forthwith its designation and essence" (III.iv.1, p. 380). The works of justice, however, being compellable, need not arise from any form of love. Pufendorf shows another side of the importance of this when he says that works of love win the hearts of others, and therefore provide for a kind of social solidarity which cannot be created by acts that will be exacted by force if not done voluntarily (III.iv.6, p. 386).

v. *Law and obligation*

God imposes moral entities on us by laying down laws that we are to obey. All the other basic concepts of morality derive, directly or indirectly, from the concept of law. We have a right to something when we may lawfully acquire and keep it (I.i.20, p. 19). Others have duties to allow us to keep, or to give us, that to which law assigns us rights.[26] Moral goodness and merit are both understood in terms of compliance with law. And law is involved in the definition of obligation, which on Pufendorf's view is central to morality.

When a superior tells a subject to do something and backs his decree by threatening punishment for disobedience, he makes a law (I.vi.4, p. 89). In so doing, he obligates the subject. Obligation "is that whereby one is required under moral necessity to do, or admit, or suffer something" (I.i.21, p. 20). The relations among law, the lawgiver, obligation, and moral necessity are as complex in Pufendorf's theory as they are in Cumberland's. The conception of moral necessity is particularly tangled; it is by comparison easy to get clear on Pufendorf's account of obligation. Obligating someone is directing the action of the other in a special way. It is different both from advising or counseling, and from threatening or coercing. When advising someone, I try to move him to do something in virtue of "reasons drawn from the matter in hand." When an authority imposes an obligation by laying down a law, on the other hand, although there ought to be sound reasons for enactments, "still these do not constitute the real ground for obedience . . . , but it is rather the power of the enactor" that creates the obligation once the superior's command is made known. An advisor leaves the recipient free to follow his advice or ignore it; one who obligates does not leave his subject free to obey or not (I.vi.1, pp. 87–8). The subject, moreover, need not understand the reasons for what is commanded or for his being commanded. He is obligated simply by being commanded by a superior who can threaten him with sanctions.

How, then, does obligation differ from coercion? Both, says Pufendorf, "ultimately point out some object of terror" in order to make someone do as ordered. Coercion, however,

---

26 At one point Pufendorf suggests that a complete imposition of rights requires a counterpart imposition of duties as well (*DJN* III.v.3, p. 391). Whether this is an assertion of the correlativity of rights and duties and if so whether Pufendorf is the first to assert it are matters of scholarly debate. See Mautner 1989.

only shakes the will with an external force and impels it to choose some undesired object only by the sense of an impending evil; while an obligation in addition forces a man to acknowledge of himself that the evil, which has been pointed out to the person who deviates from an announced rule, falls upon him justly. (I.vi.5, p. 91)

Sanctions are justified because obligation presupposes that a directive comes from one who can rightfully require certain actions of us (*De Officio* I.2.4, pp. 27–8). The superior must have "just reasons why he can demand that the liberty of our will be limited at his pleasure." So Hobbes is wrong, Pufendorf concludes, in thinking God is entitled by his power alone to lay down obligating laws (*DJN* I.vi.9–10, pp. 95–9).

Two points about this account require further discussion. One has to do with the justification of the claim that God has authority over us, and not merely the power to control us. The other has to do with the relation of threats of punishment to the moral necessity carried in obligation.

The question of the justification of God's authority is more difficult for Pufendorf than it is for Cumberland. Neither thinks that the content of God's command is what obligates; the formality of his commanding is for both what obligates. But Cumberland, like Suarez, can explain God's justification in commanding as he does by appeal to what he commands. God commands us to act as he does because he loves us and knows that these commands will be best for us: what more justification for laying down these laws could there be? It is the same kind of justification we would have for issuing a command. Pufendorf cannot say this. He thinks that we do not know God's reasons for having made us in such a way that the law of nature has the content it has. We do not know his aim in creating us. There must be some other reason that justifies God in requiring our obedience.

The doctrine of moral entities makes it difficult if not impossible for Pufendorf to give one. Although he rejects any naturalistic reduction of moral to natural concepts, the doctrine seems to entail a kind of reductionism that threatens his desire to hold that God has authority and not only power. Authority can belong only to one who is willing to use power within just limits. But if just limits arise ultimately from God's will, it is hard to see how God could be held to have authority in addition to strength. It is indeed doubtful that Pufendorf can allow that we can even mean anything nontautologous by saying that God rules justly. His voluntarism seems to force him into pure Hobbesianism.

Pufendorf does not take up the issue head on, but he anticipates it to some extent. He says that we do not call God just in any sense that might imply that God can have obligations to humans (*DJN* II.i.3, p. 146; II.iii.5, p. 186). Nonetheless God can put us under obligations. His strength is only a necessary condition, not a sufficient one, for his doing so. For someone to obligate me, Pufendorf says, it is necessary "that he should in addition [to possessing power over me] have done me some special service, or that I should of my own accord consent to his direction" (I.vi.12, p. 101). Now God has done each of us much service. He has made us with a sociable nature which enables us to enjoy the goods he has created. The very fact that he was not required to make us with that nature should lead us to praise him, not for his justice but for his goodness. The appropriate response to someone who is good to us is gratitude. And the only way to show gratitude to a being who needs nothing is to try to comply with his wishes. We ought, therefore, to seek out indications of God's wishes for us, and then carry them out. We must try to make ourselves pleasing to God.

This line of thought seems to explain why we are to consider God an authority we ought to obey, without holding that the commands themselves are justifiable independently of their source.[27] The explanation is open, however, to two objections. One is that the appropriateness of repaying benefits with gratitude must itself be a moral entity imposed by God, which raises the question of its justifiability. The other is that gratitude is only an imperfect duty and hence may not be exacted under threat of punishment. But Pufendorf cannot allow that obedience to God's commands is only an imperfect duty. The appeal to gratitude does not seem to work.[28]

Obligation carries moral necessity with it, for Pufendorf as well as for Cumberland. Why are threats of punishment central in creating obligation? The formal reason is that a law by definition contains both precept and sanction, and since law is required to give rise to obligation there must be sanctions (I.vi.14, p. 104).[29] Materially, sanctions provide incentives for obeying God's laws. Pufendorf suggests that sanctions help arouse in us a special feeling from which we ought to be moved to obey God's commands. He must have known Suarez's view that we can be moved to obedience by "righteousness" (Chapter 4.iii). But he does not himself develop the thought. He says instead that sanctions themselves give us a sufficient incentive for compliance, if this other, more refined incentive fails – as it usually does.

27 The debate on divine command ethics continues, with some revival of the strategy I attribute to Pufendorf. How satisfactory it ultimately is, even for religious believers, remains a question. See, e.g., Chandler 1985, who discusses, among others, the views on divine command ethics of Robert M. Adams in 1987.

28 I consider Leibniz's criticisms of Pufendorf on this and related points, and Barbeyrac's defense, in Chapter 12.v.

29 In the same passage Pufendorf objects to Cumberland's inclusion of rewards under the heading of sanctions. It is established usage, he says, to include only punishments.

Awareness of God's sanctions and recognition of our debt of gratitude together give rise "in the faculty of reason" to a combination of fear and reverence; but the reverence alone should "be sufficient, even without the fear, to lead one to receive the command on grounds of good judgment alone" (I.vi.9, p. 95). We must feel respect for God, who has done so much for us, and we should be moved to obey in return. Here Pufendorf seems to be suggesting that simple recognition that a law is a divine command should awaken a motive for compliance in us. He thinks, however, that most men do not pay much attention to God's commands, even when they admit that he ought to be obeyed. It takes something more than "a feeling of shame and an appreciation of what is right" to make most people obey (I.vi.12, p. 101). It takes fear, which moves the will so strongly that it makes it necessary for us to obey. We are obligated simply by the command of our superior; but the necessity in obligation comes from the fear that the threat of punishment arouses in us (I.vi.14, pp. 105–7).

Pufendorf has a good reason to wish there were some other incentive for compliance with God's law, because he has, and can have, no good account of what the sanctions for moral laws are. He nowhere indicates a willingness to share Cumberland's confidence that God has built sufficient sanctions into the course of nature to induce compliance. And he is reluctant to appeal to rewards and punishments after this life, since our knowledge of them depends on revelation (II.iii.21, p. 224).[30]

The appeal to sanctions is problematic for Pufendorf in another way as well. He holds a strong doctrine of free will. In this he is again opposing Hobbes. For Hobbes, as I noted in Chapter 5.ii, will is only an endeavor occurring in a certain position in an alternation of endeavors, wholly determined by the state of the universe preceding it. Pufendorf treats will as a power or faculty separate from desires. Its chief quality is that it is not confined intrinsically to a definite mode of action. Given all the things requisite to action, the will is able to "choose one, or some, and to reject the rest," or to do nothing. He partially accepts a weak version of the old thesis, which we have seen in Cumberland, that the will pursues what is presented as naturally good (I.iv.4, p. 56). But he refuses to go all the way with the thesis. Although the will has a general propensity toward good, it can remain indifferent in the presence of any instance of it (I.iv.2–3, pp. 53–4). "The will of individuals," he says, "exerts the force of its indifference on particular goods and evils" (I.iv.4, p. 56).

---

30 He thinks, moreover, that most men do not live by reason, but by impulse, and that they pay less attention to divine punishments than to earthly ones. So even divine sanctions alone would not suffice to constitute obligations for most people (*DJN* VII.i.11, pp. 964–5). And if divine sanctions were essential to obligation, atheists would not think they had any obligations (IV.ii.6, p. 501).

Freedom of this kind is crucial. Without it, Pufendorf holds, "the morality of human actions is at once destroyed" (I.iv.3, p. 54). Only because we possess it are our spontaneous and voluntary actions fully imputable to us (I.v.5, pp. 70–1). And Pufendorf insists that we are free to accept or reject obligations as well as natural goods. When an obligation is admitted, the will is thereby inclined to do the obligatory act, but it does not lose its "intrinsic liberty" (I.iv.8, p. 62; cf. I.vi.6, p. 91). Thus without the capacity freely to obey or disobey, there can be no obligation. Yet obligation requires moral necessity. Sanctions are supposed to create it; yet if we can freely refrain from pursuing the greatest good we are aware of, we are presumably free also to ignore the greatest harm. How, then, can the threat of punishment necessitate? And if it does not, how is there moral necessity in obligation?

I do not think that Pufendorf has an answer. But it is not entirely surprising that he should lack one. He is here confronting the intersection of moral entities and physical beings. Obligation is a moral entity. As such it has no causal power of its own. Desires, as part of our physical nature, can cause us to act in space and time; but recognition of obligation gives us a consideration or reason for action that does not operate in the field of force in which desires operate. Desires and obligations are thus incommensurable kinds of considerations for and against action. Hobbes could explain action as the outcome of commensurable desires pulling us this way and that. Pufendorf cannot. He therefore needs a separate faculty of free will to explain how moral entities can be effective in human life even though they possess no causal strength. But he offers no account of how recognition of a moral entity can have effects in the physical world. If he was the first modern to find this problem squarely at the center of his metaphysics of ethics, he was not the last.

vi. *The significance of Pufendorf's voluntarism*

The success of Pufendorf's exposition of natural law did much to make a concern with voluntarism inescapable in European moral philosophy. The voluntarism itself bears on two major aspects of moral theory. It affects both our understanding of the ontological position of morality in the universe, and our understanding of our moral relation to God.

The ontological significance of the doctrine of moral entities is fairly definite. It is a major effort to think through a new understanding of the relation of values and obligations to the physical world. It presents a new response to the developing scientific view of the world as neutral with respect to value. Accepting the concept of a purely natural good dependent on the physical relations of things to humans, Pufendorf refuses to see it as the sole kind of value, and insists that moral norms and conventional values of all kinds are conceptually independent of it. He denies the old equation of goodness with existence, and the Grotian assertion of special moral qualities built into the nature of things. He equally repudiates the reductionism of Hobbes and Cumberland, the definition of all evaluative terms by means of terms descriptive of the physical world. Moral entities involve ideas and beliefs that do not in any way represent the way things are in the world. Their whole point is to guide action. Moral entities are inventions, some of them divine, most of them human. Their ontological status gives us no reason to doubt their ability to serve their purpose.

Pufendorf's main reason for taking this line is that it alone allows us to have a proper understanding of God. Only voluntarism leaves God untrammeled. Religious voluntarists before Pufendorf might have accepted much of this. What they could not have accepted, and what makes Pufendorf's voluntarist account of the construction of morality so striking, is that humans are accorded the ability to construct functioning moral entities in just the way that God does, and just as efficaciously. It takes God to get the process started; but God has made us so that constructive willing is part of our normal rational activity. This points to the second important aspect of Pufendorf's voluntarism.

In his short book on the duty of man and citizen Pufendorf includes, as he does not in the treatise on natural law, a special chapter on duties to God (*De Officio* I.4). He tells us that we are to believe that God exists and takes providential care of us, and to worship him in public as well as privately. He also insists that we can say nothing positive about him except to show our "admiration and obedience" (I.4.4–5, pp. 41–2). His view about religious language is Hobbesian, but with him there is no question, as there is with Hobbes, about whether his voluntarism is a cover for atheism. Pufendorf was a sincere Lutheran.[31] God, for him, is beyond our comprehension. He is our creator and our ruler, whom we are to honor and obey. But he and we are not in any sense members of a single community, as Cumberland thought that we are.

It is of course clear on Pufendorf's view that God, having no superior, can never be under a law and therefore can never be obligated. Pufendorf does not discuss Cumberland's claim that despite this there is a counterpart in God to the moral necessity that binds us, but he strongly repudiates a view very like it proposed by another contemporary (*DJN* II.iii.6, pp. 187–8). The whole conceptual apparatus of our morality, therefore, since it derives from law, has no pertinence when we think of God (cf. II.i.3, p. 146).

31   See Döring 1992, pp. 115–22.

The most basic law of morality is that we are to increase our sociability. We are to do so because we are both quarrelsome and in need of assistance from one another. Since God does not share these attributes, the law holds only among humans. And since all the other laws are derived from this one, there can be none that apply to God. Not even justice can be modeled on some alleged divine justice, because "a right which is to have power among persons equal in nature" cannot be patterned after the relations between persons as drastically unequal as humans and God (II.iii.5, p. 186). Pufendorf ridicules the idea that there could be any morality common to God and us. "For who," he asks, "dare reason thus? Pay your debts, because God pays his. Be grateful, because God is kind to them that serve him. Obey your Governors, because God is subject to his superiors. Honour your parents, because God honours his. Are not these reasonings manifestly absurd?"[32]

Pufendorf makes strikingly clear the ultimate contingency of morality entailed by the voluntarist view. Once God has decided to create us with the nature we have, it is indeed necessary that he should command us to obey laws that forward our good. The laws themselves are necessary only as means to that end. And it was necessary neither that God should create, nor that he should have created beings with our distinctive nature. We do not know God's ultimate purpose in creating us as he did. Hence although God's will is in one sense the foundation of morality, in another sense morality has no foundation. It has no inherent rationality. It does not rest on self-evident principles. It is neither eternal nor necessary. It is as contingent as the constitution of the created world.

That God keeps watch on his creation does not entail that we should expect any special help from him. He has put us in the world with powers that enable us to survive and even to thrive, and this shows that he wills us to use them to create for ourselves a life superior to that of the animals. God could, of course, do more for us than anyone else, but Pufendorf takes it that his message to us is that in this life we are to rely on one another. Any advantages we have now have come to us from "men's mutual assistance" (De Officio I.3.11, p. 36; 3.3, p. 34). Reason shows us God's most general instructions. The rest is up to us.

---

32   See Kennet's translation of DJN II.iii.v, p. 123 and n. 5. The illustrations, given in the note, are added by Barbeyrac from one of Pufendorf's polemical writings.

8

The collapse of modern natural law: Locke and Thomasius

Barbeyrac tells us that Bacon was a major influence on Grotius, and Cumberland claims that his own work answers Bacon's call for empirical investigation of morals.[1] We have seen how important the empiricist outlook was for both Grotius and Cumberland; but Bacon held views that neither would have accepted. In his "Confession of Faith" he declared his belief

> that God created Man in his own image . . . that he gave him a law and commandment . . . that man made a total defection from God, presuming to imagine that the commandments and prohibitions of God were not the rules of Good and Evil, but that Good and Evil had their own principles and beginnings; and lusted after the knowledge of those imagined beginnings, to the end to depend no more upon God's will revealed, but upon himself and his light, as a God; than the which there could not be a sin more opposite to the whole law of God.[2]

Bacon was not alone in combining empiricism, voluntarism, and the belief that pride is what moves us to insist that we must be able to understand God's commands by our own lights. Pufendorf's system presents the fullest modern exposition of the implications for morality of a view like this, and Locke recommended Pufendorf's work for the education of any gentleman's son. It is, he said, "the best book of that kinde."[3]

Locke's own writings outlined a view of morality resembling Pufendorf's in important respects. They also raised furious objections. A remark by a critic indicates some of them. The critic, Thomas Burnet, though denying that he is part of a plot against Locke as Locke had suggested, endorses some common objections:

---

1 Barbeyrac, *Historical Account*, XXIX, p. 79; Cumberland, *Laws of Nature*, introd. iv.13.
2 "A Confession of Faith," in *Works*, II.III.150–1.
3 *Some Thoughts concerning Education*, sec. 186.

> I can blame none that desires such principles of human understanding as
> may give them proofs and security against such a system as this: cogitant
> matter, a mortal soul, a Manichean God (or a God without moral at-
> tributes) and an arbitrary law of good and evil. . . . the ready way to
> prevent any such storm is to give such a plain explication of your princi-
> ples, without art or chicane, as may cure and remove any fears of this
> nature.[4]

Friends as well as critics asked Locke several times to give a "plain
explication" of his moral theory, but in his published writings he did
not do so, and his rejections of his friends' requests could be testy.[5]
Though one or two of Locke's acquaintances knew that he had written
extensively on natural law when he was a young Oxford don, suggestions that he revise or release the early work went unheeded.[6] Some of
his published remarks indicate that he thought he had a comprehensive
ethical theory explaining how reason could show what moral requirements we must satisfy; yet he left his readers to infer what this theory
might be from a number of brief, scattered, and sometimes puzzling
passages. We risk serious historical distortion if we insist on piecing
together a comprehensive moral theory from writings Locke never suggested should go together. He may not have had any such theory.[7]

i. *Locke and the Grotian problematic*

Whether he did or not, we find enough in his positive assertions to
enable us to relate his views to those of the other natural lawyers we
have been discussing. Locke frequently cites Hooker in the *Second Treatise*, yet, as his strong endorsements of Pufendorf suggest, it is better to
take him to be working with the modern natural law framework than to
be using a Thomistic view. His description of the state of nature is
Grotian without being Hobbesian.[8] Grotian sociability as well as need
draw us together, the laws of nature are valid prior to the institution of a
sovereign, and although war may occur, it is neither inevitable nor

4 Burnet, *Second Remarks*, p. 11. Burnet returned to this specific charge in his
Third Remarks, p. 16, denying once again that he was part of any conspiracy and
insisting that anyone might demand that Locke reply.

5 See the letter to Tyrrell of August 4, 1690, Locke, *Correspondence*, IV, letter 1309.
His responses to Burnet, who in his first *Remarks* pressed Locke on the matter of
proof of moral principles, were also tart and unhelpful.

6 Ibid., IV, letters 1301, 1307, 1309.

7 For Locke's ethics see Colman 1983; Marshall 1994, chs. 5 and 7; Spellman
1988, chs. 4 and 7; Tully 1980 and 1993, esp. ch. 6.

8 Commentators have frequently noted Locke's intense desire to deny that his
views and Hobbes's were at all similar or that Hobbes influenced him. Page references to the *Two Treatises* are from the edition of Laslett.

frequent. At the same time there is enough discord to drive us to seek a ruler as a remedy. The discord arises because in the state of nature each of us must be the judge of whether our own actions are permissible or not (*Treatises* II.13, pp. 275–6). Locke takes it that we must set up a political order to avoid the "inconveniencies" – that is, the strife – that this causes (II.90, p. 326). Once a government is in place, other sources of discord begin to operate. In the *Second Treatise* Locke refers to money, which, by making it possible for people to accumulate great wealth, also puts us at odds with one another; and elsewhere he adduces a strong tendency in all of us both to hold views that naturally diverge greatly and to insist that other people agree with our own opinions on important matters such as religion. He does not appeal to original sin to explain discord.

Controversies among sociable beings seem therefore to set the problem that gives law its utility. Law directs rational free agents to their own interest "and prescribes no farther than is for the general Good of those under that Law. Could they be happier without it, the *Law,* as an useless thing would of it self vanish." There is no suggestion here of Hooker's Thomistic belief in our participation in the divine reason as the source of laws of nature, or of the idea that we all naturally work for the good of others as well as our own. Law does not show us our eternal roles in a cosmic harmony. It just limits our quarrels.

The reference to "general Good" here should not mislead us. Locke is not adverting to a substantive common good. He is saying that law gives each of us what we want, namely security in disposing as we please of our person, actions, and possessions (*Treatises* II.57, p. 305). He is at one with the Grotians in refusing to discuss the highest good. He argues, in fact, that such a discussion would be pointless. The argument is based on his psychology.[9] He is a hedonist about motivation, holding that only prospects of pleasure and pain can motivate us. But people take pleasure in different things. One person may like hunting, another chess, another wine. Even if everyone finds them enjoyable, not all are equally to everyone's taste. It follows, Locke thinks, that there is as little point in discussing the highest good as there is in disputing "whether the best Relish were to be found in Apples, Plumbs, or Nuts." Saying, as Epicurus and Gassendi do, that the good life consists in pleasure and the absence of pain, gives us no concrete guidance. For Locke "pleasure" is simply a stand-in for "whatever you incline toward or prefer." The greatest happiness consists, then, in having what pleases and avoiding what pains; but since "these, to different Men, are very different things" the ancient question of the summum bonum cannot be

9 I discuss Locke's psychology further in Chapter 14.vi.

answered in a way that is both valid for everyone and useful in guiding action (*ECHU* II.XXI.55, pp. 269–70).

Locke's thought on natural law is thus built around the three points that mark what I have called a distinctively modern form of the view: our unsocially sociable psychology causes basic problems that empirically discoverable law shows us how to resolve without appeal to any substantive conception of the highest good. His importance for the history of ethics does not lie, however, simply in his acceptance of the Grotian problematic. It lies rather in what he promised but did not perform in connection with it.

ii. *Elements of a science of morality*

Locke promises a science of morality. To see why he makes the promise and how he thinks it can be carried out, we must look first at the attack on innate ideas in the *Essay concerning Human Understanding*, book I. Locke there specifically denies that morality has any innate aspect.[10] Moral principles or maxims command less agreement than speculative ones, so that if disagreement shows that the latter are not innate, there is even less reason to hold the former to be so (I.III.1–2, pp. 65–6). Some speculative principles, though not innate, are at least self-evident, needing no proof. For any practical principle, however, we can rightly ask the reason; and we could not do so if such principles were innate (I.III.4, p. 68). The general agreement that virtue is praiseworthy can be explained as a result of the general awareness that virtue is useful to society (I.III.6, p. 69). Since there are many ways other than reading what is "written on their hearts" by which men can learn the principles of morals, there is no need to claim that the principles are innate in the conscience.[11] Conscience is simply one's opinion of the rightness or wrongness of one's own action, and one's opinions can come from education, or custom, or the company one keeps (I.III.8, p. 70). People frequently break basic moral rules with no inner sense of shame or guilt, thereby showing that the rules are not innate (I.III.9–13, pp. 70–5). Finally, no one has been able to state these allegedly innate rules. Attempts to do so either fail to elicit agreement or else contain utterly vacuous propositions that cannot guide action. It is no help to be told, for instance, that the principle "men must repent of their sins" is innate, unless that knowledge gives the details of what counts as sin – and no one has shown that it does (I.III.14–19, pp. 76–80).

---

10   One of Locke's targets is Lord Herbert of Cherbury, whom I discuss in Chapter 9.ii. Page references cited for the *Essay* (*ECHU*) are from the edition of Nidditch.

11   Locke thus accounts for Romans 2.14–15 in the way Pufendorf does.

Locke's points here are in accord with similar ideas in Hobbes, Cumberland, and Pufendorf. He indicates some additional agreements with them when he gives further reasons for his denial of innate moral principles. The ideas required to frame and understand moral principles cannot be innate because morality concerns laws and obligation, and these require concepts that can only be understood in terms of a lawmaker. The first lawmaker involved in morality is God. His ability to obligate us requires a life after this observable one, since it is plain that he does not make us obey him by rewarding and punishing in our present life (I.IV.8, pp. 87–8; I.III.12, p. 74). Moral principles could only be innate, then, if the ideas of God, law, obligation, punishment, and immortality were so, and this, Locke argues, is plainly not the case.

Underlying his many objections to innate ideas is Locke's belief that God gave us a faculty of reason sufficient to enable us to discover all the knowledge needed by beings such as we are. It would have been useless for him to have given us innate ideas or innate knowledge. He meant us to think for ourselves (I.IV.12, p. 91). What concerns us most nearly, Locke holds, is how to live. Our earthly as well as our eternal happiness is at stake. We must therefore be able to reason out for ourselves what is required of us (I.I.5, p. 45; II.XXIII.12, p. 302). To claim that a set of principles is innate is to claim that there is no need for further thought about the matters they cover; and this in turn is an excellent tactic for anyone who wants those principles taken on authority, without inquiry. But God could not have meant the use of our rational faculties to be blocked in this way (I.IV.24, pp. 101–2). The theme of the importance of thinking for oneself is as central to Locke's vision of moral personality as his belief that we are under God's laws and owe him obedience.

We know that the *Essay* grew out of discussions concerning morality.[12] In denying the topic any privileged place within the book Locke is underscoring the belief he shares with Hobbes and Cumberland, that moral ideas and beliefs can be explained using the terms that suffice for all our other ideas and beliefs. There is no need for any separate faculty or mental operation as their source.

Our ideas of good and evil are constructed from our experiences of pleasure and pain: good is what causes pleasure, evil what causes pain (II.XX.2, p. 229). Locke accepts the Cumberlandian distinction between natural and moral good, although he seems, with Pufendorf, not to require the law involved in moral good to direct us to natural good.[13] To

12   Aaron and Gibb, *Early Draft*, p. xii.
13   In the passages of Locke that I discuss in what immediately follows, the point is left unclear. Locke does not say that civil laws or the law of opinion must actually

call a voluntary action morally good is to mark its conformity to a law
that the lawmaker backs by attaching natural good to compliance and
evil to disobedience – that is, by offers of rewards or threats of punishment (II.XXVIII.5, p. 351). Locke then notes the sorts of rules or laws by
which men in fact usually judge actions: the divine law, the civil law,
and the law of "opinion or reputation" (II.XXVIII.7, p. 352). Ideas of
these kinds of law enter essentially into some of our moral ideas. The
divine law, the law God makes known either by revelation or by the
light of reason, is "the only true touchstone of *moral Rectitude.*" When
we judge by it we get ideas of acts as either sins or duties. The application of the laws of our government gives us the ideas of acts as either
criminal or innocent. And when we consider acts as they stand in the
general estimation of others in our society, we have the ideas of them as
virtuous or vicious (II.XXVIII.8–10, pp. 352–4).

To be subject to rules or laws, we must have wills; and experience
shows us how the will works. From the second edition of the *Essay*
onward, Locke provided a quite sophisticated view. Willing, he holds, is
simply "preferring of Action to its absence" (II. XXI.21. p. 244). And
preference, Locke holds, disagreeing with most of his predecessors, is
not determined by our beliefs about what course of action would bring
us the greatest amount of good. If it were, no one would sin, since the
prospect of eternal bliss or torment would outweigh every other. Desire
is indeed awakened only by the prospect of the agent's own happiness
or pleasure (II.XXI.41–2, pp. 258–9). As we have seen, this tells us
nothing about what we take pleasure in; it need not be only our own
benefit. More importantly, we are not mechanically moved by our
desires. We are free agents, possessing the ability to refrain from action
while we consider the different desires and aversions we feel, to decide
which of them to satisfy, and then to act on our decision.[14] Only the
person, not the will, is properly said to be free. The will is the power of
considering ideas and of suspending and deciding on action, and it

direct us to good or else forfeit their status as law. Of God's law he remarks that God
has the goodness and wisdom to direct us to good, but he does not add – as Cumberland would have added – that God must or even does always direct us to our natural
good.

14   For an extensive discussion of Locke on will, see Darwall 1995, ch. 6, which
includes consideration of Locke's views in the first edition of the *Essay*. The similarity between Locke's theory of freedom and Malebranche's is considerable, and
Locke may be indebted to him on this point despite his other, very deep, disagreements. See the stimulating essay by Vienne in Brown 1991, and Riley's introduction
to his translation of Malebranche's *Treatise on Nature and Grace,* p. 61. The idea of will
as suspension of decision was, however, common. Thus William Ames says that the
will can suspend its action without a prior judgment that it should do so (*Conscience*
I.5–6, pp. 24–5).

makes no sense to speak of a power as free (II.XXI.5, p. 236; 8–14, pp. 237–40; 21–8, pp. 244–8).[15] If we feel more uneasiness from a present lack of food than from a desire for heaven, the will makes us act to relieve the greater uneasiness (II.XXI.31–8, pp. 250–6). Nonetheless only thoughts of pleasures and pains can arouse uneasiness. Our will can be engaged only when we think there is some good or ill at stake.

Locke takes these considerations to show that the elements needed to explain our moral ideas – ideas of God, law, good, will, reward, and happiness – can all be obtained from data given by experience. We need no other ideas to build up our complex repertoire of moral concepts. One example will illustrate the point. The idea of murder involves ideas of the act of terminating human life, of doing so purposefully and voluntarily, and of the act being disapproved by most people in my society or forbidden by civil or divine law. Thus like all other complex ideas this one is made up of simple ideas "originally received from Sense or Reflection" (II.XXVIII.14, p. 358).[16]

iii. *Morality as a science*

It is a matter of considerable importance to Locke that moral ideas are complex ideas of the kind he calls "mixed modes." They are constructed by us, not copied from observation of given complexes. They

15 Some commentators claim that there is an inconsistency between Locke's hedonistic theory of motivation and the ethical "rationalism" according to which "reason alone can determine what is truly good" (Aaron 1971, p. 257), or between his hedonism and his voluntaristic view that laws arise from God's commands (Laslett, in his introduction to *Two Treatises*, p. 82). But even if the good consists in pleasure there is no inconsistency in claiming that reason must be used to tell us where the good is to be found, since it is easy to have mistaken views about what will bring the greatest pleasure to us in the long run. I find no clear and unequivocal suggestion in Locke's published work of any intuitionist rationalism about the laws of morality. And if obedience to God's commands ultimately leads to our own greatest happiness, then on a hedonistic view of motivation we can be moved to obey them, although the commands depend only on his will.

16 In *An Introduction to the History of Particular Qualities*, 1671, Robert Boyle writes: "there are some things that have been looked upon as qualities which ought rather to be looked upon as states of matter, or complexions of particular qualities, as *animal, inanimate, &c, health*, and *beauty*, which last attribute seems to be made up of shape, symmetry or comely proportion, and the *pleasantness of the colours* of the particular parts of the face" (*Selected Papers*, p. 96). Boyle here suggests a naturalistic and reductionistic account of beauty, of the kind Locke gives of moral ideas. In explaining what he means by "mode" Locke gives as one example the idea of beauty, "consisting of a certain composition of Colour and Figure, causing delight in the Beholder" (*ECHU* II.XII.5, p. 165). In Chapter 7.v, I pointed out Pufendorf's similar treatment of terms like "adultery."

are not intended to mirror or be adequate to some external reality, as ideas of substances are. They are rather "Archetypes made by the mind, to rank and denominate Things by," and can err only if there is some incompatibility among the elements we bring together in them (*ECHU* II.XXX.3–4, pp. 373–4; II.XXXI.3–4, pp. 376–7). Consequently if we are perfectly clear about the moral ideas our moral words stand for, we know the real and not only the nominal essences of moral properties (III.III.18, p. 418; III.XI.15, p. 516).

Locke's notion of mixed modes so helpfully fills out Pufendorf's theory of moral entities that it might have been designed for the purpose. Pufendorf himself, unlike Cumberland, makes no effort to explain where we get the ideas in our knowledge of moral entities, claiming only that the entities themselves are due to God's imposition. Locke emphatically rejects any explanation invoking God's immediate action on the mind. All mixed-mode ideas are our creation. They show our God-given reason doing what it was meant to do: providing us with the guidance we need through life. It is because moral ideas and terms are our creation that Locke thinks himself entitled to make his strongest claims about the demonstrability of morality (III.XI.17–18, pp. 517–18; IV.XII.8, p. 643).

Although men commonly look to the law of opinion and the civil law in framing their moral views, the true law of morality is the law God has laid down for us. That law concerns us more nearly than any other, since our eternal happiness or misery is determined by the extent of our compliance with it. How then are we to know what God's law tells us to do? In a famous passage Locke tells us what kind of answer we may expect to this question:

> The *Ideas* of a supreme Being, infinite in Power, Goodness, and Wisdom, whose workmanship we are, and on whom we depend; and the *Idea* of our selves, as understanding, rational Beings, being such as are clear to us, would, I suppose, if duly considered, and pursued, afford such Foundations of our Duty and Rules of Action, as might place *Morality among the Sciences capable of Demonstration*: wherein I doubt not, but from self-evident Propositions, by necessary Consequences, as incontestable as those in Mathematicks, the measures of right and wrong might be made out, to any one that will apply himself. (IV.III.18, p. 549)

The existence of God, considered as an eternal most powerful and most knowledgeable being, can be demonstrated, Locke tells us in IV.X, and it is obvious that as his creatures we are dependent upon him. If we then simply consider the ideas of two such beings, we "as certainly find that the Inferior, Finite, and Dependent, is under an Obligation to obey the Supreme and Infinite" as we see that two and two are more than three when we consider those ideas (IV.XIII.3, p. 651).

Locke gives an example to show how demonstrations of more specifically moral truths are to be constructed. Consider some moral concept, such as injustice. It contains as a part the concept of property, which in turn is the idea of something to which someone has a right. "Injustice" is the name given to the mixed-mode idea of violating someone's right to something. It follows demonstrably that where there is no property, there is no injustice. Here is a model for demonstrations of morality. We are left to get to work producing others (IV.III.18, p. 549).[17]

Locke allows that there are special difficulties in doing so. Moral ideas are harder to clarify and "commonly more complex," than those involved in mathematics.[18] Private interests and party allegiances lead men to quarrel about moral demonstrations, but not about mathematics (IV.III.20–1, pp. 552–3). Nonetheless Locke thinks he has shown how moral demonstrations can produce certainty, which is just "the Perception of the Agreement, or Disagreement of our *Ideas*." Even if no virtuous person ever existed, it is still demonstrably certain that a just man never violates another's rights. Of course, we must agree about the ideas to which we attach names. If God has defined certain moral names, Locke says, "it is not safe to apply or use them otherwise"; but where we are dealing only with human definitions, the worst that can happen is verbal impropriety. And if we work with the complex ideas themselves instead of using only names, we can always obtain demonstrations (IV.IV.7–10, pp. 565–8).

"Our business here," Locke says, "is not to know all things, but those which concern our Conduct" (I.I.6, p. 46). Morality provides the indispensable guidance for this task. Locke makes much of the limitations on our ability to attain speculative knowledge. But he never gave us the science of morality whose foundations he claims to have worked out.

iv. *Locke's voluntarism*

It is not hard to see how Thomas Burnet could have been led to say that Locke was presenting "a God without moral attributes." Moral goodness, on Locke's account, is what we predicate of action that complies with a law backed by sanctions. No one could impose such a law on God, so his actions could not be morally good or evil. Similarly, his acts can be neither sins nor duties, since both presuppose laws backed by divine sanctions. Locke knew of Cumberland's attempt to show that

---

17 There is a striking similarity between this sample demonstration and the sample explanation Hobbes gives in the "Epistle Dedicatory" to *De Cive*.

18 "Discourses of Religion, Law, and Morality," says Locke, are of the "highest concernment" to us and also "the greatest difficulty" (*ECHU* III.IX.22, p. 489).

there is an empirically based necessary truth grounding an analog of a law that governs God. But he does not even discuss it.

In several places, moreover, Locke insists that there is nothing in nature that corresponds to our mixed-mode moral ideas (III.IX.5, p. 477; III.IX.11, p. 481; III.XI.9, p. 513). There can be nothing in nature, then, to set a moral limit to God's will. If neither law nor nature can constrain Locke's God, then Locke is taking the voluntarist position, that God's will is the origin of moral attributes. God's power makes him, of course, a cause of pleasure and pain, and so he can be thought to be a natural good or evil. But this hardly helps matters. The possession of unlimited power merely enables God to be, at best, a benevolent despot, at worst, a tyrant. There seems to be a good case for Burnet's claim that on Locke's view the laws God has laid down for us are "entirely arbitrary."

Locke might rebut the charge if he could show that God possesses not only unlimited power and knowledge but unlimited goodness as well. And Locke does indeed hold that we are dependent on a being "who is eternal, omnipotent, perfectly wise and good" (IV. XIII.3, p. 651). He appeals to these attributes when claiming that a science of morality is possible. But his proof of God's existence does not show that God is naturally good. Put briefly, the argument is this. We know that we ourselves exist, and that we can perceive and know. The only possible explanation of this fact is that we were made by an eternal most powerful and most intelligent being (IV.X.3–5, pp. 620–1). Locke claims that "from this *Idea* duly considered, will easily be deduced all those other Attributes, which we ought to ascribe to this eternal Being" (IV.X.6, p. 621). Neither in the expansion of this proof that occupies the rest of this chapter nor anywhere else in the *Essay* does Locke show how to deduce God's essential benevolence. If the deduction seemed easy to him, it has not seemed so to his readers.[19]

---

19   Lord King's *Life* of Locke prints a manuscript (dated August 7, 1681) in which Locke argues that since God is totally perfect and needs nothing he cannot use his power for his own good, and therefore must use it for the good of his creatures (King 1830, p. 123; cited in Colman 1983, pp. 191–2). Whatever the merits of this argument, which if taken seriously would raise all the difficulties of the problem of evil, Locke did not publish it. In the *Reasonableness of Christianity* (*Works* II.528–9), he says that "The Works of Nature shew [God's] Wisdom and Power: But 'tis his peculiar Care of Mankind, most eminently discovered in his Promises to them, that shews his Bounty and Goodness." How then are God's promises to be known? If by reason, as Locke suggests in saying that "God had, by the Light of Reason, revealed to all Mankind . . . that he was good and merciful," the original problem is unresolved.

In the first *Remarks* Burnet objects that Locke had not explained how to prove that God is truthful. It is not enough, he says, to know the "Physical or Metaphysical

Locke's view of how to demonstrate moral truths makes matters worse, because it suggests that there could not be a demonstration of a moral principle that satisfies his own standards. Locke holds, as I have noted, that a principle must offer genuine guidance. It must not be trivial or vacuous, a mere verbal statement that does not enable us to pick out right acts. Although Locke says we must start our moral demonstrations from self-evident principles, he also says that there are no self-evident *moral* principles with substantial content. Demonstration consists in making explicit the ideas assembled in one complex mode and showing, perhaps by using an intermediate complex idea, their literal overlap with the ideas in another. As a contemporary critic pointed out, it is hard to see how this could yield much more than the kind of "trifling" or vacuous proposition that Locke criticizes the innatists for offering.[20] And the problem is increased by Locke's claim that we ourselves assemble the elements of moral ideas. What guarantee have we that the moral ideas we construct will inform us of God's will for us? To say, with Locke, that God may have constructed some complex moral ideas that we ignore at our peril is of no use unless we can determine which moral ideas those are; and in the *Essay*, at least, Locke does not tell us or show us how to decide.[21]

Locke's moral psychology compounds all these difficulties. On his view it is possible that we may take an interest in the well-being of others, just as we may find our happiness in a variety of pursuits and achievements having nothing to do with others. Yet his strongly worded insistence that "[i]t would be in vain for one intelligent Being, to set a Rule to the actions of another, if he had it not in his Power, to reward the compliance" (II.xxviii.6, pp. 351–2) makes him sound as if he thinks that a narrowly egoistic view of motivation is accurate for most if perhaps not all people. An untrammeled ruler giving arbitrary direction to a selfish population seems indeed to emerge as his model of

Attributes of the Divine Nature: we must also know its Moral Attributes . . . such as Goodness, Justice, Holiness, and particularly Veracity." Locke cannot prove these by appeal to revelation, Burnet continues, unless he proves God's veracity, and he has given no explanation of God's perfection that shows it to involve that attribute (pp. 5–8).

20   Henry Lee, *Anti-Scepticism*, p. 252, objects to the triviality of the conclusions Locke's method would enable us to deduce and notes that such propositions "can be of no use according to his own Principles, because they are in sense *Identical*." Berkeley makes the same point: "Lockes [*sic*] instances of Demonstration in Morality are according to his own Rule trifling Propositions" (*Philosophical Commentaries*, in *Works* I, no. 691). The point is arguable.

21   Nor could he have done so. God's mind cannot operate in the way Locke's empiricism says that our minds do. Hence God's mind must be quite basically unknown to us.

the moral relations between God and human beings. And if one allows, as Locke notoriously does (IV.III.6, pp. 540–1), that matter might think, how could one hope to obtain the certainty of the immortality of the soul that he thinks necessary to induce us to obey God's laws?

v. *Revelation and reason in morals*

Some of Locke's remarks in *The Reasonableness of Christianity* (1695) reinforce the rather grim vision of morality suggested by the *Essay*.[22] They also give us Locke's answer to an important question which is left undiscussed in the *Essay*: is knowledge of God's laws readily available to everyone? In the course of arguing that Christianity demands of its adherents only the minimal doctrinal belief that Jesus is the Messiah or Savior, Locke raises the question, "What need was there of a Saviour? What Advantage have we by *Jesus Christ?*" (p. 56). The question arises because Locke has argued that reason could have taught even those to whom the Jewish and Christian revelations were not delivered the crucial rudiments of religious truth. Reason could have shown, for instance, that the natural law requires that we forgive our enemies. So reason could teach that the author of that law – whose existence, we recall, can be learned by reason – will forgive us if we repent our transgressions and resolve to improve. But the belief that we can be forgiven is a prerevelation counterpart to the belief that Jesus is the Messiah. Accepting it would make the heathen eligible for salvation (pp. 54–5). Why, then, was Christ's actual coming necessary?

Part of the answer is that reason alone could not have prevailed on most people sufficiently to teach them God's existence, while Christ's personal presence enabled the belief to spread. Another part is that the human race needed a clearer knowledge of morals than reason alone had been able to give it. The heathen philosophers did not discover all or even the most important of the laws of nature, and it seems in general, Locke says, "that 'tis too hard a Task for unassisted Reason, to establish Morality in all its parts upon its true Foundation, with a clear and convincing light" (p. 60). But suppose that a compendium of non-Christian moral teaching had been made, including even the wisdom of Confucius, and suppose that it had included what is commanded by the laws of nature: what then? "The Law of Nature, is the Law of Convenience, too"; no wonder therefore if "Men of parts" should find out what is right simply by its beauty and convenience.[23] But as thus dis-

22 Page references to the *Reasonableness of Christianity* here are from the abridged edition of Ramsey. See Marshall 1994, chs. 8–10, for Locke's religious thought.
23   And see *ECHU* I.III.6, p. 69, for an earlier statement of the point.

covered and taught, the precepts would still have amounted only to counsel or advice from wise men about how to live a happy life. The precepts could not have been taught as laws that obligate. Only the knowledge that the precepts are the command of a supreme lawgiver who rewards and punishes could transform them into moral laws; and the heathen did not adequately possess that knowledge, which had then to be taught by Christ (pp. 62–5).

It is not evident how this position can be made compatible with Locke's view that God has given us reason enough to discover what we need to know concerning the things most important to us, morality and religion. Matters are not helped much by his assertion that now that Christ has made it clear that God lays down laws, and told us what God's laws are, we can show them to be reasonable, and so we come to think we might have discovered them ourselves. But even if reason could have uncovered and proved the whole of the law of nature, rational demonstrations would not be sufficient to move ordinary people to act morally. "The greatest part of Mankind want Leisure or Capacity for Demonstration . . . you may as soon hope to have the Day-Labourers and Tradesmen, the Spinsters and Dairy Maids perfect Mathematicians, as to have them perfect in *Ethics*" by teaching them proofs of moral laws. "Hearing plain Commands," Locke continues, "is the sure and only course to bring them to Obedience and Practice. The greatest Part cannot know, and therefore they must believe" Christ coming in glory from heaven is needed to convince most people to comply with the laws of nature (pp. 66–7).

Locke's doubts about the ability of reason to discover and to teach effectively the laws of nature do not contradict his belief that those laws, once revealed, can be rationally demonstrated. But they do require us to interpret with caution the passages in which Locke says that the law of nature is "plain and intelligible to all creatures" (*Treatises* II.124, p. 351). This is no slip into a rationalist claim that the laws are self-evident. But neither is it the claim that knowledge of the laws of nature is equally available to everyone alike. The laws are plain enough so that the day laborer and the spinster can obey, once they have been instructed. But they will not be able to see for themselves why the laws are binding on them. They will be obeying God by obeying other men.

vi. *Locke's early work on natural law*

Early in his career Locke had worked his way through a large number of traditional accounts of natural law theory and made himself familiar with the problems they raise.[24] The early unpublished work

24 See Colman 1983 and Marshall 1994.

which its first translator entitled *Essays on the Law of Nature* shows him grappling with the questions of the innateness of moral ideas, the relation of ideas of right and power in making up the complex idea of obligation, and the distinction between the advisable and the obligatory.[25] He also discusses how we come to know the laws of nature and what the justification is for God's rule over us. We need not discuss all these points here but it is worth noting his view on the last matter.

There are two reasons, Locke thinks, showing that God has authority and not simply power over us. One is his wisdom. God has aims and, being all-knowing, surely chooses the best means to them. We are in no position to dispute him. This alone, of course, might be true of a merely tyrannical deity, but Locke makes it clear that he does not view God as a tyrant. He notes that to obey a king merely out of fear of his power "would be to establish the power of tyrants, thieves, and pirates" (*Essays* VI, p. 189). To avoid charging God with tyranny Locke appeals to the principle that a creator has the right to control his creations. The principle of Creator's right is one Locke held throughout his life.[26] No one can deny that God has given us a law, Locke says, or deny that "He has a Right to do it, we are his Creatures" (*ECHU* II.XXVIII.8, p. 352). Perhaps: but neither in the *Essay* nor anywhere else does he attempt to justify it.[27] It seemed, no doubt, so obvious to him as to need no justification, but of course in his own mature philosophy he allows no self-evident moral principles.

In his early work Locke was plainly trying to avoid the kind of position to which Burnet objects. What is not clear is whether his empiricism allowed him to do so, early or late. The empiricism leads him to naturalism about moral ideas; and this leads him into some now-familiar difficulties. The ideas of good and evil in their "natural" sense are not enough for him. He needs the moral sense of the terms, and that, as we have seen, depends on the idea of law, which in turn requires

25   von Leyden, ed., *Essays on the Laws of Nature.* I follow von Leyden in referring to this work as *Essays*. Horwitz, Clay, and Clay call their translation *Questions concerning the Law of Nature.* In his Introduction to this edition, Horwitz argues that Locke here wrote "disputed questions" in a medieval style of debate still current in the Oxford in which he was teaching at the time. This may well be true, but I am not convinced by Horwitz's claim (p. 55) that it would be of major significance for our interpretation of the work.

26   See Colman 1983, p. 46, and the discussions in Tully 1980.

27   We find in the early *Essays* exactly the same transition that there is in the *Essay,* from the empirical conclusion that a powerful and wise agent created the world to the further conclusion "that there is some superior authority to which we are rightly subject" – and in just the same way the transition is not spelled out (*Essays* IV, pp. 153–5).

ideas of authority and right. If Locke thinks that the idea of power that we get by introspection (*ECHU* II.xxi.4, p. 235) suffices to account for the idea of authority, he is Hobbesian enough to warrant Burnet's worry; and he admits no other senses to give us simple ideas. He offers no explicit account of authority as an idea, nor of the idea of right, and it is hard to see how he could do so without showing quite clearly that his theory of meaning does not enable him to draw the distinction he needs between them and mere power.

In the early *Essays on the Law of Nature* it is fairly clear that Locke does not think that the fear of punishment alone serves to move us to obey God's natural laws. Somehow the simple recognition of God's rightful laws suffices to move us. But on his mature view Locke cannot appeal to this point. His final position, as I indicated, is that what moves us is always connected (however indirectly) with our anticipation of pleasure or pain.[28] A ruler's subjects can know what the laws are while remaining ignorant (as most people are) of the good obedience brings, because the laws themselves do not say what it is. What motive have they then to obey? The answer is inevitable: fear of punishment, hope of reward. The early sketch of natural law contains nothing that would help Locke escape from the unpalatable view of human moral motivation suggested in the *Essay concerning Human Understanding*.

The early work is also not much help in explaining how we come to know what it is that God commands us to do. Locke argues that we learn this from experience, not from direct revelation, tradition, innate ideas, or general consent. Experience shows us that there is a "powerful and wise creator" of all things (*Essays* IV, p. 153) whom we are naturally disposed to worship; it shows that we tend to preserve ourselves; and it shows that we are disposed to live sociably and are equipped, by our possession of language, to do so. But how exactly we are to go from

---

28   A late manuscript note indicates his awareness of the problem this set for any position like his own early one on natural law: "That which has very much confounded men about the will and its determination has been the confounding of the notion of moral rectitude and giving it the name of moral good. The pleasure that a man takes in any action or expects as a consequence of it is indeed a good in the self able and proper to move the will. But the moral rectitude of it considered barely in itself is not good or evil nor any way moves the will, but as pleasure and pain either accompanies the action itself or is looked on to be a consequence of it. Which is evident from the punishments and rewards which God has annexed to moral rectitude or pravity as proper motives to the will, which would be needless if moral rectitude were in itself good and moral pravity evil."

From an unpublished manuscript quoted in *Essays*, pp. 72–3; also quoted in Colman 1983, pp. 48–9.

there to knowledge of the laws governing our duties to God, self, and others is not made clear.[29]

vii. *Justice and love*

The *Two Treatises of Government* give us no help in working out the details of a Lockean theory of the nature of obligation or of motivation, but they point toward an elaboration of Locke's view of how we could come to know which mixed-mode moral ideas God intended us to make central to our lives and societies. This is not the main focus of the *Treatises,* but in the second of them there are indications of a line of argument that Locke's contemporaries would have found familiar. Locke there says that God made man in such a way that "it was not good for him to be alone." He therefore "put him under strong Obligations of Necessity, Convenience, and Inclination to drive him into *Society*" and equipped him with reason and speech which would make it possible (*Treatises* II.77, pp. 318–19). If these strongly marked special features of human beings indicate God's will for us, then it must also be his will that we do what is needful to carry it out. Locke suggests that in the earliest stages of human history not much in the way of morality was required. Members of families naturally accommodate to one another, and in the "Golden Age" personal and social life would have been so simple and so lacking in material goods that conflict would not have been a major problem (II.110–11, pp. 341–3). But our natural propensity to increase our level of well-being leads inevitably to greater wealth and to competition. To manage it, Locke argues, we are led to form political organizations.[30]

Locke's political philosophy is not my subject here. The point of recalling it is to indicate how it might have helped solve the problem of determining which complex moral ideas God intends us to use.[31] He intends us, Locke might have said, to use those which enable us to live as the special features of our nature show us he meant us to live: sociably and with an increasing degree of prosperity brought about in part by precisely the self-interested competitiveness that makes it

29   Locke's early *Essays* antedate Pufendorf, who uses similar arguments; but the idea of arguing from salient features of human nature to God's intentions for us and the thought that these three characteristics are our important salient features is doctrine that, as von Leyden notes (*Essays,* p. 159 n. 1), goes back to St. Thomas.

30   There are suggestions in Pufendorf of a historical evolution toward government and private property, and Locke may here be picking up some of them. See Istvan Hont, "The Language of Sociability and Commerce: Samuel Pufendorf and the Theoretical Foundations of the 'Four-Stages Theory,'" in Pagden 1987, pp. 253–76.

31   I owe this interesting suggestion to Colman 1983.

difficult for us to live together. Our reason is adequate to construct the concepts and discover the laws we need for this purpose. The related concepts of justice and of property in a broad sense thus have an obvious place in God's plans for us.

Justice is not the whole of morality for Locke, any more than it is for Grotius and Pufendorf. If an argument from the human condition to God's will makes it at least probable that God means us to organize our lives around the concepts of justice and property, the question that remains is whether a similar argument can ground the "Obligation to mutual Love amongst Men," which along with the maxim of justice Locke takes to be fundamental (*Treatises* II.5, p. 270). Locke says little about charity in his published work, and although, as I noted earlier, his psychology leaves room for us to have a disinterested and direct concern for the well-being of others, he is more emphatic about the sources of discord in our nature than about our love of one another. Actual love of others, to the point of self-sacrifice, is not such a salient feature of our constitution as Locke sees it that our nature as plainly points to charity as it does to justice. And Locke suggests no other natural source from which we might come to know that we stand under a law of love.

viii. *Voluntarism and empiricist morality*

Locke did not acknowledge his authorship of the treatises on government during his lifetime, still less say that the argument of the *Second Treatise* was intended to fill out his moral theory. He also does not say that it was his inability to give a solid grounding for the great maxim of charity that stood in the way of completing and publishing a demonstrative morality.[32] We do know from Burnet and others that his readers had more general worries than that about his views on morality. Their worries arose from his voluntarism. And we can see how Locke's political concerns could well have forced him into voluntarism and into the empiricism that is connected with it.

Locke was concerned to combat both skeptical doubts about morality and enthusiastic claims to divinely inspired insight into it.[33] All of the modern natural lawyers would have shared these aims. Both skepticism and enthusiasm work against the possibility of sustaining a decent and stable society. An empiricist naturalism seemed to Locke, as it did to Hobbes and Pufendorf and Grotius, the only response that could offer a scientific way of settling disputes and avoiding the deadlock of

32 Colman 1983, p. 204.

33 Locke added a chapter on Enthusiasm (IV.xix) to the fourth edition of the *Essay* (1700). Entries in his journal show him engaged in attacking the belief in divine inspiration as early as 1681 and 1682. See King 1830, pp. 124–8.

appeals to authority or personal preference. Only an understanding of
morality to which God is essential could be acceptable to most of
Locke's readers, and to Locke himself. Locke plainly read Grotius as
Pufendorf did, as an intellectualist, and he may have thought, with
Barbeyrac, that the position could slide over too easily into making God
superfluous. He also rejected Cumberland's way of keeping God involved. Cumberland, as I have noted, naturalized the rewards and
punishments he thought essential to law, appealing to God as the benevolent creator who reveals himself by means of them. Locke dismisses any such move quickly. God, he says, must reward and punish
"by some good and evil that is not the natural produce and consequences of the action itself. For that being a natural convenience or
inconvenience would operate of itself without a law" (*ECHU* II.xxviii.6,
pp. 351–2). This Cumberlandian view implies that no law is needed for
morality – and, if no law, no lawgiver. Only voluntarism keeps God
essential. But Locke's theory of meaning then forces him to hold that
only God's power makes him our ruler. Nothing else can meaningfully
be said.

In 1675 Thomas Traherne published *Christian Ethicks*, a systematic if
unoriginal exposition of morality. A devout poet and warmhearted
advocate of virtue rather than a thinker, he nonetheless pithily summarizes a concern raised by voluntarism quite generally. "He that ap-
prehends God to be a tyrant," Traherne says, "can neither honour God,
nor Love him, nor enjoy him."[34] Bacon would have castigated the very
phrasing of Traherne's remark, but it encapsulates an attitude that was
becoming more and more widely shared. The combination of voluntarism and empiricism was taken to lead inescapably to a vision of the
relations between God and his human subjects that is morally unacceptable. This worry underlies Burnet's complaint that Locke presents a
God without moral attributes. We shall see it later in others.

Locke's version of naturalism in ethics seems to many philosophers
now to be misguided because it gets the meanings of words wrong.
Traherne's remark suggests that the problem Locke's readers had with
it was different. Their problem was that naturalism would force on us
an unacceptable construal of our relations with God. Locke could not
portray God's dominion over us as resting on anything but his power
and skill as creator. He could admit no difference in principle between
God's rule and that of a benevolent despot except at the cost of allowing
into his scheme concepts that could not be derived from experience.

It was not the problem about proving the great law of charity, I
suggest, that made Locke refuse to publish a deductive ethic. What did
so was his embarrassment at his inability to give Burnet a satisfactory

34   Traherne, *Christian Ethicks*, p. 71.

explanation of how we could even say and mean, let alone prove, that God is a just ruler. He could not allow for the kind of relation between God and his creatures that many Christians – he himself among them – believed to exist.[35] Locke's failure drew attention to the moral consequences of empiricism more forcibly than previous empiricist ethics had done. Hobbes argued for the elements of an empiricist ethic, but his epistemology was massively overshadowed by his extremely contentious political views, and his views on religion were in any case scandalous. His work therefore raised problems more urgent than any that might arise from a connection between empiricism and voluntarism. Pufendorf, though an empiricist, did not develop a general theory of the derivation of concepts from experience. He concentrated on the development of a detailed code of natural law, usable as a guide to positive legislation. If he had a problem about the meaning of the claim that God is just, readers could pass it by and still accept his code.

With Locke it was different. Locke was more interested in the epistemology of natural law than in working out a code. As a result the connection between voluntarism and empiricism stood out more starkly in his view of ethics, fragmentary though it was, than in Pufendorf's. Locke's readers could hardly avoid seeing that if, like him, they embraced naturalistic empiricism about moral concepts, then they would be forced into voluntarism – unless they left God entirely out of morality. Locke's voluntarism, like Pufendorf's, undoubtedly had a deeply religious motivation. But one unintended consequence of his work was to make it even plainer than Hobbes had done that if strong voluntarism is unacceptable because of its moral consequences, then so too is empiricism.[36]

ix. *Thomasius: The rejection of voluntarism*

Christian Thomasius (1655–1728), though largely ignored today, is seen by German scholars as a founder of the German enlightenment.[37] He opposed witchcraft trials and other instances of what he viewed as superstition. He took the bold step of lecturing and writing on philosophy in German instead of Latin, having to invent much of the terminology as he went. He tried in this way and in others to improve the

35 Like Pufendorf Locke would have had difficulty in giving empirical grounding to belief in the immorality of the soul, which the need for sanctions made requisite for his law-based morality.

36 I discuss Descartes's voluntarism, which was not, of course, a consequence of any empiricist view, in Chapter 9.iv.

37 Schneiders 1971 is the major treatment. See also Wundt 1964, ch. 1; Beck 1969, pp. 247–56; Bloch 1986, ch. 26; Barnard 1971.

manners and morals of ordinary educated people, and to develop forms of social propriety other than those established by courts and courtiers. He favored and worked for other causes we might think of as progressive; and he kept changing his mind about the philosophy that would best underpin his endeavors. After issuing a large Latin Pufendorfian treatise on natural law in 1688, he published in 1692 a little German *Introduction to Ethics,* subtitled *On the Art of Loving Reasonably and Virtuously,* and followed it with a book about applying the art. The doctrine in these two widely read works was quite different from that in the initial treatise. His final Latin treatise, the *Fundamenta Juris Naturae et Gentium,* or *Foundations of the Law of Nature and of Nations,* of 1705, embodied yet further and more fundamental changes of view. There is no need to follow Thomasius's waverings and switches, but a brief look at some aspects of his final position is enlightening and indeed indispensable.

The two books on love show Thomasius working in terms of a long tradition of moral and therapeutic thought centered on love – love not as Christian *agapē* or *caritas* but as a purely human phenomenon not requiring to be explained by divine grace. Cumberland treated love similarly, and constructed his doctrine of natural law so as to show that morality centers on it. He also sought to avoid voluntarism; and the two aims coincided beautifully. The logic of displacing voluntarism led him to the law of love, the requirement that we maximize natural good; and if that is the moral law, we have a plain way of showing that God's commands are not arbitrary but are justifiable in terms we understand. Thomasius began as a thorough disciple of Pufendorf; and when he finally rejected voluntarism, he moved at least as close to utilitarianism as Cumberland did. "The universal norm of all action," he says, "is this: That is to be done which renders the life of man maximally long and happy" (*Fundamenta* I.6.21).

Thomasius took the Grotian problematic for granted even when he rejected Pufendorf. His objections to modern natural law theory are of special interest precisely because they come from an erstwhile adherent. They give us an idea of the effect an attitude like Traherne's must have when worked out in some detail. It is quite probable that Thomasius knew Cumberland's work, a second edition of which was published in Germany in 1683. His late treatise shows that he had read Locke's *Essay* and adopted much of what it says on natural law.[38] As

---

38 Wundt 1964, p. 31 n. 1, and Schneiders 1971, p. 301 n. 1, claim that the empiricism shown in *Fundamenta* is Aristotelian and not Lockean. Thomasius may well have been empiricist before reading Locke. But Wundt tells us that he owned

head of the new University of Halle, Thomasius occupied a commanding position in the intellectual life of Germany. His defection from Pufendorf was a highly significant response to the dominant work on
natural law.

Early in his chapter on the passions Thomasius gives us a central
indication of his reason for abandoning Pufendorf. Proper religious
feeling, he tells us, is definable as reasonable hope and fear of God, and
is also called childlike fear. Unreasonable fear of God is superstition. It
is a servile fear (I.2.32). After this it is no surprise to read later that "the
concept and representation of God as a father grounds a childlike fear,
but that of God as absolute monarch a servile fear" Only fools imagine
God as a despot:

> if a wise man should imagine God as a human ruler, he would rather
> imagine him as a father than as a ruler. For it is more suitable to God's
> perfection to seek for the best for men than to pursue his own utility
> through laws written in men's hearts in a despotic manner. (I.5.41–3)

Here the rejection of voluntarism is tied directly to God's pursuit of the
greatest good. Thomasius adds that if we think of God as "a despotic
lawgiver who obligates men outwardly through punishment," then we
must also think that no actions are honorable or shameful independently of God's will. He claims to have shown elsewhere that this
strong voluntarist claim is false, and his interest in the present work lies
elsewhere (I.5.51). It lies in his reworking of the Pufendorfian apparatus. He writes like someone who cannot shake off the old vocabulary;
but he alters the meanings of its key terms quite profoundly.

x. *Obligation and advice*

Thomasius abandons the thesis that God enforces his will by threats
of punishment. A wise God is a teacher rather than a lawgiver, he says,
and we can only learn when we have a peaceful mind, not one disturbed by fears. God, moreover, teaches by reason, and reason alone
cannot show that we should think of him as using punishments. In fact,
Thomasius says, echoing Locke's dismissal of Cumberland's attempt to
naturalize sanctions, reason "perceives that all punishments which follow in the feet of the transgressors of the law of nature which are not
due to human rule are natural and therefore are not properly called
punishments." By definition punishment involves ills attached to acts
by deliberate willed intervention into the course of nature. It is a purely

the French translation of the *Essay,* which was published in 1700, in ample time to
influence his late thought on natural law.

human institution. From the laws of nature one could only conclude that someone deserves to be punished, not what punishment is deserved (I.5.37–40, 53).

If we cannot think of God as threatening us with punishments, much in the traditional natural law view must go. In his preface Thomasius says that earlier, following Grotius and Pufendorf, he had failed to distinguish the various meanings of the word "law." Punishment is "the preeminent power of law." If God does not punish, then his directives are not law in the same sense as human laws are. Divine and human law are not really members of a common species. The word "law" applies to divine directives "only in a loose sense" (pref. 8–10).

The standard natural law distinction between advising or counseling and obligating must also be revised. To obligate someone, the legislator must have the power to make it necessary, by threat, for someone to do what the obligator wants. Thomasius retains the natural law distinction between what a teacher does in counseling and what a superior does in issuing a command. But he no longer says that what a commanding superior does is to obligate. A superior rules. And he almost says that God's directives are to be taken as counseling. God is a father, and "a father's directions are more Counsels than Rules" (I.5.41). God directs us to our good, and we can understand what that is. In terms of the standard distinction, Thomasius is saying that it is up to us to take or reject God's directives. Obedience is not our primary relation to him.

A further revision follows. Thomasius does not reject the idea of obligation. He gives an almost Hobbesian account of it. He breaks with Pufendorf's doctrine of free will and holds that we are necessarily moved by our hopes and fears.[39] A fool who threatens can exercise only strength; hopes and fears deliberately aroused by a wise man constitute obligation. But "counsel as well as rule instill fear," so both necessitate the will. "Accordingly, what is commonly said is false or not rightly explained, that counsel has no force to obligate men [*vim obligandi*]" (I.iv.58–60). Counsel binds by showing the person counseled an "intrinsic" force coming from what is necessarily connected with the act in question.[40] Rule binds by an external or outer force connected only by

---

39   At the beginning of *Fundamenta* Thomasius announces that in his earlier treatise he had made a profound mistake by accepting the doctrine of free will (pref. 6). In various places throughout the book he reverts to his newfound determinism, drawing an almost fatalistic and certainly gloomy set of conclusions from it. The matter is well discussed in Schneiders 1971, ch. 5. Thomasius claims that the doctrine of the "internal freedom of the will is the main precept of the Papistical doctrine of earning eternal salvation by good works" (I.3.1, note).

40   The intrinsic force comes not, as Pufendorf tries to make out that it does, from the rule or the superior, but from the act itself.

human choice to the act. A wise man, Thomasius says, "considers the inner duty the superior kind," and is usually governed by counsel. Fools are usually governed by rule (I.iv.62–5).[41]

Thomasius holds, with Locke, that we tend to have "wills that agree on little, disagree and quarrel and oppose in many things" (I.1.102). The state of nature is not quite a state of war, but a "state of chaos" nearer to war than peace (I.1.104; I.3.54). Hence a shared norm is needed in order that society may exist (I.4.1). We have here the elements of the Grotian problematic. Thomasius does not think obligation and sanctions unimportant. His aim is to describe their relation to morality in a new way.

xi. *Separating law and morality*

His revision of the distinction between perfect and imperfect duties shows how he does so. The Grotian distinction, Thomasius says, "is not quite right" (I.v.23). To explain how drastic his repairs are, I must first explain his fundamental positive view. His aim, indicated on the title page, is to make a threefold distinction among the honorable, the just, and the decorous or proper,[42] in order to improve the doctrine of natural law.

Justice, for Thomasius, is concerned with preventing people from damaging one another so seriously that society will not be able to continue. Its rules concern only publicly observable behavior toward other people. Justice matters because there are wicked people who tend to disturb the peace and who must be controlled. The honorable, by contrast, concerns only one's inner life. Honorable people control their passions and desires and do nothing shameful. Decorum or propriety, like justice, is a matter of one's relations to others. It concerns the ways in which one might help others or improve one's own inner condition so that one does not wish to harm them. If the honorable person is the most estimable, and the unjust is the worst, the person of propriety is of a middling sort (I.iv.87–90). In the wise person all three kinds of goodness must be combined (I.iv.91), but Thomasius gives for each a separate rule. The principle of honor is "Whatever you will that others

41 Thomasius's whole book is cast in terms of the foolish and the wise. The terminology goes back to Stoicism, but Thomasius may have in mind Hobbes's fool, who says in his heart that there is no justice (*Leviathan* I.15.4). Although the elitism implied is commonplace in natural law thinking, it is more significant that Thomasius casts the opposition as one between wise and foolish *wills* – a result of the moral psychology of the book, which makes will, not intelligence, the determining factor in human behavior. Thomasius, we might say, is trying to distinguish rational from nonrational willing.

42 In Latin, *honestum, justum, decorum;* the German translator uses the terms *ehrlich, gerecht, anständig.*

should do, do yourself"; the principle of propriety is "Whatever you will that others should do to you, do to them"; and the principle of justice is "Whatever you do not want to have done to you, do not do to others" (I.vi.40–2).[43]

The rules of justice are appropriately backed by threats of punishment. The rules of the other two domains cannot be.[44] The honorable is a wholly inner matter, hence beyond the reach of force; and Thomasius is quite explicit about propriety. "Certainly the rules of propriety regard men in their relations to other men. Nevertheless no one can be forced to propriety, and if one is forced, then it is no longer propriety" (I.v.21). Thomasius here responds to a fatal incoherence in the Pufendorfian account of obligation as applied to imperfect duties. We must perform such duties in the right spirit, a spirit of love or direct concern. Obligation, however, exists only where we can be compelled, and we cannot be compelled to feel love, gratitude, or pity.

I have pointed out that Thomasius thinks that the only punishments of which we can have natural knowledge are those inflicted by human beings. Thus justice as he understands it must be a matter of purely human legal arrangements. He also holds that although the requirements of honor and propriety cannot be enforced by sanctions, they nonetheless impose obligations. What obligates or necessitates here are inner forces – the peace of mind that attends honor, the good opinion of others that is necessarily connected with propriety – which matter more to the wise man than do the merely external obligations defining the domain of justice.

Thomasius's domain of decorum or propriety is very like the domain of the imperfect duties in Pufendorf's scheme (see Chapter 7.iv). Unlike acts of justice or other perfect duties, its acts are not needed to ensure the bare existence of society, but they do ameliorate our common life. Proper behavior, Thomasius says, awakens the kindness of others, as,

43 Leibniz also distinguishes three grades of justice, with a maxim for each: see Chapter 12.iii. I do not know how much influence Leibniz had on Thomasius.

44 An approximation to this position is present in the earlier book on love. There Thomasius says that there is "a likeness between duties of humanity and good deeds, that neither to the one nor to the other, nor to gratitude, can anyone be compelled. Indeed if someone wanted to compel someone to affability, beneficence (*Gutäthigkeit*) and gratitude (as to some extent in societies where there is a ruler he can compel his subordinates to the services of these virtues, according to opportunities and circumstances) nonetheless the services coming from force would lose the names of affability, beneficence, and gratitude, just because they were not freely offered but compelled." *Einleitung* V.26. The rejection of what is done at court is characteristic.

for Pufendorf, carrying out imperfect duties entitles one to gratitude
and fosters social solidarity. Thomasius himself suggests the identification of propriety and imperfect duty when, after asserting the inadequacy of the Grotian division, he adds: "An imperfect right extends to
no more than that which I may ask of another according to the rules of
propriety, not of justice" (I.v.23). But he immediately rejects the terminology of perfect and imperfect, holding that we are either wholly duty-
bound or wholly without duty. Moreover since the duties of honor and
propriety are more fully inner duties than those of justice, and are given
more weight by the wise man, they are in an important sense higher or
"more perfect," so that it would be absurd to call them imperfect.

> It follows from this that what a man does out of inner duty and according
> to the rules of the honorable and the proper is directed by virtue [*virtute*
> or *Tugend*]. The man is accordingly called virtuous and not just. However,
> what a man does according to the rules of justice or from external obliga-
> tion is ruled by justice and due to such behavior he is called just [*justus* or
> *gerecht*]. (I.v.24–5)

The Pufendorfian imperfect duties have been transmuted into a domain in which there are rules imposing obligations that carry motivating power although lacking external sanction. In this domain we are
ruled neither by God nor by the magistrate. Inner obligation does not
have other people as its source. Hence we can say that here we "can be
obligated to ourselves and that we can make laws for ourselves (for
example, through a vow)" (I.5.18). These obligations are higher and
more important than merely external obligations open to enforcement
by sanctions. The latter constitute the domain in which humans make
laws properly so called. The former come very close indeed to constituting a domain we are now inclined to recognize as that of morality. In it
we are self-governed.

Thomasius proclaims himself an empiricist (I.23), and acknowledges
Locke when he denies that there are any innate ideas (I.iv.16n). Yet he
makes no effort to explain how his empiricism can accommodate his
revisions of Pufendorfian and Lockean voluntarism. The impetus for
his work is not an interest in epistemology or the theory of meaning. It
comes from an interest in asserting the moral capacity of the individual,
an interest in having a theory of law and morality that replaces obedience to another with self-control and self-legislation. If he is silent
about the alterations in theories of knowledge or meaning that his
revisions might call for, he makes some drastic changes in the language
of morals.

He thinks himself original in asserting that external obligation is not
the sole kind, and that inner obligation is "the preeminent sort." He

says he had failed to realize that there are several kinds of law and that virtue is not all of a piece. Public justice and order among men require one kind of law, morality another. Pufendorf, he complains, "mixed with one another the law of nature and ethical doctrine [*doctrinam ethicam*]." He has good grounds for his proud assertion: "I am the first to have set things on the right footing" (pref. 11–12, 16).

PART II

Perfectionism and rationality

9

Origins of modern perfectionism

"Error is the cause of men's misery." So Malebranche opens his great treatise, *The Search after Truth*, published in 1674–5.[1] The contrast between this and the opening reference of Grotius's *Law of War and Peace* to controversy as the problem to be handled by morality concisely indicates the basic difference between the natural law thinkers and the rationalist moral philosophers of the seventeenth century. What united the former, I have argued, was acceptance of a problematic centering on the permanence of conflict. What unites the latter is the thesis that ignorance and error resulting from failure to use our reason properly are what stand between us and a life of harmony and virtue.

The modern natural lawyers held that by reasoning from observable facts we can find out how to cope with the moral and political problems that beset our lives. Experience gives us the evidence we need in order to infer that God exists and cares for us. Part of what we learn from it is that God has made the proper structure of our common life independent of any larger cosmic scheme. Even if there is some divine harmony in the universe, we cannot appeal to it in determining how we ought to live. Once we understand that God governs us, the observable facts about ourselves in this world provide all the rational basis there can be for working out our proper direction. The empiricism of this approach seemed to the natural lawyers to take morality out of the disputed territory over which religious wars were fought and to link it instead to facts available to science.

The major seventeenth-century alternative to modern natural law theory rejected both its empiricism and its refusal to tie morality to a divinely supervised universe. Many of those who rejected natural law theory held that God's mind and ours are fundamentally akin. On their view, our own minds give us more direct access to God's plans for us than the indirect reasoning of the empiricists allows. As we improve our self-understanding – as we perfect ourselves – we will see ever

1 See Chapter 11.v for discussion of what the main error is.

more clearly that we are part of a harmonious whole and can live on harmonious terms with ourselves and others. On this view our participation in the divine mind is the most important fact about us. It not only assures us of our eternal destination. It shapes our morals and politics as well.

The thought that our morality arises from our awareness of the divine mind was worked out in detail by the Stoics; and restatements of Stoicism were formative for seventeenth-century moral philosophy. In this chapter I first consider the presentations of Stoicism in du Vair and Lipsius, both of whom were widely read. After them the intellectualism of the Stoics was detached from their specific doctrines concerning the human good, given a new footing, and turned in new moral directions. The first of the attempts to rework elements of Stoicism was that of Edward Lord Herbert of Cherbury, who presented a strongly intellectualist ethic using what he claimed was a new method. After considering his remarkable theory I turn to Descartes. Like his neo-Stoic forerunners, he stressed the importance of intellectual self-perfection and the avoidance of error; unlike them he carefully detached his views of morality from any claims about human access to God's mind. If none of these writers worked out a full theory of morality, they gave new life to ideas that the natural lawyers had set aside.

i. *Stoicism Christianized: du Vair and Lipsius*

In the late fifteenth century the first printings of the works of Cicero and Seneca and of Latin translations of Epictetus made some of the major accounts of Stoicism readily accessible. Two sixteenth-century books helped spread Stoic teaching even more widely. Guillaume du Vair (1556–1621), a French lawyer, parliamentarian, and bishop, found time to write a lengthy exposition of *Sainte Philosophie* in 1584, and a year later published his brief and popular *Philosophie morale des Stoiques.* The Belgian Justus Lipsius (1547–1606), whose political and scholarly writings made him an influential adviser on public affairs as well as one of the foremost figures of the learned world, published *De Constantia* in 1584. The Latin text went through more than eighty editions and was translated into several vernaculars.[2] Both writers thought their work important because they believed Stoic philosophy offered effective personal shelter against the uncertainties and horrors of a deeply unsettled Europe. "I have directed all my endeavors to attain that one Haven of a peaceable and quiet mind," Lipsius says, adding, to bring out the novelty of his own focus on political matters: "I have sought out consola-

---

2 Levi 1964, p. 67. Page references to du Vair's *Moral Philosophy* and to Lipsius's *Constancy* are from the editions of Kirk.

tions against public evils: Who has done it before me?" (*Constancy*, p. 207).

The editors and translators of the classical texts of Stoicism shared with Lipsius and du Vair the belief that these works taught the best way to live tranquilly in troubled times, and that those who understand them have a responsibility to teach those still unenlightened. What philosophers can learn from their own meditations ordinary people can then acquire from custom (du Vair, *Moral Philosophy*, p. 92). "Men be generate into this world because of men, to the end that one may perfite [perfect] an other man," a translator of Cicero comments, adding that his author wrote for just that purpose.[3] The attainment of perfection is a standing concern among the rationalists, as it is not among the natural lawyers. The lawyers were concerned primarily with providing a framework for public life. With Pufendorf they held that the governance of observable action was a domain within which secular thought could reign; and they did not inquire about the highest human good. All of the rationalists, however, including even those who, like Lipsius and Spinoza, did discuss public and political issues, sought ways to achieve inner perfection and the contentment or happiness that they were certain would come with it.

Lipsius "is none of these subtle sophisticall janglers, that place philosophie in the quirks and quiddities of crabbed questioning," says his English translator (*Constancy*, p. 68). But like du Vair he could not escape some metaphysical questions. It is not only that, as a modern scholar tells us, "the foundations of Stoic ethics are to be sought . . . in cosmology or theology, and not in human psychology."[4] The sixteenth-century expositors might have wished to shun such issues; but they had to reconcile the classical teaching with their Christian beliefs. If Stoicism was to help modern Europeans cope with their lives, or if it was, as du Vair hoped, to shame them into improvement by showing how virtuously even a pagan could live (*Moral Philosophy*, p. 50), its doctrines had to be made acceptable to Christian readers. Neo-Stoicism was the result of the effort to blend two rather disparate views.

Du Vair's philosophy amounts to a mixture of Stoic commonplaces and advice, with a little theory blended in and some pages of piety to wrap it up. All things seek their proper good and we do so as well, using our understanding and our will.[5] As they are our noblest parts,

---

3 Quoted in Kirk, introduction to Lipsius, *Constancy*, p. 24.

4 Striker 1991, p. 13. This essay is the best brief but reasonably comprehensive study of Stoic ethics available. See also Inwood 1985; Rist 1969; Long 1986.

5 Du Vair has no qualms about adding a notion of will to Stoic moral psychology. Neither he nor Lipsius discusses Stoic views of the unity of the soul and of the passions as quasi-propositional.

human perfection is constituted by their perfection (p. 57). If the highest good must be attainable – and surely nature would be at odds with herself if having made us long for it she made it also unattainable – it must consist in virtue, since only that is fully within our power. People are very diverse, but nature has made us so that "the action of the mind may be as honorable and glorious in one sort as in another." Rich or poor, common or noble, anyone may attain virtue. Wisdom, which is its chief part, teaches the will to pursue what accords with nature and shun what does not (pp. 58–61). If we saw this clearly we would achieve tranquillity; but our passions get in the way. They mislead us into thinking things good which are not so. And wisdom "is so hidden in the bottom of our minds" that we need philosophy to teach us about it, and to enable us to rid our minds of "such passions as do arise in them, and with the smoke of them darken and obscure the eye of reason" (pp. 61–2).

The will occupies a key place. Through it we can control our actions by refusing to undertake or avoid any action until we come to see clearly whether it is good or bad, natural or not. The will "is able to dispose our opinion, so that it yeeld not consent but to that which it is meete it should," and can remain in suspense about doubtful matters. The skeptic regards such suspense as bringing us the chief benefit of inquiry (see Chapter 3.iii); not so the Stoic. The will's main task is to enable us to pursue only what is truly in our power. Through suspending the will, we can keep ourselves from any concern about everything else (pp. 67–9). Du Vair reflects at some length on the specious appeals we feel from riches, honors, pleasures, and other illusory goods. He urges us to shun hatred, envy, and jealousy (pp. 75–6, 80–1, 86–9), and recommends that we habituate ourselves to think of whatever happens in ways that enable us to remain tranquil.

If all this be true, he concludes, we should above all cultivate piety, or the knowledge of God. Piety unites us to God, the source of our perfection. Admitting that God is the creator of all and takes care of all things, we should accept whatever befalls us as good because it comes from him. We may pray in adoration but should never request anything except what he has ordained. He asks of us only "an innocent life," and public praise (pp. 109–12). Once we understand the honor due to God we can turn to our duties to fellow humans – to our country, our parents, our children, and others. Du Vair ends by saying that God is delighted above all else by seeing us attain the perfection he created us for; but because "our naturall forces can never bee sufficient of themselves to keepe us in this perfection" we must invoke God's favor. We must hope that he will allow our understanding to know the excellences he has given us so that through our knowledge we may control the passions and seek for the everlasting eternal good (pp. 128–9).

Lipsius gives us rather more theory than du Vair, but with no less of a Christian turn. In urging the great virtue of constancy upon us, Lipsius is urging us to live by right reason, "a true sense and judgement of things human and divine," rather than by false and frivolous opinion (*Constancy*, pp. 79–80). Reason, he says, is the remainder in man of the image of God. Though the soul is infected by the body's corruption, it is nonetheless "not without certain clear sparkes of that pure fiery nature from whence it proceeded." The sparks explain the stings of conscience; they are always there, moving us toward God, and always, like God, constant. "God by this image of his cometh unto us," Lipsius explains, "yea . . . even into us."[6] Reason is divinity within us, while opinion comes from the body and its senses, and is as mutable as they (pp. 81–3). Through right reason all of us belong to a common kingdom. Earthly patriotism is not an important virtue; our true country is heaven. This does not mean that we should ignore the sufferings of others. We may be merciful to those in need without feeling pity for them. We can help them without disturbing the calm that comes from a mind constant through its adherence to reason (pp. 93–100).[7]

The issues of free will and necessity are quite important for Lipsius. As a Christian, he is uncomfortable with the Stoic doctrine of predetermining fate, but he is not ready to give it up entirely. He allows that necessity rules all things, not least in making it inevitable that all created things should eventually decay (pp. 107–11). Repining at death is therefore pointless. And there is also destiny, but for God at least that is not an external power. Destiny is best understood as God's eternal decree, showing his providential care for us, not simply his power. From this Lipsius concludes that not all causes are natural. God works miracles and wonders, which are "besides or contrary to nature"; and contingency and free will exist as well. Is this compatible with admitting that fate rules at least the human lot? Lipsius thinks it is. Fate "is the first and principall cause, which is so farre from taking away the middle and secondary causes, that . . . it worketh not but by them: and the will is among the number of those secondarie causes, thinke not that God forceth it." Adding an Augustinian thesis to Stoicism, Lipsius argues that God foresaw from all eternity what men would do freely and of their own wills. Hence though we sin necessarily, we sin voluntarily (pp. 122–3).

6   Lipsius points to this view in the *Politickes,* saying that conscience is "a remaine and sparkle, of right and perfect reason in man, judging and naming good and evill deeds" (I.V, p. 8). Some such view as this also underlies du Vair's belief that wisdom is hidden within us like gold deep in the earth.

7   Seneca is Lipsius's most important Stoic source. He here adopts positions from Seneca's book on mercy, *De Clementia.*

When we object to what seem to us major harms, such as the ruin of
our country, therefore, we are mistakenly trying to rule the way God
rules. Since everything is sent by God, there is no chance or luck. Hence
right reason tells us to be pleased with what pleases God (pp. 101–5).
Lipsius is particularly concerned to ward off one possible misapprehen-
sion of this doctrine. If "there is no other refuge from necessity, but to
wish that, that she willeth," why not just sit by and leave it all to fate?
Because, Lipsius replies, we do not know how fate works. Perhaps our
wills are needed in order to bring about predestined results. As long as
we are ignorant of the outcome, therefore, we must try hard to avoid
evil, and keep on hoping.[8] But when you can certainly tell that your
cause is lost – that your state is about to fall, for instance – then accept
the loss as coming from God (pp. 125–7).

Lipsius thus tries to show that an understanding of providence and
necessity will enable us to remain constant and tranquil through any
calamities, public or private.[9] Next, he argues that a care for our own
profit points the same way as virtue. Here he develops Cicero's deep
belief that the honorable course of life is also the useful course.[10] One of
his chief arguments is that since all things come from God, we should
seek to understand whatever happens to us as being useful to us. In
making this out he has frequent recourse to our ignorance. We do not
understand the point of natural disasters any more than we see why
God permits tyrants to slaughter innocents (pp. 142–4). We must suppose that God uses wicked men to bring about good purposes; they are
bailiffs of his provinces unwittingly executing his punishments (pp.
145–7). Evils both natural and human strengthen our patience in addition to punishing sins. To ask if God's punishments are equitable is to

---

8   So also *Politickes* Bk. I.III: destiny is God, controlling all things for good, but
we cannot sit back and do nothing. As the marginal note says, "we ought to row (as it
were) in the barge, God himself being the steersman" (p.7). Lipsius draws on Cicero,
On Fate, a brief discussion of Stoic fate and why it should not be taken to entail
fatalism.

9   In the *Politickes* Lipsius tells us he will instruct us in civil life, which has two
guides, prudence and virtue. Virtue itself has two parts, piety and goodness; and
about goodness he proposes to say little "because it properly hath no place in this
our civile building, but belongeth to morall worke" (I.VI, pp. 10–11). But prudence
must direct virtue, and the two will always teach the same thing (I.VII).

10   See, e.g., *De Officiis* II.III.9, III.III.11. The term *honestum* is translated by the
Loeb translators as "morally right" or "morally good"; but while this points to the
Stoic distinction Cicero wants to make between what is both useful and agreeable –
the *utile* – and what is required for its own sake, it carries too strong a Kantian
overtone to be a satisfactory rendering.

want to know more than we can. No one is without sin, so all deserve punishment; and we cannot judge the severity of sins. But we can be sure that pangs of conscience always trouble the wicked deeply, and that there are rewards and punishments in an afterlife (pp. 158–60). With all this in mind we should be able to bear public calamities with a more constant mind. After all, things are no worse now than they have been in the past. And no ruler, however tyrannical, can constrain our own minds. There we always have a source of tranquillity beyond the reach of anything outside us (pp. 195–6).

Neo-Stoicism as presented in these two widely read books is essentially a personal therapy based on a metaphysics. It ties the individual mind to God's own mind. It tells us that if we look at our own reason we can both see what the highest good is and move toward attaining it. We can do so essentially because reason in us is the divine in us. If we look only to our experience of the world, we will not understand matters rightly. We must interpret events in the light of what we can work out from the sparks of God's reason buried within us. Only then will we have the right response to events beyond our control.

Cicero had sketched a Stoic theory of natural law in two works whose influence was not lessened by the fact that they were preserved only in fragmentary form.[11] Since Grotius of course knew these fragments, it is tempting to think that he was developing a Stoic doctrine of natural law for modern times. Yet I think this would be a serious mistake. We do not see him appealing to any of the metaphysics behind Stoic ethics. He refuses to say anything, in the development of his theory of natural law, about the relation of our reason and the divine mind. He sets aside, as I have noted, questions of the highest good and of the best form of state, both of which Cicero discusses at length. He does not assure us that all apparent evils are truly goods or at least matters of indifference to us; he offers no therapy; and he says nothing about individual perfection. Neo-Stoicism, like its sources in antiquity, is a perfectionist doctrine. The philosophically interesting followers of Stoicism in the seventeenth century are those who developed perfectionist views. Their perfectionism is tied, as I shall try to show, to their acceptance and development of the Stoic belief that moral concepts are not derived from experience.[12]

---

11 *De Legibus* and *De Re Publica*. See Striker 1987 for a brief discussion.

12 The Stoics did not claim that our thinking in every domain is dominated by innate concepts. For matters of fact they were willing to say that concepts have an empirical origin. But they took moral concepts to be innate, perhaps because they thought that we participate in this respect in the divine mind that informs the whole universe and assigns ends to all things in it.

ii. *Herbert of Cherbury: Cosmos and Common Notions*

Lord Herbert of Cherbury (1581/2–1648) tells us that no less a personage than Hugo Grotius urged him to publish his treatise *De Veritate* (*On Truth*).[13] It is not surprising that Grotius should have done so. Herbert argues that a minimal set of religious beliefs is adequate for everyone's salvation, opposes the kind of Calvinist predestinarianism that Grotius also fought, attempts to show that there are no grounds for skepticism, and appeals to universal agreement as the best mark of truth. It is obvious that Herbert's aim was one Grotius shared: to decrease grounds for religious strife. Encouragement is not endorsement, however, and the differences between Herbert and Grotius are, for our purposes, more significant than their agreements.

To begin with, a metaphysical view is central to Herbert's whole endeavor. Like the Stoics, he holds a metaphysics of divinely ordained harmony. The cosmos is an ordered macrocosm. We are the microcosm and are meant to bring ourselves into a kind of order analogous to the kind we see around us. An innate drive for self-preservation moves us toward this end. To reach it is to attain the kind of perfection appropriate to us individually. In doing so we will also be forwarding the common good. God moves all things toward the common good, minerals in one way, vegetables and animals in others, we humans through the special mental equipment he has given us. "Man," Herbert says, "is an image of divinity," the human mind in particular being "the best image and specimen of divinity" (pp. 149–50). We are a more than passive image. Through our wills and our basic concepts we share in the divine activity of bringing about the greatest good (p. 151).

The metaphysics is not the central focus of Herbert's inquiry. He simply takes it for granted that there are "laws of correspondence between the microcosm and macrocosm" (p. 108), that all things try to preserve themselves (p. 126), and that God has arranged matters so that the preservation of individuals and the preservation of the world are compatible. There must be a law, he says, drawn from "the universal wisdom of nature" that averts mutual destruction, for otherwise things would "all conflict with such violence that they would instantly fall into ruins" (pp. 135–6). Herbert takes this to show that there are always analogies between things of different kinds. Thus the four humors of the body correspond to the four elements in nature (p. 166). Since "the entire order of things is represented in the humors," and they are essential to our physical constitution, the whole universe is implicit in our

---

13   *Life,* p. 120. Page references to Herbert's *De Veritate* are from the translation of Carré, to his *De Religione Laici* from the translation of Hutcheson.

bodies as well as in our minds. "The infinite is everywhere and every part refers to some element of the whole" (pp. 166–9).

The presence of the universe in our minds is Herbert's main topic. His way of explaining his view is less than clear, but enough of his position is understandable for our purposes.[14] He aims to wipe out the arguments of the skeptics, and their allies the fideists, by showing that truth exists and can be known. His first point is that there are true propositions about things, the truth of things, as he calls it, and that this is so whether the things exist or not. The truth reveals itself in what Herbert calls the truth of appearance. He seems to mean that the way things appear to us or affect us internally must show us some truth about the things, however partial and distorted that truth is. Every difference in truth of things grounds some truth of appearance; and we have innate powers or faculties enabling us to recognize the differences. Because these faculties also enable us to conceptualize the differences, Herbert says they give us the truth of concepts. He insists that there is a faculty that responds to each difference in appearances. This seems to require an insane multiplication of faculties; but I take it that what he means is that there is no limit to the extent to which we can conceptualize differences among our sensory and internal experiences, and among our concepts. And if each recognizable difference calls for a faculty to produce a concept, there will be no finite number of faculties. Finally there is truth of intellect, in which we assemble all the lesser truths in one coherent system. Herbert here seems to be pointing toward a relatively small conceptual framework that unifies the indefinitely large set of concepts in terms of which we reflect on experience.[15] Only the truth of things is absolute; truth is available to us only if conditions are such that the thing conforms to our faculties (pp. 83–8). For in general, "truth consists of the proper conformity of the faculties with their objects" (p. 191).

It was not Herbert's discussion of the conditions for attaining truth that struck his readers as original but his claims about the most fundamental concepts we use in thinking about appearances. They are innate, he claims, and found "in all normal persons." He describes them variously as "derived from universal wisdom," impressed on us by nature, or given us by God (p. 106; cf. 126). But they are not accessible by

14 Descartes, thanking Mersenne for his translation of Herbert, says that he finds the book clearer in Mersenne's French than in Herbert's Latin. *Writings* III.140, letter of October 16, 1639.

15 "When freed from the contact of confused theories and arranged in systematic order," Herbert says of the Common Notions – the basic concepts – "they shine forth . . . an image of the divine wisdom. They are all intimately connected . . ." (*De Veritate*, p. 121).

themselves. They are hidden within us, revealing themselves to us only when we are "stimulated by objects" (p. 126). When some appearance given in experience conforms to some faculty within us, the faculty is activated by what Herbert calls natural instinct. Without discursive thought, and without deliberation, the instinct brings into play an appropriate faculty to respond to an experiential stimulus. The concepts that show themselves in such cases themselves stimulate the natural instinct to activate the most basic concepts or "Common Notions," to which the lesser concepts must conform (p. 122).

Now we should not suppose that experience itself is independent of and prior to the common notions activated by natural instinct. On the contrary,

> the Common Notions must be deemed not so much the outcome of experience as principles without which we should have no experience at all. Let us have done with the theory that asserts that our mind is a clean sheet, as though we obtained our capacity for dealing with objects from the objects themselves. (p. 132)

The opposition to empiricism is clear enough. But Herbert elaborates only scantily and unhelpfully on the claim that Common Notions make experience possible. He is somewhat clearer about their other functions.

First of all, the Common Notions provide a foundation for knowledge. To those who say there is nothing new in the doctrine of Common Notions, Herbert answers that "by it facts acquire a mathematical certainty. For all proof is derived from their principles" (p. 135). We cannot be mistaken about the Common Notions; sensory appearances and inner appearances also possess certainty, but to a lesser degree (pp. 103–4). Only in discursive thought, or inferential reasoning, can we make mistakes; but when we use concepts to connect appearances correctly to the common notions, then we have general knowledge of which we can be certain.[16]

Next, the Common Notions provide the focus for a methodology. Whenever anyone makes a truth-claim, Herbert says, we must ask, What kind of claim is being made? The answer will show us the faculty on which any proof of the claim must rest. If the appeal is not just to authority, it must be to the outer or inner senses, which give us access to particular truths, or to common notions, from which we get universal truths applicable to particulars, or to discursive thought, which functions to connect the two (pp. 240–1). Proof seems to be a matter of using discursive thought to move from something more or less indubitable – either particular experiential data or general Common Notions – to

---

16 I here interpret the material at *De Veritate*, pp. 232–6.

attain a new certainty. To do so correctly we must follow a definite set of procedures. Herbert takes this method of inquiry or "Zetetics" to be one of his main contributions, and explains it in considerable detail (pp. 242–84).[17] Not the least thing it shows us is that if anything can be known, then each of us can know it by using our own faculties. Authority therefore has no essential role to play in the acquisition of knowledge. This is as true in religious matters, Herbert insists, as in any others. Anyone can use the zetetic method and "by the light of his unaided powers and experience can achieve complete certainty . . . without the guidance of any instructor" (pp. 280–2).

Third, the Common Notions point the way to eternal happiness. Herbert thinks he can put the matter in one sentence: "When all the intervening faculties are in due conformity with each other, Eternal Blessedness will be in conformity" (p. 286). This is not quite as perspicuous an account of the highest good as one might wish; but it seems to mean that we will be happy when our abilities to receive appearances, to make inferences, and to subsume concepts under Common Notions are all unified in one coherent system of thought. When we achieve this, "the first faculty is connected with the last through the due correspondence of the intervening faculties," resulting in a single truth, a single conformity of the mind and its objects (pp. 286–7; cf. p. 87). The Common Notions, Herbert repeatedly says, point to the common good, and for this very reason we can be sure that "the Creator himself is revealed" in them (pp. 126, 135, 155). The command that we are to love God with all our faculties and to love him as ourselves rests on the fact that when the common notions control our thinking they control all our other faculties, and then we are in conformity with God (p. 287).[18]

iii: *Herbert: Common Notions, morality, and religion*

Herbert is commonly taken to have originated the central ideas of Deism, the rationalizing treatment of religion formulated in the late seventeenth century and disseminated widely in the early part of the eighteenth century. The Deists acknowledged the existence of God, but assigned him only the most minimal tasks after the creation. Their critics accused them of being not merely non-Christian but positively anti-Christian, since they found no place in religion for belief in the Fall, man's consequent sinfulness, the need for redemption, and God's gift of

---

17   "Zetetics" comes from the Greek root *zetein,* to seek or inquire.

18   Zeno the Stoic is said to have used the Greek for the phrase "in conformity" as shorthand for "in conformity with nature"; Herbert is perhaps echoing this in his own talk of living in conformity.

his son to save us. Herbert's claims about the essentials of religion are what gave his book, despite its considerable obscurity, a lasting influence.

Five truths, no more, sum up what the religious person must accept. First, there is a God; second, God ought to be worshiped; third, virtue and piety are the most important part of religious practice, not ceremony or doctrine; fourth, we must expiate our wickedness by repentance, which is only real if we change our behavior; and, fifth, there are rewards and punishments after this life (pp. 291–303). Common Notions make these truths apparent. And the only truly catholic church embraces all people at all times, because "it is and always has been possible for all men to reach the truths I have described" (pp. 303–5).[19]

Herbert asserts that conscience is the highest faculty and that its Common Notion should control all the inner forms of consciousness (pp. 205–6). Although he promised to write a book on what conscience would direct, he failed to do so. But in the course of working out his minimalist antiauthoritarian and anticlerical religious views he is led to spell out a number of important points about morality.

One of the most important of these is that morality has its own Common Notions. Like all such notions, they are derivable neither from experience nor from other Common Notions (p. 139). When we conduct inquiries that fall under the other Common Notions we are always asking whether something exists, and if so what its quality or essence or other attributes are. But when it comes to the "inner truths which refer to Conscience, this special question of Conscience arises, namely whether the thing ought to exist in the given way" (p. 244). Thus the concepts and principles used in thinking about morality are in a different category from all others. More precisely, they cannot be derived from the senses. "It is not from the external world," says Herbert, "that we learn what we ought to follow, what we ought to avoid. Such knowledge is within ourselves" (p. 193). Herbert is here sketching the view that morality rests on concepts that cannot be defined and that these

---

19 It is not merely the doctrinal minimalism of these articles that was shocking to contemporary sensibilities. The treatment of faith was so as well. Herbert treats faith in claims about the past, including miracles and the words of prophets, as giving only probability, offering less certainty than the Common Notions do. Faith in God's promises rests on the Common Notions, and hence on reason. (See *De Religione Laici*, pp. 90–109.) This simply ignores the idea, still alive in the early seventeenth century, that in religious matters any assurance we achieve through reason is an acquired faith which gives us less certainty than we attain from God's gift of divine faith. Chadwick summarizes this view, propagated by scholastics like Suarez, as being that "[f]aith is a higher certainty than knowledge" (Chadwick 1957, p. 34, and ch. 2 generally). For Herbert's theology, see Walker 1972, ch. 5.

give us moral truths that can only be known noninferentially. Charron had earlier suggested that the mind contains "seeds" of all the virtues, without working out a view of moral knowledge based on the idea (Chapter 3.vii). Herbert is the first to propose clearly the main epistemological tenet of what we now think of as intuitionism, although it was well over a century before the label came to be applied to such views.[20] It is significant that Herbert, like those who later thought along similar lines, insists on the human capacity for self-governance and sees his epistemology as providing a guarantee that we and God think of morality in the same terms.

Ideas derived from inner modes of apprehension give Herbert a reason for denouncing the commonplace theory that there are only five senses. If we are confined to what the five senses show us, he says, we "render obsolete a vast number of phrases of all kinds at present in our vocabulary and abolish them on the ground that there is nothing to which they can apply" (p. 113). In these "phrases" we presumably apply concepts derived from the Common Notion of conscience, whose meaning the five-senses theory cannot adequately explain.[21] But if we remember to ask what faculty is involved in any truth-claim, we will judge moral matters appropriately (p. 114). Indeed since Common Notions provide the whole basic content of morality, we find that there is great agreement about moral truths. With the exception of mathematics there is no other domain in which we find so much consensus (p. 192).

At two or three points, Herbert adduces "do not do to others what you would not have them do to you" as an example of our noninferential knowledge of first principles of morals (pp. 136, 186).[22] The claim that we have such knowledge is central to Herbert's high estimate of human moral capacities. His rejection of authority and his injunction, repeated again and again (pp. 72, 75, 80–1, 122, 280–2, 322), that each of us is to think for ourself, culminate in the claim that we must use our own reason to determine whether an alleged direct revelation from God is truly a revelation or not. The key factor is "that revelation must recommend some course of action which is good" (p. 308). Not only philosophy but justice and religion "do not depend upon the behests of priest or judge, but upon the commands of conscience" (p. 281). Each of

20 See Chapter 18.ii, and note 10.

21 At one point Herbert seems to be distinguishing the religious from the moral within the domain of conscience by assigning separate faculties to each: "there is a moral conscience, which is honour, as well as a spiritual conscience" (*De Veritate*, p. 187). But he does not develop the idea.

22 At *De Veritate*, p. 133, Herbert says that we can properly conclude that "the universe itself is governed according to this maxim" because it is a Common Notion, that is, we can tell that God himself abides by it.

us can judge religious claims, thanks to a moral capacity we share with all other humans. Learning and public status have nothing to do with our standing as moral judges.[23] Grotius suggests that moral law would bind even without God but offers no account of the presuppositions or implications of his suggestion. Herbert clearly asserts that moral knowledge sets the terms for the acceptability of religious belief; and if he fails to articulate the morality he thinks is involved, he at least offers us an epistemology to underpin his claim.

For Herbert we are all equally able to think out what we ought to do because we all have the same Common Notions.[24] The claim rests at least in part on a moral argument about how God must distribute abilities. Virtue and piety are the practical prerequisites for attaining eternal blessedness; therefore everyone needs to know what virtue requires; and God never refuses "to provide for us mortals what is essential for this life and life eternal" (p. 119; cf. p. 136). We are confronted with truth-claims from many religions. We must decide which to accept, and God requires us to judge for ourselves (pp. 289–90). With eternal blessedness hanging in the balance, he must have given us the means to make the decision. He would not have instilled in us the longing for eternal blessedness without making its attainment possible (pp. 78, 112); and our ability to make and follow our own moral judgments is the key.[25]

Herbert raises more questions than he answers. His battle against intolerance and religious authoritarianism leads him to attribute free will to us, as showing that we share in God's infinity and that like him we are independent sources of action (pp. 120, 150, 156). Our freedom must enable us to be either wicked or good, for otherwise any goodness we have would come not from us but from God (pp. 205, 164 [see also *De Religio Laici*, p. 117]). But he barely explains how freedom, "that unparalleled wonder" (p. 162), is possible in a world otherwise determined; and even his account of its nature is sketchy in the extreme. We are not free in relation to our ultimate end. Since "no one can prevent himself from desiring Eternal Happiness," our freedom concerns only the means (p. 163). But it seems that we cannot hate a clearly perceived good, and therefore that the will is as determined to pursue clear good

23   Herbert once allows that we rightly say that "with God nothing is impossible through his absolute power." He adds that God's moral attributes show that he will not alter (*De Veritate*, p. 162). I find no other reference to this voluntarist thought, and no further development of it.

24   "I measure . . . the entire race by myself, and I assert (it is an instance of a Common Notion) that the same faculties have been imprinted on the soul of every normal person in all ages" (*De Veritate*, pp. 78–9).

25   See also *De Religione Laici*, pp. 102–3.

in means as in ends (p. 200). And if this is his doctrine, we are free only insofar as we do not clearly see what is good. At the same time he says that the faculties can be misused and perverted due to free will as well as other influences (p. 203). But none of this is further explained.

Another question is raised by an ambivalence in Herbert's thought about the status of commonsense beliefs. If we all have the Common Notions and can make the judgments necessary to guide us to blessedness, should we conclude that the commonsense judgments of ordinary people are in all probability – perhaps necessarily – sound? After all, Herbert is famous for taking the *consensus gentium* to be a test of truth, as Hooker and Grotius had before him. But he says that "the same degree of intelligence is not allotted to all," and he refers from time to time to the herd or the mob: they may be "impelled to a juster pattern of living even by some confused faith" (*De Religio Laici*, pp. 115, 123) or they may need to be "harried by terrors" to pursue their own uncomprehended good (*De Veritate*, pp. 186–7). Such remarks do not suggest great confidence in the judgments of ordinary people. It is a little hard to reconcile the strong anticlericalism that says priests will have no success unless they preach what the Common Notions show to be true with the praise of priests for teaching these truths to people too ignorant to see them without help (*De Veritate*, p. 138; *De Religio Laici*, p. 123). If Herbert is "the father" of later commonsense philosophy, as some commentators have suggested, he might not have been altogether pleased with his offspring.

Herbert's positive moral doctrine, though never fully spelled out, is a species of perfectionism. Whatever the causes are that lead us into the errors that vitiate common sense – and Herbert wrote a book on the subject – none of us, not even Herbert, has yet got a full grasp of the Common Notions in their proper order and coherent system. Until we have such a grasp, we will think and therefore act wrongly. Perhaps the deepest divide between the empiricist natural lawyers and Herbert comes here. For the lawyers, our ignorance of the laws of nature is like our ignorance of other aspects of the natural world, only more harmful. It is not ignorance of ourselves in any interesting sense. Our first task is to carry out our perfect duties, regardless of our motive. We may wish to increase our love of others, but in a minimalist morality any such inward reform, even if it gives us merit, must remain second in urgency to proper external behavior. For Herbert, and for the moral innatists generally, our guide to God's mind is our own mind, and therefore moral ignorance, leading to wrongdoing, is first of all defective self-knowledge. Our prime task must therefore be, as Herbert insists it is, to perfect ourselves. Only through increased perfection will we come closer not only to our own blessedness but also to the ability to interact properly with other people.

iv: *Cartesian voluntarism*

"One of the main points in my own ethical code," Descartes declared, "is to love life without fearing death" (*Writings* III.131). He
published no single work on moral philosophy to show how this might
be accomplished. What we know of his views on the subject comes from
occasional remarks scattered in his writings, his letters, and his late
work, *The Passions of the Soul*.[26] If they do not add up to a complete
theory, they nonetheless contain striking views. Descartes has some
strong affinities with the neo-Stoics and Lord Herbert, but not because
he simply agreed with any of them.

Descartes's critical comments on Lord Herbert's *De Veritate,* which in
some respects he admired, do not indicate one of his main disagreements with it (III.139–40, 142). Herbert held that, in becoming aware of
the Common Notions, we are sharing thoughts with God. As we perfect
ourselves through improving our knowledge, therefore, we come to be
more and more like him. Descartes rejects this view because of a position he holds firmly but never fully expounds, a position that greatly
distressed a good many of his early readers. He thinks that truths of the
kind Herbert's Common Notions contain would constrain God, the
way pagan deities are tied by fate; and he is emphatic in asserting that
we must not admit that anything could subject God to such necessities.
Even eternal verities must depend on God's will, as a king's laws do in
his country (III. 23). There are eternal truths, such as that the whole is
greater than the part; but they would not be true unless God had willed
them to be so (III.103). God's will is as much the cause of essences and of
what is possible as it is of what is actual (III.343; cf. 25).

God's creative willing is completely free because he is initially indifferent to every possible state of affairs. He does not create something
because it is better that it should exist than that it should not; rather, his
willing something to exist makes its existence better. Before he wills, he
could have no reason to will as he does (II.291). Descartes goes to the
extreme of allowing that God could perfectly well have commanded
that his creatures hate him (III.343; cf. Chapter 2, note 14). But unlike Luther, Calvin, and Suarez, he says not a word about God's having commanded that we are to obey certain laws of nature. It will

26   The letters were written with an eye to publication and were widely read
after their publication in 1657. Joshua Welsh pointed out to me that in the preface to
this edition the editor, Clerselier, claims that Descartes had a profound interest in
ethics and that one of his chief aims was to show us how to guide our actions in
accordance with reason. In the brief chapter expounding a Cartesian ethic in his 1666
treatise on the human mind "according to the principles of René Descartes," Louis
de la Forge did little more than summarize and quote from the letters.

become clear that Descartes is proposing a thoroughgoing ethic of self-governance.

His refusal to make any claims about divine imposition of laws of nature goes beyond his determination not to discuss anything that is properly a matter for theologians. It is part of the same outlook that leads him to exclude all talk of final causes from physics. Descartes is no atheist, but he does not think that we can use rational knowledge of God to solve problems either in theory or in practice. His God is at least as inscrutable as the God of Luther and his predecessors, perhaps more so. Our most basic ways of thinking do not allow us to infer anything at all about how God thinks. The fact that we cannot conceive alternatives to the laws of geometry and logic shows the limits only of our minds, not of God's power (III.23, II.294). Confined thus to our own way of thinking, we "cannot share in God's plans" (I.202). Hence in physics, Descartes holds, "we must never argue from ends" (III.341).

The same is true in practice. Knowing nothing of God's purpose in making the world, we cannot suppose that he made everything in it for our benefit (I.248). We can know God's purposes only if he reveals them. If we are speaking "from the human point of view adopted in ethics," we rightly say that God made all things for his glory; but all that this means is that we must praise God as the efficient cause of all that exists (III.195). A further conclusion also follows. Whoever loves God fully will be completely resigned to whatever happens, even if it involves evil or death to himself (III.309–10; cf. 273). For Descartes as for the Christian neo-Stoics, God's providence is a kind of fate, showing us that mere fortune has no role in the world (I.379–80). But from the attitude we are to take toward life as a whole, we cannot infer any specific guidance. Descartes offers an a priori proof of God's existence, and an a priori proof to show that he is not a deceiver; he thinks of God as the creator and the indispensable continuing ground of the existence of the world; but his voluntarist insistence on keeping God untrammeled entails that although God's existence and power explain everything in general, they can never be used to explain anything in particular. What is true of physics and biology is equally true of morality. We can come to trust our faculties by considering God's perfection, but then we must do our science for ourselves. We can come to love God by considering his perfection, but then we must determine for ourselves how we are to act.

v. *Descartes: Ignorance and virtue*

Descartes tells us that he wished to avoid writing about ethics. Expressing his moral views, he thought, would cause him even more trouble from orthodox religious believers than the rest of his philosophy had already brought upon him. Moreover the regulation of other people's lives is the proper business only of rulers, not of private individuals (III.326; cf. I.142). He included what he called a "provisional morality" – *une morale par provision* – in the *Discourse on Method*; but he told Burman that he did so only "because of people like the Schoolmen; otherwise, they would have said that he was a man without any religion or faith, and that he intended to use his method to subvert them" (III.352–3; cf. 299).[27] The provisional morality is to be used while Descartes, or his reader, is withholding assent from all his beliefs, and searching for a foundation on which to rebuild them. In the meantime he has to act, and so he needs guidance.

The provisional morality starts with a skeptic's maxim: obey the laws and customs of your country. It goes on with two rules that Lipsius could have endorsed: be constant once you have chosen a course of action, no matter how uncertain the beliefs that guided your choice; master yourself rather than the world, by making yourself desire only what is fully within your power. The final rule calls for what seems a once-in-a-lifetime action: review all available occupations and choose the best. Here, however, Descartes is more decisive than he sounds. He holds that God gave us the power to separate truth from falsity ourselves, and he intends to spend his life using it. This resolution is his sole excuse for his temporary acceptance of the opinions of others. He will devote his life to seeking truth, using his new methods; only then he will know how to live (I.122–5).

If Descartes has no doubt that knowledge is requisite to right living, he is also aware that there is no easy way to attain the knowledge we need. He has strong views about the order in which knowledge can be obtained. With a provisional morality in hand, the student must first learn logic; then he must master metaphysics and its implications, moving, as Descartes shows in the *Meditations*, from knowledge of self to knowledge of God and on to knowledge of the inanimate world. Next comes study of living things, especially man. After we have come to know all this we can hope to obtain the principles of medicine and morals, the two sciences most directly beneficial to us. Metaphysics may constitute the roots of the tree of knowledge, but the useful sciences are its fruits. Thus "the principal benefit of philosophy depends on those parts of it which can only be learnt last of all" Only when we possess them will we have the most perfect moral system (I.186).

27 In the preface to the *Principles,* Descartes gives another reason for having a provisional code: we need one when "we aim to instruct ourselves" by going back to first principles, because "we should endeavor above all else to live well" and cannot let this matter wait (*Writings* I.186–7). The French *par provision* suggests not only a temporary resource, but also one that provides for one.

Descartes adds that he is ignorant of almost everything on the ends of the branches of the tree of knowledge. The remark can easily seem disingenuous: by the time he made it, he had already worked out a psychology of the passions and the rudiments of an ethics to fit it.[28] If he is being sincere in claiming ignorance of morality, it can only be because he thinks that everyone must be ignorant, at least at present. It may be centuries, he says, before we have deduced what the principles can show us (I.189). Descartes has understood enough about morality to see that none of us will ever have all the knowledge we need to live an ideal life. Whatever morality we come to, it will always be "provisional."

The Stoics were of course aware that even the wisest human, as they understood him, does not possess complete knowledge.[29] They, however, like their seventeenth-century followers, were more concerned to portray the life that would be lived by the perfect sage than they were to make recommendations about how we are to cope with our unavoidable ignorance. Descartes tells us relatively little about the life of perfect virtue. Such positive advice as he thought he could give about how to live is tailored to the human condition. Our ignorance makes essential to us the virtue that he finds most admirable. His psychology explains why we need it.

For Descartes the thinking substance that is our mind is simple. All the different mental functions must therefore be construed as ways of thinking. To a critic's suggestion that this must entail that there is no such thing as will, Descartes replies that the conclusion does not follow: "willing, understanding, imagining, and sensing and so on are just different ways of thinking, and all belong to the soul" (III.56; cf. 97). The thoughts we experience as depending on us alone are volitions, the sole actions of the mind; the perceptions that constitute knowledge are passions.[30] Some volitions, such as those directing us to think about an abstract entity, aim inward; others aim outward, as when we decide to walk (I.335). However directed, volitions, as thoughts, are about some

---

28   The remark comes from the *Principles*, published in 1647 after most of the letters on ethics had been written and when Descartes must already have done much of his thinking about the passions. See *Writings* III.289, a letter to Chanut dated June 15, 1646, where Descartes says that his small knowledge of physics has "been a great help . . . in establishing sure foundations in moral philosophy."

29   Cicero presents the Stoics as holding that natural philosophy is of profound importance to the good life "because he who is to live in accordance with nature must base his principles upon the system and government of the entire world. Nor again can anyone judge truly of things good and evil, save by a knowledge of the whole plan of nature and also of the life of the gods" (*De Finibus* III.xxii).

30   *Writings* III.182: "understanding is the passivity of the mind, and willing is its activity."

object; and their function is to unite us to or separate us from that object.

The will is as important in purely theoretical thinking as it is in practice. When a theoretical thought occurs to us, we can either accept it – make it ours – or reject it; and if we accept it, we come to believe or know it (II.39–40). When a thought about something good occurs to us, our acceptance of it is what we call desire, and the desire may effectively move our body by redirecting spirits to the pineal gland (I.343). Willing in relation to action is thus active thought about good and ill, or about perfection and its opposite.[31] We necessarily pursue what we take to be good and avoid what we take to be ill. If we see clearly and distinctly "that a thing is good for us," then, Descartes says, as long as we keep that thought before us it is impossible to "stop the course of our desire" (III.233). We can abstain from pursuing a clearly perceived good only by thinking that it is good to demonstrate, by so doing, that we possess free will (III.245).

Our liberty is thus not basically a liberty of indifference. We are indifferent to alternatives before us only when we lack sufficient clear knowledge of the goods and ills involved in them (III.233). Indifference in us is an imperfection – a lack of knowledge – though in God it is a result of omnipotence.[32] But our ability to give or withhold assent, or our freedom, is a positive power, and no imperfection. That we have this power is so self-evident, Descartes claims, that our knowledge that we possess it ranks with our knowledge of the other innate ideas. We cannot doubt our freedom, even when we see that God has predetermined all events and cannot understand how this predetermination is compatible with our freedom (I.206, III.277). When we act freely we do what we most want to do. We want to assent to clear and distinct propositions, since clarity and distinctness give us the best reasons for assent. And we want to unite ourselves with what we clearly see to be good, since, again, there could be no better reason for desiring some-

---

31   At *Writings* III.141 Descartes refers casually to "the desire everyone has to possess every perfection he can conceive of." Perfection and good are treated as convertible terms for the object of will.

32   Descartes unhesitatingly embraces the conclusion that sin is due to ignorance: if we saw clearly that a proposed action was sinful, "it would be impossible for us to sin, as long as we saw it in that fashion" (*Writings* III.234).

He is followed by Antoine LeGrand in his popular compendium of Cartesian doctrine. The essence of the will is not indifference, he says, since "will can never be said to be indifferent, except when the object is not clearly and distinctly proposed to it. . . . a Sinner knows not clearly the bad he is about to commit. . . . So that will infallibly tends toward that which appears most convenient for it, so it be made clear and manifest to him." LeGrand, *Entire Body*, part IX V.vi, p. 329.

thing. We can be indifferent when we lack reasons either to accept or reject; and acting without reason is not what we think of as acting freely. "And so," Descartes says to a critical questioner, "I call free in the general sense whatever is voluntary, whereas you wish to restrict the term to the power to determine oneself only if accompanied by indifference." We can indeed act freely in cases of indifference, but the ability to do so is not significant (III.234). It is because free will is the power to accept or reject that we are open to praise and blame and can acquire merit or demerit (I.205).

For Descartes, then, "voluntariness and freedom are one and the same thing," and the proper use of freedom is to lead us to act only from clear and distinct perceptions (II.134). But these are hard to obtain, in large part because the soul is tied to the body. The body causes us to have imperfect perceptions of objects in the world. These perceptions are confused and indistinct thoughts that what is perceived would be good or bad for us (I.358–9; III.264, 267). The desires they tend to lead to are usually desires for what is not in fact as good as it is made to seem. Only knowledge can help us; yet even though we desire knowledge when we see how good it is, we cannot always get it.

Descartes's remedy for ignorance lies in the second maxim of his provisional morality: to be as decisive as possible and to be constant in acting even on doubtful opinions, once he has made a decision (I.123). He later rephrases the rule as requiring "a firm and constant resolution to carry out whatever reason recommends," even when we know we may not have the final truth. Virtue, he adds, "consists precisely in sticking firmly to this resolution" (III.257–8). If we had clear and distinct knowledge of the good, it would give order to our action. Because we lack such knowledge, only the will's strong resolve to be constant can create order. If we are resolute, we act firmly even on beliefs we are not sure of (III.97). The free will, Descartes repeatedly says, is what comes closest to making us like God (e.g., II.40; III.141–2, 326). God is utterly constant (III.23, 273, 348). Hence when we are virtuous, we make that in us which is his image as like him as possible: we make ourselves constant. As long as we are constant and act on what seem to us after reflection the best reasons, we will never feel remorse or regret. We will have nothing with which to reproach ourselves (III.267, 269).

vi. *Descartes: Happiness, the passions, and love*

Descartes's definition of virtue as resolute constancy of will puts self-governance squarely at the center of his ethics. His definition, he claimed, was quite original (III.258). He also thought he had something new to say about happiness. Because he makes so much of the distinction between mind and body and stresses the freedom of the will so greatly, it is tempting to suppose that for him the human being is essentially the disembodied soul, or, still more remotely, the free will itself, able to accept or reject anything proposed to it. But this is a mistake. Descartes holds that we are essentially composite beings consisting of body and mind (III.189, 200, 206, 209). A primitive notion enables us to grasp the nature of the union (III.218, 226–7). It is best understood through the senses, by people who do not spend their time meditating. Cartesian morality is morality for such beings. Consequently virtue alone does not suffice for us.

Unlike the Stoics, therefore, Descartes has no wish to rid himself of the passions. They are useful in leading us to protect and nourish our bodies; and as long as they remain within the bounds set by reason, they give us pleasures, which, although minor, are not to be despised (I.343, 376; III.265, 300). Descartes nowhere treats philosophy as the study of how to die. But he wants something that such a study was traditionally supposed to give – enough detachment from the pleasures and passions of daily life to leave us tranquil in the face of disappointment and loss. This duality – appreciation of the enjoyment of life, need to be beyond the reach of its contingencies – is accommodated by a duality in his understanding of the supreme good.[33]

First, Descartes says we must distinguish between the sovereign good itself and what we feel when we come to possess it, which he calls contentment. Happiness consists only in the feeling. Our final goal ought to be to attain the supreme good; contentment will come to us as a result (III.261, 268). Next, he supposes that the sovereign good must be something that is wholly within our power. Plainly wealth, power, and other external goods are not so. If anything is, it is our thoughts (III.160; cf. 98; I.123). Hence the supreme good must be some condition into which we can put our own minds. "But knowledge is often beyond our powers; and so there remains only our will, which is absolutely within our disposal." Virtue, as resolutely willed constancy, is thus the sovereign good, but happiness, as contentment, must be added to it. Descartes concludes, a little smugly, that he has thus reconciled Zeno and Epicurus. With Zeno he takes virtue to be the supreme good; with Epicurus he accepts the ultimate importance of contentment "to which he gave the name of pleasure" (III.325).[34]

33 Descartes recommends knowledge of the nature of one's soul as a remedy against sorrow due to the death of someone beloved. It is additionally "one which I have always found most powerful . . . to prevent me from fearing my own [death], though I love life as much as anyone" (*Writings* III.215–16).

34 De la Forge gives prominence to this point in his account of the Cartesian theory of the sovereign good. He notes, following Seneca, that all humans desire happiness; and he stresses the importance of the desire for personal happiness as a

How do we know that virtue and contentment are good? Descartes does not say. He does not seem to think, as Lord Herbert does, that there is a basic concept of good that is innate in us along with the other indefinable "primitive notions" (III.218).[35] He nowhere gives a clear account of what makes something good, nor does he explain the term "perfection," which he treats as its equivalent.[36] But because the passions are to be accepted and are in any case not eliminable, the central practical problem as Descartes sees it is to keep ourselves from yielding to the specious charms that they give their objects. Of course, if we had perfect knowledge of what the passions claim to tell us – what is good for our bodies – we would necessarily desire and will it. The passions would not need to be controlled by anything outside themselves. But since we have little if any clear and distinct knowledge of what is good for us, we must control them by an exercise of will.

In his later writings Descartes seems to think he has found out how to do so. We must form the habit of thinking that only what lies wholly within our power is good. What lies wholly within our power is the exercise of our will. We can form the habit of recalling this whenever we experience a desire for something the senses present as good; then, to show that we have free will, we can suspend action and think about whether to pursue that purported good or not (III.233–4). Suspension for Descartes is not what it is for the Pyrrhonic skeptic. It is not a condition that leads to the desired life of tranquillity; it is an act that enables us to make a better decision.

What, beyond virtue and its accompanying contentment, would a virtuous agent decide to pursue? However ignorant he may have professed himself, Descartes was not without substantial convictions on the matter. His psychology is once again central, and, in particular, his view of love. When we perceive that something that affects us can cause good or evil, our basic passional response to it is love or hate. We feel love, Descartes says, when we "think of something as good with regard

---

motive. "I do not believe that the most disinterested of our anchorites would find it difficult to admit that if they did not find extreme satisfaction in following virtue, or if they expected no happiness, and hoped for no reward after death, they would not so easily have resolved to deprive themselves, as they do, of the many innocent pleasures they can enjoy in this life" (de la Forge, ch. XXVI, p. 328).

35   In the French preface to the *Principles* Descartes says that the knowledge of his own existence, of God as creator, and of God as guarantor of truth "are all the principles I use to deduce the truth of other things" (*Writings* I.184). This suggests that moral truths are derivable from principles of metaphysics and epistemology alone.

36   At *Writings* I.358 Descartes says that we call something good or ill if we think it agreeable or contrary to our nature; but it is not clear that he is endorsing what we commonly say.

to us, i.e. as beneficial to us." Thoughts about what is good or harmful to us originate all the other passions (I.350). Descartes is not proposing an egoistic view. He promptly makes it clear that when the soul willingly unites itself with an object, it feels benevolence toward the object and desires to do it some good (I.356). Because the soul is tied to the body the first confused loves we feel will be directed toward preserving our own body; but that is due not to the nature of love and desire, but to the lack of clarity in our perceptions. "It is the nature of love," Descartes says in his longest discussion of the subject, "to make one consider oneself and the object loved as a single whole of which one is but a part; and to transfer the care one previously took of oneself to the preservation of this whole. One keeps for oneself only a part of one's care," and the amount will be proportionate to the amount of good one sees in oneself as compared with the amount one sees in the greater whole (III.311; cf. 269). To be a self detached from all others would be, for Descartes, a great ill for that self.[37]

Descartes's story of the growth of love embodies one of the most important implications of his moral psychology. It is that knowledge transforms the passions. We begin by loving our own good, but when we have a friend, we think her better than ourselves, love her more than ourselves, and desire her good more than we desire our own. In the same way we can come to see that the good of our country is greater than our own, and to love it more. We will then be prepared to sacrifice even our own lives to save it. Finally, we can come to love God above all else, as we come to understand that he is the most perfect being. As I noted earlier, Descartes thinks that this love can be so complete that we will desire "nothing at all except that [God's] will should be done." We can come to have this love by our own power, Descartes says, but he refuses to discuss the question of whether such love "is meritorious without grace" (III.308–11). His claim is bold enough: through love arising from clear and distinct perceptions we can attain the enjoyment of life without suffering fear of death.

Descartes presents what he calls "generosity" as the quality that leads us "to esteem ourselves at our true value." Though we may feel esteem or contempt toward anything, depending on how we assess its worth, their most important object is ourselves. We properly esteem ourselves most highly when we find that we know that only our power of free willing belongs to us, and when we feel that we have the firm habit of willing well – of pursuing in constancy whatever we think

---

37 See the strong comments at *Writings* III.266 on the importance of thinking of ourselves as part of our family, society, and state, even though we are separate from others whose interests may clash with ours.

good.[38] Generosity involves control of one's desires, and leads one to think well of others, as being equally with oneself able to use their free will well. Generosity is thus "the key to all the other virtues" (I.384–8). The generous person will be led away from love of the kinds of goods that are made less valuable when others share them, such as wealth or glory, and toward love of the kinds of good whose value is not altered when everyone shares them, such as health, knowledge, and virtue. When the love of God leads us to think of ourselves as part of the great whole he has made, the nobler we think the whole, the more we will esteem ourselves as well (III.321–2). For Descartes there is no genuine conflict between what is good for us and what is good for all the other parts of creation, between self-love and love of others.

Although the epistemological principles he proposes "have been known for all time by everyone," no one before him has even noticed that they are the principles of knowledge (I.184). Because believing something and knowing that one believes it are different, "many people do not know what they believe" (I.122). Innatism is thus compatible with a denial of any cognitive standing to commonsense views of morality; and it is significant that, unlike Herbert, Descartes makes no appeal to common agreement as a test of truth. He does, however, agree with Herbert in stressing that we should each think things through for ourselves. Here political and philosophical motivations come together. Both Herbert and Descartes resist intervention by authorities in matters properly determined by individual thinking. Their insistence that we must each think for ourselves not only buttresses this resistance, it follows from their innatist perfectionism. The empiricist natural lawyers have no theoretical need to urge us to think for ourselves: neither Grotius nor Hobbes nor Pufendorf does so; and when Locke does, it is a political stance, not one entailed by his epistemology. But for Descartes, however little knowledge of good and ill we may now have, the only way to increase it is to increase our own cognitive capacities. Self-perfection, either through increased knowledge or, lacking that, through constant will, is the key to all of morality. And only seeing for ourselves will give us the knowledge we need.

---

38   It is not clear how Descartes can reconcile his claim that we are essentially embodied souls with his strong assertion that "nothing truly belongs to [anyone] but this freedom to dispose his volitions" (*Writings* I.384).

10

Paths to God: I. The Cambridge Platonists

Thomasius's rejection of servility in our relation to God is a late articulation in Germany of an attitude that found full voice earlier in England. "A right knowledge of God," John Smith wrote in the middle of the seventeenth century, "would beget a freedome and liberty of soul within us, and not servility" (*Discourses*, p. 28; see also pp. 362, 364, 424). "Reverence God in thyself," Benjamin Whichcote exhorted his readers, "for God is more in the mind of man, than in any part of this world besides" (Patrides, p. 333, no. 798). Ralph Cudworth quoted Athanasius in order to assert that "God was therefore incarnated and made man, that he might deify us" (Patrides, p. 101). From the 1640s on, these three formed part of a group engaged in a radical rethinking of Protestantism. They all agreed with Smith that "right knowledge of God" is indispensable to morality as well as religion. But the increase of knowledge was not, for them, sufficient for morality. What is centrally required is exercise of the virtues of love; and we are called to perfect ourselves in that exercise.

Like many others who contributed to the development of thought about morality, these thinkers were responding to religious controversies that were tearing their society apart. Sectarian Calvinism was swamping out the Thomism that Hooker had thought foundational for a national church. Battles raged over church governance, appropriate forms of ritual and worship, and the qualifications of ministers. The question of the relative importance of faith and works to salvation was under debate. Did Protestantism lead to antinomianism, the position that for the saved even the moral laws are irrelevant? There were many who drew this conclusion.[1] Could one appeal to reason and human decency to hold society together? Many held that such a view smacked of Pelagianism in modern dress. The appeal to reason was dangerously like Arminianism in its denial of arbitrary prevenient grace; it also

---

1 For a brilliant study of this strand of Protestant thought, written with considerable Catholic *arrière-pensée*, see Knox 1950.

resembled the anti-Trinitarian doctrines of Socinianism.[2] Could one insist on natural law without suggesting that one was either a papist or a Hobbesian? Everyone who had opinions seemed to be absorbed in questions of doctrinal purity. Finding biblical texts to prove one was right, denouncing those who did not accept exactly the correct formulation of saving truth, taking political action to exclude those in error from membership in one's church – these matters seemed to be overwhelmingly important. The disagreements that they occasioned and exacerbated threatened not only to destroy the possibility of a common faith among English Protestants. They were a serious threat to maintaining any common social and political life.

Whichcote, Smith, More, and Cudworth were deeply embroiled in these local battles. Unlike many of their opponents, however, they developed a stance and a philosophy that in important ways transcended the particularities of the quarrels of the times. Commonly called the Cambridge Platonists, the group's central members were divines who spent much of their lives as academics at Cambridge. The originators of the movement were not philosophers but preachers and reformers. Though they developed a complex and coherent outlook, they did not wish to present it in the kind of systematic form that philosophers often strive for.[3] They worked out their views in terms of Scripture, and argued, as did most of those whom they addressed, by interpreting biblical texts. Such theory as they presented was offered largely to show the implications of their new way of reading the texts. Their Platonism was much mediated by Plotinus and the Greek fathers of the church. Using Plato to provide help for a new Christian exegesis was an incidental, not a central, aim. The most coherent philosophical account of the group's outlook seems indeed quite Platonic, or neo-Platonic. But Ralph Cudworth's Plato, an all but overt Christian who had learned about God's revelation to the Jews from Egyptians, is not exactly the Plato of modern scholarship. The extent of genuine Platonism in the group matters far less than its attempt to put Christianity in a new light.

2   For Pelagianism see Chapter 2.v and note 26. Grotius was an Arminian; Locke was later accused of Socinianism.

3   I exclude Nathaniel Culverwell from the group, though he is frequently included. His *Discourse of the Light of Nature* (1652) is, as I have suggested earlier, almost wholly Suarezian in content. Welcomed by the Platonists for conveying Suarez's compromise antivoluntarism and for his stress on the power of reason to discover laws of nature, he shows little else in common with either the spiritual interests or the philosophical directions of the central members of the group. Patrides, sensibly, does not include him in his anthology. For discussion of Culverwell, see Darwall 1995, ch. 2.

i. *Whichcote: Morality as the core of religion*

Benjamin Whichcote (1609–83) originated the movement. In sermons and personal teaching he insisted on two conclusions: that morality is the heart of religion, and that reason and religion are the same thing.[4] From these two theses he drew a radical inference. If they are rightly understood, he claims, "we should have the very foundation of differences in the church of God taken away from us" (Patrides, p. 66). Differences of opinion on theology, church governance, and proper worship are inevitable, but they are not important enough to warrant turning society into a battleground. Protestants of whatever confession and even Catholics can be of one mind on what matters. The first thing that matters is morality.[5]

"There are but two things in religion," Whichcote writes, "Morals and Institutions: Morals may be known, by the Reason of the thing; morals are owned as soon as spoken; and they are nineteen parts in twenty, of all religion" (Patrides, p. 332, no. 586). When we recall the division of the Decalog into two tables, with the table concerning piety preceding the one on morals, we can see why Whichcote's division would immediately have appeared shocking to his contemporaries. He is no Deist. Unlike Lord Herbert of Cherbury, he aims to preserve the essentials of Christianity. Where Herbert had given conscience the primary role as a test of true revelation (Chapter 9.iii), Whichcote gave morality a place no one since Pelagius had dared to give it. His radical claim is that "the Moral Part of Religion does *sanctify* the soul; and is *Final* both to what is instrumental and instituted" (Patrides, p. 329, no. 221). Morality suffices to win salvation and must be the controlling factor in the arrangements we make about both worship and church governance; and morality is to be known by reason, rather than by appeal to authority, including biblical authority.

---

4 Whichcote himself did not publish. His sermons were published posthumously over some seventy years, as were the correspondence between him and a senior colleague at Cambridge, Antony Tuckney, and a large number of aphorisms (some of which appear in the sermons as well). These materials are most conveniently available now in Patrides and in Cragg, who give further bibliographical details.

5 On the political point of downgrading theology and emphasizing morality, see Noel Malcolm, "Hobbes and the Royal Society," in Rogers and Ryan 1988. The Platonists were opposing mainstream Protestant thought and the church powers built around it. They were, and were seen as, a group in opposition. Malcolm remarks that they seem to us to be so obviously sane and reasonable that we overlook their embattled position. They put forth the view we still accept, of their opponents as fanatics and enthusiasts, and of themselves as the only calming voice amid the fury.

The one part of religion in twenty that comes by institution – by God's positive will revealed in scripture – has, Whichcote holds, merely instrumental value. It helps soothe the troubled mind by holding out the promise of assistance in virtuous living and forgiveness for sin. The help is "medicinal," useful because of the guilt we contracted through Adam's Fall. But the moral part of religion "is necessary in itself," containing requirements dictated directly by reason (Patrides, pp. 68–9). The requirements of morality are not due to God's will; any sane person would want to abide by them even if God granted a dispensation from them (Patrides, p. 73; Cragg, p. 413). It is only if we live in accordance with these necessary moral laws that we will be truly happy. "Morality," Whichcote says, "is not a means to anything but to happiness; everything else is a means to morality" (Cragg, p. 431, no. 743).

Like Cudworth and Smith, Whichcote cites scripture to authorize his claim that we can be deified by making ourselves virtuous (Patrides, p. 70). In explaining the claim he tries to hold on to two points: that we live in God and are wholly dependent on him (Cragg, pp. 43–4) and that each of us has "a kind of sovereignty" over ourselves. The first claim is for Whichcote almost literally true: our minds and God's are not really separate. He does not develop the metaphysics involved in this, as Malebranche did later (Chapter 11.iv), but his audience would have accepted his claim that scripture teaches that we live and move and have our being in God. The claim that we can be made acceptable to God through our own moral abilities would have required more explanation.

Whichcote gives us at least the main points. The central thesis is that we are each able to know, by thinking for ourselves, how we are to live and behave, and that we each have "power to execute and perform" according to this knowledge (Cragg, p. 414). Because Whichcote is strongly opposed to voluntarism, he insists that there is something to be known at the base of morality. "Moral laws are laws of themselves," he tells us, "without sanction by will; and the necessity of them arises from the things themselves" (Patrides, p. 329, no. 221). God made us to know both him and his creation, and so made the mind with sound faculties (Cragg, p. 410). If we use them properly we are in accord with ourselves; to refuse to seek truth and to refuse to think for oneself are equally to be at odds with oneself. The important truths are readily accessible to us, moreover, and are neither recondite nor difficult. Reasoning will show us that God exists. If it did not, faith would be impossible, since faith is receiving a proposition on God's authority and so presupposes knowing that God exists. Reason also shows us what morality requires. Its first principles must be self-evident, known by "their own light," since without starting points for reasoning nothing can be known (Patrides, p. 47). Hence each intelligent agent "hath sense of

good and evil, upon a moral account" (Patrides, p. 73). Since our ability
to reason is so central to our identity, denial of what reason shows puts
us in contradiction with ourselves. From this Whichcote draws one of
his most important doctrines: the internal tie of morality to the self
(Patrides, p. 59).

When we are immoral, we act against our own principles and contradict our own reason (Patrides, p. 46; Cragg, p. 424, no. 129). We
therefore need no external tribunal to tell us we have acted wrongly.
"The unrighteous are condemned by themselves before they are condemned by God" (Patrides, p. 329, no. 232; cf. p. 44). Being self-con-
demned is what is really meant by being in hell; being self-consistent
and filled with "humility, modesty, righteousness, temperance, reverence of deity and the like" is what is meant by being in heaven. Heaven
and hell are not places; they are states of mind (Patrides, p. 46; Cragg, p.
424, no. 100). Christ's redeeming action is no more external than morality is. He "doth not save us by only doing for us, *without* us." Whichcote
thus rejects the strong Puritan separation of personal sanctification
(coming to be in a state of mind itself pleasing to God) from justification
(being acceptable to God by virtue of Christ's vicarious atonement).
Christ must be within us to make us God-like. To be saved, and so
deified, simply means to live in accordance with what we of ourselves
see to be right (Cragg, pp. 38–9).

Whichcote tells us little about the status of moral knowledge. He
says, as I have indicated, that we have a special sense of moral good and
ill – an instinctual awareness, not further explained – different from our
grasp of what is useful or harmful (Patrides, pp. 73–4). He contrasts the
absolute necessity involved in morality with the instrumental necessity
involved in God's revealed laws concerning the institutional side of
religion, but he gives no further explanation of the distinction. He asserts that whatever is in the created world is patterned after antecedent
ideas in God's mind, and suggests that there is a distinction between
truth concerning the "natures and qualities of things" and truth "upon
moral consideration." But he does not say whether the distinction reflects a distinction within God's ideas (Cragg, pp. 409–11).

Though Whichcote gives much emphasis to our rationality and our
ability to come to know the world and thinks we must forever be
striving to improve ourselves, he does not hold that increase of knowledge is increase of perfection. Where Descartes thinks that moral
knowledge is our last and most difficult acquisition, Whichcote thinks
moral knowledge is easy to acquire. The difficult thing, because of our
immersion in our bodies, is to live as it directs. That is our task. "Nothing is the true improvement of our rational faculties but the exercise of
the several virtues of sobriety . . . obedience to God, and charity to
men" (Patrides, p. 331, no. 541).

The point is of great importance. Like Lord Herbert, Whichcote argues in several sermons (e.g., *Works* III.182–3, 285) that because God holds us all equally accountable, he must have made saving knowledge available to all alike. The knowledge that saves must therefore be simple enough so that those without education can, at least in principle, come to see it for themselves. Whichcote has his reservations about the ability of the masses actually to think things out.[6] But while his first response is to urge those with little time for thought to obey their superiors, his second is to speak of the importance of educating everyone so that at least in moral matters they can each judge for themselves (Patrides, pp. 87–9).

Whichcote is firm in his belief that our shared knowledge of morality can serve as a foundation for social peace. We have a common morality because we all do, or can, participate in God's mind; but if we are to know God's mind we must consider what our own moral knowledge shows us about it. We cannot learn about it solely from the natural world, or from God's revelations about nonmoral matters. Practical reason underpins our knowledge of God (Patrides, p. 57). We must also use our knowledge of morality to understand ourselves. We cannot start from some other knowledge of human nature and derive morality from it. In Whichcote's thought, then, moral knowledge, more widely accessible than knowledge either of the natural world or of revelation, is the basic given to which theory must accommodate.

Whichcote's position seems to undercut the Lutheran and Calvinist distinction between the two kingdoms in which we are subjects. For him there is no clear sense in which we can say that the inner part of us is to be governed by God and the outer by the magistrate. "The best discharge of government is government of our selves; and there we must begin" (Patrides, p. 332, no. 659). That inner governance which is both morality and religion must lead to virtuous action, or it is nothing. Compliance with the magistrate's laws is another matter entirely. Implicit in what Whichcote says is a distinction of a kind not previously drawn between morality and law.

ii. *John Smith: Perfection, love, and law*

John Smith (1618–52) shares many of Whichcote's beliefs. He agrees that morality concerns one's inner condition, not only law-abiding external action (*Discourses*, pp. 318, 357), that heaven and hell are states of

---

6 "The longest sword, the strongest lungs, the most voices, are false measures of truth," Whichcote says (Patrides, p. 331, no. 500), recalling to his readers the shouts of the crowd in favor of crucifying Christ. Still, he is sure that the essential parts of revealed truth "are intelligible to all capacities" (Patrides, p. 81).

mind (pp. 329–30, 340), that sanctification and justification must go hand in hand (pp. 325–9), that the laws of morality do not arise from God's arbitrary will (pp. 366, 382, 396), and that we participate in God's mind (pp. 127–8, 380, 410). On various points he is fuller than Which-cote; on some matters he has slightly differing views. It is worth looking at what he says on two of these: perfecting ourselves, and the relation of love and law.

Smith takes quite literally Christ's injunction in Matthew 5.48 to become perfect as God is perfect. Life would not be worthwhile, he holds, if it were only a matter of earthly enjoyment. The point of life for us is "to live the life of God" and thus "in a sober sense" to become deified. We are to do this by bringing the highest powers of the soul together with God "in the unity of affections, will and end" (p. 407). We do not become like God by acquiring God-like knowledge. Rather we "grow most like him . . . when a true spirit of sanctity, justice, meekness, etc., runs through all our actions" (p. 408).

What is striking about Smith's thought here is not so much the identi-fication of perfection with moral perfection as the stress on will. Smith thinks moral knowledge is not hard to come by. There are innate no-tions of divine truths, moral truths among them, and if these are not smothered by lusts arising from the body they immediately become clear (p. 13). Even ignorant men feel an instinctive yearning toward union with God that is a sign of their dim awareness of these ideas (pp. 49–50). If we can only bring ourselves to act better, we will know more. This is what Smith means by saying that we learn more about God through action than through speculation (pp. 2, 4). Truth and goodness "grow both from the same root and live in one another." What keeps us from being better than we are is not ignorance, therefore, but lack of effort. "We want not so much means of knowing what we ought to do, as wills to do that which we may know" (p. 15). The will to improve would not lead us to attend to ourselves in any special way. It is just obvious that though we should love ourselves, we should love other people and God even more (pp. 387–91). We can increasingly transform our desires to fit that insight (cf. pp. 405–6). The search for our own perfection is, in Smith's eyes, an effort to increase the extent to which we act out of love of others (p. 157). Will must be informed by reason but there is no Cartesian talk in Smith of our needing metaphysical and physical knowledge before we can live as we ought.

Smith's opposition to voluntarism and his belief that God is essen-tially a loving being push him in the direction of a consequentialist view of morality. Although it would be absurd to think of God obeying anyone else, he is "not Ex Lex and without all law." Because there is "an intercourse and society as it were between God and men," there must be a law holding between them.[7] God follows his reason, and so he takes the goodness of things as a reason to bring them about. God's aim must be to bring goodness into being in the world; and the law of nature that he has inscribed within our souls tells us to do the same. The law of nature is nothing but a "paraphrase" of God's nature as it is copied in our souls: how could it tell us anything else? (pp. 154–6).[8] Not only is the law inscribed in us a law of goodness (p. 316). It is one which we need not be made to follow by threats. A law of that kind – the kind Grotius and Hobbes took as central – can exact only external observance. As such it is no part of the dispensation we now live under, after the coming of Christ (p. 318). "There needs no law," Smith says, "to compel a mind acted by the true spirit of divine love to serve God or to comply with his will." Those who see the goodness of God will obey not because of God's will but because of the perfection of what God wills – the very goodness of what is to be done or brought about (pp. 365–6).

In his brief discussion of God's justice, Smith draws what must have seemed a very radical conclusion from this stress on doing good. Justice, he says, is meant both to preserve righteousness and to bring about good. Preserving righteousness may require inflicting punishment, but never for its own sake. Punishment must reform the offender or deter others; otherwise it is unwarranted. Smith asks us to imagine a good man in charge of an isolated community of a hundred persons, of whom one turns out to be a murderer. He repents; there is no danger of recidivism, nor of his setting a bad example. Is it not obvious that the ruler would spare the "poor penitent" because equity requires it? As ruler he would have preserved the victim if he could have, so he must save the murderer's life when no harm results from doing so. In the next paragraph Smith insists that "justice is the justice of goodness," aiming at nothing more than forwarding good ends (pp. 151–3). He does not ask whether preserving equity and doing good can always go together.

If the universe were indeed created by an omnipotent and loving deity, we might not need to worry about a conflict between the two. A problem does arise, however, from the stress on love as the proper motive for obedience to the law, and Smith takes some notice of it. Why does God lay down any external law in the first place? Smith is a little embarrassed by the issue. He formulates it by asking why God makes positive laws – laws that do not spring from his eternal nature but from

7   Smith cites Cicero's *De Legibus* as authority for this point.
8   God made the world from an overflowing love: "all divine productions or operations that terminate in something without him, are nothing else but the free effluxes of his own omnipotent love and goodness" (*Discourses*, p. 140).

his own free will. St. Paul tells us that it is because of transgressions, Smith says, adding immediately that "he means thereby the *moral* laws as well as any other." Smith's question is then not really about God's decrees concerning worship. It is about what he calls "the external promulgation" of the moral or natural law, which, as we have seen, is in essence an inner law and one needing no sanctions. Why did such an inner law come to be the sort of law that is backed by threats of punishment?

The answer is that these "divine decretals" were meant to prevent disobedience to the inner law. We are not told how external laws can achieve this. But Smith's comment is revealing: "the moral law was made such a political business by an external promulgation" for the reason St. Paul gives in I Timothy 1.9. It is not the righteous but the unrighteous who need such laws (pp. 158–9). The life of the good man is under the "sweet command" of love (pp. 413, 395). It is only the others – perhaps they are "the common sort" in whose minds the innate ideas are clouded over (p. 15) – who need commands less sweet. It does not seem to occur to Smith to wonder who will rule and who be ruled in a society containing two such disparate kinds of people, or whether the unrighteous can avoid the servility arising when one must obey from fear of punishment. The identification of religion and morality enables him, as it does Whichcote, to transcend the Calvinist two kingdoms. But the thought that law is only for the unrighteous reveals a strain within the Platonists' outlook. Perhaps there may have to be two moralities, an ethic of love for the few and an ethic of law and obligation for the many.

iii. *More: Love's axioms*

Henry More (1614–87) was the one member of the Whichcote group to publish a systematic work on moral philosophy during the seventeenth century.[9] The *Encheiridion Ethicum* of 1666, translated into English as *An Account of Virtue* in 1690, is in some respects eclectic and a little eccentric. It nonetheless spells out the consequences of the views of Whichcote and Smith when those are given a philosophical form. More does not take up all the issues they raise – he rejects voluntarism, for instance, but without elaborating on the rejection or arguing for it – and the *Encheiridion* is not always as clear as we might wish. Yet its main thesis is quite straightforward, and plainly in line with the Cambridge emphasis on love and reason as together forming the center both of morality and of our relations with God.

"In morality we are as sure as in mathematics," Whichcote pronounces (Patrides, p. 330, no. 298), and More produces some twenty-

---

9 Cudworth's treatise on morality was not published until 1731.

three "moral axioms or noemas," which, he says, in a phrase recalling Whichcote, are "agreed to as soon as heard."[10] The noemas are self-evident and can serve the purpose in moral reasoning that "first undeniable axioms" do in mathematics (*Encheiridion*, pp. 27, 20).[11] More introduces them because they will make morality plain and compelling even to those unfortunately lacking in what he calls the "boniform faculty," a brief account of which opens his treatise.

What exactly that faculty is remains somewhat of a mystery even at the end of the book. But it is at least a love of the highest good as well as an insight into it; it leads us to do good as well as to desire it for ourselves; it makes us "pant after God"; and it is the supreme faculty in our minds or souls, through which we resemble God, "who is goodness it self" (*Encheiridion*, pp. 6, 106). Although we all have the faculty, some of us deny it, refusing to admit that there is such a thing as superiority in any faculty. The moral noemas are important for those who ignore superiority and act only on the strongest passion (p. 20). Sometimes such people seem to be the majority.

The noemas turn out to be more than warning signals for the morally insensitive. They are also the practical rational principles underlying each and all of the virtues. We need virtues, More thinks, because of the passions. The passions themselves are part of our nature and therefore, as coming from God, are good. They lead us to seek good in an instinctive way; but because they are blind, and focus on the agent's own good, they need to be controlled by reason. Hence arises the need for the noemas (ch. I.XII).

The noemas, which More states in chapter 4, fall into two groups. The first group (I–XII) concerns the good while the remainder (XIV–XXIII) concerns its distribution. Noema I tells us that the good is that which is "grateful, pleasant, and congruous" to any living being. In III and IV we learn that some beings are superior to others, and that goods may differ in quality, in quantity, or in both. These noemas also underlie sincerity, the virtue by which the mind is wholly devoted to the pursuit of the best and brought to pursue the greatest good with the greatest zeal. Noema V instructs us to choose the good, preferring not simply the greater to the smaller but the more excellent to the less. The seventh noema recognizes an asymmetry of good and evil: it is better to miss a considerable good than to suffer a comparable evil. Noema IX suggests that there might be a trade-off between a lesser good of more "weight and duration" than a superior good of less extent. Noemas X and XI tell

10 The term "noema" is, More says, from the Greek "nous" meaning "mind or intellect."

11 More has some rather sophisticated views about proof, laid out in his *Antidote against Atheism*, in Patrides, pp. 214 – 17.

us that, allowing for probabilities, pursuit of good and avoidance of evil should not be affected by the times at which they will occur. These plainly show the rationale of prudence; and noema XII gives the "demonstration" of that virtue, saying that a calm mind undisturbed by the passions judges better than a mind roiled by desires. Noema XIII, finally, requires that we pursue the greater good with the greater zeal.

Noema XIV, grounding justice, is simply More's version of the golden rule: if you want someone to do good to you, you are bound to do the same good for him in similar circumstances. In XVI we are told to return good, not evil, for good. Noemas XVII–XIX say that it is good for people to have the means to live well, and that the more who have the means, the better. Moreover it is better for one person to be prevented from living luxuriously than for many to be in want. There are two noemas concerned with obedience: we are to obey the magistrate "in things indifferent" and to obey God rather than men. Finally, we are to give people what is due to them, without troubling them; but we should recognize that people can forfeit their rights by bad behavior.

More has no sense that there is any tension among these axioms; he seeks no reduction of their number; and he believes in addition that being fully virtuous will make us perfectly happy. He plainly thinks that morality is wholly a matter of the pursuit of good, and that there can be no ultimate conflict or disharmony among the parts of that search. Seeing why he thinks so will bring out his relation to his Cambridge colleagues.

Although he is happy to draw on Aristotle as well as Plato, More denies both that virtue is a mean, and that all that is needed to guide us to virtue is the insight of the good or wise man. He gives arguments that sound very like Grotius's for rejecting the doctrine of the mean (pp. 146–54). But he takes an un-Grotian turn when he insists that virtue is an extreme because to be virtuous is the highest good – "the best of blessings that Mankind is capable of" (pp. 149–50). And he breaks still further with the Grotian view in explaining what is to replace the insight of the virtuous agent.

Virtue, he says, must seek out and choose, not the mean, but that which is right. How is this to be determined? Aristotle goes in a circle in trying to answer. He tells us to follow right reason; if we ask what that requires, he tells us that it requires us to be prudent; and that, in turn, urges us, again, to be reasonable. Aristotle thus fails to offer any real guidance in action. "Therefore it is necessary . . . first to inquire and find out, what is the mode and standard of this right reason?" What principle are we to use (pp. 155–8)? The principle, perhaps not surprisingly, turns out to be the boniform faculty, which is now equated with an intellectual love of all good. Because this is the divine in us, "it ought in preference to be the rule and standard of all the rest . . . this most simple and divine sense and feeling in the boniform faculty of the soul, is that rule or boundary, whereby reason is examin'd and approves her self." It is a single and simple idea, but "all the shapes and modes of virtue and well doing" come from it – including justice, temperance, and fortitude (pp. 156–8). If your boniform faculty is operating, you need not appeal to the noemas, which cover the same ground.

More thus presents a fully consequentialist ethic. He is quite willing to speak of laws of nature, even giving a rather Grotian account of the rights involved in them (pp. 112–14). But he plainly intends the laws to be explained in terms of their tendency to produce good. Divine reason, he says, has dictated to us "such laws as tend, in their own nature, to the happiness of all mankind" (p. 15). And we find in the supreme rule derived from, or constituted by, the boniform faculty, a principle that everyone can use to make moral decisions. Considering the value of things other than virtue, More dismisses subtle wit and strong memory as unimportant as long as we are filled with love of neighbor and goodwill to mankind. "For the good and perfect man is not so much actuated by a list of precepts gotten without book, as by living inwardly and printing in his mind a single and sincere sense of things." We are to pursue in singleness of mind that which is the best. And the rules for doing this are plain enough for everyone to use (pp. 161–4).

Love is thus the source of law. The law is the expression of the boniform faculty, which is what is divine within us. By living in accordance with it, we ourselves approach divinity. That is what Plato taught when he spoke of virtue as a thing divine, "and how much ally'd, and resembling unto God himself" (pp. 118–19). Unlike Cumberland a few years later, More is no reductionist. He relies on intellectual insight into self-evident axioms, or a faculty that gives us the same guidance without explicit notice of them, to ground his simplifying consequentialism, which contains within itself the explanation of all of morality and of our happiness as well. Self-evident axioms and a superior faculty come together in teaching us love.

iv. *Cudworth: A metaphysics of ethics*

Readers of Ralph Cudworth's *The True Intellectual System of the Universe* (1678) have always complained that its argument, unwieldy in itself, is so hidden beneath an incrustation of quotations and citations as to be almost invisible. His posthumous *Treatise concerning Eternal and Immutable Morality* (1731) shows that he could write with more concentration. We need to see a little of what he says in the great metaphysical work, and to draw on an even later posthumous publication, the *Treatise of Free Will* (1838), to understand the significance of his central point about morality.

That his general orientation is the same as Whichcote's and Smith's is clear from a notable sermon preached by invitation to the House of Commons in 1647. The moral quality of our lives – "willing or not-willing as we ought to do" – matters more than anything else (Patrides, pp. 96–8, 123). Those who turn themselves away from self-centered love to love the good in all things, as God loves, will find heaven within and thus need nothing more (Patrides, p. 111). They will be moved by a law of love which leaves them free in obeying it because in this obedience, even though they are under "the most constraining and indispensable necessity," there is no "narrowness and servility" (Patrides, p. 99). They are a law unto themselves (Patrides, pp. 124–5). Doctrinal differences are unimportant; following the commandment to love is the sole way to know more about God. And our chief task is to perfect not our intellects but our wills or hearts (Patrides, pp. 98–9, 108–10, 126–7). Self-reform is the path to God, making us "partakers in his Divine Form" (Patrides, pp. 101, 116–17). Intellectual disagreements will persist, but they will not matter if the "soft and silken knot of love" ties all of us together (Patrides, pp. 119–20).

Like his Cambridge colleagues Cudworth thinks that when we come to know God better through reforming our wills and loves and lives, we are coming to know God's mind directly. The aim of his *True Intellectual System* is to spell out a metaphysics that explains how this is possible. Above all else, of course, he must avert the danger of atheism. He sees the most dangerous modern form of it embodied in the kind of materialism propounded by Hobbes and the "Epicureans" generally. He is opposed also to the occasionalist element in Cartesianism – the thought that God and God alone sustains the world and its apparent activity, by exercising his power at every moment to keep things existing and working in accordance with his plans. We owe a debt to Descartes, Cudworth says, for making it clear that matter cannot think and therefore cannot do anything that evinces thought. Since much of the world looks as if it had been designed by an intelligent agent, we know that there must be more than matter at work in it. Yet we are not forced to say that God does everything. Nature is not divinity itself, but there are what Cudworth calls "plastic natures" that affect natural things, acting without consciousness but as if intelligently. They serve as God's under-ministers to do the job of maintaining order (*System*, pp. 680–1). Animal reproduction and the "mellification" of bees are examples of this (pp. 155ff.). Plastic natures are at work as much in the macrocosm of the universe as in the microcosm, "which makes all things thus to conspire every where, and agree together into one harmony" (p. 167).[12]

12   The musical metaphor recurs frequently in Cudworth: see, e.g., Patrides, pp. 118, 124.

One of the main props of atheism and mechanistic materialism is the belief that all our ideas come from experience through the senses.[13] Cudworth offers a number of arguments against this view, in order to support his own thesis that ideas are not "junior to things" (p. 679). There must be a mind that is "senior to the world," one that includes in itself thoughts of the essences of all things, of their necessary connections and of all immutable truths (pp. 736–7). It is of course God's mind, and Cudworth's platonizing theory is that unless we were in direct contact with God's ideas no one could think or speak in ways that could be understood by anyone else. It would be pure chance if experience pressed the same thoughts on any two people, or the same beliefs. But when all created minds contemplate the very same ideas or truths in God's mind, "they do all of them but as it were listen to one and the same original voice of the eternal wisdom that is never silent" (*Morality*, pp. 257–8). God's mind cannot work in the way the empiricists say our minds do, and they are wrong about human thinking as well. Although God's mind is archetypal, and ours ectypal, when we think, we share God's thoughts (*System*, pp. 734, 848).

What, then, do we learn about morality when by living in love we manage to suppress the passions and desires that muddy our thoughts and obtrude between our minds and God's? A central part of the answer – the only part spelled out at length in Cudworth's published work – is that there are special moral ideas in God's mind that guide him in his creative activity and which ought to guide us.[14] Voluntarism is, consequently, false.

Cudworth is quite willing to accept God's omnipotence, but he denies what he accuses Descartes of thinking, that it alone entails voluntarism. It is not limiting God's power to say that he can do only what is not self-contradictory. God's wisdom is as much a part of God as his will, so if the latter is limited by the former, God is still not controlled by

---

13   See, e.g., *System* III.ii. Lovejoy 1908 claims that Cudworth presents the main epistemological ideas of Kant's system. He notes that the *System* was published in 1733 in a Latin translation by J. L. Mosheim, who taught at Göttingen, so that Kant could have been acquainted with the work. There was a second edition of the Latin in 1773, and Warda lists a copy of it as among Kant's books (Warda 1922, p. 47). That Kant made no acknowledgment to Cudworth's fully developed a priorism and thought his own view revolutionary is, Lovejoy says, "only one among many illustrations of his astonishing ignorance, or forgetfulness, of all save a very few of the philosophical discoveries and tendencies of his own age" (p. 271). Lovejoy does not discuss the moral theories of the Platonists. For fuller discussion of Kant and the Platonists, see Cassirer 1953.

14   I have not been able to consult the Cudworth manuscripts in the British Library, which are said to amplify considerably our grasp of Cudworth's thought.

anything external to himself (*System,* pp. 646–7; *Morality* I.III.7, pp. 34–5). To make a more positive case, Cudworth brings in some considerations about essences and concepts. Like Suarez, he holds that essences are immutable. One might change the name one attached to an essence, but doing so would not touch the essence. Now it is essences that make things what they are; and if essences cannot conceivably be changed, then even God cannot change them. So God cannot by will alone make something that is essentially good into something that is not essentially good. God can either make something exist or refrain from doing so; but if that thing is by its nature good, then God in creating it is necessarily creating a good thing. As God cannot make a triangle without building triangularity into it, so he cannot make something good without endowing it with the essence of goodness. Will alone, therefore, Cudworth concludes, cannot be what makes good things good (*Morality* I.II.1–3, pp. 13–20).

In chapter XLVI of *Leviathan* Hobbes used his theories of language and knowledge to attack the kind of theory of meaning to which Cudworth is here appealing. Not least among the defects Hobbes sees in this ancient sort of view is its bearing on morality. It enables its adherents to "make the rules of good and bad by their own liking and disliking" – an obvious disaster from Hobbes's standpoint (*Leviathan* XLVI.11). Cudworth plainly knew Hobbes's view and saw the threat it posed to his own Platonism.[15] He adverts parenthetically to the possibility that moral terms might be "meer names without significance, or names for nothing else but *willed* and *commanded*" (*Morality* I.II.1, p. 14). Yet he does not offer anything that looks like a direct argument against the danger. It is worth seeing why he might not have done so.

Cudworth points out that Hobbes and Descartes did not think moral terms meaningless. Like atheists who deny the existence of God, they used the moral terms as if they were meaningful. But then, on Cudworth's theory, they had to have ideas in mind. And if they thought clearly they would have in mind what is in God's mind. They would see that God's idea "being commanded" is plainly not the same as his idea "being good." Of course this is not an argument to prove that they are different; but if Cudworth is right in his own theory of meaning, then it seems to be the only kind of consideration he could use to get his opponents to see their mistake. And if he is right in thinking that the only way to come to know God's mind is to do his commandments from a loving spirit, then his charge that atheists and Hobbists do not have loving spirits is not just name-calling. It is an explanation of why they make the mistakes they do about the vocabulary of morals.

15 Cudworth devotes most of *Morality* to an exposition of his neo-Platonic theory of thinking and meaning and to attacks on empiricism.

Against materialism Cudworth erects a theory of plastic natures, based on the view that the evidences of design in nature could not have come about from matter alone, and on the rejection of occasionalism. In defending the irreducibility of moral concepts, his purpose is to defeat voluntarism, whether Hobbesian or Cartesian. To do so he moves to arguments about essences and meanings that are quite general, and not tied specifically to morality as such. His other Cambridge colleagues did not use arguments of this kind. But Cudworth was plainly not satisfied with the kind of view that underlies Smith's and More's rejection of voluntarism, and with reason. Their position, which is implicit in Whichcote as well, can be put simply. The very idea of God is the idea of a perfect being; even atheists must admit as much.[16] It follows that God is wholly good. Hence he can do nothing bad, and must always act for the good. Since God is by his own nature good, in so acting he is not limited by anything external; but it is plain that his rule is not arbitrary. The upshot of this view, as I pointed out in the case of More and of Cumberland after him, is a proto-utilitarian ethic, a consequentialist view that tells us that God necessarily loves good generally and acts to bring about as much as he can, and that we ought to do likewise. John Smith spells out a further consequence, as I noted earlier. Punishment cannot be retributive; it must be either deterrent or reformative. Cudworth raises an objection to this conclusion, an objection we do not really expect.

We all share, he says, a sense that retributive punishment is "a thing really existing in nature." Civil punishments are indeed in part prospective, preventing or deterring some crimes, but "it is not true that this is all the meaning of them." They give "satisfaction to our equitable nature as rational beings." This is much more evident with respect to divine retribution, perhaps in this world and much more certainly in the next.

> And that these punishments in Hell, after death, will respect only the future, and are no otherwise designed than as iatrical and medicinal, in order to the curing and recovering of deceased souls punished . . . is neither agreeable to Scripture nor sound reason. (*Free Will*, pp. 3–4)

Consequentialism must be rejected because it forces us to the wholly unacceptable conclusion that God could not reasonably carry out retributive justice. But if consequentialism cannot be accepted, then the argument from God's goodness will not give a satisfactory reason for

16   Cf. More's *Antidote against Atheism*, Patrides, pp. 217ff.

rejecting voluntarism. Cudworth seems to think that he is forced by his moral concerns into arguments about meaning and metaphysics.[17]

At one point in the *Eternal and Immutable Morality*, Cudworth says that God's moral nature is his "essential goodness" (p. 37). But he elsewhere distinguishes among "goodness, benignity and morality" (p. 177), and he always insists on the eternal and immutable natures of the just and the unjust whenever he mentions the natures of good and evil. It is as if he would like to attribute to God two moral attributes, goodness and justice, yet hesitates to do so. There is a possible explanation for his hesitation, which may account also for the curiously skimpy nature of his treatise on morality – curious because of his belief that morality is so much more important than the metaphysical doctrines with which he engages at length in the *System.*

If Cudworth avows that God has two moral attributes, he has to answer the question of which of them takes priority. His view of eternal punishment suggests that he believes that divine retribution does not do good in the way that beneficence does. Hence justice and love might conflict.[18] But not only is such conflict theoretically inadmissible in Cudworth's harmonious universe. The question is politically loaded. The Puritans emphasized an Old Testament deity of justice and vengeance. If Cudworth were to give justice priority in God's moral nature, he would seem to have gone over to their side. But insisting on the priority of love, as he generally does, leads him into serious difficulties in explaining eternal punishment. Perhaps silence seemed the best way out.

v. *Cambridge Platonism and free will*

Cudworth's objection to Smith's consequentialist view of punishment occurs as a passing comment in his discussion of free will. Because our relation to God is such a central issue for the Cambridge thinkers, the complexities of the free-will problem could not be avoided. How can we explain our status as genuine agents, neither mere mechanical transmitters of divine activity nor servile subjects made to comply with commands we would otherwise resist, while acknowledging God's supremacy and our total dependence on him? Whichcote did not produce any extended philosophical treatment of free will. Smith's remarks on the issue are more interesting for the attitude they reveal than for the philosophical light they shed on it. More and Cudworth alone grappled

17   In Chapters 15 and 18 I discuss other responses to the problem about rejecting voluntarism that is raised by a refusal to accept a purely consequentialist ethic.

18   The Protestant Cudworth would reject the view that the soul may reform in Purgatory.

with its more difficult aspects. Although Cudworth's work was not published until the nineteenth century, we can use it to discover the difficulties seen by the most acute philosophical thinker of the Cambridge group as arising from the effort to reconcile the deification of the human, on which they all insisted, with that proper obedience to God, which none of them wished to deny.

As always in this period, the question of human free will leads unavoidably to the question of what divine free will is, or perhaps is not. Does our liberty make us similar to God, or different from him? Smith ties liberty to reason. He sees God as free not because God acts from "an absolute will," doing as he pleases in an arbitrary fashion, but because God always wills what is best, in accordance with his own nature as shown him by his own understanding. So too in us. Liberty is reason, the "liberal election of, and complacency in, that which our understandings propound to us as most expedient." To be free is to act voluntarily. It is doing what we see to be best, even in the particular situation and not only in general. When we do not see clearly what is best, we fluctuate in a kind of indifference and are in suspense about what to do. God is never in this unhappy state. Our indifference is therefore an imperfection. The perfection of freedom is to be moved by the universal good seen clearly in the particular case. It is to be moved wholly by the divine order of goodness in the universe (*Discourses*, pp. 133–4).

Why should we ever have thought otherwise? Smith blames it on the Jews.[19] Their notion of legal righteousness, now replaced by the inner righteousness taught in the Gospels, forced them to believe in a free will so absolute that it could do or refrain from any action of its own power. The law, for them, was merely the "object" on which this power was to be exercised. Compliance earned absolute merit, and nothing more was needed from God than the law's indication of his will (p. 290). Smith calls Maimonides as witness to the Jewish belief that man's ability to remain totally indifferent to good or evil, and to choose either, showed itself only after Adam's sin (pp. 292–4). Thus Adam's Fall occasioned "the rise of that Giant-like free will whereby [humans] were enabled to bear up themselves against heaven itself" and live without any need for grace (p. 296). Once we see that God is not to be served for wages, but out of love, we will see why we need not and should not claim to possess a free will of this kind (cf. p. 303).

More does not find things so simple. If there are any people who by nature always act for the best, they are indeed blessed; but they are in a small minority. More is concerned with the rest of us, who have to struggle to be good. Is there free will, entitling us to merit if we choose

19   Perhaps Nietzsche's estimate of English genealogies would have risen had he known of Smith's theory.

rightly? More's first answer is that action from free will is simply one kind of spontaneous or voluntary action. We act voluntarily when we do what we ourselves see to be best. By contrast, we act from free will when we could, even seeing what is best, either act or refrain from acting. Only some external force or our own ignorance can make action involuntary. But it is less clear what, on More's view, might deprive us of free will. His problem arises because he holds that a truly honest man really cannot choose to do something base and vicious (*Encheiridion*, pp. 176–7). It would seem therefore that in forbearing, the honest man acts voluntarily but not freely. And although More speaks of "this power of not acting, when it regards things which are base" as a perfection, he finally defines free will simply as a "power of abstaining from ill" (pp. 179–80). St. Augustine, with Luther following him, had said that since the Fall we are free only to choose what is sinful. More instead cheerfully says we are only free to resist evil – if our character is poor enough for evildoing to be an option for us.

Even this asymmetrical freedom does not leave More happy. One of the objections to allowing it arises from the theory that the will necessarily follows the greatest perceived good.[20] This of course is his own basic view; and he sees that it entails that sin arises from ignorance. That makes sin, by his own account, involuntary. But is it? Are we not all able to know the good? Here More suddenly develops doubts. "The bulk of mankind," he says, "see little of themselves [and] can never discover what is the ultimate good" (pp. 184–5). If this is their own fault, then they are culpable, as having freely willed not to develop their potential insight into the good. But the ability to learn what is good is itself a gift, for which one can claim no merit. Not having it is also not a moral fault, even though its absence makes it impossible for one to be virtuous. "But whether any are so utterly deprived of this natural aptitude," Smith confesses in despair, "is to me so hard and perplexing a question that I had rather wholly decline it, than involve myself with such mysteries of providence" (p. 186).

More's concern arises out of Smith's position. Those who are so thoroughly moved by love that they need no law are also those who cannot bring themselves to act basely. For them the kind of free will claimed by the Jews is not needed, or rather, as More puts it, we should not say of them that they have free will. But More is less willing than Smith to take these blessed few to be meritorious. Are they not so fully tied to the divine order of goodness that they have no real agency of their own? Is it only the imperfect who need freedom in order to be

20   The other objection arises from God's foreknowledge. More dismisses the problem, essentially saying, with St. Augustine, that God's omnipotence allows him to foresee even free actions (*Encheiridion*, pp. 181–3).

blamed, and perhaps to be controlled by laws and sanctions? More sees the issue but not a solution.

Cudworth thinks he needs a strong form of free will in order that "divine justice retributive, dispensing rewards and punishments," may have a justifiable sphere (*Free Will*, p. 78). One kind of freedom poses no problem. We can choose between things that do not differ in goodness or badness at all, as when we pick one coin rather than another when someone offers us money. God also possesses this power. Though he always acts for the best, much about the world is in itself indifferent – for example, whether the number of stars is odd or even, or the exact date of the last judgment (pp. 14–17, 52–4). But liberty of indifference of this kind makes for neither praise nor blame. Only where we choose what we clearly see to be the worse alternative can we be blamed. And this is where the problem lies (p. 19).

The "common psychology" is at fault. Either it makes the will always follow the understanding's judgment of good and ill, in which case the will is necessitated, not free. Or it allows the will to set the understanding to work on specific objects. But then the will must act blindly, and liberty amounts only to "mere irrationality and madness itself acting . . . all human actions." A blind will independent of knowledge would make virtue and vice as impossible as praise and blame (p. 23). What psychology must we call upon to allow freedom, and to avoid imputing all moral evildoing to God as the sole agent? (p. 32).

Cudworth's answer is suggestive if not wholly clear. The division of the mind into faculties of will and understanding is a mistake: it is the individual as a whole who knows and chooses (pp. 23–5). The soul has many powers, or levels of activity. Its plastic nature, the source of its basic life functioning, is not within its control at all; desires are not directly under our control; conscience exerts itself whether we will it to or not, and joins the will sometimes in controlling desire (pp. 30–1). The ruling principle is none of these, nor is it the understanding alone. He uses the Stoic term "hegemonicon" for the governing principle in us, or our self-power. It is, he says, "the soul as comprehending itself, all its concerns and interests, its abilities and capacities, and holding itself, as it were, in its own hand . . . redoubled upon itself more or less, in consideration and deliberation." It can be self-impairing as well as self-improving, but either way it is that through which we make ourselves what we are (pp. 36–7).

How does this reflexive hegemonicon operate? It does in the distinctively human world what the plastic natures do in the purely material world. It serves as a source of order, under God but acting independently of God. It does not make us indifferent to apparent good and ill. It enables us, however, to consider carefully before we act. Haste is thus the source of blameworthiness. We might always have suspended

choice and thought again.[21] Grant that we have this power over ourselves and you grant that we are not always determined by "antecedent
necessary causes" (p. 38). Thus in the war between conscience and the
passions, the understanding does not inevitably determine the agent
one way or the other: "the matter wholly depends upon the soul's
hegemonic or power over itself, its exerting itself with more or less force
and vigour in resisting these lower affections . . . this is not a single
battle . . . but commonly a long lasting or continued war." God praises
or blames us as the battle turns out (pp. 42–3).

Cudworth argues that the possession of a ruling power of this kind is
a necessary attribute for beings as complex as we. Without it, our
various aspects would not function together to make meaningful action
possible. In making us at all, God had to make us free; and he therefore
had to make us capable of erring and sinning. It is thus no derogation
from God's power that he created self-acting beings other than himself,
nor even that he created them with a freedom – that of choosing a
known lesser good – that he himself does not possess. God's fecundity
is such that he makes all the possible kinds of being, even those that are
self-acting; and out of them all he creates a harmonious whole, without
constantly interfering in the world he has made (pp. 77–8).

What leads us, then, to use or not use our power over ourselves?
How does the hegemonicon reflexively decide whether we shall follow
conscience or passion? On what principle does it accept or reject the
promptings to action that come before it? Free choice is not the same,
Cudworth insists, as determination by the good. Neither is it the same
as chance determination, or pure contingency. We do not make ourselves damnable by "the cast of a die" (p. 84). But on the details of the
alternative to these rejected views, showing how self-acting agency is to
be understood, Cudworth is silent.

21 Locke's views on free will in the second edition of the *Essay concerning
Human Understanding are thus remarkably close to Cudworth's, as is Locke's insistence on speaking of powers of mind rather than separate faculties. The Cudworth manuscripts were available to Locke through Cudworth's daughter, the philosopher Damaris Masham, in whose home Locke lived, but I do not know if there is
evidence for Cudworth's influence on Locke on these matters.

11

Paths to God: II. Spinoza and Malebranche

Herbert of Cherbury and the Cambridge Platonists held that what morality requires, before all else, is the pursuit of perfection; but they had different understandings of the difficulties of the pursuit. Herbert thought that we must increase moral knowledge in order to increase perfection; the Platonists saw insufficient resolution, not ignorance, as the obstacle to virtue. For them we need to strengthen our will so that we can resist temptation and live as we all know we should. Descartes also took the view that the cultivation of strength of will is the path that we must take to achieve virtue. But he presented his view as a second-best morality, an expedient needed because action is unavoidable even though we do not know that we are acting rightly. If we could now pick the fruit of the tree of knowledge, the will, guided by the intellect's clear and distinct perceptions, would necessarily – and without struggle – choose the right course of action.

Descartes could take his morality to be an interim measure because he optimistically thought that research would one day yield enough truth to direct action with certainty. Benedict Spinoza (1632–77) and Nicholas Malebranche (1638–1715) did not share his optimism. Agreeing that perfection is our goal, they held that it would be attainable only if we could know all that God knows, which we plainly cannot. Each of them, moreover, although for quite different reasons, rejected the strong Cartesian conception of free will. Consequently they had to give new accounts of how we can obtain reasonable direction for our lives when we cannot have all the knowledge we need.

Spinoza and Malebranche both accept forms of the Cartesian dualism of mind and body, reject empiricism, and hold that clear and distinct ideas are the basis of knowledge. They share, each in his own way, the Cartesian conviction that the divine order of the universe is pertinent to human action. This leads them to hold, with Descartes, that there can be no ultimate conflict between pursuing one's own good and acting for the good of all. Their understanding of the difficulties addressed by morality is thus thoroughly un-Grotian; and unlike Descartes as well as the Grotians, they see our relation to God as an inescapable part of the moral life.

Spinoza, raised a Jew, was excommunicated; Malebranche, a Catholic priest, wrote books that were put on the Index. Although their views outraged the orthodox, they were deeply religious. Christianity contains the truth, each held, but the Bible teaches it through anthropomorphic stories in order to make it comprehensible to simple people. Only reason can bring out the unassailable truth within these stories. How much of the Bible and of theology survives rewriting? On this they differed. But they agreed that only the purely rational version of the truth could provide a solid basis for virtue, happiness, and social peace. Like the Cambridge Platonists they thought we could attain these only by finding the path to God.

i. *Spinoza: Ethics in a world without ends*

The universe, Spinoza argues, is a determined whole in which every event and action is the necessary outcome of the conditions that preceded it.[1] Nothing can be other than it is; nothing can happen or be done in any way other than the way it has happened or been done. The future is as fully determined and necessary an outcome of the present condition of the universe as the present is of its past. Spinoza's metaphysics rules out any free Cartesian will, either in God or in humans.

Although no less deterministic than Hobbes, Spinoza is not, as Hobbes is, a materialistic atomist. Both mind, or substance under the attribute of thinking, and matter, or substance under the attribute of extension, are for Spinoza real and ultimate properties of substance, and everything equally possesses both of them. Stones and animals think, and God is extended just as humans are. There is, moreover, no ultimate plurality of substances. There is only one substance, and it is infinite. Under each of the two attributes we know it to have, however, substance differentiates itself into finite modes. Substance as extended is in motion, but not uniformly. What we call bodies are regions of extension that are more closely related together in motion and rest than surrounding regions and that maintain this relation in a more or less enduring fashion. Bodies thus constituted also think, and so they are paralleled by relatively cohesive groups of ideas. When clusters of these

---

1   In citing Spinoza's *Ethics* I follow Spinoza's own numbering, giving page references to the Curley translation only for the longer undivided passages. For fuller accounts of Spinoza's ethics, see Curley 1988 and Garrett's "Spinoza's Ethical Theory" in Garrett 1996, pp. 267–314. Citations from the *Tractatus* are from the *Political Works*, edited by Wernham.

extended and thinking entities together cause something else, we think of them as single things (*Ethics* II.D7).

Spinoza calls the one substance that constitutes the universe both "Nature" and "God." As extended, God is all of space and what fills it. As thinking, God is infinite knowledge of the universe grasped in all its necessity and complexity and including, in an appropriate way, even the incomplete and fragmentary thoughts that constitute our minds. In addition to being infinite, Spinoza's God is eternal, is the cause of all things, and knows all things. He is active, and produces all essences as well as all existence (I.P25). So the voluntarists also affirmed; but Spinoza's position is not quite the same as theirs. He holds that because God is controlled or moved only by himself and never by anything outside himself he is free in the only possible sense of that term. But because he is determined to his activity both in causing essences and in causing existences, "God does not produce any effect by freedom of the will" (I.P32, C1). The universe follows from God's nature as necessarily as the theorems of geometry follow from its axioms. Spinoza presents his system in a geometric manner in order to exemplify the point.

Plainly Spinoza does not think of his God in the way traditional Jews or Christians conceived of theirs. The most striking difference is that on Spinoza's conception God does not act for any ends. Spinoza is not simply saying, as Descartes does, that we cannot know God's purposes. He is rather claiming that the world that is God-or-Nature expresses God fully while being bare of value or purpose. Although it is a logically unified whole, it is nonetheless as lacking in meaning or point as an Epicurean swirl of atoms. The world as it comes from God contains nothing of what we call "good and evil, merit and sin, praise and blame, order and confusion, beauty and ugliness" (I, app., p. 440). Pufendorf explained the basic normative attributes as initially imposed on a causally determined physical universe by a free act of the divine will. Spinoza sees such properties as necessarily arising from that in us that is not divine because it is incomplete, indistinct, and finite. Our evaluative notions are due to our ignorance, confusion, and desire.

The nature of the relatively differentiated entities or modes that we perceive as separate things or minds provides the underlying explanation of our evaluative concepts. The essence of each such entity, Spinoza holds, is its effort to preserve itself in its distinctive separate being. The urge for self-preservation, which Spinoza calls the *conatus*, is present in the least complex as well as the most complex things (III.P7–8). If we consider the *conatus* as mental striving only, we call it "will"; if we think of it, more adequately, as both bodily and mental striving, it constitutes appetite. We need not be aware of our strivings, but when we are, we call them "desires" (III.P9, S). Desires lead us to have ends of which we are also aware; and these color all our thinking.

Because we are aware of our desires, and do not notice what caused those desires, we come to believe that we have free wills, and can therefore deserve praise or blame. Our desires cause us also to think of everything in terms of the ends they make us have. If we suppose that something is useful, we call it good; and whenever we find something in nature that is useful to us, we imagine that someone must have freely made it for us. This leads us to think that the cause of all things must have ends, and that our good is one of them. Then, when the many harms that nature causes distress us, we try to explain away the evil by supposing that God's ends must be hidden from us. Spinoza pokes fun at those who suppose that God must have planned to kill someone onto whose head a roof-tile falls, because they think there is no other way of accounting for the accident; and in general he treats rationalizing accounts of evil as one more symptom of the fact that every effort to see God or Nature in terms that are meaningful to us arises from desire abetted by error (I, app., pp. 441–4).

Luckily for us, Spinoza thinks, not all of our errors need be harmful. It is true that good and evil are nothing in things themselves, but we cannot help seeing the world in terms of what helps or hinders our self-preservation. And although only God knows completely what might preserve us, we can set up what Spinoza calls an idea of man that can serve as a model for us, to guide us in our strivings. The model will display the human characteristics most conducive to our self-preservation. Even our ability to imagine such a model is due to one of our defective ways of thinking, that which leads us to imagine ideas of perfection. We get ideas of perfection by forming indistinct ideas of classes of vaguely similar things. Seeing everything in terms of our ends, we imagine that some members of the class are more completely suited for them than others, and therefore better. We call these perfect and condemn those that lack some of their features as imperfect. If we imagine human beings as a class, we can say that its members are more or less perfect according to how close they come to the model (IV, pref., p. 545).

Instead of using the term "good" to refer to what we merely imagine to be useful, Spinoza says that he will use it to refer to "what we know certainly is a means by which we may approach nearer and nearer to the model of human nature that we set before ourselves" (IV, pref., p. 545; D1). Though the model must be drawn from partial and incomplete knowledge, striving toward it as a steady end would give us our best hope of success in living well. Of course, we cannot make ourselves adopt the model by an act of will. Our desire to preserve ourselves will cause us to adopt it only when we are convinced that doing so will best help us to continue in our separate being. Spinoza's book on ethics is an effort to demonstrate that it will.

An improved conception of goodness and perfection will be useful to all people alike, because all equally strive for self-preservation. Our conception of law has a different origin and a different function. It comes into being not because we are all alike finite, but because some of us understand much more than others. Most people cannot see that God does not act for purposes and that all events are determined. Hence they think that God is a lawmaker like a human monarch, laying down precepts and ordinances that need to be backed by threats of punishment directed at those who might disobey (*Tractatus* IV, pp. 77–9). The only truth underlying this imagined scheme is that some actions necessarily result in harm to ourselves, others in benefit. If we do not see this necessity, we may construe the connection as a contingent link between a command and a sanction. When God told Adam that if he ate the apple he would necessarily die, Adam might – correctly – have taken this to mean that death was a logically necessary consequence of eating. Unfortunately he misunderstood: he thought God was commanding him not to eat and would punish him with death if he did. The same misunderstanding is involved in thinking that a set of commands is the core of the Decalog. In fact it contains truths that cannot be denied without contradiction. Failing to see this, Moses and all other legislators have treated it as a set of commands backed by threats.[2] "[W]e only regard the divine laws as commandments or statutes as long as we do not know their causes," Spinoza says (*Tractatus*, notes, p. 249), and essentially the same is true of the laws with which politics is concerned.

There are, on his view, two kinds of laws. One kind is a rule in accordance with which all things sharing a common nature necessarily act, a rule following logically from their nature. The other is a kind arising from human will. Individual wills, whose doings are themselves determined, are parts of nature and so can feature in explanations of events. Wills then cause laws, understood as human commands that people can either obey or disobey because they require nothing beyond ordinary abilities. We should properly restrict the term to this meaning, and define law as "a rule of life which man prescribes to himself or others for some object." The laws politicians make are of this kind. What gives them their importance is the ignorance of the mass of ordinary people, of whom Spinoza has no very high opinion: "the real object of law is seldom obvious to more than a few; most men are practically incapable of seeing it" (*Tractatus* IV, p. 69). For the majority, helpful acts must be made necessary by laws compelling obedience through threats of punishment or offers of reward.

Like the natural lawyers Spinoza ties necessity to law and obligation; but unlike them, he thinks that the very idea that there is something one

2 *Tractatus*, pp. 77–9, and see Letter 19 to Blijenbergh in *Works*, p. 356.

ought to do is erroneous. He holds that if we had clear and distinct knowledge of the actions we now think we ought to do we would not use the concept at all. To say this is to say that those who have clear and distinct knowledge do not have obligations. When we have such knowledge, he says, what we at first took as laws "cease to be commandments, and we embrace them as eternal truths instead; that is, obedience is at once transformed into love, which derives from true knowledge with the same necessity as light from the sun" (*Tractatus,* notes, p. 249). Although he does not cite I Timothy 1.9, Spinoza, like the Cambridge Platonists, believes that those who do not understand enough will be like slaves, obeying laws from fear of sanctions. Those who understand more will act from love, and any laws they obey will be laws they have given themselves by understanding the necessity that determines all things (*Tractatus* IV, pp. 69–71). As we shall see, they are free even in doing God's will, because his will has become their own. Those who adopt Spinoza's model will strive incessantly for an increase of knowledge. In proportion as they succeed they increase the extent to which they are self-governed, acting from their own clear knowledge rather than from the commands of others.

ii. *Wisdom and the good life*

Spinoza replaces the Cartesian will, enabling the agent to stay on course in order to display his unique freedom, with a model of the wise person which he aims to explain in such a way that readers will find themselves desiring to emulate it. What, then, is wisdom? It is, for Spinoza, the intuitive knowledge of God-or-Nature.[3] To know it intuitively is to know it in a way that goes wholly beyond sensory experience. Intuitive knowledge also goes beyond careful deduction from a set of premises. Having intuitive knowledge is seeing in one mental vision the necessary connection between or among some number of propositions. We have such knowledge of the connection of propositions when we master a simple mathematical proof; and it was in fact because we possess such proofs that we could begin to seek this kind of knowledge of all things (*Ethics* I, app., p. 441). God can see intuitively all the connections that hold together everything in the entire universe. For us such complete insight is impossible, but we can move closer to it, as we come increasingly to see events and things as necessarily connected with their antecedents and consequences. The more thoroughly we understand the necessity, and the more we clearly and distinctly see how we are bound up in it, the wiser we are.

---

3   Spinoza's theory of knowledge is laid out in *Ethics* II.

Each increase in perfection is an increase in both our joy and our virtue. The two go hand in hand, or, more accurately, are not really separable. Blessedness, Spinoza says, "is nothing but that satisfaction of mind that stems from the intuitive knowledge of God. But perfecting the intellect is nothing but understanding God, his attributes, and his actions, which follow from the necessity of his nature" (IV, app. IV). And if wisdom gives us what we want for ourselves, it no less gives us virtue: "Knowledge of God is the Mind's greatest good; its greatest virtue is to know God" (IV.P28). Where Descartes saw happiness and virtue as distinct though conjoined, Spinoza sees them as constituted by the same state of mind. "Blessedness is not the reward of virtue," he says, "but virtue itself; nor do we enjoy it because we restrain our lusts; on the contrary, because we enjoy it, we are able to restrain them" (V.P42).

Happiness and virtue are tied together in Spinoza's theory by his conceptions of activity and power. An entity is active, he holds, insofar as its behavior can be understood through itself, without referring to beings outside itself. When the behavior of my body is due to your pushing me, I am passive; insofar as it is accounted for by my desires and will, I am active. If the thoughts that cause my desires and decisions are explicable only as conventional beliefs accepted on authority, I am relatively passive; if I think and act as I do because after reflection I have reached clear and distinct conclusions, I am much more active. God-or-Nature alone is totally active, since it alone is to be explained wholly through itself.

Since things necessarily strive to preserve themselves, their dissolution or death must be explained by something external to themselves. Passivity is thus a lack of power, activity is power. Growth in the clarity and distinctness of the ideas that constitute human beings insofar as they think is the conscious aspect of what on the bodily side is increase in health and strength. Both make the actions of individuals more fully explicable through themselves. Since both are measures of the extent to which individuals are able to do what they most strive to do – to persist in being – each increase of power or activity is an increase of joy.

Virtue, Spinoza says, drawing on the Latin root of the term, "is human power itself, which is defined . . . solely by the striving by which each strives to persevere in his being" (IV.P20). We act from virtue only insofar as we are determined to act by our own adequate understanding of ourselves and our circumstances. The virtuous life is thus the life of reason; and since reason seeks nothing but its own increase, Spinoza concludes that "we know that nothing can be certainly good or evil, except what really leads to understanding or what can prevent us from understanding" (IV.P27).

Insofar as we are active, our essential concern with self-preservation leads us all always to seek our own advantage (IV.P24). This makes us sound as self-interested as Hobbes's readers took him to be claiming. The deep difference between the two positions rests on Spinoza's claim that "the greatest good of those who seek virtue is common to all, and can be enjoyed by all equally" (IV.P36). Knowledge of God is the highest good, and one person's possession of that knowledge obviously does not lessen another's share. We need not compete for the true good. We would not be led into conflict if we all understood this.

Spinoza's view of rights fits into this picture. Outside society, rights are identical with powers, and all beings possess the right to get whatever their power enables them to get (*Tractatus* XVI, pp. 125–7). Understandably this leads to strife; but if all of us understood where our true good lies, we could all possess and exercise our natural right "without any injury to anyone else" (*Ethics* IV.P36, S2). It is only ignorance and error, and the passions that follow, that lead to the kind of conflict the Grotians thought normal.

Spinoza defines morality as "the Desire to do good generated in us by our living according to the guidance of reason," and his substantive moral views are all oriented accordingly (*Ethics* IV.P36, S1). It is useful to increase bodily sensitivity and health, as this increases the mind's ability (IV.P38–9). When the body's power is increased, both mind and body are in a condition of joy. Joy is thus a good, and its contrary, sadness is not. Pleasure, which arises when some part of the body is affected more than others in a favorable way, can be good or bad. It may distract us from the pursuit of knowledge, but it may simply reflect our taking proper care of our bodies. The wise will enjoy food and drink, "music, sports, the theater, and other things of this kind" in moderation. Many feelings can be good, up to a point, but can then be excessive. The wise will shun melancholy, and will avoid hatred and the kindred feelings of envy, mockery, anger, and vengeance. Pity is evil in itself as are humility and repentance, because all are forms of sadness and indicate our own weakness (and hence lack of virtue) in one way or another (IV.P50, 53, 54). The wise will therefore, contrary to Christian teaching, avoid such feelings. They will also avoid pride, though reasonable people will feel self-esteem arising from an accurate estimate of their own power (IV.P52).

The *Ethics* offers no laws or rules of behavior – their very form would be misleading – and it does not tell us what actions the wise will perform. Actions themselves are not the essential bearers of moral predicates. Considered in themselves they are simply physical motions, with physical results. What gives them their moral significance is the condition of the agent that causes them to be done. "To every action to which we are determined from an affect which is a passion [i.e., one arising from inadequate knowledge], we can be determined by reason, without that affect." Whether an act of some kind is good or bad depends not on itself or its consequences but on its cause within the agent (IV.P59, S).

What Spinoza offers instead of rules of action is descriptions of how the wise will be affected by thoughts of goods and evils. Wise people will, for instance, be indifferent to the time at which a good or evil comes to them and will always prefer a greater good to a lesser and a lesser evil to a greater. They will seek the good because it is good, not in order to avoid evil (unlike those who obey laws only from fear of punishment). They will not hesitate to avoid danger. But they will not meditate on death. They will meditate rather on the goods they pursue, chiefly, of course, on God (IV.P62–67).

As we increase our knowledge of God, Spinoza argues, we also increase our freedom – the freedom that comes when we are no longer driven by passions, but act instead from clearly understood reasons. Our affects are passions when they involve confused ideas. If we can make the idea involved in a passion clear and distinct, we will transform both of them. We cease to take the idea as presenting a state of affairs that might or might not exist, one that might or might not help or harm us. Seeing the necessity of what is coming, we will accept it tranquilly. As our knowledge increases and our inner life comes increasingly to be a life of activity, our freedom increases with it. Spinoza thinks it neither possible to attain complete freedom nor easy to increase the degree of it we enjoy. But it is the sole thing worth attempting.

iii. *Spinozistic society*

Descartes's interim ethic opens the way for a fundamental egalitarianism, since he holds that all of us equally have free wills and are capable of equal moral resolve. Spinoza denies this, and his intellectual perfectionism leads him to elitism in principle. On his view there are a few wise people who have seen enough of the truth to know at least the rudiments of what Spinoza knows more fully. They must legislate for the masses, or tell them simple stories to make them act as they ought. In his account of the significance of human society, however, Spinoza modifies his elitism to some extent.

His fundamental claim here is that no individual thing in Nature "is more useful to man than a man who lives according to the guidance of reason" (*Ethics* IV.P35, C1). To all the mundane reasons given by the natural lawyers to show why we need mutual assistance, Spinoza adds another. Those guided by reason can help one another grow in virtue, because virtuous agents find their virtue confirmed by seeing that others love what they love. Thus the wise find the company of the virtuous a good, and the choice of social life is rational on this ground alone (IV.P36). Moreover, although the wise are reluctant to accept help from the ignorant they cannot always avoid the need for it. No help is better than human help, even if given by the ignorant (IV.P70, S). The wise would therefore choose to live with the ignorant as well as with other wise agents. They can do so only if there is a government. Prior to society, the ignorant and the wise have the same natural rights. Because most people are ignorant, their rights, which are their powers, lead to strife. To form society, therefore, all alike must give up their right to all things and submit to be governed, in ways that Spinoza discusses briefly in the *Ethics* and at greater length in other works (IV.P37, S2).[4] The wise will be freer in society, living under laws made for all alike, than they would be living isolated (IV.P73). Hence even a society including the ignorant serves virtue and is therefore one of the things we can know to be good.

For the natural lawyers society is warranted because it serves the desires of all alike. People need not be virtuous in order to see the value to them of a social order in which they are allowed to pursue their own ends, even at the cost of some constraints on what they may pursue or do. For Spinoza it is only the desires that the wise and virtuous have or would have that warrant society and its constraints. His view seems at first to be unlike that of Grotius, who thinks we desire social living for its own sake. Spinoza seems, like Hobbes, to treat society as having only instrumental value. But in one of the most remarkable remarks in all of his writings, Spinoza shows why this is an oversimplification:

> Man . . . can wish for nothing more helpful to the preservation of his being than that all should so agree in all things that the Minds and Bodies of all would compose, as it were, one Mind and one Body; that all should strive together, as far as they can, to preserve their being; and that all, together, should seek for themselves the common advantage of all. (IV.P18, S)

Cartesian selves, centering on irreducibly different free wills, must seek a community of love through resolute choice. Spinozistic selves are profoundly altered by the increase of knowledge. The self the wise person seeks to preserve is radically different from the self of the ignorant person. At the limit Spinozistic selves lose their differences. Spinoza's extraordinary wish for universal community reflects both his theory that we are in fact all parts of one body and one mind – God's – and his belief that our true advantage is to be found in virtue or wisdom alone. If we all knew intuitively what Spinoza has tried to show us

---

4 Here Spinoza argues that nothing is sinful in the state of nature, and that justice and injustice, like merit and sin, arise only from socially accepted conventions.

demonstratively, we would in effect be of one mind. Spinoza's path to God is a path to our conscious awareness of our total absorption into nature.[5] If, *per impossibile,* we could fully attain the wise man's freedom, we would be like God, knowing neither good nor evil.[6]

It is easy to see why Spinoza quickly acquired a long-lasting reputation as an antireligious atheist. Though his works were read, for over a century after his death they were largely read to be refuted; and those who used them more positively saw them mainly as providing weapons for clandestine literary war against established religion.[7] He is admired and much studied now, but he had little if any influence on the moral philosophy that followed him. Malebranche's fate was nearly the reverse of Spinoza's.

iv. *Malebranche: Evil and God's general wills*

For Spinoza any appearance that there are truly separate entities in the universe is a mistake due to ignorance or error. However independent of one another particular modes seem to be, everything is connected by strict necessity to everything else. Malebranche, by contrast, is modern philosophy's great separator.[8] Wherever we understand the world by using two concepts and not one, he sees no necessity holding together what the concepts represent. Where there is no necessity connecting things, Malebranche sees sheer contingency. Only God's action makes regularity and connection. We need to understand this, Malebranche holds, in order to see how thoroughly and completely we depend on God.

The Malebranchean theory of causation called "occasionalism" is the best-known illustration of this point. Finding no logically necessary connection between any two events, and understanding causation to require necessary connection between cause and effect, Malebranche

---

5   Throughout the *Ethics* Spinoza treats the mind of the individual person as no more than the bundle of ideas that are associated with the parts of the body that constitute the physical counterpart of that individual. Yet he thinks there may be something mindlike that continues to exist after the bodily parts are all dissipated (i.e., after death). I think he does not intend this type of survival to breach his otherwise massively consistent naturalism but I do not understand his doctrine of immortality well enough to be sure.

6   "If men were born free," Spinoza remarks, "they would form no concept of good and evil as long as they remained free" (*Ethics* IV.P67).

7   See Moreau, in Garrett 1996, esp. pp. 408–21.

8   Malebranche's separatism has its roots in Descartes's principle that whatever can be conceived separately can exist separately; but Descartes does not draw from the principle the radical implications that Malebranche does.

denies that there are any causal connections in the world as we experience it.[9] Only God makes one event follow another: the earlier is not the cause of the later, but only the occasion of God's action in bringing the later event about (*Truth* VI.II.iii, p. 450). Similarly, the world does not necessarily continue to exist from moment to moment. God recreates it at each instant. And our senses do not reveal a world of material objects to us. We could have the sensory experiences that we now have even if such a world did not exist. Only belief in God gives us assurance of the existence of external objects, including our own bodies.

The only genuinely necessary connection that Malebranche allows is that between God's willing something to occur and its occurring. God therefore possesses genuinely active power, but nothing created does. We do not make our bodies move by deciding to do something. Our decision merely serves as the occasion for God to make our body act as we want. Malebranche's metaphysical stress on these ramifications of occasionalism illustrates his use of philosophy to serve his main purpose, which is avowedly the defense of the Roman Catholic version of Christianity (*Nature*, notice, p. 110; I.i, p. 113). It is a prime part of his enterprise to "make God loveable to men and to justify the wisdom of his conduct" against those who, in explaining God's power, make him "unjust, cruel, and bizarre" (letter, p. 107). Against these unnamed thinkers, who sound like voluntarists, Malebranche aims to develop a theodicy, a solution to the problem of evil that does not appeal to human ignorance or to our inability to understand God. He hopes rather to make God and God's creation, including its evil, morally comprehensible. His insistence that God alone acts makes the problem of giving a rational justification of his ways to man as hard as it can be.

The problem has two aspects. The first has confronted religious thinkers from at least the time of the Book of Job. The sun rises on the just and unjust alike, hail ruins a good man's crops, and "men are not miserable in proportion to their guilt" (*Metaphysics* XII.xi, pp. 293–5). How can a just and omnipotent deity permit this? The second is an issue that Malebranche's occasionalism makes especially acute. Whatever happens must happen because of God's will. How then can there be room for any justifiable human action in response to natural events? God's laws make the tile blow off the roof as I walk beneath: how can it be permissible for me to try to avoid being hit by it? In doing so would I not be trying to thwart God's will?

---

9 Malebranche also holds that we have no direct experience and no clear idea of the soul or mind (*Morale* I.V.xvi–xviii), and no experience of God: "the operation of God in us has in it nothing of the sensible" (I.V. xviii; I.X.vi).

Malebranche proposes to solve both problems with one basic principle. It is that God acts only through general laws.[10] He wills the relations of created things to one another in ways that display such laws (*Nature* I.xix, pp. 118–19). He does not, however, will each and every consequence arising from the joint operation of the several laws he has laid down. He wills the causal laws that make the tile fall off my roof; he wills neither that it should fall nor that I should stand patiently beneath it. In the moral realm, God's general wills are always just and good. He wills that the wicked be punished and the meritorious be rewarded. He does not, however, will that Job in particular be made to suffer. Job suffers because in his case God's general laws come together with that consequence; but the particular as such is never the direct object of God's will.[11] Natural and moral evil are thus explicable as merely particular happenings that occur because of the way God's general wills work out. Thus although God alone acts, particular evils can happen and there can be justifiable human action to alter the course of nature.[12]

To make his solution of the problem of evil possible, Malebranche separates God's will into two components. God wills that the most perfect among all the possible worlds should exist. If that were all he willed, his infinite power would enable him to intervene incessantly in the world to prevent particular evils from occurring. God, however, also wills to create only the amount of perfection that can result from his acting in the simplest manner (*Nature* I.xiii, p. 116). Simplicity is required because it is not suitable that God should tend his creation at every point. Action from general laws is alone suited to his dignity (I.xxxviii, pp. 126–7). "So do not suppose," Malebranche warns us, "that God willed absolutely to make the work which is the most perfect possible; rather, He willed to make the one which is most perfect in relation to the ways which are most worthy of him." And the worthiest ways are the simplest (*Metaphysics* IX.x, p. 213).[13]

---

10 Malebranche speaks of such laws as coming from God's "general wills." For the origins of this phrase, see Riley's introduction to the *Treatise on Nature and Grace*, pp. 3–14.

11 Jesus Christ, however, has particular wills and so can save some but not others. *Nature* II.xiv–xviii, pp. 1430–4.

12 Malebranche wavers on miracles. Sometimes he denies that they occur; at other times he says they do but are really results of laws unknown to us; still other times he allows that even God can have particular wills in some extraordinary circumstances. See again Riley's introduction to the *Treatise on Nature* and Riley 1986, to which I am much indebted.

13 The point is reiterated many times. It is a central theme of the *Treatise on Nature;* and see, e.g., *Truth* II.I.VII.iii, pp. 118–19.

In the next section I discuss Malebranche's account of why God created the world at all. In that account, as in the explanation of evil, it is important that in God's rational will the principle of simplicity takes priority over the principle of maximizing perfection (cf. *Nature* I.xiv, pp. 116–17; *Morale* I.I.xxi–xxii). Anselm and Scotus explained why Lucifer's fall is his own fault by appealing to a rank ordering among practical principles. Lucifer was not compelled to pursue whatever seemed to him the greatest good. He could have refrained from pursuing a good to which he had no just title, and chosen to act justly instead. (See Chapter 2.iii.) Luther made plain his belief that God governs us through principles that are independent of what we can see to be the production of good or the avoidance of evil, but of course he made no effort to show that God's principles are rational in our terms. Malebranche makes explicit the duality of willing in God and its bearing on us. To a far greater extent than Suarez, he brings the idea of a rank ordering of principles of action into his philosophical discussion of morality. He does so to show that, despite the existence of evil, God's will is morally comprehensible to us. We can understand God's will because in putting simplicity first God is following rational requirements that we can see to be binding on us as well (*Morale* I.I.xiv). They are the demands of what Malebranche calls Order.

v. *Order, virtue, and happiness*

The knowledge we have of how we are to direct our actions comes to us through our direct access to God's mind. Our mind's relation to our body is only contingent; its relation to God's mind is essential. Without that relation we could have no ideas. Malebranche rejects both the empiricist view that we derive ideas from sensory experience and the doctrine of innate ideas.[14] We have ideas by being aware of God's ideas, which we can perceive as they are in his mind. If this were not so, Malebranche thinks, no one could ever be sure of having the same idea anyone else has. My sensations and feelings are private, perceptible only to me. Thoughts and truths are common to all, and this can only be explained by the supposition that we all see them in God's mind. We do not always – we may not even frequently – see these ideas clearly and distinctly; but if we attend to them we can see some of them in this way, and when we do we know that we are seeing truth (*Truth*, Elucidation 10).

14 Both doctrines are impious. Innatism, like the Aristotelian doctrine that things have teleological natures, would make us too independent of God. Empiricism supposes that mere things or mere sensations have their own power to create ideas.

The ideas in God's mind stand in two kinds of relation to one another, relations of magnitude and relations of perfection. Relations of magnitude are precisely quantifiable. They underlie all exact scientific knowledge. Relations of perfection are not quantifiable, but they are related in a definite order. A human is more perfect than an animal, an animal more perfect than a rock, justice more perfect than wealth, happy existence more perfect than existence as such or than unhappy existence. Malebranche refers to the eternal ordinal ranking of ideas as Order. God acts by the simplest laws because Order requires it (*Nature* I.xliii, p. 129). We, being God's image, ought also to act according to Order (*Morale* I.I.vi). Order is the basis of morality. The acts that Order requires are our duties, and when we act from a "habitual, free, and dominant love of immutable Order," we are being virtuous (*Morale* I.III.xx). All other so-called virtues are merely helps to the acquisition of this one.

Because the Order we are to love constitutes part of God's unchanging reason, virtue is the same everywhere. Reason can teach all people the same morality, however much local customs and traditions may vary (*Morale* I.II.vii). And so far is reason not at odds with Christianity that in making the love of Order "the mother virtue, the universal virtue, the fundamental virtue," Malebranche believes he is simply clarifying Christ's law of love (I.I.xix; I.III.i.–ii). He interprets its demands in an Augustinian way. God loves all things in proportion to their worthiness to be loved, and so should we. God, as the most perfect being, is to be loved above all else; and as the sole genuine source of our happiness he alone should be loved with the "love of union." The most fundamental error we can make is to think that human beings can be sources of good for us. The error is a form of impiety. If we believe it we will also believe that we are dependent on humans rather than on God; and Malebranche thinks that his occasionalist metaphysics shows why that is such a profound and far-reaching mistake. Other people cannot really cause us any good. Our good comes only from God. Hence we should not seek union with other people. The love we are to feel toward other humans is therefore only the love of kindness and esteem, which leads us to honor and assist others (I.III). Malebranche thinks that this kind of love is important but, as his account of our duties to others makes clear, not as important as the love of God (see section vii).

Most of Malebranche's discussion of love of order is occupied with the ways in which we can make it into our dominant habit. What mainly stands in the way is our self-love. We necessarily desire and seek our own happiness above all else. Happiness consists of pleasure and the absence of pain. "It is present pleasure that makes us presently and formally happy, and pain unhappy" (*Morale* II.IV.vi; II.XIV.i; *Nature* II.xxx, p. 150). We are like God in loving ourselves most of all; but his

self-love is not only warranted because he is all-perfect, it is also necessarily governed by Order. Ours is neither warranted nor limited, even
though God has given all of us, pagans and sinners as well as virtuous
Christians, the love of perfection as well as the love of happiness (*Morale* I.III.xiv; I.IV.vii–viii, xiv). Our self-love would be appropriate if it
were subordinated to our love of Order; but "in the condition we are
now in, it often happens that our happiness and our perfection are at
odds" (II.IV.viii).

The topic of the conflict between virtue and happiness is as old as
moral philosophy, but Malebranche has a remarkably original view of
it. It was commonplace for philosophers to say that although virtue and
happiness may make superficially different calls upon us, in the end
the truest happiness is constituted or brought to us by virtue. Malebranche's radical conviction is that happiness is not at all the point of
morality. Virtue as the love of order is not only conceptually distinct
from happiness. It is not causally connected to it, not even as occasional
cause. Its primary function is to direct action in ways whose point is
quite distinct from the production of happiness.

Malebranche's position follows from his view about why God created the world. God, who rightly loves himself above all else since he is
most lovable, has no needs. He acts, therefore, only to display his own
glory. Only he himself can be a worthy expression of that glory. A finite
world cannot be. Malebranche therefore holds that "the Incarnation of
the word is the first and principal of the plans of God." God created the
world in order that it might need his own incarnation as Jesus Christ,
and its continuation in the one true church.[15] Only divine incarnation
can make the finite world infinitely lovable, as God himself is. The
universe redeemed, Malebranche says, is worth more than "the same
Universe in its initial state." Corruption, therefore, is a necessary part of
creation, since otherwise incarnation and redemption would have been
superfluous (*Metaphysics* IX.v–vi, pp. 203–5; *Nature* I.i–iii).

God's purpose, then, is to create the world that is most perfect because it most expresses his glory in the way Order requires, the simplest
way. God requires us to make ourselves virtuous and thus worthy of
our place in a world whose point is to display him. We cannot attain
what we most want – enduring pleasure – except through union with
God. God has shown us the one way to obtain it. The requirements of
Order take precedence over all other aims. Their point is to show what
any world must be if it is to express its creator properly. Insofar as we
comply with Order, we become like God and are entitled to happi-

---

15   "God, being able to act only for his own glory, and being able to find it only in
himself, cannot have had any other plan in the creation of the world than the
establishment of his Church." *Nature* I.i. See also *Morale* II.IX.viii.

ness.[16] "God is just," Malebranche asserts, "He necessarily rewards virtue" (*Morale* I.I.xix; II.XIV.iv; cf. *Nature* III.xxvii). We can thus rationally hope to achieve our end only by coming to deserve it (*Morale* II.IV.viii). The only connection between virtue and happiness is a moral connection.

vi. *Acquiring merit*

The acquisition of merit is thus of central importance to us. Malebranche has an austere view of what is required. It is not enough to comply with Order out of vanity, or ambition to shine before one's countrymen, or even natural compassion. We are virtuous only when we love Order simply because of our intellectual grasp of it. A purely rational love of Order, like God's love of it, is the sole principle of merit (*Morale* I.II.i; I.IV.xvi). "One always merits when one loves the true good through reason; and . . . one merits not at all when one only loves it through instinct" (*Nature* III.xxix, p. 187).

Our awareness of relations of magnitude in God's ideas gives us the foundation of the sciences, as awareness of Order gives us basic moral knowledge. When Malebranche distinguishes between speculative and practical truths, he is separating fact from value as sharply as Pufendorf did with his distinction between physical entities and moral entities (*Morale* I.I.vii). Pufendorf tells us that moral entities were imposed by God for the purpose of guiding free human action. Malebranche's practical truths about Order have the same function. Unlike speculative truths, practical truths move us to act (*Metaphysics* VIII.xiii). Since being moved to act is distinguishable from knowing a truth, Malebranche asks how the one is tied to the other.

There are, Malebranche says, "only two principles which determine the natural movement of the will and excite habits: light and feeling [*la lumière et le sentiment*]" (*Morale* I.IV.xvi). In the best case, the light given by our knowledge of Order moves us just as such. The best case was exemplified in Adam before the Fall. The Fall increased the power of his bodily desires over his mind, and we, his heirs, are not as easily moved by pure knowledge of Order (*Metaphysics* XII.xiv, p. 297; cf. IV.xviii, p. 97). We can now know Order without being moved by it. Feeling thus has a role in moving us to moral action. It can also be a way of becoming aware of what Order directs. God instructs us constantly about the Order he loves, not only through intellect, but also through pleasures and pains (*Morale* I.V.xix). Like Descartes, Malebranche thinks that bodily pleasures and pains advise us about what helps or harms the

---

16   Malebranche also says that God will love us in proportion as through virtue we become like him (*Morale* I.I.xiv).

body. There are other pains that warn us that we are transgressing against Order, and pleasures that tell us, obscurely, the opposite. Since pleasure is what we always necessarily seek, we can be moved by these monitory feelings even when we are not moved directly by practical knowledge.

Malebranche offers a dual account of our weakness. Because we are now sinful, we cannot contemplate Order with any pleasure. "For Order, the divine law, is a terrible law, menacing, inexorable. No man can contemplate it without fear and without horror" (*Morale* I.V.xxii). Perhaps even Adam needed, and did not always have, courage to live by Order.[17] In addition, our desires cloud our vision of Order. Our sinful nature leads us to see less pleasure in following Order than in gratifying our desires, and hence to make the wrong choice. To balance the combined effects of our fear of painful obedience and our failure to perceive the good, Malebranche calls on divine grace. Through Christ God enables some people to take enough pleasure in the contemplation of Order to overbalance the ills they fear. Although pleasure should generally be the reward of merit (*Nature* III.xxvii, p. 186), in these cases it precedes merit and makes it possible. God's action is specifically needed to enable insight into moral truth to be a motivating force for fallen beings.[18]

Feelings tend to mislead us. Because we are now sinful in nature, we cannot easily tell the monitory promptings of grace from "the secret inspirations of the passions" (*Morale* I.V.xx). Free will, however, enables us to examine our feelings with great care, so that we can prevent them from misleading us. The essential action of Malebranchean free will is to suspend choice – to enable us not to act. The claim is like one made previously by Descartes and later by Locke.[19] But Malebranche's view is significantly different from both of theirs. They see the will as simply the ability to give or withhold assent. Malebranche identifies it instead with our love of good in general, coming from God and shared with God (*Truth* I.I.ii). It therefore contains its own inherent direction. The understanding is capable of not assenting to ideas that are less than entirely clear and distinct, and the will is capable of not consenting to desires whose gratification promises less good than might be attained.

---

17   See Alquié 1974, p. 357.

18   We cannot deserve to have these monitory feelings, since we are not virtuous when we need them. Hence Malebranche treats them as a kind of prevenient grace, and part of his Christology is built on its importance.

19   Poppi, in Schmitt et al. 1988, p. 659, says that Pomponazzi held that the will's freedom comes most basically from its ability to suspend choice even where the agent's own good is at stake. I pointed out in Chapter 9.i that du Vair mentions suspension of will in connection with freedom. See also Chapter 8.ii, note 14.

If God acts only by general wills, we act only from particular wills. Desire proposes some specific object or action. When we will, we either accept or reject it. To will is thus, as Malebranche puts it, "to consent to a motive."[20]

Since the Malebranchean will is simply a general love of good, it must be guided, no matter how obscurely, by the intellect. It can never make choices regardless of its indistinct perceptions of perfection. What saves us from complete domination by our desires cannot, therefore, be Cartesian firmness in the face of ignorance. We can suspend action because in addition to desires arising from our tie to our body, all of us feel, usually very confusedly, a desire to be united to God. This desire keeps us dimly aware that no matter how great a pleasure we think we would get from union with some created being, it would not be the greatest possible pleasure. Hence we are not necessitated to consent to its pursuit. We can attend to ideas of other things that might yield greater good – ideally, of course, God – and the will can consent to them instead.

When we do not have clear knowledge of Order, or it does not move us to action, we can fall back first on graciously given pleasant feelings that show us what Order requires. We can make a habit of suspending decision until we are as clear as we can be about these feelings, and in doing so we are displaying one form of love of Order. Another remedy for our lack of moral awareness is God's provision of the incarnation. Christ's life and doctrine make evident to the least intelligent people the path that leads to God. Of course, it needs to be interpreted to them, but if they accept the teachings of an infallible church they will have by faith a certainty as adequate to their moral needs as the rational knowledge that philosophy provides.

vii. *Malebranchean morality*

Malebranche's metaphysics is intended to show us our total dependence on God (cf. *Morale* II.I.vi–viii). Unsurprisingly, he accompanies it with a morality of obedience. We are no more a law to ourselves than we are our own good (II.XIV.iv). "Nothing is greater than to obey God," he says, insisting that "it is neither base nor servile" to do so (I.II.i). As a result of his view about why God created the universe, his morality is also informed with a profound otherworldliness. He spells it out most fully in his doctrine of duties.

Acting even from the most complete love of Order does not, for Malebranche, guarantee that one is acting rightly or doing one's duty.

20 Cited in Riley's introduction to the *Treatise on Nature*, p. 59 n. 221, from Malebranche's *Réflexions sur la prémotion physique*.

An act is right in every respect only when we know what Order objectively requires and incorporate that knowledge in our reason for acting (II.I.i–ii). As we cannot always think matters through in time for action, it is helpful to learn some rules of duty. Malebranche assigns the rules to the usual categories of duties to God, neighbor, and self. Although he states quite a few, his formulations mostly do not seem able to give us the specific guidance we need. Many are concerned with attitudes or feelings – of esteem toward equals, and of respect and honor toward God's representatives and toward political superiors – without specifying any actions. In balancing the amounts of respect or honor owed to people of different degrees of relationship to oneself and of social status, matters are so complex that no rules can really be stated (II.VII.xiv). Malebranche is not suggesting that there are no objectively right acts in such cases. The implication is that only insight into Order – our own insight, or more probably that of an authority – can guide us (II.VIII.xv).

Our duties to God consist in the thoughts and feelings we should have concerning his wisdom, his power, and his love (I.V.vi). What Malebranche reiterates throughout is our need to orient our thought and our love to God as the sole source of enduring pleasure (II.II–IV). Public worship in some form or other is appropriate since we live in society, Malebranche thinks, but the forms it takes are a matter of local custom and tradition. What God wants is for our souls to be as like him as possible.

One insight governs all our duties to others. We belong to two societies, a temporary one on earth and an eternal one that arises from our participation in God's mind (II.VI.ii–iii). Order clearly shows that the second is infinitely more important than the first. Hence we are to rank duties concerning it incommensurably higher than those concerning the earthly city (II.VII.xv–xvi). We must therefore be particularly careful about what we do in showing the benevolence that we owe to all human beings. Essentially, Malebranche teaches, we should help them to eternal goods, not to earthly goods. The latter "are not, properly speaking true goods" (II.VIII.iii). We should be particularly careful never to give others anything that might enable them to sin. When their desires have gone seriously astray we may have even to humiliate or otherwise pain them. If we were not immortal, or if other people could not be made Christian, perhaps we could allowably assist them to present pleasures. But "if I serve my friend according to his desires, I lose him and I lose myself with him." In giving alms or visiting the sick "it is necessary to relate everything to the salvation of one's neighbor" (II.VIII.xiii–xv). Our duty to ourselves is to work for our perfection so that we deserve happiness (II.XIV). Similarly, we may not simply assist others to the happiness they now wish for themselves. We must help them toward perfection.

"It is in order to merit heaven that we are living on earth" (II.VIII.viii). Ascetic hedonism – pleasure to be attained through pleasure not only deferred but kept out of mind – is thus the key to his view of duties to ourselves as well as of those to others (II.XIV.v–vi). Malebranche's doctrine of duties is in thorough concord with his account of God's purpose in creating the world. We cannot rightly aim at the happiness we cannot help desiring; we may only aim to make others as well as ourselves worthy of it.

Malebranche's ethics is now almost unknown. His influence in his own times was, however, considerable.[21] Bayle greatly admired him and used some of his ideas. Hume thought him the first to start the abstract rationalist theory of morals "afterward adopted by Cudworth, Clarke, and others."[22] I have tried to show that his version of rationalist ethics contained a number of deeply original ideas about the structure and function of morality and raised important questions about the relations of virtue to happiness as well as about the possibility of purely rational motivation. His ethics was part of his pioneering attempt at a theodicy, and that, in turn, involved him in a metaphysics that we can no longer take seriously. Spinoza's work, as I remarked, came to be widely known because of the enmity it aroused. If his approach to naturalism makes him congenial to the modern world in ways in which Malebranche cannot be, Malebranche's thoughts about ethics did far more than Spinoza's to shape the actual development of modern moral philosophy.

21 See McCracken 1983 for an excellent study of Malebranche's importance for British thought.

22 Hume, *Enquiry concerning the Principles of Morals*, p. 197 n. 1.

Cudworth's occasional citations of Malebranche show a good acquaintance with his work; and Malebranche's Platonism if not his Catholicism would have been congenial to him. In the nineteenth century he was discussed at length by Martineau 1891, pp. 159–246.

12

Leibniz: Counterrevolutionary perfectionism

Leibniz (1646–1716) was usually polite to those whom he criticized, and often allowed that there was some recoverable truth in almost any view, however mistaken. Yet he rejected central positions of all his great seventeenth-century predecessors and peers. Descartes, Hobbes, Gassendi, Locke, Spinoza, Malebranche, Grotius, Pufendorf, Bayle – whatever their role in the formation of his thought, they turned out, in the end, to have made serious mistakes. Ancient and medieval thinkers were more likely to be endorsed, if often in rather vague terms. These two sides of Leibniz's attitude are linked in a famous description of his own theory, uttered by his mouthpiece in the *New Essays:* "This system appears to unite Plato with Democritus, Aristotle with Descartes, the Scholastics with the moderns, theology and morality with reason. Apparently it takes the best from all systems and then advances further than anyone has yet done" (*New Essays*, p. 71).[1] In associating his work with that of the premoderns, Leibniz was being neither eclectic nor nostalgic. He was being, in Catherine Wilson's apt term, counterrevolutionary.[2] The newest science, the most up-to-date political practices, the current religious controversies, he argued, were all to be understood and managed only in terms that embodied the deep insights of ancient and medieval thought – or only, in his modest estimate, in his own

---

1   Such comparisons are not rare in Leibniz's writings: cf. *Papers,* ed. Loemker, p. 578, where he says that his doctrine of preestablished harmony, explaining matter as confused perceptions in each soul coordinated by God with confused perceptions in each other soul, "combines what is good in the hypothesis of both Epicurus and Plato, of both the greatest materialists and the greatest idealists." And see *Metaphysics* 11, for Leibniz's favorable view of scholasticism. Citations of Leibniz's *Discourse on Metaphysics, Specimen Dynamicum, Monadology,* and *Principles of Nature and Grace* are from *Papers,* ed. Loemker.

2   Wilson 1990, p. 145. Wilson illuminatingly contrasts Leibniz to the genuinely nostalgic Cudworth.

terms. He meant to restore some old headstones that the builders of modernity had rejected.

Despite the acknowledged magnitude of his accomplishments in many fields, Leibniz is not usually thought to have been of the first importance for the development of moral thought.[3] Yet he cannot be ignored in our story, and not only because of the influence he and his admirer Christian Wolff had on Kant. Leibniz worked out a complex philosophical theory to show how voluntarism could be defeated while keeping God central to morality. It was his solution to this problem, rather than Cumberland's or Malebranche's, that set the terms in which later thinkers took it up. I have tried to show how central this issue was for earlier seventeenth-century moral philosophy. It continued to be crucial for the eighteenth century as well. Philosophers repelled by voluntarism who found Leibniz's theory unacceptable faced major problems in rethinking morality.

Although Leibniz wrote no single comprehensive work on ethics or the foundations of politics, reflection on these matters occupied him all his life. He began by thinking about issues involved in legal reform very early in his career, and he reached his mature conception of justice before the end of 1671, when he was not yet twenty-five.[4] It took him much longer to work out his final metaphysical position. His concern with overcoming the bitter confessional divisions of Europe made him think it imperative that he construct an understanding of morality and of religion acceptable to all parties alike. If his views on morality and religion tend to resemble those of St. Augustine or St. Thomas more closely than Luther's or Calvin's, it is not because his aim was to retreat to safe old thoughts. It was to develop a new way to resolve disagreements deeper and more dangerous than any that had ever existed earlier.

i. *The best possible world*

Pufendorf's refusal to use the word "good" as equivalent to "being" crystallizes one of the fundamental points on which Leibniz stood opposed to the new thought of his century. Descartes sees the physical world in wholly mechanical terms, abjures the search for final causes,

3   His political and moral thought has, however, been carefully studied: see Grua's pathbreaking works of 1953 and 1956, Sève 1989, and Riley 1996. Riley gives a more comprehensive view of Leibniz's moral and political thought than his title suggests and draws illuminatingly on much new manuscript material. I am particularly indebted to Sève's brilliant study.

4   Mulvaney 1968, pp. 54–5, 71. In *New Essays*, p. 71, Leibniz asserts that his concern with morality preceded and generated his interest in metaphysics.

and explains morality as due to God's arbitrary will. Hobbes's thesis that to be good is simply to be the object of a desire presupposes a neutral universe of moving bodies. For Pufendorf, moral entities are contingently imposed on a group of fully constituted physical objects that may preserve or endanger one another but that have no distinctive value-bearing properties. Spinoza takes our normative vocabulary to be at best a useful fiction, at worst a confusion, having a role in our lives only because our knowledge is limited. Malebranche's physical world serves as the source of occasional causes of pains and pleasures, but itself possesses no value of any sort. Leibniz was of course not ignorant of the importance of the mechanistic world view in the new science, but he rejected all of these philosophical positions, denying that the existence and disposition of what we perceive as matter could be independent of considerations of value. For him final as well as efficient causes must be invoked if we are to understand even the laws of motion (*Nature*, §11, 15; *Papers*, pp. 640–1; cf. *Specimen Dynamicum*, p. 442).

The metaphysics behind the restoration of finality and the reunification of being and value is brilliantly worked out in Leibniz's theory of the preestablished harmony of the perceptions of monads. One of its consequences is to put the harmony of the universe squarely at the center of politics and morality. As a devout Christian Grotius may have believed in the ultimate harmony of God's universe, but he does not bring it into his account of human relations. Leibniz never leaves it out. The Grotian problematic has no toehold in his theory.

The defeat of voluntarism is for Leibniz the crucial point in demonstrating that the cosmic order is rational and therefore has a normative claim on all alike.[5] Descartes does not try to lessen the shocking consequence of his extreme voluntarism, that God's will must seem wholly arbitrary from our standpoint, and that even what is to us self-evidently rational and just is so only because God made our minds incapable of thinking in any other way. Hobbes is no less shocking with his in-

---

5   In my account of Leibniz I rely very largely on the *Theodicy*, for two reasons: it is the most important systematic exposition of his views that Leibniz published, and probably the most widely read; and it is almost certain that Kant read it. In 1744 Gottsched published a new German translation, fully annotated, thus making it easily accessible to him. His edition also contains German translations of Leibniz's "Principles of Nature and Grace," "A New System of the Nature and the Communication of Substance," and first, second, and third explanations of the New System. Earlier versions of the *Theodicy* in German had been published in 1720, 1726, and 1735. (The *New Essays* was not published until 1765.) The *Theodicy* thus enables us to see what Kant would have known of Leibniz's views beyond what he read in such writings as the *Monadology* and also to see what he might have learned of earlier writers whom Leibniz discusses for his controversial purposes. See Horstmann's *Nachwort* in his edition of the Gottsched translation, pp. 543, 553.

sistence that God's authority rests solely on his power, and that the
moral terms we assign him are nothing but subservient indications of
honor. Pufendorf's version of voluntarism is somewhat less extreme
but, as I shall point out in sections iv and v, the moderation did not
placate Leibniz. Tyranny, despotism, haphazard whimsicality, and the
treatment of human beings as "earthworms," properly crushed as one
walks (*Theodicy*, pp. 58, 237, 402–3) – these are what Leibniz always
associates with the voluntarist's deity, and he uses these terms to persuade us that we cannot accept that portrayal.

His point is that voluntarism cannot allow for the basic truth that
God and we must belong to a single moral community. He repeatedly
uses the argument that voluntarists make it impossible even to hold
that God is good: "for what cause could one have to praise him for what
he does if in doing something very different he would have done
equally well?"[6] And if we cannot think him good, we must think him
"unfitted to be loved and unworthy of being loved" (*Theodicy*, pp. 236–
7, 127). Leibniz offers reasons to fear that if serious religious belief goes,
moral and social order will either vanish with it or be sustainable only
by brute force.[7] But his fundamental aim is to ensure that we conceive
God not just as an "imaginary metaphysical being" but as "a definite
substance, a person, a mind" (*Papers*, p. 158) with whom we, as persons,
stand in moral relations of love and trust.

Leibniz's notorious "optimism," his thesis that this is the best of all
possible worlds, is thus inseparable from his moral rejection of voluntarism. He utterly rejects the voluntarists' liberty of indifference. It can
never be true that God acts without a reason, since if he did so he would
need a reason for choosing the occasions on which to ignore reason, or
else arbitrariness would infect all his choices. The goodness of a state of
affairs must therefore always be a reason for God to choose it or bring it
about. Goods are comparable, and greater good gives greater reason for
acting. Since God is infallible, he must therefore always act for the best
(cf. *Theodicy*, p. 128). Against the voluntarists Leibniz insists that there is
a reason why God created this world, and that we know what it is. He

6   See also *Metaphysics* 2. It is typical of Leibniz that in the long discussion of
voluntarism in *Theodicy* beginning at section 176, p. 236, he tries to show that St.
Thomas and most Protestant apologists are on his side, and to present even Calvin as
moderate on the matter.

7   See the impassioned discussion in *New Essays* IV.xvi.4, pp. 462–3, of those
who, not fearing divine providence and future punishment, "give their brutish
passions free rein," and of the way this attitude, "stealing gradually into the minds of
men of high station who rule the rest," is "inclining everything towards the universal
revolution with which Europe is threatened." Leibniz goes on to denounce the
ferocity of religious controversy and to condemn intolerance.

created it because it is the best possible world (cf. *Nature*, §§7–8). The possibilities, moreover, despite Descartes, are fixed independently of any choice by God. "Does the will of God form the ideas which are in his understanding?" Leibniz asks, replying that an affirmative answer would totally subvert our grasp of the concepts of intellect and will (*Theodicy*, p. 428). God neither makes nor alters the possibilities. He simply chooses among them.

The thesis that this is the best possible world and the argument behind it have many consequences for Leibniz's ethics. Not least is his Thomistic conclusion that we can consider the universe to be like a well-managed organization, with everyone given a task whose execution contributes to the greatest good. It is a Kingdom of Grace, ruled by God as monarch, securely built upon a Kingdom of Nature, of which God is the architect (*Nature* 15). "In doing one's duty," Leibniz says,

> in obeying reason, one carries out the orders of the Supreme Reason. One directs all one's intentions to the common good . . . Whether one succeeds therein or not, one is content with what comes to pass, being once resigned to the will of God and knowing that what he wills is best . . . Do your duty and be content . . . because you have to do with a good master. (*Theodicy*, pp. 51–2, 55; cf. p. 154)[8]

God has, as it were, turned a part of the world over to us, so that we are like little deities in our microcosm;[9] but even if we mismanage, God "turns all the errors of these little worlds to the greater adornment of his great world" (*Theodicy*, p. 216). Spinoza's wise man is content when and to the extent that he sees that things could not be other than they are. Leibniz says rather that the sage is content because he "sees that things could not be better than they are" (*Textes* II.572).

There is a curious ambivalence about Leibniz's understanding of his optimism.[10] He argues at times as if in particular classes of happenings we can see the usefulness of an apparent evil, such as sickness (it heightens our appreciation of health) (*Theodicy*, p. 130). It sounds almost as if he were offering empirical evidence that all is for the best (cf., e.g., pp. 414–15). Yet the argument that this is the best possible world is in fact wholly a priori (p. 128). The result is that however appalling something seems to us – for instance, the condemnation of innumerable sinners to eternal torment – we must suppose that no world less awful was conceivable (pp. 126, 134). Since "*will* consists in the inclination to

8   Cf. also *Metaphysics* 4.
9   Cf. *Monadology* 83: "spirits are also images of divinity itself . . . each spirit being like a little divinity within its own sphere."
10   My reading of Leibniz on optimism and its consequences is indebted to the work of, and conversations with, Mark Larrimore.

do something in proportion to the good it contains," God must possess an absolute "antecedent will" to bring about nothing but good. But because he must create a whole world, the goodness of any one possible constituent is only a prima facie reason for creating it. God's "consequent will," by contrast, "results from the conflict of all the antecedent wills" in the way in which compound mechanical movement results from all the forces acting on a particular body (pp. 136–7). We therefore cannot conclude that any particular thing or event is good simply because it is part of the best possible world.[11] All we can conclude is that everything that happens necessarily happens because it is a necessary part of what on the whole is for the best.

To Malebranche's claim that God acts only by general wills, permitting evil but not willing it, Leibniz replies that God is never indifferent to particulars in the way this implies. In willing anything, one wills "in a sense" whatever is necessarily connected with it. But one does not will necessary effects on their own account (p. 254). God wills the specifics of this world "not only on account of what they do, but on account of what they are." They may not cause good but they are necessary parts of the whole that contains them (p. 257). Leibniz puts the core of his position in a particularly pregnant sentence: "As God can do nothing without reasons . . . it follows that he has no will about individual events but what results from some general truth or will" (p. 256).

ii. *Freedom and determination by reasons*

In such a world, is there reason for us to do any one thing rather than another? Does not my doing anything whatever, or nothing, prove that precisely that behavior was the best possible course? Leibniz, intending "in all things to consider edification" (*Theodicy*, p. 71) in his demonstration that this is the best possible world, must find an answer if there is to be any point to his attempt to move people to improve themselves and the world.[12]

In one respect the solution Leibniz offers is as blunt as St. Augustine's answer to the question of how free will can be compatible with God's foreknowledge. God foreknows what we will freely do, says Augustine; and Leibniz, adopting precisely this view, adds that the best

---

11   Hence F. H. Bradley's aphorism, "This is the best of all possible worlds, and everything in it is a necessary evil."

12   Leibniz says that the sophism of "lazy reason" is a puzzle arising in antiquity (see the discussion in Cicero, *De Fato*, 28–30, attributing a reply to Chrysippus). But in his own time it had been previously addressed at some length both by Gassendi, in his defense of Epicureanism, and by Pierre Nicole, defending a complex view of the workings of divine grace. I discuss both of these in the next chapter.

world can come about only through the causes that are needed to bring it about, such as our own actions now. If some best possible effect is certain to occur, then its necessary cause – in some cases a free action – is equally certain to occur, and God foresaw all of that in choosing to create the world containing them (*Theodicy*, pp. 57, 152–3, 161; *LCCorr*, p. 56).[13] The solution seems, however, to raise more problems for morality than it resolves. It seems to turn us into parts within a vast mechanism, parts whose behavior is wholly dictated by an antecedent choice about which we have nothing to say. Leibniz hopes to soften this by arguing that his theory that matter is confused perceptions in monadic souls whose perceptions are coordinated by God makes the mechanism a spiritual one. Yet he allows that this just means that "the human soul is a kind of *spiritual automaton*" (*Theodicy*, p. 151). That still leaves us with questions about freedom and the understanding of ourselves as agents rather than as mere loci of more or less confused perceptions. Not surprisingly, Leibniz's answers encompass God as well as us.

God cannot fail to choose the best. To hold otherwise would be to accept the voluntarist notion that God's will is indifferent, and would open the door to impiety and tyranny. Yet God is free. He is knowingly and gladly led to the good by his own inclination, neither hampered by external forces nor disturbed by inner passions (*Theodicy*, p. 386). When we realize, further, that there are different kinds of necessity we can understand the compatibility between necessity and freedom in God's choice, and also in our choices when we pursue, as we necessarily do, what seems best to us.

One kind of necessity is displayed by what Leibniz calls "eternal truths," those whose opposite involves a contradiction. The laws of geometry, for instance, hold with an absolute necessity arising from the essences of things. The other kind of necessity comes from God's choice of the best, and hence only from relations of things with one another in a complete world. Leibniz calls it "moral necessity," the adjective, in accordance with contemporary usage, indicating what comes from a will. Although the opposite of what is morally necessary is conceivable, what is morally necessary is not simply arbitrary. The laws of physics, for instance, are neither arbitrary nor absolutely necessary. God might have chosen a physical world not instantiating precisely the laws we find in ours. He chose as he did for a reason. This physical world is most harmonious with the Kingdom of Grace, which is the moral world that God also creates (*Theodicy*, pp. 61, 334, 387). What makes an act morally necessary is its being necessary to attain the good the agent aims at, whereas an arbitrary act would be one done for no reason at all. In

---

13   The similarity of Leibniz's view to that of Lipsius is quite striking: see Chapter 9.i.

acting from moral necessity, Leibniz remarks, "one is necessitated to the choice by a hypothetical necessity, when one actually makes the choice" (*Theodicy*, p. 203; *LCCorr*, pp. 56–7). We understand, up to a point, what it would be like not to do what is morally necessary. We also see why it must be done.[14]

Freedom of action exists within the domain of the morally necessary. God always acts freely; we may or may not. What makes the difference is the extent and clarity of our awareness of the good that draws us to act. There is never, Leibniz says, "any choice to which one is not prompted by the previous representation of good or evil, by inclinations or by reasons" (*Theodicy*, p. 406). A will not moved by consideration of good would be a will choosing at random, or arbitrarily and inexplicably (p. 416). Absolute indifference of will exists no more in human than in divine action, although unlike God we may be moved by perceptions below the level of conscious awareness as well as by clear and distinct knowledge of a good (pp. 406–7; 303). Leibniz's claim that we are always moved by our knowledge or belief about good is thus as a priori as his claim that this is the best of all possible worlds.[15] Perceived goodness moves, and moves in proportion to the amount of goodness involved; if we do not have a desire strong enough to make us act to obtain some perceived good, it is because below the level of consciousness other perceptions of good are at work outweighing the conscious one (p. 418).[16]

Leibniz does not call on a separate faculty of will in order to account for freedom of choice. Freedom is a matter of degree. The clearer and more distinct the perceptions are through which we are moved toward good, the more we are spontaneous, active, and free. Obscure and

---

14   Adams 1994, ch. 1, is an excellent discussion of the complexities in Leibniz's views on contingency, which I ignore here. See also Mondadori 1989.

15   And as his claim that those who try hard to do well will receive the grace needed for salvation, *Theodicy*, pp. 175–6.

It should be noted that for Leibniz it does not follow from the meaning of the terms alone that we are necessarily moved by what we think good reasons to act. We are necessarily so moved due to the principle of sufficient reason, so the truth is, in modern terms, synthetic and not analytic.

16   See *Theodicy*, p. 159: "For in so far as the soul has perfection and distinct thoughts, God has accommodated the body to the soul, and has arranged beforehand that the body is impelled to execute its orders. And in so far as the soul is imperfect and as its perceptions are confused, God has accommodated the soul to the body, in such sort that the soul is swayed by the passions arising out of corporeal representations." There is an internal relation between motivation and the representation of goodness in either case, but on the one side it is caused by clear knowledge and on the other by confused feeling.

confused perceptions constitute our passions (*New Essays*, p. 210).[17] As I noted earlier, will is simply the standing tendency toward increased perfection (cf. *New Essays*, p. 183). We can think of it as a desire that involves comparison. Because perfections are strictly commensurable, willing is simply pursuing more of it rather than less. The very notion of willing, as the voluntarist tries to project it, is for Leibniz senseless. To conceptualize the will as "alone active and supreme," deciding between the reasons offered by the understanding and those offered by the senses, one would have to admit "another understanding in [the will] itself, to understand what it is offered."[18] Much better to say that the whole soul understands reasons, feels inclinations, "and decides according to the predominance of the representations modifying its active force" (*Theodicy*, p. 421).

Goods and evils, whose representations always move us, fall into three classes: metaphysical, physical, and moral. Metaphysical good is perfection or positive reality, something of which all beings partake to some degree or other and God to the greatest degree (*Monadology* 40). Perfection is not, as Spinoza thought, simply a confused idea caused us by our finitude. It is an objective property of complex wholes (and we must remember that for Leibniz there are parts within parts to infinity even in the simplest-seeming entities). The greater the variety of the parts thus combined, the more harmoniously and simply they are combined, the greater is the reality or perfection of the whole.[19] God is the greatest reality and the most perfect being, because his intellect comprehends with perfect clarity all monads, all the perceptions within them, and all their connections; all created things are necessarily less perfect. To be less perfect is to lack some reality, and metaphysical evil is accordingly simply a privation (*Theodicy*, p. 219). Evil, as Augustine

17 Since Leibniz believes that every monad contains within itself the source of all its perceptions, every monad always acts spontaneously and, in that sense, freely. Here he tries to work out a sense in which some monads are freer because more spontaneous than others.

18 For somewhat similar objection to the concept of willing, see *Theodicy*, p. 151: "We will to act, strictly speaking, and we do not will to will; else we could still say that we will to have the will to will, and that would go on to infinity." So also *New Essays*, p. 182.

19 So *Monadology* 58, where Leibniz speaks of "the means of obtaining the greatest variety possible, but with the greatest possible order; that is to say, . . . as much perfection as possible." William Mann pointed out to me that Leibniz assumes that the two factors can be combined to produce a single product yielding comparability with other similar products in every case. There are other passages where Leibniz offers an apparently different account of perfection, linking it to "elevation of being" (*Papers*, p. 426).

held, is thus not something God created. It is only the inescapable by-product of his creation of the most perfect world.

Physical good or perfection is the kind of good appropriate to the sentient creation. It consists in pleasure, which is "the feeling of a perfection or an excellence, whether in ourselves or in something else" (*Papers*, p. 425). Pleasure is not a Lockean simple idea. In being aware of a perfection, as in being aware of anything, we are more or less clearly aware of everything in the universe, even God (*Papers*, p. 579). Pleasures are as complex as our perceptions. The more we encompass in a clear and distinct perception, the more we experience pleasure; and the more constant our perceptions, the more enduring it is. Although animals can feel pleasure, only self-conscious rational beings can enjoy happiness, which is a condition of permanent pleasure (*Theodicy*, pp. 280–1; *Papers*, p. 425). When Leibniz says that "happiness is to persons what perfection is to beings" (*Papers*, p. 327), he means that we increase the good appropriate to us – physical good – by increasing our awareness of what gives things their good, namely metaphysical perfection. Since we can contemplate the perfection of the universe at different times, we can possess a permanent happiness even if we are not feeling pleasure at a given moment.[20]

What then of the third kind of good and evil, the moral kind? "Moral evil," Leibniz says, "consists in the wrong choice," which he equates with sin (*Theodicy*, pp. 416, 411). And wrong choice, as we have already seen, is just the misguided response of the will to confused perception of degrees of perfection. Morality does not bring a new kind of good and evil into the world. "It is again well to consider," Leibniz proclaims, "that moral evil is an evil so great only because it is a source of physical evils," that is, pain and unhappiness (*Theodicy*, p. 138). Unlike the natural lawyers, Leibniz does not define sin in terms of disobedience to God's will. Even if we were to think of ourselves as disobeying God when we sin, we could really only be thinking that we are bringing about less perfection – and less pleasure – than we would if we had clearer perceptions.

For Leibniz, therefore, metaphysical good or perfection is basic: "the metaphysical good which includes everything makes it necessary sometimes to admit physical evil and moral evil" (*Theodicy*, p. 258). It is no use complaining that this shows that God does not value virtue above all else. Virtue is the noblest created thing, Leibniz says, but not the only good created thing. God is attracted by what is good in every possible thing, and if his final determination includes less virtue than is conceivable in isolation, it is because the sum of other values combined

---

20   For discussion of Leibniz on happiness, see Heinekamp 1989.

with less virtue in the world is greater than the sum combined with more (p. 198). At the same time we must remember that realized metaphysical good is what it is because of God's choice of the best possible world. Physical necessity – the laws governing the physical world God has chosen to create – "is founded on moral necessity," or God's choice of the best (p. 74); and the metaphysical perfections underlying both of these are therefore ordered by God's final end. Degrees of being are degrees of perfection and therefore of goodness. The Leibnizian counterrevolution overcomes the metaphysical foundations of modern science, and of modern voluntarist morality as well.

iii. *Love, justice, and perfection*

What, then, is the morality that Leibniz sees as being at home in this carefully designed universe? It is a morality centered on love, one in which law and obligation have a vanishingly small part to play. It is also one that is driven by our psychology: since we must act to try to increase perfection, morality can tell us only that we are to do so. Perhaps to our surprise, Leibniz sees self-love or interest at the center of the moral psychology that derives from the pursuit of perfection. Yet despite his early admiration for Hobbes's work, he is no Hobbesian. Like Cumberland, but much more clearly, he gives an account of love in general that enables him to show how knowledge can transform our self-love from a narrow and selfish concern with ourselves to an increasingly God-like concern for everyone. It is precisely because knowledge can bring about the change that our central task is to perfect ourselves by perfecting our knowledge (cf. *Papers*, p. 219). In the end everything that we are to do, according to Leibniz's morality, turns on self-perfection.

To love something, Leibniz holds, is to take pleasure in its perfection. Pleasure, as we have seen, is itself a feeling of perfection; love ties us to particular objects as its source. We can love ourselves and be pleased as we increase our own perfection. We can also love others and take pleasure in their perfection. The character of our love is not shown in its involving our own pleasure, but in its objects. "Self-love," says Leibniz, "makes all the vices and all the moral virtues, according as it is well or ill understood, and although it be true to say that men never act without interest, it is also true that there are honest and durable interests" as well as corrupt and flimsy ones (*Textes* II.575). Pleasure is durable only so far as we are able to perceive steadily a very great perfection. The conclusion to be drawn is obvious. Since God is the most perfect and happiest being, and "true pure love" is "the state which causes pleasure to be taken in the perfection and the felicity of the beloved," we will gratify self-interest most if we love God above all else (*Nature* 16).[21]

The reference in the remark just quoted to "true pure love" is significant. Leibniz uses his account of love in order, among other things, to battle a hotly contested contemporary theological claim that we are capable of a love of God so pure that we can love even our own damnation should that be God's will. Leibniz repeatedly offers his own theory to replace this one (e.g., *Papers*, pp. 420–1, 424). He would have seen in it another form of that protean enemy, voluntarism. The "pure love" he opposes cuts love off from any necessary object, leaving only arbitrary choice to direct it. To counter it, Leibniz tries to knit back together the ideas of pleasure and perfection, separated tentatively by Descartes and definitively by Malebranche. In loving we are always interested, always seeking pleasure for ourselves. But we cannot coherently think of increasing our own pleasure without increasing the amount of perfection we are aware of, which in turn entails knowing and loving God (*New Essays*, p. 500). And insofar as we love God we will love other humans as well. God, after all, loves beings insofar as they contain perfection. Humans contain more perfection than any other kinds of beings, although we each necessarily contain different amounts of it. Insofar as we know God, we think as God thinks. Hence we love as God loves; and so we love other people above all other things, and, loving them, seek to bring about their perfection and their happiness. In short, if we love God above all else we will love our neighbor as ourselves.[22] What is more, we will find our own happiness only by being in this condition of love. "It is consequently quite true," Leibniz summarizes, "that one cannot love God without loving one's brother, that one cannot possess wisdom without possessing charity, and even that one advances one's own good in procuring that of others" (*Textes* II.581). Here is the moral payoff of the preestablished harmony. Malebranche's conceptual distinction between virtue and happiness is washed out by Leibnizian harmony. There can be no ultimate conflict between working for one's own happiness and pursuing that of others.

On this basis Leibniz builds an elaborate theory of justice, which begins with a striking and highly original definition.[23] In an early essay Leibniz defended an Aristotelian account of justice against Grotius's

---

21   The perceptions in monads are always changing, in a predetermined way. Consequently, felt pleasures and pains are due to changes in perceptions of perfection, and the best we can hope for in this life is steady increase in perception of perfection, not any stasis in contemplating God. See, e.g., *Nature* 18.

22   See *Philosophische Schriften*, ed. Gerhardt, VII.74–7, for a good summary. It is interesting that here and elsewhere Leibniz puts this point in Thomistic terms of friendship with God.

23   See Riley 1996 for the fullest account of Leibniz on justice.

criticism, defining justice as the mean in affections of goodwill or hatred toward others (*Papers*, p. 75). His mature account retains the early insistence on justice as an affection but gives a new account of what that affection is. Justice, so his new definition goes, is the charity of the wise. The perfectly wise man will know the perfections of each thing and the merits of each person. His love will lead him to give most to those most deserving. Love is not opposed to justice, as the natural lawyers seemed to think; it is its completion.

Leibniz develops his account of justice by tying it to three principles of Roman law. He takes them from Ulpian's *Rules*, known only as cited in Justinian's *Digest* I.I.10: "Justice is a constant, unfailing disposition to give every one his legal due. §1. The principles of law are these: Live uprightly, injure no man, give every man his due."[24] These principles were commonplaces, used by the natural lawyers and everyone else as pegs for organizing their views on the topic. Leibniz differs on several points from the natural lawyers.

The first degree of justice corresponds to the Roman maxim "harm no one." It involves strict right, whose transgression gives ground for legal action within society, or war outside it. Leibniz associates the second degree of justice with the maxim "give each his own." It covers equity or charity in the narrower sense – the giving of goods to others in circumstances such that not giving the goods provides no ground for legal action. The degrees correspond, so Leibniz explicitly says, to Grotius's perfect and imperfect rights (*Writings*, ed. Riley, p. 172). Only the goods of this life fall within their domain. The first degree looks to preserving peace, the second degree to increasing the happiness we each take in the well-being of others. The third degree of justice Leibniz calls piety, and he ties it to the Roman maxim, "live uprightly (that is piously)" – an interpretive stretch, no doubt, but one that enables him to say that most people need a firm belief in providence and immortality in order to give charity its full scope, even in opposition to the apparent sacrifices it calls for in our present lives. From this standpoint universal justice comes to include all the virtues and duties, even those requiring us not to harm ourselves. We owe ourselves as well as everything else to God, and it is "to the interest of the universe" that we preserve our ability to act as we ought (*Writings*, pp. 172–3).

The natural lawyers saw a difference of principle between perfect duties and imperfect duties, not simply a difference of degree. For Leibniz the difference is one of degree only. Morally speaking there is a continuum between the strictest duties of the first level and the pious

24 Justinian, ed. Monro, p. 5. The three precepts are restated in the opening chapter of Justinian's *Institutes*, I.I.3: "The commandments of the law are these: live honourably; harm nobody; give everyone his due." Birks and McCleod, p. 37.

duties of the final level. All duties are duties to prevent harm and do good, and only the amount matters. In further opposition to the natural lawyers, Leibniz also sees natural law as deriving its authority solely from its purely instrumental function. "Natural law is that which preserves or furthers natural societies," he says (*Papers*, p. 428), making no mention of a lawgiver, or of sanctions, or of promulgation.[25]

Leibniz's consequentialism is thus almost complete. In his nearest approach to giving us a method for deciding what we ought to do, Leibniz says that although we can never know the details of God's will, we are to "act in accordance with [his] presumptive will . . . trying with all our might to contribute to the general welfare," and particularly to the perfection of those we can most directly affect (*Metaphysics* 4). Those we can affect are humans, and their welfare is of course their happiness.

The one apparent exception to Leibniz's consequentialism – and I am not certain that it is one – comes in his treatment of punishment. He allows a kind of punitive or avenging justice that serves no further end, "neither improvement nor example, nor even redress of the evil. This justice," he continues, "has its foundation only in the fitness of things, which demands a certain satisfaction for the expiation of an evil action" (*Theodicy*, p. 161). I pointed out that Cudworth's worry about making God wholly benevolent as a response to voluntarism concerned the justification of the eternal punishment of the damned. The same concern animates Leibniz, who could not have known Cudworth's view of the matter. It is the "principle of the fitness of things" that explains why "the pains of the damned continue, even when they no longer serve to turn them away from evil" – and why the pleasures of the saved continue, although no longer needed to sustain their virtue (p. 162).[26]

Even if Leibniz opts on the whole for unmitigated consequentialism, his is not the consequentialism of Cumberland or of utilitarianism. The good to be brought about is the good the wise person would try to bring about. Our first task is to become as wise as we can. Without that we can neither know what we ought to do, nor take sufficient pleasure in doing it to be moved to act as we ought. Like the Stoic sage, Leibniz's wise person takes account of the whole universe in calculating. Only those pleasures compatible with everything's being for the best on the whole get beyond the stage of providing merely prima facie reasons for action.

25 I discuss Leibniz's views on obligation in sections iv and v.

26 See also *Theodicy*, p. 200. At *Theodicy*, p. 418 Leibniz seems to equate morally necessary truths with truths of fitness, contrasting both with absolutely necessary truths based on the principle of contradiction. If the fitness of things is due to goods brought about, however, Leibniz has not explained how purely punitive justice can be warranted. Elsewhere he seems to take punishment to be always useful for the general good: see "Felicity" 6, in *Textes* II.579.

Not even God could make his decision about which world to realize by summing up the goods possessed intrinsically by the parts of each of his options. In Leibnizian worlds anything is what it is only through its relations with everything else. The amount of perfection or goodness of any one part, therefore, is a function of the whole of which it is a necessary part. Cumberland's God can think in terms of contingent sums to be increased by adding independent goods. But Leibniz's God must make a holistic choice (*Theodicy*, p. 128). Leibniz is a communitarian before he is a consequentialist; and he is a perfectionist because he is both.

iv. *Against Pufendorf: Law and will*

Voluntarism stimulated much of the development of new ideas in modern moral philosophy. Cumberland's new quantitative form of consequentialism was a response to it, as was Leibniz's similar principle of increasing perfection. I argue in later chapters that intuitionism and aspects of Kantian formalism also emerged from opposition to voluntarism. Cudworth, Cumberland, Shaftesbury, Clarke, Wolff, Price, and many others explained their reasons for rejecting the doctrine but they did not engage in direct debate with their opponents. There were no exchanges over morality between voluntarists and antivoluntarists comparable to the confrontations concerning metaphysics and epistemology in the *Objections and Replies* to Descartes's *Meditations* and in the Leibniz-Clarke correspondence. Given the importance of the subject for moral philosophy, the lack is regrettable. All the more important, therefore, is the nearest thing we have to such an encounter: Barbeyrac's reply to Leibniz's criticisms of Pufendorf, *Jugement d'un anonyme.*

No more suitable target for antivoluntarist criticism than Pufendorf could be imagined. If Hobbes was a more powerful thinker, he did not win the admirers and followers that Pufendorf did, and he did not display as vividly the moral gulf that voluntarism sets between God and us. Leibniz did not intend to engage in a dialogue about him. In 1706 he simply wrote out his own views on him at the request of a friend. His remarks were highly critical, and their publication eventually brought Jean Barbeyrac into the field, even if only after Leibniz's death. For the fourth edition (1718) of his French translation of Pufendorf's *De Officio*, he translated Leibniz's Latin *Monita* or warning[27] into French, breaking it up into some twenty sections and replying point by point. Leibniz had a more fully developed standpoint from which to

---

27 Leibniz says Pufendorf's readers need a warning lest they heedlessly accept his dangerous principles (*Writings*, p. 66).

attack natural law theory than its other critics then had. Barbeyrac knew the history of modern theory of natural law and the options available within it better than anyone else then living.[28]

Underlying the particular disagreements, and surfacing quite explicitly, is the issue of how God is to be kept involved in morality. The antagonists agree that morality can be understood only in a way that makes God's involvement with it indispensable. They disagree profoundly on just how he is involved; and their disagreement is directly tied to deep differences in their views of the proper moral relations between God and human beings.

The voluntarists, as we have seen, hold that an attitude of humble submission and obedience to God's commands, simply as his commands, is the only appropriate stance for us. God is infinitely removed from us in perfection and is ultimately incomprehensible. We are simply subjects, to be kept in order by commands backed by sanctions. The antivoluntarists reject this entire picture. God is a loving father, just as well as merciful. He and we think of morality in the same terms. He assures us that we live in a world that is hospitable to our endeavors, and he guarantees justice by rewards and punishments after death if not in this life.

The Leibniz-Barbeyrac exchange gives us a fuller discussion of the case against voluntarism than we have yet seen. It also gives us a clear view of what its defenders saw as one of its main strengths. Leibniz makes a number of objections to Pufendorf's views, some, as Barbeyrac points out, due to careless reading and others peripheral.[29] I shall con-

---

28   For details of the publication history of Leibniz's attack, see Bobbio 1947, which also notes various replies made to Barbeyrac. I am grateful to Dr. Fiammetta Palladini for bringing this article to my attention and for sending me her own valuable article of 1990 on the subject. She also sent me some material in which the Leibniz-Barbeyrac debate continued. In 1721 a young scholar named Balthasar Branchu published his observations on Roman law, attaching to them at the end an essay vindicating Leibniz against Barbeyrac's attacks. Barbeyrac, in the 1734 preface to a new edition of his translation, reports that Branchu sent him the book, that he was pleased with the hope of learning from his critic, but that he found nothing to correct in his views, as Branchu understood neither him nor Pufendorf – "a harsh judgment," as Meylan 1937 remarks at p. 131 n. 2.

29   The most important is Leibniz's charge that for Pufendorf natural law concerns only "outer" behavior and not the inner life at all. As Barbeyrac points out, what Pufendorf actually says is that natural law is "for the most part" concerned only with what others can observe of our actions. This is because it is largely concerned with enforceable rights, which do not reach as far as the inner life. But, Barbeyrac insists, Pufendorf has numerous passages stressing the importance of one's motives and urging one to improve one's character. Leibniz, as I have noted, sees morality in the first instance as a matter of having the appropriate motivating

centrate on the two conceptual problems at the core of the "debate."[30] One concerns the relation between God's will and morality. The other concerns differences over moral justification and its relations to moral motivation.[31]

Pufendorf's claim that God creates moral entities by a fiat of will, Leibniz plainly thinks, is the major error in his entire treatment of natural law. Against it he reiterates an argument he uses elsewhere – that the voluntarist can make no sense of the fact that God is praised because he is just. Leibniz is not making the point that linguistic philosophers of our century, believing they follow G. E. Moore, would have in mind. He is not simply claiming that voluntarism mistakenly makes the sentence "God is just" vacuous. His point is rather that we can think that God is just even though he has no superior over him. We think, that is, that someone can be just or law-abiding without the existence of a superior imposing law on him and sanctioning him. But the voluntarist thinks justice requires such a superior. Voluntarism is therefore mistaken about the concept of justice. The consequences are morally horrendous, and the only alternative is Leibniz's own view (L, pp. 465–7; cf. *Writings*, pp. 71–2).

Leibniz adds a new criticism. The voluntarist allows that superiors whose commands impose obligation must have not only power to enforce their orders but "just reasons to justify their power." If a binding law can come only from an authoritative superior, but the authority of a superior can be warranted only by reasons drawn from a binding law, "a circle is created, than which none was ever more manifest." And if there are reasons for the order the superior gives, Leibniz fails to see why sanctions are needed to make the act morally necessary. Sanctions might cause fear, but they will neither make the act more justified nor improve the character of those threatened (L, pp. 484–8; cf. *Writings*, pp. 73–5).

Barbeyrac takes up the first criticism in two sections. In both he

---

feelings and as requiring self-perfection first of all. Whatever the underlying issue here Barbeyrac does not move it much beyond the level of assertion and counter-assertion.

30   Barbeyrac pretends that he does not know who wrote the attack. After the first long paragraph of his reply he consistently refers to Leibniz as "the anonymous writer" and to Pufendorf as "the author" or "our author." According to Meylan 1937, p. 109, Barbeyrac had met Leibniz in Berlin and thought him full of "jealousy of others who distinguished themselves in the Republic of Letters."

31   In the following references to the *Jugement d'un anonyme*, I identify Leibniz's criticisms as L and Barbeyrac's replies as B. For the Leibniz citations, I also give page references to *Political Writings*, ed. Riley. Barbeyrac occasionally differs from Riley in his translation of Leibniz's Latin.

comes close to accepting Leibniz's position, although at first he seems to be denying or qualifying the premise that God is praised because he is just. God's justice and man's are similar, Barbeyrac says, but there is a great difference between them. We might expect him to go on by denying the Leibnizian assumption that God and man are just in a univocal sense, and possibly by making the point that Pufendorf himself suggests, that God is praised not because he is just but because he is benevolent. Strikingly, Barbeyrac does not do so. "God is just by his nature. He can neither act nor wish to act except justly. It is a happy impotence in him, a glorious necessity, coming uniquely from his infinite perfection."[32] Barbeyrac adds that men are plainly different, needing an obligation imposed "by some external principle" to become just (B, p. 459). But he seems to concede that God can be thought just, and that he is governed by necessity, even though, of course, he has no superior.

Concession seems even plainer in the second comment on the matter. Barbeyrac insists that Pufendorf always speaks of God as "sovereignly just," and as one who "inviolably follows the rules of justice conformable to his infinite perfections." He does not think that all law "emanates from the will, still less from the arbitrary will of a superior." True enough, God is independent; no one, for instance, can have rights against him. Pufendorf, however, is concerned with law, not for God but for "dependent beings." Law as produced by will is suitable only for such beings – and even then it is not *arbitrary* will that creates our law. "God could not," Barbeyrac says, "without affronting his perfections and being false to himself, prescribe other rules to men than those of justice which are founded on their nature" (B, p. 468).

Barbeyrac's reply to the charge of vicious circularity relies on his claim that God is necessarily just. God has a right to command "based on reasons which carry their justice with them." If God commands for good reasons, we have a duty even if sanctions are left out of the picture, Barbeyrac insists, so Leibniz's criticism gets no hold on Pufendorf. But Barbeyrac interestingly admits that his author was not clear enough about the important distinction between what gives God the right to command and what "puts him in a position to *command effectively*." Pufendorf's failure to emphasize the point is, however, he suggests, only a "little fault" (B, pp. 489–91).

Coupled with Barbeyrac's own failure to explain the nature of the law God obeys, the necessity under which he obeys it, or how his perfections give rise to it, these concessions sound like an abandonment

---

32 Barbeyrac did not publish his translation of Cumberland into French until 1733 but we must surely suppose that he had read him by the time he wrote his reply to Leibniz. Here he sounds quite Cumberlandian.

of voluntarism. They give up the claim that justice by its very nature requires compliance with the will of a superior, and with it the claim that moral necessity arises only from sanctions backing a superior's command. Moral necessity understood in those terms now relates only to created beings. The concerns that drive Barbeyrac to his concessions are fairly clear. Leibniz tries to associate Pufendorf with Descartes's extreme voluntarism (L, p. 466; *Writings*, p. 72); Barbeyrac does not respond to this at all. He emphasizes instead that for Pufendorf the maxims of natural law have their foundation in the nature of things. Once God has made things with those natures, he "cannot without betraying himself prescribe anything contrary to them" (B, p. 461; cf. p. 468). Barbeyrac simply does not speak, as older voluntarists did, of God's absolute power, the power that enables him to choose to create beings with whatever natures happen to please him. He plainly wants to escape all association of God with arbitrariness (B, p. 477). The moral revolt against voluntarism, as forcing us to a morally untenable view of the relations between God and human beings, here seems to win a decisive victory.

v. *Against Pufendorf: Justification and motive*

Of course, we have not heard the whole story. Barbeyrac has his own objections to Leibniz's position. They center on the relation between justification and motivation in moral action. Although they involve a certain amount of embarrassment for Barbeyrac himself they ultimately add up to a challenge to Leibniz's understanding of morality. They thus bring out another way in which moral convictions, rather than purely epistemological or metaphysical beliefs, shaped the debates about moral philosophy.

One way in which Barbeyrac puts his point is by claiming that Leibniz cannot show God to be indispensable to morality. If Pufendorf avoids the extreme of thinking that "justice depends on a purely arbitrary volition of God," Leibniz does not avoid the other vicious extreme of thinking justice "completely independent of the will of God." He falls into the trap of making virtue independent of religion and so he keeps company with those, like Pierre Bayle, who believe that even atheists can admit obligations (B, p. 480). Barbeyrac here fails to see, or to admit, that Leibniz's God, as the guarantor of the harmony of the universe, is as central to morality as the voluntarist God, though not, of course, in the same way. Ultimately this issue leads Barbeyrac to the claim that Leibniz's understanding of moral justification and moral motivation is defective, and that this is due to moral inadequacies in his position.

Barbeyrac's counterattacks center on the Leibnizian theory of obligation. The theory itself is basically quite simple. Obligation, Leibniz says, just is moral necessity (*Theodicy*, pp. 387, 386). Moral necessity is "the necessity which constrains the wise to do good" (*Theodicy*, pp. 395, 390), the necessity attaching to the acts required as means to attain ends, either God's ends or a wise man's ends. Like Leibniz's account of law, the definition of obligation is meant to deny that it presupposes the existence of a superior who imposes laws or sanctions in order to make agents behave in certain ways. Locke, says Leibniz, is quite wrong on the subject. He thinks "that moral good or evil is an instituted good or evil – something imposed on us" by God to give us an added inducement to comply with his will. But no contingent sanction is needed to constitute obligation. The perceived good or evil that God has connected with various actions, in creating the best possible world, already makes it necessary for us, or obligates us, to do what is good or avoid what is evil. Leibniz thus partially agrees with Cumberland. He agrees that by making nature reward and punish us as it does, God has indicated his will and thereby obligated us to act as he commands.[33] But he does not accept Cumberland's claim that God's telling us his will is required to turn our knowledge into an obligation. For Leibniz we are obligated by the knowledge.

We are to take quite literally Leibniz's implication that for a good man it is impossible not to do what is morally necessary. "Right," Leibniz says in a remarkable passage, "is a kind of moral possibility, and obligation a moral necessity. By moral I mean that which is equivalent to 'natural' for a good man: for . . . we ought to believe that we are incapable of doing things which are contrary to good morals" (*Writings*, pp. 170–1). A good man possesses wisdom and therefore sees the best; seeing it clearly, he cannot fail to be moved by it. He is necessarily moved by it or, in other words, he is obliged or obligated to do it. In a fragment Leibniz works out rudiments of a deontic logic: an act owed is necessary, a permitted act is possible, an illicit act impossible (*Textes* I.605).[34] The agent's view of the normative status of actions as the agent sees them not only shows the agent's evaluation of them; it also provides the explanation of what the agent does.[35] To be justified in acting is to have a good reason for acting, and a good reason for acting explains why one acts. A justification is simply an explanation relying on

---

33 Leibniz, *New Essays*, pp. 250–1, commenting on Locke, *ECHU* II.xxviii.4–6, where Locke attacks Cumberland.

34 See also Sève 1989, pp. 108–22, and references there.

35 Leibniz explains Ovid's famous passage about seeing the better and doing the worse by saying that in such cases, the morally good – what the good man would aim at – is overwhelmed by the "agreeably good," that is, by what the passions at the moment make us think good. There are not two wills within us, but there are mixed perceptions (*Theodicy*, p. 220).

true beliefs about perfection. Justification and motivation are therefore inseparable.

Given this account of obligation, it is easy to see how Barbeyrac can charge that it leaves God out of morality. Leibniz, he says, thinks that obligation arises directly from "the nature of things" and our awareness thereof. Atheists might notice the relations that obligate. And if those relations are, as Leibniz says, "no less founded in the immutable nature of things . . . than are the principles of arithmetic and of geometry" (L, p. 466; cf. *Writings*, p. 71), then they would hold even if God did not exist.[36] Pufendorf objected to a claim like this that Grotius made, and Barbeyrac does make a similar complaint about Leibniz's view. But his deeper criticism is directed against the assumption that, more than any other, makes Leibniz's moral outlook possible: the assumption that all reasons for action, and hence all motives, arise from considerations of just one kind. For Barbeyrac this is false. He holds that moral law brings into our deliberations reasons for action that are different in kind from, and incommensurable with, the kind of reason that is tied to our desires. He believes that Leibniz wholly ignores this point.

Leibniz makes it unduly easy for Barbeyrac to make this objection stick. Because Pufendorf confines the sphere of natural law wholly to this life, Leibniz says, he cannot explain the motivation to act justly. It is sheer folly for someone to "risk riches, honors and his very existence on behalf of his dear ones, of his country or of justice, when by the ruin of others, he could think only of himself, and live amidst honors and riches" – unless there is an afterlife in which the just are rewarded (L, pp. 441–3; cf. *Writings*, pp. 67–8).

Pufendorf never so confined natural law, Barbeyrac replies, and he goes on to charge Leibniz with having "neither exact nor well-connected ideas of the nature and the inherent strength [*la force propre*] of Duty." Unlike Pufendorf Leibniz does not grasp "the impression that simply seeing the law should make on the heart of any reasonable person." Pufendorf understands that genuine sacrifice may be required by morality, and holds that we can be moved by the thought of duty, with no concern for rewards or punishments after death. Since Leibniz does not see this, he cannot claim to be really in agreement with those ancient pagans "who distinguished so well between the honest and the useful." Their morality, Barbeyrac adds, is surely purer and nobler than Leibniz's (B, pp. 444–5). He returns to this point later. It is a mistake to

---

36 It was, of course, careless of Leibniz to compare the eternal truths of morality with those of arithmetic and geometry. The former depend on God's choice of the best, the latter presumably hold for all possible worlds. But since Barbeyrac is pretending he does not know who wrote the "Judgement" he cannot take the distinction into account.

reduce talk of duty and obligation to talk of utility. We are permitted to ignore or even harm our own interests, so long as no others are affected, but we are not similarly permitted to ignore our duty (B, p. 472).[37] Barbeyrac is charging that because Leibniz's theory of obligation cannot accommodate a conceptual point embedded in our practice of praise and blame, it gets our morality wrong. On this matter voluntarism is morally superior to Leibniz's rationalism.

Leibniz has overstated, or misstated, his own view. Despite his remark about the folly of self-sacrifice, he does not think that we are all necessarily selfish. As he says in the *Theodicy*, "I require a man to be virtuous, grateful, just, not only from the motive of interest, of hope or of fear." But his explanation of this requirement still seems to leave room for Barbeyrac's objection. A man should be virtuous, says Leibniz, from the motive "of the pleasure that he should find in good actions" (*Theodicy*, pp. 422, 417). To say this is to say that the motive in selfish actions and that in just or dutiful actions are in one important respect the same. In both cases we pursue what we take to be the greatest perfection available to us, in the expectation that success will be pleasant for us. The selfish person is shortsighted, the charitable person is wise. Otherwise they do not differ.

For Barbeyrac, moral action is different. In acting from awareness of law we need not think that the amount of good or perfection for ourselves or for others will be increased. Moral requirements – God's commands – do not require that we bring about the best results. Barbeyrac does not claim that this is the best possible world; and he does not think morality requires the presupposition that it is. When we act because we are aware that there is a law requiring us to do so, we must be acting not from a desire to increase perfection, but from a special motive. Morality requires obedience to its laws no matter what the consequences. The radical difference between the justification of moral action and justifications resting on pursuit of good or perfection is tied to the radical difference in our motivation. I pointed out (Chapter 7.v) that Pufendorf gives only the most tentative sketch of a position like this. Barbeyrac is developing his hints.

The difference between Leibniz and Barbeyrac can be put this way. Leibniz thinks that there can be only one kind of motivation – the kind that arises from cognition of perfection. Since he thinks all perfections are commensurable, he has to hold that all practical justification must be of the same kind. His theory of motivation, which is part of his

---

37   There is a strong similarity between this argument and Grotius's claim (Chapter 4.vii) that Aristotle is wrong about justice because it is not *unjust* to take less than is due to one (provided one may consider oneself alone), however imprudent it may be.

general epistemology and his metaphysics, drives his grasp of morality. Barbeyrac holds that we distinguish two different kinds of justification. One kind shows that some act is a means to our ends. Another kind shows that some act complies with one of God's laws. Since it is clear that these justifications are incommensurable, it follows that there must be different kinds of motivation that enable us to respond to them. Barbeyrac's understanding of morality drives his theory of motivation.

Like Pufendorf, Barbeyrac offers no positive account of the inherent strength of duty, or of how awareness of "the beauty of virtue" (B, p. 447) can motivate us. But he is quite insistent that the motivation cannot come solely from reason's awareness of the nature of things. Reason is, in the end, only ourselves reasoning; and "no one can impose on himself an indispensable necessity of acting in such and such a manner." What I impose I can remove. Necessity holds only if I cannot at my own pleasure escape from it. If I can release myself there is "no true *obligation*" (B, pp. 472–4). Only the command of another imposes necessity.

Leibniz might well reply that I cannot release myself from the necessity of pursuing what my reason tells me (correctly or not) is the greatest available good or perfection. But Barbeyrac's point concerns a concept specific to morality. Pursuing the good as the good is not the same as performing an act because it is a duty, or because we are obligated to do it. The motive required for morally proper action is not one's own pleasure, not even if one has a natural inclination to take pleasure in the good of others (B, p. 478). It is duty. Barbeyrac is insisting that a moral point is involved here. Those who by a "happy bent" of their nature find it easy and pleasant to do their duty we consider as lucky rather than meritorious. We think that the man who has to struggle to overcome inner obstacles and who succeeds is "undeniably more just and praiseworthy than another whom it costs almost nothing to be a man of good will" (B, pp. 478–9). When Barbeyrac sums it up by saying that "the anonymous writer always confuses suitability with obligation and interest with duty" (B, pp. 482–3), he is claiming that Pufendorf's voluntarist view is more accurate about morality than Leibniz's.

By presenting the laws of morality as God's commands, to be obeyed above all and obeyed as commands rather than as advice about the good, Pufendorf in effect asserted that the claims of morality are incommensurable with those of prudence and take priority over them. Fully moral action must therefore be motivated by a unique kind of motive, although it is possible to do what morality requires for prudential reasons. Whatever his other concessions to Leibniz's criticisms, Barbeyrac rightly held on to these points as central to the morality of the voluntarist position he was defending. Leibnizianism denies both the incommensurability of prudential and moral reasons and the need for a unique kind of moral motive. Leibniz's position was at least coherent; it is not clear at the end of the day that Barbeyrac's was. He could see the main outlines of what had to be said if morality is the way Pufendorf and he thought it is, but not how to work out a theory that could put all the points together.[38]

38   I wish to thank the participants in the 1994 Berlin Conference on Pufendorf for helpful discussion of an early version of these sections on Leibniz and Barbeyrac. I am particularly grateful to Dr. Fiammetta Palladini for a long letter in which she pointed out a mistake of some importance in the original paper.

PART III

Toward a world on its own

13

Morality without salvation

Many of the writers with whom I have been concerned so far held that morality is tied in some way or other to salvation. If they did not think that morally decent behavior would by itself lead to or guarantee salvation, they took it to be at least a necessary condition of salvation, or a sign of it. Either you had to behave decently in order to become qualified for saving grace, or you could earn eternal life by moral goodness, or if you were of the elect you would show it by morally good behavior. Even the natural lawyers, reticent on principle about such matters in their jurisprudential treatises, had salvation somewhere in mind: witness Pufendorf's claim that dedication to performance of imperfect duties in the right spirit may win us merit – and not only in this life (Chapter 7.iv). Extreme antinomians, indeed, may have held that if you are saved, then anything you do counts as good, and morality is quite beside the point.[1] But such views drew philosophical consideration, if at all, only to be rejected. Philosophers with serious religious convictions tended to think that there had to be some connection between morality and salvation.

For atheists, of course, there was no issue here. The so-called libertines in France during the first half of the seventeenth century proposed a wide variety of unorthodox standpoints, with atheistic morality among them.[2] Innovative, bold, and often amusing as they were, they did not put their views into the form of philosophical essays or treatises. Hobbes and Locke, both claiming to be religious believers, held that only a minimal number of truths had to be accepted as the saving faith, and neither said much about the relation of morality to salvation. The first modern thinkers to explore systematically the possibility that morality might or should be understood as having little or no connection with salvation were not unbelievers. Accepting Christianity in one form

---

1   In Chapter 10, note 1 I have referred to the Knox 1950 study of this subject.
2   See the texts reprinted in Adam, and the studies by Spink 1960, Pintard 1943, and d'Angers 1954.

or another, they still found it necessary to ask, How should morality be understood if not as part of the path to salvation?

In this chapter I discuss three different ways in which religious believers approached the issue. Gassendi, Catholic priest and great champion of Epicureanism, Pascal and Nicole, subtle defenders of Jansenism, and Bayle, the unsurpassably learned Huguenot controversialist, had very different reasons for considering the question. Each thought his work would help to purify and protect religion as well as morality. Later readers often turned their ideas to different uses.

i. *Gassendi's rehabilitation of Epicureanism*

Epicurus was given a bad name by his opponents in antiquity because he allegedly held that crude beastly pleasure constitutes the highest good, and then lived just the sort of life one might expect to follow. His materialism and his denials of immortality and of divine providential care gave Christians strong additional reasons for finding his position unacceptable. Yet those seeking less austere guides to life than the teachings of the church or the Stoics had quietly been finding Epicureanism helpful at least since the Renaissance recovery of the texts.[3] The development of Democritean atomism in Epicurus's own work, and still more in that of his follower Lucretius, made Epicureanism in physics attractive to those fighting against Aristotelian final causes. The question was whether Epicureanism could be made safe for Christianity. Pierre Gassendi (1592–1655) devoted a lifetime to arguing that it could.[4]

Raised a Catholic and trained for the priesthood, Gassendi developed an early interest in the new science. He found himself deeply repelled by the orthodox theology he was assigned to teach in his first job and put off by the intellectual authoritarianism of his superiors. As alternatives, he turned to Pyrrhonic skepticism as well as to Epicureanism. His first book, published in 1624, was an attack on Aristotelianism. Of the ambitious plan to present seven sections, with the final one

3 The citizens whom Thomas More presents in his *Utopia* (1516) live by an Epicurean ethic, though More himself was a devout Catholic. And nearly a century earlier the Italian humanist Lorenzo Valla had published a defense of Epicureanism in his *De Voluptate* (*On Pleasure*).

4 Sarasohn 1996 is the fullest study of Gassendi's ethics. She discusses influences on Gassendi, his relations with Hobbes, and the use Locke made of his work, as well as his own moral and political thought. See also her earlier Sarasohn 1982 and 1985. Jones 1989, ch. 6, gives a helpful survey of Epicureanism in the Renaissance; ch. 7 is a good overview of Gassendi. In both chapters Jones focuses, as he also does in the fuller Jones 1981, on science and methodology rather than morality.

to be devoted to Epicurean morality, only the first part was realized.[5] Insofar as the book has any positive outcome, it is a skeptical one. The arguments for skepticism are mostly the familiar Pyrrhonian ones; but Gassendi is not attacking all knowledge equally.

The propositions of faith are specifically exempted, whether or not they are to be called knowledge. The target is essentially the Aristotelian view that real knowledge must be strictly deduced from self-evident, intuitively certain, principles (*Works*, ed. Brush, pp. 85–6). But Gassendi argues that the senses are also unreliable, attempts to rebut the claim that skepticism is self-defeating, and in general seems supportive of the view that nothing is known (pp. 102ff.).

Gassendi said he was initially attracted to philosophy by Cicero's promise that it can show us how to live "without vexation." The scholastic Aristotelianism he had to teach failed to keep that promise (pp. 18–19), but Gassendi early came to think that Epicureanism could. The seventh installment of his critique of Aristotle was to expound "Epicurus' doctrine of pleasure" (p. 25). By the end of his life, after many delays, he felt that his version of it was nearly ready for publication. His enormous *Syntagma Philosophicum* was in fact published posthumously, assembled by devoted admirers from a mass of papers.[6]

Following Epicurus and other ancients, Gassendi divides the work into three main parts: Logic or Canonic, Physic, and Ethics.[7] The Physics is an immense compilation of facts and theories about geography, the contents of the earth, plants, the variety of animals, and the psychology of animals and humans. It concludes with a defense of the immortality of the soul, refuting Epicurus's objections to it. The Logic has a more direct bearing on our concerns. In it Gassendi makes clear that he has abandoned skepticism, though he still plainly feels its pull, and he never claimed to attain absolute certainty for any of his results.[8] He has come up with the basis for a modest program for learning about the world as we experience it and for using reason to obtain at least

5   The church let Gassendi know it was upset by his first volume. Such displeasure could be serious: in 1624 the death penalty was threatened for a group of three young men who wished to hold a public disputation against Aristotelian theses. See Pintard 1943, p. 153; Tack 1974, p. 119.

6   It was preceded by a long study of the life and teachings of Epicurus, which began with a carefully established text of the writings as presented in Diogenes Laertius, and went on to a translation, a biography defending Epicurus's character, and a detailed commentary. The work is one of the landmarks of classical scholarship.

7   For Epicurus, see Diogenes Laertius X.29–30.

8   He has some interesting things to say in reply to Pyrrhonic concerns about the criterion and circular reasoning, e.g., *Works*, ed. Brush, pp. 345–8.

highly probable knowledge of aspects of the world that are not directly available to us through the senses. He rejects the deductive model of knowledge that he takes to be Aristotle's, and argues instead that we can trust our senses well enough to use what they convey to us as starting points for finding out what makes the world appear to us as it does.

Gassendi is basically proposing that we find out about what is in fact hidden by asking what best explains the apparent. For example: people perspire; therefore, although the skin looks solid, it must have tiny holes in it, because otherwise nothing could pass through. Microscopes may some day enable us actually to see them. Meanwhile we can take our experience as providing us with signs, like visible sweat, and use reason to think out what is hidden (*Works*, pp. 326–35).[9] Similarly we can infer that there are souls in living human bodies because there are aspects of what people do that could only come from souls. And we can infer that there is a God from "effects perceived by the senses, which could not be produced by anything but God and which therefore would not be observed unless God were present in the world, such as the great order of the universe " (p. 336).[10]

A methodology follows, which shows Gassendi's familiarity with the Galilean science that came from Padua. When discovering a truth, we must be shrewd in "finding a middle term" to connect a subject to a predicate. The middle term is most likely to be found among things we already know. It "may be called a sign since it leads us to the knowledge of something hidden." We can find it either by analysis of the subject, or by synthesis, beginning from the predicate. If we find our middle term by analysis or resolution, we test our theory by using composition or synthesis. And we use the senses and reason in judging our success (pp. 367–71).

In teaching practical arts or sciences, as distinct from teaching theoretical knowledge, we must begin with the goal, and we start by explaining the parts into which we have resolved it. Hence in teaching ethics, Gassendi says, "it is first made clear what constitutes the good life and the proper means of achieving and maintaining it are explained to be honorable morals, or virtue" (p. 374). Although Gassendi does not mention his methodology in presenting his ethics, his treatment of the subject does in fact follow his own precepts.

Morality is the practical science of leading a good or happy life, and as such it is the most important part of philosophy (*Discourses*, pp. 1–

---

9   The example, without reference to the microscope, goes back to antiquity.
10   See also Gassendi's "Objections" to Descartes, *Writings* II.215, arguing that the main rational evidence for God's existence is the order and organization of the world and its parts.

3).[11] What stands in the way of achieving our goal is, first of all, ignorance of what constitutes happiness. Not knowing this, we do not know
how to act virtuously. Gassendi then shows us how we can attain this
much-needed knowledge. We can observe that all people desire pleasure, and only pleasure. Some philosophers have held that we desire
riches, or health, or other things. But the desire for pleasure is in fact
what moves us to seek all these things, since we desire health, strength,
beauty, and so on because they are pleasant. The pleasant is not a good
different from the honest and the useful: it is simply "part of the common stock which renders the others good and desirable," since they are
desired only as they are pleasurable. Pleasure is so firmly a part of all
our aims and desires that "we have not a liberty of refusing it" (p. 88).
Even when we desire the honorable for its own sake, we are seeking
pleasure. What is "honest" or "honorable" (*honestum*) is what people
honor or what they praise; and we take pleasure in being praised (or at
least in being praised by the better sort of people) even if we get no
further benefit (pp. 94–7). Our desire for pleasure, then, and our inability to desire anything else, are signs pointing to an analysis of the
concept of the highest good as pleasure. "From hence therefore we may
infer that 'good' and 'pleasant' are but different names for the same
thing" (p. 91). The Epicurean conclusion is the best explanation of the
appearances about human behavior. As such it is a reply to skepticism
about morality.

On most basic points Gassendi's version of Epicurean morality follows the master's so closely that no account of it is needed here.[12]
Gassendi is well aware that he must work hard to make the theory
acceptable to Christian readers. It is worth noticing some of the issues
he takes up in doing so. Not surprisingly he goes to much trouble to
refute the charges brought against Epicurus of sensuality and debauchery. The charges are due, he thinks, to Stoic spite. Epicurus was personally a great deal more likable than the Stoic teachers, and his doctrine,
unlike theirs, is one that people can actually live by. Hence he attracted
many who might otherwise have tried to follow the Stoic teaching.
Unable to refute him, the Stoics, burning with envy, turned to slander.
Gassendi devotes a good many pages to pointing out, quite correctly,
that Epicurus recommended an austere and simple life, and was a
model of it himself (*Discourses*, pp. 45ff.). The Epicurean will not pursue

11   Despite his view of its importance, Gassendi treats morals last in the *Syntagma,* and more briefly than the other topics. Of the six volumes of Bernier's abridg-
ment of the *Syntagma,* which I mainly use here, the ethics occupies only the last.

12   I agree with Tack 1974 (p. 216 n. 389) that Rochot is mistaken in claiming that
Gassendi seriously modifies the Epicurean position in morals (Rochot 1944, pp. 98–
9).

pleasures when they are mixed with, or followed by, pain, as are most
sensual pleasures. He will seek tranquillity and the absence of pain, and
his material needs will be few. As a result, Gassendi aims to show, the
search for personal pleasure, properly understood, will in fact lead to
the kind of life that is commonly praised as honorable and upright.
Even the Stoics sought pleasure, though they tried to hide this fact
behind technical verbiage (pp. 82ff.). We are not, he insists at the start,
"concerned with that Happiness mentioned by the Sacred Penmen"
who tell us of the joys of divinely influenced total devotion to God, nor
with "such a life as we can't imagine a better." We ask only what
"natural felicity" is, the kind we can sensibly expect to enjoy in this life,
in human society (p. 6). Gassendi does not point us toward the greatest
possible pleasure. The enjoyment of moderate pleasure is a perfectly
acceptable ultimate goal.

Along with the rehabilitation of pleasure Gassendi attempts a rehabilitation of self-love. The effort is clearest in his account of piety.
There are those who insist that God is to be loved for himself alone with
no concern for one's own pleasure. Some people, hoping to show that it
is possible to live this kind of life, "boast and believe they perform all
this. Truly, I don't envy, nor shall I contradict them," Gassendi says, but
if they are so selfless it is owing to a direct supernatural gift of God.
Gassendi however is concerned with the kind of piety and virtue that is
natural, "according to which, Man performs all that he doth with some
respect to himself." Holy Scripture itself teaches that we are to love God
because he is good to us. He forgives our sins, he grants favors, and he
promises heaven. Hence in loving God there is nothing wrong with
"having in view those everlasting delights which such are to enjoy who
have loved and honoured God" (*Discourses*, pp. 111–12; cf. 337–8). If
supernatural grace is needed for selflessness, then it is irrelevant to an
ethics concerned with the natural – and that is what we need to think
out.

All the virtues are treated as means for the attainment of pleasure, in
accordance with Epicurus's own view. In treating justice, for instance,
Gassendi confines himself largely to giving a long passage from Epicurus's own writings, including the passages claiming that justice presupposes a social contract.[13] Yet he precedes it with one significant
addition. Citing the Roman lawyers, he defines justice as a constant and
perpetual will to give each his right, and goes on to discuss right as a
faculty belonging to individuals by which they are entitled to act as they
please, or to enjoy and protect their possession of something. Right in
this sense, he says, seems "more ancient than justice." Even if men
lacked the will or desire that constitutes justice, there would still exist

---

13   Diogenes Laertius X.150–1.

the rights the just person respects. Without any pause he couples this claim with the Epicurean thesis that justice derives from utility, adding that deriving right from Nature is the same as deriving it from utility since what is useful is what is natural (*Discourses*, pp. 308–12, 24–6). Plainly the finer points of the relations of natural law and utility do not concern him, any more than the relation between desiring one's own pleasure or happiness and desiring that of all.

ii. *Free will and the incomprehensibility of God*

Gassendi's treatment of directly religious matters helps us to a better understanding of his aim. Early in the book he dismisses Epicurus's denial of providence, and asserts that there is judgment and reward or punishment after death (*Discourses*, pp. 14 ff.). At death, he allows, the part of the soul connected to the body ceases to function, and with it pleasures and pains. But "the spirit or understanding" is not thereby eliminated. As he explains at the end of the part of the *Syntagma* concerned with physics, there is room for immortality even on the atomist view. But on an issue where most Christian thinkers insisted on a definite answer, Gassendi reverts in the end to his original skeptical stance. This is the matter of free will.

Gassendi devotes most of the final part of his account of morality to the issue. His own theory is simple. The intellect discerns, as best it can, what is good and what evil in the options before us. The will moves us to act for what seems best, as the intellect presents it. If the will opts instantly for a perceived good, it is plainly acting spontaneously. To count as free, the will's choice must come after "some Reasoning, Examination, Judgement or Choice preceding" (*Discourses*, pp. 373–5). Freedom comes into the picture with deliberation because the intellect may fail to see one course of action as decisively better than another. When it is thus indifferent, so is the will. And the understanding can always consider whether the act now before it is better than any other: it is not "fixed to a thing," not tied to pursuit of only one type of good. We turn our attention away from a proposed action and consider another (Gassendi does not ask what moves us to do this), and if no clear balance appears to the mind, the will is also indifferent. Its freedom is its indifference (pp. 379–82). None of this is in Epicurus or Lucretius.

To explain the experience, given memorable expression by Ovid, of seeing the better and pursuing the worse, Gassendi appeals to Aristotle's views about how the mind can fluctuate in its opinions (pp. 383–9).[14] He bemoans our weakness "here below," and the inconstancy that

14   At this point Bernier adds, without any warning, several pages of his own

results from it. Only in a future life will this be remedied – but, he hastily adds, we should not dwell on supernatural matters (pp. 382–3).

Not dwelling on supernatural matters is important to Gassendi's ethics, though in the *Discourses* he does not explain why. But in his "Objections" to Descartes's *Meditations,* he is not at all reticent about a problem we must face if we allow such issues to arise. Our judgment is faulty, he says, because we cannot help giving assent to the clearest ideas available to us, even if in fact they are false. God could have equipped us better. He could have given us "the kind of faculty which would never lead [us] to assent to falsehood." The universe would plainly have been better with all its parts perfect than it now is with many imperfect parts. The imperfection is that the human understanding does not do well what God intended it to do. Even if we grant that he did not mean us to know everything, "this still leaves room to wonder why he gave man a faculty which is uncertain, confused and inadequate even for the few matters which he did want us to decide upon." Was God unwilling, or was he unable, to make us with intellects perfect for their purpose (Descartes, *Writings* II.214–18)? Brought thus to the problem of evil, Gassendi simply suggests that we cannot understand our moral situation in relation to the divinity.

The same point emerges from Gassendi's encounter with the mechanistic determinism of Democritus. Such thoroughgoing determinism, he says, seems to make deliberation useless (*Discourses*, pp. 399ff.). He rejects the Epicurean thesis, spelled out by Lucretius, that an inexplicable swerve in the movement of atoms through space breaks the causal chain and accounts for human freedom.[15] Such a swerve could be at best just another determined motion and would alter nothing. Epicurus should be praised for trying to rescue human liberty, but he did not succeed (pp. 405–8). The best Gassendi himself can do is to adopt a thesis he attributes to St. Thomas: God, who is destiny, created both unfree causes that act necessarily and free causes that act independently (p. 410). Gassendi discusses some problems that arise with this solution: is God's foreknowledge compatible with freedom? What about predestination? Is there any point in deliberating if God already knows what we will do, or has determined what it will be? Gassendi

opinions on free will, which flatly contradict those of Gassendi. The will can ignore what the understanding shows it, it is not, as Gassendi, quoting Cicero, had said it is, with the will as it is with a pair of scales, and we can always just stop action even in presence of a belief about the greater good (*Discourses*, pp. 389–91). There is no foundation in Gassendi's *Syntagma* for these views, although they have, of course, a certain interest of their own. Bernier makes another long addition at the end of *Discourses* III.III.

15 Lucretius, *De Rerum Naturae* II.243–62.

does not answer any of the questions. Whichever way we look, the matter is too difficult for us. As with the problem of evil, Gassendi takes the line the voluntarists took.[16] We must say that God is incomprehensible and that this is a mystery above our reach (pp. 414, 419). Gassendi is untroubled by God's incomprehensibility, and by the fact that we cannot know whether or not God's morality is ours. In his writings on physics Gassendi accepts a voluntaristic position about the absence of limits on God's powers. God, he holds, can change the essences of things.[17] He did not seem worried by any implications of this for morality. Like Hobbes he was content to see morality as instituted for our earthly life; what lies beyond is not accessible to reason.

We are immortal, there must be freedom so that there can be meaningful deliberation and responsibility, God presumably is our judge – but he seems to have made us less perfect than he might and we cannot understand the whole business. Despite our imperfection and our faulty moral capacities, we can, with fair probability, show even the skeptic that we have a coherent morality. We can infer it from signs given in experience. It does not point very intelligibly beyond this world, but it works here. Apparently we need ask no more of it.[18]

16   I am indebted here to Margaret Osler, "Fortune, Fate, and Divination: Gassendi's Voluntarist Theology and the Baptism of Epicureanism," in Osler 1991, pp. 155–74.

17   I owe this point to Osler 1994, ch.2, esp. pp. 52–6, 163ff.

18   Jones 1989, ch. 8, sketches the fortunes of Epicureanism in seventeenth-century England, noting the appearance of Walter Charleton's *Epicurus's Morals* in 1656 and the exposition of Epicureanism given in Thomas Stanley's *History of Philosophy* of 1655, the first such history in English. In the anonymous, brief and almost entirely useless biography of Stanley prefixed to the 1721 edition, we are told that he was following the example of "the learned Gassendus" in writing his history. He gives Epicurus about a hundred pages, while Pythagoras – the true originator of moral philosophy – gets eighty, Plato sixty, and Aristotle forty. In treating Epicurus, Stanley elaborates on Epicurean points much in the manner of Gassendi. But he shows Epicurus holding to the materiality and mortality of the soul, the declination of atoms as the source of free will, and the parity of right and justice. Charleton is more readable but no more original. In France there were several propagators of Epicureanism besides Gassendi, among them J.-Fr. Sarasin, poet and essayist, whose "Discours de morale sur Épicure," written in 1645–6, draws on Gassendi's early work. It opens with a rejection of the traditional views of the swinishness of Epicureanism and goes on to claim that Epicurus recommended a life as austere as that praised by the Stoics.

In 1717 Anthony Collins praised Epicurus as a great freethinker, notable for his possession of innumerable virtues, in particular friendship. Our own religion does not make the capacity for true friendship a great virtue, Collins says, and so our veneration of Epicurus for possessing it should be all the greater (Collins 1717, pp.

iii. *Morality and the hidden God*

Gassendi, an admirer of Charron and Montaigne and like them a fideist, resisted their more general skepticism by defending a rudimentary empiricism; but he did not think that reason, even aided by and starting from sensory evidence, takes us very far. Much graver doubts were raised about human capacities generally by a thinker far more concerned about religion, Blaise Pascal (1623–62).

After St. Augustine's powerfully articulated objections to Pelagianism there were few if any Christian thinkers to argue that human beings could win salvation by being morally good, unassisted by any form of divine grace.[19] Luther and Calvin were both extreme Augustinians on this matter, insisting that morality alone, no matter how dedicated to it the agent might be, could never remove the taint of original sin. A morally good character or will could never even lead us, let alone entitle us, to enjoy the divine presence.[20] The teaching that only God's freely given grace, mediated through Christ, could purify us was thus strongly identified with Protestantism. But in the seventeenth century an important group of French Roman Catholics developed a very similar view. They were avowed followers of Cornelius Jansen (1585–1638), a Flemish cleric. Bishop Jansen's *Augustinus* (1640) was a lengthy polemic against neoscholastic theory and particularly against all forms of Pelagianism. His French admirers formed a powerful group, not least because among their members were two of the most brilliant controversialists who ever lived – Pascal and Nicole.[21]

Whether the two were full-fledged Jansenists or not, they were certainly powerfully influenced by Jansen and his followers. Both developed versions of the Augustinian view that grace given prior to merit is needed for salvation and that not all people – indeed relatively few – are given it. Both, therefore, believed that most people most of the time live in a state of corruption due to Adam's original sin. Luther and Calvin, holding similar views, reiterated a stern morality of law and sanction for sinners, and reserved a morality of love for the elect – the righteous

---

129–31). Apparently Epicurus's standing was by then high enough to allow his spotless life to be used as a reproach to Christian morality.

19   See Chapter 2.ii.

20   Augustine argued that if freely willed moral goodness sufficed for salvation, then Christ would have come in vain, and that is unthinkable.

21   See Abercrombie 1936 for a good overall account of the Jansenist movement, including, on pp. 126–53, a substantial summary of the *Augustinus.* Similarities between Jansenists and Calvinists were noted at the time; some Huguenots thought the Jansenists were secret Calvinists, and the Jesuits agreed, attacking them as "Calvinists in disguise" (see Rex 1965, pp. 52–3).

for whom the law was not intended. Pascal and Nicole agreed that charity is the mark of the saved, but Pascal suggested, and Nicole developed, a strikingly original view of the morality that operates among those who are not chosen.

Pascal thought morality to be of an order of importance incomparably lower than that of salvation, and tried to say in the *Pensées* how of two incomparables one could be lower.[22] No amount of a "lower" can make any difference to the amount or value of a "higher." Adding units to a number makes the number greater: they are of the same order. No addition of lines increases the size of a plane, no increase in number of planes increases a volume. They are of different orders. Similarly, no amount of earthly power increases the value of a mind, and no increase in the amount of someone's brilliance increases the amount of his charity. So "all bodies together and all minds together and all their products are not worth the least impulse of charity. This is of an infinitely superior order" (*Pensées* 308).

Christianity teaches charity and nothing else (270). Charity is a love which only God can enable us to have, and he does not enable many to have it. God is ordinarily hidden, and "men are in darkness" as a result (242, 427). Reason alone will not reveal him to us; we can even notice how wretched our lives are, and feel we are fitted for something grander, without finding him. He reveals himself rarely, and only when he does are we excited to the love that leads us to want to serve him.[23]

If "[t]here are few true Christians" (179) because God rarely shows himself in the world, what makes it possible for human beings to live together? Pascal makes a few suggestions about what a truly Christian moral order might be like. We would hate ourselves because we are not worthy of love, and would love God alone, loving ourselves only as God is within us (564, 373). We would see ourselves as members of an organism. Each part, while aware of its own existence, would subordinate its "individual will" (*volonté particulière*) to the "primal will [*volonté première*] governing the whole body" (360, 368–74).[24] A merely rational knowledge of God will not bring us into this condition, even if proofs of God's existence could convince us (and Pascal doubts that they are much use). "What a long way it is between knowing God and loving

22 Here I follow Baird 1975, ch.1. I refer to Pascal's *Pensées* by giving the Lafuma number, the first number listed in the Krailsheimer translation, which I use. I do not know whether Pascal was acquainted with the medieval discussion of Lucifer's fall and the thought that emerged from it of the priority of justice to good. See Chapter 2.iii.

23 See the fourth letter to Roannez, *Oeuvres*, p. 267.

24 For the importance of Pascal's thoughts here in the development of the concept of a general will, see Riley 1986, pp. 14–26.

him!" he exclaims (377). Simple people have belief without arguments because God gives it to them (380). But since "All men naturally hate each other" (210) and too few are rescued from this condition to constitute the community of love, what are we to do?

The answer turns on our concupiscence. Everyone without exception desires personal happiness, and nothing else motivates us. God is in fact man's only good, but, ignorant of this, we seek happiness in things that rapidly tire us, leaving us bored and in frantic need of diversion. Our frequent boredom and our endless search for amusement are in fact signs of our wretched, fallen condition, showing that we are pursuing the wrong goals (148, 132ff.). We cannot now avoid this futility. "The mind naturally believes and the will naturally loves, so that when there are no true objects for them they necessarily become attached to false ones" (661). Having turned away from our true good, we can make anything into our good (397). Those who get on in the world learn "that the only way to succeed is to appear honest, faithful, judicious . . . because by nature men only like what may be of some use to them" (427). Our concupiscence, our misdirected desire for happiness, rather than insight into true good or God's directions, gives rise to what we think of as morality and what we take to be good. We live in our imagination, which establishes a second nature in us, giving us its standards for good and ill, right and wrong, and leading us to attribute to them an order of value which they cannot conceivably possess (44).[25] Pascal puts it quite concisely: "We have established and developed out of concupiscence admirable rules of polity, ethics and justice, but at its root, the evil root of man, this evil stuff of which we are made is only concealed; it is not pulled up" (211). The admirable rules may keep us in order, but they will not save us.

Pascal detests philosophers. They all fail miserably to locate the highest good and they cannot understand human nature. Criticizing them from the superior standpoint of Christian insight, he has no interest in creating yet another philosophical position. In the *Pensées* Christian apologetic is his interest, not ethical theory, and he is consequently very brief on the latter. His approach to morality in his brilliantly devastating attack on Jesuit casuistry, the *Provincial Letters,* may be different from, or even inconsistent with, that in his own apology.[26] But even if he had

25 Pascal rejects Montaigne's view that the laws of one's country are to be obeyed merely because they are the established laws. Rather, he thinks, men obey because they think the laws just; and this belief, however deluded, must be sustained (*Pensées* 60, 61, 66, 86).

26 Baird 1975, ch. V, discusses some of the difficulties Pascal faces in working out a coherent theory of morality, given his view of the incommensurable orders of value.

elaborated more fully and more coherently on his ethics than he did, philosophers concerned with the moral and political issues of the times would have found it difficult to use his work. He is so single-mindedly in pursuit of a defense of Roman Catholic Christianity that he seems to exclude not only the heathen but also all other Christians from the number of those who can possibly have any saving gift of love and consequently of true morality.[27] True, he says that we must never suppose of any living human that he or she is hopelessly irredeemable (427). But because he thinks that politics is an affair of the flesh, existing on the lowest order of value and significance, he thinks it also a matter of sheer power, manipulating human imagination to disguise itself as something higher.[28]

Humans may be great because they can become fit for company with God; but most of them remain in the wretched condition to which original sin reduced them. If Pascal allows that "our dignity consists in thought" and that thinking well is the basis of morality, he also holds that reason is unable to reveal our true condition to us. Only through "its simple submission" to the truths of faith can we come to know ourselves (200, 131). As far as eternity is concerned, our only hope lies in giving up all hope that we can do anything for ourselves.

iv. *Nicole: The ingenuity of self-interest*

Pierre Nicole (1625–95) has a more complexly graduated outlook on the human condition. Assistant to Pascal in the research behind the *Provincial Letters*, coauthor with Antoine Arnauld of the widely used textbook known as the *Port Royal Logic*, writer of theological treatises and pro-Jansenist polemic, Nicole also produced, from 1671 on, a series of volumes of "moral essays" which were widely read until well into the eighteenth century.[29]

---

27 "We know God only through Jesus Christ. Without this mediator all communication with God is broken off. . . . Apart from that . . . it is impossible to prove absolutely that God exists, or to teach sound doctrine and sound morality" (*Pensées* 189). As no one can usefully know God who does not acknowledge Christ (191), the basis for natural law theory is wrecked. Moreover only Catholics understand that God is hidden in the sacramental bread (Letter to Roannez, *Oeuvres*, p. 267); and it must be accepted that the pope is the head of the one true church (*Pensées* 569).

28 For a good discussion of Pascal on politics, see Keohane 1980, pp. 266–82.

29 Locke translated three of them, though he did not publish the translations. For Nicole's readership, see the "Conclusion" to the compact and comprehensive study by James, to which I am much indebted. Abercrombie 1936, pp. 244–73, gives an account of Nicole's involvement with Jansenism; and he remarks that though the moral essays were "exceedingly popular, . . . [t]he serious excellence of Nicole's

Assuming a casual and informal manner, he presents a variety of
general principles to be used in thinking about morality and politics.
His is a more humane mind than Pascal's, and a less despairing vision
of the human condition. He is concerned to mitigate the harshness of
Jansenist teaching, in order to keep his readers enrolled among those
who try to sustain a religious life. I will concentrate on just one of his
themes, the consequences of the fact that God hides himself from all but
the few.

Why does God do this? One reason, Nicole explains, is that although
God is really the cause of everything that happens, if he let this be seen
we would never exert ourselves in working or thinking. More importantly, God aims to hide himself in his work so that only those will come
to know him who deserve to. If God did miracles all the time or managed all events overtly, everyone would know that God exists. And
then there would be no room for the life of faith. We can only be prudent
and humble if we have to struggle for worldly goods and for faith
(*Oeuvres*, pp. 161–3). God has given us various abilities to act on the
world. We should use them and not sit back expecting him to provide
for us by miracles.[30] The ordinary course of nature is his hidden provision for us.

It follows, for example, that although God could miraculously teach
each of us our moral shortcomings by direct inspiration, he expects us
to find them out for ourselves in the ordinary way, by self-examination
(p. 167). The same principle explains our suspicion of deathbed conver-
sions. God could of course save someone who had lived as a reprobate
until about to die, but that is not the ordinary way of grace (p. 169). We
should show gratitude to people who help us because, although it is
God who makes them do so, he is hidden in his benefits and wants us to
honor the secondary instruments he uses (p. 238). Nicole draws some
further, rather surprising, conclusions as well.

Supernatural grace is necessary, we all know, if we are to act and
worship from charity. But anything we do from charity can also be done
out of self-love (*amour-propre*), in the form of servile fear. The acts due to
the different motives are essentially identical, and we cannot tell

contribution to moral philosophy has never received due recognition" (p. 275).
(Abercrombie, incidentally, thinks that Nicole had no part in writing the *Port Royal
Logic*.) Marshall 1994, pp. 180–6, gives an excellent discussion of Nicole's views of
morality and their influence on Locke. Raymond 1957 is also helpful.

30   The point is also Malebranchean. Perhaps this principle suggested one of the
arguments Locke used against innate ideas, to the effect that God equipped us to
make all the ideas we need from what experience shows us. Innate ideas would be
redundant.

whether we ourselves or others act from charity or cupidity. The opacity of our own desires and motives is a blessing, Nicole says, for if we could really tell that we were among the unregenerate, we would fall into the sin of despair, and if we knew we were saved, we would become proud and so be lost.[31] Ignorant of everyone's state of grace, we must simply suppose that we are all alike obligated to do as the law commands. If we try to obey, we must quietly await the final judgment in another life to learn what has moved us. "And this will suffice," Nicole comments, "to yield us a human peace which is not sensibly distinguishable from the peace of God." Because God hides himself, the tranquillity sought by the ancient philosophers has the same value in our lives here as divinely granted tranquillity (pp. 172–4). Nicole thus gives us reasons for not feeling the deep anxiety about our own state of grace that Pascal's position might well awaken.

In a remarkable essay, "Of Charity and Self-Love," Nicole further obscures the line between enlightened self-love and charity by arguing that the former mimics the latter in its effects on social life. Descartes had remarked, in a letter to Princess Elizabeth, that "God has so established the order of things . . . that even if everyone were to relate everything to himself and had no charity for others, he would still commonly work for them as much as was in his power" – at least if he lived at a time when "morals were not corrupted" (*Writings* III. 273).[32] Nicole develops the thought, despite his belief that human morals are corrupt at their core. Charity and self-love, though totally different in themselves, lead so entirely to the same results "that there is virtually no better means to ascertain where charity should lead us than to uncover the paths taken by an enlightened self love" (*Oeuvres*, p. 179).[33] Nicole thus reverses Hobbes's advice about a method of ethics: instead of recommending use of the maxim "Do not do to others . . ." as a way of finding out what is required by natural laws based on self-interest, he suggests using considerations of fully instructed self-interest to find out what charity requires (pp. 179, 190). The whole essay might be read as an expansion of one of La Rochefoucauld's maxims: "Interest speaks

31   A similar view about our inability to know ourselves is expressed in the *Port Royal Logic*, where Arnauld and Nicole describe the human mind as "ordinarily weak and obscure, full of clouds and false lights." Passage cited in Rex 1965, p. 42.

32   Pufendorf expresses a similar thought: because we are so interdependent, the more a man loves himself, "the more he will endeavor by kindly deed to get others to love him" (*DJN* II.III.16, p. 213).

33   In quoting from this essay I use the translation by Elborg Forster in my *Moral Philosophy from Montaigne to Kant*, pp. 369–87, though I continue to give the reference to Jourdain.

every sort of language, and plays all sorts of roles, even that of dis-interest."[34]

Our corrupted nature leads us to unbounded desires for power, possessions, and pleasures. We want to rule everyone else. But once we realize that everyone has these desires, our self-love causes us to mod-erate our desires and to be willing to cooperate with others. The most common specifically human desire, moreover, is desire for the love of others; and we are aware that "nothing attracts as much aversion as self-love does" (p. 185). We thus not only moderate our demands on others, we try to conceal their source. We present ourselves as possess-ing the virtues that make others love and esteem us. Charity, for exam-ple, would make us love justice and hate injustice, because God himself is justice. Enlightened self-love leads to the same result. It makes us respect the possessions of others and their spheres of action. It teaches us to avoid the coarse vanity of self-praise and to behave with a mod-esty that can offend no one's pride (pp. 186–7). We will be alert to our own faults, will receive reprimand graciously, and, although naturally "malicious, jealous, envious," will ungrudgingly praise the good qualities of others (pp. 191–3). Self-love makes us patient of insult, grateful to benefactors, obedient to our political superiors: in short it causes us to imitate the Christian virtues so fully that if everyone lived a life of enlightened self-interest, "they would have to do little more than change their ends and their intentions to become as pleasing to God . . . as they would be to men" (p. 200).[35]

In addition to showing how enlightened self-love gives rise to the manners and morals of common life, Nicole appeals to it to explain the commercial side of society. "One gives in order to be given. This is the mainspring and foundation of all the business transacted among men." Self-interest makes us attentive to every detail of the needs and wishes of others – witness the hotel business – because there is money to be made from it. Cupidity is even superior to charity in this respect (pp. 397–8). Thus "all of life's needs are somehow met without involving charity" (p. 181). Every one of us is pursing our own private ends, not thinking of the good of other individuals, let alone of society as a whole; yet the outcome is so like the organic community of love envisaged by Pascal that no mere human can tell the difference. God is not to be thwarted. If fallen humanity cannot create an order of grace on earth, it

---

34   LaRochfoucauld, *Maximes*, in *Oeuvres complètes*, p. 408, no. 39 in the edition of 1678. La Rochfoucauld shared many Jansenist views with Pascal and Nicole.

35   The important French jurist, Jean Domat, codified French law on the basis of Nicole's theory. See his *Traité des lois*, 1689, IX.3; for discussion see James 1972, pp. 151ff.; Keohane 1980, pp. 304–6; Kelley 1990, pp. 215ff.

cannot help but mimic it. There is no need that we should know that we are doing so.

v. Bayle: Religion and the virtuous atheist

During the eighteenth century advanced thinkers took Pierre Bayle (1647–1706) to be one of the first who struggled to cast off the yoke of religion and to equip others to do so as well. His *Historical and Critical Dictionary*, first published in 1697, was amazing for the breadth and detail of the erudition it contained and even more so for the innumerable shocking and scandalous suggestions it made, usually in lengthy footnotes to more or less innocuous main entries. It is not only that various anti-Christian doctrines, such as Manichaean dualism, are presented as offering reasonable solutions to problems to which Christian theology has no answer. At least as outrageous to the sensibilities of the time was Bayle's treatment of various sacred figures. Consider only his treatment of King David, "one of the greatest men in the world and a man after God's own heart," a model religious ruler and prefiguration of Christ. David is described in the notes as a bastard lecher who carried out unauthorized terrorist raids on helpless people, was quite willing to betray his own people, worked to gain a kingdom by the vilest treachery, had no qualms about making someone lose his soul in serving him, and engaged in unjust wars. Biblical figures, Bayle explains, must be examined "in terms of the ideas of morality" because to fail to do so would be to open the way to endless injustice.[36] Again and again religious thought and much of religious action are examined by the light of reason and reasonable moral standards, and shown to be abject failures. It is not hard to see why one might take Bayle for a raging atheist.

By the time the *Dictionary* appeared, moreover, Bayle was already notorious for having argued at length that atheism might not be as bad a thing as respectable people took it to be. His argument appears in the long-winded *Thoughts on the Comet* of 1682, aimed at showing that a recent comet should not be understood as a sign of God's displeasure and an omen of disasters to come. Bayle's strong Malebranchean streak comes out clearly here.[37] He argues that God acts by general laws and

36 See the *Historical and Critical Dictionary*, s.v. David and Manicheans. In the notes to "Paulicians" at pp. 169ff., Bayle continues the discussion of the problem of evil, saying that it is incomprehensible how an all-powerful, just, and benevolent deity could allow evil in his universe. This is the sort of remark that provoked Leibniz to write the *Theodicy*.

37 For a good brief review of the uses to which Bayle put Malebranchean doctrine, and the changes in his attitude toward it, see Riley's introduction to his

does not send miraculous messages in order to make himself and his will known. In particular, Bayle says, God does not send comets to convert atheists. If atheists were converted by a comet, they would become not good Christians but idolaters – and God would hardly try to drive out the crime of unbelief with the worse crime of idolatry (*Oeuvres* III.70–1). This leads him, in the course of an extremely convoluted digression on atheism, to make some of his most upsetting statements.[38]

The common belief that atheism is the most abominable condition one can imagine, Bayle says, is a mere prejudice. It supposes that without fear of punishment after death, people will live vicious lives of uncontrolled sensuality. But in fact experience shows that belief in God does nothing to control vicious desires (III.86–7a). The first step in Bayle's argument is his claim that people do not really live according to the principles they profess. The words Ovid gave Medea about seeing the better and pursuing the worse "represent perfectly the difference between the enlightenment of conscience and the particular judgment that makes us act" (III.87b). Bayle has no doubt that conscience shows us clear moral principles.[39] But our "unregulated desires" are what win the day. Religious belief is no different: look at the pagans, believing in innumerable deities as dispensers of prosperity or misfortune and nonetheless committing "all the crimes imaginable." If people lived by their beliefs, how could we understand Christians, who, despite having an unmistakable revelation supported by miracles and taught by marvelous preachers, live "in the most enormous disorder of vice" (III.88a)? What is more, it is not even true that those who flaunt the morals taught by their religion fail to believe in God. To give just one of Bayle's many examples, the Crusaders were not covert atheists, but they committed unspeakable crimes (III.89b, 90a).

Atheists and idolaters, Bayle continues, are moved, like everyone else, by their passions and habits. If an idolater's desires are worse than those of an atheist, he will act worse. After all, huge numbers of Christians are "drunk almost all their lives" because they like wine; and atheists might not like it so much. Debauchery is a matter of taste, not

---

translation of Malebranche's *Treatise on Nature and Grace*, pp. 81–91. The *Oeuvres diverses* cited in the text is the multivolume work edited by Labrousse.

38 "The famous examples of virtuous atheists are invoked to prove the seventh proof of the seventh proof of the fourth answer to the first objection to the proposition that comets are not signs of misfortune." Sandberg 1966, p. 28.

39 He was teaching this as early as 1675, as witness the syllabus for his course on philosophy (*Oeuvres* IV.259–60), where he says that despite the Fall, some moral principles are still evident to us, and that conscience shows us the principles of natural law.

conviction (III.93a). Thus it seems to Bayle that "a society of Atheists, in respect of their morals and civil actions, would be quite like a society of Pagans." They would of course need stiff law enforcement, but so does everyone, we Christians included (III.103b). Most people are virtuous – if they are – only due to social pressure (III.104–5). Atheists would be just as susceptible as anyone else to public honor and dishonor, reward and punishment; and so one would see in a society of atheists plenty of people who fulfilled their contracts, helped the poor, opposed injustice and were faithful to their friends. Even a belief in the mortality of the soul would not alter their behavior in these matters (III.109–10).[40]

All this sounds, of course, rather like the work of someone trying to unseat the dominance of religion. But that is not Bayle's aim. He is a devout Huguenot, and his target is not religious belief as such but the Roman Catholic faith of those in France who persecute his coreligionists. He himself, after being briefly a convert to Catholicism, returned to his Huguenot heritage and as a result of these changes had to live the rest of his life in exile. In the *Thoughts on the Comet* he is arguing that atheists are not nearly as bad as believers in corrupt religion. Crusaders are worse than atheists, precisely because they use their religion as an excuse for their worst crimes. The Catholic Church is in effect a church of idolatry and superstition, licensing far worse behavior than anything a godless atheist might wish to do.

The prime example is persecution. After the revocation of the Edict of Nantes in 1685, Huguenots were subjected to appalling pressure to convert to Catholicism. One of Bayle's most passionate and influential books was a direct response. The "Converters" appealed to the words of Christ, "Go out into the highways and hedges, and compel them to come in, that my house may be filled" (Luke 14.23). In his *Philosophical Commentary on These Words of Jesus Christ* (1686)[41] Bayle points out strongly that persecution cannot bring about the sort of inner religious devotion that would alone be pleasing to God (*Commentary,* pp. 35–7; II.371–2a). The point is of course important, but for us the most significant part of his argument concerns the proper way of interpreting the text used to justify persecution.

He announces at the opening that his mode of interpreting the text is entirely new. Leaving textual criticism, philology, history, and mysteries entirely aside, he bases his reading on just one principle: "any literal interpretation which carries an obligation to commit iniquity is false"

40 Tuck 1993, pp. 97–9, says that in the sixteenth century the Venetian political theorist Paolo Sarpi argued that a morally decent community of atheists would be possible.
41 I cite page numbers from the *Philosophical Commentary* translated by Tannenbaum, followed by the page reference to *Oeuvres diverses,* vol. II.

(*Commentary*, p. 28; II.367a). He then brings out numerous ways in which persecution is iniquitous, unjust, and destructive of any moral order in society. Among them he emphasizes the incoherence of the persecutors' principles. They are willing to have the French king destroy heretical subjects but not to allow subjects to destroy a heretical king (*Commentary*, p. 48; II.376a). They allow persecution of those they take to be wrong about religion, but would not allow persecution of early Christians by pagan rulers. They think violence permissible in their own religious cause but not in that of any other. But this, Bayle exclaims, is a doctrine so abominable that he doubts whether the devils in hell would wish human affairs conducted by it (*Commentary*, p. 47; II.375b). He offers numerous other arguments, but we must concentrate on the basic principle.

Bayle is quite clear about the revolutionary implication of his insistence on using moral standards to judge the meaning of Scripture. It is that "reason, speaking to us by the axioms of the natural light . . ., is the supreme tribunal. . . . Let it nevermore be said that theology is the queen and philosophy only the handmaiden . . ." (*Commentary*, p. 29; II.368a). Reason shows us undeniable principles both of metaphysics and of morals. God must have given us this insight into his mind – Bayle is here again being Malebranchean – to serve as infallible guide to what his written message is saying. Without such a test we cannot know whether a message comes from God or from the devil. Lord Herbert had outlined this point in his difficult Latin in 1624 and Whichcote had been saying similar things to small English audiences for three decades by the time Bayle propounded these doctrines, but it was Bayle whose inexhaustible energies and vivid polemical style earned such views a hearing for the first time in France and everywhere else in Europe.

Is he dethroning religion when he makes reason the queen?[42] Not at all: he is in fact appealing to a principle of scriptural interpretation first put forth by a Huguenot divine. In 1682 Pierre Jurieu published an examination of the doctrine of the Eucharist, in which he argued against the Catholic view that the bread and wine at communion must be taken to be literally the flesh and blood of Christ. The doctrine is based on the scriptural words "This is my body." But, Jurieu says, we know there are some passages in scripture that require figurative interpretation. If a passage is absurd, or if it is ridiculous and full of contradictions, one must explain it figuratively. And there is a third rule, coming from St. Augustine: "when a text seems to command us to commit a crime it must be taken figuratively." The Catholic doctrine of the Eucharist fails

42   For this paragraph I am wholly indebted to Rex 1965, pp. 145–52, one of the most illuminating passages of a brilliant book.

to respect this canon, while the Protestant doctrine does not, and the interpretation required by morality must dominate.

Bayle's defense of toleration thus rests on good Huguenot doctrine. It is neither atheistic nor designed to eliminate religion from society. It is aimed at showing that nations must learn to allow different religious communions to flourish within them, contrary to the strongly established traditional demand for religious uniformity. They must allow what was called liberty of conscience, taking conscience in its traditional sense as the inner voice that conveys God's will to us. Bayle even gives a new sense to that phrase. He distinguishes the certainty the intellect can have if it withholds its assent unless the ideas it considers are completely clear and distinct from the certainty that conscience can give us. "In matters of religion," he says, "the rule for judging is not at all in the understanding but in the conscience; that is to say that one must accept objects not according to clear and distinct ideas but according as conscience tells us that in accepting them we are doing what is agreeable to God."[43] It is morality that must tell us what religious doctrines to accept, not the other way round.

The natural light of reason, Bayle holds, delivers axioms so clear that no one can doubt or deny them. One of them is that one must act according to one's conscience. Otherwise one's assent to religious assertions is forced, unreal, and unacceptable to God. But consciences plainly vary; and Bayle could not figure out how to solve the resulting problems. Suppose the conscience of a converter tells him to persecute heretics. What becomes of undeniable axioms forbidding this? In the "Third Clarification" appended to the *Historical Dictionary*, Bayle puts forward a fideistic view: "the Christian religion is of a supernatural kind . . . its basic component is the supreme authority of God proposing mysteries to us, not so that we may understand them, but so that we may believe them with all the humility that is due to the infinite being" (*Dictionary*, p. 421). Thus when he says that the party of reason will always win in disputes with theologians, who will always have to "take refuge" in the "supernatural light" (p. 410), he is not abandoning religion. Fideist skepticism may look like religious skepticism, but we have already seen that it is not, not even if it detaches morality and the possibility of a decent moral life from religion.

To judge a picture properly, Pascal says, one must be neither too far away, nor too close. There is just one right standpoint. "In painting the rules of perspective decide it, but how will it be decided when it comes to truth and morality?" (*Pensées* 21). He himself had no doubt. "The argument of the ungodly in [Charron's] *Wisdom*," Pascal says, "is based

---

43 Cited in Sandberg 1966, p. 65, from *Nouvelles lettres critiques* II.334.

solely on the assumption that God does not exist. 'Granted that,' they say, 'let us delight in creatures.' It is a second best. But if there were a God to love they would not have reached this conclusion" (*Pensées* 618). To those who think that the hidden God only *seems* to be absent from his creation, love of human beings may well be a second best. Nonetheless Pascal, Nicole, and Bayle suggest that the pursuit of the good that unredeemed humans seek can be enough to enable the world to get along on its own. If we can never know our own motives, and if our own efforts to improve them are in any case hopeless, perfection cannot be an issue. The point of morality is then not to show us how to reconcile ourselves to God or to earn salvation from him. Perhaps its point is, as Gassendi thought, simply to teach us how to preserve and increase human happiness. Without an otherworldly standpoint for judgment, that may be more than a mere second best.

14

The recovery of virtue

Carl Friedrich Stäudlin, the first historian to group modern moral philosophers by nationality, claimed that during the eighteenth century British writers on ethics had done more to advance the subject than had the French or the Netherlanders, and allowed that they had had considerable influence even in Germany. In his treatment of the British moral philosophers, he assembled, I believe for the first time, those we now consider canonical, though his emphases – two pages on Hobbes, seventeen on Adam Smith – are not ours.[1] Stäudlin rightly noted that the issues with which they were engaged had emerged from a more cosmopolitan debate. If this point has often been ignored, it is partly because in the eighteenth century the British tended to carry on their discussions largely with reference to one another. It is also due to the fact that Selby-Bigge's anthology, *British Moralists*, first published in 1897, made their writings more readily available than those of their continental counterparts. For these among other reasons, the British moralists have been studied more thoroughly than any comparable group of modern moral philosophers. In presenting the British debate in this and the following chapters I make no effort at a comprehensive discussion. I try to show only how some of the issues generated in the earlier European debates developed in the much envied free and politically stable environment of Britain.

---

1 Stäudlin 1822, pp. 774–5. He does not treat Bentham, who was still alive when he wrote. Adam Smith himself, in his 1756 *Letter to the Edinburgh Review*, claimed that British moralists from Hobbes through Hutcheson had contributed more to original thought on their subject than had the French, who were taking up their work, or the Germans, of whom he had a generally low opinion (*Essays*, pp. 250, 243). Sir James Mackintosh's *Dissertation on the Progress of Ethical Philosophy* (1830) ranges more widely but devotes most of its attention to the British. Blakey's *History of Moral Science* (1833) is more comprehensive than Stäudlin on the British but extremely weak on continental writers. In Whewell's *Lectures on the History of Moral Philosophy in England* (1852), the only non-English philosopher discussed is Hutcheson.

i. Virtue and law

It is sometimes said that the study of virtue and the virtues was neglected during the formative years of modern moral philosophy.[2] Given the prominence of virtue in the ethics of Hume and Kant, the charge is a little puzzling. We can understand it only by supposing that those who make it have some particular type of virtue-centered theory in mind and are deploring the absence of anything like it in early modern thought. Aristotle's ethics is the one that the friends of virtue are likely to take as the paradigm of a virtue-centered theory. If they do, it would be, strictly speaking, incorrect to say that Aristotelian moral theories were absent from the scene. Luther allowed that the *Nicomachean Ethics* contained good advice about how to behave in worldly matters; and throughout Europe professors of different religious persuasions lectured on it, edited it, and published commentaries on it well into Kant's lifetime. Perhaps, however, this is not enough. Such works, we might all agree, did not contribute to the distinctive outlines of modern moral thought. Hence, if Aristotle provides the only model of a virtue ethic, the complaint brought by the friends of virtue is understandable.

Along with the lament about the decline of real concern with virtue, there often comes an explanation of the decline. Aristotelian teleology was being displaced quite generally during the modern period, so it is easy to suppose that the demise of Aristotelian ethics was a consequence of the abandonment of teleology in science. But this would be a mistaken account. Whatever the fate of teleology in physics, Christian teleology was widely used by seventeenth-century thinkers to explain the point of the various dispositions, feelings, and abilities that go to make up our nature as moral beings, and sometimes to show our true goal or our function in the universe as well. That sort of teleology did not disappear in the eighteenth century, nor did the belief that without knowledge of God's ends we could not know how to direct our actions. "[I]f God's Aim in producing me be entirely unknown; if it be neither his Glory . . . nor mine own Good . . . how know I what I am to do here?"[3] Edmund Law's question was commonplace, and so were reassuring answers to it. If a virtue ethic requires teleology, supplying it was not a problem.

2 See, e.g., Philippa Foot, "Virtues and Vices," in *Virtues and Vices* (Oxford, 1978), p. 1.; and G. H. von Wright, who says that "Kant's famous *dictum* that formal logic had made no appreciable progress since Aristotle, could be paraphrased and applied – with at least equally good justification – to the ethics of virtue." *The Varieties of Goodness* (London, 1963), p. 136.

3 Law's preface to his translation of King 1739, p. viii.

Christianity itself, however, suggested serious moral misgivings
about an ethics centered on virtue. Luther was vituperative about Aristotelian ethics insofar as in its concern with virtue it meddles with the
inner life. Thomas Reid pointed more dryly to an opposition between
virtue ethics and Christian ethics. "Morals have been methodized in
different ways," he remarked, "The Ancients commonly arranged them
under the four cardinal virtues of prudence, temperance, fortitude, and
justice. Christian writers, I think more properly, under the three heads
of the duty we owe to God, to ourselves, and to our neighbor."[4] Christianity, Reid believed, teaches a morality of duty, not of virtue, and it
understands duty in terms of acts complying with law. Some aspects of
Roman Catholic teaching testify to the long history behind Reid's view
of Christian morals. I indicated in Chapter 2.ii that St. Thomas subordinated the virtues to the laws of nature. Moreover from the earliest days
of the practice of confession in the sixth century through the great
flowering of casuistry in the sixteenth and seventeenth centuries,
Catholic moralists were preoccupied with specific acts that might or
might not be sins, and with the appropriate penalties for them if they
were. If ever there was an ethics of acts and quandries, it was here.[5]

The rejection of Aristotelian approaches to virtue was due, in a word,
to perceived religious and moral shortcomings in any such approach.
For beings with natures like ours, Christians were likely to think, only a
law-centered morality would do. The commonest position in the seventeenth and eighteenth centuries was that virtue is secondary to laws or
rules. John Locke articulated what had long been a commonplace: "By
whatever standard soever we frame in our minds the ideas of virtues or
vices . . . their rectitude, or obliquity, consists in the agreement with
those patterns prescribed by some law" (*ECHU* II.xxviiii.14, p. 358).[6] In

---

4 Reid, *Active Powers* V.II. The contrast between Christian and heathen did not
end with Reid. "Many have heard so much of the *danger* of trusting to good works
. . . that they . . . consider that the less they think about them the better. The word
virtue sounds to them heathenish." *Miscellaneous Remains from the Commonplace Book
of Richard Whately, D.D.*, ed. E. J. Whately, (London, 1865), p. 239. "It is true that the
classic origins of the doctrine of virtue later made Christian critics suspicious of it.
They warily regarded it as too philosophical and not Scriptural enough. Thus, they
preferred to talk about commandments and duties rather than about virtues." Josef
Pieper, *The Four Cardinal Virtues* (Notre Dame, 1966), p. x, referring to what he
evidently regards as a still-living attitude.
5 See Edmund L. Pincoffs, *Quandries and Virtues* (Lawrence, 1986), especially ch.
2. For the history of casuistry, see Mahoney 1987, pp. 30–1 and ch. 1 generally, and
Jonsen and Toulmin 1988.
6 Pufendorf, *DJN* I.IV.6, p. 59, defines virtues as dispositions leading us to act to
preserve ourselves and society. Since those are the aims of the laws of nature as well,
the difference between his view and Locke's is not great.

the previous century the Puritan divine William Perkins had the same thing to say: "universall justice, is the practice of all vertue: of that, whereby a man observes all the commandments of the Law."[7] Even Aristotle was made to fall into line with this view, as is shown by the notes of an early seventeenth-century Cambridge tutor taking his students through the *Nicomachean Ethics*: "the other day we proposed a definition of virtue," he says, "it is a constant disposition of the soul to live according to law."[8] As late as 1785 William Paley was treating virtues as the habits of following the rules through which we apply the divine command to maximize happiness (*Principles* II.7).

We have seen that the perfectionists followed a different line of thought. For them the knowledge needed to bring the soul or mind into a proper or praiseworthy condition is not ultimately knowledge of moral laws. It is knowledge of the order of the universe, or of the degrees of perfection of being. Their central moral question concerns not right actions or binding laws, but the best condition of each person's mind. The perfectly virtuous or wise person has a mind brought into conformity with a rational objective order by knowing it. Those who are perfectly wise or virtuous desire what is truly good and do what is right. Our first endeavor must be to approach ever nearer to that perfection. Character is central to the perfectionists and right action secondary, while it seems that right action is dominant in natural law theories and character secondary. By some accounts, that suffices to enroll the

---

7   William Perkins, *Whole Treatise*, in Perkins, ed. Merrill, ch. VI, p. 231. Merrill does not give the date of this treatise; Perkins died in 1602.

8   Quoted in Costello 1958, pp. 65–6.

Eighteenth-century examples abound. Morality, says Diderot's *Encyclopédie*, "is the relation of human actions to the law that is their rule," and adds, not surprisingly, that "A virtuous man is one who has the habit of acting conformably to his duties." S.v. "Moralité," 10.1765. Christian Wolff, illustrating what a verbal understanding of something is, says: "if I think these words concerning virtue: it is a disposition to direct one's acts according to the laws of nature – then I understand virtue through words" (*Ethics* 316).

Samuel Johnson provides another eighteenth-century example. Although in numerous essays he speaks of the virtues as means between extremes, he has no clear view about them. In the review of Soame Jenyns, *A Free Inquiry into the Nature and Origin of Evil* (1757), he espouses a version of what we call "rule utilitarianism," and he seems to think of its rules as the laws of nature laid down by God and revealed through conscience. These are at the core of morality for him (Johnson, p. 371). He does not mention virtue or the virtues in the 1748 allegory "The Vision of Theodore, the Hermit of Teneriffe," which he once said he thought was his finest work. That tale shows Reason guiding us with the aid of Conscience, which is the emissary of religion; habits are almost always bad; and it is clear that man's natural dispositions, uncorrected, would do no one any good (Johnson, pp. 147–60).

perfectionists among the exponents of an ethics of virtue, and to exclude the lawyers.

The natural lawyers, however, did not ignore character. As I have tried to show, their theory of imperfect duties carries, among other things, their effort to allow for a part of the moral life in which motives matter and sensitivity to the nuances of particular cases cannot be explained as rule following. They reject rules in the domain of imperfect duties; and although they replace Aristotelian cognitive insight with discretion, they plainly insist on the importance of having the kind of good character that the imperfect duties require. It is a source of merit, even with God. If the lawyers thus confine their approach to something like a virtue theory to only part of morality, the perfectionists are far from saying that virtue suffices. Most people will never be near enough perfection, on their view, to be allowed to act on their own insight alone. For different reasons then, perfectionists and natural lawyers alike conclude that the vast majority of people cannot live a life of Aristotelian virtue. They will always need to be directed by others, moved by external threats as well as guided by laws.

ii. *Virtue in Utopia*

In discussing Machiavelli's views I pointed out that his term *virtù* could not be translated by the word "virtue." But by a curious twist Machiavellian political views helped to give rise to an ethical theory that centered on virtue in something closer to its conventional moral sense. Shaftesbury's *Inquiry concerning Virtue or Merit*, first printed in 1699, is traditionally taken, with good reason, as giving a new direction to systematic thought about morality. I shall argue that Shaftesbury's work must be understood in the light of his involvement with the renovated Machiavellianism current in his time.

Historians have shown us how Machiavellian classical republicanism came to England and Scotland, and played a role in British political thought during the troubled years of the seventeenth century and the early part of the eighteenth.[9] The central mid-seventeenth-century figure is James Harrington, whose *Oceana*, published in 1656, portrayed in utopian form what the classical republic would look like if it were

9   Among the major investigations are Baron 1955 and Pocock 1975. For the importance for American history, see Robbins 1959; Bernard Bailyn, *The Ideological Origins of the American Revolution* (Cambridge, 1967); Gordon S. Wood, *The Creation of the American Republic, 1776–1787* (Chapel Hill, 1969). For the importance of classical republicanism in the Scottish Enlightenment, see Hont and Ignatieff 1983, especially the essays by Pocock and Ignatieff.

created in England, taking account of the special features of English history and geography.

Like Machiavelli, Harrington sought a form of government that could assure a country of liberty as well as stability and endurance. A government of laws, not of men, was his aim, and the secret of attaining it lay, he thought, in getting the right procedures for law making. Let the few, who are able to invent new policies and strategies for handling the changing world, propose what the state should do; and let the many, who can tell what is for the common good, decide whether to adopt those proposals or not. The result will be a just, free, and enduring commonwealth. To assure its endurance two fundamental laws are required. One lays down that all holders of office, including those in the body that proposes laws, should rotate in office, and be chosen by secret ballot. The other governs ownership of the land. Those who are to hold the elective office of lawmaker must have a material base on which to build their lives. They must study warfare and government, and they must have time to devote wholly to the commonwealth. They must therefore have wealth, but not more wealth than is needed to sustain the functions they are to carry out for the state. Hence, while anyone may be allowed to increase his holdings and win election to high office, there must be strict laws against excessive acquisition of land. Harrington calls these "the agrarian," and sees them as the true foundation of the republic. The commonwealth, he says, "is founded upon an equal agrarian; and if the earth be given unto the sons of men, this balance is the balance of justice" (*Oceana*, p. 322). The people do not need to own land in order to earn their livings. Since legislative proposals must always win their approval before going into effect, the people can be assured of decent sustenance for themselves even without such ownership.

The natural principle of the commonwealth is justice (p. 203). And Harrington is sure that the rotation of office holding, the agrarian, and the division of the tasks of ruling into proposing laws and approving them, together create "the balance of justice." He has, however, so little to say about justice itself that his modern editor did not find it necessary to give an entry for the topic in his exhaustive index. Yet there is a strong view of justice implicit in *Oceana*. It is allied to a more general view of right and wrong, which, again, Harrington barely sketches.

Harrington sees the soul as torn between reason and passion. He offers what sounds at first like a conventional view about the relation they have to vice and virtue:

> For as whatever was passion in the contemplation of a man, being
> brought forth by his will, is vice and the bondage of sin; so whatever was

reason in the contemplation of a man, being brought forth by his will into action, is virtue and the freedom of soul. (p. 169)

What Harrington means, however, is far from conventional. It is that if a disposition to rationality governs each of us, then what it leads us to do will count as virtuous, while if passions govern, what results counts as vice. The right and wrong of action are determined by the inner condition of the agent, not by law and not by consequences. What is true in individual action holds also in the commonwealth. Reason is identified with concern for the interest of the whole, and passion with private interest; and only what is done from reason will count as right (pp. 173, 280–1).

Harrington's view of justice expands his thesis about the nature of virtue and vice. He does not think that justice poses any difficult theoretical questions. There is a simple procedure for procuring justice. If the aim is to divide goods so as to "give the upper hand in all cases unto common right or interest, notwithstanding the nearness of that which sticks unto every man in private," consider that even simple country girls know how to do it.

> For example, two of them have a cake yet undivided, which was given between them. That each of them therefore may have that which is due, "Divide," says one unto the other, "and I will choose, or let me divide, and you shall choose." . . . That which great philosophers are disputing upon in vain is brought unto light by two silly girls: even the whole mystery of a commonwealth, which lies only in dividing and choosing. (p. 172)

It is not the equality of the resulting portions that interests Harrington; it is the procedure. It guarantees that the cake will be shared in a way that both parties are willing to accept. Either girl is willing to divide or to choose first, and each will be content with whatever share she gets as a result. Equal shares will result in this case, and because they are the result of a procedure both parties can accept, equal shares are fair shares.[10]

Dividing and choosing then become Harrington's metaphors for proper government. "Dividing" is thinking out the fine points of public policy, separating one option from another. Choosing is balloting, choosing one proposed policy rather than another. Harrington thinks that in any group of people, about a third will naturally have more

10   At p. 416, defending his example against a critic who sneers at it, Harrington explicitly says that "either office . . . was communicable unto either of the girls." In the commonwealth, offices are not as readily interchangeable; what matters is having procedures acceptable to all parties.

ability than the others at devising solutions to problems and long-term policies. They constitute a "natural aristocracy," whose task is to counsel the people (not command them). The remaining two-thirds, or their representatives, can speak for the interest of the commonwealth. They are to make the choice as to what advice to accept. As long as these tasks are carried out by different groups, each will get "that which is due" with regard to the common right or common interest (pp. 172–4).[11] The just policy or act is that which emerges from a procedure all parties accept.

If Harrington is brief about justice, he has even less to say about the nature of the individuals who will be his citizens. He assumes that once the structure of the commonwealth is in place, the proper actions will be generated regardless of the human material used in carrying on its operations. He does not ask what is going on in the minds and hearts of his citizens. Once people are rightly organized they will acquire the virtues of good citizens. It does not matter whether they participate willingly because they think a fair procedure has been used to set up the republic, or because they think that they are living a better life than they could in any other kind of society.[12] But certain virtues are needed by the commonwealth, and are created by it.

Courage and wisdom are the virtues most in demand, because the commonwealth depends most on its armies and its councils. Whoever has these virtues has "arrived at the perfection of human nature." Whatever men might be like under other kinds of government, the commonwealth "driveth her citizens like wedges: there is no way with them but through" (p. 311). Virtues are forced upon us by the political structure of the community, and we stay virtuous as long as the commonwealth sticks with its fundamental procedural laws. This is hardly an Aristotelian view either of how the virtues are acquired, or of what they are.

It is not surprising then to find that Harrington has little to say about character. He discusses the education to be given the ruling class, but unlike Plato he does not go into detail (pp. 298–310). He does not discuss the virtues as such. His thinking throughout is dictated by the principle that if the basic procedures for making law and policy in the commonwealth are sound, its citizens will be so as well. We can see this in passage after passage.

11   Cf. Harrington's *The Prerogative of Popular Government* (1658), in *Works*, p. 416. There will also need to be a magistrate to see to it that accepted advice is executed: thus elements of monarchy, aristocracy, and democracy are combined in a republic.

12   See Pocock 1975, pp. 389–90.

"Give us good men and they will make us good laws" is the maxim of a demagogue, and . . . exceeding fallible. But "give us good orders, and they will make us good men" is the maxim of a legislator and the most infallible in the politics. . . . the errors of the people are occasioned by their governors. If they be doubtful of the way or wander from it, it is because their guides misled them; and the guides of the people are never so well qualified for leading by any virtue of their own, as by that of the government. (p. 205)

Similarly, Harrington's insistence on the importance of a sound agrarian law does not come solely from attachment to egalitarian principles of fair distribution as such. It comes from the belief that the agrarian is the sole basis on which the central procedures for governing the commonwealth can be sustained. Large differences of wealth will give rise to faction and thus threaten "the balance" – the proper working of the governmental machinery. The rotation of officials is motivated by the same thought: this mechanism, working via elections, is vital for harmony and stability (cf. pp. 230–1).

A commonwealth that is internally equal hath no internal cause of commotion [sc. social discontent], and therefore can have no such effect but from without. A commonwealth internally unequal hath no internal cause of quiet, and therefore can have no such effect but by diversion. (pp. 274–5)[13]

When the "manners" (or as we would say, morals) of the population become corrupted, this is "from the balance," that is, due to slippage in the structuring of power or wealth in the city. And when by good fortune a leader was found for Oceana who brought about the proper balance, "the manners of the people were not thereby corrupted, but on the contrary fitted for a commonwealth" (p. 202).[14] Oceana's inhabitants are political animals shaped by the community. Harrington does not think that he needs any discussion of individual psychology.

iii. *Harrington's hollow citizen*

Now one might say that, after all, Harrington is concerned with politics, and hence need not bother himself with the inner makeup of

13 Pocock 1975, p. 390, points out that "internal" causes are those arising among the landed class. Servants and their discontents are listed as among "external" causes.

14 Harrington is arguing that not all change is corruption: some changes are improvements. But behind the argument there is the belief that "manners" change when and because structure changes.

his citizens. This would be more convincing if he were not writing in strong opposition to the antirepublican and possibly promonarchist views of Thomas Hobbes.[15] And what drives Hobbes to some of the conclusions Harrington finds most repugnant is precisely a view about individual psychology. Harrington thinks that if there comes to be a commonwealth with the structure he recommends, it will never suffer from internal dissension and will be powerful enough to protect itself from outside enemies. But he does not try to show that the individual psychology of the people who would be his citizens would permit the existence of an enduring classical republic. If Hobbes is right about the motivations he attributes to everyone, the Harringtonian republic is in trouble.

As we have seen, Hobbes holds that individual desires inevitably set men in competition, and that the management of that competition is an unavoidable task of the state – indeed, its central internal task. Harrington does not explicitly reject Hobbes's Grotian view of the major problem confronting society but he does reject Hobbes's view of its roots in human motivation. Yet he does not argue for his position directly, and even in his occasional explicit confrontations with Hobbes he does not explain why he takes a different view of the problem of order. He contents himself with reiterating his own view. Thus after citing Hobbes as saying that the prosperity of ancient commonwealths was due not to their laws but to their emulation of great men, Harrington replies: "as if so great an emulation could have been generated without as great virtue, so great virtue without the best education, the best education without the best laws, or the best laws any otherwise than by the excellency of their policy" (p. 178).

What Hobbes takes as man's natural condition is for Harrington what people become when they are "corrupt." They then have unlimited desires for power and wealth and find luxury and political servitude more tempting than liberty and the austerity it requires (cf. pp. 202–3). If men are not corrupt, however, they are content with what they see is the fair share of goods allotted to them. They will not seek limitless wealth, power, or glory. But if Hobbes is right, then even in a well-ordered civil society men do not get rid of their original infinite desire. For them, fair shares coming from just procedures will not be enough. They care for justice and the commonwealth only because political stability is the condition for their own flourishing. When men are governed by no one but themselves they can pursue only their

---

15   Whether or not Hobbes supported the king or Cromwell is not to the point here. Pocock 1975, pp. 397ff. indicates various matters, especially their anticlericalism, on which Harrington and Hobbes were agreed or nearly so. See also Pocock's introduction to Harrington's *Works*.

private interests. *Oceana*'s portrayal of a self-governing armed citizenry living together under a government that has no standing army – Harrington here carries forward a central feature of Machiavelli's thought – must have seemed to Hobbes not so much a sketch of an ideal of government as a description of an improbable temporary lull in the war of all against all.[16] The classical republic is impossible, on a Hobbesian view, because people cannot understand themselves as the uncorrupted citizens of that society are said to. Harrington thinks that the commonwealth may be perfect even though "the citizen be sinful" (p. 320). He relies solely on the mechanisms of ownership and government to control behavior. He offers no account of how the strong self-interest of his citizens comes to be tempered enough so that each is content with a fair share and is attached to the commonwealth that provides it. This lack in Harrington's theory would naturally seem to be an important defect to anyone wishing to use his view as a guide to practice.

iv. *Shaftesbury's politics*

Harrington makes occasional reference to law, right, and obligation, but the concepts play no real role in his thought. This is neither accidental nor due to his being absorbed in utopian details. It is central to the whole classical republican outlook. In that outlook, as Pocock says, " 'virtue' cannot be satisfactorily reduced to the status of right or assimilated to the vocabulary of jurisprudence."[17] An Englishman opposed to natural law thought and deeply concerned with politics at the end of the seventeenth century might naturally turn to Harrington and the neo-Harringtonians. And if he were of a philosophical cast of mind, he might naturally think of trying to remedy the weak point in the Harringtonian structure – the absence of an individual psychology or a theory of virtue in the individual, an absence that leaves the whole view open to criticism by those less sanguine about the plasticity of human nature than Harrington was, and more pessimistic about its actual state. The third earl of Shaftesbury, I suggest, was just such an Englishman.

In the four decades or so that elapsed between the publication of *Oceana* and the first appearance of Shaftesbury's work, much happened to the problems facing classical republicans and to the doctrines they produced in response. Harrington, like Hobbes, had been strongly anticlerical, and republican anticlericalism persisted, but the understanding

16   The late Harringtonian Neville discusses the need for law enforcement and has altogether a more "realistic" picture of the daily problems of the state. But then he is analyzing contemporary England, not portraying an ideal. See *Plato Redivivus*, ed. Robbins, p. 125.

17   Pocock 1985, p. 41.

of corruption took on new forms and became more important. Corruption came to be thought of as stemming not from landlessness or maldistribution of land, but from commerce, the wealth it engendered, and the elaborate culture that wealth made possible. Commerce and culture both seemed a threat to the austerity in which the virtuous citizens of a republic must live. Neville's *Plato Redivivus* was the most notable production of the neo-Harringtonian school.[18] In it Neville makes numerous changes in Harrington's doctrines, but like his friend and master he omits any discussion of the psychology of the individual, and still thinks of the structure of the commonwealth as essentially determining the individual character of its citizens.

To see the place Shaftesbury had in this discussion we must look away from arguments and toward facts for a moment. Shaftesbury's grandfather, the first earl, was a major figure in post-Restoration politics, whose views importantly involved the reformulation of Harringtonian principles so they could address the problems of his own times.[19] He was also the patron of John Locke, by whom our Shaftesbury was tutored. In the 1690s the younger man's relations with Locke were still cordial, but Shaftesbury was developing views on morality and religion that were not consonant with Locke's. Locke, we know, saw morality as necessarily backed by threats of punishment and offers of reward, and as originating in God's will. Shaftesbury was reading the Cambridge Platonists, who strongly attacked voluntarism and who held that our natural love of others makes virtue inherently so pleasant to us that no sanctions for it are needed. His own earliest publication was a selection of sermons by the leader of the Platonists, Benjamin Whichcote, with a preface stressing the importance of love in Whichcote's position and attacking Hobbes.[20]

Shaftesbury was associated with the politically and intellectually active gentlemen gathered around Viscount Molesworth, a group that was the center of post-Harringtonian republican or, as it was also called,

18   Pocock 1975, p. 417.

19   See Pocock's introduction to Harrington's *Works*, pp. 129, 132–3.

20   Voitle 1984, p. 119, shows that Shaftesbury eventually took a strong stand against Locke's views on morality. He cites a letter of 1709 from Shaftesbury to a younger friend: "'twas Mr. Locke that struck the home Blow (for Mr. Hobb's character and base slavish principles in Government took off the poison of his Philosophy). 'Twas Mr. Lock that struck at all Fundamentals, threw all Order and Virtue out of the world, and made the very ideas of these . . . *unnatural* and without foundation in our minds." There seems to be no hard evidence showing exactly when this break with Locke became definite in Shaftesbury's mind; but it must have at least begun to take shape during the period when he was writing the *Inquiry concerning Virtue or Merit* – that is, in the later years of the 1690s.

commonwealth thinking.[21] He admired Molesworth, and as Molesworth was advocating a strongly republican political program for contemporary England, his company would have reinforced Shaftesbury's opposition to the kind of natural law theory that was central to Locke.[22] In politics during this period he thought of himself as a commonwealthman or republican and, his biographer tells us, so he remained until his death.[23]

Shaftesbury's first independent book, the *Inquiry concerning Virtue, or Merit*, was initially published in 1699 in a version edited by John Toland. Toland, who was also a member, or at least a hanger-on, of the Molesworth circle, sympathetic to commonwealth thought, produced, among many other things, an edition of Harrington's works. Shaftesbury's son claimed that he was not authorized to print the *Inquiry*, and it is true that Shaftesbury himself later repudiated the edition.[24] But it is not clear that it was unauthorized at the time it was published. Some evidence suggests that Shaftesbury may have encouraged Toland's publication of the *Inquiry*; as much as six years later he was urging that a French translation be made from that version.[25] It thus seems possible

21   See Robbins 1959, ch. 4, esp. pp. 125ff. See also Voitle 1984, pp. 70–1, who says that Shaftesbury associated with the Old or Country Whigs, especially those who admired Harrington and Neville, and that when young he probably knew Walter Moyle and Charles Davenant; "his closest friends among the group were . . . Molesworth . . . and Toland." For more details, see Worden 1978, pp. 28–9, 40ff. My attention was drawn to Worden by Sullivan 1982.

22   In a letter of 1709 to Molesworth, published in *Letters from the Right Honourable the late Earl of Shaftesbury to Robert Molesworth, Esq.* (London, 1721), Shaftesbury says: "You have long had my heart, even before I knew you personally" (Letter 8, p. 26). What he admired was Molesworth's very republican analysis of the politics of Denmark, *An Account of Denmark* (1694). Because of that book, Shaftesbury says, Molesworth became "my Oracle in publick affairs," and in the letters he treats him as his adviser on private matters. See also the introduction to Worden 1978, p. 40; and Voitle 1984, pp. 118–21. For an interpretation of Shaftesbury as a political writer, see Klein 1993. Klein sees Shaftesbury as starting from a Harringtonian orientation but moving away from it. He bases his reading on essays written after the *Inquiry* (p. 285), which was, however, the main theoretical work.

23   Voitle 1984, pp. 206, 236. For a good brief account of republican thought and activity at the end of the seventeenth century see Goldsmith 1985, pp. 4–21.

24   See *Characteristics* II.273–4, and the title page of the *Inquiry* given at I.235. Citations from the *Inquiry* are from the first volume of *Characteristics*, edited by Robertson.

25   Worden 1978, p. 44 and n. 192. Champion 1992, p. 214, describes a more mixed reaction on Shaftesbury's part. Allowing that the author tried to have a French translation made from it, he notes that Shaftesbury tried to purchase and destroy all the printed copies. The *Inquiry* is strongly opposed to Locke's views of morality, and

that Toland and republican circles more generally might have thought that Shaftesbury's *Inquiry* would be a valuable addition to their armory. The philosophy itself suggests that Shaftesbury thought so as well. We must go round about in order to see just how.

v. *The diversity of the passions*

Shaftesbury had more than politics in mind when he wrote the *Inquiry*. He had it in mind to provide an answer to skepticism about morality and to construct some weapons for a battle against certain kinds of religion.[26] These two enterprises are linked to his political concerns, and his approach to all of them is importantly conditioned by his understanding of the problem of imposing order on the passions.

The main modern European line of thought about the passions up to Shaftesbury was a Socratic or neo-Stoic view. In one way or another, it is central to the moral psychologies of Spinoza, Malebranche, and Leibniz. The intellect represents something as a good that an agent might attain, thereby awakening or calling into action a desire. Philosophers of this persuasion differed, not surprisingly, about the goods that reason represents. They agreed, however, that if the good thus presented is greater than any other the agent calls to mind, the agent will pursue it. Agents may, of course, be mistaken in thinking something a good, but they will pursue illusory goods with as much intensity as real ones because it is belief that dictates behavior, not truth as such.

Hobbes worked out an alternative to this Stoic approach to the passions. For him, as we have seen, desires and impulses do not respond to perceived good. Rather they are the sources of good in the world. In themselves, desires and passions are simply forces moving us toward or away from one thing or another. Although caused or elicited by thoughts about such things, they are themselves nonrepresentational. We call the objects toward or away from which they move us good or evil; but those predicates result from, and do not explain, our desires. Hobbes was strongly inclined to think, moreover, that our passions are directed at self-aggrandizing ends. He consequently saw no way of bringing them under control internally. Only an external power could be a sufficiently credible threat to our lives to cause us to bridle them. For the Socratic theorists, on the contrary, since the passions are essentially representations of goods and ills, improvement in belief necessarily brings improvement in desire. We can come to see our own good

Locke was, of course, still alive and well in 1699. It is worth adding that it was Toland who published Shaftesbury's letters to Molesworth, cited in note 22.

26   On Shaftesbury's place in the anticlerical battles of the period, which were not reducible to antireligious struggle, see Champion 1992, esp. ch.7.

in the good of others, and by enjoying their perfection for its own sake we become less self-interested. Internal control of the passions is thus possible: what is needed is simply knowledge of the outcomes of yielding to different desires.

Locke took a Socratic line about desire in the first edition of the *Essay*. The will, or preference, he there says, is determined by belief about what is good. "Good, then," he says, italicizing the whole sentence, "the greater Good is that alone which determines the will" (*ECHU* II.xxi.29 of the first edition, in the footnote on pp. 248–51). I pointed out in Chapter 8.ii that he changed his mind for the second edition (1694). The changes show his acceptance of the Hobbesian view that desires are wholly nonrepresentational urges or forces. But he went beyond Hobbes in breaking the tie between desire and good. As I have indicated, Locke thinks that the good is the cause of pleasure. But it is present felt uneasiness, not the prospect of future good, that Locke thinks determines the will. We feel uneasiness in proportion to the amount of the pain of an evil, and so we always desire to avoid it. But we do not feel an uneasiness about an absent good that is proportionate to the amount of good or pleasure it promises. Locke thus does not follow Hobbes in holding that to be good is simply to be the object of desire. We may simply not care for, or may not desire, some goods that we could obtain and would enjoy. The passions and desires urge us on regardless of our judgments of good, and their different strengths are shown in the different degrees of uneasiness each of us feels at the thought of various absent goods (*ECHU* II.xxi.29–46, 54–7). The amount of uneasiness we may feel concerning any absent good is moreover idiosyncratic. What moves me may not move you; I may take as a part of my happiness some good to which you are quite indifferent. (And, as I noted, this is why Locke thinks it pointless to seek a common summum bonum.) But because we inevitably try to avoid evils, we can be controlled by threats of punishment; and, as we have seen, it is such threats that Locke relies on to move us to obey the laws of morality.

Shaftesbury's theory of the passions develops out of Locke's. He agrees that there is no single common factor that explains the origin and strength of our desires. There is also no common factor in their objects. Spontaneous desires are at work in all animals, some of them helping the animal itself, some helping or harming other members of its species, still others beneficial or detrimental to different kinds of sentient creatures. Rational agents are moved not only by "sensible objects," as brutes are; they can be moved by "rational objects," by abstract concepts of the good of the species, or of "justice, generosity, gratitude, or other virtue" (*Inquiry*, pp. 255–6, 259–60). Shaftesbury thus stresses the multiplicity and variety of our motives. Does interest alone explain our action? No, he says, if you look you will see that "passion, humour, caprice, zeal, faction and a thousand other springs, which are counter to self-interest, have as considerable a part" (*Characteristics* I.77). The theory that we all pursue our interest, or our pleasure, or our happiness, tells us nothing unless it also tells us where we find our interest or happiness or pleasure. To say that the diligent student or devoted artist is as much in pursuit of pleasure as the debauched gambler is to misuse language (*Characteristics* II.32–3):

> [W]hen will and pleasure are synonymous; when everything which pleases us is called pleasure, and we never choose or prefer but as we please; 'tis trifling to say "Pleasure is our good." For this has as little meaning as to say, "We choose what we think eligible"; and "We are pleased with what delights or pleases us." (*Characteristics* II.29; cf. I.80–1, 83–4)

If the passions have neither common source nor common object, how are they to be controlled?

vi. *Moral feeling, voluntarism, and skepticism*

Hobbes took our overriding fear of death to impose some order on our passions. For Leibniz, the objective amounts of perfection provide for inner order. The will is itself only a general desire for the greatest good or perfection. It can therefore move us by weighing our different desires, or representations of perfection. But no positive ordering principle seems available for the Lockean inner world. The Lockean will, though an active power different from motives, has no rational ordering principle of its own. The strengths of uneasinesses or desires are not necessarily proportional to the amounts of good in the ideas that cause them. The springs of action are thus nonrational; and all the will does is to give the uneasinesses time to fight it out.

In his ethics Locke invokes God's laws backed by threats of punishment and reward to produce more order in human affairs than civil laws and a concern for public opinion can create. Aside from its unpalatable implications for religion and human relations, it is not clear that this can work for Locke. Distance in time weakens the present uneasiness caused by threats (*ECHU* II.xxi.63, p. 275); and plainly people are not strongly moved by the promise of heavenly rewards. Locke devotes much space to warning us about the dangers of miscalculation in deliberating about what to do. But he never explains what moves us to suspend action and deliberate.[27] And he does not tell us how we can

---

27 Leibniz criticized him for this in *New Essays* II.21.47. Collins 1717, p. 39, makes the same point: "suspending to will, is itself an act of willing: it is willing to

bring ourselves to feel a dominant uneasiness in the absence of our greatest good once we see where that is. If he is right, personal order as well as social stability seems to be attainable only through some sort of external pressure. It is understandable that later thinkers, even if they accepted much of Lockeanism, should have sought to explain human action in ways that show how we can ourselves control what we do.

Shaftesbury is the first major thinker to try to do so. Influenced by Whichcote as well as by Harrington, Shaftesbury detested Locke's insistence on the need for control by sanction-backed laws. Nonetheless, he makes the Lockean view of the passions central to his whole outlook and uses it to construct a new understanding of morality. Part of what enables him to do so is his insistence that there are generous passions within us, desires for the good of others that are wholly self-oblivious. The other major element in his theory is his view of the moral faculty, which he sometimes calls the moral sense.[28]

defer willing about the matter proposed." The objection still seemed worth making to Priestley in 1777: "a determination to suspend a volition is in fact another volition, and therefore, according to Mr. Locke's own rule, must be determined by the most pressing uneasiness." Priestly, *The Doctrine of Philosophical Necessity Illustrated* 1777, sec. I, p. 57.

28 E.g., at *Inquiry*, p. 262. The corresponding passage of the 1699 edition does not contain the phrase.

Shaftesbury was not the first to suggest that a special sense is what enables us to make moral distinctions. Thomas Burnet does so in his first *Remarks* on Locke (1697). He fails to find, he says, that the distinction between good and evil or virtue and vice is made by the usual five senses. If the distinction is a delusion, it is one he cannot shake off. And he continues: "This I am sure of, that the Distinction, suppose of gratitude and ingratitude . . . is as sudden without any Ratiocination, and as sensible and piercing, as the difference I feel from the Scent of a Rose, and of Assa-foetida. 'Tis not like a Theorem, which we come to know by the help of precedent Demonstrations and Postulatums, but it rises as quick as any of our Passions, or as laughter at the sight of a ridiculous accident or object" (pp. 4–5). See Tuveson 1960, ch. 2, who draws attention to an interesting passage in the *Third Remarks* in which Burnet argues that we all possess "a principle of distinguishing one thing from another in Moral Cases, without Ratiocination" which he compares to our ability to distinguish colors. Burnet makes it clear that he does not think moral good and evil can be understood in terms of natural good and evil. "This inward Sense . . . ," he says, "is simple and irrespective as to those Natural Evils or Goods, They are not its proper Objects." His claim is that a principle of this sort is "seated in the Soul of Man, as other original Principles are" and like them it develops as we mature (pp. 7–9). Burnet allows that the principle may fail to develop fully, or be dimmed in some people; but the same is true, he holds, of the truths of Christianity, so that if Locke adduces these facts against the belief in a natural conscience, he must let them stand against religious belief as well.

Tuveson takes Burnet to be the originator of the idea of the moral sense in ethics.

Shaftesbury draws a sharp distinction between two kinds of judgments we make about the goodness of active beings. There are living creatures whose passions and affections lead them to act in ways that tend directly to bring about some good either for themselves or for others. We call these creatures "good" when they bring about good to others because of a direct disposition to do so, rather than incidentally or as a by-product of seeking their own good.[29] We attribute a quite different kind of goodness to beings able to reflect on the affections they find within themselves and to form rational objects of affection, in particular those concerned with the good of others. Reflection on such affections, Shaftesbury says, gives rise to "another kind of affection towards those very affections themselves, which have been already felt, and are now become the subject of a new liking or dislike" (*Inquiry*, p. 251). This new liking or disliking is moral approval and disapproval. Only beings capable of having this reflective feeling can be virtuous or vicious.[30]

That the moral faculty gives us a feeling, on Shaftesbury's view, is quite clear. It is however a special kind of feeling, and not only because of its felt quality (about which Shaftesbury says little). It is special because through it we become aware of an objective order. The object of the moral feeling is passions and desires – our own, or those of others, which Shaftesbury assumes we have no difficulty in knowing. Moral feeling concerns the whole set of someone's active impulses. It approves some such sets and disapproves others. The approval and disapproval themselves are feelings, but they reveal that the set of passions being considered either is or is not harmonious. " 'Tis a due sentiment of morals," Shaftesbury says, "which alone can make us knowing in order and proportion, and give us the just tone and measure of human passion" (*Characteristics* I.181).

The two aspects of moral sentiment – its objectivity as revealing harmony, its subjectivity as feeling – enable Shaftesbury to cope with

Shaftesbury might well have read the first two pamphlets prior to working out his *Inquiry* but the third pamphlet appeared in the same year. But he also, of course, knew the work of the Cambridge Platonists, and would have noticed More's "boniform faculty" as well as Whichcote's claim that everyone has a "sense of good and evil, upon a moral account," discussed in Chapter 10.i and iii.

29   With Cumberland and Pufendorf, Shaftesbury holds that there is an objective natural good for each kind of creature, something that benefits them as they are naturally constituted (*Inquiry*, p. 243).

30   The reflexive nature of moral approval calls to mind Cudworth's ruling power, the "hegemonicon . . . redoubled upon itself" which is essential to our moral agency (Chapter 10.v). But the work of Cudworth's in which this view appeared was not published until the nineteenth century.

what he sees as two major threats to stability and decency in society, enthusiasm and skepticism.[31]

The worst enthusiasm, in Shaftesbury's view, is voluntarism in religion. Calvinist religion, which is Shaftesbury's main target, is as lacking in measure and order as the will of its deity. Its voluntarism makes it impossible for us to think of God in moral terms. In direct opposition to Locke, Shaftesbury tells us that anyone who believes in a just and good God "must suppose that there is independently such a thing as justice and injustice, . . . right and wrong . . . If the mere will, decree, or law of God be said absolutely to constitute right and wrong, then are these latter words of no significancy at all" (*Inquiry*, p. 264). To deny this is to give oneself the liberty to say that it is perfectly just to make one person suffer for someone else's fault, or arbitrarily to assign some people to eternal torment and others to bliss. The worship of a deity of that sort, Shaftesbury adds, is bound to be harmful to one's character. Worshiping any intelligent being who is not necessarily good is worshiping a demon, not a God (p. 241).[32] Leibniz's kind of objection to voluntarism is here given a more passionate, as well as an anti-Christian, expression.[33]

Shaftesbury repeatedly points to an analogy between moral distinctions and our judgments of the arts. His appeal is to our own experience. We all agree, he thinks, that "harmony is harmony by nature," even if people make absurd judgments about, say, music, or architecture. " 'Tis the same case where life and manners are concerned. Virtue has the same fixed standard" (*Characteristics* I.227–8). The mind "feels . . . the agreeable and disagreeable in the affections; and finds . . . a harmonious and a dissonant" as truly there as in music (*Inquiry*, p. 251). The undeniable reality of harmony undercuts voluntarist views of God and morality. And Shaftesbury, unlike the teachers of this sort of religion, has no need to set himself up as an authority in such matters. Just

31   One of the two main interlocutors in *The Moralists*, beginning as an avowed skeptic, comes to share the vision of self propounded rhapsodically by the other; and in the comments on this essay in the *Miscellaneous Reflections*, Shaftesbury carefully points out that the former is a skeptic while the latter "passes for an enthusiast" (*Characteristics* II.334n, and cf. p. 24).

32   Shaftesbury's own account of what it takes for a being to have moral attributes implies that the voluntarist's God cannot have any. For the voluntarist, God merely acts, and what he does is good. He cannot therefore be acting in order to bring good to us. Moreover since he merely acts in a way that turns out to be for our good, but does not reflect on his desire to do so and act because he finds it approvable, his is not moral action. To act this way is to act the way a naturally docile mule acts. We may be glad to own one, but we do not praise its virtue (*Inquiry*, pp. 249–50).

33   Leibniz admired Shaftesbury's work, with some reservations: see his 1712 "Remarks on the . . . *Characteristics*," in *Papers*, ed. Loemker, esp. pp. 632–3.

as we grasp aesthetic harmony through an inner feeling, so are we all able to judge alleged religious dictates by our moral feelings. Shaftesbury thus agrees with Bayle (whom he knew and admired) in holding that no command to do anything immoral could come from God. Conscience, if it is anything, is moral sentiment: "to have awe and terror of the Deity does not, of itself, imply conscience" (*Inquiry*, p. 305). God, therefore, can do no evil. Moreover, if we believe in God we cannot think there is any real evil in the world. Leibniz was not the only optimist.

If the reality shown to us by our awareness of harmony undercuts voluntaristic religious enthusiasm, our ability to discover harmony through feeling helps Shaftesbury respond to moral skepticism. It does so because it means that we need not look outside ourselves to find moral order. Moral feeling tells us whether our passions are harmonious or not, and we can understand right and wrong action as deriving from that harmony or disharmony.

> Whatsoever is done through any unequal affection is iniquitous, wicked and wrong . . . For wrong is not such action as is barely the cause of harm . . . but when anything is done through insufficient or unequal affection (as when a son shows no concern for the safety of a father; or, where there is need of succor, prefers an indifferent person to him) this is of the nature of wrong. (*Inquiry*, p. 253)

Harrington's thought that virtuous action is action motivated by "reason" or a concern for public good is here put to a new use. By making morality center on feelings assessing feelings, Shaftesbury obtains a way to reply to the Pyrrhonian skeptic. In moral judgment we judge an inner condition by an inner faculty, which everyone possesses. Neither of these is open to any variety of skeptical doubt. "Let us carry skepticism ever so far, let us doubt, if we can, of everything about us," Shaftesbury exclaims:

> [W]e cannot doubt of what passes in ourselves. Our passions and affections are known to us. They are certain, whatever the objects may be on which they are employed. Nor is it of any concern to our argument how these exterior objects stand: whether they are realities or mere illusions; whether we wake or dream. (*Inquiry*, pp. 336–7)[34]

Moral skepticism is not refuted by arguments showing that we do know the moral laws or the perfections of the universe. Nor is moral skepticism evaded by being insulated from real life and ignored for

---

34   And see *Inquiry* p. 260: "If there be no real amiableness or deformity in moral acts, there is at least an imaginary one of full force."

practical purposes.[35] It is rather neutralized by accepting that even if all we have, in morality, are appearances, the appearances suffice.

Or at least they might. Shaftesbury in fact leaves the door open to skepticism by insisting that the capacity to appreciate moral harmony is as much in need of education or training as the capacity for aesthetic judgment. Nature has happily enabled some people to act and feel with grace and harmony even though they have had only the rudest of upbringing. "'Tis undeniable, however, that the perfection of grace and comeliness in action and behaviour can be found only among people of a liberal education" (*Characteristics* I.125; cf. II.129). Shaftesbury must thus think of himself as an educated writer educating the sentiments of others, lessening the danger that their feelings will miss the mark. Moral and aesthetic feeling can fail to reveal objective harmonies. But Shaftesbury does not worry about the possibility of skepticism that seems to loom here. To allow that one might be mistaken is, after all, only to refuse to be a dogmatist. Shaftesbury reminds us that even St. Paul refused to dogmatize about his vision of Christ; and we can live with less than demonstrative certainty in moral matters (II.201–3).

Acts are not right, then, for Shaftesbury, because they are in compliance with anyone's commands. They are not inherently right or wrong, and they are not made right by bringing about the greatest amount of perfection. The moral quality of actions depends on whether the set of passions that leads the agent to do them is morally approved or disapproved. The virtuous agent is the agent whose character elicits moral approval, and the right act is simply the act the virtuous agent does.

Shaftesbury thus presents at least the rudiments of what might be called a method of ethics. It is not what Sidgwick thought a method had to be – a rational procedure by which we determine what it is right for an individual to do or what an individual ought to do.[36] But it is a regular procedure, and it is presented as one that can in principle be used by everyone. The importance of procedure in his theory makes Shaftesbury's view a new departure in the history of ethics. It is not the strengths or objects of our desires that make us virtuous in acting as they urge. It is their constituting a harmonious whole, as shown by reflection. The moral sense, when well educated, does indeed reveal objective harmony to us. But our moral assessments do not derive from our possession of objective knowledge. They come from the procedure of reflecting on our own direct desires and passions and noticing the special feeling we obtain from such reflection. We are virtuous if our passions move us only when we are aware that they have passed the

35 Burnyeat 1984, pp. 225–32; cf. Burnyeat 1980.
36 Sidgwick 1907, p. 1. For discussion, see Schneewind 1977, pp. 198–204.

test of feeling. Only our own feelings can do the job. When we are virtuous, we are self-governed.

vii. *Virtue, happiness, and the complete citizen*

Shaftesbury's realization that an anti-Stoic theory of the passions requires a new kind of theory of assessment of the passions makes possible for him a new way of handling the age-old question of whether the virtuous agent is also the happy agent. The question is raised in the second part of the *Inquiry*. Having shown us what virtue is in itself – acting from passions which as a group embody a harmony approved by the moral sentiment – he asks "what obligation there is to virtue, or what reason to embrace it" (*Inquiry*, p. 280).[37] He argues, in a Platonic manner, that only inner harmony brings happiness. The particular mixture of passions from the overall gratification of which we obtain most happiness is the mixture approved by the moral feeling as harmonious. The motive or obligation to be virtuous is therefore not external to virtue but arises from within it. The virtuous balance is additionally one in which generous and benevolent desires are dominant. Because the obligation or reason to embrace virtue is that we will be happiest if we do so, and the balance of motives approved by the moral sense is also that which contributes most to the well-being of others, there is no real conflict between private and public interest. No sanctions are needed to bring about this congruence. It is due to the way our psyches are constituted.[38]

Here is the psychology for a classical republic. Self-interest has a proper place among our passions, when it is neither too strong nor, as it might well be, too weak. But we find our greatest joy in acting from concerns for the well-being of others. Shaftesbury, consequently, does not see society as principally engaged in keeping the peace among individuals in conflict with each other in pursuit of their private good, and secondarily seeking to help the needy.[39] Perhaps as a result, he has

37 See Darwall 1995, ch. 7, for a full discussion.

38 Shaftesbury's views here echo Bacon, who holds, as Hooker also did, that everything has a double nature: "the one, as every thing is a total or substantive in itself; the other, as it is a part or member of a greater body." We can see this in natural objects but "this double nature of good . . . is much more engraven upon man, if he degenerate not; unto whom the conservation of the duty to the public ought to be much more precious than the conservation of life and being." *Advancement of Learning*, in *Works*, I.III, p. 313.

39 In fact he sees our sociable instinct as itself responsible for the factions out of which socially pertinent conflict arises: selfish men do not throw themselves wholeheartedly into political parties. The Grotian problematic, he seems to be saying, is

little or nothing to say of justice, though he speaks of it occasionally; and he does not mention law or rights at all. The Grotian problematic of controversy and strife has no place here.

A well-ordered republic of different but harmoniously self-ordered parts is, at the social level, what the well-ordered virtuous agent is at the personal level. Shaftesbury does not think it easy to attain either kind of order. As individuals we are ourselves parts of nature, governed by "Humour and Fancy" or by our strongest passions (cf. *Characteristics* I.122–3). Buffeted and driven in every direction, we must, he says, "hold our fancies under some kind of discipline" or be literally insane. We are rational only insofar as such control exists (I. 208ff.). What can provide it? Shaftesbury says at one point that it is philosophy:

> 'tis the known province of philosophy to teach us ourselves, keep us the self-same person, and so regulate our governing fancies, passions, and humours, as to make us comprehensible to ourselves and knowable by other features than those of a bare countenance. (I.184)

But it is not Locke's kind of philosophy that does this – not one that leads us to spend time simply analyzing ideas. It is a philosophy that reminds us rather of Montaigne, a philosophy that shows me whether I can keep my approvals constant and bring myself to esteem the same things from one time to another (I.194). It is the philosophy that reveals my moral faculty to me and teaches me that it is the part of myself through which self-control and with it a unified self become possible.[40]

The parallel between morality and taste emerges clearly in this connection. Virtuous agents try to shape themselves so that their inner lives will have the kind of harmony that wins moral approval. Within ourselves, we are active insofar as the mind "superintends and manages its own imaginations, appearances, fancies . . . modelling these as it finds good" (II.103). The moral feeling is what enables us to unify our complex and changing affections. By responding to it, each of us can be an artist of the most important sort – not one working on stone or paint, but one working on a soul or mind. The wise man, Shaftesbury says, "becomes the architect of his own life and fortune, by laying within himself the lasting and sure foundations of order, peace and concord" (II.144).

simply a result of "the abuse or irregularity of that social love . . . which is natural to mankind" (*Characteristics* I.77). As such it is just one more illustration of the lack of balance in the passions which the moral feeling detects.

40   Shaftesbury's interest in this issue is evident in several places: see *Characteristics* I.112–13, 119–21 for concerns about unity of the self, and II.99–105, for exploration of the notion of unity more generally. See also Rand's *Life* for many personal thoughts on the subject.

The moral faculty that enables us to become self-governed by achieving a unified self is for Shaftesbury different in kind from the ability to think about personal happiness or our own greatest good. Moral judgment concerns the harmony of our passions. Judgments about happiness have a different subject matter. They concern how much we will enjoy life. Moral judgment is superior to prudential judgment. You cannot be virtuous if you act from a motive out of harmony with the rest of your soul, no matter how much you might think you would enjoy doing so. This is not because moral judgment is working on the same question as prudential and coming up with a more accurate, because more comprehensive, answer. As in Malebranche, the two are conceptually distinct. But in telling us which passions we may gratify, morally speaking, the moral sense is also showing us how to become one person rather than a bundle of conflicting passions

Is Shaftesbury here betraying his own conviction that disinterested affection for the public good is required for virtue? Is he trying to bribe the reader into becoming virtuous, by showing that it pays? I think not. He is, rather, trying to show that the natural world – the realm in which the natural good of happiness exists – is such that it makes sense for us to act morally within it.

Shaftesbury's cheerful belief that the most virtuous inner harmony is also the most enjoyable life is of a piece with his belief that the universe itself is a harmonious whole, a harmonious system of harmonious systems. "Nothing indeed can be more melancholy," Shaftesbury says, "than the thought of living in a distracted universe," a world that would not cohere with our sentiments or, still worse, would be contrary to them. His point is not simply that we need to be rewarded for our virtue. It is that if our virtuous efforts seem to be in vain, we can get discouraged. The atheist can indeed be virtuous, but in hard circumstances he is apt to become disaffected and splenetic at the frustration of his virtuous efforts. The theist, however, believing that the universe backs his efforts, develops "the highest constancy in any state of sufferance" despite the hardships virtue may impose. If virtue were our natural ill, it would imply a "blot and imperfection in the general constitution of things." Hence virtue is complete only when it develops into piety; and the believer in a moral deity possesses a constancy and benignity that the atheist must lack (*Inquiry*, pp. 276–80). In the same way, the universe will be coherent only if virtue leads to happiness.

A neo-Harringtonian might plainly be tempted to adopt Shaftesbury's views. But there are important respects in which Shaftesbury differs considerably from the classical republicans. Despite his non-Stoic view of the passions, Shaftesbury's thought is Stoic in important respects. He detaches virtue from the agent's occupation, from the structure of his society, and to some extent from his material possessions.[41] The virtuous agent is not created by the political structure he inhabits. He brings his character to it. As a consequence of this and of the quasi-aesthetic nature of moral perception, the cultivation of the individual is of great importance for Shaftesbury. In essays other than the *Inquiry* Shaftesbury stresses the importance of freedom of thought and criticism in maintaining a free and nondespotic government.[42] He thinks that a vital role is played by literature in sustaining the questioning attitude toward authority which is essential to such a political system. In short, while Shaftesbury favors a classical republic, he certainly does not endorse rude simplicity or unpolished manners. He aims to capture the classical republic for high culture.

The Harringtonian republic would have a civic religion, which Shaftesbury's doctrine would endorse. Beyond that, it is not clear that the societies we could make for ourselves and the lives we could lead within them have any need of divine involvement. We need no commands, no histories, no divine voices to guide us. We are sustained by the belief in a well-ordered universe of the sort a benevolent deity would assure; but in a pinch we could do without it. Shaftesbury's virtue ethics has exactly the consequences that led Reid later to say that Christianity should teach an ethic of law and duty instead. It is no wonder that Shaftesbury was taken up so warmly by the Deists.

41 On this point there is a tension between the Stoic tendency in Shaftesbury, making the agent self-sufficient in his virtue, and the aesthetic tendency, for which the leisure to cultivate the moral sensibilities – and the wealth this implicitly supposes – is important for the achievement of complete virtue.

42 See particularly the *Essay on the Freedom of Wit and Humor,* and the *Soliloquy or Advice to an Author.*

15

The austerity of morals: Clarke and Mandeville

Attempts to avoid the morally unpalatable consequences of Locke's empiricist ethics were at the core of the development of British moral philosophy during much of the eighteenth century. Shaftesbury kept a deity in his universe to ensure its moral harmony, but he most emphatically held that there was no need to appeal to divine laws and threats to explain how people can live decently. He tried to show that Locke's voluntarist ethics is undercut by our possession of a moral faculty that enables us to govern ourselves. Desires and passions are, for him as for Locke, blind forces caused by, but not containing, representations of goods and ills. The moral faculty gives us a special feeling of moral approval that is aroused by a harmonious balance of the motivating forces in the soul and then in turn reinforces that balance. If this was a way around Locke, it posed problems even for those who shared Shaftesbury's moral revulsion at Locke's reductionist ethics of command, threat, and obedience. Shaftesbury sometimes presents the moral feeling as a mere sentiment, causally interacting with ideas and feelings; but more deeply and persistently he treats it as revealing eternal truths. The one reading points toward a naturalistic view of morals which the other reading denies. Theories of both kinds were proposed early in the century.

Samuel Clarke (1675–1729) shared with Shaftesbury a high estimate of human moral capacities, but he understood them in a diametrically opposed manner. He proposed a mathematical model of morals, in which rational cognition provides both guidance and motivation, and feeling is at most a hindrance to virtue. He gave a decisive place in our psychology to a strong conception of free will, for which Shaftesbury had no room. And although like Shaftesbury he opposed Calvinist voluntarism, he offered a defense, based on his moral theory, of far more of Christianity than Shaftesbury cared to advocate.[1]

---

1 Vols. III and IV of Clarke's works are largely taken up with theological debate.

An alternative way of avoiding a Lockean theory of morality was sketched, if not unambiguously advocated, by a thinker who had a very different opinion of human moral capacities. Bernard de Mandeville (1670–1733) had a view of what people are actually like that led him to think both Shaftesbury's noble sentiments and Clarke's rationality ludicrously inappropriate as sources of morality. He suggested instead that morality emerges as a human invention designed to protect us against the unbridled selfishness that dominates our nature while still leaving ample scope for the gratification of our desires. He and Clarke, along with Shaftesbury, set the terms for the next several decades of debate.

i. *Free will and reasons for action*

Clarke's Boyle lectures of 1704, on the existence and attributes of God, and those of 1705, on the obligations of natural religion, are explicitly aimed at Hobbes and Spinoza, whose materialism and necessitarianism amount, he insists, to atheism.[2] Clarke also seeks to go beyond Locke and Leibniz. He thinks both of them propose views of free will that do not enable us to defend human moral responsibility. And in different ways each of them opens the door to views of God that Clarke finds morally unacceptable. His first set of Boyle lectures provides the necessary metaphysical antidote to these errors.

Clarke begins by arguing that there must of necessity be one eternal, nonmaterial, unchanging, infinite being who is the cause of all other things and who himself is a self-activating agent. This being must be free, because "Intelligence without Liberty . . . is really . . . no Intelligence at all. It is indeed a Consciousness, but it is merely a Passive One; a Consciousness, not of Acting, but of being Acted upon" (Lectures I, IX, p. 548). God's freedom does not entail that his choices are arbitrary. They are constrained by a special kind of necessity arising from a

He was not orthodox in his views on the Trinity. Despite his brilliance and his excellent connections, his deviant views prevented him from achieving the bishopric, let alone archbishopric, that might otherwise have been his. See Ferguson 1976.

2   The first set of lectures is titled *A Discourse concerning the Being and Attributes of God*, the second *A Discourse concerning the Unchangeable Obligations of Natural Religion, and the Truth and Certainty of the Christian Revelation*. See Jacob 1976, Ch. 5, for general discussion of the European impact of the many series of lectures given on Boyle's endowment. Jacob stresses the extent to which the Boyle lecturers tried to put Newtonian science at the service of an inclusive conception of the requirements for membership in the English church.

The lectures are cited as Lectures I and Lectures II, with page references from volume 2 of Clarke's *Works*. Sermons are cited by number. Sermons I–CXIV are in volume 1 of *Works*, CXV–CLXXIII in volume 2.

unique sort of "fitness" which requires that things be as they are to preserve "the Beauty, Order, and Well-being of the Whole" (IX, p. 550). This is not an "absolute necessity" entailing that there is a contradiction in supposing the contrary (III, p. 528). Alternatives are conceivable even if unfit. To act as one does because the fitness of things makes such action necessary is "consistent with the greatest Freedom and most perfect Choice. For," Clarke continues, "the only Foundation of this Necessity, is such an unalterable Rectitude of Will, and Perfection of Wisdom, as makes it impossible for a Wise Being to resolve to Act foolishly; or for a Nature infinitely Good, to choose to do what is Evil" (IX, p. 551). Clarke in effect uses his idea of fitness to elaborate on Cumberland's way of explaining how there can be laws governing God even though God has no superior. (See Chapter 6.iv.)[3]

It is a mistake, Clarke holds, to base the view that liberty is a conceptual impossibility on the premise that every event, including volitions, must have a cause. Those who argue in this manner "ignorantly confound Moral Motives with Physical Efficients, between which Two things there is no manner of relation." Avoid this confusion, Clarke is saying, and you will see that choices made from motives are free, even though they are morally necessary (Lectures I, IX, p. 553).

So far, God's freedom: now for ours. God is proved to be omnipotent, and from this it follows that he can give creatures the power of initiating movement, or acting (Lectures I, X, p. 555). When we act, we experience ourselves as we would if we possessed the power of self-motion (X, pp. 557–8). This no more demonstrates that we actually have such a power than sensory experience proves the existence of an external world. But the bare possibility that we might be without the power, like the bare possibility that the material world might not exist, should worry no one.[4] Since the power of self-motion coupled with intelligence is liberty, Clarke thinks he has done enough to show that our wills are free. What remains is to dismiss arguments against it as all due to the "Fundamental Error" of failing to distinguish clearly between "moral Motives, and Causes Physically Efficient" (X, pp. 565ff.).

Clarke's treatment of morality shows that he considers motives to be

3   As Sharp 1912, p. 384, says, Clarke, in Lectures II, cites Cumberland for support more than any other modern moral philosopher. Although Clarke rejects Cumberland's naturalizing move, the affinities of their views are strong.

4   *Remarks upon a Book, entitled, A Philosophical Enquiry concerning Human Liberty*, 1717, in *Works* IV.734. Against Malebranche, Clarke simply points out, as Reid did later, that our possession of self-moving power does not make us independent of God. He freely gives us the power, and he can take it away. See Reid, *Active Powers* I.II, p. 517b: "All our power is, without doubt, derived from the Author of our being; and as he gave it freely, he may take it away when he will."

reasons, different in kind from felt desires and not dependent on them. God is guided by reasons given by his knowledge of certain self-evident axioms about the eternal fitnesses of things; we can and ought to be guided by them as well. Knowledge of the axioms, just as such, serves as a motive to us. We do not need additional considerations of punishment and reward to be moved to do what "right reason" moves us to do (Lectures II, I, p. 628). Thus the earlier argument to show that intelligence entails agency is transposed to human beings to support the claim that we can act from reasons arising not from desires but solely from knowledge of moral truths.

Clarke's liberty is not a Hobbesian absence of external impediments. We possess this liberty even in prison (Lectures I, X, p. 566). It is an inner power different in kind from desire. It is not an expresssion of a Cartesian will, which necessarily assents to clear and distinct representations and can choose only where there is confusion and indistinctness.[5] It is neither the Leibnizian tendency to seek the greatest perfection nor the Lockean ability to suspend action. What is it then? Clarke regrettably devotes more effort to refuting his opponents than to developing his own position. He is content to say that liberty consists in a person's "having a continual Power of choosing, whether he shall Act, or whether he shall forbear Acting." He does not tell us anything about how we choose whether to act or forbear. And he does not tell us how the motives constituted by our knowledge of eternal fitnesses relate to the urges and impulses due to our needs and desires. What he does make clear is that morality depends on our ability not only to have but also to be moved by knowledge of eternal truths. That ability is at the core of what he calls the "Power of Agency or Free Choice (for these are precisely Identical terms)" (X, p. 566).

In the phrase just quoted, Clarke makes what I believe is the first use of the term "agency" in its modern philosophical sense.[6] Bishop Bramhall, controverting Hobbes a half century earlier, had supported views like Clarke's.[7] But Clarke brings a new consideration into his defense of liberty. For Leibniz, desires can be controlled directly by reason because they are themselves implicitly rational. Lockean desires, as I explained in the previous chapter, are not themselves inherently rational and

5 Assent to truth is a passive operation of the understanding, Clarke says, and it does not "determine" the active power. See *Works* IV.716–18, 722–3.

6 The *Oxford English Dictionary* shows only one earlier use, in 1658, which is not clearly a philosophical one. It then gives a citation from Jonathan Edwards dated 1762, although Berkeley, Hume, and Price had all previously used the term. In 1731 Edmund Law, referring to Clarke, described the word as "generally including the power of beginning Thought as well as Motion" (King, *Essay*, p. 156n).

7 See John Bramhall, *A Defense of True Liberty* (1655), in his *Works*.

cannot be directly controlled by reason. Clarke agrees with Locke on this point. Leibniz and Locke think of the will as determined by the strength of various desires. Clarke does not mention strength when he speaks of moral motives and the kind of necessity they involve. Moral motives are the wrong kind of thing to have that sort of property.[8] Pufendorf held a similar view about his moral entities; but although Pufendorf saw the pertinence of distinguishing between reasons and causes to the issue of free will (Chapter 7.v), Clarke seems a little clearer in using such a distinction in his argument. Knowledge of moral axioms and the desire for happiness are incommensurable, yet both enter into explanations of our action. Strength of desire is one kind of determinant of action. Knowledge of normative truth must be a different kind, playing a unique role in our decisions. We experience ourselves as deciding which of these incommensurable kinds of consideration to follow. More clearly than Pufendorf, Clarke sees free agency as providing the only possible explanation of how we can do so.[9]

ii. *Mathematical morality*

Clarke grounds the morality from which we derive distinctive reasons for action in a doctrine of "necessary and eternal" relations of things to one another, which he puts in terms of "the fitness or unfitness of the application of different things or different relations one to another." Whatever the fitnesses are – I return to this later – God knows them. His will necessarily *does* determine itself in accordance with them, and our wills *ought* to determine themselves by them as well (Lectures II, I, p. 608). Clarke does not say whether he intends this as a definition of "ought," but it plays the role of one in his theory. His only argument for it seems to rest on the claim that we were made in God's likeness. Since God, who has no superior, obliges himself to conform to the fitnesses, it is "very evident" that we should do so as well (I, p. 612). God's self-governance is thus the model for our own. This point, like all the rest of Clarke's theory, supposes that we cannot deny the existence of the eternal fitnesses themselves.

___

8   See, e.g., *Works* IV.723, 734.

9   The sixteenth-century Jesuit Luis Molina, trying to resolve the intricate issues concerning the respective parts played by God's grace and human choice in determining salvation, offered a careful analysis of human freedom. One kind of freedom is that which belongs to the human will: a man is free who "given everything that is required for him to act, is able to act, and is able not to act, or is able to do one thing in such a way that he is equally able to do the opposite" (cited in Abercrombie, p. 94). I do not know whether Clarke knew Molina's ideas; but Molinism was widely debated in the seventeenth century.

Locke promised a science of morality as demonstrable as mathematics; Clarke tries to give at least its rudiments. Like Whichcote he thinks that "In *Morality* we are as sure as in Mathematics" (Patrides, p. 330). But he does not simply ask us to allow that it is obvious that people should help one another. What he thinks obvious always involves comparisons couched in moral terms. Thus he says that it is obvious that it is more fit to help others than to harm them at random. This is as obvious as that the whole is greater than its parts. It is obviously more fit that the Creator should direct all things to constant ends than that he should allow things to "go on at adventures," producing complete confusion; and it is more fit, even before "positive bargains" (a slap at Hobbes), that people should fulfill contracts and act justly than that people should pursue their own advantage without scruples (Lectures II, I, p. 608–9). The comparisons presuppose, of course, that the reader is willing to think in terms of what is more or less fitting. Once Clarke has that much in hand, it is plausible for him to say that "nothing but the extremest stupidity of mind, corruption of manners, or perversion of spirit, can possibly make any man entertain the least doubt" that there are the specific fitnesses he adduces (I, p. 609).

From these comparative fitnesses Clarke thinks himself entitled to conclude that some things are in themselves fit and reasonable to be done. They do not receive their "obligatory power" from any external source, although penalties may be imposed upon those who will not comply without such threats (I, p. 611). The voluntarist theory of natural law is thus rejected. Sanctions have no role in obligating. Moral necessity arising from the rational justification of choice provided by the fitnesses is all the necessity needed to constitute obligation.

A look at the specific fitnesses Clarke thinks evident will show why he thinks we cannot rationally deny them. He accepts the traditional set of duties: to God, to self, and to neighbor. Since God is infinitely superior to us, we are to honor, worship, and serve him (I, p. 618). What Clarke calls our duty to ourselves is indeed a duty concerning ourselves – we are to preserve ourselves and keep ourselves ready to do whatever God requires of us – but it is owed to God. He "appointed us our station here," and we are to serve in it until called away by him (I, pp. 622–3). We have a twofold duty to our neighbor. First there is a duty of equity: we are to treat any other as we, if we were in like circumstances, "could reasonably expect he should deal with us." This is the principle underlying the virtue of justice, which is "the top and perfection of all the virtues" (I, pp. 621–2). The second branch of duty to neighbor is "universal love or benevolence." We are to go beyond doing "what is just and right," and are to try always to promote the welfare of all men, as far as it is in our power. The best way for us to comply with this requirement is to feel "universal love and benevolence" (I, p. 622).

Although Clarke separates moral necessity from absolute and from physical necessity, he gives us no account of its special nature. We can get some insight into what he has in mind, however, by taking the four basic fitnesses as making explicit what is implied in giving reasons to justify our actions. Clarke himself points in this direction: inequity, he says,

> is the very same in action, as . . . contradiction in theory; and the same cause which makes the one absurd, makes the other unreasonable. Whatever I judge reasonable or unreasonable for another to do to me; that, by the same judgment, I declare reasonable or unreasonable, that I in the like case should do for him. (I, p. 619)

Equity requires only consistency in bringing reasons to bear on cases. It is purely formal, saying nothing about what the agent takes or should take to be reasons for action. In seeing this eternal fitness, I am seeing that I am not allowed to count as a reason in one case what I deny to be a reason in a relevantly similar case. Here we have a principle for permissions that is missing from Leibniz.

The principle of benevolence tells us something about a substantive reason that we are to use. Given the way Clarke states the reason, we can see how he can present this eternal fitness as a conceptual truth. God sees, he says, that the goodness of some state of affairs is always a reason in favor of bringing it about, that its justificatory weight as a reason is proportionate to the amount of goodness involved, and that there is no other kind of substantive reason. We are to be as like God as we can. Then it would be self-contradictory to think it rational to bring about less good when one might bring about more. Clarke might also wish to argue that if I take the goodness of something I might obtain as a reason for acting to get it, then by the principle of equity a like good available to another provides a reason for me to try to obtain it for that other; but although there are later philosophers who take this line, there is nothing in his text to show that Clarke himself does.[10]

The eternal fitness of cultivating love derives from the moral necessity of doing what the greatest possible love would lead us to do.[11] Since love is required as a means, its fitness is an instance of what is involved in the eternal fitness of prudence: a requirement to avoid a contradiction involving reasons tied to ends. It is contradictory to have a reason to bring about some end and not to admit that one has reason

10   In the first edition of *The Methods of Ethics*, 1874, pp. 357–60, Sidgwick uses Clarke's statements of the principles of equity and benevolence to introduce his own versions of these two basic "axioms."

11   Clarke here lays the ground for a reformulation of the distinction between perfect and imperfect duties; but he never discusses them.

at least as strong to use or cultivate the means required to bring it about. Clarke assumes without argument that our loving others is the best means to bringing about everyone's good.

I believe we can see the eternal fitness of obeying and worshiping God as drawn, like the other fitnesses, from the nature of giving reasons, though my interpretation here is quite conjectural. If we agree that action ought to be guided by reasons, it seems self-contradictory to prefer less well grounded reasons to better reasons. But God knows the best reasons, and intends us to be directed by them. So it would be self-contradictory to claim to have reason not to follow his guidance. Moreover, it seems plausible to say that those who want to guide themselves by reason have reason to show gratitude to those who are unusually good at seeing the reasonable course of action and who share their insight. There would be something irrational in having reason to want to know the best reasons while not admiring those who could provide them. Granting this, then it would be self-contradictory to deny that God deserves the greatest admiration.

The fitnesses governing our duties to our neighbor sound very Cumberlandian. Every good gives a reason to act, and we are to maximize the amount we bring about. But where Cumberland claimed that his principle grounds a better method than Aristotle gave for individual decision making, Clarke sees a problem. "What is for the good of the whole creation, in very many cases, none but an infinite understanding can possibly judge. . . . But truth and right . . . is what every man can judge of, when laid before him." Here he seems to be saying that anyone can see the fitness in the particular case; but only God sees how individual actions fit into the larger scheme of things. We are to do as much good as we can in our "respective spheres" (Lectures II, II, p. 637), where we can understand how our action affects the natural good or ill of others. Presumably we are simply not to worry about ramifications beyond our grasp (cf. II, p. 630). Clarke does not bring God's will into his explanation of moral necessity; but God is essential to morality because he guarantees that our acting for the best reasons available to us will not turn out to have been unreasonable on the whole.

iii. *Morality and rational agency*

Moral necessity, then, is best understood as absolute or mathematical necessity in cases where the reasons for conclusions are reasons justifying action, not reasons grounding theoretical truth. Clarke's principles seem to be undeniable, as he says they are, once one gives the kind of rational justification of one's actions that he considers. To give any reason at all is to be committed to the principle of equity; to think that increasing the amount of good in the world is always a reason for action is to be committed to maximizing good results. Clarke does not explore the ways in which the two principles grounding duties to others might interact. But if he is not thorough in working out the details of his theory, he is at least securely in possession of the rudiments of an original position. His is not the rationalism of the continental perfectionists, for whom the rationality of morals was a matter of calculating the best results.[12] Nor is Clarke an "intuitionist" if by that term is meant one who holds that we just see a number of substantive moral principles to be true. But he is the first to claim that morality is based on principles that do no more than make explicit the formal requirement of consistency for anyone who gives and expects reasons.

Could we, then, escape the requirements of morality by refusing to give reasons for our actions? Clarke gives only the barest suggestion of an answer – but it is an intriguing one. The eternal fitnesses not only give us cognitive guidance. They also, Clarke holds, give us a motive for compliance. If we see the fitnesses plainly, we will acknowledge that they are "truly amiable" in themselves (Lectures II, I, pp. 627–8). Our own judgment of what is right, Clarke says, is "the truest and formallest obligation" and need not, at least in principle, be backed by sanctions (I, p. 614). Why is it that we are able to be moved by awareness of the fitness of things? In a sermon on the nature of human action, Clarke says that like the animals, humans are "self-acting" or initiators of their own motions. But man in addition can act for a foreseen end. What is more he must so act: "a man cannot indeed but have some view and design in everything he does. Even when he abandons himself most implicitly to the brutal guidance of mere appetite and passion, still he does it with some view" (Sermon XXXIX, p. 244). God made us rational agents, like himself. To be a rational agent is not only to be able to be moved by reasons; it is to be unable to escape being moved by reasons, at least to some extent. We pursue and must pursue what we think to be good; and if we justify our acts to ourselves by thinking of them as good, then we fall under the further demands of the eternal fitnesses, to which, as rational agents, we are able to respond.

Clarke is thus trying to think his way to the view that it is our rational agency as such that both makes moral principles binding on us and enables us to be moved by them. In doing so he runs afoul of a problem that he barely touches on. We can, regrettably, know what we ought to

12 The rationality of morality, and hence its necessity, is for Leibniz the rational necessity of using the means needed to bring about an end one necessarily has. Leibnizian "moral necessity" is always based on the principle of sufficient reason. We may think that refusing to use appropriate means to one's end is irrational in a formal way, perhaps even self-contradictory, but Leibniz did not explain the necessity in formal terms.

do and yet not do it. We cannot withhold assent to a "plain speculative truth" but we can refuse to will what we plainly see to be right (Lectures II, I, p. 613). Clarke contents himself with reiterating that we ought not to neglect our duties, and blaming our immorality on our corruption. If that hardly gives us a philosophically satisfying account of weakness of will, it is perhaps not much worse than Leibniz's way of explaining how we can see the better and do the worse – that we have subconscious perceptions of good that move us contrary to our best conscious thoughts about perfection.

iv. *Morality in the best possible world*

In some of his sermons Clarke presented serious philosophical discussions – not as densely packed as Butler's a generation later, but each containing a tightly reasoned examination of a topic with many theoretical ramifications, and only a minimum of edification. The motivation for some of the views Clarke defends in philosophy emerges very clearly in some of these discussions. One theme appears repeatedly: opposition to voluntarism. Clarke associates voluntarism with the Calvinist doctrines of "absolute Predestination and unconditionate Decrees" and holds that, in making God's goodness and justice different from ours, it makes him incomprehensible.[13] Clarke adds another complaint. Voluntarists place too much stress on the purely positive duties of religion, forgetting that "the end and design of all Religion . . . is the practice of virtue." Doctrine for Clarke, as for the Cambridge Platonists and for Shaftesbury, is to be judged by a moral test, and voluntarism fails (Sermon XL, pp. 250ff.; CX, p. 703).[14]

Clarke thus feels as strongly as Leibniz does a moral need to defeat and replace voluntarism, but he rejects Leibniz's way of doing so because of what he saw as defects in the Leibnizian account of freedom. Leibniz cannot really allow for the kind of freedom of choice that morality presupposes, Clarke thinks, because he leaves God no room for genuine rational choice. Leibniz's God is a spiritual automaton, as by his own admission we are. Clarke's innovations in what he sees as the structure of morality arise from his morally motivated abhorrence of voluntarism, together with his conviction that absolute freedom of will

---

13 Sermons X, XIV, and XVI contain these points as do many others.

14 Clarke was one of his generation's leaders among those defending a "latitudinarian" view of the Church of England, holding that it should set only minimal doctrinal standards for membership and should place little importance on theological disputes. See Gascoigne 1989, pp. 117–20, for a compact account of Clarke's place in Cambridge, which is indicative of his general standpoint.

is required if morality is to have purchase on us. He needs to show how God can have completely free choices that are yet not entirely arbitrary.

Although Clarke thinks that God must always do what is best and wisest on the whole (Lectures I, XII, pp. 573–4) his position about what is best is not Leibnizian. In his correspondence with Leibniz, Clarke in effect denies the principle of the identity of indiscernibles.[15] He is thus in a position to argue that even if God acts for the good, and indeed for the best, some things are in themselves indifferent. In such cases, Clarke says, God is surely not prevented from willing. Here his position is the same as Cumberland's (Chapter 6.iv); but it is Newton with whom he explicitly associates his views.[16] It is as a Newtonian that he asserts that God can place atoms and stars here rather than there in space, even though there be no reason to prefer any one location to another (LCCorr, pp. 20–1; 30–1). To argue as Leibniz does that there must always be a sufficient reason to determine the will and that "a mere will without any motive is a fiction" is to commit oneself to fatalism. It turns the will into a passive mechanism.

> But intelligent beings are agents; not passive, in being moved by the motives, as a balance is by weights; but they have active powers and do move themselves, sometimes upon the view of strong motives, sometimes upon weak ones, and sometimes where things are absolutely indifferent. (LCCorr, pp. 45, 51)

Now if God is a free agent who could have done something he did not do even if everything prior to his action were the same, is not his action arbitrary? It is to limit precisely this danger that Clarke introduces the principle of equity. As I noted earlier, it is a principle that in effect constrains what is morally permissible. It assures us that when God chooses among options all equally good, he cannot choose inequitably. If he gives a good to one person, he should give the same good to anyone else equally deserving. Souls might, for Clarke, be identical as far as their merit is concerned. The principle of equity says that God cannot justifiably save one soul that is wholly undeserving of salvation without saving others equally undeserving. The predestinarian Calvinism that Clarke so detested is thus ruled out. Leibniz himself rejected voluntarist predestinarianism (Theodicy, p. 328). But that did not prevent him from arguing that a world might be best in which many souls are eternally damned, with their sufferings more than made up for by

---

15 For instance, he says that "the perfectly solid parts of all matter, if you take them of equal figure and dimensions . . . are exactly alike" (LCCorr, p. 45).

16 Clarke was an important early expositor of Newtonian science, and Newton himself collaborated with Clarke in writing the letters to Leibniz in which much of Clarke's position is set out.

the enjoyable perfections of everyone else (*Theodicy,* pp. 379–80). Clarke's principle of equity seems to entail that such a world could not be best on the whole. Regardless of how much good it contained, it would be unjust.[17]

v. *Morality and the need for Christianity*

Clarke does not tell us how we are to go about applying our understanding of the eternal fitnesses in particular cases. Were he to do so, however, he would be sketching a method of ethics in which we would come to know the right act by knowing what makes it the right act. Compliance with the requirements of the eternal fitnesses is not simply a sign or token of rightness. In principle we can all equally be aware of those fitnesses, and are able to see what they require in each instance. We can also do what is required simply because we see it to be so. For Clarke God remains necessary for morality, as I said, because God assures us of the ultimate harmony of a universe too immense for us to understand. But if morality matters more than ceremony or abstract belief, and if reason can do so much to lead us to morality, Clarke has a problem in showing the need for the Christian revelation. His solution to the difficulties depends on two claims, one about morality and moral psychology, and one about the ultimate weakness of reason in most people.

Morality, for Clarke as for Malebranche before him, is not conceptually tied to the agent's happiness at all. Moral virtue is essentially constituted by living as the eternal fitnesses direct and from awareness of them. Among the fitnesses, equity is only a formal requirement, saying nothing about our own happiness. We cannot allow ourselves to do our duty to God because we hope for reward, even if we are allowed to ask him for favors. The requirement of prudence tells us to pursue not our own well-being but our fitness for doing our duty. Granted, the requirement of benevolence requires everyone to consider the happiness of others, and we might hope that if everyone is virtuous, then we will be benefited. But no such thought is to enter into our motivation for developing universal love.

17 By denying the principle of the identity of indiscernibles and allowing the existence of equally good states of affairs, Clarke opens a rationale for his claim about the relative importance of morality and ritual in religion. If Leibniz were right, God's positive precepts concerning ritual would be as fully grounded in his reason as the moral precepts. But the positive precepts concern things themselves indifferent, Clarke holds, and where God has not plainly spoken concerning them, we are free to decide about them for ourselves. We need not agree; hence there is no basis for ferocious controversies among Christians over such matters. Sermons LXVIII, pp. 420–5, and CXI, p. 708.

As if to emphasize the austerity of his account of the distinctness of morality from happiness, Clarke rejects the Stoic thesis that virtue alone constitutes happiness. Virtue is certainly worth choosing just for itself, he says, but "it does not follow that it is therefore entirely self-sufficient, and able to support a man under all kinds of suffering." Even if a few of the old Stoics may have been able to give up their lives for the sake of virtue alone, "'tis plain that the general practice of virtue in the world can never be supported on this foot." Indeed it is not even reasonable to ask people to sacrifice their lives with no hope of recompense (Lectures II, I, pp. 629–30).

Clarke is neither tempted nor disturbed by psychological egoism. He notes Hobbes's position about what makes the state of nature so awful, and dismisses it by saying simply that Hobbes is portraying "a state of the greatest, most unnatural . . . Corruption that can be imagined" (I, p. 635). His belief in the possibility of a motivational response to pure rational insight moves him well beyond any egoistic psychology. But he insists that the rational side of our nature is only one part of it. Without the hope that virtue will make the virtuous agent happy, most people will not be capable of acting in accordance with the eternal fitnesses of things. Clarke never defends, or even states, any principle to the effect that we must be able to do whatever we ought to do, but some such thought underlies his defense of the religious outlook. Had the Stoics not been so arrogant about human self-sufficiency, they might have been led to expect a future life, with punishments and rewards; but they were too blinded by pride to see what reason points out (I, p. 631).

The reasonableness of Christianity concerns Clarke at least as much as it did Locke. "Christianity," he says, "presupposes the truth of natural religion" (LCCorr, p. 6), and he holds that even the efficacy of divine grace is to be understood as the gift of the ability to understand the arguments that should move one to belief (Sermon XXX, p. 187). With a rational morality at the core of religion, what room is left for anything more than the deists would have admitted? Clarke devotes far more of his second set of Boyle lectures to arguing for the truth and necessity of the Christian revelation than he gives to demonstrating the unchangeable moral obligations which are, he thinks, at its core.[18] Having proved to his own satisfaction that the morality of Christianity is embodied in eternal moral truths, he then goes on to argue that most people cannot understand and appreciate these gifts of reason. The widespread weakness of reason, a sure sign of human corruption (Lectures II, XV, pp.

---

18   See the summary of the argument at Lectures II, pp. 596–600. In Lectures II issues of moral philosophy as such are discussed only under the first proposition; under the remaining fourteen Clarke argues for the truth of specifically Christian doctrines and the need of a revelation.

730–1), is clear evidence that there was need for a revelation; the Christian revelation best fills that need; and if this does not convince the reader of the truth and certainty of its message, nothing will.

Reason can in fact do only part of the job. It can show us that God exists, and we can infer from his attributes that he wants his creatures to be as happy as possible. Hence we can be sure that "the good of the universal creation does always coincide with the necessary truth and reason of things" (Lectures II, I, p. 630). We also know that God wills that we should conform to the eternal fitnesses of things, as he himself does. Hence he must consider disobedience grounds for punishment, and obedience grounds for reward (II, p. 637; III, p. 641). Although happiness and misery must initially have been meant to accompany virtue and vice in this life, they no longer do so. Clarke suggests that this is due to human corruption and depravity, but in any case the fact provides a powerful reason to suppose that there must be a future life in which justice will be done (III–IV, pp. 642–52). Without that hope virtue could not be widely practiced. Yet most people are so enslaved by lusts and desires, so swayed by prejudice, so governed by superstition, that they cannot follow arguments like these. So although "the great obligations and the principal motives of morality are indeed certainly discoverable and demonstrable by right reason," most people must be instructed about them and about the future rewards and punishments they lead us to expect (V, pp. 652–6). Moreover such instruction must come from someone who can speak with *authority*. Reason alone and the philosophers have never been able to do so (VI, pp. 656–7). Clarke is a little more optimistic than Locke about the power of reason in at least a small elite, but he follows Locke's lead as regards the vast majority.

The morality of natural reason, then, cannot reach the world it should govern, and "[f]or these reasons there was plainly wanting a divine revelation" (VII, pp. 666ff.). Clarke goes to great lengths to demonstrate that the Christian revelation supplies, more perfectly than any other, exactly what is needed. Not the least of the reasons for accepting it is that it centers on an authoritative teacher on whose word even the simplest will accept the truths that enable them to act morally. Happily that authority has been passed on to others, who have carried it down the ages. So long as reason remains weak in the many, the clergy will be there to see to it that virtue has its champions (V, pp. 655–6).

vi. *Mandeville: Morality naturalized*

There is no evidence that Clarke read Shaftesbury's *Inquiry* prior to working out his own view, though he might have seen the "unauthorized" edition of 1699. His position is in obvious respects opposed to

Shaftesbury's, despite their shared aim of destroying voluntarism. Both of them tried to show us how to understand ourselves as moral agents capable, at least in principle, of seeing for ourselves what morality directs, and of being moved to do it without externally imposed rewards and penalties. Both saw moral virtue as conceptually distinct from self-interest, and both invoked further assumptions, about psychology and divinity, to connect the two. And both of them supplied their admirers with weapons against a new provocateur whose work raised a loud outcry on the continent as well as in England – the notorious Bernard Mandeville.

An émigré Dutch physician who wrote in English, Mandeville was a journalist and a wit as well as a social analyst. His books have been condemned and his morals castigated since the public began finding them too intriguing to be ignored. He outraged his contemporaries with paradoxes about morality and economics that fascinate us as much by their ambiguity as by their apparent depth. What he wrote was not so much moral philosophy itself as an examination of the social effects of morality. Yet his work revolved around a major issue in moral theory itself – the relation between morality and personal well-being. He simply took for granted the kind of conceptual distinction between the two that Malebranche, Shaftesbury, and Clarke tried painstakingly to articulate. Then, in various forms of writing, from doggerel to discourse to dialogue, he envisioned the social realities in which the distinction gets embodied. What is society like if morality is one thing, and the pursuit of the agent's own happiness something altogether different, and if we do not assume that God will see to it that they coincide?

Clarke gave the lectures in which he spelled out his way of understanding the relations between morality and personal happiness during the year in which Mandeville published his own first thoughts on the question. But Mandeville owed little to philosophy. He was, perhaps – we know next to nothing of his life – vexed by the smug, overbearing attitude of the numerous societies for the suppression of vice that had sprung up in the latter part of the seventeenth century and that were busy preventing the mostly impoverished Sabbath breakers, drinkers of gin, and frequenters of prostitutes from enjoying such pleasures as they could afford.[19] He had previously published a few fables of his own as well as a translation of some of La Fontaine's. In 1705, with *The Grumbling Hive; or Knaves Turn'd Honest,* he embarked, unwittingly, on a venture that occupied the rest of his life.

The tale his roughly rhymed verses tell concerns a large beehive that,

19   On the importance of these societies for Mandeville, see Goldsmith 1985, ch. 1, and Speck 1975, who dates them from 1678 and says that by 1700 there were some twenty in London, and more elsewhere.

under a limited monarch, throve because of its "millions endeavoring to supply / each other's lust and vanity." Mandeville described how counterfeiters, gamblers, whores, and quacks contributed, along with "the grave industrious," to the gross economic product of the hive. Lawyers, doctors, priests, government officials, merchants, soldiers, and judges all cheated, deceived, shirked their duties and took bribes – and this too helped increase the hive's wealth, trade, and military power. "Thus every part was full of vice / Yet the whole mass a paradise" until a fit of moralism hit the bees. Suddenly they all objected to the corruption. "The least thing was not done amiss, / Or crossed the publick business; / But all the rogues cry'd brazenly, / *Great Gods, Had we but honesty!*" Jove, irked, granted their wish and turned everyone completely honest. With the end of all immorality, the luxury trades vanished, the suppliers of liquor, whores, and gambling went bankrupt, jails and locksmiths had no more business, and even the clergy had to live frugally. Population declined; and the army, though now valiant, was too small to withstand foreign forces. The hive finally had to move to a hollow oak tree. The moral was plain: "Then leave complaints: fools only strive / To make a great an honest hive / . . . Bare virtue can't make nations live / In splendour; they, that would revive / A golden age, must be as free, / For acorns as for honesty" (*Fable* I.17–37).

Debates about virtue and corruption, and about the commercial importance of luxury and its immorality, were a staple of English cultural activity in the early decades of the eighteenth century. Mandeville's poem might have remained no more than a minor contribution to that discussion had he not expanded his thoughts, perhaps to make them clearer, into an essay on his poem, along with extensive comments. Mandeville followed this 1714 volume with a second on the same topic and with others expounding the desirability of government-run brothels, the undesirability of free schools for the poor, and usefulness of Christianity in making men good soldiers. None of his views made him popular with the orthodox, but refutations and condemnations by judicial bodies seemed only to assist his works, especially *The Fable of the Bees,* with its infuriating subtitle, *Private Vices, Public Benefits,* in reaching an astonishingly large audience all over Europe.[20]

Mandeville is readily understood as telling his readers that they hypocritically condemn the means to ends they value. Prosperity, worldly power, the availability of many forms of enjoyment – all these goods result from what the official teaching of the society proclaims to be vices. If you don't want to live austerely in a hollow oak, if you enjoy, however secretly, the goods produced in response to the demands aris-

20 See Hundert 1994, 1995, on Mandeville's enormous impact on European thought.

ing from ordinary human passions and desires, why do you stigmatize
the demands? It is bad enough that societies for the suppression of vice
spread the mistaken economic view that sin is bad for the national
economy. Worse still is their masking their effort to prevent all of us
from enjoying life, in the name of some incomprehensible virtue that
even they themselves do not really possess.

Cynicism about ostentatious virtue and an interest in unintended
consequences are certainly present in Mandeville's thought, but neither
of these captures the deeper problem about morality that he explores.
Mandeville takes a naturalistic position about human action. Man is an
animal driven by passions that "as they are provoked and come upper-
most, govern him by turns whether he will or no" (*Fable* I.39). Concerned only for our own good, we find it difficult to live together in
society. On this view, which is not far from that of the modern natural
lawyers, an obvious question arises: what naturalistic account can be
given of how we come to have "morality" at all?

Mandeville answers with a story about the origin of moral virtue. He
tells it not about Jews or Christians but about "man in the state of
nature" with no divine guidance (*Fable* I.40). In that condition some
who had unusually strong desires for power concocted a fable by which
they gained the power they wanted. They understood that people cannot be governed by force alone. They appealed, therefore, to vanity and
pride to convince everyone that some people are superior to others, and
should be obeyed. Those who control their natural passions, they
started saying, are morally superior to the "abject low-minded people"
who seek only immediate enjoyment. The fable-makers touted "lofty,
high-spirited creatures" who used reason to oppose their strong inclinations, and "aim'd at not less than the publick welfare and the
conquest of their own passions." Since everyone is always looking for
some way to show their superiority to others, most people swallowed
this story, and so became tractable to the rule of those who taught it
(I.45–7). Even those who did not really believe it were cowed into
pretending that they did. Hypocrisy abetted flattery, as shame and
pride were manipulated by ingenious schemers to generate our present
system.

One of the aspects of Mandeville's story that has most interested
later commentators is his belief that the unintended consequences of
actions, taken together, often have features that would have been unknown and surprising to those whose individual acts brought them
about. The knaves and scoundrels in Mandeville's hive never intended
to bring about the general good, but they did so. Mandeville sounds
like Nicole in this respect, and like him has often been treated as significant because he seems to anticipate the "hidden hand" economic theory

of Adam Smith.[21] The unscrupulous politicians, seeking only their own power, benefit the whole society as much as the individually knavish bees do. We do, after all, want to live in society, we cannot do it if force is the only resource to keep us in order, and morality is meant to serve the well-being of all alike. In giving us this much, the original politicians bring us the first rudiments of the morality we eventually learn that we need, ultimately, for salvation.

In all this, Mandeville says, we should see the workings of providence, bringing it about that natural man should be led by his frailties to the social condition for which God intended him and should get the first knowledge of what religion later taught him more fully (*Fable* I.57). The remark may have seemed like cynical window-dressing for a fully naturalistic account of the origins of morality. But there were other things to be seen in Mandeville's work as well, and the attack on the *Fable of the Bees* by William Law, a prolific and powerful advocate of heartfelt Christianity, brings out one of them. Law holds a rather Clarkean view of morality as resting on eternal and immutable truths. Our reason enables us to know them and to be moved to action by the knowledge. Mandeville, Law notes, plainly denies this, and the denial has disastrous consequences. In holding that we are moved only by our passions, he denies the centrality of reason as our guide. But our rationality is not only what makes us capable of virtue; it "brings us into a kind of Society with God and all other intelligent Beings. For our Reason gives us a share in that common Light, which all intelligent Beings enjoy, and by making us Partakers of the same Things, so far makes us of one society" (*Remarks*, p. 16). If Mandeville is right, then God and we do not form a moral community. Law thinks that naturalism has the same objectionable outcome as voluntarism.

vii. *Morality against nature*

What, then, is the morality we come to have as a result of the schemes of politicians? Mandeville surprises the reader by insisting on an extremely austere answer. Everything done out of passion without regard to the public good is to be considered vice. Virtue requires that "man, contrary to the impulse of nature, should endeavour the benefit of others, or the conquest of his own passions, out of a rational ambition of being good" (*Fable* I.488–9). All the passions are suspect. Even those

21   As Kaye shows in his introduction to *The Fable of the Bees,* Mandeville was very well acquainted with French work on topics that interested him and knew Nicole's essays. For Mandeville's posthumous reputation, see the epilogue in Hundert 1994.

that seem amiable, like pity and mother love, "center in self-love," and cannot be relied on to produce concern for the common good (I.56, 75). Hence only a "rational ambition" can be a fitting motive to virtue. And it is the motive that matters, not the results (I.87). Consequently, without self-denial there is no virtue. Shaftesbury's belief to the contrary is simply "a vast inlet to hypocrisy" (I.156, 331). "There is no virtue that has a name," Mandeville proclaims in the preface to the *Enquiry into the Origin of Honor,* "but it curbs, regulates, or subdues some passion that is peculiar to human nature." This explains why we can no more say that God is virtuous than we can attribute hands and feet to him.

In replying to his critics Mandeville frequently asserts the earnestness of his commitment to morality as he describes it. He insists that he is not trying to praise vice or undermine virtue. He is trying to force us to see that we must make a choice. "Tho' I have shewn the way to worldly greatness, I have, without hesitation, preferr'd the road that leads to virtue," he replies to Bishop Berkeley's vehement attack, adding that the usefulness of vice does not prevent it from being evil.[22] Why then does he write a book so shocking to accepted opinion? Because he thinks us prone to self-deception, easily taking our frailty for goodness (I.282); and because, unlike Berkeley, who thinks it for the good of society that human nature should be praised, he thinks "the real meanness and deformity of it to be more instructive."[23]

Commentators have long been puzzled by the rigor of the morality Mandeville presents. Was he sincere, they ask, in his protestations of belief in this austere view, or did he adopt it as merely a marvelous standpoint from which he could lash his targets? Was he trying to debunk morality, was he trying to purify it, or was he simply ambivalent? I do not think we need to try to settle this issue, which may in any case be undecidable. We can see the philosophical importance of Mandeville's work without doing so.

Morality, Mandeville thinks, makes demands on each individual that

22   *Letter to Dion,* pp. 31, 34. "Vice is always bad," he says in the latter passage, "whatever benefit we may receive from it." Berkeley's attack is in *Alciphron,* Dialogue II, in *Works* III.
   Mandeville describes the speaker who is his mouthpiece in the dialogues that make up part II of the *Fable* as one who on reading the original work found people as insincere as it claimed they were, who was a believer in Christianity convinced, among other things, of "the severity of its precepts," who is quite willing to admit his own deep inability to control his passions but who finds mere verbal gratitude to heaven insufficient to prove genuine commitment to morality (*Fable* II.16–17).

23   *Letter to Dion,* p. 48. In the preface to the *Fable* he says he does not believe his book will do anything to change the way people act, unless it persuades people to look at themselves before charging others with vice and hypocrisy (*Fable* I.8–9).

go against any and all of the passions, desires, and inclinations the individual naturally has. Yet morality has an indispensable function: it makes life in society possible. The prereligious inventors of morality were right in thinking that force alone will not hold us together. There must be some socially oriented control which we come to internalize. But what we have come to accept as morality is so austere that people cannot comply with it. We are forced, therefore, into hypocrisy. We comply externally with those of its demands that cannot be flouted without detection, and we condemn those less successful than we at hiding transgressions. We all want our passions gratified. We also all agree, at least in public, that hypocrisy and sham are disgraceful. Must morality be so severe that it makes its own demands unsatisfiable? After all, it is – at least at the start – a human invention.

If Mandeville had found human nature as well suited to society as Shaftesbury found it, he could have allowed the scheming politicians to invent a morality of benevolence or utility, or a Leibnizian morality in which each could come to take pleasure in the good of others. Then, of course, he would have had no paradoxes and no satire. He also could not have brought out the problem about morality that seems to be at the root of his concern. If morality is one thing and bringing about our own good another, and if we do not simply appeal to a divinity to connect the two, how are we to understand their relation? Mandeville's vision of human nature is that of Hobbes or Pufendorf, not of Shaftesbury. He does not possess the consoling belief, which religion gave Malebranche and Clarke, that what is for the good of all is always for the good of each. He may have thought a rigorist morality the only morality that could make society possible. It takes such a morality to direct us to the common good; at their best, our passions have the good of others as a goal only sporadically. But how can reason be a motive? Unlike Clarke he has no faith in a free will tied to our agency that might yield the answer. We are moved by the strongest passion whether we will or no.

Mandeville's paradoxes arise from his acceptance of the Grotian problematic and his rejection of the solutions the Grotians had proposed. Hobbesian force alone cannot guarantee stability, morality is not simply an indirect means to happiness, and Mandeville will not appeal to God to guarantee the congruence of morality and interest. A morality capable of overruling passion is required for society to exist, but we have no motive capable of bringing us to comply with it. We can each see that we would all benefit if everyone were virtuous, yet each of us has powerful reasons to pretend to morality while cheating wherever we can. Hypocrisy may be the best reply to this dilemma; and then, of course, if we start complaining about hypocrisy (as our morality requires that we do) and the gods take us seriously, we will be lucky if we can stay together even in the hollow oak.

16

The limits of love: Hutcheson and Butler

Which comes first in morality, law or love? Moral philosophy after Grotius was deeply shaped by this issue. No one denied that both law and love have a place in morals, and even those who put law first could, with Pufendorf, allow that love, as the only source of merit, has a unique importance. The priority of law is often associated with a voluntarist view of God, and the priority of love with opposition to voluntarism. Law comes first for those whose main concern is with social order, while those who give the prize to love focus on individual character. The natural lawyers did not think they needed to say much about love once they had made theoretical room for it in imperfect duties. The theorists of love had to be a little more explicit about law. In particular they had to show how to understand concepts embedded in ordinary morality that seem tied to a law-centered approach – concepts of rights and duties and obligations. But Cumberland seemed as able as Pufendorf to give definitions from which to derive his system. How could one get a purchase on the disagreement? One might, of course, show that some particular theory contained internal problems; but to get beyond that, one would need to have a way of assessing the initial premises.

The debates among British moral philosophers in the eighteenth century produced, among other things, some ways of discussing and evaluating the starting points for ethical theory. In this chapter I discuss two further stages in the long controversy about the relative importance of love and law in morality, stages which also marked some new developments in the growth of self-consciousness about methodological aspects of moral theory. In his early works the Presbyterian minister Francis Hutcheson (1694–1746) presented a new version of the view that love is the basic factor in morality. Part of his case against Mandeville on one side, and against Clarke and his admirers on the other, involved claims about the *kind* of grounds on which any theory about morality must rest. Joseph Butler (1692–1752), an Anglican minister who became bishop of Durham in 1750, likewise took pains to spell out his views about the kind of evidence that could tell for and against an account of morality. In arguing that there are limits to love that Hutcheson failed to see, Butler framed, for the first time, some methodological as well as substantive issues that proved to be of lasting significance in modern moral philosophy.

i. *Carmichael: Pufendorf in Scotland*

I begin by taking a step backward, to consider briefly the thought of a teacher whom Hutcheson admired, Gershom Carmichael (1672–1729).[1] His annotated edition of Pufendorf's compendium, *De Officio Hominis et Civis* (1718), which Hutcheson used both as student and as teacher, was influential in bringing modern natural law theory into Scotland. But Carmichael did not bring it in unmodified. Agreeing with Pufendorf that revealed religion and its morality should have no part in natural law theory, he maintains that natural religion must have a more important role than Pufendorf allows. He thinks that once he shows how natural theology provides the foundations for morality, he will have given an adequate reply to what he thinks is Leibniz's most telling criticism of Pufendorf: that he disconnected morality too much from religion.[2]

Carmichael reconnects them by tying our natural desire for our own happiness to our ability to please God. We can easily learn, he thinks – this is among the lessons of natural theology – that God did not make us for ourselves alone. We were made to display his glory. Since we always seek our own happiness, therefore, we should take to heart the fact that God wills us to act in ways that display love and veneration toward himself. God commands certain actions as "a symbol of love and devout inclination" toward himself, and forbids others as showing "contempt, neglect, or hatred." If we obey these commands knowingly and willingly "because they are such," we are said to be morally good, and deserving of reward (suppl I.I–X).

We are to calculate the consequences of our actions so that we never do less good than we might. Our merit will depend not only on our actually knowing what God wills in the case at hand but also on the

---

1   James Moore and Michael Silverthorne, to whose article on Carmichael (1983) I am indebted, have allowed me to see their translation of selections from Carmichael's writings on natural theology and on ethics, which tell us much about his views. Charles Reeves's privately printed selections from Carmichael, edited by John N. Lenhart, are the only publicly available translations of his work of which I have any knowledge. See also Thomas Mautner, "Carmichael and Barbeyrac: The lost correspondence" in Palladini and Hartung 1996.

2   The comments are made in Carmichael's preface to his Pufendorf edition, translated by Moore and Silverthorne 1983. Other citations of Carmichael refer to the translation by Charles H. Reeves.

degree to which our will is devoted to doing it (suppl. I.XV–XVIII).
God's will is promulgated not only by express revelation but through
nature as well. The investigation of his will carried out by students of
natural law can be called either ethics or moral philosophy; the knowledge the discipline yields does not differ from natural prudence (suppl.
I.XIX–XXI).

Underlying all specific laws is the requirement to show a fitting
attitude of love toward God. We do so by obeying his commands simply as such; and disobedience is accordingly a sign of contempt for him.
Our most immediate duty flows from this: it is to worship God. Our
indirect duties, showing how we are to act toward beings other than
God in order to show our love of God, are summed up by saying that
we should be kind toward "the whole system of rational creatures"
insofar as this is not contrary to loving God and to acting for God's
glory (suppl. II.I–III). Rational creatures are those who are images of
God. To our knowledge only humans are so. It follows that within the
limits of our abilities we must each "procure the common Good of the
whole human race, and, so far as this is allowed, the proper good of
individuals." Two precepts elaborate this duty. We are to act for our
own good so far as doing so harms no one else. But as pursuit of private
advantage leads us into conflict with one another, another duty arises:
"that any man at all, to the best of his ability, must foster and promote
the social inclination and social life" whether in himself or in others. We
are not allowed to subordinate this duty to the duty of pursuing our
own interest.[3] The rest of the laws of nature all follow from these three
basic laws of worshiping God, pursuing one's harmless advantage, and
cultivating sociability. They do not follow, as Pufendorf mistakenly
held, from the requirement of sociability alone.

To this amalgam of Cumberland and Pufendorf, Carmichael adds a
number of hortatory paragraphs about the importance of controlling
our passions and of knowing ourselves in order to do so. His stress on
developing the ability to suspend action until the passions cool, and to
reflect carefully, might show his serious study of Locke (to whose political thought he expressly notes a debt) or of Malebranche. In either case,
Carmichael makes clear a concern for the inner dimension of the moral
life, which the text he was annotating does not elaborate (suppl. III).

Carmichael sketches the derivative laws of nature in terms of rights.
Sociability itself he somewhat surprisingly describes as a matter of
balancing one's own rights against those of others; and he goes on to

3 Suppl. II.V–IX. Carmichael promptly adds that sociability requires the vigorous pursuit of one's own advantage, even if this leads to some conflict. Unless we
each look out for ourselves, no one will know what is for our good. Suppl. II.XVI–
XVII.

consider a variety of kinds of rights, and their functions in pacts, property, marriage, slavery, and civil government.[4] Yet he offers no account of what rights are or of their connection with the common good. Pufendorfian specifics are left merely juxtaposed to the basic doctrine that in morality we are to act lovingly toward others out of the desire to show our love and veneration of God.

ii. *Hutcheson's morality of benevolence*

Carmichael was closely connected with Robert Molesworth and his republican circle and enabled Hutcheson to meet Molesworth, who became an early patron and encouraged him to publish his first work in ethics.[5] There are some explicitly republican political views in Hutcheson's later works, and the view of virtue spelled out in his earlier writings, like Shaftesbury's own theory, portrays human beings as well suited to be citizens of a classical republic.[6] If Hutcheson shared some political motivations with Shaftesbury, however, he deplored his negative attitude to Christianity and dismissed his elitism (*Inquiry*, pref., p. xix). He aimed to recast Christian morality to fit a world understood in bare Newtonian terms, without any of Shaftesbury's Platonic harmonies; and he argued that morality requires only the most natural of feelings, not sensibilities calling for leisurely cultivation. Orthodox theologians in Scotland charged him with heresy, but he provided a view that many leaders of the Scottish enlightenment found persuasive.[7]

4   "Appendix containing abridged Ethical Theses," Carmichael, pp. 31ff.

5   In 1725 Hutcheson published *An Inquiry into the Original of Our Ideas of Beauty and Virtue*, two separate essays bound in one volume. The fourth edition, from which I cite, appeared in 1738. In 1728 he published another double volume, *An Essay on the Nature and Conduct of the Passions, with Illustrations of the Moral Sense*, which reached a third edition in 1742. Citations of the essay on the passions are from the reprint of this edition, but in citing the *Illustrations* I use the edition of Peach. Hutcheson's much fuller *System of Moral Philosophy* was published posthumously in 1755. There is scholarly disagreement about the relation of the late *System*, and also a late Latin work intended for Hutcheson's classes, to the early work. I consider only the early work both because it seems to me to be more coherent and original than the late, and also because it seems to be this work that influenced Kant (Chapter 22.v).

6   Hutcheson explicitly acknowledges Molesworth in his preface to *Inquiry*, pp. xvii–xviii. See further Scott 1900; Leidhold 1985, pp. 35–6. Robbins, 1969, p. 49, refers to Hutcheson as a disciple of the commonwealthmen along with Walter Moyle. See also Robbins 1959, esp. pp 185–96.

7   On Hutcheson and religion, see W. I. P. Hazlett, "Religious Subversive or Model Christian?" in Smyth, n.d., pp. 17–21.

His theory is remarkably simple in its essentials. With Shaftesbury, he holds that the kind of goodness we praise as "moral" is possible only for reflective beings who have a disposition to feel approval or disapproval of impulses and motives. Unlike Shaftesbury's moral faculty, the Hutchesonian moral sense approves of only one basic motive: benevolence, which for Hutcheson is a stand-in for Christian *agapē*, or disinterested love, directed to others regardless of any merit on their part.[8] We approve of temperance, prudence, courage, and justice only because we think that they are dispositions people need in order to forward the good of others (*Inquiry II* II.I). Virtue is thus benevolence, as approved by the moral sense. The virtuous agent will perform actions that tend to make other people happy. Both agents and actions gain their moral significance from the agent's motive, not from the acts or results due to it. Happiness is naturally good, but its moral goodness is due to its being what the morally approved motive causes.

Hutcheson is emphatic in holding that approval is not proportioned to the amount of happiness the agent produces. As Carmichael had taught, the degree of virtue depends only on how much benevolence people feel, and how earnestly they express it. The more benevolence they feel and the more they act from it, the more virtuous they are. No subtle judgments of the balance of many dispositions are needed. Moreover it does not matter how good one is at calculating consequences, or how extensive are one's abilities or one's material resources for bringing about good. All that matters is the degree and seriousness of one's love of others.[9] From all this, Hutcheson says, we can draw "the most joyful [inference] imaginable," namely "that no external circumstances of fortune, no involuntary disadvantages, can exclude any mortal from the *most heroic virtue*" (*Inquiry II* III.XIV, p. 198).

This is a joyful inference because, among other things, to be virtuous is also (as in Shaftesbury) to be happy. All other sources of pleasure, Hutcheson argues, pale into insignificance beside the pleasure of making others happy (*Inquiry II* VI). Hutcheson's citizens will thus find happiness in serving the republic. But the republic will not be quite as Harrington or Machiavelli envisaged it. The prince, the statesman, the general are not the only ones who can display heroic virtue. It is just as open to "an honest Trader" (*Inquiry II* III.XIV, p. 198). Harrington al-

---

8   Leidhold has done more than previous commentators to stress (rightly, in my opinion) the Christian aspect of Hutcheson's idea of benevolence.

9   In a rejection of Carmichael as well as of the French theorists of pure love, Hutcheson argues that morally good actions need not be done with the thought of God in mind. We can be directly concerned with the good of those we benefit, not with showing our love of God. *Illustrations* VI, pp. 175, 190ff.

lowed for commerce but feared it as a source of corruption. In Hutcheson's classical republic, it benefits others and so it has become virtuous.

In saying nothing, so far, of justice, rights, obligations, and laws, I have been following Hutcheson, who waits until the final section of the *Inquiry* to discuss them. He sees these law-related concepts as all tied to the promotion of "the public natural happiness of rational agents" (*Inquiry II* VII.V, p. 275). He does not, in his early work, give an analysis of justice as such; but he plainly thinks of it as being valued solely because it is instrumental in bringing about the greatest happiness.

This can be seen by looking at his accounts of other terms from this part of the language of morality. We may call human laws just when they conform to God's laws, he says, but what we mean by calling God's laws just is that they display something that is absolutely good, namely benevolence. We think that his laws "are contrived to promote the public Good in the most effectual and impartial manner" (*Inquiry II* VII.V, p. 275). To attribute justice to our laws, then, is indirectly to say that they promote the public good. Similarly with the notion of a right:

> Whenever it appears to us, that a faculty of doing, demanding, or possessing anything, universally allowed in certain circumstances, would in the whole tend to the general good, we say, that one in such circumstances has a right to do, possess, or demand that thing. (*Inquiry II* VII.VI, p. 277)

Hutcheson thus gives an explicit account of the connection between love and law at which Carmichael merely pointed. Rights, duties, and justice, for Hutcheson, are simply channels through which love gets expressed. The only point at which Hutcheson finds a need for a sterner moral notion is the point at which the moral sense is "exceedingly weakened, and the selfish passions grown strong." Then laws backed by sanctions may be needed to give people "a steady sense of obligation" that will move them to act for the public good (*Inquiry II* VII.I p. 269). Hutcheson's position here is like that of John Smith, the Cambridge Platonist (Chapter 10.ii). Obligation in the sense central to natural law theory comes in where love fails.[10] Hutcheson does not seem to

---

10   Hutcheson says that the term "obligation" has three senses. He explains them by giving three ways in which we can be "obligated" to pursue benevolent actions: (1) by a "determination" to approve and perform actions, regardless of our own interest; (2) by a motive from self interest to pursue our *enlightened* private advantage; (3) by a law backed by sanctions, needful when our moral sense is "exceedingly weakened" or our selfish passions have become excessive (*Inquiry II* VII.I, pp. 267–70). Hutcheson thus accommodates the New Testament statement (I Timothy 1.9) that the law is not for the righteous but for the unrighteous. He would have approved of Zwingli's position, cited in Chapter 2, note 20.

think it will fail very often – particularly not if everyone can be brought to understand clearly how much happier benevolence makes the agent than anything else.[11]

Like Shaftesbury, then, Hutcheson rejects the problematic of the natural lawyers. Although he allows self-interest a legitimate place in the life of the virtuous agent, and does not see it as a sign of our sinfulness, it need not run up against our benevolence.[12] Morality therefore does not have to serve first and foremost to control controversy and strife. Morality is rather the expression of our ability to love one another and therefore to look after one another's needs. And when strife enters our lives, it is to be handled by an aspect of morality that is not different from the expression of direct concern for the needs of others, as the natural lawyers said it was. Strife is to governed by principles derived from our care for others.

iii. *Morality and sentiment*

It is a rather nice picture, but can it be made plausible? The contemporary challenge to his view that Hutcheson took most seriously came from Mandeville. To rebut Mandeville's views as well as to support his own, Hutcheson thinks he must prove three connected theses. He must show that there is an idea of virtue that is different in nature from any idea concerned with self-interest. He must show that benevolence alone is what we approve of morally. And he must show that benevolence or unselfish concern for others is a natural and effective human motive. Only then will he have supplanted the Mandevillean view that virtue is either a sham constructed for political purposes by and for beings whose motives are all selfish or else a condition so hard to attain that people cannot really be expected to do so.

Hutcheson relies on Lockean theory and Lockean tactics. He is sure that we all already know the data he needs in order to prove his points. Everyone has the experiences that are the "originals" of our ideas of morality and motivation. We have but to notice certain quite ordinary and commonplace facts about how we feel toward others, or what we approve of, or the ideas that words stand for, to be able to see that the Mandevilleans are quite mistaken. Hutcheson does not argue for his

11 The philosopher – might we add, the clergyman? – is to teach this to everyone.

12 Self-interest is more than that. It is a necessary spur to industry, which benevolence alone does not provide. And industry, even if egoistically motivated, produces goods that benefit others. Hence, "self-love is really as necessary to the good of the whole, as benevolence" (*Inquiry II* VII.VIII, pp. 284–5).

Lockeanism. He simply proceeds on its basis to pile up examples of the relevant kind of experience and to draw the appropriate conclusions.

He begins by reminding us that we have different feelings toward different kinds of things we think good or bad. We do not feel the same way toward a fertile field as toward a virtuous person, although both produce good outcomes. An accident may cause us great harm, as may someone's malicious act but, again, we have different feelings about them (*Inquiry II* I.I, pp. 116–17). The second kind of feeling is what we call moral approval or disapproval. We can easily see that these moral feelings cannot be resolved into feelings derived from interest. If they could, we might be bribed to feel one or the other; but the most a bribe could get would be pretense (*Inquiry II* I.I, pp. 123–4; II.II, p. 135).

This special moral approval, Hutcheson holds, is the root experience from which all moral ideas originate. Since there must be a special sense to account for any unique kind of simple idea, he concludes that there must be a moral sense to account for our experience of approval. A sense is only the tendency of the mind to receive, involuntarily, an idea from the presence to it of some object (*Inquiry II* I.I, p. 113). It is mere prejudice to suppose that all our simple ideas must come from the traditionally recognized senses (*Inquiry*, pref., p. xiii).[13]

Just as everyone has the experiences from which moral ideas arise, so we all have experiences that show that we have disinterested desires and passions. In the *Inquiry* and at greater length in the *Nature and Conduct of the Passions* Hutcheson appeals to "reflection upon our own hearts" to remind us that we do desire the good of others, such as our children, with no thought of profiting from it. He also argues that benevolent feelings like these are natural, since we cannot make ourselves feel them at will (*Inquiry II* II.II, pp. 139–42). The benevolent passions are only part of a wide array of desires and affections with which nature equips us. Malice, anger, avarice, envy, gratitude, affection for parents, and concern for the needy, have different strengths in different people. They are given us for different purposes: some make us dangerous to aggressors, some make us industrious, some make us generous. With Locke and Shaftesbury Hutcheson notes that the strength of a desire is not a simple function of the amounts of good, whether to oneself or to others, that one thinks would result from satisfying it. "Thus lust or revenge may conquer the calm affection toward private good, and sometimes are conquered by it" (*Passions* II.ii., p. 30). We all want many things, but we do not act from some desire for our own total good or the good of all mankind or – contra Leibniz – for the greatest available amount of perfection as such. Even when we have such conceptions,

13   A century earlier Lord Herbert had protested against limiting the senses to the traditional five, in order to make room for moral knowledge. See Chapter 9.iii.

Hutcheson says, "we do not serve the individual only from love to the species" any more than we desire grapes only because eating them will increase our own total happiness (*Illustrations,* p. 124). Since the passions are simply causal forces urging us in different directions, no straightforward calculation of amounts of good will suffice for their guidance or for their control. Hutcheson thinks that the moral sense provides what is needed.

The deliverances of that sense are themselves feelings – pleasant feelings of love toward persons showing benevolence or unpleasant feelings of hatred toward those lacking it or showing harmful desires. The feelings are accompanied by a desire to give or refuse help according as we approve or disapprove. Once we are aware of benevolence at work, in others or in ourselves, the moral sense provides us with a new feeling about it.[14] From the moral sense we obtain no new information either about the actions to which benevolence leads or about the agent. Before the moral sense operates, we must know what the "external motion" is that constitutes the action, as well as its likely effects, and we must know "the affections in the agent" to which this action points as its cause. But the approbation itself, Hutcheson says, "cannot be supposed an image of any thing external, more than the pleasures of harmony, of taste, of smell" (*Illustrations,* pp. 163–4).[15]

It is a matter of observable fact, Hutcheson holds, that the loving feeling of approbation is caused in us always and only by our perception (possibly erroneous) of benevolent feelings in others, or ourselves. Things might have been otherwise. God might have made us without any moral sense, or he might have given us a moral sense that responded positively to spiteful and malicious motives.[16] Part of the evidence of God's goodness is that we are constituted with a moral sense that reinforces benevolent motives tending to the good of everyone alike, as well as with a direct and natural enjoyment of doing good to others (*Illustrations,* pp. 136ff.).

Were we without any moral sense, we would continue to be moved

14   Hutcheson is of course aware of the empirical difficulty of knowing other people's motives, but he does not raise any general problems about our knowledge of other minds.

15   Hutcheson often speaks of a "perception" of approbation, or of the mind receiving an idea of approbation. This is Lockean terminology. Any immediate reception of an idea is a perception, even the reception of physical pleasure or pain. Talk of an idea or a perception does not carry the implication that what is in the mind is representative of anything. Hutcheson knew Leibniz's views and did not accept them.

16   God might likewise have made our aesthetic sense, the pleasure we take in regular forms, quite different (*Inquiry I* VIII.4–5, pp. 100–2).

by our strongest passions, whether benevolent or otherwise. "The *universal Benevolence* toward all men, we may compare to that principle of gravitation, which perhaps extends to all bodies. . . . And that attraction or Force by which the parts of each Body cohere, may represent the self-love of each individual" (*Inquiry II* V.II, pp. 221–2). We have enough generous passions so that we could continue to form a social world even without the moral sense, though we would not do it as well as we do with morality. Moral approval has effects in our lives because it is itself pleasant, because we enjoy being the object of it, and because when we are approved we tend to get help from our approvers (*Inquiry II* II.VI). Approval thus reinforces the benevolent feelings and helps keep the moral world in balance.[17]

Hutcheson believes that his arguments for a unique idea of moral goodness and for a love-centered ethic of virtue reveal the falsity of skepticism. Experience shows that there really are benevolent as well as selfish feelings, and disinterested approval and disapproval, not just selfish calculation. These facts suffice to show, against Mandeville, that virtue and vice are realities. In them we have all the certainty we need about morality. The facts also enable us to be comfortable with the pure contingency of God's will toward us. We say that someone is good when we approve of him for his benevolence. God has plainly been benevolent to us, having made us benevolent and additionally having made us love benevolence. He is all the more lovable because there was no necessity for him to have made us this way. We therefore need not say that God's will is the source of morality. Indeed, to say that would be to turn the assertion that God is just and good into "an insignificant tautology" (*Inquiry II* VII.V, p. 275). Gratitude should lead us to want to obey the God whom we must feel is good to us. Hutcheson is content with the contingent experientially based assurance that God chose to act lovingly; he calls on no rational principle for assurance of God's love. As Richard Price saw clearly, Hutcheson is fully a sentimentalist in morals.[18]

17   See the further Newtonian metaphors in *Inquiry II* II.III, p. 137; VII.VIII, p. 285.

18   See Price, *Review*, pp. 13–15, 63, 215ff. n. Norton 1974, 1977, 1982, and 1985b, and Haakonssen 1990, defend the view that Hutcheson is a moral realist, that, as Haakonssen puts it, "[m]oral perception is *not* a subjective affective experience." On Norton, see Winkler 1985 and Norton's reply, Norton 1985b. Haakonssen cites *Inquiry II* I.VIII, pp. 129–31, which does not, I think, bear out his claim. He argues that Hutcheson aimed to show "that morality is an empirically ascertainable part of the world and . . . this excluded the possibility that morals could be relational in character" (Haakonssen, 1990, pp. 72–4). But relations can be empirically ascertainable. Hutcheson does indeed argue that morality is not constituted by a (nonobservable?)

iv. *Reason, motive, and calculation*

Hutcheson did not reject rationalism without argument. Clarke's version of moral rationalism seems to be his main target. Unlike the theories of Malebranche and Leibniz, Clarke does not overtly rest his ethics on a complex metaphysics. Like Hutcheson's sentimentalism, it rests on claims put forward as things everyone already knows. Additional versions of neorationalism appeared in the two decades between Clarke's Boyle lectures and Hutcheson's first work on ethics. Hutcheson devoted his second work on ethical theory largely to attacking them.

Is reason the basis of morality? Reason is simply "our power of finding out true propositions" (*Illustrations*, p. 120), and it is obvious that there are innumerable truths about any action. When we think of acts as reasonable, we are going beyond that triviality. Hutcheson asks us to notice that there are two ways in which we do so. Some truths show what there is about an action that excites someone to do it; others show what leads us to approve of doing the action. He calls these exciting and justifying reasons, and he attributes the distinction to Grotius (*Illustrations*, p. 121).[19]

Hutcheson's own theory requires this distinction in a way that many earlier theories, such as Leibniz's, do not. For Leibniz a justifying reason is simply an exciting reason we have considered and accepted. Only perceptions of amounts of perfection enter into the process of deliberation; the perception of what will yield most perfection gives us both the strongest and the most reasonable ground of action. For Hutcheson,

---

relation to divine law. He thinks its origin is in the empirically observable relation between the feeling of approval and the motive of benevolence. Seeing benevolence, which is objectively real and which is virtuous because we feel approval toward it, is not the same as seeing an objective quality of virtuousness that belongs to benevolence regardless of our response to it.

19   His reference is to *DJBP* II.I.i.1 where Grotius says: "Let us proceed to the causes of war – I mean justifiable causes; for there are also other causes which influence man through regard for what is expedient and differ from those that influence men through regard for what is right." Grotius's reference to both kinds of reasons as causes indicates that he is not in fact making quite the distinction Hutcheson has in mind.

Leibniz cites Grotius's distinction in his 1693 preface to his *Codex Iuris Gentium*, in *Political Writings*, p. 167. Barbeyrac used the distinction in philosophical argument, giving it a role, as I pointed out in Chapter 12.v, in his 1718 defense of Pufendorf. Carmichael's references to the Leibniz-Barbeyrac exchange make it almost certain that Hutcheson had read it.

what moves a good agent is love of others, while what arouses approval is awareness of the agent's motive – and self-approval is not necessary for virtuous motivation (cf. *Inquiry II* I.VIII, pp. 129–31).

Given the distinction, Hutcheson mounts a twofold attack on rationalist moral theory. What *excites* us, he argues, is always in the last analysis a desire. No truth about any fact will move us unless we care one way or another about the fact – welcome it or reject it. And welcoming or rejecting, he takes it, results only from desires and aversions, from the passionate side of our nature. As for justification, truths alone will not suffice here either. Justification is inseparable from approval. That an act is a good means to an end does not justify doing it unless the end itself is justified, or approved. What then makes us approve ends, especially ultimate ends? It is not enough to say that an end is God's. We must ask why we approve of God's ends to see where justification enters (*Illustrations*, pp. 128–9). And so it is with any other ultimate end. No truth about any end is the same as approval of the end. Because he rejects reductionist definitions of moral terms, Hutcheson concludes that what *justifies* is no more a deliverance of reason than what excites (*Illustrations*, pp. 130ff.).

We need not follow Hutcheson through the many acute and interesting arguments with which he applies this radical critique to existing theories and defends it against objections. We do need to see one important way in which he opens the door for reasoning within the domain of morality. Knowledge of facts is of course involved in finding out what motives lead someone to act. More interestingly, we can use reason to get precise estimates of what to do and of how virtuous people are.

Hutcheson does not think that we have reasons for approving benevolence. God just made us so that we do. Unlike Clarke, therefore, he does not think benevolence good because it is the best means for assuring that men will do as they ought. Approval, however, gives benevolence moral priority over all other motives. When more than one benevolent course of action is available, we can calculate which will do more good. Greater benevolence is shown in doing more rather than less good. Reason has a moral role because benevolence and its results can be quantified.

If two acts will bring equal amounts of good to each individual affected by it, then we show more benevolence by doing the act affecting more people. Hence "that action is best, which procures the greatest happiness for the greatest numbers" (*Inquiry II* III.VIII, pp. 180–1). If two people have equal abilities to do good, the one who does more shows a greater amount of benevolence and is more virtuous. When self-interest concurs with benevolence in bringing us to act, we must subtract the amount of good due to the former in order to calculate the

amount of virtue (*Inquiry II* I.III, pp. 187ff.).[20] With these remarks
Hutcheson proposed a Christian mathematics of love that was later
taken over for other purposes.

v. *Butler: The complexity of human nature*

In his history of English moral philosophy, William Whewell described Bishop Butler as having done what pioneers in a science always
do: improve our knowledge of the facts while developing the concepts
with which we understand them. He did better on the facts, Whewell
added, being content with a degree of conceptual fuzziness that pre-
cluded an adequate theory.[21] It was a shrewd assessment, even if Butler
would not have agreed about the importance of the kind of theory
Whewell envisaged (and later went on to produce). Butler saw differences where others saw uniformity, complexity where to others things
seemed simple. Moreover it is not by chance that he wrote out his
ethical views in the form of sermons.[22] His aim in reflecting on the
issues of moral philosophy was to lead those he addressed to improve
their behavior. Whatever was not essential for that purpose could be
ignored. The moral life, he thought, can be lived quite well without
answers to most philosophical questions. After all, the Scripture is not
"a book of theory and speculation, but a plain rule of life for mankind"
(XII.3), and its teaching must surely be sufficient. To be virtuous, however, we do need, if not to understand our own nature, at least not to
misunderstand it completely. Bad philosophy can, consequently, endanger morality. When it does, only good philosophy can set things to
rights.

Some of the *Sermons* contain so much good philosophy that it is easy
to ignore the others. Concentrating on the most philosophical parts of
the work we see what is new in Butler's thought without seeing what is

20   In the first edition of the *Inquiry* Hutcheson devoted several pages to mathematical formulas expressing theorems like these. Let M = amount of good produced,
A = agent's ability, and B = agent's benevolence: then M = BxA. For mixed motives,
let S = self-interest; then M = (B+S)A or BA+SA, hence BA = M-SA; and B = (M-SA)/
A. B, of course, gives a direct measure of virtue. (For these and other formulas see the
excerpts from the first edition given in Selby-Bigge I.110–13.)

21   Whewell 1852, pp. 108–9, 112–13.

22   Butler's *Fifteen Sermons* were first published in 1726. The *Analogy of Religion,
Natural and Revealed*, a substantial and devastating attack on the deists, appeared in
1736. To it are appended two important short dissertations, "On Personal Identity"
and "On Virtue." I cite the sermons by sermon and paragraph number, following the
paragraphing of the Bernard edition. The preface to the second edition (1729) I cite as
"pref." with the paragraph number, and the *Dissertation on Virtue*, in Vol. II of the
Bernard edition of the *Works*, as *Virtue*.

not.[23] We fail to see, for instance, that the sermons handle the traditional topics called for by Christ's summary of the law. The first three sermons are a philosophical prolegomenon. The next seven concern our duty to ourselves; they are followed by two on our duty to our neighbor, and three on our duty to God.[24] Butler's brief discussion of the ultimate good is also usually overlooked. Our dissatisfaction with earthly goods, our restlessness, and our search for amusements, he tells us, show that only something beyond this world can truly satisfy us, that only the vision of God can be our highest good (XIV.9, 14).[25] The philosophically richer sermons do not contain Butler's discussions of the erring conscience. Nor do they show Butler's strong insistence that because the universe is divinely managed we should be content with our lot despite our inability to understand why God acts as he does (XV.6–8); his rejection of voluntarism and of servility of mind toward God (XIII.2, 9); and his insistence nonetheless that "[r]esignation to the will of God is the whole of piety" and that "the whole attention of life should be to obey [God's] commands" (XIV.3; XIII.10; XV.18). It takes the sermons as a whole to reveal that if Butler moved moral philosophy in new directions, it was in order to reformulate some quite old-fashioned views.[26]

He proceeds by appealing, not, as Clarke did, to "the abstract relations of things" but to the facts of human nature, and by asking what pattern of life accords with them (pref. 12). In an important way his method resembles Pufendorf's. He takes the salient features of "the inward frame of man" (III.2n) as showing us God's intentions for us (I.5; II.1; VI.1; XV.14). Unlike Pufendorf Butler thinks readers will be more readily convinced to live morally by reviewing their own nature than by studying a complicated quasi-legal system. But he never denies that things have "abstract relations," and there is much in what he says to suggest that he himself accepts some version of natural law theory. The

23   Philosophers from the nineteenth century on have concentrated on the preface, Sermons I–III, on human nature, and Sermons XI–XII, on love of neighbor. These with the *Dissertation on Virtue* are still the most frequently reprinted of Butler's writings.

24   Sermons I–III give an overall view of our nature, while Sermons IV–X, more hortatory in tone, take up particular parts of that nature to illustrate "what should be our general aim respecting ourselves in our passage through this world" (VI.10). At II.16 Butler uses the traditional categories of duty in raising the question of how things would look if we had no conscience.

25   The view is at least as old as St. Thomas. Is there an echo of Pascal here? Butler had read him; see Barker 1975.

26   Among recent commentators Penelhum 1985 gives the fullest treatment of Butler's work. Penelhum also rightly insists that those interested in Butler's ethics should study the *Analogy* carefully as well as the sermons. See also the important chapter on Butler in Darwall 1995.

first sermon displays the evidence that we were meant to be sociable – the Grotian starting point – and the next two are preached on the favorite text of natural law theorists, Romans 2.14, concerning our being a law unto ourselves. Butler shows us morality from inside the consciousness of the ordinary untheoretical moral agent, claiming that fully adequate guidance is embodied in that experience. Our moral experience is what we would expect it to be if some version of a natural law theory were true.[27]

The main point to be established is that our experience shows us inner hierarchy and authority (pref. 14). In the soul as in politics, hierarchy requires differentiation; and Butler accordingly begins by arguing that there are many kinds of desires and passions. At the simplest level we find ourselves with desires aimed directly at, say, food, or revenge, or the well-being of our child. We do not have such desires because of a prior thought that their objects are good. We simply find ourselves desiring certain things, without thought of the further consequences of getting them. Butler does not speak of desire in Lockean terms as uneasiness; but he is following Locke's lead in rejecting the rationalist Stoic theory of the passions and affections.

Butler sees even more complexity in the soul than Shaftesbury and Hutcheson do. In addition to the particular passions, he claims that we find within ourselves two general impulses, one toward the good of others and one toward our own good: benevolence and self-love.[28] Our particular passions may move us to act in ways resulting in benefit or harm to ourselves or to others. Benevolence moves us intentionally to avoid harming others and to help them, self-love gives us a similar impetus concerning ourselves. We as often ignore the latter as we do the

27   In the *Analogy,* where it is more appropriate for Butler to discuss abstract philosophical issues, there are further indications of his natural law orientation. All our evidence, he thinks, shows that God "manifests himself to us under the character of a righteous governor" over servants, rewarding and punishing (*Analogy* I.III.2). When he opposes the fatalists by defending freedom of the will, responsibility, and the justness of punishment, he reiterates that in moral discernment we learn that we are under the laws of God, and are liable to reward and punishment as we comply or disobey (*Analogy* I.VI.10). He asserts an antivoluntarist view of God's commands, though he expresses his dislike for prying into such things (*Analogy* I.VI.11n). There is, he says, "a thing of the utmost importance, which I do believe, the moral fitness and unfitness of actions, prior to all will whatever" (*Analogy* II.VIII.11). He also insists that the moral law "is as much matter of revealed command as positive institutions are, for the Scripture enjoins every moral virtue." But the moral law is in addition written in our hearts (*Analogy* II.I.26). Thus his view is that morality is a matter of law, not only of fitness, and therefore presupposes a lawgiver.

28   Butler here picks up a distinction made by Malebranche between individual and general passions: see *Truth* V.7, p. 374.

former, Butler says (I.14), but we cannot deny that we feel both of them. Finally, there is a "principle of reflection" within us, shown in our approving and disapproving our passions and desires, both particular and general, and in the actions due to them (I.8; *Virtue* 1). This principle, and no other, asserts its own authority over all our other impulses (pref. 24).[29]

All these claims, Butler says repeatedly, concern facts observable by anyone.[30] He returns both to his assertion of the complexity of our nature and to the factual warrant for it several times (see, e.g., V.1n; XI; XIII.5; *Virtue*). The facts, he declares, plainly refute Hobbes's misleading reductions of all desires to desire for personal power or benefit, and his consequent denial that benevolence exists.[31] The insistence that we need no theory to see that Hobbes is wrong is part of the general point that God has provided all of us with adequate instruction about how we are to live. We have but to look to see it.

vi. *Conscience*

What is it, then, that we are to see in order to realize that within ourselves there is more than a power struggle among the passions, that there is authority as well? (pref. 26).[32] Butler appeals to our ability to see that some actions are natural, and some unnatural. It is natural for an animal goaded by hunger to rush into a well-baited trap, but it would be unnatural for a man to do so, no matter how hungry he was. More generally it is natural for a man to deny gratification to an impulse, however strong, when to yield to it would seriously harm him. Considered in this light, self-love is plainly superior to a harmful passion, even if the latter is stronger. We think of self-love as having a different kind of superiority: it possess authority. We do not need even to con-

---

29   Malebranche in *Truth* V.10, p. 397, and V.11, pp. 399ff., says that every passion seeks its own justification, a point that Hutcheson repeats in *Inquiry II* II.iv, p. 140, explicitly referring to Malebranche.

30   A statement from the footnote to Sermon I.6 is typical: "If any person can in earnest doubt, whether there be such a thing as good-will in one man towards another . . . let it be observed, that *whether man be thus, or otherwise constituted, what is the inward frame in this particular*, is a mere question of fact or natural history, not provable immediately by reason. It is therefore to be judged of and determined in the same way other facts or matters of natural history are" (italics in original).

31   Butler's "refutation of psychological egoism" has been analyzed innumerable times. For an excellent discussion see Penelhum 1985, ch. II.

32   Here Butler carries on a line of thought suggested in Henry More's discussion of the superiority of the "boniform faculty" in the *Encheiridion*, p. 20, noted in Chapter 10.iii; and in Clarke's claims concerning moral reasons, whose weight in deliberation is not a function of their causal strength (Chapter 15.i).

sider the idea of conscience, the most general reflective principle, to have a clear grasp of the idea of authority (II.9–11). But a little more consideration will show that conscience possesses exactly the kind of superiority over all our passions and active principles that self-love has over our interested passions. As in politics there is a distinction between power and authority, so it is within the self. The supreme authority within us is conscience. Its authority is "a constituent part of the idea, that is, of the faculty itself. . . . Had it strength as it has right; had it power, as it has manifest authority, it would absolutely rule the world" (II.14).[33]

Our moral vocabulary, and common features of our moral responses, such as the difference we perceive between harming someone by chance and deliberately injuring him, show the existence of this supreme faculty (*Virtue* 1); and its presence within us explains how we can be, as St. Paul taught, a law unto ourselves. The precept, "Live according to nature" makes sense because our nature is normative, ruled by "the voice of God within us" (VI.7). This is orthodox enough and is made more so because Butler calls the authoritative faculty the conscience. But in explaining conscience he completely abandons the Thomistic account with its apparatus of synteresis as the repository of principles and syneidesis as enabling us to subsume particular cases under laws. That view was standard among the great seventeenth-century moralists of the Church of England, like Sanderson and Jeremy Taylor, and even among Puritan casuists.[34] Butler quietly drops it. Conscience is not a repository of laws, and it does not assess external actions but "will and design, which constitute the very nature of actions as such" (*Virtue* 2). Although our intention of consequences is part of "design," the actual outcome is not. Conscience tells us only whether all the parts of our inward frame are functioning within "the constitution of man" as they are meant to, none being excessive or defective in strength relative to the others (III.2; XII.11–12).

Before turning to see how Butler spells out the work of conscience in judging the proper proportions of our passions and affections, I must comment on several further points about conscience itself.

First, it is through conscientious direction of our inward frame that we come to have the unity that alone makes each of us a morally unified

---

33   Henry More uses political language in presenting himself as combatting those who "allow no such thing as Superiority in the Faculties, but assert Obedience to that Passion in particular, which shall happen to usurp above the rest" (*Encheiridion* I.iv, p. 20).

34   See Sanderson, *Conscience,* I, particularly sec. 11 explaining syneidesis and synteresis; and Jeremy Taylor, *Ductor Dubitatium,* who omits the technical terms but keeps their substance, at I.I.I.6, in *Works* XI. p. 372.

person who is more than a single physical agent. Conscience turns into a functioning system what would otherwise be only a bundle of urges striving for dominance within the limits of a human body. It takes the place of an Aristotelian *telos*, showing us not our ultimate end but the shape we are to give our character for its own sake (III.2n; pref. 14). Butler agrees with Shaftesbury in holding that because many of our desires are not good-based they can only be steered toward unity by a higher-order principle, which itself does not direct us simply to do or obtain as much good as possible.[35]

Second, we are moral agents because our awareness of the authority of conscience enables us to know that we can be held responsible for ourselves. Conscience always anticipates a higher judgment on us than it itself can give, and suggests rewards and punishments dependent on our virtue or vice (II.8; *Virtue* 3). Even atheists, should there be any, can see from this that they are liable to divine punishment if God exists. They can see what they ought to do, and it is violating a known obligation, not knowledge of the penalty for transgression, that makes one justly punishable (pref. 27–9).[36]

Third, behavior is natural, or suitable or correspondent to our nature, in virtue of being conformable to a principle of superior authority (III.9; pref. 39). In admitting that we ought to visit a dentist to prevent a bad toothache, even though we detest going to dentists, we are recognizing the superior authority of self-interest. We similarly recognize the even higher authority of conscience when we see that we ought to make some important sacrifice for our children or our country. But what gives these principles their authority? Authority cannot be founded on the naturalness of behavior because it is the source of naturalness. What, then, does it rest on?[37]

Butler's answer is not one that we are likely to find philosophically satisfactory, but it is perfectly in keeping with his whole position. The makeup of conscience shows that it "was placed within to be our proper governor" (II.15). The very fact that the claim to supreme authority is part of the nature of conscience gives us reason to suppose that God intends it to guide us. What better foundation for its authority could there be? "Conscience is God's vice-gerent," says Whichcote, "the God dwelling within us" (Patrides, p. 335). Butler would agree. His frequent comparison of the constitution of the self to a political constitution makes it clear that the authority of conscience is the authority of God's

---

35 See Darwall 1995, ch. 9.

36 Butler here agrees with Suarez, *De Legibus* II.ix.3 (*Selections*, p. 225), who finds the same doctrine in Gerson, and with Culverwell, p. 52.

37 This issue is discussed at length in Sturgeon 1976; see Penelhum 1985 for commentary.

deputy. It is no part of Butler's plan to explain God's authority in sermons on morality. He does not even take a decisive stance on the issue Hutcheson raises, of whether morality derives from sentiment or reason. He is indifferent whether the moral faculty be called "conscience, moral reason, moral sense, or divine reason; whether considered as a sentiment of the understanding or a perception of the heart; or which seems the truth, as including both" (*Virtue* 1; cf. II.1, 8).[38] Butler nowhere claims that the awareness of all these data about the self give us conclusive proof that we are to obey conscience. But the facts point clearly enough at this conclusion to convince any reasonable person (XV). We can be virtuous without further theoretical insight into morality.[39]

There is finally a question about whether the deliverances of conscience can be mistaken. Standard treatments of conscience prior to Butler generally included a discussion of the erring conscience. Puritan divines, seeking to defend conscientious disobedience to clerical or royal ordinances, argued that conscience binds as much when it errs as when it is correct.[40] Hobbes was well aware of the political danger of this doctrine, as was Locke when he defined conscience as nothing more than a man's opinion of his own action. Living under a stable government, not plagued by questions of divided allegiance, Butler discusses the issue as a matter of personal morality, not of politics. He often seems unduly optimistic about moral error. "In all common ordinary cases," he says, "we see intuitively at first view what is our duty, what is the honest part" (VII.14). Consequently there is not much point in trying to articulate rules. "Let any plain, honest man, before he engages in some course of action, ask himself, Is this I am going about right, or is it wrong? . . . I do not in the least doubt but that this question would be answered agreeably to truth and virtue, by almost any fair man in almost any circumstances" (III.4).

Is Butler then blind to the horrendous misjudgments people often make, and act on? By no means; but he blames them primarily not on an erring conscience, but on personal faults that warp our judgment about the facts (pref. 31). Superstition and partiality to oneself all too often lead us astray (III.4). Butler presents Balaam, torn between religious duty and self-interest and deluding himself into thinking he could ac-

38   There are other passages in which he appears more decided. Thus at Sermon XII.9 he attributes to "rationality . . . both the discernment of what is right, and a disposition to do it."

39   I return to the question of the foundations for the authority of conscience at the end of the chapter.

40   See the passage from Ames, *Conscience* I.IV.6, cited in Chapter V.iii, for a widely held view.

commodate the one to serve the other, as only one among great numbers who try to convince themselves that things are not as they are (VII.12, 15–16). He devotes a whole sermon to David's moral blindness in arranging the murder of Uriah to conceal his relations with Bathsheba, as a striking illustration of the fact that "many men seem perfect strangers to their own characters."[41] In the worst cases, Butler says, partiality to ourselves "reaches to the understanding, and influences the very judgement." Because most of life cannot be guided by precise rules there is ample room for this kind of wrongdoing. Even if recalling the golden rule before we act may help a little in such cases, the damage done by corrupting the very source of moral insight is worse than wicked action springing from admitted selfishness (X.2, 6, 9, 14–15). Butler does not offer any general remedy.

vii. *Self-love, benevolence, and morality*

We can best see what a properly functioning conscience does by looking at specific issues. Some of our particular passions lead us to acts that benefit ourselves, others to acts that help our neighbor. General principles of self-love and beneficence move us to plan the satisfaction of these desires so as to bring about the greatest good, either to ourselves or to others. Conscience shows us the proper balance within ourselves, and indirectly the balance of goods we are to bring about. The whole scheme bears the marks of providential design. But what about dispositions that lead us to do evil to others (I.11)? Butler does not deny that we have them; he adds that we likewise have passions that cause us to harm ourselves; and he devotes a number of sermons to discussing both kinds.

Two points govern Butler's analyses. No passions seek evil as such, either to self or to others (I.12); and the "proper use" of any passion is a function of the end or good for which it was given (IV.7). Consider, then, resentment – an apparently perverse passion for a benevolent God to have given us. Yet it must be good, and Butler not surprisingly shows us how. Sudden anger serves to help us resist "violence and opposition," and may even help deter it. Settled anger, or resentment proper, arms us against "injury, injustice, and cruelty" rather than against mere harm (VIII.6–8). Like all natural passions, then, it can bring about a good, or it can be abused. The office of conscience is to show us when our resentment is too strong or too weak. In effect it tells us when we have enough for it to be the virtue of righteous indignation, and when we have so much that it becomes a vice such as vengefulness.

41 For an important discussion of the complexities of commentary on the story of King David, see the study of Bayle's *Dictionary* article on him in Rex 1965, ch. 6.

I pass over Butler's treatment of other particular passions to come to
the general principles of self-love and benevolence. As the text for his
two sermons on the issues, Butler takes the Gospel statement in Romans
13.9 that the commandments are summarized by the saying, "Thou
shalt love thy neighbor as thyself." Butler confronts two problems
about the limits of love. Are not self-love and love of neighbor in conflict? And is it true that all the commandments are contained in the
command to love?

The problem posed by self-love comes first. If anything is a moral
peculiarity of his own times, Butler says, it is the popularity of the belief
that one's own interest is to be pursued without limit. Against this he
asks whether that pursuit may not be self-defeating (XI.1). In arguing
that it is, he relies on his earlier distinction between particular passions
and the principle of self-interest. The latter is nothing but a drive to
increase one's own happiness. The drive cannot itself constitute happiness, which consists rather in "the enjoyment of those objects, which are
by nature suited to our several particular appetites, passions, and affections." Devotion to increasing the impulse of self-interest would lessen
happiness by taking our attention away from its sources, our other
interests. If we do not have such specific concerns there will be nothing
whose attainment we will enjoy, and therefore nothing for the drive to
increase our happiness to work with (XI.8–9). Of course someone might
say that because one gets pleasure from gratifying a desire one is always self-interested when one does what one wants. But this, Butler
says, "is not the language of mankind." To speak in such terms is to
deprive ourselves of the ability to distinguish between particular passions whose intended end is some benefit to the agent and particular
passions whose immediate object is something else (XI.7; pref. 35). I
may desire to do good for a friend even at the cost of ruin to myself. It
would be a distortion of language to say that this desire is as self-
interested as, for instance, the desire to take advantage of a friend's
trust to double my wealth.

Butler concludes that conflict between self-love and benevolence is
no more unavoidable than conflict between self-love and any other
desire. If I desire to help others, I will get happiness from doing so
(XI.11–12). Butler thinks that gratifying appropriate benevolent impulses is one of the greatest sources of happiness (I.6; III.7), although he
does not elaborate the point as Shaftesbury and Hutcheson do. Like
them, he asserts repeatedly that virtue and self-interest perfectly coincide (I.4; III.9). He is, however, far more concerned than they about the
disruptive power of particular passions (III.8). Particular passions can
wreck one's own life and gravely harm others. Butler sees self-interest
as a countervailing virtue. He insists that it is a properly *moral* virtue,
and that we disapprove morally of imprudence (*Virtue* 6–7). In a per-

plexing passage he seems to concede even more to self-interest. Virtue is the pursuit of the right and the good, to be sure; but it may be allowed that "when we sit down in a cool hour, we can neither justify to ourselves this or any other pursuit, till we are convinced that it will be for our happiness, or at least not contrary to it" (XI.20).

Is Butler here attributing to self-love an authority greater than that of conscience? Or is he saying that virtue will turn out to be justified even to someone who considers the matter only from the point of view of self-interest? Interpreters disagree strongly. I am inclined toward the second reading. Butler refers to this sermon as one in which he has removed "prejudices against . . . the love of neighbor" (XII.1). If the psychological prejudice is removed by the analysis showing that benevolence is at least not contrary to self-love, then, he suggests, there is nothing to fear from a justificatory prejudice. It seems unlikely that a writer as careful as Butler would have failed to see so flat a contradiction as the other reading involves.

Since we have both benevolent and self-interested impulses, the task of conscience is to show us the proper proportions they are to have to one another (XII.9–11). Humans are not called on to love as universally as God does. We are to love our neighbor, not all the creation or even all mankind (XII.3). Moreover, as our concern for ourselves should not be all-engulfing, so too our concern for others is bounded. Benevolence must acknowledge that each of us has the responsibility for our own well-being. We cannot be expected to do everything for others (XII.14–19).

Familial affection and friendship, attention to one's special obligations, respect for social rank, temperance and the other ordinary virtues may seem at first to limit benevolence still further, though they really spring from it (XII.27–31). But there is a genuine limitation to general benevolence. Butler sketches it in a footnote. We approve, he says, of certain dispositions and actions that do not bear directly on happiness or unhappiness. Treachery, indecency, and meanness of mind draw our disapproval and contempt, fidelity and strict justice our approval, "abstracted from the consideration of their tendency." He offers an explanation. We are in no position to judge what is for the good of the whole. God, of course, is; and it is possible that even if the good of the whole is his aim, he may "have laid us under particular obligations, which we may discern and feel ourselves under" despite our inability to see that fulfilling them benefits others. Our moral approvals and disapprovals give us some evidence that God has in fact done this (XII.31n).

The second *Dissertation* is more emphatic in arguing that "benevolence, and the want of it, singly considered, are in no sort the whole of virtue and vice." Butler gives some cases to show that the thesis that benevolence is the whole of virtue leads to moral judgments we simply do not accept. The thesis implies, for example, that it would be right to take property from its owner and give it to another whose benefit would outweigh the owner's loss. It implies that we are indifferent as to whether family members or strangers receive benefits from someone as long as the benefits are equal. But we disapprove of certain acts without even considering the benefits and harms they cause. It follows, Butler thinks, that even if God's whole moral character is benevolence, "yet ours is not so." To think otherwise, he adds, is terribly dangerous.

> For it is certain, that some of the most shocking instances of injustice, adultery, murder, perjury, and even of persecution, may, in many supposable cases, not have the appearance of being likely to produce an overbalance of misery in the present state, may sometimes even have the contrary appearance.

Hutcheson's view – though not named, he is plainly the target – would then lead us to think such acts not wrong (*Virtue* 8–10). We cannot accept any general thesis so plainly irreconcilabie with our conscientious convictions. Hutcheson's own method leads to his refutation.

viii. *God and morality*

For Butler, then, as for the natural lawyers, no single principle is adequate to spell out morality as we are to live by it. If our trust in the divine administration of the universe leads us to think that somehow all virtues conduce to good (XII.32), conscience nonetheless places limits on the role of love in our lives. We must be just, honorable, and truthful no matter what the consequences. We must be prudent and benevolent as well. Neither in the *Sermons* nor in the second *Dissertation* does Butler explain matters any further. As Whewell said, he offers no theory. But we find clues to his position in the *Analogy,* and since they help us to a fuller understanding of his moral outlook, it is worth following them.

In the *Analogy* Butler rejects the idea, hypothesized in the twelfth sermon and the *Dissertation,* that we should think of God as moved only by benevolence. Were we to take that view, he says in a phrase that strongly recalls Leibniz, we would have to think that "veracity and justice in him would be nothing but benevolence conducted by wisdom." But we lack evidence for this view. Although we can at best make guesses, it may be that God is moved not by the simple disposition to make us happy, but by the complex disposition to make the good and honest man happy. Perhaps God is pleased with the "moral piety of moral agents in and for itself, as well as upon account of its being essentially conducive to the happiness of his creation" (*Analogy* I.II.3). Perhaps, in short, God wills our happiness only on condition of our being virtuous, and our being virtuous requires our being just and veracious as well as benevolent. Like Malebranche and Clarke, Butler thus seems to be working toward a way to reject voluntarism without adopting the sweeping consequentialism of Cumberland and Leibniz.

I return now to the question of the basis for the deliverances of conscience. It is perhaps more evident at this point that conscience, whether it directs us to increase our benevolence, or to set it aside in order to be just or truthful, is showing us God's will. It is moreover showing us not only *what* he wills, but *why* he wills it. Conscience, God's voice in us, transmits what God sees to be the eternal truths about desirable character. It is fit that finite agents should be happy, and also that they should be just and truthful. "Moral precepts," Butler says, "are precepts, the reasons of which we see; positive precepts, are precepts, the reasons of which we do not see" (*Analogy* II.I.21).[42] Conscience, finally, does more than enable us to see what God sees. If we understand conscience fully, we understand that God commands us to comply with it. Fully conscientious agents will know why they ought to do what they ought to do; but in complying, they will be obeying not themselves but God.

42   I was mistaken about this point in Schneewind 1991, and am indebted for this correction, as for much else in my understanding of Butler, to Professor Wendell O'Brien, who drew my attention to the passage I have just quoted from the *Analogy*.

17

Hume: Virtue naturalized

I have argued that the voluntarist natural lawyers tried to keep God essential to morality while confining his role in it to his initial willful act of creating it. Machiavelli and Harrington did without God in establishing their principles, though they thought a stable republic needed a civil religion. Montaigne explored the possibility of morality without religion, and his follower Charron made some effort to create a systematic naturalistic theory. Although Hobbes worked out such a system quite fully, he retained a marginal role for God in transforming the dictates of prudence into genuine laws; and however tempting it is for us to read Spinoza as a wholehearted naturalizer of morality, his own understanding of the universe was profoundly religious. Mandeville gave a natural history of morality, only to add to it an account of a demanding principle that has something to do with the divinity. No one believed he meant that part of what he said, and in any case it is plain that he was more interested in outraging public sentiment than he was in presenting a serious and thorough naturalistic philosophical account of human life.

David Hume (1711–76) intended to give just such an account. He made very clear, moreover, his belief that religion is morally and politically detrimental to society and human happiness. He did not urge the establishment of a civil religion for the masses. He hoped, rather, that the light of advancing knowledge would cause religious belief to disappear.

Hume was raised as a Scots Calvinist, and in his youth took seriously the exposition of religion given in a popular seventeenth-century devotional manual, *The Whole Duty of Man*.[1] Its preface urges the care of the soul upon its readers. Care is especially needed because Adam broke the first covenant with God – the agreement that all things would be Adam's if he refrained from eating the fruit of one tree. As a result all his descendants are "both ignorant in discerning what we ought to do,

---

1 Probably but not certainly by Richard Allestree.

and weak and unable to the doing of it" (XIII). There is hope for us, however, because in the second covenant God promised to send his son to redeem us. We have but to obey Christ as our King and never to rebel against his laws; thanks to him some of us may be given the ability to comply (XVII, XXI).[2] A series of Sunday homilies spells out the details of this whole duty. Hume when young checked his morals against the list; when a little older he preferred to measure himself by the teachings of Cicero, Seneca, and Plutarch.[3] In his mature thought he aimed to replace Christian duties with a naturalized ethics of virtue, modeled on the thought of the ancients but even less mindful than they of the gods.

Hume was long viewed as dangerous to religion and morals, an extreme skeptic to be attacked rather than studied. Scholarly work in this century, and changes in philosophical opinion, have transformed him from pariah to paragon. The literature on him is enormous, the number of interpretations almost as large. My aim in this chapter is less to add to the number than to relate Hume's views to some of the philosophical discussions of morality that he knew and took into account. In presenting Hume's position I draw largely on the account of it in the *Treatise of Human Nature* (1739–40), which is more fully elaborated than that in the later *Enquiry concerning the Principles of Morals* (1751).

i. *Moral philosophy as a science of sentiment*

Pufendorf opened his major work on natural law with a chapter on the status of morality in the universe. Hume similarly begins his treatment of morality, in book III of the *Treatise,* with a prolegomenon on the topic. Thereafter he departs from precedent, making no use, for instance, of the threefold scheme of duties to self, to others, and to God. His abandonment of these categories is part of the enterprise of getting religion out of morality. The way he argues for his views is shaped by his determination to present them as the outcome of scientific investigation. To put himself in a position to do so, he takes, quite deliberately, an antireligious moral stance about the role of desire in morality.

The title page of the *Treatise* announces that the book is "an Attempt to introduce the experimental Method of Reasoning into Moral Subjects." The term "moral" is used to contrast the sciences that study human beings with the natural sciences that deal with the rest of the universe; morality in the narrower sense is only a part of what is to be

2   Unlike the sermons to which Hume listened when he was a boy, *The Whole Duty* is not explicit about the doctrines of election, prevenient grace, and predestination. See N. K. Smith, introduction to Hume's *Dialogues*, p. 4.
3   Mossner 1954, pp. 34, 64.

investigated. Hume regrets that deliberate experiments cannot be carried out in this domain, but is sure even so that experience will provide him with all the material he needs.[4] We cannot explain the most basic facts. Once we find them, however, we may hope to develop a science as certain as, and more useful than, any other science we possess (pp. xviii–xix). What then are the basic facts that a theory of morality needs to take into account? And what sort of theory can we expect from studying them?

To get to his reply, Hume first asks how we "distinguish between vice and virtue, and pronounce an action blameable or praiseworthy" (p. 456). Do we make the distinction by reasoning? Or do we make it noninferentially, by some impression – some sensation or affection or sentiment arising in the mind immediately upon its perception of an act or agent? Hume's answer is like Hutcheson's (Chapter 16.iv). He dismisses rationalism with a short but powerful argument. "Morals excite passions, and produce or prevent actions. Reason of itself is utterly impotent in this particular. The rules of morality, therefore, are not conclusions of our reason."[5] The first premise seems obvious: why all the fuss about moral rules and precepts unless they affect our behavior (p. 457)? The second premise arises from his analysis, in book II, of the roles of desire and reason in producing action, which I discuss in the next section. Hume drives his point home here with some additional Hutchesonian considerations about reason.

Reason, Hume says, tells us only about truth or falsehood. Now passions and actions are "original facts . . . compleat in themselves." They are neither true nor false, and they can be neither contradicted nor affirmed. Although they are consequently the wrong kind of thing to be reasonable or unreasonable, they can be laudable or blamable. So the latter two terms cannot mean what the former two mean (p. 458). Reason can give us beliefs about means, but no one thinks they are themselves moral beliefs, or the whole subject of moral assessment (pp. 459–60). If morality is to be demonstrated, and brought, as some claim it can be, "to an equal certainty with geometry or algebra" (p. 463), it must be a matter of relations of ideas, or analytic truths. But none of the kinds of relations of ideas are found always and only in morality. Even if they

---

4   There are several points, e.g., *Treatise* II.II.ii, at which Hume gives a number of "experiments" designed to help the reader see the accuracy of one of Hume's positions. They are of course experiments in thought only, but they exemplify many aspects of what J. S. Mill later described as scientific methods, such as concomitant variation.

5   Malebranche might well have agreed that what Hume says is true of human beings in their sinful, fallen condition. Only Adam seems to have been able to be moved directly by the light of his knowledge of Order. See Chapter 11.vi.

were, there would still be the problem of showing that recognition of such relations would have the motivational effect that morality must have. Rationalists like Malebranche and Clarke allow that the knowing a moral principle is one thing and being moved by it another. From this Hume draws an anti-Clarkean, but quite Malebranchean, conclusion: if moral knowledge and moral motivation are distinguishable, there is no necessary connection between them. The only kind of proof appropriate for a claim about what moves everyone is empirical. So no moral principle can be proved a priori because, as Hume reminds us he has shown in book I, there can be no a priori proof that anything moves anything to act. And morals must move us to act (pp. 464–6).

If the rationalist, in desperation, says that a matter of fact discoverable by reason is the core of morality, Hume asks to be told what it is. Looking at a murder, for instance, he finds facts about motions and passions and volitions, but no moral facts – at least not until he looks within. Then he finds a fact: a feeling of blame. All we can mean when we speak of virtue and vice is feelings of approval and disapproval (pp. 468–9).

Morality is thus "more properly felt than judg'd of" (p. 470). The task of a science of morals then becomes clear. If "the distinguishing *impressions*, by which moral good and evil is known, are nothing but particular pains or pleasures," the question is, What causes us to have the pains and pleasures that are the feelings of moral approval and disapproval (p. 471)? There are evidently many kinds of things about which we feel approval or disapproval. It would be poor scientific method to suppose that each sort of thing we approve of evokes approval due to its own peculiar constitution. So we must ask what the objects of approval or disapproval have in common that is not shared by morally neutral objects. When we find it, we will have found the basis of morality (p. 473).

In a famous passage Hume remarks that many philosophers describe the way God or human affairs are in fact constituted, and then draw inferences about how things *ought* to be. He adds that he fails to see how an inference from *is* to *ought* can be valid. Those who try to draw it do not explain their procedure, Hume doubts that they can, and adds dryly that the "vulgar systems of morality" are all subverted by this point (pp. 469–70). Hobbes's reductive account of obligation falls to the criticism, as do the theories of Pufendorf and Locke, with their claims about the possibility of an empirically based deductive science of morality. So too do any other views – Butler's included – resting on an inference of what we ought to do from observable distinctive features of human nature. If the motivation argument eliminates moral rationalism, the "is-ought" argument cuts against any empiricist attempt to provide rational justifications for moral claims by appeal to facts about human nature.

In his own work Hume makes no use of the kind of deductive argument he condemns. He claims to discover principles of morals, and to show how they are related to what is the case. His principles are not meant as starting points from which we can rationally justify our moral beliefs. They are meant only to explain certain feelings we all experience as being caused by a small number of specific features of the characters and actions we pronounce praiseworthy or blamable. If he is right, we can understand how some of our beliefs about what is the case cause moral approval and disapproval and lead us to have convictions about what we ought to do. He thinks we should expect no deeper explanation of morality (*Principles of Morals*, p. 219n). A science of the moral sentiments is all we can look for, once we see that in morality neither purely rational nor empirical justification is available. If Hume makes moral judgments in his writings, he does not think they are epistemologically privileged. They are causally explicable in the way everyone's moral pronouncements are.

ii. *Desire, belief, and action*

When Hume insists in his first premise that morality moves us to action, he is doing more than laying the ground for his criticism of rationalism. He is denying the Calvinist and Lutheran view of the relation of moral principle to human motivation. The moral law cannot, as the Reformers held, be intended to show us that we cannot do what we ought to do. (See Chapter 2.iv, vi.) The desires arising from our nature as it now is set the limits to what morality can demand. No alleged morality that was unable to move us by itself could be a morality valid for us. Whatever morality asks of us is something we are already moved to do. Leibniz would have agreed. His morality is even more strongly a function of the desires from which we act than Hume's is. But Leibniz's world is divinely chosen to have the best outcomes, whereas Hume's is not; and the two philosophers understand desire in radically different ways. The difference here underlies Hume's sentimentalism.

For Leibniz all thoughts are representations, and desires are among the less clear and distinct. They represent, confusedly, amounts of perfection, and in representing perfection move us to strive for it. Leibniz's theory is essentially that of the Stoics. Plutarch tells us that the Stoics

suppose that the passionate and irrational part [of the soul] is not distinguished from the rational by any distinction within the soul's nature, but the same part of the soul (which they call thought and commanding-faculty) becomes virtue and vice as it turns around and changes in passions . . . and contains nothing irrational within itself.[6]

6 See Long/Sedley, I.61B.9, p. 378.

Hume's assertion that the passions are complete in themselves is his rejection of this theory. And if passion, which is not rational, must be what moves us, then reason cannot directly guide or control what we do.

Like Shaftesbury and Hutcheson, Hume accepts the Lockean view of passions and desires as nonrepresentational forces moving us in one direction or another. All the passions, Hume says, involve perceptions of what he calls indifferently good or ill, pleasure or pain (*Treatise*, p. 276). Most are caused by the belief that something is good or bad, which comes from our having felt pleasure or pain from it. Others "arise from a natural impulse or instinct, which is perfectly unaccountable" but which makes us think its object good (p. 439). Whichever way we come to think something good, the idea is involved in all desires. To say this, however, is not to say that the passions depend wholly on thoughts of good and ill. Those thoughts do not explain the difference between strong or weak desires, or between calm and violent passions (pp. 418–19, 437). And they do not alone determine the will.

There is in fact no formula that accounts for our willing. The will is a simple impression, Hume says, felt "when we knowingly give rise to any new motion of our body, or new perception of our mind" (p. 399). Metaphysicians say it is determined by some single factor. But experience shows otherwise. "Men often act knowingly against their interest: For which reason the view of the greatest possible good does not always influence them. Men often counteract a violent passion in prosecution of their designs and interests: 'Tis not therefore the present uneasiness alone, which determines them" (p. 418).[7] Reason thus can control neither the passions nor the will by informing them of the amounts of good that would result from gratifying our desires. The most it can do is to tell us when the objects of desire are available, and to find means to get what we want (p. 459). "Reason is, and ought only to be the slave of the passions" (p. 415), Hume concludes, echoing Hobbes's view that reason

7   Thus Hume dismisses Locke's theory of present uneasiness as what motivates us, while accepting his criticism of the view that the thought of the greatest good motivates. The other metaphysician may be Mandeville, but it may be Leibniz. In the correspondence with Clarke, which could hardly have escaped Hume's attention, Leibniz reiterates his view that motives are the mind's dispositions to act. "And therefore to pretend, as [Clarke] does here," he continues, "that the mind prefers sometimes weak motives to strong ones, and even that it prefers that which is indifferent before motives: this, I say, is to divide the mind from the motives, as if they were without the mind . . . and as if the mind had, besides motives, other dispositions to act, by virtue of which it could reject or accept motives" (*LCCorr*, p. 59). Hume's moral sentiment, like Shaftesbury's and Hutcheson's, is precisely something other than a motive which rejects or accepts motives.

is but the scout for passions; and with this he has in hand the second premise of the argument to show that morality is centrally dependent on feelings.

The will plays no essential role in Hume's theory of action.[8] And it seems that although he must show that moral approval and disapproval are involved in causing our behavior, he cannot easily explain how they function. The desires and passions seem to be what move us. What role do the moral feelings play? Simply this: approval reinforces, and disapproval damps down, whatever motives or character traits cause them. Approval not only makes those who give it willing to help us, it also gains us their esteem or love. Like Nicole, Hume thinks that we all enjoy being loved. Hence we try to cultivate the qualities that make us lovable.[9] It is a mark of our sociability that we do so. And insofar as our strong concern for our reputation (p. 501) is an interest in having the moral esteem of others, it is also a sociable desire. "Morals excite passions, and produce or prevent actions," then, not by bringing us knowledge in the indistinct form of pleasure (as Malebranche held) but by causing us to be moved differently than we would be if no one had any moral sentiments.

For Hume as for Pufendorf, the point of morality is not to inform us about the world, but to move us. Hume's way of working this out gives him a way of bypassing moral skepticism. There is no room for skeptical doubt about morals, on Hume's view, because in responding morally we make no epistemological claims about which we could be mistaken. Without disputing the Pyrrhonist view that all we have are appearances, Hume is in effect claiming that the appearances will give us all we need, not just for personal guidance, as Montaigne thought, but for social life as well. Hutcheson and Hume are at one with Shaftesbury on this matter. When we reflect on our responses to the appearances of good and ill – our desires and motives – another feeling arises that backs some and rejects others. Shaftesbury, as I pointed out in

8   When at *Treatise*, p. 408, Hume ridicules those who try to prove that they have a "free" will by acting capriciously, he is attacking Descartes's view that we can control ourselves by forming the habit of thinking admiringly of our unique capacity to choose independently of antecedent causation. In such cases we act from a new desire, not from no desire. In discussing liberty of will in the *Enquiry concerning Human Understanding* VII.I, Hume devotes several paragraphs to attacking Malebranchean occasionalism, claiming that its assertions about the power of God's will are undermined by, among other things, the fact that we have no impression, and hence no idea, of how a mind causes a body to move (pp. 69–73).

9   Hume does not think we can alter our character to any considerable degree, so it may be that our desire for moral approval will lead us to control only our behavior (*Treatise*, pp. 608–9).

Chapter 14.vi, leaves a door open to skepticism here. Hutcheson and Hume close it. The method of ethics they think we all possess involves only a spontaneous feeling about motives, not a trained sensitivity. Montaigne might have protested that our sentiments are much more varied than Hutcheson and Hume allow; but that is a matter for factual – Hume might say scientific – investigation.

It is sometimes said that Hume develops his moral theory from the standpoint of a spectator rather than an agent. He takes as central not questions like "What should I do now?" but questions like "Was she a good person in acting as she did?" Hume admittedly does not offer an account of deliberation (as Hobbes did), still less provide rules for decision making. But if the point is meant as a criticism, it begs the question against Hume. It assumes that human agency has some privileged position in the universe, or at least in the moral universe; and he would not have agreed.

He addresses the point in discussing causality in connection with the mind. If causation requires that we perceive a connection in the ideas of the cause and its effect, then not even God is a cause. If we insist that we know, even without having any idea of power, that God causes all things, then we must allow him to be the cause even of our volitions and hence of our misdeeds. Philosophers have tried to avoid the conclusion by excepting our volition from God's power. But "[i]f nothing be active but what has an apparent power, thought is in no case any more active than matter." And if we say that objects that are constantly conjoined are therefore causally connected, then causal connections between matter and thought will not be impossible or even unusual (pp. 248–50). If human agency is nothing more than desire or will followed by bodily motion, as Hume thinks it is, then it is just another species of constant conjunction in the natural world.

Hume's starting question, like Hutcheson's, is not about spectators or agents but about the presence of morality in a Newtonian universe of bodies in motion. Given Hume's naturalistic assumptions about what we can observe, the question is, How is it that some bodies are moved by moral thoughts and utterances? The answer bears out Hume's denial that there is something special about agency. All the facts about morals can be explained without invoking it. So far we have seen how there can be morality at all.[10] The bulk of Hume's theory concerns its contents – the specific feelings that create the moral world.

10 Pufendorf held that God's will, and ours, could impose moral entities onto a world of force and motion. Hume holds that it is not our will but our distinctive moral taste that is thus productive. It gilds natural objects with colors "borrowed from internal sentiment" and thereby "raises in a manner a new creation" (*Principles of Morals*, p. 294).

iii. *Laws of approval*

The search for the qualities that cause approval and disapproval begins by specifying the objects of those feelings. Neither laws, nor lawmakers, nor actions, nor the outcomes of actions are the primary concern of praise and approval. The object of "conscience, or a sense of morals" (*Treatise*, p. 458) is motives. In his earlier discussion of the passions Hume has already argued that there are causal connections between motives of a given character and actions of a definite kind (pp. 403–4). This fact explains our apparent approval of actions: we do indeed speak of actions as virtuous or vicious, but only because actions are signs of motives (pp. 477–8). Hume offers little evidence to show that motives are the primary object of the moral sentiments (p. 478); and his only suggestion as to why they are is the Malebranchean suggestion that motives are enduring enough, and actions too transient, to arouse such sentiments (p. 575; cf. p. 411).

A survey of the character traits that we do in fact approve produces a long list. Whatever moves people to be just, respect property, honor contracts and promises, and obey the government wins our approval. So too do chastity and modesty, at least in women. We esteem the well-regulated pride that shows itself in "[c]ourage, intrepidity, ambition, love of glory, magnanimity" (pp. 599–600); we think there is merit in "generosity, humanity, compassion, gratitude, friendship, fidelity, zeal, disinterestedness, liberality" and other benevolent qualities such as parental affection (p. 603). Hume refuses to acknowledge any difference between the approval we give these traits and that which we feel toward "[i]ndustry, perseverance, patience, activity, vigilance, application, constancy." Great men, he tells us, are praised for "their prudence, temperance, frugality, assiduity, enterprize, dexterity" (p. 587). Add to this that we value wit and eloquence as well as good humor (pp. 609–11), and it is clear how varied is the collection of approvals, and corresponding disapprovals, calling for explanation.

The explanation, as we would expect from a good scientific account, derives the effects from relatively few causes. The traits we endorse all lead to acts that contribute to human well-being or good. Some, such as benevolence and justice, lead us to do what is useful not to ourselves but to others. Virtues like industry and frugality make agents useful to themselves. Wit and eloquence are immediately agreeable to those to whom they are displayed, and good humor is enjoyed by its lucky possessor regardless of its effects on others. We have, then, an inductive argument to show that approval is caused by character traits that are useful or immediately agreeable, either to others or to the agents themselves (p. 591).

In the course of giving the evidence for his view of the underlying causes of approval, Hume also displays the mechanism that explains why we have a pleasant sentiment of approval on noticing that something helps or pleases other people, even those with whom we have no personal connection. Both his theory of the actual makeup of the sentiment of approval and his theory of sympathy are involved in the explanation.

Although Hume names and describes the moral sentiment in various ways, approval and disapproval are for him essentially feelings of love and hate (p. 614). He sometimes says that moral approval is a kind of esteem; but "love and esteem are at the bottom the same passions, and arise from like causes" (p. 608n; cf. p. 357). Love, we learn in book II, is a simple feeling and cannot be defined. We can, however, discover its objects and causes. It is always directed at some person other than oneself. What is misleadingly called self-love has nothing in common with the real feeling of love (p. 329). Genuine love is aroused when one person observes another who possesses some pleasing quality, such as beauty or charm or talent, which matches and elicits the pleasing quality possessed by the feeling of love itself (p. 330–1).

Love is thus the feeling that arises when we take pleasure in the pleasurable qualities of another. As such it has no end or aim. If we happen to think of the happiness of the person we love, then we will find ourselves moved by benevolence toward that person and will desire his or her well-being. Yet we can love someone for a long time without that thought occurring to us. Humean love is thus essentially contemplative, neither acquisitive nor erotic nor selflessly generous like Christian *agapē*. Yet Hume believes that we often do think of the happiness of those we love. When we do, benevolence normally follows (pp. 367–8).[11]

Hume adds a qualification of considerable importance to the theory that our judgments of virtue and vice are essentially feelings. There are variations in the felt quality of pleasures and pains, he notes, and only some of them are "of that *peculiar* kind, which makes us praise or condemn." We must be thinking of someone's motive or character disinterestedly, without considering its impact on us, in order to have the specific feeling that "denominates it morally good or evil" (p. 472). By concentrating our sympathies on those who are most directly affected by the person we are judging, we gain a fixed point that will allow

11   "I see no contradiction," Hume remarks, "in supposing a desire of producing misery annex'd to love, and of happiness to hatred" (*Treatise*, p. 368). Hume's approval has similarities to what Descartes calls favor, which is "aroused in us by some good action of the person toward whom we bear it . . . a kind of love, not desire, though it is always accompanied by the desire to see good come to the one whom we favour" (*Passions of the Soul* 192, in *Writings* I.397).

everyone to feel the same way (pp. 581–2). Disinterestedness is not a defining feature of moral feeling, but a causally necessary condition of its occurrence. If it gives morality a coolness that we normally think of as belonging rather to reason than to feeling, we should not be deceived. The moral sentiments are among the "calm desires" that are better discerned by their effects than by their sensible quality (pp. 583, 417).

When I possess something that has unusually pleasing qualities, it arouses pride in me; and I, as possessing such a thing, am the sort of person who arouses love in others. The bearing on virtue and vice is clear: "these two particulars are to be consider'd as equivalent, with regard to our mental qualities, *virtue* and the power of producing love or pride, *vice* and the power of producing humility and hatred" (p. 575). *The Whole Duty of Man* taught a different lesson about pride: "The sin of it is so great that it cast the angels out of heaven. . . . it was not only the first but the greatest sin" (VI.4).[12] Hume makes pride the natural accompaniment of qualities that awaken moral approval. Humility, for Christians the virtue of docile submission to God, is for Hume caused by qualities that lead to disapproval, which is itself a form of hatred.

With this understanding of approval, the stage is set for the operation of sympathy. Sympathy is an animal capacity enabling the feelings of others to reverberate within us. Because of it, we can grasp what the beneficiaries of justice or generosity feel, no matter how remote from us they may be. Benefactors appear in a pleasing light to the beneficiaries, whose view we spectators sympathetically share. We can love benefactors because of their pleasing quality of benefiting others. Sympathy, in short, puts us in a position favorable to feeling love; we are equipped by nature to feel the peculiar kind of love that we call approval or esteem; and as we are thinking of happiness in the circumstances that generate the feeling, we naturally desire some good for the virtuous agent and some harm for the vicious one – or in other words, thoughts and desires of reward and punishment naturally follow the moral sentiments (p. 591). Sympathy and the moral sentiments together generate the distinctively moral aspect of the world.[13]

---

12   The view is at least as old as St. Augustine: "Whence doth iniquity abound? From Pride. Cure pride and there will be no more iniquity. Consequently that the cause of all diseases might be cured . . . the Son of God came down and was made low" (*On St. John Evangelist* xxv.16).

13   Hume sometimes speaks as if sympathy alone were a source of approval (e.g., *Treatise,* p. 577) but this is hyperbole. Sympathy could give us concerns for strangers, but unless we had the moral faculty we would not have the thought that such a concern is a virtue. We would have no moral concepts at all.

iv. *Artificial and natural virtues*

Hume's insistence on the priority of motivation is as central to his discussion of the contents of morality as it is to his sentimentalism about its nature. He organizes his analysis of what morality calls for by a division of the virtues into the artificial and the natural. The division is best understood in the light of the natural law distinction between perfect and imperfect duties.

Hume acknowledges a debt to Grotius in his second *Enquiry*, and there is no doubt that he was familiar with Pufendorf and other natural law writers as well.[14] The coincidence between Hume's two categories of virtue and the Grotian dichotomy is too striking and too detailed to be accidental. The artificial virtues, for Hume, include justice, fidelity to promises, and allegiance to government.[15] Hume himself describes the natural virtues as the virtues of beneficence (*Treatise*, p. 603), and includes meekness, charity, clemency, moderation, and equity among them (p. 578). Hume's artificial virtues, like perfect duties, cover the domain of clear and definite claims that may be enforced by law. This is obvious in the case of justice and of duties owed to government in Hume's view of them, and becomes so with regard to promising when we note that Hume views it chiefly as concerned with "the interested commerce of mankind" (p. 522), that is, with contracts.

One of the arguments Hume uses to show that justice must be artificial appeals explicitly to the fact that in its domain clear and sharp distinctions are required: "all natural qualities," Hume says, "run insensibly into each other, and are, on many occasions, indistinguishable" (p. 530). This is true of "all kinds of vice and virtue" as well – or almost all kinds:

> [W]hatever may be the case, with regard to all kinds of vice and virtue, 'tis certain, that rights, and obligations, and property, admit of no such insensible gradation, but that a man either has a full and perfect property, or none at all, and is either entirely obliged to perform any action, or lies under no manner of obligation. (p. 529)

14 See the discussion in Forbes 1975, esp. ch. 1.
15 He also includes chastity and modesty, which he treats as arising from the man's desire to feel assured of his paternity of a child if he is to let it inherit his property. Pufendorf treats the issue as part of the natural law governing sexuality and marriage. Like Hume he ties it to the male desire to have legitimate offspring, but he does not stress the connection with property as Hume does. See *DJN* VI.I.10, pp. 855, 857; VI.I.18, p. 872; and VI.I.21, pp. 878–9, where Pufendorf says that people marry chiefly to have children.

If you admit that justice has this preciseness, Hume holds, you must agree that it is artificial, not natural.

Hume takes over yet a further aspect of the Grotian tradition. For Pufendorf the perfect duties are those which are indispensable for the existence of society; for Hume the artificial virtues are the ones required if any society beyond the level of the family is to exist, that of justice, concerning itself with property, being the most important of all (pp. 491, 497). Hume's natural virtues, like the imperfect duties, serve rather to ameliorate or embellish personal relations as they are in large societies. Both sorts of virtue, like both sorts of duty, produce good results. But instead of taking the distinction between the precise and the imprecise, or that between the enforceable and the unenforceable, to be the core of the difference between the artificial and the natural virtues, Hume takes the distinction to be that the good arising from the natural virtues is normally brought about in every case of their exercise, while the good arising from the artificial virtues comes about only as a result of the existence of a general practice of exercising them, and so may not come about in each particular case.[16]

A series of post-Humean philosophical works has brought out the depth and importance of the distinction between acts that bring benefits only if there is a general practice with which all or most others comply, and acts that bring benefits even if no others do similar acts. Hume's introduction of it is one of his most brilliant achievements. From a historical perspective it is probably best to describe it as his attempt to show how perfect as well as imperfect rights and duties can be explained by a virtue-centered theory. He seems to have been convinced that the Grotian tradition, in distinguishing between perfect and imperfect duties, had brought to our notice a definite pattern in moral approvals and disapprovals. Since these feelings are Hume's data, he has to explain the pattern. A theory making virtue rather than law the central concept of ethics is called for by the data showing that character traits are the objects of approval. This theory, Hume holds, can also give a better account of the artificial–natural distinction, and what it means for morality, than the theory proposed by the natural lawyers who initially noticed the facts.

The key to his theory is a narrative showing the ability of human nature to evolve its own directives and controls. Hume's theory of the

16 This is one important reason for calling them "artificial." Their exercise involves in each case the thought that others will similarly exercise them, and that these others will have the thought that I and others will exercise them, and so on. This is not true of the natural virtues, which need not involve the virtuous person's awareness of participating in a social practice. Hume emphasizes that it is natural for humans to develop the artificial virtues.

moral sentiments already carries the message that morality need not be imposed upon us from without. His thought is that we ourselves could have "*invented* the . . . fundamental laws of nature" once we came to see that such laws were needed to make society possible (pp. 543, 520).[17] He presents his account as a response to a problem posed by his principle that "virtuous actions derive their merit only from virtuous motives" (p. 478). There is no problem about the natural virtues. When we approve of parents looking after their children, and of the well-off caring for the needy, we are approving spontaneous parental affection or generosity. Perhaps building on the work of Shaftesbury, Hutcheson, and Butler, Hume does not seem to think it needs to be argued that people have such other-directed concerns. But how does it work with the artificial virtues?

No one doubts that we approve of acts of justice. Hence there must be some motive that leads to them. What can it be? Not, Hume argues, a "sense of morality or duty." There is such a motive, but it is a kind of stopgap, or second best. If people usually have a certain virtuous motive and someone notices that he lacks it, he may "hate himself upon that account" and do what the motive normally leads to in order to acquire the motive by practice. But if there were no motive for such acts in the first place, neither approval nor a sense of duty concerning them could be generated (p. 480).

Hume can find no natural, spontaneous motive that picks out all and only acts of justice. What we do under the heading of observing contracts and respecting property, and similar matters like keeping promises, forms no such unity as what we do in expressing our love of our children or our kindness to strangers. Self-interest certainly could not serve as the appropriate motive: it is more likely to cause injustice. Justice is owed to all, but no one has a love of humanity as such; and because we often owe justice to people who are strangers or even enemies, private benevolence cannot serve the purpose. There is in short no natural motive to follow justice. Unless we allow a sophistry in nature, therefore, we must see if there can be some other kind (pp. 481–3).

17 Hume is no Mandevillean. He thinks, as I note later, that the laws of nature are, as Mandeville says, invented without any appeal to morality, and that the first motive to them is self-interest; but they can be given moral significance only because we naturally have moral sentiments which give meaning to a shared moral vocabulary and because sympathy enables us to have a special kind of unselfish motive. See *Treatise*, pp. 578–9. Cudworth makes a similar point against those who argue that politicians have devised religion to support their own power. They could not do so, he points out, unless there were something credible about religion in the first place (*System*, pp. 690–1).

Hume uses a conjectural history to show why and how justice arises. We need to cooperate with others to provide ourselves with all the things required for the continuation and enjoyment of life. Such things are scarce relative to our desires, but plentiful enough so that exchanges can benefit everyone involved. Although no one is wholly selfish, no one is generous enough to give others all that they need or want.[18] Socially acknowledged security in keeping what one has, and the ability to transfer commodities when one wishes, obviously have a point in these circumstances (p. 494). Together they come close to defining the difference between physical possession and property; and property is, for Hume, the core of justice.

Justice originates when individuals slowly become aware that stability of possession would be beneficial to each of them individually but is possible only if all steadfastly refrain from disturbing one another's transferable goods. The individuals involved must be roughly equal in strength and therefore able to defend what they possess. If some were overwhelmingly powerful, they could with impunity take what they wanted (cf. *Principles of Morals*, pp. 190–1). But among equals this would not serve the purposes each person has. As awareness of this complex of conditions spreads and comes more reliably to control the behavior of one's fellows, there arises what is in effect a convention of respecting possessions. We begin to expect certain actions from one another, without any explicit discussion of how we will behave. Only then are the conditions present which enable ideas of justice and injustice to arise, and with them the ideas of property, rights, and obligations (*Treatise*, pp. 489–91, 497–8). Self-interest, redirected by the realization that one's own interest cannot be forwarded unless one controls one's avidity for possession when others do so as well, is thus the motive out of which we initially act when we act justly.[19]

The practice we now call "justice" thus comes into being without any activity of the moral sentiment. Its name acquires positive moral connotation only when agents reflect on their common behavior and through sympathy with the benefits others enjoy are moved to approve of the disposition in each agent from which such good consequences flow (*Treatise*, pp. 498–500). This approval gives rise to the second motive to justice, the "moral" obligation (p. 498); I shall return to it shortly.

What is striking about Hume's account is that there is no reference in it either to a goal or *telos* of human nature, or to law. Others had

18   Compare this with Pufendorf's account of the complementary roles of perfect and imperfect duties, discussed in Chapter 7.iv.

19   Knud Haakonssen has provocatively disputed this view and offered an alternative interpretation, admittedly hypothetical, of what Hume has in mind. See Haakonssen 1981, ch. 2, esp. pp. 33–5.

dropped Aristotelian ideas of virtue before Hume, and, as I have noted, they could still keep a place for virtue. But they defined the virtues in terms of habits of obedience to law. Hume does not do so. The natural virtues, benefiting their objects in every instance, normally need no rules or laws to guide them. Even in the case of justice, none are needed initially. Hume sees justice as eventually requiring us to obey the laws or customs concerning property that are current in our society. Individuals may, however, possess goods before there are customs or laws. We can see, therefore, that the latter serve only to codify and clarify the convention of respecting possession and to make it more easily teachable to the young.

What makes justice possible, then, is not an ability to form habits of compliance with rules but the ability to extend our sense of self so that we come to take an interest in the interests of others with whom we form a cooperating society. We come, that is, to have an interest in the good of others, which, though mediated and indirect, is akin to the kind of interest displayed in the natural virtues. Hume's directly loving virtues have nothing to do with law. Even the virtue that needs law does not need it in order to exist. Positive laws simply specify and communicate conventions through which everyone benefits.

Hume's larger aim in supplanting natural law with virtue is to free our understanding of morality throughout from any need to appeal to supernatural origins or maintenance. Natural law theory invokes divine wisdom to explain the fit between moral laws and human good, and divine commands and sanctions to explain the nature of obligation. Hume argues that an understanding of how we are naturally suited to live with one another in our particular sort of world enables us to do without such a picture. The moral sentiments give everyone alike all the guidance we need, and since we naturally have or develop the motives needed to engage us in virtue, there is no need of sanctions. We invent the very notion of law involved in justice, and make the laws ourselves. Morality calls for nothing that transcends the natural world in which we live; and, within it, our common human nature makes us all self-governing.

v. *Obligation*

Hume may have been prompted to his theory of justice by Butler's critique of Hutcheson's view that benevolence is the whole of virtue.[20] Butler pointed out that not every act of justice helps someone (Chapter 16.vii). Hume responds that it is the whole practice of justice that makes

---

20 Hume greatly admired Butler and hoped he would be willing to read the *Treatise* in manuscript, but apparently failed in his efforts to meet him.

everyone better off than anyone would be without it. If this is a Hobbesian move, it is made in an anti-Hobbesian manner, by showing that justice can exist without the need for a sovereign. The ingenuity of the theory should not, however, blind us to a problem. Hume's view of the motive that leads us to act justly is obscure. It is not obvious that he can improve his account.[21]

The difficulty is that although perceptions of good do not determine the will, they seem to be a necessary condition of its activation except where the direct passions are involved, those springing from an inexplicable instinct (*Treatise*, p. 439). Acts of justice are not motivated by such passions. In a fully developed system of justice we must obey our country's laws or customs concerning property, perhaps at some loss to ourselves. On Hume's view, moreover, we will be aware that sometimes no one benefits when we act justly. There can also be cases where injustice seems best on the whole. Should we not approve, for example, of a poor but honest laborer keeping money he has found, if returning it to its wealthy, selfish owner will not increase the happiness of the latter, who did not even know he had lost it? No one suffers, someone gains, and the practice is not harmed. But Hume is committed to requiring the return as just (cf. pp. 531–3). What motive can serve if all motives must involve some perception of a good?

Butler never offers an account of what can move us to comply with the directives to follow justice and truth regardless of consequences. Other philosophers did have views on the subject, which Hume would have known. Samuel Clarke holds, as I pointed out in Chapter 15.iii, that awareness of basic moral principles generates its own motive for compliance, which is not a good-based motive. He relies on beliefs Hume rejects about freedom and necessity. Clarke thinks that God is free to act according to the eternal fitnesses or not to do so, and so are we. This is a freedom of indifference, and Hume rejects it (pp. 407, 411). Clarke also thinks that both God and we are morally necessitated to act according to the eternal fitnesses. This sort of necessity is compatible with freedom, although physical necessity, which is of a different kind altogether, is not. But Hume thinks his own theory of causation shows "that there is but one kind of *necessity,* as there is but one kind of cause, and that the common distinction betwixt *moral* and *physical* necessity is without foundation in nature" (p. 171).

Clarke was trying to restate a natural law view of obligation as moral necessity, but there is no place for it in Hume's morality. Yet, if Hume is

---

21   In what follows I am indebted to some intensive and profitable discussions with Stephen Darwall concerning an early version of material now in Darwall 1995, ch. 10.

not to revise common views of justice drastically, he needs something like a direct obligation to follow a rule simply because it is the proper rule.[22] Bishop Berkeley had published an account of morality as involving such obligations in a widely read sermon entitled "Passive Obedience." He there appeals to rules in order to show how his basic principle of bringing about the greatest amount of good can be applied. We must never make our own exceptions to the rules of morality, Berkeley holds, because we cannot think well enough about consequences to see what we ought to do in individual cases. Unquestioning civil obedience is required because this matter in particular "is of too nice and difficult a nature to be left to the judgement and determination of private persons."[23] Hume rejects the view. " 'Tis certain . . .," he says, "that in all our notions of morals we never entertain such an absurdity as that of passive obedience" (p. 552). Where Berkeley thought justice straightforwardly useful, Hume took it to be of a nice and difficult nature. But his requirement of compliance with the rules of justice does not rest on our inability to see where the good lies. He does not want rule-obedience to be the kind of rule-engendered compliance that leads to Berkeley's politics. He requires compliance because compliance itself generates the good that eventually causes us to approve it. The problem arises when we see that compliance is doing no good.

Hume talks of obligation from time to time. He never takes it to involve the will of another who directs and sanctions our actions, as the natural lawyers do. Rather, like Shaftesbury, he takes it to refer only to a determining motive.[24] Thus he speaks of interest as "the *natural* obligation to justice," and when he asks what the *moral* obligation is, he is asking what role the moral feelings have in moving us to be just (p. 498). Discussing the obligation to keep a promise, he remarks that "when any action, or quality of the mind, pleases us *after a certain manner,* we say it is virtuous; and when the neglect, or non-performance of it, displeases us *after a like manner,* we say that we lie under a moral obligation to produce it" (p. 517). The moral obligation to act justly is simply our disapproval of ourselves when we lack the appropriate motive in the

22 Hume may also be trying to avoid Hutcheson's threefold distinction of senses of "obligation," and its biblical association with the claim that law is for the unrighteous, not for the righteous. See Chapter 16, note 10.

23 *Passive Obedience* 19, in *Works* VI. Berkeley extends to political obedience the kind of inability to think out consequences that Cumberland uses to support the existing distribution of property.

24 Shaftesbury asks "what obligation there is to virtue," meaning thereby "what reason to embrace it," and as the discussion shows, he means motivating reason (*Inquiry* II.I.1). On the issue of obligation in British moral thought, see Darwall 1995.

appropriate strength to do so.[25] It is the sense of duty that fills in gaps in first-order motives. But as we have seen, there must be a first-order motive to act justly in order for the need for a gap-filling motive to arise. Explaining what that is, in the case of justice, is as difficult for Hume as it was for Pufendorf.

vi. *Hume and the classical republic*

Since Hume's account of an ethics of virtue was shaped in part by Hutcheson's, the question naturally arises whether Hume also means to provide a virtue theory suitable for the politics of a classical republic. It may at first seem that he does. His virtues are all oriented either to the well-being of the community or to the benefit of its individual members. There is no appeal to rights or to laws divinely imposed and sanctioned. Virtuous agents will themselves benefit from their virtue. Is not Hume as much a theorist of the republic as Shaftesbury or Hutcheson?

The answer is that he is not. Though his view of the two kinds of virtue enables him to show that both can operate only due to some sort of concern for the well-being of others, the distinction incorporates a main thesis of the natural lawyers. Hume puts justice squarely at the center of the needs of society for the same reason the natural lawyers do: a tendency to conflict is an ineradicable part of human nature, not alterable by any social structure. Hume sees its source in "the avidity . . . of acquiring goods and possessions," which is "insatiable, perpetual, universal, and directly destructive of society" (p. 492; cf. p. 532). People's personal interests tend to be opposed (p. 529), and the institution of property increases the very tendency to conflict that it functions to control. If Hume sees justice as the virtue without which society cannot exist, he sees it also as an enduring locus of conflicts, which the republicans claim can exist only in a corrupt society. But in the *Treatise*, at least, Hume does not suggest that property corrupts.

Like the natural lawyers, then, Hume sees two spheres of moral life, one concerned with the control of conflict, the other with the expression of direct concern for the good of others. Unlike Hutcheson, he refuses to see the former as directly derived from the latter. While insisting against Hobbes that benevolence is an effective force at least in small and intimate groups, Hume nonetheless plainly thinks that the acquisitive and competitive strains in human nature are ineradicable. Society must adjust them and protect against them, in ways for which the Harringtonian republic seems to make no adequate provision. Justice cannot be treated simply as "the result" when society consists of properly bal-

---

25   This is Hutcheson's first kind of obligation: *Inquiry II* VII.1, p. 267.

anced orders, because there will be no balanced orders, there will not even be society, unless justice is first brought into play. Hume is thus in this important respect no Hutchesonian.[26]

Despite his acceptance of one part of natural law thinking, Hume's position on justice is even further away from the natural lawyer's position than I have already indicated. Pufendorf may have been an apologist for the rulers who employed him, but the kind of theory he expounded could be used to justify the possibility of appealing to God's laws to criticize the laws of any specific regime.[27] Hume provides no basis for such criticism. The "laws of nature" that we invent to make property possible, in Hume's system, are not a specific set of statable rules. They amount to nothing but the recognition that for society to exist property must be safe and transferable. Beyond that, all is local convention. And one convention is as good as another, if both do the job. In Hume's theory of justice there is no conceptual room for the question whether a stable society's laws concerning property are just or not.

vii. *Morality and religion*

Hume is quite conservative about property. Yet his descriptive science of ethics is in fact profoundly revisionary. The revisions that would follow from its acceptance as the common self-understanding of ourselves in society include changes in our list of virtues and vices. We will see why Hume thought an experience-based moral science more useful

26 There is another significant point about Hume's view of the virtues with implications for his relations to the classical republican tradition. He offers an account of the possible genesis of a large society in which justice and the other artificial virtues are practiced. The account makes no appeal either to a social contract – the favorite device of the natural lawyers – or to a divine or semidivine legislator, of the sort to whom the classical republicans appeal. Hume's avoidance of any need for the implausible classical republican legislator is on a par with his better-known dismissal of what he took to be the equally implausible social contract.

In his "Idea of a Perfect Commonwealth" (*Essays*, pp. 512–29), Hume points out what he takes to be political difficulties with Harrington's *Oceana*. I have mainly been concerned with the relation of Hume's view of morality to republican views.

27 Glafey, enumerating those who will find study of natural law useful, begins with the ruler (*Regent*), who will learn from it "the true limits of his power" over subordinates. He cites Barbeyrac on Pufendorf as one of his authorities, adding that subordinates who are not satisfied that their ruler stays within the bounds of natural law may turn away from him with the worst of consequences (Glafey, pp. 1–2). He also thinks that those who make or improve laws in a republic should study the laws of nature, so that their enactments will be obeyed and approved by subordinates (pp. 6–7).

than natural science only if we grasp the alterations in our thoughts and feelings to which it could lead.

In book I of the *Treatise* Hume confines natural science to tracing the regular connections of events within our experience. He does so by reconstructing the concept of causation so that it can itself be seen to function only in connection with experiences of reiterated sequences. There are two other concepts sometimes thought to be needed for the natural and moral sciences: that of a physical object continuing through time unobserved, and that of an enduring mind or mental substance. Both concepts might be used in efforts to acquire beliefs that transcend experience, but Hume finds it impossible to make sense of them. We seem to be unable to do without them in daily life, but once we reflect on them we cannot rid them of internal incoherence.[28] Moral convictions, like causal beliefs, do not allow of any strict rational proof. Nonetheless morality survives reflection upon itself.

Hume makes the point clearly at the end of the *Treatise.* Reflection on the large role sympathy plays in generating our moral ideas and beliefs shows us that they spring from a "noble" source, which "gives us a just notion both of the *generosity* and *capacity* of our nature." If we reflect on sympathy and on the sense of morals itself, we do not find incoherence. On the contrary, by the same principle that explains our approval of ordinary virtues we are led to approve of both of these parts of our nature, and also of the causal principle behind approvals. All are useful and agreeable. In morality, at least, "nothing is presented on any side, but what is laudable and good" (p. 619).

Our religious beliefs are in yet a third category. In the *Dialogues* Hume attempts to destroy every rational defense of religion; in the *Natural History of Religion* he offers an account of how such completely nonrational beliefs develop. They are due to ignorance of the causes of the events on which our happiness depends and our consequent fear at being unable to control our lives.[29] The solider and more comprehensive our beliefs about causation, therefore, the fewer the occasions for unfounded fears, and the less religious belief. The light of knowledge will drive out the shadows. As the darkness recedes, so will the approval given to character traits which are harmful or disagreeable, but which superstition claims are pleasing to the gods. "Celibacy, fasting, penance, mortification, self-denial, humility, silence, solitude, and the

---

28   See Norton 1982 and Baier 1991 on the inability of the mind to "bear its own survey" on these matters and the remedy Hume proposes.

29   This is the general theme of the *Natural History;* see, e.g., pp. 30–1, 40, 43, 47. It also shows that Hume can argue that some moral beliefs have a more durable basis in feeling than others. See Shaver 1995 for development of this point.

whole train of monkish virtues" will be transferred to the list of vices as superstition dies away.[30]

The great utility of the moral sciences lies in their leading us to just this result. They enable us to understand why a descriptive natural science of causal connections, and a morality of useful and agreeable motives have nothing to fear from the advance of knowledge. Religion and the harmful morality associated with it, by contrast, are likely to lose their hold on us. If Hume is in many respects Hutchesonian, he is so, therefore, only on the surface. Hutcheson is trying to show that the morality to which our nature gives rise is, when properly understood, just what Christianity – properly understood – itself teaches.[31] When he appeals to pagan writers like Cicero, his purpose is to enroll them among those who unwittingly testify to Christian truth. When Hume turns to Cicero, it is rather to see how morality was conceptualized before Christian religion began to influence our thought about it. Hobbes thought the scholastic moral theologians were right about the substance of the laws of nature, and wrong only in the explanation they offered. Hume allows that Hutcheson gives a better account of the data than Hobbes; but the facts do not show what he thought they did. The virtues are simply our adaptations to the circumstances in which we live. Some of those circumstances require us to develop laws, others do not. The set of virtues we need is purely contingent: if we were big-hearted beings living in a world overflowing with milk and honey, justice would be quite pointless.

One of the implications of this view would have been quite plain to any religious readers Hume might have had. They would have seen that on Hume's view of morality, only a voluntarist understanding of God would be available. To hold that morality rests on "eternal fit-nesses" is to imply, as Hume points out, that immutable moral stan-

---

30 *Principles of Morals*, p. 270. The *Natural History of Religion* portrays most religion as socially harmful. Polytheism is less dangerous than monotheism though both lead to superstitious practices. Belief in the absurdities taught by all religions is weak, Hume optimistically thinks, "and scarcely ever approaches . . . to that solid belief and persuasion, which governs us in the common affairs of life" (p. 60). There is also "a kind of contradiction" between two principles that lead to religious belief, which is like the contradictory principles that lead us to the concepts of mental and physical substance: "Our natural terrors present the notion of a devilish and malicious deity: Our propensity to adulation leads us to acknowledge an excellent and divine" (p. 66).

31 In his *Historical Account* Barbeyrac gives a concise statement of a commonplace that applies, *mutatis mutandis*, to Hutcheson: "the intire Conformity of the Christian Morality with the clearest Dictates of right Reason; is one of the most convincing proofs of the Divinity of the Christian Religion" (XXXII, p. 87).

dards "impose an obligation . . . on the Deity himself," and of course he rejects all such theories of morals (*Treatise,* p. 456). God, moreover, is not our equal and does not share with us in the circumstances of justice. In relation to him we are like those rational but feeble creatures whom Hume imagines, who are too weak to make resentment of us effective. We might be gentle to such beings, but we could not enter into relations of justice with them (*Principles of Morals,* p. 190). Pufendorf had made exactly this point about the limitation of justice to human relations (see Chapter 7.vi). And Hume is plainly aware of the voluntarist implications his view would have for believers. His treatment of the problem of evil, in the *Dialogues concerning Natural Religion,* makes this evident.[32] His speakers argue that we cannot admit that evil exists and also have any justifiable views about God's moral attributes. Rather than proposing a solution to this problem Hume's discussion exacerbates it. If in the end he allows us any rationally grounded religious belief, it is belief in a deity so attenuated and so incomprehensible as to have no resemblance to the God of either Leibniz or Clarke, let alone to the God of Christianity.[33]

Hume lets his readers know that, if there is to be any religion, it must be of a kind most of them would reject. His antireligious aims were not hard to see. One of his acuter critics described him as one who destroys "all the *Foundations of religion, revealed and natural;* and with a Pen truly Epicurean, dissolves at once all the *Fears* of the *Guilty,* the *Comforts* of the *Afflicted,* and the *Hopes* of the *Virtuous.*"[34] There is, however, some tension between Hume's descriptive scientific procedures and his revisionist, antireligious aims. If the monkish virtues will be driven out by the increasing realization that they do not serve human happiness, why cannot similar revision occur within other parts of morality? Cumberland argued that the present distribution of property had better be left standing, because, given the vast complexity of the consequences of any alteration, we cannot count on reason to hit upon a better arrangement

32   See M. A. Stewart, "An Early Fragment on Evil," in Stewart and Wright 1994, for evidence that Hume was concerned with the problem of evil from the early stages of his philosophical work, not only after the *Treatise.*

33   *Dialogues* X and XI contain the discussion of the problem of evil; in XII Hume suggests that the cause or causes of the world probably have some remote analogy to human intelligence. Whichever speaker represents Hume's own position, if any one of them does, the voluntarist religious implications of empiricism are made plain. See also *Principles of Morals,* p. 294, where Hume says that the standard of rational truth is unalterable "even by the will of the Supreme Being," while the moral standard, arising from an animal constitution, "is ultimately derived from that Supreme Will," which made each kind of being have the nature it has.

34   John Brown, *Thoughts on Civil Liberty* (1766). I owe this quotation to the excellent article by Crimmins 1983, p. 540.

than the one we happen to have. If Hume is sometimes critical of such views of property as radical egalitarianism (*Principles of Morals*, pp. 193–4), he provides no overt procedure for improving the justice of any kind of distribution of goods. But he also says nothing to show that the artificial motive moving us to be just would not respond to the kind of information an economist might develop, comparing the benefits and harms produced by our present laws with those of some possible alternative.

Hume is no utilitarian. He does not think that we either do or should appeal to one single principle in making our moral judgments. He does not say that the point of morality is to bring about a maximum of pleasure and a minimum of pain. He does not think that there is a rational procedure for reaching practical conclusions by the use of which we could settle all disagreements. He offers his theory as an explanation of our moral judgments, not as a warrant for them, and certainly not as a calculus of reform. His theory could, however, easily be turned in that direction; and his attack on the monkish virtues points the way.

18

Against a fatherless world

Kant proclaimed in public the importance for moral philosophy of the work of Shaftesbury, Hutcheson, and Hume. He gave no similar recognition to the work of later British writers on ethics, although he read and admired Adam Smith's *Theory of Moral Sentiments* in its translation into German in 1770.[1] Smith and two of his contemporaries, Richard Price and Thomas Reid, rejected the enterprise of working out an ethics for a world left on its own, without providential care. They, like the man of benevolence described by Smith, would have found "the very suspicion of a fatherless world . . . the most melancholy of all reflections" (*Theory*, p. 235).[2] Kant would have agreed. But we have no reason to suppose that he knew of the moral philosophy of either Price or Reid; and in any case they, like Smith, developed options that Kant did not take.[3] They are important here because their response to the post-Humean situation in moral philosophy helps us to understand the problems that Kant would also have seen.

i. *Sentimentalism, skepticism, and the new rationalism*

Shaftesbury, Hutcheson, and Hume were taken by their readers to be proponents of a sentimental theory of morality, making feeling central

1 See Kant's "Announcement of the Program of his Lectures," *Gesammelte Schriften* 2.311 (*TP*, p. 298). For his admiration for Smith, see 10.126, letter of July 9, 1771; 15.1, no. 767; 15.2, no. 1355; XIX, nos. 6628, 6798, 6894. See also the editors' introduction to Smith's *Theory*, p. 31.

2 So also Price, *Dissertations*, p. 97: denying Providence is "making the universe in a manner forlorn and fatherless." They echo Shaftesbury's remark that "the thought of living in a distracted universe" would be utterly melancholy. See Chapter 14.ix.

3 On Kant's knowledge of Reid see Kuehn 1987, ch. IX. The lives of Price and Smith overlapped almost exactly; Reid was born earlier and died later than they. Smith knew Price and Reid personally; they knew and occasionally commented on one another's work.

and reason peripheral to moral judgment and moral principle. The few earlier writers who had challenged the ability of reason to give us effective moral guidance had drawn a skeptical conclusion with real practical implications. In doubting or denying that morality has any rational justification, their point was to show that morality has no inherent motivating hold on us. Suppose that Christian moral doctrine, or something like it, represents the content of morality: then, said the skeptics, you may or may not find that way of life to your taste. If you do not, there is nothing in it that will motivate you to live as it directs. Thus Montaigne holds that he must be guided by his own inner form, which is unlikely to be the same as that of anyone else. Of course he will comply with the laws of his country – but not, as I pointed out, because of any thought that they are just. He claims that he can be fully and perfectly the being he has it in him to be without necessarily paying attention to morality as standardly understood. And he has no interest in reshaping morality so that it turns out to be something more closely suited to his own individual nature. Morality just does not matter much.

For the British sentimentalists no such practical skeptical conclusion follows from the thesis that morality lacks any rational justification. Their aim is to show that even without such a rationale, morality has a motivational hold on us. It moves us because it is tied to our nature – not to our supposed nature as rational pursuers of the good, but to our nature as moved by nonrational Lockean desires. Shaftesbury and Hume do not take Christian moral doctrine as giving the fixed content of morality. For them that morality may have to be reshaped into something to which we cannot be indifferent. Shaftesbury's morality can move us because it alone promises us harmony among our desires. Hume's morality moves us because it is our approval of desires and motives we either naturally have or naturally develop. No virtue will be part of a morality we can care about unless it ties into our sentiments. Hutcheson, too, insists that morality moves us because it is essentially our approval of our own naturally existing benevolent motivation. As I pointed out in Chapter 16.ii, he is defending a Christian view. If his sentimentalism carries a deep departure from the austere Presbyterian Calvinism in which he was raised, it still does not invoke any skeptical doubts about the reality of the motives and feelings on which it rests.

Traditional rationalists saw morality's hold on us as coming from its being instrumental to or an intrinsic part of our flourishing as essentially rational beings. This enabled them to claim that rational morality gives us what we really want. That connection was broken by Malebranche, who held that although we want pleasure, morality requires us to comply with the order of value in God's ideas. It was broken again by Clarke and by Mandeville. Both of them allowed that most men are dominated by selfish desires, though Clarke calls this the corruption of our nature and Mandeville does not; and both required a virtue that can move us regardless of its effect on the agent's own flourishing. Clarke is thus driven to claim that reason alone can move us to act virtuously, even contrary to our desires; and Mandeville's mankind can almost never act as morality directs.[4]

The work of the sentimentalists made it possible to dismiss the egoistic motivational theory underpinning Mandeville's paradoxes. They argued that desire for our own exclusive good is only one motive among many, along with feelings of concern for others. Hume went to some pains, moreover, to explain how feelings of approval could shed their initial ties to those close to us and become impartial. Feeling, not reason, enables us all to approve the same virtues. We are also all moved by our own inner constitution to practice them. Practical moral skepticism is no part of sentimentalism. The theory thus seemed to give the rationalists everything they could want – except a rational foundation for morality. The sentimentalists differ from the rationalists only in insisting that reason could not give morality the motivating force that, as all agree, it surely has. Sentimentalism thus changed the question for advocates of the rationality of morals. As a look at Adam Smith's moral theory will show, an antirationalist could be neither an egoist nor a skeptic, but the defender of as generous and as serious a morality as a rationalist could hope for. The question is why rationalist thinkers like Price and Reid thought that they had to reject this new position. What is at stake in the post-Humean controversies about reason in morals? Is it simply a matter of the epistemology of morals?

ii. *Price's intuitionism*

We find one answer in the work of Richard Price (1723–91), whose first book, *A Review of the Principal Questions and Difficulties in Morals,* was published in 1758. In defending a new form of rationalism, he is rejecting the theological voluntarism he thinks is implied by Hutcheson's view. Morality must rest on necessary truths if we are to be assured that we and God share a common set of principles; and without that, Price thinks, we cannot love God and try to live in friendship with him (*Review,* p. 266).

To defend his rationalism Price thinks that he must, with Butler, reject the sentimentalist thesis that benevolence is the whole of virtue, even in Hume's attenuated form. Like Clarke, he holds that what enables to act as morality requires is our possession of a kind of free

---

4   Adam Smith treats Mandeville as a destructive practical skeptic, in contrast both to Epicurus and Hobbes, and to Hutcheson (*Theory,* pp. 307–13, 315).

agency that is incompatible with determinism. God's continuous providential care of his universe is also indispensable for Price's scheme.
The whole system is meant to defend not only his version of Christianity but also his profound and active concern to see liberty increase
throughout the world. After explaining how Price thinks the philosophical points hang together, I shall look briefly at the perspective his
political thought gives us on his ethics.

"The human mind," says Price,

> would appear to have little order or consistency in it, were we to consider
> it as only a system of passions and affections, which are continually
> drawing us in different ways, without any thing at the head of them to
> govern them, and the strongest of which for the time necessarily deter-
> mines the conduct. But this is far from being its real state. (p. 215n)

The Lockean vision Price calls up of the mind's lack of any internal
principle of order is falsified by the "moral faculty" that appropriately
governs "all our other powers" (p. 215n). To explain the operations of
the moral faculty Price finds that he must reject Lockean epistemology
and assert, with Cudworth, that reason is not, as it is in Locke and
Descartes, a purely passive power. It is an active power, and as such it is
what enables us to be genuine agents.

The key part of Price's rejection of Locke's epistemology lies in his
claim that reason is itself a source of simple ideas. He is driven to this by
what he takes to be the inadequacies of Hutcheson's account of moral
approval. If Hutcheson were right, approval would be nothing but a
sensation derived from the way our mind operates, telling us nothing
about "the real characters of actions" (p. 15).[5] We need not agree. Reason does what sense cannot. It generalizes and compares where sense is
confined to particulars. Reason discerns; sense merely suffers. Many of
our ideas – of solidity, substance, duration, space, infinity, contingency,
necessity, causation, power – cannot be explained as originating from
purely sensory information. Hume sees this but draws the wrong conclusion. The right response is not to deny or redefine the ideas as he
does, but to admit the creative power of reason and the narrow bounds
of sense (pp. 21–35).

Price offers some arguments to support the claim that moral ideas are
among those given us by reason. If we appeal to common sense, it will
be as obvious that moral ideas involve truth and falsity as that ideas of
number, causation, and proportion do. We assume that judgments
about gratitude or treachery are as true or false as those about equality

5   For Hutcheson, feeling approval is one way of taking pleasure in someone's
action. It resembles, he says, liking a piece of music rather than contemplating a
truth. See *Illustrations*, p. 136.

(pp. 41–4). One of the "universal apprehensions of mankind" is that moral terms stand for real properties of objects. Suppose it is replied that mankind thinks the same about terms for secondary qualities and is mistaken about them. Price replies that there is a difference. It really *is* absurd, he claims, to speak of a colored body, but not so to speak of a right action. Thus we treat moral and secondary properties differently. If we did not, we could not speak, as we do, of people making mistakes about right and wrong, or about what ends are valuable (pp. 46–9).

From these considerations, which a Humean might well not find compelling, Price immediately draws a strongly antivoluntarist conclusion: "Right and wrong, it appears, denote what actions *are*. Now whatever any thing *is*, that it is, not by will, or decree, but by *nature and necessity* . . . No will, therefore, can render *any thing* good and obligatory, which was not so antecedently, and from eternity" (p. 50). This and this alone enables us to show rationally that God has a moral and righteous nature. On Hutcheson's view, our moral faculty is a mere instinct contingently planted in us. If so we have no reason to suppose that God has a moral sense like ours. Indeed we could not conclude that God has "any moral character at all" (p. 236).

Price stresses the point that moral truths are necessary truths. He thinks that only their necessity enables us to have knowledge of God's principles (p. 237). A wicked or characterless being might produce the amount of good we observe in the world. Moreover, we must know about eternity; a mere empirical inference would not tell us. Only rational necessary truths about God's nature will (pp. 238–43; cf. *Dissertations*, p. 23). Sentimentalism about morals would bar us from such knowledge.

Given, then, that we have rational ideas of right and wrong, Price argues that they must be simple ideas. No one has managed to define them; and unless they were simple, we could never come to a final approval or disapproval of anything, but would be stuck with "an infinite progression of reasons and ends." He is perhaps a little cavalier with this argument because he takes Hutcheson to agree with him about the simplicity of the ideas, disagreeing only about their rational origin. For Price they come from our "INTUITION of truth" (*Review*, p. 41). Here, Price's strongly Platonic turn is at work. In our intuitive awareness of a truth, "the very object itself [is] present to the mind." Otherwise there is no explaining how millions of people can think the very same thing (p. 39n).[6]

Price's appeal to common sense rests on a view about the necessity of trusting the deliverances of our faculties. The sentimentalist position implies, he thinks, that our moral faculty always deceives us. It presents

---

6   On Price's Platonism, see Zebrowski 1994.

as properties of acts what are only our own feelings. We cannot think in this way of any faculty and hope to have knowledge anywhere. If we cannot prove our faculties to be veridical, we cannot even ground general doubt about them, since to have reason to doubt we would have to use those very faculties. Price concludes that "what things *seem* to us, we must take them to *be*" (pp. 48, 91ff., 97).[7] The consequence is that we are to take "the natural and unperverted sentiments of men" on moral matters as "instances of *immediate duty intuitively* perceived" (p. 140).

The bearing of this on Price's substantive moral outlook is considerable. Since we must trust our immediate intuitions of right and wrong, we cannot hold that benevolence or a concern for general well-being is the whole of virtue (pp. 131–2). In supporting his position Price supplements Butler's list of counterexamples, and dismisses Hume's use of the idea of a general practice to support the claim that utility is the source of all approval, even in cases of justice. We would disapprove of injustice, Price says, even if no one remained to be harmed by it. An attempt to explain away our commonsense views here is like the attempts some theorists have made to explain our apparently benevolent desires as originating in self-interest.[8] We should avoid the misleading love of simplicity and admit that our immediate approval of veracity, gratitude, candor, and justice shows us that there are many independent principles of conduct (pp. 134–8).

Given Price's insistence on a plurality of moral principles, we should not think of him as a Platonist in ethics, however important Platonism is for his epistemology. Pursuit of the good is not, on his view, the sole basis for rational action. His theory on this matter has a striking similarity to Malebranche's. He does indeed reject the Malebranchean view that God works always through general laws and does not extend to particulars.[9] But he insists, with Malebranche, that God is not moved solely by concern for the good. In place of Malebranchean order Price substitutes principles of justice. "Happiness is the *end*, and the only end conceivable by us, of God's providence and government," Price insists.

> But he pursues this end in subordination to rectitude. . . . *Justice* and *Veracity* are right as well as *goodness*, and must also be ascribed to the Deity. . . . *justice* is not merely a mode of goodness, or an instance of its taking the most effectual method to accomplish its end. (pp. 250–1; cf. p. 252)

7   Price's line of argument is suggested in the final paragraph of Butler's dissertation "Of Personal Identity" in *Works* II.

8   The theorists Price has in mind are John Gay and David Hartley, whose work I discuss in Chapter 19.i. Later his Unitarian ally Joseph Priestley held similar views, undeterred by Price's criticisms.

9   *Dissertations*, pp. 9–10, 15–17.

Justice and goodness thus provide different kinds of reasons for God's actions and ours, and reasons of justice take precedence. What leads Price to go beyond Clarke in relating justice and the good in this way is an antivoluntarist concern with the problem of evil. Like Leibniz, Price says that only a voluntarist or an atheist could think that this is not a perfect world. God's moral principles are ours, and he is all-perfect. Nonetheless it seems to us that more good might exist than we can find. We therefore need an account of how the deity could refuse to cause some good he might bring about. To solve the problem we need a more complex view of the perfection of the universe than Leibniz's. Price turns to a view that is strikingly similar to Malebranche's (Chapter 11.iv).

We cannot deny God's providence, and if God cares for any one event in nature, then he takes all the care that it is possible to take for all events (*Dissertations,* pp. 17–18). Admittedly there is much suffering and evildoing in the world. But once we see that morality requires God to be just before he is benevolent, we can also see that his care of the world is governed by moral principle. "Rectitude, under the government of a being of perfect rectitude," Price declares, "I may be sure, shall take place invariably, universally and for ever; and this is all I ought to wish for" (*Dissertations,* p. 96). If unmerited suffering occurs in this life, we may be sure it will be recompensed in another, just as the apparently successful scoundrel will get his due there. The voluntarist thinks punishments and rewards are essential to the very constitution of moral obligation. Price disagrees: rational necessity suffices to obligate, all by itself. But sanctions are essential to show that God ensures the fairness of his world by making up for the individual costs of acting justly (*Dissertations,* pp. 132–3). The priority of justice to the good is asserted here for the same reason that led Malebranche to give priority to order over pleasure. It serves to make God's providential care morally intelligible.

Price himself speaks, as we have seen, of moral intuitions; and that fact, together with his pluralism of ultimate principles, is what makes Price the first of Lord Herbert's successors to develop a systematic intuitionism.[10] What exactly does Price think we intuit? Unsurprisingly, the principles of duty to God, self, and neighbor. One intuitive principle

10   In the introduction to his edition of the *Review,* Raphael says that Price was "the first to apply the word 'intuition' to moral judgement" (p. xiv). John Balguy cites an earlier approach to this use of the term. He quotes an objector who wonders whether, if Balguy sees a certain moral connection "immediately, or as it were intuitively," everyone else should expect to see it as well. The "as it were" suggests that this use of the term is new to the objector. Balguy, *Tracts,* p. 114.

of our duty to others, that of benevolence, tells us simply that "it is *right* to promote and pursue" public happiness (*Review*, p. 151). This shows us the form of all intuitively known necessary principles: it is right to worship and obey God, right to promote our own good, right to be truthful and grateful and just as well as beneficent. All of them come together in one general idea, Price says, and they should be considered "as only different modifications and views of one original, all-governing law" (*Review*, pp. 138–65). But this Platonic thesis of the unity of the virtues, or of the laws governing them, does not for Price entail any simplification of the moral life. There are no doubt clear cases of right and wrong. But Price stresses instead the difficulties of applying our intuitive insight to instances, particularly when different principles come into conflict (*Review*, pp. 166ff.). Whatever we intuit, on Price's view, it is not the rightness of a definite act in specific circumstances.[11]

iii. *Intuition and motivation*

Price allows that awareness of moral truth is always emotionally colored. But the moral feelings are aroused by knowledge of moral truth, not a replacement of it. No new sense is needed to account for feelings of approval and the pleasure we take in contemplating virtue. Despite Hutcheson, our cognitions cause them. And these feelings have a definite moral function. It is not that our moral ideas are confused and indistinct; but reason's deliverances would be too slow and weak, in many cases, to move us to act properly, were they not seconded by feelings or what Price calls instinctive determinations. We need both "a perception of the understanding, and a feeling of the heart" to prompt us effectively (*Review*, pp. 61–2).[12]

Price uses this apparatus when he discusses the virtuous agent's motives. The virtuous agent must first possess liberty, "the power of acting and determining." By this Price means, not that an agent's actions must be uncaused, but that the agent must be the cause of them. There cannot be a *"foreign* cause" for what I think of as my own volition.

---

11 Whewell 1852 does not discuss Price, perhaps because Price was Welsh. Yet in his own moral theory Whewell is closer to Price than to any other predecessor, particularly when one takes into account Price's suggestions about progressive improvement, which includes improvement in our understanding of the ideas of each of the heads of virtue or duty.

12 Price here tries to correct Butler, who says, as I noted in Chapter 16.vi, that moral awareness may be considered as "sentiment of the understanding or a perception of the heart; or which seems the truth, as including both" (*Dissertation on Virtue* II.1, in *Works* II).

It is absurd to suppose that "I determine voluntarily and yet necessarily." Price thus thinks the Hobbesian view is obviously false. If we do not allow "*agency*, free choice, and an absolute dominion over our resolutions," there is no room for morality (pp. 181–2).

The second requisite for morality is intelligence. Self-motion or activity can exist without intelligence, but intelligence cannot exist without liberty. Since we are plainly intelligent, we must have liberty, or so Price suggests, without spelling out his argument at any length (pp. 183–4). Liberty and reason together make an agent capable of virtue, and Price argues that only the motivation arising from the belief that a given act is morally right, or morally good – only the intention to do the act as one that is called for by morality – constitutes the agent's virtue. He has no doubt that we all "continually feel, that the perception of right and wrong excites to action." Excitement to action "belongs to the very ideas of moral right and wrong." The feelings that normally accompany moral insight are not necessary for motivation. Morally appropriate action will ensue from seeing that the ideas apply to a case "whenever there is nothing to oppose it." Price thinks that there is no sensible question to be asked about "why a reasonable being acts reasonably" (pp. 185–7).

Liberty, for Price as for Clarke, is an all-or-nothing attribute, not something we can have in varying degrees (pp. 209–10). When Price takes up – what Clarke does not discuss – the relations of moral and nonmoral motives, he opens up a difficulty for himself. The two kinds of motive can cooperate in leading to an action, and they can conflict. The strength of our nonmoral motives always threatens to overwhelm or outweigh the moral motive, but we can strengthen the latter indefinitely. Thus Price seems to allow, as Clarke does not, that reasons and desires operate in the same field of force. The "spring of virtue," he says, which should repel the forces of temptation, may be "relaxed or broken" (p. 207).

Price agrees with Butler in criticizing Shaftesbury for treating motives only in terms of commensurable strengths. Shaftesbury failed to see that moral motives claim an *authority* over the others (p. 190n). Yet Price does not show how authority can be factored into the field of forces in which moral motives may lose. He sees an incommensurability in considerations prompting us to action, but he does not treat the will as that which explains how we can decide among incommensurable potential motivations. He treats it instead as that through which we are able to respond to reasons of a kind that override considerations coming from desires. Hence he does not explain how we can be acting freely when our moral reasons are not strong enough to win the day against nonmoral or immoral reasons.

iv. *Morality and providential care*

As a Welsh Dissenter making a career in England, Price must have suffered from prejudice and legal exclusion from political office. If his personal experience helps explain the fervor with which he defended both the American and the French Revolutions, his moral philosophy certainly gave him a basis from which to argue.[13] However complicated he might think particular moral issues to be, he had no doubt about the need to extend liberty, and particularly religious liberty, further than it currently reached, even in England. Conscience, which he treats as God's voice within us (*Review*, p. 147), requires freedom so that it can be obeyed; and Price combined this requirement with his belief in divine providential supervision of every detail of life to produce an astonishing conviction of the apocalyptic importance of the American Revolution. The world, he believes, must show signs of major improvement before the last coming of Christ; and "next to the introduction of Christianity among mankind, the American revolution may prove the most important step" in that improvement. It will do more than any event hitherto to spread liberty and to show the world "that nothing is fundamental but impartial enquiry, an honest mind, and virtuous practice" (*Writings*, p. 119). He deeply deplored the acceptance of slavery in America, and held that if the Americans would get rid of it, their revolution would herald an approaching millennium (*Writings*, p. 150).[14]

Of the many bearings of Price's millennialism, I can note only one.[15] It shows more clearly than anything else how important God and God's providence are for his ethics. We must follow conscience; we often do not know the consequences of our doing so; but we may be sure that all will work out as it ought because God is there to supervise everything (*Review*, p. 244). There must be an afterlife because virtue is not suitably rewarded nor vice suitably punished in this life; moreover, the present course of events must be treated as a moral education, leading us to greater virtue even here (*Review*, pp. 260–1; *Writings*, pp. 118, 154–5, 157).[16] Price rejects the idea of "the greatest possible happiness" as a

---

13 His tracts on these subjects, frequently reprinted and popular beyond all expectation, earned him honors from both the United States and France, as well as the enmity of Edmund Burke.

14 Price says nothing about a need to improve the position of women.

15 See *Dissertations*, p. 137n, where Price argues for progress, including progress beyond nationalism to world peace, as part of his hope that more and more humans will turn out to be saved for eternity and not damned. For a full study of his millennialism, see Fruchtman 1983.

16 Price does not think we are to strive for perfection (*Review*, p. 221).

suitable goal for human endeavor, in part because he thinks we cannot form a coherent notion of it: a greatest happiness is no more possible than a longest duration or a largest number (*Dissertations*, pp. 110–12; 120n). But if each of us does our best to follow our conscience and to obey the different parts of the law of virtue, God will see to it that the greatest justifiable happiness for all will ensue. For Price, as for Hooker and Butler, we are agents in a great cooperative venture, guided and supervised by God. Moral principles are independent of his will; but God is indispensable for morality because the proper functioning of the moral world depends on his goodness and his power (*Writings*, pp. 163–4, 173).

v. *Adam Smith: Sentimentalism restated*

Adam Smith's *The Theory of Moral Sentiments* (1759) was more successful than Price's *Review*, which appeared only a year earlier. Eloquent and charming, as Price's book was not, and enlivening its discussion of theory with vivid sketches of the virtues and vices and morally pointed historical anecdotes, it went through six editions in its author's lifetime and was translated into French and German.[17] For later readers Smith's great work on economics, *An Inquiry into the Nature and Causes of the Wealth of Nations* (1776), has been more important. Even philosophers have paid less attention to Smith's ethics than to Price's, and most historians, if they have discussed Smith's moral treatise, have done so only for the light it sheds on the ideologically crucial economic work. It was once supposed that Smith abandoned his moral theory when he came to write the later work. This error has now been dispatched once and for all.[18] Smith's economics rely on the moral philosophy of *The Theory of Moral Sentiments*. If he was thinking out the one as he worked on the other, it was still the ethics that he completed first. We are entitled to examine it by itself.

Considered thus, it helps us with the question with which I began the chapter: what was the significance of the post-Humean rationalist efforts to base morality on reason? It helps us with a second question as well. Sentimentalism has never gotten a more sophisticated exposition than Smith gave it. After Smith, indeed, it received no major reformulations at all. That kind of theory ceased to be influential; Smith's work may help us understand why.

17   For the reception of *The Theory of Moral Sentiments*, see the editors' introduction, sec. 3(a).

18   For a most useful review of earlier thought on the relations between *The Theory of the Moral Sentiments* and *The Wealth of Nations*, see the introduction to *Theory*, sec. 2(a). See also Fitzgibbons 1995.

Opening his historical study of moral philosophy in part VII of *The Theory of Moral Sentiments,* Smith says there are two questions to be answered about the principles of morals. We need to know what virtue is, or what "constitutes the excellent and praise-worthy character." We must also discover through what "power or faculty in the mind" we come to prefer one sort of conduct to another and call one right, the other wrong (p. 265). His own system answers both questions, starting with the second.

The basic power of mind leading us to distinguish right from wrong is, for Smith, the power of feeling; but reason has an important, if subsidiary, role. By a process he describes with great care, we all come to have feelings of approval or disapproval directed in the first instance at the desires and feelings of others (pp. 7–18, 92–3). In large part these approvals and disapprovals are common to all normal people. Hence inductive reasoning enables us to formulate rules that summarize what we feel approval of and what we do not. It is appropriate to think of the rules as God's laws or commands. In the absence of the moral feelings we can use the rules to guide conduct (pp. 161–8). Independently of moral approval we are naturally motivated to follow them; but the reinforcement given our natural motives by feelings of approval, in others as well as in ourselves, is essential for making our compliance with them reliable (p. 262).

On the feelings of approval on which all of morality rests, Smith differs markedly from his sentimentalist predecessors. He rejects both Hutcheson's claim to have located a moral sense and Hume's to have identified a specific feeling of moral approval. Hutcheson allows, Smith points out, that no sense can be described in terms of its proper objects. The sense of sight is not some color, nor does hearing have a pitch or volume. But, Smith says, we would think that the moral feelings of someone who felt approval of cruelty and treachery were themselves depraved and evil (p. 323; cf. p. 158). Hutcheson is thus mistaken; and how odd it would be if no one prior to Hume had noticed and named a special feeling that is supposed to be among the commonest experiences of human beings! (p. 326).

Approval arises from our basic capacity for sympathy, the power enabling us to feel within ourselves a counterpart to what other people are feeling. In becoming aware of your feelings, I can put myself in your shoes and feel as you do. I can also note how I myself would feel in the situation you are in. To say that I approve of your feeling is to say only that were I in your situation, I would feel just as you do. Or, more precisely, when I notice that I would feel what you do, and as strongly, I feel a new emotion; and this new emotion, arising from my noticing the match between your feelings and what I would feel, is approval (pp. 16, 46n). Later Smith adds a caution. Approval is not one unique feeling; it is a family of feelings, with "no common features . . . between them" (p. 325).

Sympathy can be reflexive as well as directed to others. It shows us what others would feel about our own feelings, including our approvals. Hence we come to understand the level of feeling that everyone would share and so approve. The faculty enabling us to become aware of what feelings, at what strength, would be approved by all is what Smith calls the man within or the impartial spectator.[19] Although the onlooker's appraisive response provides the initial data for morality, Smith thinks it not difficult to explain the decision-making feelings of the agent as well. When thinking about what to do next, we divide ourselves into two beings. We are both prospective agent and onlooker (p. 113). As agents, we have feelings prompting us to this or that course of action. The man within shows us whether others would or would not sympathize with those feelings, and we can act accordingly.

Disapproval can be enough to check action, and approval can help move us, because, Smith holds, one of our chief desires is to be esteemed and approved of by others. Smith goes beyond Nicole on this point, saying that we want to be worthy of the esteem and approval of others (pp. 114–19, 126). This means simply that we want praise by others to show feelings that everyone would approve. Thus our being moved by our moral convictions as well as our having them depends on the impartial spectator, constructed by our abilities to sympathize (pp. 131, 137). Hume is wrong, Smith thinks, in claiming that beliefs about what is useful or immediately agreeable underlie morality. "I affirm," Smith says, "that it is not the view of . . . utility or hurtfulness which is either the first or the principal source of our approbation" (p. 188). The source is rather our understanding of which desires and feelings everyone can share. Nature made us sociable by making us desire to act only from desires into which everyone can enter (p. 116).

Utility does, however, play a major part in Smith's view of morals. Just as his theory resembles the views of Nicole and Mandeville in its stress on our desire or need to stand well with others, so it does also in its emphasis on the unintended consequences of that desire. Nicole held that self-love mimics the work of charity, Mandeville that it provides the drive for the hypocritical morality that most people practice; Smith

---

19   The phrase "the impartial spectator" is used in the first sentence of the dedicatory letter prefixed to the 1711 republication in book form of Addison and Steele's journal, *The Spectator.* Hume speaks of "impartial enquiry" and the "impartial enquirer" but does not use the phrase Smith made famous. Smith uses it early in part I (*Theory*, p. 26) but modifies the theory it carries as he goes along. I have not noted all the developments; see especially *Theory*, pp. 134–5, where the need for impartiality is stressed.

argues that sympathy does the work of utility. The impartial spectator approves of many motives and desires besides that of benevolence; hence the rules we form by induction from our sentiments do not reduce to the instruction to maximize the good. Even considering benevolence alone, we approve of those who limit their benevolence to family, friends, and native land (pp. 219ff., 227ff., 236–7). When we properly understand this fact about what the man within tells us, Smith's position turns out to be a familiar one:

> The happiness of mankind, as well as of all other rational creatures, seems to have been the original purpose intended by the Author of nature. . . . But by acting according to the dictates of our moral faculties, we necessarily pursue the most effectual means for promoting the happiness of mankind, and may therefore be said, in some sense, to co-operate with the Deity, and to advance as far as in our power the plan of Providence. (pp. 166; cf. pp. 77–8, 236)

None of us intends, when acting morally, to bring about the greatest happiness; but the directives of the impartial spectator, and the divine laws summarizing them, turn out to instruct us in the part we are to play in realizing that end. This is not human wisdom. God, "the great Superintendant of the universe," is responsible (pp. 87, 277; cf. pp. 236, 290). Moreover, what Smith calls "success in every sort of business" as well as the trust and love naturally attendant upon virtue are God's way of sanctioning his laws in this life – though admittedly they may need to be supplemented by further rewards in another life (pp. 166–9). Smith sounds much like Cumberland on this matter, but Price is closer to Smith's position. Cumberland thinks, like Hutcheson, that benevolence is the whole of virtue; Smith, with Butler and Price, rejects the view. He resists the philosopher's temptation, which ensnared Epicurus, of trying to account for all appearances from a few principles (p. 299). Smith's God aims at the happiness of all rationals, and the man within is "his vicegerent upon earth" (p. 130). Even so, we must live with an irreducible plurality of laws and of their corresponding virtues, and be moved by many motives other than benevolence, including, sometimes, a sense of duty (pp. 171, 305).

The visions of morality that Price and Smith come up with are thus surprisingly close. For both of them morality requires us to comply with a set of rules or laws that are not themselves obtained by considering how to bring about any single end or goal. Both think that regard for the rules can motivate us (p. 162). They agree that no single principle suffices to give appropriate moral guidance. Both hold that in fact compliance with the requirements of morality will bring happiness to those who deserve it. The guarantee of this union of morality and happiness lies, for both of them, in God's providential construction of our moral

powers and his supervision of our lives. Neither wishes to draw any
sort of fatalistic conclusion from the belief in God's providence. Price
believes in free will; Smith is a determinist who finds no need even to
mention the matter, but he hesitates no more than Price in giving an
account of merit and demerit that would be valid in God's eye. The
Welsh Dissenter and the Scots Presbyterian are alike strongly opposed
to state control or support of any specific religion.[20] No doubt they had
disagreements on specific moral and political issues. But morality alone
does not suffice to explain why Price should have felt so strongly that a
rational defense of morality is necessary, while Smith is so contentedly a
sentimentalist. The crucial difference between Price and Smith here
comes at the intersection of religion and morality.

Smith lectured on natural theology while he was professor of moral
philosophy at Glasgow (from 1752 to 1764), considering "the proofs of
the being and attributes of God, and those principles of the human
mind upon which religion is founded." Unfortunately we know nothing about what he said.[21] We learn only a little from the *Theory of Moral
Sentiments* about Smith's grounds for confidence in the providential
design of our nature and oversight of our fortunes. Explaining why he
believes that God's end is the happiness of all rational beings, he suggests two kinds of ground: "abstract consideration of his infinite perfections" and "examination of the works of nature" (p. 166). Here and
there he gives a few suggestions about the empirical evidence for God's
providence, but he says nothing about the kind of a priori proof that
would be needed to derive it from his perfection.

As I have noted, Price is deeply concerned about the need to ground
a rational defense of our religious convictions. In an appendix to the
Review he gives an a priori proof of God's existence, and he uses his
rationalist morality to argue that God's decisions must have moral
grounds that match our own. He plainly doubts the ability of "examination of the works of nature" alone to give us the assurances we need
about God's will, assurances that take us beyond experience in this life.
Smith, despite his long friendship with Hume, does not show any
worry about the adequacy of empirical theology, and his early contempt for Platonic metaphysics suggests a strong empiricist bias.[22]
More significantly, Price fears voluntarism; Smith gives no sign that it
ever bothered him. Both are strong defenders of what Price calls self-

20   For Smith, see *Wealth of Nations* V.i.g.
21   The quotation is from John Millar's report on Smith's teaching, as given in
Stewart's *Account of the Life and Writings of Adam Smith, LL.D.,* in *Works* III.274. For
our ignorance, see the introduction to *Works* V.4.
22   The attitude is clear in the essay "The History of the Ancient Logics and
Metaphysics," in *Essays*; see, e.g., p. 125.

governance and Smith self-command; but Price has theological worries about it that Smith apparently does not share. Is our self-governance compatible with God's being a tyrant whom we must obey, or does it need a God who commands simply what we can see for ourselves to be reasonable? Only the latter will give Price the morality he insists on. What drives Price's rationalism is the belief that sentimentalism is inadequate to rule out a universe governed by the voluntarist God in which human dignity cannot be sustained. Price's epistemological war is fought in the name of a deep moral value.

vi. *Moral philosophy dissolved*

Unlike any of his predecessors Smith presents a serious historical survey of his subject as part of his treatise on moral philosophy. In the course of it he asks what effect "the reasonings of philosophy" might have on our moral feelings and conduct (p. 293). The question arises during his critique of Stoicism. He greatly admires the awe-inspiring virtue of self-command – our ability to control our feelings – and sees the strength of Stoicism in its commitment to that virtue. But he rejects its praise of apathy and is highly critical of its favorable view of suicide (pp. 281–92). Can the reasonings on which these abhorrent views rest really alter the judgments of the inmate within the breast? Smith allows that Stoic reasoning might indeed sometimes pervert our unphilosophical feelings, though on the whole he thinks it more likely to encourage us to "actions of the most heroic magnanimity and most extensive benevolence" (p. 293). The point has an importance beyond that of the assessment of Stoicism. "To direct the judgments of this inmate," Smith holds, "is the great purpose of all systems of morality"; and if Stoicism misdirects those judgments, then it fails very badly.

How well does Smith's own theory serve this purpose? It is sometimes objected that precisely because his theory aims at being a science, it offers at best a psychological account of why we judge morally as we do. It cannot direct our sentiments because, so the objection goes, the theory fails to ground our judgments or to give any reason why we should consider them authoritative.[23] But the criticism misses the force of Smith's theory of approval. To ask for a justification of a set of moral judgments just is to ask whether the impartial spectator would approve of them. An affirmative answer is all the justification for morality there can be. Smith thinks that we cannot escape from our moral sentiments to some other level of warrant.

Smith himself, however, raises a question about the ability of moral philosophy to direct the judgments of the inner man. He has no doubt

23 So for example ch. 11.1 in Campbell 1971.

about the theoretical power of his view. He claims that it does much more than account for both the existence and the effectiveness of moral rules. Sympathy with the feelings of agents, those affected by what they do, and mere onlookers explains why some virtues are amiable and others, especially self-command, awesome. The theory lays bare the origins of the distinction between the precise and enforceable duties of justice and the far less specifiable and unenforceable duties of beneficence. It clarifies gratitude and resentment and their ties to our convictions about punishment and reward; our acceptance of inequalities of rank and wealth; our propensity toward self-deceit and its remedy; our beliefs about perfection; and our need to disregard mere differences in the time at which a benefit will be enjoyed. Not least, Smith thinks that his theory remedies the defects he finds in all the other views history shows us.[24]

Suppose then that his theory does what he thinks a science should do: reveal a "connecting principle of nature" and thus bring order into "this chaos of jarring and discordant appearances."[25] What does it do to guide our sentiments, and thereby direct our actions? Since most people live by the practical rules of morality and are not directly guided by actual feelings emerging from the man within the breast, we might think that moral philosophy should help us to articulate those rules. Smith, however, gives a quite negative assessment of the ability of theory to help with this task. His view results in part from his acceptance of the modern natural law distinction between perfect and imperfect duties, which he, like Hume, recasts in terms of virtues.

What Smith calls "the general rules of the virtues" are, he says, in almost all cases, so "loose and inaccurate" that they cannot provide complete guidance. We cannot state exceptionless rules for the virtues of prudence, gratitude, charity, and friendship. The general rules of the virtue of justice, however, are different. They can be given with "the highest degree" of accuracy (pp. 174–5). The most that writers can do to forward the practice of the virtues of beneficence is to portray "the sentiment of the heart, upon which each . . . is founded" – a task requiring delicacy as well as eloquence. It is easier to describe the actions to which each virtue would prompt us. Cicero and Aristotle have done well at this. Their works may "inflame our natural love of virtue," and may lead us to have more finely differentiated sentiments than we would otherwise have. This kind of treatment of the rules of morality is

24 For instance, the defect in Hume's theory shown by Hume's remark, *Treatise*, p. 416, about its being as reasonable for him to prefer the death of innumerable unknown persons to getting a scratch on his finger. Smith criticizes this harshly at *Theory*, pp. 136ff.

25 History of Astronomy, in *Essays*, pp. 45–6.

what is properly called ethics. If it is a science not capable of much precision, it is still one which is capable of "producing upon the flexibility of youth, the noblest and most lasting impressions" (pp. 328–9). Recalling the origins of Smith's *Theory* in his university lectures, we see the function of his own portrayals of virtues and vices.

A problem arises because many moralists are not content thus to refine and exhort the young. They would like ethics to be more precise. They take the virtue of justice as their model and try to work out detailed rules for agents to follow in carrying out all their obligations. The result is casuistry, the effort "to prescribe rules for the conduct of a good man" (pp. 329–30). The casuists were not content with spelling out the demands of justice for individual actions. Prodded by the needs of those who heard confessions and probed every secret thought for deviation from orthodoxy, they tried to regulate veracity and chastity as well. They tried, in short, "to direct by precise rules what it belongs to feelings and sentiment only to judge of." Their works are useless and tiresome, and their enterprise should be abandoned. What needs to be done is to work out an adequate articulation of the virtue of justice. This is the task of jurisprudence; it and ethics are the only useful parts of moral philosophy. At the end of his book on the subject, Smith announces that he will turn next to questions of justice, where the important work begun by Grotius has not yet been completed (pp. 339–42).

From what we can see of Smith's work on this subject, in the notes students took of his lectures on jurisprudence, it is clear that though the moral philosophy of *The Theory of Moral Sentiments* is presupposed, the details owe nothing to it and do not add to our philosophical understanding. When he introduces natural rights, for instance, Smith simply says that their origin is "quite evident" and that they need no further explanation.[26] Jurisprudence, then, the only part of moral philosophy capable of systematic rational development, is not philosophical. Casuistry is to be dismissed; and ethics is essentially a matter of rhetoric. On Smith's view there seems to be not much that philosophy itself can do to direct the judgments of the impartial spectator. Others, we know, expected more from moral philosophy. Smith may well have led them to think that they would have to look elsewhere than to sentimentalism for what they wanted.

vii. *Reid: The active powers*

Smith's friend Thomas Reid disagreed deeply with him, but not because his theory failed to guide the sentiments. Reid took moral philosophy to be a theoretical enterprise, not a practical one. He held

26 *Lectures on Jurisprudence* (B), in *Works* V.401, 459.

that "wherever we find any disagreement between the practical rules of morality, which have been received in all ages, and the principles of any of the theories advanced upon this subject, the practical rules ought to be the standard" (*Active Powers* V.iv, p. 646a).[27] About what makes for a happy life, by contrast, wise men may well know more than ordinary folk; but even here their advice has little influence on anyone, themselves included (III.iv, pp. 216–7). Theory does not correct practice, according to Reid, and his interest in moral philosophy is accordingly concentrated on the epistemology and metaphysics of ethics.

Reid shows us the reason for his approach in his *Essays on the Intellectual Powers of Man*, published in 1785.[28] He there develops an epistemology intended to defend commonsense convictions about our knowledge of ourselves and the world we live in. Against Hume and others who have been deeply misled by the Cartesian theory that in perception we are immediately aware only of ideas in the mind, Reid claims that perception gives us knowledge of external objects and of their causal connections. Where Locke and Hume held that we have immediate acquaintance only with particulars, Reid argues that we have intuitive awareness of general concepts, which are simply given us along with our mental powers, and of basic truths or axioms. Without these we could not reason about the world our senses show us and so could not develop the sciences we have.

Human beings need to reason because of our inability to see, as God does, all the connections among truths (*Intellectual Powers* VII.1, p. 476a). Locke argued that moral truths can be demonstrated; Reid rejects the view. He does not do so because he thinks that sentiment is adequate to explain morality, but because demonstration is not the appropriate concept to use in understanding its rationality. Locke gives examples of abstract connections between concepts: for instance, where there is no property, there is no injustice. But morality has to do with moral obligations binding concrete individuals, and since we cannot know what Locke would call the real essences of individuals, we cannot demonstrate these. We cannot demonstrate our own existence either, although we have no doubt of it. We simply have a faculty that enables us to see that obligations exist in certain cases. Without it we could not be accountable agents (*Intellectual Powers* VII.II, pp. 479b–481a). The

---

27   The point is also made in Reid's lecture notes, *Practical Ethics*, p. 111. Page references to *Active Powers* and *Intellectual Powers* are from *Works*.

28   The most fundamental ideas are adumbrated in early "Philosophical Orations," given at graduation exercises in 1756 and 1759, in terms reminiscent of Lord Herbert of Cherbury: see *Philosophical Orations*, p. 951, where Reid urges philosophers not to busy themselves in overthrowing common notions but instead to build on them.

moral faculty or conscience is an intellectual power (*Active Powers* III.III.VIII, p. 599a). Like other basic cognitive powers, it must show us first truths, which are intuitively known, and must also enable us to deduce conclusions from them. All reasoning must be grounded on truths known without reasoning, and morality is no exception. Indeed, if someone lacks intuitions and is unable to see that some things are right, others wrong then he cannot reason about morals (*Intellectual Powers* VII.II, p. 480a; VII.III, p. 482a).

It is more than a happy accident that morality depends essentially on intuitive knowledge of principles. "If the rules of virtue were left to be discovered . . . by reasoning of any kind, sad would be the condition of the far greater part of men, who have not the means of cultivating the power of reasoning." But virtue is required of everyone, and "the knowledge that is necessary to all, must be attainable by all" (*Intellectual Powers* VII.II, p. 481a). Of course we must use reason to apply the "axioms of morals" to cases, and all of us are fallible in doing so. The foundations, however, are secure, and readily grasped (VII.II, p. 481b).

In the *Essays on the Active Powers of Man*, published in 1788, Reid defends his claims about the rationality of morals in several ways. He argues for a moral psychology that explains how the knowledge we obtain from the moral faculty can be effective in guiding our action. Then he attempts, as Price did not, to state the axioms that are intuitively known. Like Price, again, and perhaps more successfully, he argues against Hume's sentimentalist thesis. I begin with Reid's claims about the axioms of morals and their rationality.[29]

viii. *Defending the obvious: The intuitive axioms*

In making the basic self-evident truths explicit Reid is presenting the rudiments of a system of morals, which is not the same thing as a moral theory.[30] Because even native powers of intuition require education and development, it may be helpful to articulate the principles of morals and illustrate their bearing on typical cases. A system of morals is not to be geometrically ordered. Rather, like a system of botany it collects particular knowledge and makes it more memorable. I pointed out in Chapter 14.i that Reid disapproves of the way the ancients "methodized" morality, in terms of virtues, and that he thinks it more Christian to use the headings of duty to God, self, and neighbor (*Active Powers* V.II, pp. 640a–642). He also thinks it more appropriate to start

---

29 For a fuller account of Reid's moral philosophy, see Haakonssen's introduction to *Reid's Practical Ethics*, or, alternatively ch. 6 in Haakonssen 1996.

30 He is also, of course, replying to Locke's complaint that innatist theorists of morals never tell us what principles are innate: Locke, *ECHU*, I.II.14, p. 76.

from duties than from rights, as the writers of natural jurisprudence tend to do. Morals teaches us duty, jurisprudence rights; rights presuppose duties, which are prior (V.III, p. 643a). And duties – the sets of acts to which we are morally obligated – depend in turn on the laws or axioms we know by intuition.

There are three groups of axioms. Those in the first group spell out, roughly, general conditions concerning morality: that there are moral differences in human conduct, that only voluntary and avoidable actions are subject to moral appraisal, that we ought to try hard to discover our duty and then to do it (V.I, p. 637b).

The axioms in the second group are more substantive. Two concern our duty to ourselves. We are to prefer a greater good to a lesser, regardless of when it will occur; and we are to comply with "the intention of nature" as we learn that from studying our nature – for instance, by following conscience, which has the marks of being given us as authoritative guide (III.III.VIII, pp. 597–8a). Next come two axioms about our duty to others. We are not to live for ourselves alone, but should do as much as we can to benefit the various societies to which we belong. We should treat others as we would judge it right for them to treat us. This is the essence of justice; Reid emphasizes that it presupposes our ability to see what is right and what is wrong, at least in the conduct of others (V.I, p. 639). Finally, we owe "veneration and submission" to God.

The third group of axioms helps us when there are conflicts between the requirements of the different virtues. Virtues are "dispositions to act according to a certain general rule" and as such they cannot conflict; but sometimes we cannot satisfy the rules of all the virtues at once. Then some rules take precedence over others, and Reid thinks the ranking self-evident. It is obvious, for instance, that we are to repay debts before giving gifts (V.I, pp. 639b–640).

General agreement about principles does not by itself show them to be rational intuitions. Philosophers from antiquity onward have agreed about "the practical rules of morals" while disagreeing about the proper explanation of them (V.IV, p. 646a). The need for a defense of their rationality is a relatively recent development, Reid thinks, arising from "the modern system of ideas and impressions." After philosophers made the distinction between primary and secondary qualities and described the latter as mere sensations in our minds, it was not long before they sent aesthetic and moral qualities along the route of colors and tastes (V.VII, p. 670b). Reid's attempt to show that acts can be really obligatory and agents really virtuous is part of his effort to defeat the modern epistemological system.

Reid offers several arguments against Hume's sentimentalism. I consider only one, which elaborates a line of thought suggested by Cumberland. Ordinary thought and language suppose that moral differences really characterize actions and agents and do not express merely our own emotions or desires concerning them.[31] Reid makes the point forcibly. When I say that your conduct was right, this is not identical with saying that your conduct gave me a special feeling, since one is about your conduct, the other about me. You can contradict my first assertion without giving me offense, but if you deny my second assertion you are charging me with lying. All languages allow for expressions of the first sort. But if "moral approbation is merely a feeling without judgment" then everyone who uses such language is either speaking without meaning or is breaking every rule of grammar and rhetoric by speaking of himself while pretending to speak of something else. "Such a consequence," Reid says, "I think sufficient to sink any philosophical opinion on which it hangs" (V.VII, pp. 673–4a).[32]

ix. *Freedom and morality*

Arguments such as these belong on Reid's view to the theory of morals, which gives an explanation of "the structure of our moral powers" (V.II, p. 642b). Although this complex subject has little bearing on daily knowledge of duty, it gets most of Reid's attention in the *Active Powers*; and, on his view, little wonder that it should. Given that we must trust our faculties (III.III.VI, p. 591b), that the principles of morals are self-evident and easily available to mature people, and that from them the whole "system of morality" follows so easily that anyone "who wishes to know his duty, may know it" (V.I, p. 640b), the moral philosopher can really have little new to say about morality.[33] One of the main differences between Reid and the natural law theorists whom, like Butler, he follows in important respects, is that Reid does not claim that our knowledge of moral requirements is to be derived from our knowledge of human nature. Like the natural lawyers, he thinks our

31 For Cumberland's similar point in *Laws of Nature* 5.xvi, pp. 214–15, see Chapter 6.v. I was not aware of this passage when I discussed Reid's arguments in Schneewind 1977, p. 67.

32 Hume himself appeals to ordinary language as a guide to our moral sentiments, noting that "every tongue" possesses eulogistic and dyslogistic words (*Principles of Morals*, p. 174).

33 I do not wish to understate Reid's commitment to teaching his students to be more sensitive moral agents. As Haakonssen 1990 shows, in discussing natural jurisprudence he covered many topics of importance to the moral life. It is quite compatible with his printed views that he should do so, since, as he says, those who have thought more about these matters than most people do may be able to enlighten others (*Active Powers* V.II, p. 642a).

nature shows us God's intentions for us; he claims that we are to comply with the intention of nature; but in making the axioms self-evident he denies that people need to have any special knowledge of our nature in order to have moral knowledge. He thinks nonetheless that the theory of morals is "a very important part of the philosophy of the human mind" (V.II, p. 643a). What makes it so important is not simply the evidence it gives that we possess desires for the good of others as well as self-interested desires, but its engagement with the question of whether or not we are real agents, or, as Reid puts it, whether we have genuinely active powers.

In discussing this issue, as he does at great length, Reid is responding to the worry that in a universe of the kind modern science shows us there is no room for anyone but God to be truly active. In his reply he develops Clarke's line of thought. The belief that some things act and others are acted on is one of the fixed points of commonsense belief that Reid refuses to doubt (I.III, p. 519a). The idea of power is simple. It is not acquired through sense or reflection but is known only indirectly, through that which we observe it to bring about (I.I, p. 514). If Locke was mistaken in many ways about power, he was correct in holding that "the only clear notion or idea we have of active power, is taken from the power which we find in ourselves to give certain motions to our body, or a certain direction to our thoughts" (I.V, p. 523a). Given that we have wills, how do we fit in with the causally ordered world in which we live? Reid never challenges the commonsense belief that every event or change must have a cause (IV.II, p. 603a). But he does raise questions about the commonsense way of speaking of one natural event as causing another. We must not take such language literally, any more than we now take it literally when we say that the sun is rising. Because we cannot obtain knowledge of causation or power through our senses – here Reid accepts Hume's view – all that we really know about nature is lawlike sequences of events. That is enough to gratify our curiosity, teach us what to expect, and show us how to make things happen (I.VI, p. 526b; IV.III, pp. 606b–607a). Regularities do not constitute causes, whatever Hume may think, but where nature is concerned they give us all we need. God might move natural things directly, or through intermediaries, or by means of an initial command; it is unimportant as well as impossible to decide. "It is only in human actions, that may be imputed for praise or blame," he says, "that it is necessary for us to know who is the agent"; and here we can tell often enough.

What matters is the act of will, or volition. Desire and appetite can take almost anything imaginable as their objects, but will can take as its object only "some action of our own," either thinking or bodily movement, which we have a thought of and believe to be in our power (II.I, pp. 531a–533a). To will it is to determine ourselves to do such an act. Only actions coming from the will are voluntary (II.I, p. 531a; IV.I, p. 601b). Reid cheerfully allows that neither he nor anyone else knows how determinations of the will control thoughts or make the body move (I.VIII, p. 528a). The central question, for him as for Locke, is, What determines the will?

Reid thinks that in cases of free volition the person whose will is involved is the cause of the volition. He here comes to his central claim about human active power. We simply possess the power to determine our wills to this or that, to act or refrain. Because causation is the exertion of a basic active power, and not constant conjunction, Reid offers no account of what this kind of determining is, and thinks that there is no room for further inquiry about causes. We can ask why someone made the choice they made. But that, as we shall see, is not necessarily asking what caused the agent to determine her will as she did. It may be a question about her reasons (IV.I–II, pp. 601a–604a).

A conception of the agent as a special sort of cause is thus central to Reid's account of liberty and morality. Agency is not always involved in explaining our behavior. But when our agency explains why we determined our will as we did, then, Reid says, we are free, and for the actions that ensue we are fully accountable.

It is no surprise that Reid does not accept the Humean position that motives determine the will necessarily. Like Clarke, he argues that motives are not efficient causes at all. A motive "is not a thing that exists, but a thing that is conceived," and so it is not the right kind of entity to enter into causal relations (IV.IV, p. 608b). The necessitarians suppose the world to be composed of inert matter, never acting and always acted upon. Since they think the behavior of intelligent beings is part of such a world, they think motives work on will in proportion to their strength and direction. But if we consider rational beings as genuine agents, then we must say that motives *influence* action as advice does, but not that they cause it.

Among the motives that influence action are those coming from the rational principles of action. We know that we are influenced by the thought of our own good on the whole; and without reason we could not even have the concept of such a good (III.III.II, pp. 580b–581). We can also be moved by the thought of our duty, which, because duty is a simple concept, cannot be reduced to that of interest. We have no ground for doubting that our judgments here also influence us. If we could not govern ourselves by such rational principles, we would be left to drift at the mercy of the passions which, Reid thinks, contain no inherent order (III.III.V, pp. 586b–587). But we are not in this hapless state. Moral knowledge and free will collaborate to make us self-governing agents.

x. Reid's legacy

Reid notes that God's "disinterested goodness and rectitude" are what make him an object of devotion, rather than of fear, and that we are to obey him on principle and not out of "servility" (III.III.IV, p. 585b). Otherwise the old worry about a voluntarist deity seems absent from Reid's pages. Though he argues against psychological egoism, he is not seriously concerned about it. Nor is practical skepticism a live danger. No one – not the pleasure-seeking Epicureans, not even the notoriously skeptical Hume – genuinely doubts the reality of moral distinctions (III.III.V, pp. 587b–588a; cf. III.III.VII, p. 594a). What we see of the divine government of the world around us makes it evident that for God benevolence is not the whole of virtue (IV.XI, p. 633b). So also for us: since we must trust our faculties, and our intuitions show us a plurality of moral principles, we cannot suppose morality to be solely a matter of benevolence. Moral perplexity may arise because of the plurality of basic principles, but on the whole "the path of duty is a plain path" (V.I, p. 640b).

What most exercises Reid the philosopher is the theoretical defense of commonsense claims to knowledge. The attack on Hume's sentimentalism is part of this defense. So too is Reid's attempt to explain how it is that we can be self-governing agents in the world science shows us. Hume's naturalizing necessitarian view must be rejected. Reid sees it as the one theory that endangers morality. On the system of necessity, the world is simply a great machine, which God operates through mechanical principles. It leaves no room for moral government. Laws and punishments can be only so many levers for causing motion in us. Necessitarianism depresses our estimate of ourselves too much, tempting us into fatalism. True, we must not "exalt the powers of man too high" either. We must never forget our dependence on God (IV.XI, pp. 635b–636a). But when we are assured that we possess free active power, we rightly see ourselves as not merely God's tools but as his trusted servants. Within our sphere, we have a proper realm of self-government and so we "may be said to be made after the image of God" (IV.V, pp. 615b–616a; cf. IV.IV, p. 612a). If moral philosophy is needed to defend this understanding of our place in the universe, then the purely theoretical insight it can give us is worth pursuing.

However differently they interpret the dictates of our moral faculties, Price, Smith, and Reid agree in taking them as God's directives. Our ability to see for ourselves what we are to do and to be motivated to do it without need of externally imposed sanctions makes us fully self-governing. But our self-governance is compliance with an order we do not make. It is moreover God's governance of the universe that entitles us to be confident that, even without the knowledge – impossible to attain – of all the consequences of our actions, we act for the best when we follow the moral directives he gives us. We can be self-governing as individuals because we do not live in a fatherless world. The well-being of the whole is, in the end, God's responsibility and not ours.

Price and Smith were widely read during their lifetimes, but their views of morality did not exert much influence on later generations. In the nineteenth century sentimentalism dropped out of sight.[34] Interest in it was revived only in the twentieth century, first by positivists and then by philosophers concerned with explaining the connections between moral conviction and moral motivation. And if Price's appeals to self-evident principles helped shape Reid's views, it was Reid's intuitionism and defense of common sense that lasted. From it there arose British, American, and French schools of thought that were influential well into the nineteenth century. It seemed to offer the best hope for grounding Christian opposition to Bentham's promise of a wholly secular hedonistic method of ethics. Reid's intuitionism lived on by generating the versions of the view that Mill so strenuously opposed and that Sidgwick tried to reconcile with the utilitarianism that was its chief enemy.[35]

34 With the exception of Thomas Brown; see Schneewind 1977, pp. 78–80.

35 For the history of these controversies in nineteenth-century Britain see Schneewind 1977; Haakonssen 1996; and Stefan Collini, Donald Winch and John Burrow, eds., *That Noble Science of Politics* (Cambridge, 1983).

19

The noble effects of self-love

The article on "interest" in Diderot's *Encyclopaedie* opens with an account of the ambiguities of the word, expounds the view that proper self-love is the source of all the virtues, and deplores the efforts of Nicole, Pascal, and La Rochefoucauld to paint self-love as vicious. The Encyclopedist thinks that Lord Shaftesbury demands an impossible disinterestedness and moreover that he "does not sufficiently see that the noble effects of self-love, the love of order, of moral good, of benevolence, can influence only few of the actions of men living in a corrupt society."[1] Many eighteenth-century writers held that self-love might have generally noble effects even in a corrupt society. What is more, it might do so without causing us to be benevolent.

The new advocates of self-love opposed the sentimentalists no less than the rationalists. They did not, like Nicole, think our egoism a result of sin, and try to show how God could overcome it behind our backs. They were aiming neither to support an absolutist politics by showing that without it selfish human passions would lead us to self-destruction, nor to unmask all apparently generous and benevolent desires. They were not arguing that self-love, by increasing our concern for our long-term interest, can act as a countervailing force against the eruptions of the passions.[2] They saw a psychology and morality of self-love as the sole theory able to make sense of our motives and actions and to guide them intelligently. What divided the new egoists among themselves was their understanding of the universe in which self-love should direct us. The first English theorists who defended egoism after – and despite – the criticisms of Butler and Hutcheson took us to live in a divinely ordered universe. The French egoists did not accept this comforting thought. In addition they oriented their thinking, as the English did not, around the belief that the social world was profoundly corrupt. Some of them also thought it could be improved, and that

1 *Encyclopaedie,* vol. 8 (1765), s.v. *"Interest,"* p. 819a.
2 See Hirschman 1977.

philosophy could help. Jeremy Bentham brought these French concerns for reform into an otherwise complacent English philosophical setting. The results are still with us.

i. *Association and utility*

In a compact essay entitled "Concerning the Fundamental Principle of Virtue or Morality," published in 1731, a clergyman and sometime Cambridge don named John Gay (1699–1745) set out a line of thought that initiated the new egoism.[3] He presents himself as a Lockean convinced by Francis Hutcheson's description of the phenomena of morality. We approve of virtue immediately and without thought of its results, we choose it for its own sake, and we act appropriately with no consideration of self-interest. But Gay thinks that this cannot be the whole story. He thinks that there must be a deeper explanation of our approvals and motives; and he offers one, built around a theory about the association of ideas (pp. xiii–xiv).

His basic thought is simple. In morality we are like the miser: originally he loves money for what it gets him, but eventually, forgetting why he first took pleasure in money, he loves it for itself. A similar mechanism produces our apparent intuitions of moral laws or of meritoriousness. First we frequently see that certain classes of actions benefit everyone affected by them. Because we ourselves are among those who gain from such acts, we feel self-interested approval of them. We come to associate beneficial acts, and those who do them, so closely with our feeling of approval that we overlook the increase of our own happiness, which is the real cause of the approval. We then mistakenly explain our apparently immediate approval of beneficence in terms of innate simple ideas or instinctive simple sentiments (pp. xxx–xxxi).

Our apparently benevolent motives come about in similar fashion. Not only do we feel approval or love of those who benefit us, but we want them to approve of us, because if they do they will benefit us. We know that people will approve of us if we pursue our own good in ways that deliberately include their good as means to ours (pp. xxiv–xxv). Hence we encourage in ourselves those of our desires that get others to approve of us. Eventually we forget that we acquired those desires in

---

3   The essay was published as a "Preliminary Dissertation" prefixed to Edmund Law's 1731 translation of King's 1706 Latin treatise on the problem of evil. I cite from this edition. Though Gay's view agrees on some points with King's, and, more importantly, with Law's, it does not do so on all. See Law's note, at pp. 66–7. Given the divergences it is unclear why Law printed the essay as he did. Perhaps he simply found it convincing; he later went on to patronize William Paley, the most successful of the exponents of theological utilitarianism.

order to benefit from having them, and treat them as part of our original nature. As the miser comes to love his money for itself, so we come to enjoy helping others, forgetting our initial interest in doing so.

Gay's reductionist psychology enables him to work out a new theory of virtue and obligation. The notion of virtue is a Lockean mixed-mode idea. It is "the conformity to a rule of life, directing the actions of all rational creatures with respect to each other's happiness; to which conformity everyone in all cases is obliged" (p. xvii). In addition to knowing what virtue is, we must know how to tell which acts are virtuous. We must know the criterion of virtue. Gay derives it by considering the ideas of being obliged and being obligated. Both terms refer to "the necessity of doing or omitting any action in order to be happy." Thus nothing can oblige us but our concern for our own happiness. Gay brings in the will of a law giver only indirectly. Virtue, by definition, *always* obliges. But only God can make us happy or unhappy in all cases. Hence his will must be the ultimate source of morality, and so its first criterion.

How, then, are we to apply the criterion? God, being perfect and needing nothing, must have willed our happiness when he created the world. The happiness of mankind is therefore an indicator of God's will, and therefore a proximate criterion of virtue. What is right or fitting for that end is another proximate criterion; right reason, judging such matters, is another. All moral theories reduce to the same thing (pp. xix–xx).

Gay thus works with Hutcheson's sentimentalist critique of ethical rationalism. He agrees that our moral convictions necessarily move us to action. He then gives his own twist to the view by arguing that we are moved to act only by desire; desire arises only when we take pleasure in something; to take pleasure in something is to consider it part of our happiness; and to act for the sake of what we consider part of our happiness is to be moved by self-interest. It looks, of course, as if Gay simply does not notice the attempts Hutcheson made to show the fallacy of this reasoning. But in fact his associationism enables him to think that the criticisms do not touch his own version of egoism. He does not deny that we feel immediate approvals and benevolent motives. But they are not, as Hutcheson holds, simple. They are associations of simpler ideas. We merely fail to notice their origin, or their complexity.[4] Gay thinks his theory is better empiricism than Hutcheson's because it requires fewer unexplained entities.

---

4   Gay does not talk of feelings and desires as confused and indistinct cognitions of the good. It remains unclear in his work what exactly the relation is between the felt simplicity of benevolent desires and approval and the self-interested origin of these feelings.

Hume's use of associationism was quite different from Gay's. Hume did not on the whole use it to claim that certain ideas were "nothing but" a combination of others. Moral approval, love, will, and benevolent desires are all, for Hume, simples. Associations may explain their causes and effects but are not identical with them. Gay's kind of reductionist associationism was elaborated at length by David Hartley (1705–57), whose treatise, published in 1749, bears a title – *Observations on Man, His Frame, His Duty, and His Expectations* – that suggests how he aimed to link psychology, morality, and religion. A self-proclaimed follower of Newton as well as of Gay (*Observations* I.5–6, 115), he says that Newton's work suggested locating the physical substrate of the ideas whose associations explain all our mental life in tiny vibrations of the nerves that he calls "vibratiuncles" (I.60). These cause sensations, which in turn generate simple ideas and pleasures or pains; and various combinations of these give rise to all other contents of the mind.

Groups of ideas associated with feelings of pleasure and pain generate the passions, which in turn become love and hate and move us to act (I.381ff.). Complex pleasures and pains, such as those due to sympathy, the moral sense, and the feeling for God, or theopathy, all start from sensible pleasures and pains (I.428ff.). Hartley portrays normal moral development as moving from the "gross self-interest" with which all of us begin, through a "refined self-interest," which is gratified by the pleasures of sympathy and the moral sense, and on to a "rational self-interest," which finds pleasure in devotion to God (I.471–2). Hartley's point, like Gay's, is not that we consciously think that loving neighbors will be more pleasant than crudely forwarding our own prosperity, and that loving God will be even more enjoyable. Rather, we come to have such strong associations between helping others and our own enjoyment that any separate thought of the latter disappears. This, Hartley thinks, is "proof from the doctrine of association, that there is, and must be, such a thing as pure disinterested benevolence; also a just account of the origin and nature of it" (I.487). There is a counterpart explanation of the pure disinterested love of God.

The moral upshot is clear. We are able to pursue only what we think will forward our own pleasure, and we can learn that the more we take pleasure in the pleasures of others, the pleasanter our own lives will be. The pleasures of sense, imagination, honor, and short-term self-interest should therefore be ruled by the pleasures of benevolence, piety, and the moral sense (II.223, 254, 272, 289). We are to carry this to the point at which "theopathic" pleasures lead us to "self-annihilation . . . and the pure love of God" (II.292–3). Even our benevolence will be partial and imperfect until we locate ourselves in God's standpoint, and "view everything from thence" (II.321).

Hartley does not tell us to use a single consequentialist principle to guide our actions. We never know all the results of what we do, and we cannot determine which act "would contribute most to augment happiness and lessen misery." Even when we know that benevolence toward all brings us our own greatest happiness we must be guided by less general rules (II.303–4). We should follow scripture and our moral sense, weigh consequences, put ourselves in others' shoes, take care of family, friends, and good religious folk before we help others, be truthful, and obey and revere the civil magistrate (II.304–10). The moral sense should be our monitor when quick decisions are called for, but it should in turn be guided by piety and benevolence (II.349–51).

ii. *God and the greatest happiness*

Both Gay and Hartley present a Christian ethics of love, but where Gay sees God as the one who obliges us to be virtuous and so to act lovingly to all, Hartley sees love of God as the great pleasure, which, once we feel it, will attract us to act lovingly to all. Both aim to defend Christianity by using a morality they think their readers accept to strengthen a piety they see as under fire. The apologetic intent is even clearer in John Brown's attack on Lord Shaftesbury's deistic ethic, "On the Motive to Virtue," the second of his three *Essays on the Characteristics* of 1751.

Brown thinks, with Hartley, that everyone agrees about morality. Virtue requires that we engage ourselves to "the voluntary production of the greatest Happiness" (*Essays*, pp. 136–7). Theorists of feeling and of intuition seem to disagree with this. But their views are utterly imprecise, and cannot serve as a real test of virtue (pp. 116–18). Sentimentalists and rationalists alike are forced in the end to call on consequences for real guidance, and common sense agrees. Brown's formulation simply makes explicit what everyone already knows (pp. 133–5).

The problem is that "the only motive" by which we can be led to practice virtue "must be the Feeling immediate, or the Prospect of future private happiness" (p. 159). The natural effects of virtue and vice do not suffice to ensure the coincidence of moral requirement and effective motive, nor will the rewards of honor (pp. 197–8, 202–3, 209). If some people naturally enjoy benevolence, others do not, and, despite the hopes of Gay and Hartley, character training is not going to fill the gap (pp. 207–9). Since human law does not reach the heart, it cannot enforce performance of imperfect duties. The only way to ensure "an entire and universal Coincidence between private and public Happiness" is to convince everyone that an omniscient God will make us happy or miserable according as we do or do not live virtuously (pp. 209–10).

Brown goes out of his way to deny that this view of the motive to virtue is base, slavish, or servile, as Shaftesbury had claimed it is (pp. 213, 219). In his third essay, indeed, he suggests that Christianity shows that the true self is the self that loves others, so that divine sanctions bring us not merely to an external compliance but to the highest human perfection (p. 329).[5] But the strong impression left by the essay on virtue is that virtue is one thing, happiness another, and that in the natural course of events they do not go together, not even for a perfect self. Malebranche, Clarke, and Mandeville had all laid out something like the problem Brown poses; none had presented it in exactly his terms. But Brown simplifies the issues. He sees no basic problem of incommensurability. Only one motive is available, and only one moral end is justified. Although the motive does not naturally lead us to seek the end, the two are made to come together by God.

The fullest and most widely read exposition of the theological solution to the problem of making motive and end agree was William Paley's. His *Principles of Moral and Political Philosophy,* published in 1786, served for decades as a textbook at Cambridge and was frequently reprinted.[6] Paley thought that the simplicity of the Gospel had been covered over with superstitious accretions and that, as he affirmed in the book's dedication, "whatever renders religion more rational renders it more credible." If we understand matters properly, then Dr. Johnson's dictum will be true: "religion will appear to be the voice of reason, and morality will be the will of God." The natural lawyers, Paley complained, write too much about specific legal issues and international affairs to serve the purpose of a system of ethics, which is "the direction of private consciences in the general conduct of human life." They also put too great a distance between the teaching of reason and that of Scripture. Paley proposed to set this to rights, giving us a system in which the basic principle is applied to the problems of the times. He emphasizes in his preface that his theory of "the necessity of *general rules*" gives unity to what might otherwise appear to be unconnected topics.

Paley begins with the first of Gay's questions, that concerning the criterion of virtue. Dismissing the law of honor, the law of the land, and the Scripture as being unable to give us complete guidance, he also denies the competence of a special faculty to fill this role. Whether called moral sense, conscience, or intuition (and all of these amount to

5   This point is stressed in Crimmins 1983.

6   The text seems not to vary among the editions. I cite by book and chapter number, since the chapters are each short. On Paley at Cambridge, and his relation to the latitudinarian tradition of the Cambridge Platonists and Samuel Clarke, see Gascoigne 1989, pp. 238–45.

the same thing), no such faculty is necessary to account for our moral judgments. As these terms suggest, we do indeed approve of virtue even where it does not benefit us personally; but this is because we begin by approving of what *does* benefit us. The sentiment then accompanies the thought of the acts even when we do not benefit from them. Once some people acquire this habit of disinterested approval, it spreads to others by imitation and teaching. Because a special moral faculty cannot afford us a way of reasoning about morality, Paley dismisses questions about it as trivial (*Principles* I.2–5).

His own criterion involves his account of happiness. John Brown complained that sentimentalists and rationalists alike give us no exact principle. Paley is exact. Any condition is happy, he says, in which the aggregate of pleasure exceeds the aggregate of pain. What we refer to when we speak of human happiness is simply "the greatest quantity" of excess of pleasure over pain "ordinarily attainable in human life." All pleasures, from the most sensual to the most refined, are comparable. They "differ in nothing but continuance and intensity." We can therefore compute amounts and calculate what sort of life is happiest.[7] Insisting that men differ too much for any single "plan of happiness" to work for all, he holds that most of us will find happiness in the exercise of our social affections, the use of our faculties for some end that engages us, prudence, and health (I.6).

The importance of these points becomes clear from Paley's definition of "virtue" as "the doing good to mankind, in obedience to the will of God, and for the sake of everlasting happiness." When we act virtuously we take human happiness as our goal, the will of God as the basis for our rule, and the desire for our own eternal happiness as our motive (I.7). There are two stages in Paley's argument for taking the happiness of mankind as the sole proper moral goal. First, we can see that God wills that we should pursue it. He had either to be indifferent to our happiness, or to will it, or to will our misery. There are so many evidences of "contrivances" in nature that make for human happiness that we cannot doubt God's benevolence, and hence his will for our happiness (II.5). This view is the presumption of the whole system. But more is needed to make the argument complete.

---

7   In much of this chapter Paley is following Maupertuis's *Essai de philosophie morale* of 1749. Pierre Louis Maupertuis (1698–1759), a French scientist who directed Frederick the Great's Prussian Academy from 1744 until he died, is the first writer I have found who explicitly claims that amounts of pleasure and pain can be summed in terms of duration and intensity. Insisting on the commensurability of all pleasures and pains, he argues that there is less pleasure than pain in life, and turns this eventually into an argument in favor of Christianity. See Maupertuis, pp. 231–5, 236–7, 240, 275.

Morality involves obligation; and being obligated, Paley says, is the same as being obliged. One is obliged when one is "urged by a violent motive, resulting from the command of another." Persuasion and temptation are thus not the same as obligation, though in both we are strongly moved (II.2). God, we have seen, commands us to follow a definite course of action, and, since he punishes and rewards, his will gives us the requisite violent motive (II.3–4). It is thus the source of obligation in morality, as the natural lawyers had held. God's benevolence is the source of the basic rule itself, but the goodness of consequences does not alone give rise to obligation.

Paley holds that since God's will makes certain acts obligatory, it also makes other acts right. Can we then say of God's actions that they are right? He sees that his own view seems to make such an assertion a merely "identical proposition," and plainly it is not one. He explains why by appealing to rules. Once we have moral rules, we associate "right" and "wrong" with them, rather than with God's will; then we can ask whether God's will conforms to these rules; and since the answer is affirmative, we can meaningfully and truly say that God's acts are right (II.9). Subsidiary rules with which we come to associate the notion of rightness thus enable Paley to avoid all worries about the voluntarist foundation he gives his basic principle. Such rules also have a major part to play in applying the basic principle. One reason for this has to do with our psychological constitution.

"Man is a bundle of habits," Paley thinks, and most people most of the time act from habit. No realistic account of virtue can require more. The first exercise of virtue then lies in forming the right habits. Habits can lead us to act virtuously without any thought either of our own good or of the good of mankind or of God's will. Such action, however, will not lead to our eternal happiness. Christianity has not told us "the precise quantity of virtue necessary for salvation," but there are some rules to bear in mind. We cannot expect eternal happiness if we are never prompted by regard to virtue or religion, that is, by concern for the good of others or the will of God. We must not allow ourselves knowingly to practice a vice at the expense of our duty. We are not meritorious if we merely abstain from evildoing; we must do positive good, if we are to avoid eternal punishment (I.7). Paley's ethics is thus an ethic of character. The more we form ourselves so that we act habitually out of concern for mankind and the will of God, the more we will deserve what we most basically desire – our own everlasting happiness.

There are moral as well as psychological reasons for making rules central in daily life. Without mentioning Butler, Paley allows that there are obvious examples of useful acts that no one would think right (II.87). And without mentioning Cumberland or Clarke, he adds that rules must be used because "you cannot permit one action and forbid

another, without showing a difference between them." He does not give
any rationale for this claim, but goes on immediately to say that if
generally permitting acts of a given kind would be harmful, all acts of
the kind must be forbidden. Even God must act by general rules; otherwise his threats and promises would not be efficacious, since they
would be random (II.7). Calculating rightness of action requires calculating "general consequences."[8]

Like Hutcheson, but with less discomfort, Paley assimilates the vocabulary of right to his consequentialist principle. Both right acts and
rights belonging to persons are explained in terms of God's will, and
thus indirectly in terms of general consequences (II.9). Thus people
have imperfect rights when it would be generally useful to give them
some service or object but generally harmful to allow them to extract it
by force (II.10). Mankind has general rights because it is clear that God
intended much of his creation to benefit all men alike. Our specific
rights and duties are discussed when Paley considers the rules of commonsense morality. He makes no effort to show that compliance with
the rules brings either to the agent or to everyone else the greatest
quantity of happiness ordinarily attainable. He is content to show that
some happiness results from living by ordinary moral beliefs.

For him these are the beliefs of moderate Christians in a highly
hierarchical and class-based society. But he is not afraid, on occasion, to
show that his principle does more than validate existing norms. Thus he
objects to hunting because it harms agriculture (II.11), and he is vehement in his condemnation of slavery (III.3). He was not the only one to
hold such views in the England of his time; but he does not have any
general reformist attitude. His views on property make this evident. He
starts his discussion with a description that suggests a radical conclusion, but then he does not draw it. Imagine, he says, a flock of pigeons
gathering grain in a field, where all but one are heaping the grains up
for the idle one. The lazy pigeon keeps all for himself and gives the
gatherers only the chaff. Imagine that if a specially hungry pigeon takes
away from the heap a nourishing grain, the others tear him to pieces.
Well, all this is "nothing more than what is every day practiced and
established among men" (III.1). We call it the practice of property. There
must be some striking utilities tied to such a system, and indeed there
are. It increases the amount produced; it prevents "contests"; and it
improves "the conveniency of living." Inequality of some sort is un-

---

8   Since the ancient philosophers overlooked this, Paley explains, they had to
invent a distinction between the *honestum* and the *utile* in order to allow that consequences make all the moral difference between acts, while not being forced to allow
gross immorality (*Principles* II.8).

avoidable but, Paley says, if there is great inequality that fails to serve these purposes, it should be corrected (III.2).

We seem to be a far cry from Cumberland's defense of the existing system of property on the grounds that no one can calculate the costs and benefits of alternatives. But having made his bold claim, Paley draws no radical or even reformist conclusions from it. He shows not a trace of indignation about the way that great inequalities of wealth make a small minority happy at the cost of making the majority wretched. On the contrary, he thinks that happiness is "pretty equally distributed among the different orders of civil society" (I.6). He never says who is supposed to use his account of the criterion of virtue as a test. He does not suggest that everyone should use it in daily life, and he does not ask the philosopher to teach the legislator how to improve the laws. In short he does not tell us how to base a method of ethics on his principle. And if examination of accepted rules only confirms our existing moral habits, as Paley thinks, then his purified rational religious morality turns out to be not much more than an apology for the status quo.

iii. *Egoism and reform: Helvetius and d'Holbach*

Hartley held that we should reverence the magistrate. The exponents of the noble effects of self-love in France did not feel the same way. They belonged to a group of writers whose work outraged the authorities. Censorship, persecution, exile, and prison were their lot. In 1770 the French Parlement condemned Baron d'Holbach's books to be burned; it would have burned the author as well, could it have done so. The indictment that led to the condemnation makes quite clear what the authorities feared. The author, wrote France's chief legal officer, Chancellor Seguier, is part of a confederacy "against religion and the government . . . With one hand, they have tried to shake the throne; with the other, they aim to topple the altars. . . . It is particularly religion against which these innovators have aimed the most harmful blows. . . . this dangerous sect has employed every resource; and to extinguish corruption they have poisoned, so to speak, the public wells." They infect every form of literature; their influence reaches far beyond Paris and the wealthy, to the workshops and the cottages, where "the burning breath of impiety desiccates souls and consumes virtue"; they deprive the poor of hope for a better life in another world and replace it with a strong sense of the miseries of their present condition, leaving them no hope but annihilation.[9]

9 Chancellor Seguier's *requisitoire* for a parliamentary decree is reprinted in vol. II of d'Holbach, *Système de la nature;* the quotations are from pp. 403–7.

Seguier was not mistaken. The so-called *philosophes,* intellectuals who dominated French thought and whose work spread rapidly throughout Europe, were a self-conscious avant-garde who agreed in calling themselves enlightened and who thought that the spread of the light of knowledge would bring about the end of the ancien regime. They hoped, at the very least, for profound reforms of what they saw as corrupt, inefficient, and oppressive structures of authority of church and state in their own country and throughout the continent. They reworked economics, history, and psychology as well as moral and political philosophy to support their often conflicting theories, and used poetry, drama, and fiction as well as more theoretical forms of writing to disseminate their views. Their greatest collective work was the *Encyclopaedie* edited by Diderot and d'Alembert between 1751 and 1772, a work whose publication the government forbade for some years because it seemed too dangerous. Their greatest publicist was Voltaire, who moved out of France to Switzerland to assure his personal safety. Their most profound intellectual opponent in France was Jean-Jacques Rousseau, who began as one of their number and was a contributor to the *Encyclopaedie* before breaking with them personally and theoretically. I discuss Voltaire and Rousseau in Chapter 21. Here I consider two thinkers who saw in self-love the only hope for bringing about the happiness of mankind: Claude Adrien Helvetius (1715–71), the most systematic moralist among the *philosophes,* and Paul Henri Thiry, Baron d'Holbach (1723–89), one of the most prolific of them.

After great difficulty with the censors and at some personal risk Helvetius published *De l'Esprit* in 1758. It is a general study of mind or thinking, sketching very briefly the thesis that sensation is the source of all our thoughts. To judge, Helvetius holds, is only to sense. No active soul is required to explain the contents of the mind. Passion and ignorance, and not a separate Cartesian will, are the sole sources of error. Self-interest governs our actions and causes all our appraisals both of actions and of thoughts. Education, so Helvetius argues at length, is a potentially powerful means of improving the way men think.

The aim of the exercise is anything but theoretical. Helvetius's targets are evident throughout his book, despite his occasional cautious bows in the direction of religious orthodoxy. In a country where education is controlled by the church, he argues that ignorance is the great source of the misery of millions. Living under a court and a nobility whose profligacy was as notorious as the taxes that supported it were unbearable, he argues that politicians who are not devoted to the well-being of the many can easily dupe an ignorant populace. When he gives arguments both for and against luxury to illustrate how one-sided views lead to error, the attack shows not only where his heart is but what the main theme of his book is.

Helvetius's defenders of luxury point to the amount of employment that arises from the habits of the wealthy. Its critics say that "luxury constitutes no one's happiness, and that in supposing an overly great inequality of wealth among the citizens, it supposes the unhappiness of the greatest number of them" (*Esprit* I.III, p. 35). A footnote elaborates on another side of this Mandevillian debate:

> In civilized countries the art of legislation has often consisted only in making an infinity of men concur in the happiness of a small number, in order thereby to keep the multitude in oppression and to violate in them all the rights of humanity. . . . However the true legislative spirit ought to occupy itself only with the general happiness. . . . Are we not right to suspect that the extreme felicity of some few is always attached to the unhappiness of the greatest number? (I.III, p. 35n)

Combining a moral demand for the happiness of the greatest number with a psychology of self-interest, Helvetius promptly denies that self-interest must be vicious, as La Rochefoucauld had insinuated. "It is . . . easy to see that self-love, or love of oneself, is nothing but a sentiment written in us by nature; that the sentiment transforms itself in each man into vice or virtue according to the tastes and passions that move him; and that self-love, differently modified, produces equally pride and modesty" (I.iv, p. 45). We are all invariably moved by interest taken in the broadest sense, Helvetius says many times, so that the real question is, In what specific ends do we find our interest? "The humane man is he for whom the sight of the unhappiness of another is an insupportable sight, and who, to avoid this spectacle, is as it were forced to help the unhappy one. The inhumane man . . . is he for whom the spectacle of the wretchedness of others is an agreeable spectacle" (II.ii, p. 59n).

Helvetius betrays no awareness of the British objections to treating all motives as instances of self-love. And though he thinks our tastes and habits can be educated so that we find our interest where the humane man does, he offers no complex theory of association. He does, however, have one thought that moves him well beyond the ambit of the British exponents of the new egoism and makes his work a turning point in the history of ethics. He does not think that we live in a divinely ordered universe in which God's hidden providence or heavenly rewards make it always to the interest of each to work in this life for the interest of all. He thinks, on the contrary, that it is up to us to make our social world into one in which self-interest will lead us all to care for the happiness of others.

He puts the point quite simply. Despite all the variations in what is counted virtuous by men in different countries and times – a variation to be explained by different ideas of what is in the interest of their society – there is one core meaning to the term "virtue": it simply means "the desire for the general happiness" (II.xiii, p. 119). Since Helvetius thinks that the largest group with which we can learn to concern ourselves is our own country, he defines virtue in action, which he calls "probity," as "the habit of actions useful to one's nation" (II.xiii, p. 123).[10] Now men tend only toward their own happiness; "consequently one can only make them virtuous by uniting personal interest to the general interest." The point has an urgent practical bearing: if Helvetius is right,

> it is plain that morality is only a frivolous science if one does not blend it with politics and legislation; from which I conclude that, to make themselves useful to the universe, philosophers should consider objects from the point of view from which the legislator contemplates them. . . . It is for the moralist to indicate the laws of which the legislator assures the execution. (II.xv, p. 139)

Taking the same view of the problem about virtue and motivation that the English egoists take, Helvetius thus assigns to human beings the task Brown leaves with God. He wants no halfway measures. Men tend to have loyalties to small groups; since this gives them interests opposed to the interests of all, they must be brought to a concern for the nation. We need an official "catechism of probity" that men can use to render their virtue steadier. Through it the legislator will point out who deserves esteem, who contempt, and wean people from their attachment to old laws and customs (II.XVII, pp. 144–6). "The whole art of the legislator consists thus in forcing men, through the feeling of love of themselves, to be always just toward one another" (II.xxiv, p. 196). At the beginning the philosopher will need to prod and instruct the legislator, but in the long run everyone can be educated to understand the relations between his own interests and those of the nation. Consequently if the legislator passes the proper laws, he will make everyone virtuous. In doing so he will not have tried the impossible task of making men sacrifice their own pleasures to those of others; he will have altered men's pleasures, linking them so firmly to the general interest that each will be "almost always necessitated toward virtue" (III.xvi, p. 298).

Helvetius published only one further book, the posthumous *On Man* (1772), in which he elaborated and defended his views on education

---

10   "Probity" is simply French for the English "morality" or "virtue" in general. Thus Shaftesbury's remark, "If we are told a man is religious, we still ask, 'What are his morals?' " in Diderot's French translation of 1745, reads as follows: "M.*** a de la religion, dites vous; mais a-t-il de la probité?" A few lines later he uses "probité" to translate "virtue." (See the opening paragraph of Shaftesbury's *Inquiry* in Diderot, *Oeuvres complètes* I.302).

and commented briefly on morality. Scholars are not sure how many books were written by the German-born Baron d'Holbach. Living in Paris on inherited wealth, the jovial host for a group of important *philosophes* and sympathizers, he put apparently limitless energy into anonymous or pseudonymous publications attacking every aspect of the established religion and defending a wholly secular morality. His *Système de la nature* (1770), one of the works ordered burned for the crime of *lèse majesté* against king and God, was his most systematic account of his materialist and sensationalist replacement for a dualism of soul and body. The passionate preface makes clear d'Holbach's conviction that religion and political tyranny support one another, and that both survive only because of ignorance of the truth about nature and man. His books are an attempt to spread what he saw as the light of knowledge and thereby to dissipate the shadows in which alone oppression can operate.

D'Holbach's fullest account of the moral philosophy appropriate to his deterministic metaphysics is given in *La morale universelle* (1776). Adumbrated briefly in the earlier *Système de la nature*, the same theory is elaborated at length in the *Système social* (1773). He gives a reformist twist to a Mandevillian story. The first legislators, he says, invented religion to keep the people docile; the practice continues. But governors no less than subjects are victims of prejudice and ignorance. Both sacrifice happiness needlessly. Morality is needed to guide politics, politics to strengthen morals. "The object of morality," d'Holbach says, "is to make men know that their greatest interest demands that they practice virtue; the end of government should be to make them practice it" (*Social* I, introd, pp. vii–viii). The view is not of course new, but d'Holbach handles the philosophical details in his own way.

Unlike his English predecessors, he does not think that all the different moral systems amount to the same thing in the end. Claims about intuition and moral sense and eternal fitness simply obscure the truth that only the bearing of actions on happiness is morally significant, and that only experience can teach us what that bearing is (*Morale* I, pref., pp. xi–xx; *Social* I.IX, pp. 91–103). D'Holbach is willing to use the idea of order to explain his view, but not as Malebranche does. What he calls order is closer to what Leibniz calls perfection, but it has no ties to any metaphysics of perfection. Order is simply "the accord found when the parts of a whole concur to one end. Moral beauty results from moral order, which is the accord of the wills and actions of men concurring for their happiness" (*Social* I.IX, p. 97).[11] Happiness, for d'Holbach, is essentially constituted by pleasure. He says that only the pleasures

---

11   D'Holbach continues with what must be a deliberate echo of St. Augustine's great passage about the peace of an ordered whole, in *City of God* XIX.13.

that conform to order are morally acceptable, but he means simply that pleasures are not to be pursued if they come at the cost of an excess of pain, either for us or for others (*Morale* I.I.IV, pp. 12–14). Moral order is not for him a Malebranchean check on the pursuit of pleasure. It is the order that brings about "the constant happiness of the beings with whom we live" (*Morale* I.II.II, p. 75).

Although d'Holbach speaks of virtue, he sees morality as basically concerned with duties and obligations. Duty he defines as "the suitability of means to the end one proposes"; moral obligation is nothing but "the necessity to do or avoid certain actions in view of the well-being that we seek in society" (*Morale* II.I, pp. 1–2). Experience shows that the end we all always seek is our own preservation and enjoyment (I.I.II, p. 4). Given that we need society in order to flourish, morality has only one virtue to recommend: justice. Justice as a virtue is the disposition to accord men their rights; and their rights are "the free use of their wills and their faculties to procure what they need for their own happiness." Hence it is unjust, d'Holbach concludes, to do anything that harms the rights, liberty, or well-being of anyone in society (II.IV, pp. 84–5). From this we can see how to derive from experience all the moral rules we need, thus turning morality into a useful science.

To those who claim that the variety of rules we see in different societies and at different times shows that there is no universal morality, we need only say that the variety is due to the ignorance and prejudice under which mankind has had to live up to the present. There is, of course, some understandable but removable ignorance of what will in fact lead to human happiness. But for d'Holbach there is a sinister cause at work as well. Our morals "are corrupted because those who should have guided [men] to happiness . . . have thought it necessary that they should be blind and unreasonable, in order the better to subdue them" (*Morale* I, pref., p. xxi). The fault lies with religion; and d'Holbach's explanation of this point links him closely to a series of thinkers who would have viewed with alarm and dismay most of the rest of what he says. He thinks religion has a disastrous effect on morality because he sees religion as centering on a crude variety of voluntarism. His opposition to voluntarism is not, as is that of Cumberland or Leibniz, an effort to show that we can know more of God's morality than the voluntarists allow. It is an effort to unmask the psychology of those who teach any religious morality, and to expose the harm they do.

What do the theologians say when we ask what virtue is? They say that it is "the will of the incomprehensible being who governs nature" (*Nature* II.9, p. 256). They give, in short, the voluntarist answer; and the reason it is so harmful is simple. When we ask how we are to come to know God's will, we get a hodgepodge of confusing replies. The upshot is that we must rely on the priests themselves to tell us. We get no stable principle, the same for all people at all times; we get "caprices of the imagination" (II.9, p. 259). Religious moralists would have us think morality the most problematic of sciences, whose principles could be known only by a few deep metaphysicians. But to derive morality from such systems is in fact to subordinate it, he repeats, to "the caprice of each" (II.9, p. 265). The results are disastrous.

"Nature says to man," d'Holbach declaims, "you are free, no power on earth can legitimately deprive you of your rights: religion cries out that he is a slave, condemned by his God to weep all his life under the iron rod of God's representatives." Religion tells man to obey his ruler no matter how tyrannical; it threatens the ruler himself if he is not completely devoted to the priests. Thus "religion corrupts princes; princes corrupt the law; all institutions are perverted" (*Nature* II.9, pp. 270–1). Ideally the legislator ought "to invite, to interest, to compel each individual, out of his own interest, to contribute to the general interest" (*Morale* I.VII, p. 37). When society is corrupted by its leaders and guided only by their caprices, it forms men who are avaricious, jealous, and dissolute; it discourages talents, neglects virtue and truth, tramples justice underfoot, and rewards moderation only with poverty (*Nature* II.9, pp. 272–3). Only the morality of nature can cure this appalling situation.

D'Holbach is well aware that it will be difficult to set matters to rights. In an uncharacteristically melancholy passage he laments that men "float continually between virtue and vice . . . in contradiction with themselves." Glimpsing the true value of an upright and honest life, they wish to live accordingly; but they promptly see that such a life gains nothing, and "can even become an obstacle to the happiness that their heart never ceases to seek. In corrupt societies," he concludes sadly, "it is necessary to corrupt oneself to become happy" (*Nature* II.9, pp. 271–2).

iv. *Bentham: Making morality in a world on its own*

Jeremy Bentham (1748–1832) would not have agreed. There is a widely circulated story, whose provenance I have not been able to trace, to the effect that when he was asked why he devoted his life to such arduous labors of law reform, he replied that, though as self-interested as others, he simply enjoyed it. He certainly did not expect a reward in heaven for his labors. He was repelled by religion early in his life and attracted to legislation when he was barely twenty.[12] He held back the

---

12   On Bentham and religion, see Steintrager 1971; for his early interest in legislation, see Bowring 1843, p. 27. Halevy 1928 gives a valuable brief account of

publication of his best-known statement of the principles on which he
proposed to reform the laws of England until he was prodded by
friends after the publication of Paley's ethics to let it go. The *Introduction
to the Principles of Morals and Legislation* (1789) did not have the success
that Paley's book had. A second edition did not appear until 1823, and it
was only with the decline of Paley's reputation and the rise of a new
generation of thinkers that Bentham assumed the place we now think of
as securely his, that of the founder of what we now call (though Bentham did not) utilitarianism.[13]

We associate the term with a phrase Bentham made famous, "the
greatest happiness of the greatest number." Hutcheson's formula for
the moral end was put very nearly in those terms; translated into
French, his work was read by the Italian penal reformer Cesare Beccaria, who wrote of "the greatest happiness divided by the greater
number"; mistranslated, this came out as the famous formulation in the
1767 English version of Beccaria's *On Crimes and Punishments,* from
which Bentham got it.[14] Bentham used the phrase in his own first
published work, the *Fragment on Government* of 1776, which was a critique of Blackstone's *Commentaries on the Laws of England.* He did not
use it again until the 1820s, and then with reservations.[15] But the idea it
captures – that we can use a precisely quantified ultimate goal to generate definite moral guidance – is one that informs all his work.

From the beginning Bentham used the idea of a calculable morality
to support his efforts at legal criticism and social reform. In his early
years he was not as radical as he later became.[16] He attacked Blackstone
early on, however, because in the *Commentaries* he found only description, and no assessment, of the English legal system. Blackstone en-

Bentham's intellectual development, and Mack 1962 gives a longer one, correcting
Halevy on some points.

13   See Schneewind 1977, ch. 4, for the early reception of Bentham's work.
Bentham used the word "utilitarian" to label his doctrine in 1802 (Bowring 1843, p.
320) but the noun form seems to have been used only later and not by Bentham.
References to Bentham's *Introduction* are from the edition of Harrison.

14   Hutcheson, *Inquiry II* 3.viii, p. 181, says: "so that that action is best, which
procures the greatest happiness for the greatest numbers" (cited in Chapter 16.iv).
Shackleton 1988 argues that it must have been the English translation of Beccaria of
1767 that provided Bentham with the phrase, as it does not occur precisely in the
Italian, or in the work of Priestley where Bentham reported having found it, or in
Helvetius. Smith 1993 points out that Helvetius did use the phrase; but he cites *De
l'homme,* which was not published by 1768, the time at which Bentham says he came
across it. For Bentham's own report, see Mack 1963, p. 103 and n.

15   See Rosen 1983, pp. 201–3.

16   See Crimmins 1994 for a persuasive discussion of Bentham's move toward
radicalism, making it earlier than other scholars do.

dorsed it, with all its faults; and Bentham found this unacceptable.[17] A lawyer by training, he was interested in moral philosophy for the service it might provide in bringing contending parties to agree on matters of law. Unlike Grotius, he did not have to deal in the first instance with controversies between hostile countries of opposed religious confessions. He made the kind of clean sweep of past philosophical guides to action that Montaigne had made, but much more brusquely; and he made it not to find personal tranquillity but in order to provide a procedure for settling moral issues that everyone could use in public as well as in private and that would get its results only from objectively determinable facts.

To indicate his objection to all previous "systems . . . concerning the standard of right and wrong" (*Introduction* II.14), Bentham uses the word d'Holbach used to pillory the basic weakness of theological morality: caprice (II.11n). The only fact on which all previous theories take moral judgments to rest is the bare fact of the feelings of approval or disapproval of the person judging. But approval just as such amounts to the caprice of the person judging. Moral sense, common sense, understanding, rule of right, eternal fitness, law of nature or reason or right reason, truth of things – all, Bentham says, reduce to this: whether the speaker feels sympathy or antipathy toward the act in question (II.14n).[18] Resting morality on the will of God is no better. No one now appeals to revelation for political advice; and to say that what is right conforms to the divine will is true but empty, because "it is necessary to know first whether a thing is right, in order to know from thence whether it be conformable to the will of God" (II.18). With this Bentham takes the greatest happiness principle, as he calls it (I.1n), out of the hands of the religious moralists to whom, in Britain, it had previously belonged.

Bentham describes his own principle as a sentiment of approval and disapproval (I.2). His view differs from the invocation of mere feeling in all other systems because his alone "points out some external consideration, as a means of warranting and guiding the internal sentiments of approbation and disapprobation" (II.12).[19] The Benthamite external

17 On Bentham's critique of Blackstone and its historical setting, see Lieberman 1989; for Bentham on common law, see Postema 1986.

18 Bentham had a theory about language and meaning to back up this reductionist claim and others that he makes; see *Bentham's Theory of Fictions*, which gives numerous passages relating the view to language concerning morality and motivation. I have found no similar theory in d'Holbach to support his thesis that religious morality reduces to the capricious judgments of priests.

19 Bentham's argument against other principles is a greatly expanded version of an argument suggested by Hobbes in *Leviathan* 46.11, and noted in Chapter 10.iv,

consideration is the quantity of pleasure and pain produced by the action we judge. Pleasures and pains are the ultimate constituents of individual interests, which in turn make up the interest of the community. The moral question is neither how we actually come to make our judgments nor whether when we reflect we can privately sustain wholly unwarranted feelings. The question concerns public justification. Bentham thinks that a person addressing the community can justify moral judgments only on the basis he proposes. An act is to be approved just to the extent that it promotes the happiness of those it affects; the more happiness it brings, the more we are to approve (I.2, I.6). He defends the greatest happiness principle by arguing that everyone will agree that some such principle is needed and that none other is available.

Appeal to publicly verifiable facts is needed because the alternatives are unacceptable. It seems out of the question to ignore the interest of the community, especially in political matters. Bentham thinks no one can state an alternative principle that gives weight to interest without making it the sole test of morality. Are we then to judge without principle, or merely on the basis of our feelings? But if each person is to judge, the result would be an anarchy so complete as to destroy the objective character of morality, reducing moral judgments to expressions of taste. Are we instead to be guided by only one person's feelings? Bentham does not show much concern for religious voluntarism, but his denunciation of this option uses language always used by antivoluntarists. It is, simply, "despotical" (I.14.6; cf. II.15n). Bentham's principle is the sole principle we can all agree to use to settle our disputes without fighting.

Helvetius and d'Holbach had nothing much to offer in the way of justifying their basic principle. Bentham says that his principle cannot be proved, and he does not claim that it is self-evident. His principle is as universal in scope as Leibniz's, but his mode of supporting it is new. He does indeed claim that it arises as the requirement of reason applied to practice. But this is not because other practical principles are, as Clarke thought, self-contradictory. It is because his is the sole possible basis for decision making that can be publicly defended. It is, Bentham thinks, the only one that can serve the purposes for which we need such a principle.

The greatest happiness principle has another advantage. It is the only principle that people can be reliably motivated to follow (I.14.10; III). Bentham holds that although language suggests that motives differ widely, the only facts behind the language are pleasures and pains. Nothing moves us but anticipation of one or the other, as a consequence

---

to the effect that appeals to essences and forms enable philosophers to set moral rules according to their own tastes.

of action (X.5–7, 10). He apparently thinks this grounds the claim that we can be moved to accept the greatest happiness principle and not any other; but he never explains clearly just why. He does not claim, as a hedonistically inclined Leibnizian might, that we are necessarily moved to pursue the good no matter who will enjoy it, and wherever we see we can bring it about. He knows that we sometimes take pleasure in the well-being of others. In treating us as pursuing the greatest positive balance of pleasure over pain for ourselves, he is not claiming that we are all necessarily selfish. He is noting that we are not all so moved by affection for others that we naturally tend to the pursuit of the greatest happiness of the society. Hume, whom Bentham admired, argued that there is no natural motive to justice; Bentham extends the point to morality more generally and then, misleadingly, puts it in terms of a divergence between duty and interest that must be overcome.[20]

It must be overcome by our own action. We will pursue the morally proper goal just in case legislation makes it plain to us that it is to our own interest to do so. The task of the legislator and the magistrate is "to promote the happiness of the society, by punishing and rewarding" (VII.1). With Helvetius and d'Holbach, Bentham thinks that proper laws are the central tool through which we can make it to each person's interest to act in ways that bring about the greatest happiness of the greatest number. The French egoists devoted themselves to theory and propaganda; Bentham spent most of his life working out precise instructions about the laws and institutions that were needed to do the job.

The plans he developed or encouraged seemed to show that the greatest happiness principle could deliver, as Bentham promised, a way of settling disputes and guiding social change. He was concerned with projects such as ensuring clean water and effective sewage, where it could be plausibly claimed that the balance of utilities was obvious. He never called for any serious scientific investigation of actual balances of pleasure and pain (nor, indeed, have utilitarians since then). He never fully explained, moreover, how individuals were to get from the principle of utility a method for making private decisions, and philosophical debate since then has shown the difficulties that stand in the way of doing so. If a morality of self-governance requires that individual agents be able to reason out for themselves what they ought to do, then it is unclear that Benthamism can ground such a morality. It is an interesting fact that later utilitarians tried to find a way in which their theory could do so.

---

20 For Bentham's expression of a debt to Hume, see the *Fragment on Government*, ch. I.36 and the long note.

The Benthamite doctrine raises a further problem about self-governance. Bentham thinks we live in a moral world on its own. We cannot count on a deity who will make the world harmonious for us, either in this life or in another. It is up to us to make the moral world harmonious. But we cannot do so by becoming virtuous individually. We can do so – as d'Holbach's sad admission makes clear – only through a properly structured community. Bentham portrays a morality that needs no obedience to or sanction from anyone or anything outside of the people it is to govern. But he also presents a morality in which only those who happen to have a strong taste for the greatest happiness can be moved to be moral without the threat of sanctions. As in the Harringtonian classical republic, those of us whose tastes do not run this way cannot act virtuously unless we live in a society that has overcome corruption by instituting the proper legal order.

v. *De Sade: Self-love in a corrupt society*

"In all of life's events," says one of de Sade's speakers, "at least, in all those wherein we have freedom . . . we experience two impressions . . . one invites us to do what men call good – and to be virtuous – the other to elect what they call evil – or vice . . . we must find out why we are of two minds and hesitate" (*Juliette*, p. 147). The Marquis de Sade (1740–1814) went out of his way to reveal some of the problems with views like those of Helvetius and d'Holbach.[21] He was no kinder to the apologists of the old regime and its religion, or indeed to anyone aiming to defend virtue and morality of any kind. His views are specially tied to those I have just been discussing, however, because he shares the atheism, the hatred of organized religion, and the psychological egoism of Helvetius, d'Holbach, and Bentham. Agreeing with them further in seeing human beings as nothing but parts of a fully determined nature, he nonetheless speaks at times, as does d'Holbach, as if nature has lessons for us. But if they were all nature's pupils, de Sade learned things that the *philosophes* and reformers did not.

Philosophical disquisitions and remarks are scattered throughout the thousands of pages of de Sade's interminable descriptions of sexual orgies and tortures. Like his obsessive fantasizing about different ways to unite or disassemble various humans and their parts, his justifications of the absolutely untrammeled pursuit of individual enjoyment

---

21 For the idea of discussing de Sade's views in this connection, as well as for some details, I am indebted to the Domenech's treatments of him in his informative *L'éthique des lumières;* see esp. pp. 214ff. Smith 1993 discusses Helvetius's actual and possible replies to problems such as those de Sade later raised, some of which, Smith notes, had been raised quite quickly by his critics.

also play with only a limited number of possible positions. We need not ask whether they all fit together into a single whole. His general view is not hard to discern.

Though he does not refer to them, de Sade is opposed to a basic idea shared by Helvetius, d'Holbach, and Bentham. They all think that in a well-ordered society the legislator will have made it to the interest of each individual to act in a way that forwards the well-being of others. If everyone is aware of this, then, because we all always pursue what we think to be to our own interest, we will act in ways that benefit others. Self-interest well understood will produce virtue. The problem, which d'Holbach stated explicitly, is that we live in a corrupt society. The legislators have not done the job the *philosophes* require of them. Hence self-interest, well understood, does not here and now rationally require everyone alike to act for the greatest good. Rationality leaves it up to the individual. As Bentham suggested, it depends on one's tastes. Those who like law reform will act for the public good; those with other tastes, not finding their interest in such disinterest, will act otherwise; and quite rationally so.

The humane man described by Helvetius may find the sight or thought of the unhappiness of others so insupportable that it is in fact to his interest to benefit them. Like the Mandevillian rescuing a child from the fire in order to assuage his own distress, he will cheer himself in so doing, and may think the relief well worth the material cost. Helvetius also imagines an inhumane man, for whom the sight of the misery of others is an agreeable spectacle. His pursuit of pleasure will lead him in quite different directions. This is the person who fascinates de Sade. He spells out in exhaustive detail what will please such a man, or woman. The activities that de Sade depicts so obsessively make a certain kind of sense, given his own psychological and social views.

Let us begin with the individual psychology. Each pursues what he takes to be his own greatest pleasure. For the Sadean hero, the degree of pleasure increases with its violence and enormity (*Juliette,* pp. 146, 174). Sex of any sort, preferably combined with inflicting or undergoing bodily harm, will thus yield the greatest pleasure. If we are to take the teaching of nature seriously, so that we view the natural consequences of actions as rewards and punishments enforcing her laws, then for such persons a law of nature requires Sadean joys. The enormous difficulty of abstinence, admitted by all moralists, shows plainly which way nature points (*Bedroom,* p. 220). Acts in themselves, therefore, are indifferent; if we think or feel otherwise – if we feel pulled toward virtue – we merely show the bad effects of having been raised to accept the prejudices of our corrupt society. We should train ourselves out of feeling remorse rather than alter our behavior (*Juliette,* pp. 170–2). Nature destroys as often as she creates; she plainly needs the one as much as she needs the other; we are but doing her bidding if we maim or kill others, when that is how we get our greatest pleasure (*Juliette*, pp. 172–3; cf. *Bedroom*, pp. 238, 345). Keep in mind that "there is no possible comparison between what others experience and what we sense." We do not feel the agony of others, but a minor pleasure of our own touches us. Hence "we should . . . prefer this most minor excitation which enchants us, to the immense sum of others' miseries, which cannot affect us. . . . are we not all born solitary, isolated?" (*Bedroom*, p. 283).

Do we not, however, have sentiments of love and affection and concern for others? Yes, but they expose us to terrible losses. "Never listen to your heart . . . the heart deceives, because it is never anything but the expression of the mind's miscalculations" (*Bedroom*, pp. 340–2). We should not be fooled into thinking that those who act from benevolent impulses are better than those who are more overtly interested. "The virtuous sentiment . . . stinks of commerce: *I give unto you in order that I may obtain from you in exchange.*" If it is true, as Helvetius and d'Holbach teach, that all voluntary acts spring from self-interest, then "man does not practice virtue save for a purpose, . . . the advantage he hopes to reap therefrom, or the gratitude that puts others in his debt." There can be no such thing as disinterested virtue whose aim is to do good without a motive (*Juliette*, p. 144). We do well, then, to avoid love, which ties us unprofitably to the well-being of the one we love (*Juliette*, p. 502; *Bedroom*, p. 285).

It did not escape de Sade that people might object to what his heroes and heroines do. After all, he was frequently imprisoned for engaging in such activities himself. He has two responses. First, he simply declares that nature intends the strong to act one way, the weak another. The rich man can buy the right to enjoy life in his own way. Nature meant the weak to be slaves. Pity for them interferes with nature's intended order. The poor and weak are like the strong in seeking only their own good; the strong are just better at getting it. Of course the weak think otherwise (*Juliette*, pp. 174–9). The second response is to sketch a view – I do not know how seriously he took it – of a social order in which the Sadean life could be lived within the framework of law.

He imagines a classical republic in a France that is now, thanks to the great revolution, free of king and priest. We are each to be as free as possible, constrained by the fewest possible laws. And what laws do we need? We will no longer recognize duties to God, since we deny that God exists. Hence we will have no more laws dictating worship and, as a result, no more religious persecution (*Bedroom*, pp. 308–9). The sole duty to self that de Sade considers is that of not committing suicide; but he repudiates it entirely (p. 337). Duties to others require us to pay attention to four matters: what affects a man's reputation, his property, his person, and his life (p. 311). Reputation can look after itself: the vicious deserve to be exposed and virtue will eventually be known. As for property, in a republic there should be no great inequalities of wealth. Property would cause no problems were it not unjustly distributed; as it is, if the poor steal from the rich, they are righting injustice. We should perhaps punish one who is incautious enough to let himself be robbed, but we should not burden the poor thief with yet further hardships (p. 314). Protection of the person of others gets predictably short shrift. We will be so far from supporting modesty and chastity that the state should provide at public expense for places to which anyone, woman or man, may summon anyone else for whatever sort of gratification seems pleasantest, even if it involves sodomy or incest. We fail otherwise to recognize nature's voice in the strength of our desires (pp. 320–7). Finally, do we need a law against murder? No, let each look out for his own life: only thus will the republic have the kind of hardy and fearless citizen it needs for its defense (pp. 331–7).

De Sade's ideas are in effect brilliant caricatures of the moral and political theories of his time. He sometimes thinks of his exemplary figures as noble, but he is proclaiming not so much the noble effects of self-love as what he thinks are its inevitable consequences in a corrupt and godless world. Insofar as he intended his work to be a critique of the thought of the *philosophes,* he was both too late and too bizarre to be an influence on them, or on later philosophers who followed their lead. He leaves us, however, with – among other things – a powerful if unpalatable indication of one serious flaw in the thought of the advocates of self-love.

PART IV

Autonomy and divine order

20

Perfection and will: Wolff and Crusius

In the 1720s the theological faculty at the University of Halle was up in arms about the philosophy of Christian Wolff. Their outrage was compounded when they learned that he planned to publish in Latin an expanded version of the metaphysical system he had first written in German. The new book would allow the whole world to learn that antireligious theories were taught at Halle, bringing the university into terrible disrepute.[1] If the theologians thought that foreigners would not read metaphysics in German, their judgment was sound. Even thirty years later Adam Smith could say that "the Germans have never culti-vated their own language; and while the learned accustom themselves to think and write in a language different from their own, it is scarce possible that they should either think or write, upon any delicate or nice subject, with happiness or precision." He added that although the achievements of German academies are known abroad, "it is seldom that the works of any particular man are inquired for."[2]

Smith's comments reflect a widely held opinion of Germany. It was seen by non-Germans of the eighteenth century as an amorphous con-glomerate of innumerable small or medium-sized states, picturesque perhaps but making no contribution to intellectual life. Non-Germans did not think German a language worth knowing.The Germans rapidly translated into their language almost everything of note written in French, and much of what was published in English. But unless they themselves wrote in French, few of them were read abroad until the latter part of the century.

From the end of the seventeenth century onward, German writers and thinkers who agreed with the foreign estimate of German cultural backwardness made strenuous efforts to change things. They created periodicals like the English *Spectator*, designed to polish the manners and broaden the minds of a growing group of reasonably well-to-do

---

1 Hinrichs 1971, pp. 410–11.
2 Smith, *Essays*, "Letter to the *Edinburgh Review*," p. 243.

merchants, lawyers, and civil servants.[3] They tried, without much durable success, to reform the universities.[4] They worked hard at improving the German language itself, using foreign models for poetry, drama, and fiction, and then moving beyond such models with the help of their own increasingly sophisticated and innovative writers and literary critics.

The point was not simply to stand higher with cultivated Frenchmen. It was to bring greater freedom to the lives of those whose successes in commerce and administration made them chafe at the subordination their highly hierarchical societies imposed. Lutheran pastors and Catholic priests kept a stern eye on morals; aristocrats and courtiers exacted deference as well as taxes. It was not clear what the subordinates got in exchange. Clarification, or *Aufklärung*, which we might think of as demystification, was a cultural endeavor with a political point.[5] Creating the ability to speak clearly and precisely in one's own language about morality and politics was a crucial part of the enterprise of enlightenment.

i. *Wolff: The need for system*

No philosopher did more in this endeavor than Christian Wolff (1679–1754). Where Christian Thomasius helped his native language to handle philosophy by using French and English words with German endings tacked on, Wolff created a whole vocabulary to replace the Latin that still dominated the universities. Thomasius struggled unsuccessfully to work out a coherent view of natural law and morality. Wolff produced an entire philosophical system, beginning with logic and methodology and working through ontology, philosophical psychology, the universal principles of practical philosophy, and then their specification in morality, politics, international law, economics, cosmology, the teleology of nature, and the teleology of the parts of animal and human bodies. From 1712 to 1726 he published his views in compact books in German; then he elaborated them at enormous length in Latin. Some of his works found their way into translations or French summaries, and of course his Latin treatises were available to anyone with the patience to read them.[6]

---

3 See Martens 1968 for an interesting study of these journals.
4 See McClelland 1980, Turner 1974, and Paulsen 1919.
5 In the first sentence of his essay "On the Question: What Is Enlightenment?" Moses Mendelssohn says: "The words 'enlightenment' [*Aufklärung*], 'culture,' 'education' [*Bildung*], are still new arrivals in our language." They belong in the language of books. The essay was published in 1784. Bahr, p. 3.
6 For a full view of Wolff's life and work, see Ecole 1990. Wolff wrote copiously

Wolff is quite explicit about why he writes his philosophy in German. A firm knowledge of morality is needed for happiness and an assured conscience, and such knowledge requires certainty about basic principles. Admittedly some people are much better than others at producing demonstrative knowledge; but the latter can benefit from the work of the former. "And it is for this reason," Wolff says, "that I publish in German my thoughts on philosophy, in which I derive basic knowledge of truth, so that even those who have not studied can obtain it, and I rejoice when I see that my efforts are recognized and useful."[7]

And why, we might ask, does it take a professor to teach us the basic principles of morality? The answer is that moral knowledge, though of the first importance in practical terms, depends on metaphysical and psychological knowledge, which itself must be derived in the proper order from the appropriate starting points. Wolff's 1703 doctoral dissertation was the first methodological treatise produced by a German. In his metaphysics he refers back to his logic to explain the order of his argument, in the ethics back to the metaphysics for his principles, and so on through the series of expositions, as he reminds us each time he expounds the later stages.[8] The whole constitutes a modern Protestant scholastic system. Wolff had many followers, but his was the last full articulation of the claim that rational knowledge of the way the uni-

on mathematics and science from 1703 onward, and continued writing in Latin while publishing his German philosophy. The "German logic" – *Vernünftige Gedancken von den Kräfften des Menschlichen Verstandes* – was published in 1712. It was translated into Latin, French, Italian, Dutch, and eventually, in 1770, into English. The German accounts of metaphysics, ethics, and politics were not translated into English.

Mme. du Châtelet put a good deal of Wolff as well as Leibniz into her *Institutions de physique* in 1741. Two Huguenots residing in Berlin produced fuller accounts of Wolff's work. Jean Deschamps published French summaries of the foundations of the system in 1741 and 1743, and abridgments of the two Latin volumes on psychology in 1747. J. H. S. Formey's six-volume *La belle Wolfienne*, which appeared between 1741 and 1753, covered most of Wolff's teaching. From 1740 on, Formey also edited a journal, the *Bibliothèque Germanique*, designed to familiarize French readers with German thought, which, in Formey's hands, meant largely Wolffian thought. See Barber 1955, ch. VIII, for more details on the French reception of Wolffianism.

7 *Vernünftige Gedancken von der Menschen Thun und Lassen* (*Reasonable Thoughts on Human Action*), 1720, 288–9. As this work is commonly known as the "German ethics" I cite it hereafter as *Ethics,* giving the paragraph number. I use the word "philosophy" for Wolff's term *Weltweisheit* or "worldly wisdom," which he introduced in apposition to the German for "theology," namely *Gottesgelarhtheit* or "learning concerning God."

8 See, e.g., the introduction to *Vernünftige Gedancken von dem gesellschaftlichen Leben der Menschen,* cited here as *Politics.*

verse forms a cosmos through God is essential to bringing harmony into our own lives and to living with others in social unity.

Was Wolff's synthesis original? His view was deprecated as "the Leibniz-Wolff philosophy" by its critics.[9] He was undoubtedly much influenced by Leibniz, explicitly accepting his doctrines of monads, the principle of sufficient reason, and the preestablished harmony. But he was more nearly an eclectic than a Leibnizian, holding that empirical knowledge is as important as rational knowledge, and seeking to include truths no matter what system first turned them up.[10] In practical philosophy in particular, which was one of Wolff's most enduring concerns, he went far beyond his master. If there is a "Leibniz-Wolff" philosophy, its ethics and political theory are largely of Wolff's own making.

Empirical or "historical" knowledge comes from the senses and shows us what actually exists. Mathematics gives us knowledge of quantities. Philosophy is the discipline that shows us the reasons why things exist, or, more precisely, it explains what is possible and then shows why there exist among the possibles the things that actually do exist. Thus although philosophy is, as we would say, essentially a conceptual discipline, its principles "must be derived from experience" (*Discourse* 34). Philosophy should give demonstrative proofs showing how facts given in experience are connected through the principles of possibility and the reasons of things. Thus understood, philosophy is useful. "Things which we know philosophically," Wolff says, "are applied to the problems of human life with greater success than the things which we know only historically" (41).

There are three divisions of philosophy. Theology deals with God, psychology with the soul, and physics with body.[11] Each shows what is possible through its main subject. Thus psychology shows what is possible through the soul. From experience we learn that the soul has both cognitive and appetitive faculties; philosophy shows what they make possible (*Discourse* 58–60). Only then can we begin "practical philosophy," which is "the science of directing the appetitive faculty in choosing good and avoiding evil" (62). Through his demand for system, Wolff achieves what Hume later got only by special arguments about

9   See Carboncini 1969; Corr 1975.

10   The methodological views are explained in the German Logic and more fully in the *Preliminary Discourse on Philosophy in General,* cited as *Discourse* followed by the section number.

11   Wolff was the first to use the term "Psychologia" in the titles of books – his *Psychologia Empirica* and *Psychologia Rationalis* – in what was roughly the discipline we think of as psychology.

the relative permanence of acts and motives: making the psychology of action the determinant of morality.

ii. *Wolffian psychology*

Wolff's brief account of psychology is given in his German Metaphysics, the *Vernünftige Gedancken von Gott, der Welt und der Seele des Menschen (Reasonable Thoughts on God, the World, and the Soul of Man).*[12] The soul, he holds, is a simple, non-corporeal substance. Like any existing thing its essence is constituted by its power; and because it is simple, it can have only one power (*Metaphysics* 742–5). Basically this is the power of representing the world as the world impinges on the soul via the body associated with it. Representations (*Vorstellungen*) can have different degrees of clarity and distinctness. The more we can distinguish a representation from others like it, the clearer it is; the more of the parts making it up we can clearly perceive, the more distinct it is. Whether clear or dark, explicit or obscure, representations all essentially carry propositions about the world (198–9, 206, 209). The senses, imagination, memory, reflection, understanding, desire, and will are all to be understood as different ways in which the soul represents the world (747).

Wolff's position thus entails that each specific instance of each kind of mental activity, from sensation to conceptual reasoning, from desiring to willing, is constituted by two factors: its definite propositional content and the degree of its clarity and distinctness. Since there is only one power in the soul, and content and degree of clarity and distinctness are the only dimensions of manifestations of that power, there is nothing else from which mental states can get their identity. Sensations, for instance, may be clear representations – I see clearly that green is not red – but they are indistinct (*undeutlich*), since I do not see exactly what

12   Since this work is usually referred to as the German metaphysics, I cite it as *Metaphysics* followed by the section number. The Leibnizian character of Wolff's thought is clear at many points: see, e.g., secs. 765–6, where he accepts the thesis of preestablished harmony.

A. G. Baumgarten's *Metaphysica* (1739 and many later editions), a textbook from which Kant regularly taught, contains a comprehensive outline of the Leibniz-Wolff philosophy. It was translated into German by G. F. Meier in 1766 for use in his own classes.

Wolff's account of the psychology is presented at much greater length in his *Psychologia Empirica* and *Psychologia Rationalis*. The first summarizes the facts about perception, memory, imagination, attention, the various forms of thinking, dispositions, pleasures, affects, volitions, and the commerce of the soul and the body; the second shows how they are all made possible by the essence of the soul.

constitutes the difference between red and green (214). Yet there is some
set of truths about that difference, and if I perceived colors distinctly I
would know it. Memory and reflection, involving reiterated operations
on representations, enable us to have clearer and more distinct concepts, to form judgments, and to make inferences. To see how passions
and will arise from representations, we must bring in a new consideration.

Like Leibniz, Wolff sees the world and everything within it in terms
of perfection and imperfection. "The harmony of the manifold" is
Wolff's definition of the perfection of things (152). Complex entities
contain a number of parts working harmoniously together to attain an
end. The more parts they contain, and the simpler the principles of their
organization toward the end, the more perfect they are. This world,
Wolff argues, is the most perfect of all possible worlds, since all its parts
work together as fully and as simply as possible to express God's glory,
that is, his infinite perfection (982, 1045, 1049–51).

The doctrine of perfection is important for understanding the passions and desires. When we recognize, or think we recognize, perfection, we feel pleasure. To feel pleasure indeed just is to have an intuition
of perfection (ein Anschauen der Vollkommenheit) (404).[13] In speaking of
intuition, Wolff refers to an uninferred representation, without intending to imply that no error is possible. We can get pleasure from mistaken
as well as accurate representations of perfection (405). And the amount
of pleasure we feel must be absolutely proportional to the amount of
perfection we intuit.[14] Pleasure and displeasure or pain (cf. 417–18, 421)
are tied to good and ill, through the central definitional claim that "what
makes us and our condition more perfect is good" (422). Thus the
intuitive awareness of good is what brings, or more accurately constitutes, pleasure. And pleasure and pain, so understood, are the building blocks out of which the passions are constituted.

We can clearly tell pleasure from pain, but both of them remain
indistinct representations of perfection, or good and ill (432–3). Insofar
as they are indistinct, they give rise to sensuous desire. Such desire is
"an inclination of the soul toward something of whose goodness we
have an indistinct conception" (434). Just as we can tell green from red
without being able to see what makes each the color it is, so we can tell

13   "Voluptas est intuitus, seu cognitio intuitiva perfectionis cujuscunque, sive
verae, sive apparentis." Psychologia Empirica 511. Wolff says we owe the idea to
Descartes.

14   As Ecole 1990, I.269, notes, Wolff sometimes speaks of pleasure and pain as
consequences of intuitions. If he means to treat pleasure and pain as nonrepresenta-
tive states of mind, he is departing from his basic theory rather seriously. In either
case, however, the feeling will be proportional to the perfection perceived.

that we like the taste of a specific wine without being able to say what it is in the wine that makes it more perfect than a wine we dislike. Our pleasure represents the good confusedly and indistinctly; and the inclination to drink is, Wolff says, thereupon necessary, since the soul is necessarily inclined toward whatever pleasure represents to it as good (878).

The specific passions are essentially characterized by the kind of good or pleasure that constitutes them, taking into account also the relations in which we stand to that good. Desire and aversion arise directly, Wolff says, from pleasure and pain (434, 436). When we are disposed to take pleasure in the happiness of another person, we are said to love that person. Such love can give rise in turn to notable happiness or unhappiness on our part, according as the other fares well or ill (449–53). Wolff is careful not to suggest, as Leibniz sometimes does, that in loving another we are seeking our own enjoyment or benefit. When passions rise to a noticeable degree of strength, Wolff says, they are called affects (441). Affects pull us this way and that, and we remain their slaves as long as they stay indistinct (491). But we can escape this passive slavery by improving the quality of our representations. We can think something good through clear and distinct representations as well as through obscure and indistinct ones. The clearer and more distinct our thoughts, the more perfect we ourselves are. The effort to attain more perfection is essential to our being. Hence insofar as we are moved by indistinct representations, we are doing less of what we essentially will, and therefore are passive. As our ideas become more distinct, we are acting more as we essentially will to act. Since distinct ideas give us more power than indistinct, they make us more active (115, 744, 748, 755–6). The more active we are, the less we are enslaved.

Our essential striving toward perfection or good in general constitutes our will (492). Will and desire are not different in kind from "the representing power of the soul" (879). A representation of something as perfect just is a representation that inclines us toward it. Will differs from desire only because in willing we compare amounts of perfection presented by different ideas and move toward the greatest. What finally moves our will is our reason for acting; and Wolff follows Leibniz in stressing that the will has no power of choosing in the absence of a reason or motive (*Bewegungsgrund*).[15] It may seem that we can make choices where we are wholly indifferent, but this is never the case, although often the cognitions of perfection that move us are below the level of consciousness (496–8, 508–9). Moreover, we never choose what seems to us the worse in preference to what seems the better, though,

---

15 Wolff gives *motiva* as the Latin equivalent for *Bewegungsgrund*.

again, we may not be aware of the sensuous desires influencing us (503–7).

The mind has no dispositions to act other than its motives. Hence we always necessarily act for what we represent as the greatest good or perfection available to us. Both Leibniz and Wolff think, moreover, that God has created the best possible world. It seems therefore that not only are we determined to act by our representations of goods and ills, but that these representations could not have been other than they are, and therefore that we could in no sense act in any way other than we do. How, within this framework, can we be free? Wolff gives essentially the answer we have already seen in Leibniz.

Freedom is "the ability of the soul through its own power of choice [*Willkühr*] to choose, between two equally possible things, that which pleases it most" (514–19).[16] Contrary to vulgar prejudice, freedom does not require the ability to choose either of two alternatives without any reason for a preference (511). On that view, Wolff says, all moral truth is destroyed. Morality requires that representations of good and bad have a reliable effect on human action.

> If you throw that out the window, then all certainty in morality collapses, since one cannot influence the human soul except through representations of the good and the bad. Even in the commonwealth, obligation as based on punishment rests on the fact that man does not want ill and does want good, and avoids what he thinks good in order to escape a greater ill. (512)

Our being determined to action by the reason that most strongly moves us is thus essential to, not destructive of, morality – a point Hume made later, in somewhat different terms.

iii. *Wolffian ethics*

Wolff connects his metaphysical psychology of perfection to his ethics through an account of obligation. "To obligate [*verbinden*] someone to do or omit something," he says, "is only to connect a motive of willing or not willing to it." For instance, the magistrate's threat of hanging for theft obligates someone who fears the gallows not to steal (*Ethics* 8). What we are obligated to do is thus what it is necessary for us to do. Because by nature the availability of increased perfection necessarily moves us, we are always obligated to pursue it. Hence there is a basic law guiding our behavior: "Do what makes you and your condi-

---

16 Here again, as in Leibniz, the possibility invoked is bare logical possibility. What is not actual is conceivable but not metaphysically possible under the rule of the principle of sufficient reason.

tion, or that of others, more perfect; omit what makes it less perfect." Because this law arises from the nature of things, it is the law of nature (12–16). Our own reason can teach it to us; consequently "a reasonable man needs no further law, for because of his reason he is a law unto himself" (24).

Because God created the world, we can view the specific links of actions with perfections as showing what God obligates us to do; and then we consider the guidance we obtain from the law of nature as a divine law. God's law cannot deviate from the natural law, which would obligate us, Wolff adds, even if God did not exist (5, 29). And he adds a point that emphasizes both his Leibnizian opposition to voluntarism and his insistence on human worth. The reasonable man needs no external rewards or punishments to move him to act as he sees he ought. Doing the good because it is good, he is therefore "like God, who has no superior who can obligate him to do what is good . . . but does [it] simply because of the perfection of his nature" (38).

Although Wolff echoes Grotius's famous phrase about God and obligation and stresses the importance of our social nature, he is no Grotian. The problematic of conflict is as absent from his thought as it is from Leibniz's. The real perfection of any one person is tied to that of all others: "whoever seeks to make himself as perfect as possible seeks also what others seek and desires nothing at their expense" (43). Holding, as Spinoza does, that God is the greatest perfection and cannot be attained, he sees the good life as progress toward our own perfection. Honoring God and serving others are inseparable from the achievement of our own perfection. To be virtuous, moreover, is to be disposed to comply with the law of nature that requires us to aim at perfection. Since psychology teaches us that as we attain more perfection we feel more pleasure, Wolff thinks that he has demonstrated that our happiness lies in virtue (40–66).

With perfection, obligation, motivation, and happiness thus all unified, the questions that remain concern how we are to know what to do, and what, specifically, we are obligated to do. "Conscience" is the term Wolff uses for our general ability to know what is good or bad in action, and what we ought or ought not to do (73, 78). He gives new accounts of the many distinctions used in traditional discussions of conscience but says little about how we are to gain the information conscience needs. We are slaves if we allow conscience to be determined by the indistinct perceptions constituting sensory pleasures and pains, free if clear and distinct perceptions guide us (81; cf. *Metaphysics* 519). Even with care, we can be mistaken, since it is the consequences that determine whether actions are good or bad (*Ethics* 100). But mistakes are excusable, though we will suffer pangs of conscience if we have not been careful in judging.

Conscience, as Wolff treats it, judges all our actions, not just those considered specifically moral. The difficulties in the way of accurate conscientious judgment are therefore considerable. All our actions must aim to increase the perfection, which is the happiness, of ourselves and others. As I said earlier, Wolff thinks that men of learning can discover rules for the rest of us to follow (*Ethics* 150). We need general rules or "maxims" to judge particular cases, as Wolff has shown elsewhere (*Metaphysics* 337). But though he thinks it easier to know one's own maxims than those on which other people act – and not very hard to find those out either – he does not spell out any method by which either we or our learned betters can discover them (*Ethics* 198–203).

Wolff, however, knows what they are, and tells us. He puts his morality in terms of duties, and like Pufendorf divides them into duties to self, God, and others. A duty is simply an act in accordance with law; and since there is no law without obligation, we can say that duties are acts we are obligated to perform (*Ethics* 221). The account of duties to God occupies nearly two hundred pages of the German ethics, but the principle is simple. We can do nothing to benefit God; we can only honor him. We honor him by performing from love of God's perfections all the duties required of us by the law of nature which, of course, is God's law for us (650–4). The more clearly we know God, the more we will love him and, loving him, honor him. And the more we honor God the more blessed we will be. "So a man who wishes to be blessed must think of God in all his actions" (671).

Duties to self are spelled out in detail. For Wolff, here differing from Clarke, they are truly duties *to* oneself, and not merely concerning oneself. What obligates us to them is not the service to God and others for which we must keep ourselves in trim. It is the perfection we can attain for ourselves. We must care for our own soul as well as for our own body; we must improve our knowledge and our will, thus increasing our own virtue; we must improve our condition, thus giving ourselves increased means to pursue yet further perfection. The German ethics devotes the many pages of its part II to the details. Maxims concerning health and good manners toward patrons and other benefactors concern Wolff no less than recipes for controlling unruly desires and keeping one's mind clear in the heat of passion. One is reminded that Wolff, like his Scottish university counterparts, was teaching raw country boys with little background and no social polish.

In philosophical ethics, as Wolff defines it, we consider man as he is by himself, living with no external authority over him. Politics considers man in society, so that rights and duties concerning others are treated in a separate volume, *Vernünftige Gedancken von dem gesellschaftlichen Leben der Menschen*, known as the "German politics." In the German ethics only some fifty pages are given to duties to others, contrasted with over two hundred given to duties to self. More than methodology is involved in the imbalance. Wolff's statement of the principle behind it is quite clear: "Man must undertake for himself as well as for others such acts as make more perfect the inner condition of soul and body as well as outer conditions. Hence duties toward others are the same as duties toward self. What we owe to ourselves, we owe to others" (*Ethics* 767). The long discussion of duties to self has in effect made it unnecessary to go into much detail about our duties to particular other persons considered simply as persons, though the German politics spells out at length our role-related duties as spouses, parents, and citizens.

On Wolff's view the only way we can improve ourselves is by increasing our stock of clear and distinct ideas. All mental contents are representations; subject matter aside, they vary only in clarity and distinctness. If we are not improving these dimensions of our minds, we are becoming less perfect. It is part of our essence to strive for greater clarity and distinctness. Only what agrees with this drive is that "agreement of the manifold" that constitutes perfection (*Metaphysics* 157). It is thus morally necessary for us to strive always and only for what is in effect self-perfection, even if we do not ourselves always see this clearly. Increase in our own perfection is the only change that will improve our behavior toward others. The priority of self-perfection is thus required by the Wolffian psychology.

Since the basic law of nature requires that what we must do for ourselves we are equally bound to do for others, Wolff thinks we must consider ourselves as being united to others. "We are obligated to see others," he says in the German ethics, "as if they were one person with us" (*Ethics* 796). The same principle guides the theory of politics. Societies arise when two or more people join together to promote their "common best." In this regard, "they are not to be viewed otherwise than as one person, having accordingly a common interest" (*Politics* 6).

The lesson Wolff derives is that amounts of good are the sole considerations to be weighed in making decisions. I need not help another to a good he can procure for himself, though I am bound to help him where he needs assistance. If, however, the damage to myself would be greater than the benefit to him, the obligation to help ceases. Similarly, a promise binds only because of the good the promised act will bring about; promising as such adds nothing to the obligation to do the act, and if it turns out that I would obtain more good from breaking my promise than you would get from my keeping it, I should break it (*Ethics* 769–72, 1003–6).

Since I am to will the perfection, and hence the pleasure, of others, I must receive pleasure from their receiving pleasure. This means that I am obligated to love others and, indeed, to love them as I love myself

(*Ethics* 774–5). Wolff develops this point into a Leibnizian definition of justice. We are not merely to love others, but to love others wisely. But to do good according to rules of wisdom is "what we customarily call justice." Love and justice thus come together through wisdom (1022–4).

iv. *A note on Pietism*

One of Wolff's editors allows that he was "the most prolix and boring author of his century, even of modernity as a whole."[17] Even so, his books were in great demand; and during his early years as a teacher at Halle, from 1706 to 1723, he attracted so many students that he earned the enmity of those, especially on the Theological Faculty, from whom he seemed to be stealing them. In 1721 Wolff delivered an oration on the ethics of the Chinese, in which he claimed that Confucius had discovered all the important truths about morality (and therefore agreed with Wolff), although he lacked adequate knowledge of God and knew nothing of Christ. One of the theologians used the oration as the occasion to denounce Wolff. The leader of the Pietists, August Hermann Francke (1663–1727) took the complaints directly to King Frederick William I, and in 1723 the king prohibited Wolff from teaching philosophy and then banished him from the kingdom, under threat of death.[18]

More than personal envy was driving the theologians. Religious conviction was also involved. Halle, with Christian Thomasius as one of its leaders, was not only the first modern Prussian university. It was also the major early eighteenth-century home of the leaders of a personal and emotional form of Lutheranism known as Pietism. The work of Philipp Jakob Spener (1635–1705) gave new impetus to an existing revival of Lutheranism, and Spener's admirer Francke, who spent the latter part of his life in Halle, made it influential throughout Prussia. He and his colleagues took Wolff's views to pose a serious threat to religion and morals. We must look very briefly at their position.[19]

Spener saw the terrible sufferings of the Thirty Years' War as a divine chastisement of the German people for falling away from true religion. They had not carried forward the reformation that Luther began. They had allowed themselves to think that Christianity required no more

17 Marcel Thomann, in his preface to Wolff's *Grundsätze des Natur- und Völcker-rechts* (Hildesheim, 1980), p. v.

18 For a brief chronology of the controversy and its literature, see Ecole 1990, I.19–20, 81–92. Hinrichs 1971, ch. V.2, gives a full and illuminating history of the whole affair, which I follow here.

19 For what follows I rely largely on Hinrichs 1971, ch. 1; see also Stoeffler 1973, chs. I and II.

than knowledge of the chief doctrines together with occasional confession and communion. But it requires much more than that: it requires deep repentance for one's sins, and a conversion that alters one's whole life. For the Pietists this did not mean a one-time experience of justification before God. If they did not teach justification through works, they warned sternly that we can be sure of our acceptance only by seeing that our behavior has changed for the better. Every day we must feel and act as good Christians do. Ultimately this means that the whole world must be freed from corruption and brought to perfection. The historical destiny of the Germans, so Spener thought, is to complete the Reformation by bringing about the Kingdom of God on earth. The work must start within the soul of each and every individual.

Underlying this missionizing attitude is a rejection of Calvinist views of predestination. As Francke puts it, "we are certainly not to think that God the Lord has only a few elect" (Erb, p. 150). God offers grace to all. It is up to us freely to accept or refuse his offer. Taking seriously the Lutheran doctrine of the priesthood of all believers, the Pietists urged all Christians to help one another toward repentance, conversion, and steadfast adherence to the right path of life. If conscious striving can help us attain grace, laxity can cause us to lose it. We cannot be truly perfect because justifying perfection is only ascribed to us by grace due to Christ's intercession. But there is a kind of perfection we can approach. "A person can come to a human strength in Christianity so as to kill the old habits in himself and to conquer his flesh and blood . . . one person is always more perfect than another" in this way.[20] This kind of self-improvement is an endless task for each of us.

Given this outlook, the formation of character was understandably a major concern. Hence education was of the first importance to Francke and his followers. The Halle Pietists founded orphanages and schools in order to have opportunities to shape poor and rich alike from their earliest days. They valued learning for its utility in preventing misguided interpretations of the faith, not for its own sake. Spener taught that "the apostles wrote their epistles for the most part to uneducated and plain people, who could not have understood them by heathen science and philosophy, but who by the grace of God understood them for their salvation without these." We should not reason about Scripture but should try to live in obedience to its precepts (Erb, pp. 55–7).

Calvinism, like Lutheranism, held that one should labor within one's calling. But where the Calvinist was apt to see worldly success as the sign that he had received grace from God, the Pietist held that worldly

---

20 Francke, "On Christian Perfection," in Erb, *Pietists*, p. 115.

success was more likely to lead to sin. Like the English Puritans, by whom they were influenced, the Pietists believed that we should avoid drink, dancing, gaming, and elaborate clothing, live an austere life, and work hard. The aim of our work should not be to increase wealth. It should be to improve our own spiritual condition and that of others.

Improvement, then, comes ultimately from grace and involves having a love that is beyond nature. Morality requires more than abstention from harming our neighbor: "we must actually love him with a sincere affection." Thus morality, for the Pietist, is not a matter of external behavior, although there is an external morality by which even the heathens could live. But as Luther taught (see Chapter 2.iv), we do not have within ourselves the strength to live in an inwardly righteous way. Because of the Fall, we naturally love only worldly things, and we cannot overcome this corruption. "In vain," Spener declares, "does the law encounter it with her impotent discipline. In vain does she display her rewards and punishments. These all serve only to show us our guilt and danger, but cannot work our deliverance" (Erb, pp. 132–3).

The Pietists' general doubts about the efficacy of rational knowledge to procure a saving faith led them to attack Wolff's method. Their belief in austerity and self-denial as central to the life of the believer led them to be furious about Wolff's stress on the importance of enjoying life in this world, and his praise of dance, opera, fine clothing, good food, and the amenities in general. They accused him of denying divine providence, a charge tantamount to that of atheism. They thought that the doctrine of the preestablished harmony turned human beings into mere machines. Wolff's view on these matters, they held, amounted to no more than Spinozistic fatalism. That was precisely the doctrine they did not want the world to know that Halle allowed to be taught. What convinced the king ultimately to move against Wolff was the conclusion that the Pietists said followed from his theory, that a rebellious minister or faithless soldier could plead that his behavior was fated and therefore not blameworthy.

When the Pietists learned that Wolffian ministers were preaching from the pulpit in Königsberg, they launched an attack on the Wolffians there, and with similar success. But the king eventually changed his mind about the Pietists and their accusations. Among other things, Wolff had been elected to the French Academy, the first German since Leibniz to be so honored. In 1740 Frederick William's successor, Frederick the Great, engineered Wolff's return to Halle. Wolff had claimed during the controversy that his rational arguments were useful in protecting those whose religious feelings were wavering. By the time Kant was a student in the Pietist school in Königsberg, there were teachers who claimed to be both Pietists and Wolffians.

v. *Crusius: The significance of free will*

During Wolff's lifetime his most impressive philosophical opponent was Christian August Crusius (1715–75), a Lutheran pastor as well as a professor of philosophy. His remarkable book on ethics, the *Anweisung vernünftig zu Leben* (*Guide to Reasonable Living*), was published in 1744, a year prior to his metaphysical treatise, *Entwurf der nothwendigen Vernunft-Wahrheiten* (*Sketch of the Necessary Truths of Reason*). Crusius has a highly systematic philosophy, using in the earlier work the positions defended in the later one. His philosophy lays the groundwork for a specifically Lutheran apologetic. He deliberately opposes Leibniz and Wolff on almost every major issue, claiming, from his titles onward, that reason is on his side, not theirs. He is, however, not entirely on the side of the Pietists either.

Reason, Crusius argues, shows us far less than the Wolffians think it does. Like Descartes, he accepts the possibility that a more perfect mind than ours can think in ways we cannot. What to us seems contradictory might not be so to a perfect mind, but we are confined to our own limited and possibly erroneous grasp of what is conceivable. We must also assume that when we think one thing cannot exist without another, or cannot coexist with another, then things behave as we must think they do. But we cannot prove these principles, and a more perfect mind might see things otherwise (*Sketch*, pp. 24–7).

It is of course God's mind that provides the telling contrast with ours; and Crusius insists that there are un-Wolffian limits to our understanding of God. The difference between finite and infinite mind is not one of degree. The inner essences of the two are so different that the finite can have no relation to the infinite (*Sketch*, p. 225). Our minds possess some perfections, but God's are so infinitely superior that it is not as if a created being "could be, so to speak, a little divinity." We understand God only negatively, denying limits on his perfections; not even a direct revelation could enable us to understand him fully in positive terms (pp. 439–41). God can and does leave room for us to exercise such powers as we have, but Crusius does not allow, as Leibniz and Wolff do, that we are God-like in our own sphere.

The way is thus open for a voluntaristic view of morality, of the sort that Luther presented, and Crusius does indeed develop such a position. But his is a carefully modified voluntarism, designed to avoid the chief charge against the view – that it is morally unacceptable, reducing humans to a servile position under a tyrannical deity. There can be no moral requirements binding Crusius's God, who is the source of all moral laws for us. Crusius argues, moreover, that the most important requirement of morality is that we obey the laws God gives us out of a sense of our dependence on him and from a desire to obey him. To show how we can respond to this requirement, which concerns motivation and not simply behavior, Crusius works out a moral psychology in which freedom of the will, in a very strong sense, is central. And by assigning more significance to human freedom than any of his German predecessors had, he thinks he can turn the edge of the Leibniz-Wolff objections to voluntarism. The moral philosophy that results from Crusius's attempt to rationalize Lutheranism is one of the most original products of the eighteenth century.

If Crusius opens his *Guide to Reasonable Living* with a psychology of will, it is not in order to make the content of what morality requires depend on human nature, as his voluntarist predecessors do. It is rather to show that our nature is able to respond to commands embodying God's ends, not ours. The will is one of the active powers God has assigned to some created beings. It is "the power of a mind to act according to its representations," or the effort to make real something represented (*Guide*, p. 2; cf. *Sketch*, p. 866). Just as "understanding" is a catchall name for various powers concerned with acquiring knowledge, so will as active power contains various strivings, some constant, some intermittent. These include our desires, which are thus aspects of the will (*Guide*, pp. 7–8). Desire is not essentially due to need or lack, and it is not, as it is for the Wolffians, confused or indistinct cognition. It is one form of the will's exercise of its activity. The will enables us to reject or adopt any desires that are aroused by representations. To adopt a desire is to decide to realize what is represented – to make it exist, or to come to possess it. The understanding moves only from one idea to another; the will takes us beyond the realm of thinking, and so is neither a part of the understanding nor simply derivable from it (*Guide*, pp. 9–11; *Sketch*, pp. 867–9). The Wolffians are thus mistaken in thinking will and understanding to be only one power.

Acts of will, or volitions, for Crusius, always bring to the representations that elicit them an otherwise absent thrust toward realization. Beings who can think must have wills because otherwise their representations of the world would be pointless.

> All minds must have wills. If they had none, they could not act according to their representations [*Vorstellungen*], and these would then be useful neither to them nor to others but quite in vain. But it is altogether contrary to God's perfection to create something useless and in vain. (*Guide*, p. 7; *Sketch*, p. 886)

The Cambridge Platonists assumed that reason's function in guiding practice is more important than its function in discovering truth. Crusius here gives a general argument for the primacy of the practical. The argument and the assumptions on which it rests – that representations alone do not move to action, and that God does nothing in vain – are central to Crusius's thought. Their importance is shown in his way of explaining of human action.

Pleasure and good as well as desire are explained in terms of will. Pleasure is what we feel when we are in a condition we have willed (*Guide*, p. 25). The good itself is simply what is in conformity with a will, or with desire (*Guide*, p. 29; *Sketch*, pp. 326–7). If goodness is thus relative to agent's impulses, as it is in Hobbes, perfection is different. Things are more or less perfect as they are more or less able to be causes of other things, or as they have more or less power (*Sketch*, pp. 296ff.). Thus it is God's infinite power that makes him the sole infinitely perfect being. But God has a standing desire for perfection – a tendency to self-affirmation and to the production of other perfections – and therefore what is perfect is also, for God, good. We too always desire perfection, so that for us as well the perfect is in fact the good, although the concepts are different. Crusius thinks it pointless to say, as Leibniz and Wolff do, that we always will the good. Goodness presupposes the desiring aspect of the will, and does not explain its activity. And since, like Locke, Crusius thinks that desire is only contingently aroused by any particular representation, it is no surprise to find him insisting that there are innumerable kinds of objects of desire, and refusing to try to explain them in terms of self-interest or any other single factor.

Many of our desires originate from other desires, as the desire for a means does from the desire for an end. Since this cannot go on forever, there must be basic desires, and at least some of these must be essential to the mind. Basic desires, given us by God, cannot be wicked and must be shared by all. There are also contingent desires, implanted in us by our parents or the present condition of the world. No general account of these desires can be given. But from them there arises the desire for happiness. Like Butler, Crusius thinks that in desiring happiness we aim only at the gratification of our specific, contingent, desires. Without them there would be little in which we would take pleasure (*Guide*, pp. 119–29).

The desire for happiness is not among the basic desires. Crusius identifies just three of these. The first is the desire to increase our own appropriate perfection (*Guide*, pp. 133–4). Against the Wolffians Crusius argues that the desire for perfection is the origin, not of all striving, but of the desires for truth, clarity, good reasoning, the arts, bodily improvement, freedom, friendship, and honor (pp. 135–44). The second basic desire is a wholly disinterested desire for union with what-ever it is in which we find perfection (p. 145). This leads us, among other things, to feel a general moral love, or desire to help others (pp. 148ff.). The third basic desire is "the natural drive to recognize a divine moral law" (p. 157). This drive is evident in our active conscientiousness (*Gewissenstrieb*), a sense of indebtedness that moves us to do our duty and carry out our obligations. There is no common denominator for all these strivings. They move us toward incommensurable ends.

All desires, as forms of will, require representations. Innate desires must therefore carry innate ideas with them. Crusius thus departs from Pufendorf and Locke on a crucial point. But he immediately says that we are not directly conscious of these ideas. It is from their effects in experience that we learn of them. Efficacious regardless of our knowledge of them, they are needed to make intelligible the workings of our consciousness and the relation of the mind to the world (pp. 109–15). The innate ideas essential to active drive of conscience are the ideas involved in God's laws for us. These laws direct us to act in ways that may often conflict with other desires.

If we are to act in opposition to desire from our awareness of God's laws, Crusius thinks, we must be free. He has three arguments to show that we are so.[21] One is that we experience ourselves as originators, capable of acting or changing course or not acting at all (pp. 51–2).[22] Another is that we know that there are divine moral laws and that we are obligated to obey them; but we could not be so obligated, were we not free (pp. 53–4). If these arguments remind us of Clarke, Crusius's central argument is much more unusual.

Without free agents in a world, Crusius says, everything in that world would really be done by God himself. Hence "created beings would obtain through their reality no other relation to God than what they already had in the mere condition of possibility, namely, that their being and essence depended on him." This would mean that God could have no formal purpose in making a possible world real. But God does nothing in vain; hence any real world must contain free agents (p. 53).[23] Because of free will, created beings can come into kinds of relation with God – moral relations – that would otherwise be impossible. Because moral relations are what justifies God in making any possible world

21   Crusius is eclectic in making it his general practice to give several arguments for most if not all of his conclusions. Even in proving God's existence Crusius does not rely on a single argument, and certainly not on an isolated a priori argument. His method is to appeal to empirical data as well as to a priori considerations to show that whatever thesis he is supporting gives us (as we might say) the best explanation. He does not think we obtain apodictic certainty; but this is the best we can do with our limited cognitive powers.

22   Crusius adds that we can choose between indifferents – equally good means to our ends, for instance.

23   The argument is directed against Leibniz, who in *Theodicy*, p. 151, says that God's creative decree "changes nothing in the constitution of things: God leaves them just as they were in the state of mere possibility."

real, morality, rather than the display of God's power or his glory, is the necessary condition of existence (*Sketch,* pp. 505–8, 638, 669–70). Malebranche, as I pointed out in Chapter 11.v, held that only the incarnation warranted God's creation of the world. Crusius thinks God's reason lies rather in the importance of human agency. The intellect is for the sake of the will because of the unique significance of finite free will in the created world (*Sketch,* p. 886).

vi. *Freedom and virtue*

Crusius makes several points about the freedom that enables us to obey God's laws. Freedom is not just the absence of external hindrances to doing what we will. Nor is it acting for what we perceive as the greatest available amount of good or perfection. If there were only Leibnizian freedom, Crusius thinks, "all our virtue would be turned into a mere piece of luck," since it would depend on our having a constitution enabling us to acquire knowledge and on our being situated so as to get it (*Guide,* p. 46).[24] If we are truly free, then even given constant antecedents and circumstances we can determine ourselves to act in any of several ways, or not act at all. "A willing that one could in identical circumstances omit or direct to something else is called a free willing" (*Guide,* p. 23; cf. pp. 44–5; *Sketch,* pp. 140–5), Crusius says, and he explains how such willing operates:

> Whenever we freely will something, we decide to do something for which one or several desires already exist in us. . . . Freedom consists in an inner perfect activity of will, which is capable of connecting its efficacy with one of the currently active drives of the will, or of omitting this connection and remaining inactive, or of connecting it with another drive instead of the first one. (*Guide,* pp. 54–5)

What allows Crusius to make this claim is his distinction between physical causes and motives, which are reasons justifying proposed actions. He argues that the Leibnizian principle of sufficient reason systematically and inexcusably overlooks this distinction, collapsing radically different kinds of reason (*Grund*), the physical and the moral, into one (*Guide,* pp. 204–6).[25] Crusius feels no hesitation in allowing cognitive reasons a role in moving bodies in a material world. Physical

---

24 Crusius thinks Leibniz does not avoid fatalism. If his "hypothetical necessity" is to offer real alternatives of action, then the ends involved must be chosen by genuinely self-determining agents of a kind for which Leibniz leaves no room (*Sketch,* pp. 203–10). He also accuses Leibniz of altering the meaning of "free" to suit his philosophy (p. 752).

25 The matter is discussed at length in *Sketch* I, ch. v; and see *Sketch,* pp. 865–6.

determinism admittedly plays a large part in explaining the behavior of inanimate objects, but total determinism is unacceptable. It allows neither for morality nor for miracles (*Sketch*, pp. 723–5). Mind, however, is spiritual substance, and both God and we must be able to alter the course of events. Indeed, in the end, only God and we possess truly active powers (*Sketch*, pp. 776–7). If determinism cannot account for these things, so much the worse for it.

Among the basic desires, conscientiousness occupies a place of singular importance. It is "the natural drive to recognize a divine moral law," not as merely theoretical knowledge but as involving a drive to obey the law out of a sense of our dependence on the lawgiver. Conscience shows us certain indebtednesses (*Schuldigkeiten*) or obligations (*Verbindlichkeiten*), which involve quite distinctive motivations. To be obligated is not, despite Wolff, simply to be given a motive to act, since we can be motivated to act badly or to do morally indifferent deeds. It is not to be compelled, either inwardly or outwardly, since compulsion excludes obligation. Acting out of fear or hope is not acting from obligation, because from fear or hope we may well do what we have no obligation to do. Finally, acting from obligation is not acting from love. In love we act as we prefer to act; but indebtedness may require us to act contrary to our preferences. The drive of conscience is thus a unique motivation to obey the commands of one's supreme ruler (*Oberherr*) (*Guide*, pp. 157–61).

Because some people disobey conscience, we might think that not everyone has one. Crusius therefore offers several proofs that everyone has a conscience. One argument of particular importance is directed against the Wolffians. God will judge all men by their obedience to his law, but most men cannot reason very well. God must therefore have given men a simpler way to become aware of the law.[26] We find it in the immediate dictates of conscience. They enable people of average understanding to grasp, even "in the hardest and most confused cases, what would be right, what wrong," perhaps without seeing the reasons why (*Guide*, pp. 162–6). Crusius thus thinks of conscience as providing a method of ethics available to everyone alike, even if it does not show the rationale for the guidance it gives.

As I noted earlier, Crusius thinks that the will must contain innate representations of the law that the basic drive of conscience obligates us to obey. Only the most basic law need be innate. From it, we can figure out the details. Now there is a rule from which we can gather most of what conscience shows us are our duties. It must therefore be the innate rule. It tells us to "do what is in accordance with the perfection of God

26 Lord Herbert of Cherbury holds a similar view, backed by similar reasoning; see Chapter 9.iii.

and your relations to him and . . . with the essential perfections of human nature." (Like Wolff, Crusius adds that we are to omit the opposite.) The fundamental drive of conscience is, as he has already told us, the unique motive that leads us to conform to perfections "out of obedience to God's will because of our dependence on him" (*Guide*, pp. 167–8).

Like the will as Leibniz and Wolff explain it, then, the Crusian will contains within itself its own rule for making choices among the alternatives presented to it by desires and drives (*Guide*, p. 54). But like Locke, Crusius thinks, as I have explained, that our drives urge us toward incommensurable goals. Hence, the Crusian will is not only unlike the Leibnizian will in being different in kind from desire; its operation is much more complex. It does not direct us to maximize perfection, or anything else. It tells us to follow a moral code as well as rules of prudence. Crusius gives a new precision to this distinction.

Consider prudence first. Our striving toward our own perfection gives rise to particular desires, as representations of possible objects happen to cause them. Desiring these various represented objects, we desire also to have clearer ideas of what we want; since we cannot get what we want without continuing to live, we desire to preserve ourselves; because we, like God, do not want to act in vain, we want what we desire to be attainable, and we want our striving for it to be efficient (*Guide*, pp. 116–26). All these desires about desires are inherent in the will. They are rules of prudence [*Klugheit*], or "the skill of choosing and applying good means to one's ends" (p. 200).

Virtue [*Tugend*], by contrast, is "the agreement of the moral condition of a mind with the divine laws." Those laws are set for us by God and arise from his ends, not ours. Crusius distinguishes virtue from prudence by explaining two kinds of duty. A duty is an act that it is morally necessary to do – that is, an act that must be done in order to attain certain ends. Wherever we have a duty, we have an obligation. When we do what it is necessary to do to obtain some end of ours, we carry out a duty of prudence, and we fulfill an obligation of prudence. When we do what it is necessary to do to bring about one of God's ends, we perform a duty of virtue. The necessity of acts of this kind lies in a law coming from God's command, and hence "the obligation . . . can be called legal obligation, or the obligations of virtue, or true obligation in a narrower sense" (*Guide*, pp. 199–202). Without the basic drive of conscientiousness, plainly, virtue would be impossible. We would act just to satisfy personal desires, or out of love of others, "which is not yet obedience" (pp. 218–20).[27] But we are virtuous only insofar as we freely

---

27 Crusius argues further that prudential motives need not lead us to comply

will to act from the ever present motive of acknowledging our dependence on God by obeying his laws, disregarding any empirically given ends of our own.[28]

vii. *Morality and God's will*

Actions springing from obedience due to a sense of dependence on God possess what Crusius calls "the *form* of virtue." The *matter* of virtue is action that respects the perfections of things divine and human (*Guide*, pp. 220–2). We can discover the particulars of the matter of virtue by listening to our conscience. This is what most people, including scholars, do. If conscience is not infallible, neither are our five senses, yet we rely on them nonetheless. But we should try to transform conscientious feelings into clearly understood conclusions in order to protect ourselves against partiality arising from self-love or corruption. We can do so by learning about the perfections of things and God's intentions (pp. 222–7, 449–50). Thus philosophy can have a role to play in the moral life.

Crusius discusses duties to God, to neighbor, and to self. Since all duties arise from laws God has commanded us to obey, they all fall under the law of nature taken in a broad sense. Metaphysics shows that God made nothing in vain (*Sketch*, p. 505). Hence both a posteriori and a priori considerations can be used to show us what he intends and commands. We have already seen that the existence of beings with free will gives God the only reason he can have for creating any world. That such beings should exist and flourish is therefore, Crusius thinks, God's aim in creation. But the physical world would have no point unless reasonable free agents could know and enjoy it. If it is made for the service of man, God's aim, and man's as well, must be first of all to see virtue develop. We are to use the world and enjoy its pleasures only insofar as virtue allows (*Guide*, pp. 251–6; *Sketch,* pp. 506–9, 669–70). Crusius thus comes in his own way to a conclusion that Malebranche explained in somewhat different terms (Chapter 11.v).

The duality and order in the human end is matched by, and is indeed due to, a similar duality in God. God has an absolutely free will,

---

with God's laws. If virtue is treated as just one end among others, one might choose to disregard it from time to time, as one does with other desires. No doubt virtue is the best means to happiness if everyone is virtuous; but as that is not the way people are, the merely prudential obligation to virtue fails. Thanks to the drive of conscience, however, each of us, even in a corrupt society, has adequate motivation to act virtuously.

28   Crusius thinks there are two kinds of praise and condemnation, one given to things without freedom, and one – moral praise and blame – reserved exclusively for free agents (*Guide*, pp. 46–8).

through which he always wills to sustain his own perfections and sometimes wills to act beyond himself. When he creates, he takes delight in his creations, and thus loves them. We may therefore infer that there are two basic drives in God's will: that toward perfection, which leads him to create; and that to love and be good to whatever he creates (*Sketch,* pp. 498–501). These two aims, Crusius says, "fit together only if God first puts reasonable minds into the world in conditions in which they can exercise free virtue, and afterwards distributes happiness in proportion to virtue" (*Guide,* pp. 257–8).

God's end for us cannot be knowledge, since intellect is for the sake of will. Nor can our happiness alone be his end. Crusius is too aware of natural evils to share Wolff's cheerful outlook, or Cumberland's. Although all physical things are meant for our service, God gives them to us raw and unfinished, and does not even endow us with skills and knowledge. We must develop our mere potentials for the latter, and transform the former with "sour toil and work." These facts make it clear that God intends us to have only such happiness as we can earn for ourselves. If we are God's "objective end" in creation, what that means for us is that "virtue is the goal of life." It is a goal we are all equally able to pursue (*Guide,* pp. 260–2).

Our duties to God consist essentially in honoring God, since we can do nothing else for him. Obedience is of course the main point. We are also to increase our knowledge of God, keep it vivid, and, since it shows us his perfections, let it lead us to love him ever more. Eventually all our duties should be done out of love. We can even think of our chief duty as being that of coming to love God above all else. When we do, our obedience will be fully voluntary (*Guide,* pp. 388–96; cf. pp. 294–5).

Our duties to others require us to act in accordance with their perfections, but action alone is not enough. The love we owe God obligates us also to love all men, as objects of his love. The facts of human nature show us what such love entails. God has made us sociable, by making us need one another's assistance; he has given us immediate feelings of love toward one another, making life outside society intolerable; and he has shown us how tied we are to one another by making our very lives begin in other human beings. It follows that we should not view the welfare of other people simply as a means to our own, but should "will it as a final end." Moreover, seeing all men as the "absolute ends of God," we should accord equal rights to all, treating them always and only as we think we could with right demand to be treated were we in their place. If we do all this we will love others as ourselves (*Guide,* pp. 442–9).

Supposing, then, that a system of duties can be derived from Crusius's basic law (and he himself develops one in some detail), the question remains of the exact relation between God's will and that law.

Crusius makes some remarks indicative of a wish to remove certain standard grievances against voluntarism. Thus he goes out of his way to say that the sanctions of punishment and reward are not essential to moral obligation. Fear and hope are not moral motives, and God's laws are binding independently of them, even though God must punish transgressors and reward the obedient to ensure that his lawgiving is not in vain (*Guide*, pp. 237–8). A highwayman can compel us to hand over our money, but his will creates no obligation to do so. God creates obligations because he provides goods for us. We have to thank him for these, not just out of prudence but "because of the drive of conscience" (pp. 208–9).

That we owe God obedience out of gratitude is of course the view suggested by Pufendorf, and Crusius is open to the same question: whence the conscientious obligation to show gratitude? If the answer is simply that God commands it, we have no answer to our basic question; and if it is an obligation independent of God's will, the door is open to the possibility that all obligations might be thus independent. Crusius considers and rejects that possibility. It might be advantageous were it true that morality could rest solely on our social nature, and on perfection or happiness. Atheists, in that case, would be as obligated to virtue as the rest of us. But the obligation of prudence, which alone would be left, is not enough to "block all the loopholes in particular cases." General happiness might be attained even if some did not contribute to it. To guarantee that all are obligated to do so, which is surely what morality requires, we need "true laws," and that means commands from a superior backed by sanctions (*Guide*, pp. 454–8; *Sketch*, pp. 515–16).

What accords with God's will is morally good, simply by according with that will. Crusius attempts to deflect criticism by saying that "the morally good is not at all arbitrary, because the will of God . . . is not a free but a necessary will" (*Guide*, pp. 216–17). This is a puzzling remark, and we must see in what sense Crusius thinks it is true. He cannot mean that God himself has a morally good will, in the sense of a will in conformity with the command of a superior.[29] But there is a way in which we can see that it is necessary that God should give commands to his free created beings. We must start from the assumption that God does nothing in vain. If so, then he cannot will that his creations should fail to attain the end for which he created them. He must therefore will that physical nature serve free beings, and that free beings develop their

29   The "moral designs" of God are those that he wills to have carried out by free and reasonable created agents, so that in this sense too God cannot have a will that is morally good. Or if, as Crusius also says, "the morally good is what agrees with [God's] laws," then it is not informative to say that God has a morally good will, as earlier critics of voluntarism had frequently pointed out (*Guide*, pp. 30–1).

virtue. What allows God to create, and not merely to consider, the world is, after all, only the fact that obedience freely chosen out of a sense of dependence creates relations to God that otherwise could not exist; hence bare freedom is not enough but, as with all our potentials, it must be developed.

Crusius is here taking the line that Barbeyrac attributed, with some justification, to Pufendorf. God is free to create or not to create. Nothing in his nature requires either. But once he wills to create free beings, he must give them laws that are suited to their possible perfections. And he must make a world that helps them, either positively or at least by not acting against them (*Sketch*, pp. 505–10). It seems thus plausible to claim, as Crusius does, that God's basic law must be that we are to do what is in accordance with the perfections of God and our fellows. God's will can avoid arbitrariness even though it is not determined by the good, but by its own act determines what shall count as good (pp. 518–19).

For Crusius it is important to make clear that God's will is not determined by God's pursuit of perfection, as the Wolffians thought. Leibniz held that there is a single most perfect world. Crusius denies this. It is not possible to include all perfections in one world, and not possible to prove that there is only one that includes more than any other. If such a world were possible, Crusius adds, God would have to choose the one best. In that case he would not be free: what kind of choice is it when there is only one option? And then, lacking the power of freedom himself, he could not create us with freedom. God is free, not (as the Wolffians hold) because he knows and wills the best, but because in any constant set of circumstances he can act one way or another, or not at all. All we can say of the world is what the Bible says (Genesis 1.31) – that it must be very good (*Sketch*, pp. 742–53).[30]

Our assurance that the world is very good must rest largely on a priori grounds. Physical suffering and moral evil are all too evident; these, and the eventual condemnation of large numbers of free agents to eternal punishment, are all foreseen by God, even if he did not desire them as part of his creation (*Sketch*, pp. 488–96, 504). How can we be sure that the whole of which they are part is "very good?" Our virtuous willing must accord with the perfections of created things as well as with God's; God's willing determines what exists, and thus is controlled, as voluntarists have always held, by nothing external to itself. It is however necessary to God's willing that he do nothing in vain. Can

---

30   The similarities here and elsewhere between Crusius's positions and some of Clarke's are striking, but I have found no reason to think Crusius knew of Clarke's work.

that internal necessity assure us that God's willings are more than the expression of arbitrary power?

Crusius does not say what it means for God not to act in vain, but we can see what the idea is. Self-contradictory thoughts are not thoughts of something, and so cannot be in God's mind at all (*Sketch*, p. 483). Being infinitely powerful, God cannot fail to achieve any goal he freely sets himself. Since God cannot set himself thinkable but unattainable goals, acting in vain must, for God, be acting in a way that frustrates his own aims. God cannot, in a word, will in any self-defeating way. We might ourselves raise questions about how far such a principle of willing could go in determining plans of action, but for Crusius the question must be somewhat different. Given what he holds about the limits of human knowledge and the ultimately inscrutable nature of God, he should really wonder whether we can properly draw any comfort from God's necessary inability to act in vain.

21

Religion, morality, and reform

Expressing one's opinions during the eighteenth century involved considerably more risk in France than in Germany or Britain. In Prussia a king could exile a professor; in England the orthodox could block a promising ecclesiastical career; in France the government could jail, torture, and execute those it disliked. Censors kept a watchful eye on French publications. The standards for licensing were intended to serve the needs of the royal government and the hierarchy of France's Roman Catholic Church. The licensing laws failed, however, to stop the flow of criticism. Attacks on all aspects of the established regime were published anonymously, or outside the country, or inside it with falsifications about the printer. They were addressed to the public at large, not only to the learned. We do not know how many readers they reached.[1] But it seems clear that the more oppressive the political and religious authorities were, the more numerous and vehement became the books denouncing them. Writers went to prison or left the country, but they did not stop criticizing the powers whose threats could literally endanger their lives.

The chief concern of those who wrote about morality in prerevolutionary France was not with theory but with the hope, or threat, of change. In England, Scotland, and some of the German states, clergymen and professors produced original and important moral philosophy. In France the clergy and the professoriate were staunch defenders of existing institutions; original thought came from others.[2] If French moral philosophy in the eighteenth century seems for the most part less sophisticated and systematic than that produced by the British, it is

---

1 See Darnton 1995 for an attempt to get at the numbers and the impact of subversive books.

2 For the conservative nature of instruction in moral philosophy in French universities during the seventeenth and eighteenth centuries, see Brockliss 1987, pp. 216ff., 292ff., 300–1.

partly because the French had a much more pressing practical need to examine their existing religious and political institutions.

Although some of the critics of the old regime were avowed atheists, many were not. Believers and unbelievers alike could be as strongly opposed to untrammeled clerical domination as to royal despotism. But the critics did not think in terms of violent revolution. If they shared any belief it was that what most needed to be done to change things was to dispel ignorance and superstition by educating the public. Like social critics in many other parts of Europe they saw themselves as driving out the darkness of the past with the new light shed by Newtonian physics, history, critical study of Scripture, and advances in the understanding of physiology, medicine, and psychology. The aim of an encyclopedia, Diderot laid down in the one he was editing, is to gather and systematically explain all the knowledge mankind has acquired, transmitting it to future generations so that our successors, "becoming better instructed, would become at the same time more virtuous and happier."[3] In this chapter I discuss only a few of the many writers who hoped that enlightenment by itself would bring about fundamental change.[4] It is not hard to see how their ideas could be taken up by people who held that enlightenment without political action is futile.

i. Voltaire and voluntarism

François Marie Arouet, who renamed himself Voltaire (1694–1778), was probably the most effective anti-Christian campaigner of the eighteenth century, and an outstanding defender of those who suffered injustice because of alleged transgressions against the symbols and the dogmas of the established faith. If he used the ideas of others rather than originating his own, no one used them more effectively. Because he professed belief in God and in the importance of religion while relentlessly attacking all revelation, his own personal convictions have been a matter of debate almost since he started writing.[5] His understanding of morality is also hard to sort out. He wrote a great deal, he changed his mind on many matters, and he did not have a philosopher's concern for system, coherence, and precision. I doubt that he had a completely consistent moral theory. What he did have was a coherent attitude toward morality and its involvement with religion. Morality, for him, is

3   "Encyclopédie," in *Oeuvres*, ed. Versini, p. 363.

4   For a comprehensive survey, discussing also the views of some of the defenders of the old order, see Domenech 1989.

5   See the summary of two centuries of views on Voltaire's religion in Pomeau 1965, pp. 7–15.

a human device needed to make social life possible; yet God is indispensable to it. The problem, of course, is how to link these two convictions.

The last two chapters of Voltaire's early *Treatise on Metaphysics* show us his first efforts to solve the problem.[6] He suggests a naturalistic account of morality. Sexual needs draw people as well as animals together, but we do not form well-organized societies by instinct as the bees do. Not all our desires, moreover, are self-interested; along with selfish impulses we feel a natural benevolence, which leads us to come to the aid of others – if helping does not cost us too much. Driven by numerous desires, not least the desire for precedence and power, we threaten one another's well-being, but we also produce all the goods and services that make human society so complex and enjoyable. It is quite probable, Voltaire says, "that God gave us these needs, these passions, so that our industry would turn them to our advantage." It is up to us to control those who misuse his gifts (*Traité* VIII, in *Mélanges*, pp. 193–5).

Laws are what enable us to do so. They vary enormously from country to country, but everywhere virtue and vice, moral good and evil, are "what is useful or harmful to society." Virtue, then, is simply the habit of doing what pleases men. Despite the differences in the laws enforced in different societies, there are natural laws which all men are obliged to admit. If God did not dictate them literally, he gave man "certain sentiments that he cannot get rid of," and it is these that are the "eternal ties and the first laws" of human society. Because the good of society is the "only measure" of moral good and evil, the variability of moral judgment reflects changed circumstances: incest, normally forbidden, would be good were it the only way to preserve the species. And anyone who decides to act only from self-love, ignoring morality, will need a small army to protect himself. Pride makes us unable to bear the sort of contempt that criminals display. We find out about crimes and punish them. Mutual fear of humanly inflicted punishment is thus what God has given us to link us together. A sound education will perpetuate these feelings in everyone. Consequently no one should need the aid of religion in order to be a decent human being (IX, pp. 196–202).

Utility, benevolence, pleasing others, innate sentiments, laws, fear of punishment, feelings instilled by education – however morality is explained, it is explained by natural facts; and they are facts about our responses to the world. Without our way of responding there would no more be virtue or moral good in the world than there would be heat or

---

6 Written in 1734, frequently revised but not published until after Voltaire's death. I cite from *Mélanges*, ed. van den Heuvel, giving chapter and page numbers.

any other secondary property. The one source of morality that Voltaire explicitly excludes is direct instruction by God. If some law had "fallen from heaven" clearly teaching us God's will, that would indeed be the moral law. "But as God has not deigned, to the best of my knowledge, to get so involved in our conduct, it is best to stick firmly to the gifts he has given us" – our natural endowments, mixed as they are (IX, pp. 198–9).

Voltaire frames his views about morality in a strong claim about the incomprehensibility of God. That there is a God is the most probable view we can take, that there is none "the most absurd" (II, p. 171). Relying on Samuel Clarke, Voltaire thinks that if God exists, then his freedom is demonstrable. But Voltaire goes on to say that God's freedom, omniscience, infinity, and creative activity are alike incomprehensible to us (VIII, p. 192). Departing even more seriously from Clarke, moreover, he holds that we do not have any moral comprehension of God. We have, he says, "no other ideas of justice than those we have made ourselves of actions useful to society, and conformed to the laws we have established for the common good." But that idea concerns only relations among humans and can have no "analogy" with God. "It is as absurd to say of God," he concludes, "that God is just or unjust as to say that God is blue or square" (II, pp. 169–70).

The portrait of morality here, however blurred some of its lines, is familiar enough. It is that of the natural law voluntarists. Voltaire shares their empiricism. He studied Locke and adopted most of his epistemology. He did not care to notice that however useful Clarke might be in supporting free will, Clarke's theory of eternal moral fitnesses is wholly at odds with his own empiricist view of moral law. He shares the voluntarist sense of the infinite distance between God and man, denying the continuity of the great chain of being.[7] And he comes back many times to the kind of account of how our passions and salient features point to God's moral laws that we have seen in the *Traité de metaphysique*. Perhaps the most compact statement is in the article on "Laws" in the *Philosophical Dictionary*:

> When Nature created our species, and gave us instincts – self-regard for our own preservation, benevolence for the preservation of others, love which is common to all species, and the inexplicable gift of being able to combine more ideas than all the other animals put together – after giving us our portion, she said to us: "Now do the best you can." (*Dictionary*, p. 364)[8]

7 See Voltaire's note to his "Poem on the Disaster at Lisbon," in *Mélanges*, pp. 1389–90.

8 See the comment by Pufendorf cited at the end of Chapter 7.vii.

When Voltaire's moral thought is seen in this light, it is clear that *Candide* is (among other things) a voluntarist tract.[9] As the case of Crusius makes clear, voluntarists have no moral need to hold that this is the best possible world. They take Leibniz to deny God's freedom by denying him any real choice, a point Voltaire suggests in the opening stanza of the "Poem on the Disaster at Lisbon." In the preface to the poem he dismisses those who condemn Leibniz's "best world" thesis for its religious implication that man is not fallen or corrupt and therefore not in need of a redeemer. He chooses instead to stress the ancient truth, that there is evil on the earth. To take literally the maxim that all is good, Voltaire asserts, is to deny any hope that life in another world will be happier, and in that sense the maxim is "only an insult to the miseries of our life." Our minds, he adds, are so weak that "no philosopher has ever been able to explain the origin of moral and of physical evil" (*Mélanges*, pp. 302–4). Voltaire makes no exception for himself.

What he does insist on is our ability to tell whether what seems evil to us really is so. Candide, Voltaire pointedly remarks, "had been brought up never to judge anything for himself."[10] The thesis of the best possible world requires us to take the word of a metaphysician that what seems ill to us is really good on the whole; and *Candide*, like many of Voltaire's other writings, exposes the thesis to the ridicule that is perhaps the only way of bringing a dazzled reader back to confidence in the soundness of normal human judgment.[11]

It is all the more important for Voltaire to make this point because he needs to distance his version of the incomprehensibility of God from Pascal's. Voltaire makes quite clear his utter revulsion at Pascal's treatment of man as a mysterious duality, half angel and half brute, made restless and bored by his degrading worldly activities yet still capable of receiving divine grace. We are indeed mysterious, Voltaire allows, but no more so than matter or the rest of the universe; and God has not wholly withdrawn from us.[12] The "Poem on the Natural Law" makes

9 For discussion of interest in Leibniz in France and the way in which Pope's popular *Essay on Man* helped reawaken it, see Barber 1955. Barber also gives a useful review of Voltaire's relations to Leibnizianism and Wolffianism, but he does not discuss the implications of optimism or of its rejection for moral philosophy.

10 *Candide*, p. 85.

11 In the *Philosophical Dictionary* under "Tout est bien" Voltaire turns the tables on rationalist complaints about the tyranny of the God presented by the voluntarists. "The system of *All is good* merely represents the author of nature as a powerful and malicious king, who does not care if it should cost the lives of four or five hundred thousand men . . . provided he accomplishes his work" (p. 122).

12 *Lettres philosophiques* 25, in *Mélanges*, pp. 106–11.

the latter point clear. "What!" Voltaire exclaims, "the world is visible and God is hidden? What! the greatest need that I have in my wretchedness is the only one I cannot satisfy?" No, I cannot fail to know at least one thing: I know what God has ordained for me. God "has given me his law, because he gave me existence" (*Mélanges*, p. 276). Reason enables me to find out what the law is; the remorse I feel at transgressing his law makes me obedient. Reason and remorse come from God, not from education. Call them what you will, Voltaire declares, reason and remorse exist "and they are the foundations of the natural law" (p. 272).[13]

Voltaire's campaign for religious toleration draws on his voluntarist insistence on God's incomprehensibility and is supported by his view of morality as God's law binding on all. He says little about how God remains indispensable to morality. Of course God is its creator, as he is ours. But Voltaire offers no account of obligation along voluntarist lines, nor does he discuss Pufendorf or moral entities. Although he says that it is our reaction that introduces morality into a world of fact, his expressions of this position are too variable to make for great precision. He thinks that belief in God as sanctioning morality in another life is necessary to frighten the masses into reliable conformity; he suggests at the end of the "Poem on the Natural Law" that he does not himself believe in the eternity of punishment for the wicked; but exactly what more he thinks about the need for justice in another life is unclear. A strong-minded atheist might find the Voltairean idea of a naturalized morality acceptable while holding that the religion is excess baggage.

ii. *La Mettrie: Atheism let loose*

That, of course, was the position of Helvetius and d'Holbach. But they were not the first atheistic moralists in France. In their own century they were preceded by Julien Offray de la Mettrie (1709–51). If Voltaire thought a minimalist religion offered the best hope for toleration, La Mettrie went a step further. Only a universe without religious belief can be happy, he suggested in 1747, because only there will all religions be cut off at the roots. In such a world there would be no more theological wars, and no more "soldiers of religion." The "sacred poison" would work its way out of our systems and all would be well (*Oeuvres* I.97).

Or at least all would be somewhat better. La Mettrie had hopes for social improvement, but no program, and no way of providing a basis for one. A physician and an empiricist, he had a bad reputation for loose living and for flattery of Frederick the Great, the enlightened despot on

13 For similar assertions about morality and human ignorance of God, see *Le Philosophe Ignorant*, chs. XVII–XIX, XXI–XXIII, XXVI, XXXI–XXXVIII, in *Mélanges*.

whom in his last years he depended. He was an embarrassment for the enlightened thinkers who came after him. His naturalistic morality pointed to problems they themselves had to face. His failure, or refusal, to be concerned with these issues only increased the discomfort of those who, like Diderot, drew on his work while condemning his philosophy.

La Mettrie finds no empirical evidence for the existence of a human soul or for a deity. Descartes, he notes, had seen that animals are machines; but in hope of deceiving the church, he had pretended not to realize that matter can sense and therefore think, and that man is as much a machine as animals are. If nature, itself unable to see, can produce eyes that see, why should not unthinking causes produce a world in which intelligence exists? After all, many clever people have stupid parents. La Mettrie makes shrewd conjectures about the evolution of human animals from simpler forms, through generations of varieties that failed to cope with their surroundings. His atheistic materialism is sometimes masked with remarks to the effect that faith alone reveals God to us. But he is no fideist. His ethics is an attempt to see what sort of morality is possible given the facts about the wholly natural animal, man. God does not enter the picture.[14]

"In a century as enlightened as ours," La Mettrie says, "it is finally demonstrated . . . that there is only one life and only one happiness," happiness on earth (*Oeuvres* II.249).[15] But no two organisms are exactly alike, and no two people find happiness in exactly the same kind of life. External causes of happiness matter far less than internal causes, and the latter are "unique and individual" (II.241). It is natural for all of us to have pleasant and unpleasant sensations and to seek the most enduring of the pleasant ones.[16] But it is no more natural for us to be virtuous than it is to be richly clothed. The ignorant and the wicked can be as happy as the learned or virtuous.

La Mettrie's naturalism thus leads him to disconnect morality from happiness as sharply as Malebranche did. He sees virtue not as an "absolute," but simply as the disposition to serve the well-being of the

14   La Mettrie's best-known work is the brief and trenchant *Man a Machine*. Similar views are vehemently expressed in the *Traité de l'âme*, in his *Oeuvres philosophiques* I.

15   I draw heavily on La Mettrie's *Discours sur le bonheur*, which is usefully discussed in the edition by Falvey.

16   La Mettrie accepts Maupertuis's views about the commensurability of pleasures and pains (Chapter 19, note 7), taking them to differ only in duration and vivacity. Typically, he explains that "vivacity" matters because no part of the sovereign good is as important as the pleasures of love (*Oeuvres* II.239). The technicalities are unimportant for La Mettrie, but he was trying to keep in favor with Maupertuis, who had close ties to Frederick the Great.

community. If we all lived alone, there would be no need for it. Our sexual and other desires, however, bring us together, and our emotions lead us to give moral names to the merely political devices needed for a common life. We therefore think they are somehow more than means to sociability. It is true that virtue brings happiness to some; but although those who lack the taste for it will lack this source of happiness, they will have others, and can find happiness in living simply for themselves (II.251–3). La Mettrie points out that "one who takes great satisfaction in doing ill will be happier than whoever takes less satisfaction in doing good." Since pleasure is the content of happiness, each individual's constitution determines whether happiness comes from virtue or from vice. There are many happy criminals because virtue is "foreign to the nature of our being," an ornament of happiness but not its foundation (II.263, 284). What, then, can lead us to it? Vanity, says La Mettrie, which is the source of most of our actions. Virtue may come from a beautiful soul, but it will be exercised only if it is recognized and flattered. Vanity does more for man than even the best-regulated self-love (II.253).

Education can help make people take pleasure in serving others, but it cannot do everything. As things stand, moreover, education tends to destroy happiness. It instills in us feelings of remorse for antisocial action; and remorse is worse than useless. It comes after actions which its anticipation is powerless to prevent. We cannot change our natures. Our wills are determined by what we think will yield us pleasure and pain, and consequently some people cannot avoid acting in antisocial ways. They suffer already since they cannot enjoy the pleasures of virtue. If anything can keep them from crime, it is the threat of the gallows. Remorse makes the virtuous miserable without preventing the vicious from doing ill. Once we admit that it is not a natural feeling, but a social artifice, we may cease instilling it and thus increase the overall amount of pleasure.

La Mettrie is quite willing to say that pleasure is the sovereign good and to allow that all of us seek it. Nonetheless he does not think that we agree in any substantive way about the good. And if we all also seek at least enough society to gratify our desires for sex and praise, those goals would hardly enable us, as La Mettrie sees us, to agree about what laws should govern us when we live together. Voltaire held that we can discover laws of nature, to which political institutions should conform, by discovering God's ends for us. We can learn about these final causes, he held, where there is uniformity throughout the relevant domain of facts. Thus eyes were made for seeing, but noses were not made for holding eyeglasses.[17] La Mettrie, denying that there is any pertinent

---

17 *Philosophical Dictionary,* under "Final Causes," pp. 71–2.

uniformity in human nature, sees no place for natural teleology or natural law. There is at most a feeling that "teaches us what we ought not to do from what we do not want others to do to us." It is a sort of natural dread or terror which is beneficial to the species (I.93). Animals have it too, just as they feel remorse (I.87–90).

We should not think that La Mettrie means to restore the old Roman idea of the law of nature as applying to "all creatures of the sky, earth, and sea."[18] He is simply bowing ironically toward a commonplace moral term. Although he expressed deep anger at attempts to repress and control natural individuality, he nowhere suggests any constraints on the laws rulers use to try to control those with criminal physiologies. The character of a despotic ruler, on his view, is as much a natural fact as the character of an ordinary criminal, and as little to be altered. He is not, he tells us, prescribing anything: he is merely explaining. Where earlier writings on happiness such as Fontanelle's popular essay *Du Bonheur* (1724) were meant to guide the reader, La Mettrie's essay on the same subject is mainly meant to give an account of the way in which the drive for happiness functions in individuals and society.

The facts, however, are pertinent to social change. La Mettrie alternates between writing as a physician and experimentalist and writing as a critic. He is ambivalent (if we take all his comments at face value) about the usefulness of philosophy. On the one hand, he argues that philosophers should be allowed freedom of thought. They are not dangerous. Their work is impotent to change public opinion or behavior, because the masses are too stupid and too strongly indoctrinated to respond to criticisms like his about remorse. On the other hand he thinks quite highly of his own work and its potential to reform at least a thoughtful ruler. But he does not make it at all evident what grounds he can adduce for taking his objections to current practices as expressing anything more than his own personal tastes.[19] La Mettrie thus poses for the enlightened reforming writers who followed him something like the problem that Montaigne posed for Grotius. Like Montaigne's skepticism, La Mettrie's atheistic naturalism seems to leave no place for impersonal standards that might settle the profound disputes racking the times for which he wrote. Even some fellow atheists were left unsatisfied by the line of thought that Helvetius and d'Holbach offered in reply.

18 Justinian, *Institutes*, I.1.1.
19 La Mettrie's fullest discussion of the role of philosophy is in the *Discours Préliminaire*, in *Oeuvres* I.9–49, which is carefully analyzed in Thomson 1981, part II.

iii. *Diderot: Morality without theory*

Voltaire wrote his poem on the natural law as a reply to La Mettrie's dismissal of it and of remorse; nearly three decades later Diderot still thought he had to denounce La Mettrie, in a passage of astonishing virulence. "The apologist of vice and the detractor of virtue," as Diderot called him, held man to be perverse by nature and then "made his nature the rule of his duties and the source of his happiness."[20] Diderot learned much from La Mettrie's medical materialism and his insistence on the biological determinants of action and feeling. But he had to distance himself from a writer who had come to be seen as a toadying drunken atheist – and also as the archetype of the philosophical reformer.

In matters of theory it was not easy for Diderot to create the distance because he came to share La Mettrie's atheism and his deterministic materialism. He also developed a deep appreciation of the ways in which variations in individual temperament lead people to have highly idiosyncratic views of happiness. He drew on these positions in criticizing Helvetius's thesis that education alone is responsible for individual differences and that good education could therefore turn everyone into a good citizen.[21] But since he shared many political aims with Helvetius and d'Holbach, he understood the need for a generally acceptable principle that might guide the changes he hoped to help bring about in France and elsewhere.[22]

Morality was one of Diderot's most enduring concerns, engaging him from his copiously annotated early translation of Shaftesbury's *Inquiry concerning Virtue* (1745) to his late extended commentary on Seneca (1778–82). But he wrote no formal treatise on the subject. He presented his views in dialogues and commentaries and arguments with imagined opponents. If these discussions always contain shrewd and insightful points about central issues arising for a secular morality,

20   *Essai sur les règnes de Claude et de Néron*, bk. II.6, in *Oeuvres*, ed. Versini, pp. 1118–19. On the critical response to La Mettrie's *L'homme machine* in France, see Vartanian 1960, chs. V and VI; he mentions, without going into detail, that there was an enormous outcry against the book in German-speaking countries.

21   Helvetius expounded this view in his posthumously published *De l'homme*, 1772. See Diderot's detailed attack on this book in his *Refutation suivie de . . . Helvetius*, in *Oeuvres*, ed. Versini, pp. 777–923.

22   Diderot criticized La Mettrie for being, among other things, a hanger-on of a despot; yet he himself served, to his considerable financial benefit, as philosopher in waiting to Catherine the Great of Russia, and urged reforms upon her without success. The issue was a very touchy one for him personally, as is made evident by the pages of self-defense toward the conclusion of his commentary on Seneca in the *Reigns of Claudius and Nero*, written at the end of his life.

they quite intentionally do not add up to a theory. Diderot did not aim at elaborating one. It is plain, nonetheless, that he had a coherent outlook on morality that set him apart from his fellow atheists.[23]

Diderot's nearest approach to a philosophical statement of a basic principle of morals and politics comes in one of his earliest published writings on the subject, his *Encyclopedia* article "Natural Right."[24] Justice, Diderot says, is the obligation to give to each what is due to him; but how does the idea of obligation arise? Suppose that we are free agents, driven to contend with one another by our restless passions, yet aware that we are tempted to treat others as we ourselves would wish not to be treated. What might we say to one whose passions are so powerful that if he is to find his life worth living he must gratify them at our expense? Diderot assumes that this being – he is thinking of Hobbes's man in a state of nature – will see that if he allows himself to treat others as he pleases, others may treat him as they please. He is willing to reason; even evil men admit that to refuse to reason is to forfeit one's status as human. How, then, are we to talk to this "violent reasoner?"

Diderot thinks the violent reasoner wishes to be just as well as happy; if not, we would simply have to smother him. And if he wants to be just, he will admit that there must be an impartial tribunal to allocate goods between himself and others. Where are we to find it? Not in anything coming from God: we must, says Diderot, appeal to mankind. Mankind "has no craving other than the good of all. Private wills are suspect; they may be either good or bad. But the general will is always good." The general will is thus to determine what we may do in all the walks of life. It directs us to make all our actions to cohere with "the general and common interest" (*Writings*, pp. 19–20).[25] And how do we find out what the general will requires? Diderot's answer is not very helpful. We see its direction in the laws of civilized nations, the social practices of savages, the agreements that hold among thieves, and the emotions of indignation and resentment felt even by animals. More specifically, the general will is "a pure expression of the understanding," telling us, when the passions are silent, what each of us may ask of

---

23 Much of Diderot's writing remained unpublished during his lifetime; some of his work circulated only in a manuscript newsletter that went to a small circle of select readers; and many of his printed works were published anonymously. It would have been difficult for an eighteenth-century reader to obtain an overview of Diderot's thought on the issues of moral philosophy.

24 The article was published, marked as Diderot's, in vol. V, 1755. Diderot's earlier philosophical writings center on problems of religion and metaphysics.

25 Diderot thus uses a Malebranchean phrase to attribute to humans a kind of willing that Malebranche held to be appropriate only for the divine will.

each and every other human. From this "regard for the general will of the species," we can see what laws ought to be made. The matter is obvious to those who think about it; and anyone who refuses to reason should be treated as an unnatural being (*Writings*, pp. 20–1).

Seek happiness with justice in this life: if this is a moral principle, it is the one Diderot would support. His discussions and his fictions show, however, that he does not think that it or any other statement of a rule gives us determinate and complete instructions about how to act. For one thing, he thinks it is not even obvious what constitutes happiness. Nowhere does Diderot bring out this point as thoroughly as in the dialogue *Rameau's Nephew*. The nephew might have been created to illustrate La Mettrie's thesis of diversity. Diderot (as the other speaker) may find happiness in acting to help others, but the nephew does not. That kind of happiness, he says, "would only make me die of hunger, of boredom, and perhaps of remorse" (*Oeuvres*, ed. Billy, p. 457). Decent people like Diderot act and judge one way, eccentrics and scoundrels another. If virtue requires a special sense, the nephew thinks he must be missing it. Perhaps it has been spoiled by his living mostly "with good musicians and bad people" (p. 489).[26] Lacking the order imposed by virtue he is still as content with his life as Diderot with his. After all, no life is without its drawbacks. The existence of people like the nephew shows that one person's happiness may require the misery of others. Are we to take account of all kinds of happiness equally and, if not, how are we to decide what goes into public well-being?

The younger Rameau forces Diderot to consider the issue of the motivation for behaving morally. This topic is central to one of his most engaging discussions, the "Conversation of a Philosopher with the Maréchale de ***," written in 1774. You are an atheist, says the Maréchale to Diderot, why are you not also a thief and murderer? Are you not inconsistent in being honest? No, Diderot replies, I am luckily so made that I take pleasure in doing good; and besides, experience shows that virtue is the best path to a happy life.[27] As for a life after this, Diderot does not believe in it, nor would he welcome it. The terms of entry to it are too risky for anyone to accept – contra Pascal, who is not mentioned – and it is surely not reasonable to ask us to worship a deity who would condemn to endless punishment someone whom he had

26   One of Diderot's earliest important publications was his annotated translation of Shaftesbury's *Inquiry concerning Virtue or Merit* (1745). He had not at that time broken wholly with religion, and he was strongly sympathetic to Shaftesbury's view.

27   In the *Refutation of Helvetius*, Diderot offers a number of objections to simplistic egoistic psychological theories. People take pleasure in such a wide variety of things, he says, that to say that we always pursue our own interest is either blatantly false or else uninformative. Versini, pp. 799–801, 804–8.

created too foolish to recognize his existence.[28] Religion offers no assistance with social problems either: hell is too far off, temptation too close, for fears of the one to outweigh the promises of the other. Besides, people rarely act on their beliefs. Diderot says he has never seen a truly consistent Christian (*Oeuvres*, ed. Versini, pp. 929–43). What is needed, he suggests, is to arrange affairs to ensure that "the good of the individual is so closely linked with the general good that a citizen can scarcely harm society without harming himself" (Versini, p. 936). There will still be those whose temperament makes them evil, but society will get along adequately. Religion only makes things worse: it introduces hatred, strife, and all the horrors of persecution and religious war. If a misanthrope wanted to make everyone miserable, Diderot asks, what better could he do than invent the idea of "an incomprehensible being, whom human beings could never understand, and to which they would attach more importance than to their lives?" (Versini, p. 933).[29]

That morality neither should nor in fact does depend on religion is a theme to which Diderot frequently recurs. Religion for him seems always to center on the deity of the voluntarists, who is a tyrant and who provides a model for earthly despotism.[30] When Socrates proclaimed that our actions are not good because they please the gods, but that they please the gods because they are good, he enunciated "a principle which detaches morality from religion" (*Writings*, p. 211). The Tahitian sage who expresses secular wisdom in the *Supplement to Bougainville's Voyage* points out the difficulties of attributing good and evil to the will of the "great craftsman" who, according to the European priest, made the world. Can he and his priests, or your magistrates, the Tahitian asks, "make harmful actions good, and innocent and useful ones evil?" If so, you depend on their whims, which might change or even disagree; and then, unable to satisfy all of them, you could not be at once a good man, a good citizen, and a good believer (*Writings*, p. 51).

The Tahitian sage recommends simply following nature, attending especially to the effects of action on the general welfare and the agent's own happiness. The Frenchmen in this dialogue are particularly struck by the Tahitian emphasis on the importance of sexual satisfaction; and one of them comments that civilization introduces an artificial man alongside the natural man, causing an internal warfare that makes happiness quite impossible (*Writings*, pp. 52, 71). Diderot is not, however,

28   A similar point is made in the *Pensées philosophique* XXIX, in *Oeuvres*, ed. Versini, p. 28.

29   Diderot had expressed the same view of the harmfulness of the invention of religious belief in the astonishingly Nietzschean final paragraph of the *Addition aux pensées philosophiques* of 1762, in *Oeuvres*, ed. Versini, p. 48.

30   See the *Encyclopedia* article "Hobbisme," in *Oeuvres*, ed. Versini, p. 445.

advocating sensualism. Although he rejects Seneca's austere Stoic interpretation of living according to nature, (Versini, pp. 1199, 1209–10), he insists that we are reasonable as well as passional, and that we need the laws reason can show us. "There is but one duty," Diderot says, "it is to be happy; there is but one virtue: it is justice" (Versini, p. 1189; *Writings*, p. 211). Diderot is acutely aware of some of the problems that would arise from taking the sole moral principle to be that one should increase happiness as much as one can. He tells the story of a conscientious executor of an estate who discovers a wholly unknown will left by a well-to-do priest whose desperately poor relatives expect to be rescued by an inheritance. The will leaves the money to a heartless millionaire: should the executor destroy the will or follow its instructions? Should a doctor save the life of a sick criminal who, once healed, will do great harm to others? If we are to "work with might and main for the public welfare," as Diderot's spokesman says, we should destroy the will and let the criminal die. But is Diderot willing to let everyone have the discretion he assigns to the executor and the doctor? Who is to decide, once we cease to obey the law? But what if the law is unjust?[31]

Diderot offers no universal answer here, as he offers none about the problem of motivation. His is a world of uncertainties and incomplete solutions, not a world governed by a deity who makes sure all disharmonies are somehow resolvable or resolved. Although the wicked usually have a feeling about what is just or unjust, the police must protect us from those who ignore it as well as from those who lack it. Perhaps not many are moved by a feeling for justice like Diderot's; even so, self-interest well understood will lead most people to act decently in a society in which the laws usually serve the general well-being. Diderot thinks that writers like Voltaire and himself should advise rulers. Good advice requires shrewd understanding of what might make things better in given historical circumstances. Theory has little to do with it. His remarks on the general will amount to an appeal to all of us to work together toward a just happiness. With no divinely given assured principle or outcome, we must nonetheless keep trying.

iv. *Rousseau: The origins of morality*

In the first part of his life Jean-Jacques Rousseau (1712–78) was an admirer of Voltaire, a contributor to the *Encyclopedia*, and an intimate

31 See the "Discussion of a Father with His Children, or the Danger of Putting Oneself above the Laws," in *Oeuvres*, ed. Billy, pp. 759–81. In the "Supplement to Bougainville's Voyage" Diderot puts a similar point concisely: "Anyone who on the strength of his own personal authority violates a bad law thereby authorizes everyone else to violate the good" (*Writings*, p. 74).

friend of Diderot's. In 1749 he even wanted to go to prison with Diderot so as not to be separated from him; but in the late 1750s he broke with the *philosophes*, and Diderot soon came to consider him a wholly untrustworthy person as well as a philosophical opponent. Rousseau's change of mind did not make him indifferent to social and political issues. His portrayals of human misery are sensitive and powerful, and in his mature work he presented what he thought was the sole hope for political improvement.[32] He had major disagreements with both his former allies and the religious defenders of existing society about the causes of suffering. The church explained it by the sinfulness of human nature, inherited from Adam; the *philosophes* tended to blame ignorance and the misdirection of self-interest that is its consequence. Rousseau repeatedly denied both positions by saying that man is originally neither sinful nor selfish, but good. He also rejected the individualism of these diagnoses of social ills. Individual and society, he held, must be considered together. "Those who want to treat politics and morals separately," he proclaimed, "will never understand anything of either of them" (IV.524; *Emile*, p. 235).

Rousseau's position begins from a conjectural historical explanation of our present state, which is meant both to account for its wretchedness and to show how morality might have entered into the world. The narrative constitutes a formidable attack on the natural law theories of Grotius, Hobbes, Locke, and Pufendorf.[33] It opens the way to a critique of existing theories of political legitimacy. It underpins a rejection of the view that the point of morality is to guide us to happiness. It also leads Rousseau to reject the enlighteners' central claim that the spread of reason and knowledge will improve morals, increase happiness, and bring freedom to everyone. He argues instead for the paradoxical thesis that what the *philosophes* considered progress is inseparable from tyranny in politics and corruption in private life.

Like the natural lawyers Rousseau begins with human beings in a state of nature.[34] He sees them as essentially solitary. They are moved

---

32   For a compact statement of his vision of suffering, see Note IX to the *Second Discourse*, in *Oeuvres complétes*, ed. Gagnebin and Reymond, III.202–7; and *Discourses*, trans. Gourevitch, pp. 207–13 (hereafter Gourevitch). In citing Rousseau's works in the text, I give the volume and page number of *Oeuvres* followed by a reference to a translation where appropriate.

33   On Rousseau's relations to natural law thought, see Derathé 1950 and Wokler 1994.

34   In summarizing Rousseau's hypothetical history I follow the *Discourse on the Origins of Inequality* (1755), in *Oeuvres* III, and his own summary in his *Letter to Beaumont* (1763), in *Oeuvres* IV.934–7.

by a strong impulse to preserve themselves; they have no desire to harm others; they feel and act on pity for those like themselves whom they see to be suffering. They couple without love, and when their offspring can fend for themselves, they cease to be concerned about them. Languageless, they are without general concepts and without forethought. Their desires are of the simplest. Those who survive are so hardy they barely suffer physical pain. Because they cannot anticipate death, their only fears are about immediate threats to their existence. When fed, sheltered, and sexually satisfied, they are happy.

The natural lawyers, Rousseau complains, have inserted into the state of nature desires and fears that can only exist in complex societies. People are too indifferent to one another to engage in a Hobbesian war of all against all. Envy, greed, and rivalry all require concepts the natural man does not have. Without language there could be no rights and no laws. But prior to any activity of reason people feel and respond to two principles: self-love, or interest in their own well-being; and pity, or "repugnance at seeing any sentient Being . . . perish or suffer," which fills the place of morality. People are thus initially good – not harmful to others, and helpful in cases of need. Eventually, however, natural self-love and pity give rise to natural right. For this to occur, nature must, Rousseau says, be smothered; and then reason must "reestablish on different foundations" the "rules" of these original motivations (III.125–6, 156; Gourevitch, pp. 132–3, 162).

The development occurs because of the human faculty of "perfecting oneself" (III.142; Gourevitch, p. 149). Animals are only machines cleverly made to preserve themselves; but humans, despite La Mettrie, are more complex. They can resist their desires and change their natural ways of behaving. Somehow language and abstract concepts emerge, and with them the possibility of comparison, forethought, and invention. New desires lead people to develop new knowledge, which in turn makes possible more complex desires. Sexual desire develops into preference for one person rather than others, causing rivalry and the urge to shine in the eyes of the beloved. With this the stage is set for the developments that make men wicked by making them sociable (III.162; Gourevitch, p. 168).

Rivalry makes men wish to stand out by possessing more of whatever is admired than their fellows have. No longer content to live in the moment, some begin to acquire more goods than others. Then someone encloses a piece of ground and calls it his own. Others naively accept his claim; and with this a destructive cycle is unleashed. Possessors make others work for them. With the leisure they obtain for themselves, they start to pass time seeking luxuries. Ever more curious about how to gratify their new desires, they foster the growth of knowledge. What people come to want above all is to be admired by others.[35] Natural love of self, or *amour de soi,* when socialized in this way, turns into what Rousseau calls *amour propre,* a self-centered motivation that, unlike its original, is satisfied only by superiority over others. Social conflict is then inevitable, as are deceit and hypocrisy. Everyone seeks their own advantage while pretending to act for the benefit of others. Nicole saw hypocrisy as one of the means God uses to bring social good out of individual evil. For Rousseau it is one of the worst features of our present society. Perfectibility leads us first to corruption.

Although some people acquire power over others in the state of nature, there seems to be no room within it for morality. In the opening chapters of *On the Social Contract* Rousseau explains its origin. He does so by asking how power can be made legitimate. Paternal authority, he says, though admittedly natural, does not extend to societies. The right of the strongest is no more than power, lasting only as long as the strength is overwhelming. Slavery can arise only from a surrender to power, which gives no legitimacy. Like Pufendorf, Rousseau thus sees no basis in nature for any conception of legitimacy. But where Pufendorf invokes divine imposition of moral entities to explain normativity in a natural world, Rousseau appeals instead to human convention.

He gives a naturalistic account of the need for a convention. It arose when groups of people found that they could not continue to preserve their lives if they understood their relations only in terms of power. A new way of life had to be invented. But the only forces people have are their individual powers. They had therefore somehow to aggregate them and "make them act in concert" to create an endurable situation.[36] They did so, Rousseau says, by making a contract with one another, bringing about "a form of association that defends and protects the person and goods of each associate with all the common force." When everyone involved agrees to the contract, a "moral and collective body" is formed out of previously private individuals (III.351–64; *Contract* I.i–vii). "This passage from the state of nature to the civil state," says Rousseau,

> produces a remarkable change in man, by substituting justice for instinct in his behavior and giving his actions the morality they previously lacked. Only then, when the voice of duty replaces physical impulse and right

35 Rousseau here echoes Pascal: "We are not satisfied with the life we have in ourselves and our own being. We want to lead an imaginary life in the eyes of others, and so we try to make an impression" (*Pensées* 806).

36 As Masters points out in his note 29 to the *Social Contract* I.viii, Rousseau uses strongly Newtonian imagery here. He is stressing the transition from a world of natural forces to another kind of world, the world of moral entities created by will.

replaces appetite, does man, who until that time only considered himself, find himself forced to act upon other principles and to consult his reason before heeding his inclinations. (III.364; *Contract* I.viii)

The practical problem to which the social contract is the sole solution is complex (III.360; *Contract* I.vi). Its solution is the work of reason. We are able to respond to reason, and to take ourselves out of a world of purely physical interaction, because of central emotional aspects of our nature. Rousseau sometimes speaks of them as the foundations of morality.

v. *The transformation of human nature*

Adam Smith thought Rousseau's views very like those of Mandeville, although "softened, improved, and embellished" (*Essays*, pp. 250–1). He sees that in the *Social Contract*, as in Mandeville's *Fable*, morality enters nature as a human invention that enables different agents to cooperate in satisfying their own desires. But Smith does not note that Mandeville portrays the pursuit of social eminence and luxury, and its attendant pretenses, as the normal and even desirable condition of society, while Rousseau, like Machiavelli or Harrington, sees them as constituting corruption. More importantly, for Rousseau, in contrast to Mandeville, the creation of a moral society requires the transformation of human nature (III.381; *Contract* II.vii).

One such transformation occurred as people gradually left the state of nature for the rudimentary groups that developed into the corrupt societies in which we now live. Although his critics thought Rousseau was urging us to return to our original condition, he always denied that such a return is even possible.[37] Our only hope, on his view, lies in a further alteration of our nature. We must become capable of acting in accordance with the directions of what he calls "the general will" (*volonté générale*).

Rousseau first used this Malebranchean term, revived by Diderot's article on natural right, in an early *Encyclopedia* essay on "Political Economy." The body politic, he says, is a moral being with both will and intelligence. Its will is the general will, "which always tends toward the preservation and welfare of the whole and of each part." As the voice of justice, it is the source of laws both for politics and for "the morality of all human actions." Government ought to obey the general will in legislating, and citizens should obey it in their private lives. The general will works through law, here described as a "celestial voice" telling each person the "precepts of public reason" and urging each to follow them

37 See, e.g., *Oeuvres* III.207; Gourevitch, p. 213; and the letter of September 10, 1755, responding to Voltaire's attack on the *Second Discourse*, in *Oeuvres* III.226–9.

and "not to be in contradiction with himself."[38] In the *Social Contract* Rousseau makes it clear that in accepting the general will as our own will, we pursue a new good. It is a common good, the good of living in a society in which each can not only pursue his ends but can avow them publicly as well. In such a society the hypocrisy and deceit which are one of the worst aspects of corrupt society are overcome. To attain this benefit, however, each of us must limit our ends to those compatible with everyone else's pursuit of their acceptable ends. When we do so, our agreement to the contract transforms us individually as much as it changes the group in which we live. We each cease to be a physically isolated being and become part of a moral whole (III.381–4; *Contract* II.vii).[39]

As citizens we do not cease to have private wills swayed by our personal desires, but we need not continue to be enslaved by our corrupt passions. Living in accordance with the general will, we are not simply caused to act by our desires: we choose which of them to satisfy. Rousseau admits that the private will in each of us always threatens to overwhelm the general will; but social sanctions support the latter. If they compel us to act from the general will and so to act virtuously, we are only being forced to be free. "For the impulse of appetite alone is slavery," Rousseau asserts, "and obedience to the law one has prescribed for oneself is freedom" (III.364–5; *Contract* I.vii–viii). As this suggests, Rousseau thinks that experience shows us a duality in our nature. "Man is not one," he declares; we are divided within ourselves. Reason shows us one sort of good, the senses and our passions allure us with another. We are not passive in the face of the alternatives. We possess will; and though we cannot refrain from willing what we think is our own good, we will freely when our will responds to our own judgment of the good, and is not moved by anything external to ourselves. Our possession of this Leibniz-like will, Rousseau thinks, shows man to be "free in his actions and as such animated by an immaterial substance" (IV.586–7; *Emile*, pp. 280–1). Our possession of free will is part of what makes us like God; and if it enables us to sin, it also enables us to earn the satisfaction with oneself that comes from acting rightly. "It is in order to deserve this satisfaction," Rousseau says, "that we are placed on earth" (IV.583–7; *Emile*, pp. 278–81).

We need more than reason and will to enable us to conquer our passions by acting on the terms of the general will. Reason shows us the good that would come from accepting the social contract. But for Rous-

38 "Political Economy," in *Oeuvres* III.245, 247–8; *Contract*, pp. 212, 214.
39 Rousseau again echoes Pascal on the desirability of being part of an organic community; see Chapter 13.iii.

seau as for Malebranche, knowing the good is not the same as being moved to pursue it. Before we can act as reason directs, we must come to see that justice and goodness are not "pure moral beings formed by the understanding." They are "true affections of the soul enlightened by reason," and so arise as a development of our natural feelings. "By reason alone, independent of conscience, no natural law can be established . . . the entire right of nature is only a chimera if it is not founded on a natural need in the human heart." And Rousseau adds:

> Even the precept of doing unto others as we would have them do unto us has no true foundation other than conscience and sentiment. . . . Love of men derived from love of self is the principle of human justice. The summation of all morality is given by the Gospel in its summation of the law. (IV.522–3 and n; *Emile*, p. 235 and n)

Desire as well as knowledge must be present if the will is to have a choice to make. Reason may teach us to know good and evil, but only conscience makes us love the one and hate the other (IV.288; *Emile*, p. 67).

Rousseau elaborates this point helpfully in the *Letter to Beaumont*. We naturally feel a love of order, he remarks, which, when it is "developed and rendered active, bears the name of conscience." This is the natural love that renders man essentially good. We must become enlightened to know order, but once we know it, this love urges us toward it. Conscience is not active until we come to see ourselves, not as isolated beings, but as beings essentially related to one another – the way we see ourselves under the general will. If we think of ourselves only as separate beings, we will be caught forever in the sad history of corruption revealed in the *Second Discourse* (*Oeuvres* IV.935–7). Conscience is thus a Malebranchean love of order, activated in the individual by the social contract.

Speaking through the Savoyard vicar in the most extensive philosophical remarks in *Emile*, Rousseau devotes a number of passionate pages to expounding the glory of conscience. Asking himself what rules he as a free agent ought to follow, the vicar replies that the rules of morality are "written by nature with ineffaceable characters in the depths of [his] heart." He learns this from conscience, "the voice of the soul." Conscience is apostrophized as a "divine instinct, immortal and celestial voice, certain guide of a being that is ignorant and limited but intelligent and free; infallible judge of good and bad which makes man like unto God" (IV.594–5, 600–1; *Emile*, pp. 286, 290).[40] Conscience

40 As early as the *First Discourse*, Rousseau had spoken of conscience in a similar way. The principles of virtue, he there says, are "engraved in all hearts." To

makes morality plain to everyone alike. Thanks to it, the vicar says, "we are delivered from all that terrifying apparatus of philosophy. We can be men without being scholars. Dispensed from consuming our life in the study of morality, we have at less expense a more certain guide in this immense maze of human opinions" (IV.600–1; *Emile*, p. 290). Conscience guides us, not least, in testing what would-be religious teachers have to say. It shows us that we do not need revelation, to say nothing of theology, but it also responds positively to Christianity – and to no other doctrine (IV.608–27; *Emile*, pp. 296–308). Conscience thus makes it possible for even the simplest person to pick out the true faith from among the many religions clamoring for adherence.[41]

Conscience itself is not, however, cognitive. "The acts of the conscience," the vicar declares, "are not judgments but sentiments." They are our felt response to ideas that "come to us from outside" and tell us which of them to follow and which to shun. "To know the good is not to love it; man does not have innate knowledge of it, but as soon as his reason makes him know it, his conscience leads him to love it. It is this sentiment which is innate." Rousseau thus follows Malebranche in holding that there must be desire for the good as well as knowledge of it if we are to choose it. But he does not accept Malebranche's claim that our knowledge of order is knowledge of God's mind. He points instead to differences between God's mind and ours (IV.593; *Emile*, p. 285). He says, indeed, that "whatever is good and in accordance with order is so by the nature of things, independently of convention. All justice comes from God." But he promptly adds: "if we knew how to receive it from on high, we should need neither government nor laws" (III.378; *Contract* II.vi). Rousseau is concerned with justice as it can operate on earth to solve our practical problem. The source of order in society is, for Rousseau, not God's mind but the social contract. If reason enables us to conceive of the contract, our changeable nature brings forth a love through which we feel the attraction of justice and can freely will to set the public good ahead of our private good.

---

learn its laws one needs only "to return into oneself and, in the silence of the passions, to listen to the voice of one's conscience" (III.30; Gourevitch, p. 27). See also Rousseau's remark in his reply to criticisms of the *First Discourse* made by Stanislas of Poland: "We have a guide within, much more infallible than all the books, and which never forsakes us when we are in need. It would suffice to guide us in innocence if we were willing always to heed it" (III.42; Gourevitch, p. 37).

41 Rousseau says he could not understand it if "what every man is obliged to know is confined to books" and if even those who involuntarily lack revelation are punished for their ignorance (IV.620; *Emile*, p. 303).

vi. *Toward the classical republic*

Rousseau's account of the totalizing transformation brought about by the social contract makes it appear that for him any social condition other than a civil society wholly compliant with the general will is completely amoral, remaining in the domain of nature and power. But this is not his thought. There can be, as it were, enclaves of morality in the natural, precivil condition as well as in the generally corrupt and appalling societies in which most of us now live. The *Second Discourse* describes how "some crude idea" of mutual engagements might have arisen before a social contract (III.166; Gourevitch, p. 172).[42] The exemplary education Rousseau sketches for Emile plainly takes place in a less than perfect society, since the pupil is surrounded by people filled with corrupt desires. He must be brought up to avoid these, and to remain as "natural" or precivil as is possible in civilized circumstances. He will then be guided by love of self, avoiding the corruption of *amour propre*. It is only very late in his education that Emile comes to morality. Until then, Rousseau never tires of telling us, the tutor has made no appeal to authority (IV.639; *Emile*, p. 316). Authority and obligation enter the picture only when Emile's natural feelings of pity develop into a more than occasional concern for others. In particular he must come to love his God-like tutor enough to agree to obey him. He can do this because, having learned to understand his own self-interested desires, he knows that what the tutor will order him to do will always be for his own real good, even if he himself does not recognize this in particular cases. "I want to obey your laws," Emile says,

> I want to do so always. This is my steadfast will. If ever I disobey you, it will be in spite of myself. Make me free by protecting me against those of my passions which do violence to me. Prevent me from being their slave; force me to be my own master and to obey not my senses but my reason. (IV.651–2; *Emile*, p. 325)

The authority that has thus entered Emile's life via something like an individual contract (IV.653; *Emile*, p. 326) still comes from someone else, so his moral education is not complete. Up to now, the tutor tells him, using a distinction of Shaftesbury's,

> I have made you good rather than virtuous. But he who is only good remains so only as long as he takes pleasure in being so. . . . Who, then, is

42 So also in the *Letter to Beaumont:* "when by a development of which I have shown the progress men begin to cast their eyes upon their fellows, they begin also to see their relations and the relations of things, to take in ideas of suitability, of justice and of order; lovely morality [*le beau moral*] begins to be noticeable to them and conscience acts" (IV.936).

the virtuous man? It is he who knows how to conquer his affections; for then he follows reason and his conscience; he does his duty; he keeps himself in order. (IV.818; *Emile,* pp. 444–5)

Emile learns to do this by postponing his marriage to Sophie. He does so at first at the tutor's insistence, but ultimately he chooses to do so, in order to learn his duties as citizen before assuming the position of one by marrying. Once he has made this choice, he has moralized his life. He has achieved in the private sphere what is accomplished in the public by the creation of civil society to replace the state of nature.

Speaking as Emile's tutor, Rousseau makes it clear that it is not easy to live a virtuous life in a society like the one his pupil inhabits. The life of virtue, he thinks, can best be led in a small republic. His attachment to a version of the republican ideal of self-government by virtuous men living as free and equal citizens in a society that eschews refinement and artistic elegance was perhaps never more fervently expressed than in the prosopopoeia of Fabricius in the first *Discourse.* Called upon to contemplate Rome in its glory, its buildings covered with marble, its populace rich with craftsmen, artists, and philosophers who discourse of virtue, Fabricius says:

> what has become of the thatched roofs and the rustic hearths where moderation and virtue used to dwell? . . . When Cineas took our Senate for an Assembly of Kings he was not dazzled by vain pomp or studied eloquence. . . . What, then, did Cineas see that was so majestic? O Citizens! He saw a spectacle which neither your riches nor all your arts shall ever succeed in exhibiting . . . the Assembly of two hundred virtuous men worthy of commanding in Rome, and of governing the earth. (II.14–15; Gourevitch, p. 10)

The republic that Rousseau advocates is far from Harringtonian. He professes indifference in principle to the "administrative" form of government, so long as the commonwealth is ruled by the general will (III.379–80; *Contract* II.vi). He never abandons a vocabulary of law and rights, and although he appeals to a quasi-divine legislator for aid in the institution of his republic he of course sees its central founding moment as a contract. Yet he agrees with Harrington rather than with Shaftesbury in thinking that the ideal republic will austerely avoid the refinements and luxuries that only wealth makes possible. Perhaps he thinks that in such a republic the path of duty will be plain to everyone. He gives no answer otherwise to the vicar's question of how we are to know the rules we should follow.

If Rousseau envisioned a moral Utopia, he never sounded sanguine about actually achieving it. "From knowledge to ignorance is but a single step," he says in the *First Discourse*, "and Nations have frequently gone from one to the other; but never has a people, once corrupted, been known to return to virtue." At least no such return seemed possible to him "short of some great revolution almost as much to be feared as the evil it might cure" (III.56; Gourevitch, p. 51). And Rousseau did not preach revolution. He is aware that his attack on the arts and sciences makes his own copious publication a little embarrassing. But he holds that "the same causes that have corrupted peoples sometimes help prevent a greater corruption" (II.971–2; Gourevitch, p. 108). Thus he thought the educational reforms he proposed in *Emile* might help people raise their children better and he hoped his work might change what people admire, thereby helping to save the few existing societies small enough to preserve some elements of virtue (*Oeuvres* I.935). And unlike Voltaire or La Mettrie or Diderot, he not only condemned the corrupt society around him. He sketched a healthy society that might replace it, and spelled out principles to which social critics more outraged or simply more practical than he might appeal in calling for drastic action.

vii. *Providence without intervention*

Voltaire the theist found evil incomprehensible and concluded that God is so as well. Diderot the atheist refused to discuss the problem of evil. His response to those who did was to "give the finger to heaven [*montre le ciel du doigt*]," and leave them to their squabbles (*Oeuvres,* ed. Versini, p. 1178). Voltaire expected no aid from his deity in solving earthly problems. Stories about punishments and rewards after death are necessary to keep the populace in order, but we can say no more about providence than that. For practical purposes we live as much in a world on its own for Voltaire as we do for La Mettrie or for Diderot.

Not the least of Rousseau's grounds for breaking with his colleagues was his religiosity. He rejected not only the atheism whose near avowal in the *Letter on the Blind* had gotten Diderot sentenced to prison, but also what he took to be Voltaire's comfortless voluntaristic theism. "I am a Christian," Rousseau insisted, "and sincerely Christian, according to the doctrine of the Gospels" (*Oeuvres* IV.960). Yet his own religious views were so unorthodox that when he published them as the "Confessions of a Savoyard Vicar" in *Emile,* his book was condemned and burned, and he himself forced to flee France to avoid prison.[43] The vicar thinks Jesus exemplifies a purer morality than the world ever saw before; and morality, which requires worship of God, is the essential part of religion. All else, including what separates Protestant from Catholic and Muslim or Jew from both, is unimportant. If the Gospels teach the

43   See Cranston 1991, pp. 358–60.

finest practical lessons, they also contain much nonsense. The differences among the world's many faiths are trivial. Any religion is acceptable that teaches the morality we all instinctively feel, along with decorous worship (IV.620–35; *Emile*, pp. 303–12). No wonder that the Catholic French establishment had the book burned.

Voltaire's poem on the Lisbon earthquake drew from Rousseau a passionate letter defending the thesis that "the whole is good or everything is good for the whole." He phrases this "optimistic" belief carefully to avoid the implication that every particular within the whole is good. His is the Malebranchean view that God's providence is "only universal." God does not "disturb himself about the manner in which each individual passes this short life" (*Oeuvres* IV.1069). Experience does not prove general optimism, Rousseau admits, so we must derive it from God's existence and the attributes that flow from his necessary perfection (IV.1068). In *Emile* he says that God's goodness is a necessary consequence of his intelligence, will, and power. Since he is good he is just; and, without argument, Rousseau connects these two attributes to a divine love of order, which God both produces and preserves in the creation (IV.581, 588–9; *Emile*, pp. 277, 282).

Against Voltaire Rousseau is also passionate in defense of immortality. If the arguments for it are feeble, so much the worse for them:

> I have suffered too much in this life not to expect another. All the subtleties of metaphysics will not make me doubt for a moment the immortality of the soul and a beneficent providence. I feel it, I believe it, I want it, I hope for it, I will defend it to my last breath. (*Oeuvres* IV.1075)

The vicar makes it clear that immortality is required to assure us of God's justice, since the good often fail to flourish in this life (IV.589–90; *Emile*, pp. 282–3). But this is not the major concern of Rousseau's defense against Voltaire's voluntarist dismissal of the problem of evil. His main focus is on this life, not a future one. He opens *Emile* by saying that all is good as it leaves God's hands and that all degenerates in man's; and the vicar complains that he sees order throughout the natural world but none in the moral world (IV.583; *Emile*, pp. 37, 278).[44] The thesis of God's general providence allows room, as Malebranche explained, for individuals to try to prevent particular evils.[45] It also gives Rousseau the conceptual space he needs to defend God by assigning the responsibility for human suffering almost entirely to human beings

44   For a history of connecting the ideas of order and disorder in the natural and moral worlds, see Macklem 1958.

45   Rousseau himself stresses this point in his "Letter to Philopolis" (Charles Bonnet), a reply to an attack on the *Second Discourse*. See *Oeuvres* III.235–6; Gourevitch, pp. 234–5.

themselves. Human freedom relieves God formally of responsibility for what we do (IV.587; *Emile,* p. 281). But Rousseau's theory of history, explaining what we have done with our freedom, carries the great weight of his theodicy. It shows precisely how we ourselves cause the evils from which we suffer. Even a providential God leaves our fate in our own hands once he has created a good universe. What Rousseau gets from his faith seems to be essentially consolation.[46]

In a note to the *Second Discourse* Rousseau describes himself as "convinced that the divine voice called all Mankind to the enlightenment and the happiness of the celestial intelligences," which is to be attained, if at all, "by practicing the virtues which they obligate themselves to perform as they learn to know them." Such men will be entitled to an eternal reward, the thought of which will spur them on through the difficulties of earthly life (III.207; Gourevitch, pp. 213–14). The remark brings out some of the larger significance of Rousseau's narrative of decline and recovery. Rousseau finds written in his soul the words "Be just and you will be happy." Our troubled history is God's way of enabling us to create the circumstances in which our divinely given conscience – that love of order which we share with God – can become operative and motivate us to be the moral agents God wants us freely to become. "O let us be good in the first place," Rousseau exclaims, "and then we shall be happy. Let us not demand the prize before the victory, nor the wage before the work" (IV.589; *Emile,* pp. 282–3). Morality for Rousseau as for Malebranche shows us how to deserve happiness, not how to obtain it. Hence for Rousseau, as for all the antivoluntarists, God's existence provides more than consolation. It gives the theoretical assurance that we live in a world in which a harmonious outcome to our personal and social struggles is possible. The classical republic is the nearest we can come to a city of God on earth. Beyond that, those who strive for virtue may hope for a heavenly reward.

46 Cranston's term; Cranston 1991, p. 193. See *Oeuvres* IV.590; *Emile,* p. 283.

22

The invention of autonomy

At the core of the moral philosophy of Immanuel Kant (1724–1804) is the claim that morality centers on a law that human beings impose on themselves, necessarily providing themselves, in doing so, with a motive to obey. Kant speaks of agents who are morally self-governed in this way as autonomous. He took the term from the political thought of the seventeenth and eighteenth centuries, in which it was used in discussions of the idea of states as self-governing entities.[1] I have indicated that the idea of moral self-governance goes back at least as far as St. Paul's assertion in Romans 2.14 that the gentiles are "a law unto themselves." Kant understood the idea in a radically different way. His view of morality as autonomy is something new in the history of thought.

I do not propose to summarize Kant's mature moral philosophy or to engage in exegesis or assessment of it.[2] Assuming the reader's familiarity with his view, I address two topics that have received much less attention in the literature than the structure and adequacy of the theory. In this chapter I offer an account of how Kant came to take the first major step toward his view of morality as autonomy. In the next chapter I discuss some of the ways in which Kant's mature moral philosophy is related to the views of his seventeenth- and eighteenth-century predecessors. There have been a number of valuable treatments of the development of Kant's moral philosophy, to which I am indebted.[3] As

1 See Chapter 1.i, note 2, for the German term. The *Oxford English Dictionary* lists only the political application of the term prior to importations of Kantian vocabulary.

2 I have tried to do so in Schneewind 1992a.

3 See Henrich 1957, 1960 (sec. III), and 1963, and esp. Schmucker 1961. Henrich 1992, ch. 1, reiterates some of his earlier points and stresses, as other commentators do, that throughout his life Kant kept changing his mind on key points. Busch 1979 is also helpful, though concentrating on the development of Kant's political thought. Schilpp 1938 and his German predecessors Menzer 1897, 1898, and Küenberg 1925

these studies show, the issues are very complex. Without attempting anything like full discussion of Kant's early writings, I try to bring out sources of Kant's original views of morality in his attempts to think through problems that had engaged him in earlier parts of his philosophical work.

i. *Toward the moral law*

The idea that we are rational beings who spontaneously impose lawfulness on the world in which we live and thereby create its basic order is, of course, central to the whole of Kant's philosophy. In its practical aspects it has engaged attention and attracted adherents since its first publication. How did Kant come to invent such a revolutionary view, and to think that it could explain morality? We do not know the whole story. As the Kant biographer Vorländer complains, in almost everything that concerns the development of Kant's thought "we are frequently left with conjectures, where we would rather know solid facts."[4] But there are a few solid facts, and they enable us to catch glimpses, at least, of Kant's starting point and of some of the steps he took on the road to his mature moral theory.

Traditional views of the development of Kant's moral philosophy accepted the idea that his work could be divided into precritical and critical periods, the break coming cleanly with the *Inaugural Dissertation* of 1770. It was supposed that during the precritical years Kant's ethical thinking reflected his pietistic upbringing and the influence of Shaftesbury, Hutcheson, Hume, and Rousseau. These philosophers were held to have led him to think of morality as based on sentiment; and since the critical ethics is so different from this view, it was said that Kant decisively altered his position because of the epistemology he developed in answer to Hume's general skepticism.

Very little of what Kant published prior to 1770 deals with ethics, so it is understandable that what he did say about it in those writings exercised a strong influence in creating this picture.[5] In the *Inquiry concerning the Distinctness of the Principles of Natural Theology and Morality*,

---

did not have all the material we now have. Rossvaer 1979, pp. 21–37, gives a useful discussion of the early ethics. Ward 1972 seems to have used only what was available in English. Velkely 1989 has less to say about Kant's ethics in particular than about the role of reason in his theory generally. De Vleeschauwer 1962 is mainly interested in Kant's views on epistemology and metaphysics, and the biographers Gulyga 1981 and Ritzel 1985 share this focus.

4   Vorländer 1977, I.80, echoed by Ritzel 1985, p. 3.

5   In Chapters 22, 23, and 24, references to Kant's works will be given in the text. I give the volume and page number of the *Gesammelte Schriften* followed by reference to a translation where I have used one.

published in 1764, Kant says that it is a recent discovery that "the faculty of representing the *true* is *cognition*, while the faculty of experiencing the *good* is *feeling*" (2.299; *TP*, p. 273). In the *Observations on the Feeling of the Beautiful and the Sublime*, written in 1763, Kant tells us that true virtue must be supported by basic principles which are not mere speculative rules but "the consciousness of a feeling . . . the feeling of the beauty and the dignity of human nature" (2.217; *Observations*, p. 60). The appeal to feeling here sounds like some of the sentimentalist statements Rousseau gives to his vicar; and the "Announcement of the Lectures for 1765–66" praises the British moral sense philosophers for their penetration in the "search for the fundamental principles of morality" (2.311; *TP*, p. 298). But in the *Inaugural Dissertation* of 1770 it is clear that Kant does not accept the view of morality suggested by these passages. There Kant includes moral concepts among those "which are cognized not by experiencing them but through pure understanding itself" (2.395; *TP*, p. 387). Kant is equally definite in a letter to Lambert written in the same year. "I have resolved . . . this winter," he says, "to put in order and complete my investigations of pure moral philosophy, in which no empirical principles are to be found, the 'Metaphysics of Morals.' It will in many respects pave the way for the most important views involved in the reconstruction of metaphysics" (10.97; *Correspondence*, p. 59).

On the surface, then, the case for a drastic shift from precritical to critical ethics seems clear. But it is now generally agreed that the story is in fact much more complex. Kant devoted a great deal of thought to ethics prior to 1770. By 1765 he had, in fact, come to think that a formal principle of avoiding practical self-contradiction must be at the center of morality. He had also begun to have some sense of the complexities of elaborating and defending such a view. In getting to this point, his responses to German philosophers, particularly Wolff and Crusius, were more important than the earlier accounts allowed. The nature and importance of his reflections on the British moralists and on Rousseau therefore call for some reassessment. After 1765 there remained many problems for Kant to work out. Not the least of these was the problem of moral motivation and its connection with the rational first principle of morals. Kant saw that his new understanding of morality needed to be reconciled with his generally Newtonian view of the physical world.[6] The need to solve this problem was at least as significant in driving Kant on to develop the critical standpoint as his concerns with Hume's skepticism and the epistemological problems of modern science.

---

6 Kant was introduced to Newtonianism as well as Wolffianism by his most important philosophy teacher, Martin Knutzen. See Erdmann 1876 for what is still the fullest study of Knutzen.

This in outline is the story that now seems to make the best sense of the available evidence. The central point is of course the claim that Kant had arrived at the essentials of his distinctive view of morality by 1765. The clearest evidence for this comes from an extensive series of Notes (*Bemerkungen*) written by Kant on, or inserted into, his own copy of his *Observations on the Feeling of the Beautiful and the Sublime*. Written no later than early 1765, some of the Notes were published in 1842 and were widely used by scholars. The full text did not appear until a century later; it alters the picture significantly.[7]

Various Notes show Kant exploring positions that he later develops more fully. Thus he distinguishes two sorts of objective necessity in action, one conditional and the other categorical. "The first is hypothetical and if the individual appetites which are considered as conditions for an action are . . . actual, it is a necessity of prudence . . . The categorical necessity of an action is not so involved as this."[8] Morality is identified with objective necessity, which cannot rest on any advantages the act brings about (155.18; 125.3). Neither can it rest on the will of God. Kant asks whether we can make moral distinctions only if we know the will of God who is its creator, and he is ready with a negative answer. "Piety is only a kind of virtue," he says, and he claims that to subordinate morality to religion is to engender hypocrisy and idolatry, but to control religion by morality makes people "good-hearted, well-meaning, and just" (23.12, 18.18; 137.3, 109.9; 153.9, 122.11). What, then, is morality, if it is not pursuit of good results or obedience to the divine will?

It is obedience to what Kant calls at one point "the laws of freedom" (136.16; 109.5). He plainly sees freedom as crucial, although there is at least one question about it that he does not try to answer: "How freedom in the real understanding (the moral not the metaphysical) may be the highest principle of all virtue and also of all happiness" (31.10; 25.14). He does try several times to formulate freedom's laws, some-

7   The Notes were published in *Gesammelte Schriften* 20, ed. G. Lehmann, in 1942. See 20.471–5 for his remarks on the editorial problems involved. In *Bemerkungen*, Rischmüller gives a new critical edition, which is nearly an *editio diplomatica* and includes a useful introduction and extensive elucidatory and interpretive notes of considerable value. I identify individual Notes by giving the page number and the number of the first line of each cited item. I cite Lehmann's edition first and then Rischmüller's edition, using the bracketed page numbers that are part of her text rather than the numbers of pages of the book. To give the reader some sense of how rough the Notes are, I have added only a minimal amount of punctuation and capitalization.

8   "The goodness of a free action . . . is either conditional or categorical. The former is the goodness of an action as a means [;] the latter as an end . . . this contains practical necessity that problematic" (149.22; 120.2).

times using the idea of avoiding self-contradiction. "Whatever will is to be good if it is taken universally and reciprocally must not cancel itself" (67.5; 53.1). He also has in view the problematic relation of private and public or general will, as a cryptic Latin Note suggests: "The intention of action out of an individual will is moral solipsism. The intention of action out of the general will [*voluntate communi*] is moral justice" (145.4; 116.1). Morality is a matter not of external behavior but of inner perfection, which must arise from "the subordination of the totality of powers and sensibilities under the free will." Awareness of the goodness of the will must therefore differ wholly from awareness of its good results. "This will," he continues, "contains both the merely private and also the general will or man observes himself immediately in consensus with the general will" (145.16; 116.19).

One of the fullest of Kant's efforts to articulate the structure of moral willing comes in a convoluted Latin passage:

> if an action viewed according to the will common to men is in contradiction with itself it is externally and morally impossible (unwillable). Suppose I go to seize another's grain[.] if I consider that no one will acquire anything if he himself will be robbed of what he has acquired I will something privately and oppose the same thing publicly. For to the extent that something is fully dependent on the will of someone it is impossible that it should objectively contradict itself. The divine will would contradict itself were it to will the existence of men whose wills were in opposition to its own. The will of mankind would contradict itself if men were to want what by their own common will they would find abhorrent. In cases of conflict the general will is more weighty than the private. (160.26; 129.11)

If Kant has not yet articulated the categorical imperative, these Notes are enough to show that he has reached the first stage of a new understanding of morality – an understanding that forces upon him questions it took him the rest of his career to answer.

ii. *On Rousseau's influence*

The Notes show us Kant's fullest explicit response to Rousseau.[9] Kant was not an uncritical admirer, but he never ceased to hold a

---

9 Rischmüller argues convincingly against the view that the Notes show Kant's first reaction to *Emile* and the *Social Contract*. Claiming that Kant's French was not good enough to allow him to read it with ease (p. 271), she points to the publication of German translations of these works almost immediately after their appearance, and adds that Hamann and Herder kept Kant up to date on Rousseau's work. The Notes are therefore, she holds, to be read as a considered response to the two *Discourses* as well as to the later theoretical works. She also dismisses as *Klatsch* the

number of Rousseauian views that he here first discusses.[10] The most important single point that Kant attributes to Rousseau is his conversion to a new, and permanent, attitude about the importance of honoring the moral status of ordinary people. "One must teach the young," he says, "to honor the common understanding from moral as well as logical grounds" (44.6; 35.19). Kant speaks more personally when he says that "The belief in inequality makes people unequal. Only the teaching of Mr. *Rousseau* can bring it about that even the most learned philosopher with his knowledge uprightly and without the help of religion holds himself no better than the common man" (176.1; 141.1). This is not the only point at which Kant seems to see himself in some of what Rousseau says. There is an amount of emotion in some of the Notes that is unmatched anywhere else in his writings.

> When I go into the workshop of a manual worker I would wish that he could not read my thoughts. I shy away from this comparison[.] he would see the great inequality in which I find myself in relation to him. I perceive that I could not live for a day without his industriousness that his children will be raised to useful lives. (102.7; 81.8)[11]

Knowing Kant's humble origins, we can hardly avoid hearing a confessional tone here, and again in one of the most frequently quoted of the Notes:

> I am myself a researcher by inclination. I feel the whole thirst for knowledge and the curious unrest to get further on, or also the satisfaction in every acquisition. There was a time when I believed that this alone could make the honor of humanity and I despised the rabble that knows nothing. *Rousseau* set me to rights. This dazzling superiority vanishes, I learn to honor man and I would find myself more useless than the common

famous tale that *Emile* so excited Kant that to read it he skipped the daily walks by which his fellow-residents set their watches. Rischmüller, 150.

10   Some of the Notes are explicitly critical, e.g., those at 29.4, 24.1 and 29.10, 24.9, saying that it is a waste of a life to spend it tutoring a single child and that Rousseau's views must be adapted to schooling for many. Others are implicitly critical, e.g., 14.5, 8.37: "Rousseau. Proceeds synthetically and starts from the natural man I proceed analytically and start from the civilized." In the *Distinctness* essay (written prior to the Notes), the line of argument concerning analytic and synthetic methods makes it clear that Kant thinks Rousseau's method is fundamentally mistaken. Cf. 2.276–7, 290; *TP*, pp. 248–9, 263.

11   Compare this with the passage in *Emile* on the importance of letting one's pupil learn to do the work he is shown in the workshops he is to visit to learn about human interdependence. "[A]n hour of work," Rousseau adds, "will teach him more things than he would retain from a day of explanations" (*Oeuvres* IV.455–6; *Emile*, pp. 185–6).

laborer if I did not believe that this observation would impart to all else a value to restore the rights of mankind. (44.8; 35.21)

Honoring the moral capacities of common people entails, as Rousseau's vicar so passionately made clear, giving up the intellectualist morality of Leibniz and Wolff, in which Kant was raised. It also means abandoning the Wolffian claim that the philosopher must educate ordinary people into morality. And if everyone equally can know what is required by morality, there seems to be no useful role for moral philosophy in helping to realize the rights of man. It is thus understandable that, as these Notes show, Kant was troubled by doubts about the value of philosophy and of learning generally.

One Note suggests a palliative: "Among all the ranks there is none more useless than the scholar as long as there is natural simplicity and none more necessary than he in the condition of oppression through superstition or force" (10.18; 5.10; cf. 105.13, 83.20). Kant makes frequent use of Rousseau's hypothetical history in describing his own times. Perhaps he thought that it could justify the kind of career he wished to follow. But his own attitudes still upset him:

> One always talks so much of virtue. One must however wipe out injustice before one can be virtuous. One must set aside comforts, luxuries and everything that oppresses others while it raises me so that I am not one of all those who oppress their kind. All virtue is impossible without this conclusion. (151.7; 121.1)

Kant might have learned to honor the common moral understanding from his religious upbringing, or from Crusius, who argued that God must have given everyone the capacity to know what morality requires because he will judge all of them.[12] But it seems to have taken Rous-

---

12   He might have learned it also from the Swiss polymath and poet, Haller, who was Kant's favorite poet after Pope. Haller wrote a series of "Swiss Poems" in the 1720s and 1730s from which Kant quotes in his own works, both early and late. Among these is one written in 1729 called "Die Alpen." In it the poet sings, if that is the correct word, the virtues of the simple folk who live in poverty on the higher reaches of the Alps. Unlike the wealthier city residents, these untutored peasants retain the rugged honesty of their ancestors. They have no luxuries to tempt them out of the narrow path of integrity. As long as their simplicity is unspoiled, they will live harmoniously, guided only by reason and nature. In another poem, "Die Verdorbene Sitten" (Corrupted Morals), 1731, Haller takes the theme still further, pessimistically wondering if even in Switzerland there remain any of the pure and simple hearts he earlier praised. (These poems are in Haller, *Gedichte*.) In the Notes, Kant says that it is hard, once one's inclinations have been developed in civilization, to picture the goods and ills of other conditions. If I am now threatened with boredom

seau's powerful writing to change Kant's own feelings.[13] However he did it, Rousseau converted Kant permanently into a defender of the moral capacities of ordinary people.[14]

On another personal matter the Notes are also quite clear: Kant's hatred of servility and of the class hierarchy that requires it from inferiors. He resents the nobility whose members always despise the "rabble," although the workers and the oppressed actually support them (10.12, 5.5; cf. 17.12, 11.32). In a series of Notes he deplores the status of lackeys and decries subordination to others. Interestingly, he ties his objections to this to human agency. To be at the beck and call of another is to deny or give up one's ability to direct oneself; hence subordination involves "a certain hatefulness and a contradiction that immediately shows its injustice" (91.9–94.15; 72.2–73.19). And in one passionate Note Kant gives his newfound Rousseauian feelings a more positive turn:

> In our condition when universal injustice stands firm the natural rights of the lowly cease[.] they are therefore only debtors[.] the superiors owe them nothing Therefore these superiors are called gracious lord He who needs nothing from them but justice and can hold them to their debts does not need this submissiveness. (140.12; 112.8)[15]

unless I have ever-increasing satisfactions, I imagine the same of "the Swiss who pastures his cow on the meadow" (26.5; 21.5).

13   Cf. 30.4, 24.25, and especially 43.13, 35.1, with Rischmüller's commentary at *Bemerkungen*, p. 188.

14   Everyone who writes about Rousseau and Kant notes the statement by Kant's early biographers that the sole picture on the walls of his house was a portrait of Rousseau. It is not noticed that one of the biographers adds that "in fact [the engraving] was certainly a present from some friend or other, in consideration of whom Kant felt its preservation to be a duty" (Hoffman 1902, p. 256). We should thus not infer too much from Kant's keeping the picture up; but there may well have been more than politeness involved. Could it have been gratitude for an account of Kant's early attitudes toward common people that explained these feelings as due not to personal sinfulness but to the corruption of the society in which he lived? The Kant editor Lehmann believes Kant was undergoing some kind of personal crisis at around the time he read Rousseau; see Lehmann 1969, 417–18.

15   See also *Reflexionen*, no. 6736, probably from about the same period as the Notes: "Many people take pleasure in doing good actions but therefore do not want to stand under obligations toward others. If one comes to them submissively they will do everything. They do not want to subject themselves to the rightful in people, but to view such simply as the object of their good-heartedness. It is not all one under what title I get something. One must not give me, merely because of my request, what properly belongs to me" (19.145).

With these strong feelings in mind, we can see one of the most frequently quoted of Kant's notes as showing a problem of which he was plainly aware.

> Newton first of all saw order and regularity unified with great simplicity where before him disorder and badly sorted multiplicity were to be met and since then comets run in geometric paths.
> Rousseau first of all discovered beneath the multiplicity of forms assumed by humans their deeply buried nature and the hidden law by which providence through his observations will be justified. Previously the reproach of Alphonsus and Manes was valid. After Newton and Rousseau God is justified and now Pope's theorem is true. (58.12; 44.24)[16]

If Newton showed the hidden law revealing a divine order in the natural world, Rousseau did something analogous for the moral world: he explained the present disorder in the moral world of which his vicar complains so eloquently, and did so in a way that shows it to be our fault, not God's. But the only advice he offers for creating order seems to be the formation of a social contract. And that in turn seems to contradict the vicar's insistence that morality must be something we can each come to know individually, by looking within ourselves, regardless of book learning. Rousseau thinks that a legislator of God-like abilities is needed "to give laws to men"; he might have to pretend to have divine authority in order to convince the masses to obey (*Oeuvres* III.362–4; *Contract* II.vii). Rousseau no more tries to reconcile these claims than he tries to answer the vicar's request for moral guidance.

Kant seeks a moral law that will make good the deficiency. Like Rousseau, he is concerned with the moral world. "The single naturally necessary good of a man in relation to the will of others," he says, "is equality (freedom) and in relation to the whole unity. Analogy [:] repulsion through which the body fills its own space as each does its own. Attraction, through which all parts bind themselves into one" (165.20; 134.8).[17] He does not offer an answer to the question of how the moral

16 Alphonsus was a king of Castile who was an astronomer and who claimed that he could have given God some good advice about making the heavens more orderly. Leibniz among many others mentions his criticism of God in order to dismiss it in *Theodicy* 193; cf. 241–5. Manes is the founder of the dualistic Manichaean religion. Rischmüller has an extensive discussion of this Note, on pp. 200–11. As I show in section iii, Pope's theorem as Kant read it is that whatever is, is good; it comes from his *Essay on Man*.

17 Herder records Kant as telling his students in 1764 that "the unselfish feeling is similar to the power of attraction and the selfish to the power of repulsion. Both in conflict constitute a world" (27.4; *LE*, pp. 3–4). See also *Pure Reason*, A808 = B836. In the *Metaphysics of Morals* Kant makes a similar comment: "In speaking of laws of

law can actually bring order into the moral world. But he is not satisfied with Rousseau's belief in a conscience that has but to learn morality from reason to be moved by it. Perhaps "inner moral grounds" can enable one to act rightly if one is not strongly tempted by desire or a feeling of injustice to act otherwise, Kant says, but often it will take the thought of supernatural rewards to make morality effective, and then one has gone outside of morality (28.3; 22.8). It took him a long time to find an answer to this question.[18] Kant's dissatisfaction with what he saw as Rousseau's omissions or inadequacies seems to have directed his thought as much as his acceptance of the Rousseauian estimate of the moral standing of ordinary people.

iii. *Theodicy and morality*

With the hindsight given us by our understanding of Kant's mature thought we can understand how his moral decision to honor the common understanding might have led him to see a need for an action-guiding principle of morality that did not require the calculations of consequences demanded by the Wolffian ethic. Nothing can explain the creative leap that enabled Kant to invent the new principle he needed. But a look at Kant's earlier work shows that he was not unprepared to think about the issues that Rousseau made him consider. Although his early published work all concerned scientific and metaphysical questions, an interest in the problem of evil led Kant to some thoughts that pointed in the direction he eventually took in ethics.[19]

In 1753 the Berlin Academy announced a competition for a prize to be awarded in 1755 for the best essay on "the system of Mr. Pope, which is summarized in the assertion: All is good." Contestants were asked, among other things, to compare this view with "the system of optimism, or the choice of the best," that is, with the view of Leibniz

duty (not laws of nature) . . . we consider ourselves in a moral (intelligible) world, where, by analogy with the physical world, *attraction* and *repulsion* bind together rational beings (on earth)." Love draws men closer, respect keeps them at a distance; both "moral forces" are needed for "the kingdom of moral beings" to continue (6.449; *MM*, pp. 243–4). See Macklem 1958, app. II, for earlier uses of physical forces as metaphors for morality, and Probst 1994 for numerous historical and literary parallels.

18   Gueroult discusses Kant's changes of view in essays on the moral theory contained in the first *Critique* and on the transition from that position to the one in the second *Critique*; see Gueroult 1977, pp. 15–36, 37–48. I agree with Henrich 1992, p. 21, that it was only when working out the *Foundations* that Kant came to his final motivational theory.

19   In this section I am much indebted to Henrich 1963, pp. 408–14.

(17.229n; *TP*, p. lv). I have pointed out how frequently the problem of evil appears in philosophical works. It was a matter of general cultural concern; and the popularity of Pope's *Essay on Man* had revitalized the issue, which attained unforeseeable notoriety from the Lisbon earthquake of November 1755. Among the earliest Kant manuscripts are some which show that he thought of writing for the contest.[20] He did not submit an essay, but the fragments show that by 1754 he had begun to think about issues concerning perfection and the nature of possibility that were to occupy him for more than a decade. The problem of evil, as raised by the academy's question about Leibniz and Pope, occasioned Kant's move in a new direction.

Leibniz holds that the world, created to display the glory of God, has the most extensive purpose conceivable, since God's glory is infinite. He also thinks that no simpler way of organizing more, and more complex, entities for this purpose is imaginable. Perfection is an objective characteristic of entities united for a purpose, and is greater or less depending on their number, the scope of the purpose, and the extent to which they serve their purpose. Hence this is the most perfect world possible. Nonetheless it contains evil. As Kant states the Leibnizian position, God desires a world without "irregularities and imperfections, which upset those who are of good disposition"; but he cannot have what he wants (17.233; *TP*, p. 79). He can only examine the possibilities spread out before him and then choose, balancing the goods and evils of one world against those of another. He is, Kant says, like a sailor forced either to throw some of his freight overboard or to lose his whole ship (17.236; *TP*, p. 81). Unable to alter the possibilities that determine what entities can be united in what ways, God chooses the actual world, knowing prior to its creation that it will not be everything he wants it to be.

The problem with Leibniz's view, as Kant sees it, is not that it fails to excuse God from willing evil. The problem is that it is incompatible with the important claim that God is infinite and independent of everything outside himself. What can bring it about, Kant asks, that entities cannot be united into a systematic whole, even though their perfections taken singly must win God's approval? It seems on this view that there is some sort of fatality controlling God (17.236–7; *TP*, pp. 81–2). Like many a theological voluntarist, Kant thinks this simply unacceptable. But he is not trying to defend a conventional voluntarist position. He aims to defend Pope's thesis, against Leibniz.

Pope put the essential point in a famous couplet:

20 For what Kant might have known of Leibniz's writings, see Chapter 12.i, note 5.

> And, spite of Pride, in erring Reason's spite,
> One truth is clear, "Whatever is, IS RIGHT."

In the German translation by Brockes, used by the academy and by Kant, Pope is made to say that everything that is, is *good*. He thus apparently denies what Leibniz allows, that there is any evil.[21] And Kant thinks that Pope has a way to show the claim true. Making the *Essay on Man* into rather more of a technical treatise than seems plausible, Kant says that the perfection of Pope's system lies in the fact that he "even subjects every possibility to the dominion of an all-sufficient original Being; under this being things can have no other properties, not even those which are called essentially necessary, apart from those which harmonize together to give complete expression to His perfection" (17.233–4; *TP*, p. 80). God, in short, must determine the possibilities as well as the actual world.

In these fragments Kant does not say how this striking move – which Leibniz explicitly rejected (see Chapter 12.i) – would yield Pope's thesis that all is good. But the thought must be that perfection, or metaphysical goodness, is not, as it is for Leibniz, an objective feature of complex wholes. Perfection must rather be a relation between a will and what it brings about. A perfect entity must be one that perfectly reflects the will of the being who created it. Leibniz's project fails because he holds that God's initial will is for complete good and then admits that the independent possibilities rule this out. Hence the created world thwarts its maker's will. There can be a perfect world, then, Kant thinks, only if God grounds possibilities so that nothing he creates can counter his will.

Kant used the thesis that God grounds possibility in his 1755 *New Elucidation of the First Principles of Metaphysical Cognition* (1.395–6; *TP*, pp. 15–17). He elaborated it at greater length in the essay dated 1763, *The Only Possible Argument in Support of a Demonstration of the Existence of God*.[22] In the later essay Kant also makes quite explicit the claim suggested in the early fragments about the relational nature of perfection. He remarks that although he uses the idea of perfection in an

---

21   Alexander Pope, *Essay on Man* I.293–4. The translation by Brockes (1740) reads as follows:

> *Trotz unserm Geist, der öfters irrt, trotz unserm Stolz und Übermuth,*
> *So ist die Wahrheit offenbar: das alles das, was ist, ist gut.*

22   The essay was written and actually published in 1762. See *TP*, p. lix. Kant discusses the essay in the *Lectures on Philosophical Theology*, pp. 65–9, trying to work its argument into his critical framework. He also refers to it in his late ethics lectures, the *Metaphysik der Sitten Vigilantius*, 27.718, *LE*, p. 441, retracting the early claim to be considering a valid argument.

I am indebted to Paul Guyer for discussion of these points.

unconventional way, he does not do so lightly. He has devoted "careful investigations" to the concept, and has finally become convinced that in a proper understanding of it there is "a great deal capable of clarifying the nature of the mind, our own feeling, and even the fundamental concepts of practical philosophy." Allowing that the term "perfection" is used in a variety of ways, Kant has become convinced that the core meaning of the term, involved even in aberrant usages, "always presupposes a relation to a being endowed with cognition and desire" (2.90; *TP*, p. 134).

Kant's undeveloped suggestions about possibilities and perfection recall claims I have noticed by earlier philosophers. Descartes held the strong voluntarist thesis that God created essences as well as eternal truths. Crusius gave a relational account of "good," defining it in terms of willed choice, although he left perfection an objective quality, identifying it with causal power. He also denied that this is the best possible world and defended a form of voluntarism. But in the *New Elucidation* Kant makes clear his rejection of Descartes's view of God (I.396; *TP*, p. 17). And in a brief essay in 1759 he rejects both voluntarism and Crusius's attack on optimism. He argues in support of the anti-Crusian claim that there is a single best possible world; voluntarism he simply dismisses as not worth wasting time controverting.[23] He does not confront voluntarism head on in the *Possible Argument* essay either. But his new relational idea of perfection moves him a step in that direction.

God's will, Kant says, cannot be the sole aspect of his nature that grounds possibilities, because "a will always presupposes the internal possibility of the thing itself" that it wills. So it must be God's whole infinite nature – his understanding as well as his will or desire – that is the ground of possibilities. These two aspects of God collaborate in the determination of possibilities, because, as Kant says in an obscure sentence, "the same infinite nature is related to all the essences of things as their ground; at the same time it also has the relation of highest desire for the greatest consequences which are thereby given, and the latter [the desire] can only be fruitful if the former [the essences] are presupposed." God's desire to express his entire nature is anticipated in the way the possibilities are constituted. Kant makes this explicit in saying that "the possibilities of things themselves, which are given through the divine nature, harmonize with his great desire." And he adds emphatically that "goodness and perfection consist in this harmony" (2.91; *TP*, p. 135).

Pufendorf rejected the equation of being and goodness. Kant denies that reality and perfection are identical and explicitly rejects the Leib-

---

23   See "An Attempt at some Reflections on Optimism," 2.30, 33; *TP*, pp. 71, 75. Kant refers favorably to this essay in his *Lectures on Philosophical Theology*, p. 137.

nizian view that harmonizing many things into a unity would constitute perfection (2.90; *TP*, p. 134). What makes the world perfect is that it realizes God's desire. Kant thus replaces the Leibnizian conception of perfection with a conception modeled on Crusius's understanding of goodness (Chapter 20.v). He now takes perfection to be the relation between the conscious desire to bring some state of affairs into being and the existence of a state of affairs that fully realizes the desire.

In the *Possible Argument* essay Kant gives us an idea of how this would work out in a theodicy. He is considering, he says, mainly the course of natural events. In this realm it is plain that Pope's thesis, not Leibniz's, is true, since whatever is, is as a result of God's willing and so is perfect by definition. So "all the changes which take place in the world and which are mechanical in character and thus necessary . . . must always be good, for they are naturally necessary" (2.110; *TP*, p. 152). The problem of physical evil is resolved: there simply is none. Kant touches only very briefly on moral evil. He raises the question whether human freedom requires God to be constantly fixing up the world to keep it functioning harmoniously, and assures us that the statistical regularities appearing in large numbers of free actions show that this is not needed. Although he thinks that neither freedom nor the contingency of free acts is adequately understood, he is sure that "the laws of freedom" do not bring indeterminacy into the order and harmony of the world (2.110–11; *TP*, pp. 152–3).

Despite the sketchiness of the account of moral evil in the *Possible Argument* essay, Kant is moving in it toward the positions we have seen him holding by 1765. He has come to the point of conceiving of a kind of non-Leibnizian conscious agency which is not determined to action by anything outside itself, not even possibilities. God cannot be limited or determined by anything external, and yet God is moved to very determinate choices. In being so moved he cannot be guided by a preexistent goodness. A state of affairs can be good, Kant now holds, only if someone wills or desires it; and willing and desiring presuppose the possibility of the object of will or desire. So when God's nature grounds possibilities, it cannot do so by looking to something independently good for guidance.

Second, a clear and definite problem emerges for Kant. How, without appealing to consequences, does God decide what essences to create? A traditional voluntarist might have said, with Descartes, that God must be incomprehensible here.[24] But as the "Reflections on Optimism"

---

24   Cf., e.g., the remark in the Conversation with Burman, *Writings* III.348: "we must never allow ourselves the indulgence of trying to subject the nature and operations of God to our reasoning."

(2.29–35; *TP*, pp. 71–6) makes clear, Kant rejects voluntarism.[25] He thinks that there must be a principle at work in the divine nature, and indeed only one principle; but he gives us no idea of what it might be (2.125–6; *TP*, p. 166). Whatever it is, however, it must allow God's creation to be the outcome of his own inmost nature. It must explain how God acts – and God acts autonomously.

iv. *Theodicy and freedom*

Kant's statement in 1763 that freedom is not adequately understood marks a change in his thinking. Earlier he held a definitely Wolffian view of freedom. But one of his first major works contains the makings of a problem with this view of freedom; and Kant's continued brooding about theodicy may have led him to want to revise it. The problem emerges in the *General Natural History and Theory of the Heavens* of 1755, written during the period when Kant was thinking about Pope and Leibniz.

In its scientific aspect the *Natural History* is an attempt to show that a mechanistic account can be given of the formation of the entire system of heavenly bodies. Kant's famous hypothesis is that the particles of matter are so constructed as to group themselves into larger and more complex units, and then to separate. This is an antioccasionalist view.[26] God is active in creating the individual atoms; but he has so made them that over infinite time they form themselves into countless galaxies and solar systems and then undo themselves, in an endless and sublime spectacle of orderly change. Newton's laws give the rules according to which the atoms move. Without invoking knowledge of the inner essence of the atoms, the laws thereby explain how their internally determined motions generate the great beauties, utilities, and harmonies of the natural world, so stressed by proponents of the argument from design.[27] Such harmonies do indeed yield proofs of God's existence, Kant says, all the more so since they emerge from an untended mechanism. They make evident

> that the essential characteristics [of nature] cannot possess any independent necessity, but that they must have their origin in a single under-

---

25 In his ethics lectures as recorded by Herder just a little later, Kant says that to require obedience to God simply because God wills it is to make him into a despot (27.9; *LE*, p. 5).

26 Kant is opposed here not only to Malebranche but to Descartes, who thinks it is absurd to attribute to the particles of matter properties enabling them to attract one another and so to influence what is happening at a distance. Letter to Mersenne, April 20, 1646, in *Writings* III.285.

27 Cf. *Distinctness* 2.286; *TP*, p. 259.

standing. . . . There is, then, a Being of beings . . . from which nature
derives its origin, including the very possibility of the essence of its determinations. (1.333–4)

The *Natural History* is thus a partial theodicy as well as a scientific
theory, and the thought of the theodicy fragments is embedded in it.

In this harmonious and useful universe, resulting from mechanical
laws and displaying God's construction of the possibilities so that all is
perfect, what of man? The natural world involves decay and destruction as well as growth and integration.[28] But humans are different. We
are, in the first place, immortal, and can hope that after "the transformation of our being" we will be "liberated from dependency on finite
things" and able to "find in fellowship with the Infinite Being the enjoyment of [our] true felicity" (1.321–2; *Natural History*, pp. 142–3). In the
second place we can be virtuous. And in the last two sections of the
Natural History, Kant speculates about the way in which humans and
others like us might be placed in the universe. It would be arrogant,
Kant says, to suppose there is no life like ours on other heavenly bodies:
that would be like lice on the head of a beggar supposing their sphere
was the only inhabited one. What will other rational beings be like?
Kant conjectures that there will be important differences (1.355–6).
Those closer to a sun than we will be in heavier and more rigid bodies,
those further away less burdened by the flesh.[29] Lighter beings will be
more intelligent, more moral, and consequently longer-lived than heavier ones. We on Earth, he says, are midway between the very light
inhabitants of Jupiter and the much heavier ones of Mercury. So we are

28 In the *Possible Argument* essay, Kant expressly singles this out as an occasion
for declaring his commitment to his new principle of perfection: "Even if, as Newton
maintained, it is naturally inevitable that a system such as the solar system will
eventually run down and arrive at a state of complete stagnation . . . I would not
follow him in adding that it is necessary that God should restore it again by means of
miraculous intervention. For, since it is an outcome to which nature is of necessity
destined as a result of its essential laws, I assume from this that it is also good"
(2.110n; *TP*, p. 152n). Here Kant engages with one of the arguments in the Leibniz-
Clarke correspondence and tries to reconcile Leibniz and Newton. The *Natural History* had already tried that reconciliation on a larger scale. Several of the earliest of
the *Reflexionen* on religion show that Kant continued to worry about special intervention by God and the meaning of providence in its absence. See 19.617–23, nos. 8081
and 8082.

29 Kant was not the first to speculate about the physical features of inhabitants
of other planets. Wolff in his *Elementa Mathesos Universae* had tried to estimate the
height of the beings who live on Jupiter by calculating the size of eye needed to cope
with the brightness of sunlight there, and then inferring what size body would
accommodate such eyes. I owe this point to Barber 1955, p. 153n.

in a middle position: tempted by the flesh, we are still able to resist its solicitations by the exercise of our intelligence.

Kant refuses to speculate about whether we will ever be wholly rid of temptation and the vice that comes from it. But he ends by remarking that he cannot believe the immortal soul will always be confined to earth, a minuscule corner after all in an infinite universe. Perhaps after death we will get to gratify some of the curiosity roused in us by the thought of the immensity of the world and become space travelers.[30] Will we not at least be able more fully than on earth to get beyond all concern for finite things, and find satisfaction simply in pleasing the highest being? Kant disclaims any knowledge, but goes on to say:

> In fact when one has filled one's mind with such considerations and with what has just been said, then the sight of a starry sky on a cheerful night gives a sort of pleasure which only noble souls can feel. In the universal stillness of nature and peace of the senses, the buried power of knowledge of the immortal soul speaks an unnameable language, and yields concepts not yet unfolded, which may well let themselves be felt but not described. (1.367)[31]

These somewhat bizarre speculations make evident Kant's concern with the moral position of rational beings in an infinite Newtonian universe. They also suggest a problem for Kant's theodicy. Can there be a moral world that, like the physical world, is the result of the independent action of its constituent units? If souls are of a vastly higher order of value than physical things, as Kant holds in the *Natural History*, it surely cannot be that order and harmony emerge from the interaction of the latter but not of the former. By the time Kant read the Savoyard vicar's unhappy reflections on this question, he himself had been thinking about it for years.

The kind of order traditionally required in a theodicy is one in which the virtuous are rewarded with happiness, and the vicious are punished. In 1755 Kant was still thinking along the lines laid down by Christian Wolff, and the basic structure of Wolffian thought raises a problem about the emergence of that sort of order in the universe of the *Natural History*. Kant's Wolffian view of moral freedom, expounded in the *New Elucidation*, involves him in the difficulty. He rejects the idea that freedom could be simple indifference about the alternatives open to one. That would lead only to random behavior, and could not account for responsibility. Instead he proposes an account of freedom as

---

30   The contrast between this attitude toward the infinite spaces and Pascal's horrified dread of them is worth noting.

31   See Probst 1994 for discussion of this passage in connection with an extended examination of the counterpart at the end of the second *Critique*.

spontaneity, which he construes as acting from one's own perception of the good. "Spontaneity," says the Kantian figure in the discussion,

> is action which issues from an *internal principle*. When this spontaneity is determined in conformity with the representation of what is best it is called freedom. The more certainly it can be said of a person that he submits to the law, and therefore the more that person is determined by all the motives posited for willing, the greater is that person's freedom. (1.402; *TP,* pp. 25–6)

It is possible, on this view, that the virtuous are always happy. Wolff certainly thought they were. But in the universe of the *Natural History* a problem remains. It is that the chances of becoming virtuous are not equal. Agents who are more intelligent, or who, on Kant's view, are embodied in less dense matter, have a much better chance of correctly perceiving the good and of achieving virtue and its rewards than the less intelligent, or denser. Surely no one merits being created more or less intelligent, or being born in either the denser or the less compact parts of the universe. Kant knew Crusius's trenchant remark that Wolffian freedom renders virtue a matter of luck, and he could not have overlooked Rousseau's insistence on the importance for theodicy of believing that God rewards virtue. Yet on the Wolffian view Kant held in 1755, there would be an arbitrariness in God's actions that would render it impossible to justify his ways to man. Nor would this be removed even if the statistical regularities of actions done under the laws of freedom permit us to assert that in other respects the moral world is orderly and harmonious.

Kant thus seems morally driven to find a new account of freedom; and he may have seen a suggestion of one in Rousseau's declaration that "obedience to a law one has prescribed for oneself is freedom" (*Oeuvres* III.365; *Contract* I.viii). God prescribes a law for himself; and Kant's new view of God's way of deciding how to constitute possibilities opened up a way for him to handle the moral side of the problem of theodicy. Attributing moral evil to man's free will is, of course, as old as St. Augustine. But Kant is moving toward a new idea of the relation of will to good. He no longer thinks that the will pursues only what is presented as good. That view raised the problem that Anselm faced in considering the fall of the Devil (see Chapter 2.iii). Kant avoids it by adopting what is, in effect, Anselm's solution. We can indeed will what we think good; but we can also will in accordance with a moral law. Moral evil, then, cannot be due to ignorance of what is already good or bad. What comes from God's decisions is necessarily perfect: analogously, everything resulting from autonomous choices of humans would necessarily be morally good. And if the human will, like God's will, is not necessarily determined by external factors, then our exercise of our will is our own responsibility. If we are not always good, we cannot call in nature as an excuse.[32]

v. *Reason and sentiment*

Kant's early Wolffian orientation as well as his thoughts on possibility and perfection do not suggest that he would have had a sentimentalist bias when he began to consider morality. Yet the remarks I quoted in the first section from essays Kant wrote in the early 1760s suggest a strong sentimentalist bent. What are we to make of it?

German translations of Hutcheson's two early books on ethics were published in 1762, and Kant owned copies of them.[33] His prior explorations of the idea that perfection and goodness require a relation to will or desire might have led him to see Hutcheson as thinking along similar lines. I argued in Chapter 16.iii that Hutcheson attributes moral distinctions in the human world to the sentiment with which we react to certain facts about motivation. He does not suggest that in so reacting we are perceiving, however confusedly and indistinctly, any unique moral property of the motives to which we react. The moral feeling that we are caused to have by noticing benevolence simply brings moral distinctions into a world otherwise without them. Kant might well have found this a tempting way in which to develop his own view, except that, unlike Hutcheson, he began by considering how God decides on possibilities and actualities. God could not have made his initial decisions about possibilities out of a reactive feeling, since there could be nothing determinate for him to react to. It seems unlikely, then, that Hutcheson would have led Kant to think that moral judgments result from feeling rather than reason.

In the *Illustrations on the Moral Sense*, Hutcheson elaborated on another point of equal significance – the difficulty of showing how reason alone could move us to act (Chapter 16.iv). Kant plainly felt the force of the problems Hutcheson displayed in the work of Clarke and other intellectualists, and it is these that moved him closest to sentimentalism.[34] In the early *Observations on the Beautiful*, his Hutchesonian assertions are most marked when he is discussing "the grounds of motivation" (2.221; *Observations*, p. 66). He suggests that "vices and moral crimes" can be "tested by reason" (2.212; p. 53). But he discusses moral-

---

32   Kant considers only much later, in *Religion within the Limits of Reason Alone*, the problem of why we fail to make the free choices we ought: see 6.39–40, 44–1, 83; *Religion*, pp. 34–5, 40–4, 78.

33   Warda 1922, p. 50. Hutcheson's late *System* was also translated, by Lessing, but Kant did not own a copy.

34   Here I follow Henrich 1957.

ity only as it affects the beauty or sublimity of character. True virtue, he thinks, "is alone sublime," but it is rare (2.215, 227; pp. 57, 74). And it is motives that are the problem. After saying that moral principles are not speculative rules but the awareness of the feeling of the dignity of human nature, Kant goes on to discuss other motives available for those who lack this feeling. Such people, who form the majority, can be brought to act with a semblance of morality either out of sympathy with others and a desire to please them, or out of a sense of honor, a concern for what others will think of them. They may be admirable in various ways, but they are nonetheless not sublime because they are not virtuous (2.217–20; pp. 60–3).

Kant shows far more awareness here of the richness of human feeling than those who read only the later formal ethical writings usually give him credit for. Admitting the existence of a variety of unselfish and even noble motives, he nonetheless worries about their inconstancy and the fact that most of them can easily lead us to act wrongly. Only a strong feeling of universal affection can control more specific generous feelings and thus enable us to act justly; and "as soon as this feeling has risen to its proper universality, it has become sublime, but also colder" (2.216; *Observations*, p. 58). The "principles" for which Kant expresses admiration here are thus cold and unchangeable as well as universal in application. Kant is indeed a sentimentalist about motivation in this work, but the sentiment he appeals to is a very rational one.

Kant has no occasion, in the *Observations on the Beautiful*, to discuss the principle by which we judge what is just or unjust; and we can see from the other major work he wrote at the same time that he did not have a clear idea of what it might be. In 1762 he entered a Berlin Academy competition with an essay on *The Distinctness of the Principles of Natural Theology and Ethics* (*TP*, pp. lxii–lxiii). The scant four paragraphs he gives to morality contain his first published effort to deal explicitly with principles of moral judgment (1.298–300; *TP*, pp. 272–4). It is significant that although he thanks Hutcheson for starting us toward some "lovely observations," he concentrates on what he calls, in a most un-Hutchesonian manner, "the primary concept of obligation." His compact and not wholly perspicuous discussion is framed by the disagreement between Wolff and Crusius about the concept. Their views were being expounded by popularizers like Johann Christoph Gottsched, whose Wolffian *Erste Gründe der gesammten Weltweisheit* went through some eight editions from the 1730s to the 1780s, and Christian Fürchtegott Gellert, a beloved university teacher whose edifying lectures on Crusian morality were published posthumously in 1770. Kant himself taught from the Wolffian manuals of Alexander Gottlieb Baumgarten, and there were many other textbooks that retailed, or, like August Friedrich Müller's, mixed in various degrees, the opposing views of the two major German thinkers of the midcentury. Kant was trying to get beyond them.

He does not claim to get very far in the *Distinctness* essay. On the contrary, he begins by saying that he aims to explain why we do not understand the concepts of free action and justice as they are in God or "even when they occur in ourselves" (2.297; *TP*, p. 271). The topic of the essay is the attainability of certainty about basic principles. Kant holds that both formal and material principles are required in all full demonstrations (2.294–5; *TP*, pp. 268–9). What principles might give us certainty, then, in morality?

Kant rejects one kind of basic principle out of hand. Nothing asserting the necessity of a means can be a first principle of morals. The necessity of means, in fact, "does not indicate any obligation at all." Only a principle of *necessitas legalis,* legal necessity, could be a principle of moral obligation. The term is Crusius's.[35] And Kant takes a further Crusian step. Still thinking in terms of means and ends, he says that obligation exists only for acts that are "subordinated to an end which is necessary in itself." This suggests, as Crusius held, that obligation depends on an end that is independent of the agent's own desires. But Kant does not quite say this. When he shows us what might serve as foundations of moral knowledge, he uses both the Wolffian and the Crusian principles as examples. Either "do the most perfect" or "obey God's will" could be basic as long as each commands acts for their own sake and not as means. This kind of rule must be indemonstrable, Kant adds, because only practical propositions concerning the necessity of means can be proved true – and then, of course, only on the hypothesis that one accepts the end.[36]

At this point Kant abandons Crusius and declares the Wolffian principle to be the first formal principle of action. How, then, are we to give it the content it needs, the details about what is perfect? Kant says we must call on feeling, because feeling is our mode of experiencing the good. He also says that the immediate ugliness of opposing God's will provides another material principle, which must, however, be subordinated to the formal principle of perfection. It is in connection with such material first principles that "Hutcheson and others" have given us a starting point, which they call moral feeling (2.298–300; *TP*, pp. 272–4).

The *Distinctness* essay thus plainly shows that Kant was considering sentiment as the source of part of the grounds for moral judgment, and

---

35 See Crusius, *Anweisung,* or *Guide,* 162, p. 301, discussed in Chapter 21.vi.

36 Kant here seems to think that the principle of using means to an end is provable because analytic, and that moral principles do not identify the predicate and the subject.

not only, as the *Observations on the Beautiful* suggests, as a motive. Yet the way in which feeling is allowed to contribute to our guidance is significant. Kant is now saying that a feeling of good, which would naturally arouse desire, must be subordinated to a formal principle that provides the necessity involved in moral obligation but by itself cannot yield specific guidance. He is not allowing the feeling of the good to be our guide by itself, as Rousseau's vicar sometimes seems to do. In placing formal constraint on these feelings, he is responding to a problem about the role of feeling in morality that comes directly from Rousseau.

The problem is one to which he expressly adverts in the lectures on ethics attended by Herder in 1764. "It is often difficult," Herder reports him as saying, "to distinguish the natural from the acquired conscience. Much that is acquired is taken for natural" (27.42; *LE*, p. 18). Rousseau's vicar tells us that conscience is an infallible guide, but then says that he must make us "distinguish our acquired ideas from our natural sentiments" (*Oeuvres* IV.599; *Emile*, p. 289). Human nature, Rousseau thinks, is so transformed and corrupted by its historical development that "none of us knows this first nature any more" (IV.407–8; p. 151). The vicar allows that one must "know how to recognize" conscience when it speaks, and that because it speaks to us in nature's language, "which everything has made us forget," there are very few who hear it (IV.601; pp. 290–1). It may be, as Rousseau says, that "the heart receives laws only from itself" (IV.521; p. 234); but if the heart is corrupt, how can its responses reliably guide the actions of even the simplest peasant?

Kant shared for quite some time the belief of Hutcheson and Rousseau that reason alone, as traditionally understood, cannot move us to action.[37] But feeling by itself could not have seemed adequate in explaining how each agent can play an appropriate part in constituting a moral world. Feelings, Kant thinks, especially our corrupted ones, vary too greatly from person to person and from time to time to be the source of moral order. Only reason is able to yield the necessities required in the laws of a world. But this kind of reason must be equally accessible to everyone; and it must have the immediacy of feeling, while being more than feeling. The rational faculty at work here must be also able to move us as well as to show us the paths we ought to follow. It must therefore be as much a part of us as the passions and desires it is meant to correct and control. But it must somehow be a deeper part of us, a part of "the

---

37   This is clear in the early Notes, as I indicated earlier. In the first *Critique* Kant says that without a future life in which virtue is rewarded, we would have to consider moral laws as "empty figments of the brain" which could not be "springs of purpose and action." *Pure Reason* A811–13 = B839–41.

unchanging *nature* of man" as Kant put it in announcing his lectures for 1765 (2.311; *TP*, p. 298). Like freedom, it cannot be bound in the network of time and change. A reason such as this must exist, because without it no account can be given of the distinctive obligations that constitute morality. But what explanation can be given of it?

vi. *Morality and the two worlds*

If Kant had no sure answer to this question, he at least had a conjecture. He published it for the first time in 1766 – as a joke. It occurs in his sardonic examination of Swedenborg, the *Dreams of a Spirit-Seer.* Nothing can be known about spirits, Kant roundly asserts, adding that we hardly even know what the word *Geist* means (2.320; *TP*, p. 307). He also says quite firmly that we would do well to treat people as mentally ill if they make any claims about spirits, rather than argue with them (2.348; *TP*, p. 335). Despite this, however, and as if to show us how easy it is to generate plausible fantasies in this realm, he sketches a view of the spirit world and its relation to the world we perceptibly inhabit.

What makes the view plausible, Kant says – so plausible that it tempts even him – is that there is *life* in our world, and spirit must be its principle. Now life consists "in the inner capacity to determine oneself by a power of choice [*nach Willkür*]" (2.327n; *TP*, p. 315). We should think of spirits, then, as acting voluntarily, and since they cannot occupy space, they must all be in immediate communication with one another, forming an immaterial world. If an intelligent spirit were in contact with the right kind of matter, that would form a person, while nonintelligent spirits bound to matter might form animals or even plants (2.330–2; *TP*, pp. 317–19). And at this point, in a jocular passage, Kant throws caution to the winds. Why, he asks, should I be concerned with proving what I say? Why not assert, in the best academic tone, that all this is as good as proved, or that it will be proved some day? That saves the trouble of thinking! (2.333–4; *TP*, p. 320). And he forthwith gives us his view.

Spirits, he asserts, are regularly in touch with the bodily world. This may explain the fact that "among the forces which move the human heart, some of the most powerful seem to lie outside it." We cannot think of our selfish needs without "feeling ourselves bound and limited by a certain sensation" that makes us attend to the fact that something like an alien will is active within us and must agree with what our desires prompt us to do before we can act on them. "This is the source from which the moral impulses take their rise," Kant says, which "often incline us to act against the dictates of self-interest." Kant specifies the moral impulses as "the strong law of duty, and the weaker law of benevolence," his way of referring to the perfect and imperfect duties of the Pufendorfian tradition.[38] Thus we learn that "in our most secret motives we are dependent on the rule of the general will," which brings about, in the realm of thinking beings, a moral unity and a systematic constitution according to purely spiritual laws. When Newton called the mutual attraction of particles "gravity," he pointed to a real cause, without getting into metaphysical disputes about its nature. If we call the alien check we feel on selfish action "moral feeling" we will in the same way be naming without explaining what we experience within us (2.334–5; *TP*, pp. 321–2).

Kant finds these ideas charming, not least because they help us remove the apparent disorder that exists in the moral world, and with it the disparity between the moral and the physical worlds. The latter arranges itself in order, according to the laws of matter; and if these speculations are true, we can see how the moral world would have a similar order. For the morality of an action would be purely spiritual, and its real effects would be perceptible in the world of spirits. Then, even in this life, man's moral condition would immediately determine his occupying an appropriate place in the universe, although his doing so would not be visible during our earthly life. But the reward coming to the good after death would be a result of the continuity of life, and would thus not require any special divine intervention in the workings of the universe. Kant thinks this a most desirable feature of the view (2.335–7; *TP*, pp. 322–5).

Well, it was not meant seriously. But joke or not, we tend to read it now in the light of what we know of Kant's mature views. The extent to which it carries forward his earliest speculations is equally striking. Looking back to Leibniz's kingdoms of nature and grace, it elaborates Kant's long-standing effort to see morality and what it presupposes as part of a theodicy. The lightly sketched metaphysical view in it responds to the problems of disorder in the moral world that Rousseau's vicar voiced. It continues Kant's attempts to understand moral feeling, using not so much the Hutchesonian version of it as another one, hinted at in a Note: "The moral feeling is the feeling of the perfection of the will" (136.16; 109.5).[39] Much more clearly than the earlier writings, it shows that although Kant thinks, as Hutcheson did, in terms of a moral world, he refuses to accept Hutcheson's deterministic naturalism about

---

38 For brief discussion of the development of Kant's thought on this issue see Chapter 23.vi and note 26.

39 See also 147.10, 118.1: "The inner sense, if it is adduced as a logical principle of judgment of moral law, is an occult quality; if as a power of the soul whose ground is unknown, a phenomenon." Both these Notes suggest the difficulties of holding that Kant was a straightforward adherent of a "moral sense" theory of moral judgment.

it (see Chapter 16.iii). Where Hutcheson saw self-love and benevolence as the forces that, like Newtonian attraction and repulsion, keep the human world in order, Kant now puts in their place the moral force of a free spiritual world controlling the self-interested powers of those in the natural world.

Kant's early speculations equipped him well to try to think coolly about Rousseau's passionate claims. It was not only Rousseau's thesis about freedom and self-governance that led him toward the view of morality as autonomy. It was even more the moral conversion to honoring the common man's moral insights, worked in him by Rousseau's magical prose. He was convinced by the moral sense theorists that there is a grave problem about how reason can provide moral motivation; but his early Wolffianism and then Rousseau's stress on the corruption and variability of human feelings kept him from ever wholly accepting the idea that moral sentiments could guide us into creating an orderly moral world. Rousseau called for a transformation of the self to explain how a moral world could come into being. Kant thought the ordinary person should be honored even if he acted badly, and to explain why he tried to root morality in an unchanging aspect of human nature. In trying to make it explicit he invented a principle of self-governance that he thought was capable of explaining how we could give ourselves moral guidance. "To the extent that the will is capable of action it is a good," he says in one of the Notes,

> but this goodness can also be considered as the will alone. . . . [I]n great matters to have willed is enough[.] And this absolute perfection is called moral to that extent whether something results from it in actuality or not nor is it for this reason something indeterminate. (148.8; 110.21)

23

Kant in the history of moral philosophy

Stäudlin held that Kant single-handedly created a revolution in moral philosophy. "When Kant came on the scene," he said,

> it had become the ruling tendency in Germany to derive not only morality but religion and Christianity from the principle of happiness. Everyone started with the natural drive to happiness and found in it a guide to all duties and virtues . . . Kant let his dissatisfaction with this be known in 1763. . . . Since the year 1785 [with the publication of the *Foundations*] he has begun a new era in the history of moral philosophy . . . a revolution in the philosophical investigation of morality.[1]

Stäudlin's belief, and ours, that Kant was a profound innovator is by no means unwarranted, but his statement is less than helpful in showing exactly where and how he altered moral philosophy. Numbers of philosophers had indeed claimed that happiness would guide us to all duties and virtues. But Kant was not revolutionary in rejecting such views. As we have seen, and as Stäudlin knew perfectly well, others, even in Germany, had done so.[2] Stäudlin was a Kantian, trying to ensure recognition of his master's originality. I hope to be somewhat less partisan in discussing what Kant did with the problems and options that his predecessors and contemporaries considered part of moral philosophy.

1 Stäudlin 1822, pp. 960–1. The 1763 publication to which Stäudlin refers is the *Distinctness* essay, discussed in the previous chapter. The essay was in fact not published until 1764; see *TP*, p. lxiv. For a different estimate of Kant, see the English historian Blakey, who thinks that continental thinkers on the whole have "a disposition to adopt extravagant theories, and wild and fanciful conjectures," and that Kant is totally unintelligible: "if it were possible to extract all the verbal jargon of the schools, from the Christian era down to the fifteenth century, into one book, it would come far short of the obscurity of the *Critical Philosophy*." Blakey 1833, II.299, 313.

2 Stäudlin 1822 himself notices Gellert's Crusian lectures just a few pages earlier, at p. 954.

It is quite unlikely that Kant had read all of the material I have so far discussed. I find no evidence, for example, that he had read Pufendorf or that he knew Malebranche's *Traité de morale*. Brucker's massive history of philosophy was the source of much of his knowledge of the past of his subject, but Brucker scants ethics in favor of religious thought, metaphysics, and theories of knowledge, and has much less to say about modern moral theorists than about the ancients. Nonetheless Kant shows familiarity with most of the issues of the period from Montaigne to himself. When his own contributions changed the terms of discussion, it was not by accident.

i. *Equality with God*

The Kantian conception of morality as autonomy was not invented just out of the blue. Kant was raised on the Wolffian view that knowledge can make at least some of us self-governing, and in the writings of Rousseau as well as the British moralists he had seen richer and more egalitarian conceptions of self-governance. His own work emerged from consideration of several alternatives to earlier conceptions of morality as obedience. Those conceptions were almost without rivals until the late seventeenth century. They had two essential components. One concerns the proper human stance in relation to God. As created beings we are required to show deference and gratitude as we obey our Creator's commands, which cover morality as well as religious worship. The other concerns human moral abilities. Most people are unable to think well enough to give themselves adequate moral guidance; most people are also too weak-willed and too strongly driven by their desires and passions to behave decently without credible threats of punishment for transgression and promises of reward for compliance. The majority, therefore, must defer to the exceptional few whom God has enabled to understand, follow, and teach his moral orders. And even these few, like everyone else, must live their lives in humble submission to their ruler, God.

Philosophers working out conceptions of morality as self-governance made repeated efforts to overthrow both of these assumptions. It is artificial to separate the debates about theology from those about moral psychology, but it is useful. I begin with the more theological aspects because, as I argued in the previous chapter, that is where Kant began.

In earlier chapters I have argued that controversies over voluntarism, the doctrine that God creates morality by a fiat of will, were central to the development of modern moral philosophy. Because of its importance in the theologies of Luther and of Calvin, and in the philosophical thought of Descartes, Hobbes, Pufendorf, and Locke, the issues voluntarism raised could be avoided only by unbelievers like Hume, the radical French thinkers, and Bentham. Everyone else held that God must somehow be essential to morality. Those opposed to the voluntarist explanation of God's role in it were united in their *moral* rejection of what the theory implied about the kind of community that is possible between God and human beings, and consequently among ourselves. Voluntarism, they held, makes it impossible for us to love God. Hence it excludes a central Christian moral requirement. And if love of God is impossible, then the common moral understanding of our relations to one another is unavoidably affected. A morality of tyranny and servility can be avoided only if God and man form a moral community whose members are mutually comprehensible because they accept the same principles.

The opponents of voluntarism thus had to show that morality involves principles that are valid for God as well as for us. God and we must be able to have a common understanding of the rationale or point of the principles as well as of the actions they require. As the work of Cumberland, Leibniz, Clarke, and Price makes clear, the only principles that seemed capable of satisfying this requirement are so abstract that they are, in effect, principles that spell out the essential conditions of practical reasoning as such. The antivoluntarists also had to explain how we and God can have relevantly similar motivation for action of the required kind; and the motivation must be such that, in acting as we ought, we, like God, are acting freely. Finally, because the critics of voluntarism agreed with their opponents that the denial that God is essential to morality is tantamount to atheism, they had to provide an explanation of how God can be indispensable in sustaining morality even though he is not its creator.

A remark in the preface to the *Foundations* gives us a telling indication of Kant's alliance with the antivoluntarists. Kant says that it is "self-evident" (*leuchtet von selbst . . . ein*) from the common ideas of duty and of the moral law that there must be a pure moral philosophy, independent of anything empirical.[3] Everyone will admit, he says, that if there is a genuine moral law, then it "does not apply to men only, as if other rational beings had no need to observe it" (4.389; *Foundations*, p. 5).[4] If he did not know Pufendorf's specific denial that there is any law common to God and man (Chapter 7.vii), his study of Crusius and of Leibniz's *Theodicy* would have taught him that voluntarists would have

3   Earlier, in the first *Critique*, Kant had explicitly rejected voluntarism, saying that we may not regard moral laws as "accidental and as derived from the mere will of the Ruler" of the world. *Pure Reason* A818–19 = B846–47.

4   See also the comment in the student lecture notes, that "virtue is more to be imputed to us than to angels, since they do not have so many impediments thereto" (2.27.292; *LE*, p. 84).

denied these points. He might have argued for them; it is surely surprising that he could have thought them self-evident.[5] An unquestioned assumption that the moral community must include God would, however, make it seem self-evident to him that there must be a moral law that applies to all rational beings, not to humans only, and a pure a priori moral philosophy to explain it. Kant is plainly making that assumption.

Another indication of Kant's antivoluntarist moral stance is his attitude toward servility. As I pointed out in the last chapter, the early Notes show how strongly Kant objected to the thought of the dependence of one rational being on the commands and desires of another, seeing it as somehow contradicting our essential free agency. The mature Kant does more than condemn servility, as the antivoluntarists always do. He explains what is wrong with it. Humanity in our own person requires us to respect ourselves, and to pursue those ends which are our duties "not abjectly, not in a *servile spirit*," but always aware of our dignity "as a person who has duties his own reason lays upon him" (6.434–7; MM, pp. 230–2).

If these are small pointers to Kant's agreement with the antivoluntarists, his account of the basic moral principle as a principle of pure practical reason, together with his thesis that the principle motivates rational agents to comply with it, make it plain that he stands with them on the central issues. His account of God's indispensability to morality is also common among the opponents of voluntarism. From Hooker through Leibniz and Wolff, they assign God the task of assuring us that we live in a morally ordered universe, one in which virtue is, ultimately, rewarded and vice punished. Only in such a world does morality make sense for free and intelligent but needy and dependent creatures. Kant describes God as having this function when he discusses the religious outlook that moral agents will have. They will believe in a Kingdom of God, "in which nature and morality come into a harmony, which is foreign to each as such, through a holy Author of the world." The antivoluntarists thought that they could give theoretical grounds for

5 The commentators, to the best of my knowledge, have not taken up the issue. Most do not discuss the preface in detail. Rüdiger Bittner gives it a careful examination, in "Das Unternehmung einer Grundlegung zur Metaphysik der Sitten," in Höffe 1989, pp. 13–30. He argues that neither Kant's exclusion of all empirical grounds for the moral law, nor his extension of its validity to all rational beings follows from the necessity he attributes to it; but he does not take up the claim that it is self-evident that there must be a pure moral philosophy and a pure morality binding all rational beings (p. 25). Ludwig Siep, in "Wozu Metaphysik der Sitten?" in Höffe 1989, pp. 31–44, also discusses the preface but, again, without considering the relevant lines.

their belief in divine order. Kant defends the older view on new grounds, resting the belief in divine order on the requirements of autonomy itself (5.128–9; *Practical Reason*, pp. 133–4).[6] But this radical reversal should not conceal the deep similarity of his position to the older one.

The Kantian morality of autonomy is decisively opposed to voluntarism because the rationality of the moral law that guides God as well as us is as evident to us as it is to him. But Kant's thesis that the moral law is the law of God's *will* shows clearly that he is also deeply indebted to the voluntarists.

In his early attempts at theodicy Kant worked with the voluntarist idea that to be good is simply to be what God wills. He gave up on the thought that God creates all possibilities; but he never abandoned the account of goodness inchoately expressed in the early fragments. In the mature theory this point emerges in Kant's identification of practical reason with a free will governed by the moral law. Here the early thoughts about creating possibilities are still at work. "The concept of good and evil is not defined prior to the moral law," he says in the second *Critique*, ". . . rather the concept of good and evil must be defined after and by means of the law" (5.62–3; *Practical Reason*, p. 65). It is not, he goes on to insist, "that the concept of the good as an object of the moral law determines the latter and makes it possible, but rather the reverse, i.e., that the moral law is that which first defines the concept of the good – so far as it absolutely deserves this name – and makes it possible" (5.64; p. 66).

To be good is, thus, to be willed by a will governed by the moral law. Our will is such a will, and so is God's. Kant transposes onto human practical reason the relation he tried to work out earlier between God and the goodness of the outcomes of his choices. His astonishing claim is that God and we can share membership in a single moral community only if we all equally legislate the law we are to obey. The mature Kant does not hesitate to make an explicit comparison between human agents and God. When we try to bring about a harmonious totality of all ends, a totality made possible and governed by the moral law, we may think of ourselves "as analogous to the divinity."[7] Leibniz held that in our own sphere we are little divinities, but he could not have accepted Kant's theory that will originates morality. Crusius flatly denied the Leibnizian claim that we are God-like; and he would have been out-

6 Unlike Clarke and others who argued for immortality on the ground that injustice in this life must be redressed in another, Kant rests our belief in immortality on the requirement that we approach moral perfection.

7 "Concerning the Old Saying: That May Be True in Theory, but It Won't Work in Practice," 8.280n; *Political Writings*, p. 65n.

raged by Kant's view that our will gives us a law that must also be law for God. Clarke would not have said that we can be God-like; but he thought that we are self-governing because we share moral knowledge with God and are moved by it as he is. For Kant, however, it is not knowledge of independent and eternal moral truth that puts us on an equal footing with God in the moral community. It is our ability to make and live by moral law. The invention of autonomy gave Kant what he thought was the only morally satisfactory theory of the status of human beings in a universe shared with God.

ii. *From self-governance to autonomy*

Montaigne opened the way to modern moral philosophy by rejecting every conception of morality as obedience that he knew, but his rejections were as personal as his style of governing himself. The psychological assumptions of the morality of obedience were more formally challenged as early as 1625, when Lord Herbert of Cherbury argued that everyone could know what morality requires. His argument was repeated, in essentials, by a number of later philosophers.[8] In the middle of the seventeenth century the Cambridge Platonists began to offer a more hopeful picture of our desires than that of Hobbes or the Calvinist Puritans. Later thinkers – some, like Shaftesbury, influenced directly by the Cambridge philosophers – elaborated on the point. Eventually a variety of new views of human moral psychology were worked out in order to underpin conceptions of morality as self-governance.

Herbert's argument is that since God will judge us by how well we comply with the requirements of morality, and since God is a just judge, he must have given all of us the ability to know what we are to do. Against the motivational assumptions behind conceptions of morality as obedience, philosophers argued that we are not selfish by nature, and that we have benevolent desires or the capacity to take disinterested satisfaction in the well-being of others, which is what morality requires us to forward. Clarke tried to move beyond the contingencies

8 See Barbeyrac, *Historical Account* II.3–4. J. G. Heineccius, whose treatise on natural law, first published in Latin in 1737, was translated into English by George Turnbull in 1743 has the same view: "Every principle of science must be true, evident, and adequate; wherefore the principle of science, with respect to natural law . . . must be evident, and that not only in this sense, that it is intelligible to the literate; but universally, to the unlearned as well as the learned, all being equally under obligation to conform themselves to the law of nature . . . a too subtle principle of natural law is suspicious, since all are . . . without excuse, even the illiterate, and those who are strangers to subtle refined philosophy, if they offend against the law of nature." Heineccius I.LXVIII, I.45–6. Crusius also uses the argument; and see Chapter 21, note 41, for Rousseau's appeal to something like it.

of desire by tying motivation directly to immediate awareness of the laws of morality. Price and Reid follow him in holding that everyone equally can know what morality requires and thus have some psychologically moving reason for acting properly. They do not, however, think that we give ourselves the laws of the morality we are to follow. Even if we need neither outside instruction nor outside motivation, our moral knowledge is knowledge of an order independent of us, and our psychology enables us to bring ourselves into conformity with it. We are self-governing, for these thinkers, but not autonomous.

Hume and Rousseau go beyond these views and move much further toward conceptions of morality as autonomy. Hume, omitting God entirely from his theory, and thinking of morality as "more properly felt than judg'd of" (*Treatise*, p. 470), has no place for arguments about equal abilities to know moral truths. He assumes, however, that the moral sentiment of approval and disapproval is present in everyone alike. Moreover everyone is moved, at least most of the time, by motives we approve, and when these fail a substitute for them, a "sense of duty," arises to fill the gap. We construct elaborate practices where we need them to enable our lives to run smoothly; these artifices generate their own motivation naturally; and although we speak of them as laws of nature, Hume reminds us that these are laws that we invent (*Treatise*, p. 543). We think and talk as if acts or people really have moral attributes, but Hume argues that this is simply because our moral feelings project themselves onto an otherwise neutral world (*Principles of Morals*, p. 294). In being moral, therefore, we are not following any external order. Rousseau goes even further toward portraying us as autonomous. Our own reason enables us to invent a response to a crisis in our previous, wholly natural mode of existence. When the social contract creates a new idea of the common good the thought activates in each of us an innate love that enables us to control our private desires and to act as moral members of a moral whole. We come to be free because we can break away from slavery to our natural desires and live under a law we have given ourselves.

Are these conceptions of morality as autonomy? Kant would not have thought so. On Hume's view we are wholly determined to feel and invent and act as we do. Whatever harmony exists in our common life is caused in it by a happily harmonious nature. Since the existence and the content of morality are determined by the whole of the universe of which we are parts, his theory would not, for Kant, make us fully autonomous. Rousseau's theory, given his beliefs in God, soul, and immortality, is not naturalistic. But it is in its Leibnizian way as deterministic as Hume's. For Rousseau, moreover, if we are autonomous, it is only as members of a special kind of society. We are not individually autonomous by nature. Like Hobbes, Rousseau thinks we do not have moral reasons for agreeing to the contract. But where Hobbes thinks that any ongoing society must be understood as having agreed to have a sovereign, Rousseau seems to think there can be societies – corrupt ones, to be sure – whose members have not moralized themselves by agreeing to a social contract. Moreover it is unclear exactly what moral guidance Rousseau's contract as such provides for its signatories. What Rousseau tells us about Emile does not help here. He shows us how Emile grows into personal self-governance but says nothing to indicate that his freedom gives him any new moral guidance. Rousseauian self-governance is empty as well as only contingently available.

Kant embeds his conception of autonomy in a metaphysical psychology going beyond anything in Hume or Rousseau. Kantian autonomy presupposes that we are rational agents whose transcendental freedom takes us out of the domain of natural causation. It belongs to every individual, in the state of nature as well as in society.[9] Through it each person has a compass that enables "common human reason" to tell what is consistent with duty and what inconsistent.[10] Our moral capacities are made known to each of us by the fact of reason, our awareness of a categorical obligation that we can respect against the pull of desire. Because they are anchored in our transcendental freedom, we cannot lose them, no matter how corrupt we become. Kant sees his theory as the only way to defend the conviction Rousseau gave him of the importance of honoring the common moral understanding.

iii. *Will and desire*

For Kant we can have no empirical understanding of the aspect of will that grounds our autonomy. As noumenal, it is ultimately inexplicable. At the same time the will is part of our psychological makeup; and in working out what it must be in order that it can be open to the moral law, Kant drew on elements from many of his predecessors.[11]

For Leibniz and Wolff the will is not a faculty different in kind from desire. It is simply the desire to attain the greatest perfection available. Its sole task is to compare the objects of differing desires. The comparison once made, the will is determined to move us toward the object

---

9 *Pure Reason* A810 = B838: "the moral law remains binding for every one . . . even although others do not act in conformity with the law."

10 Kant does not appeal to Herbert's argument about God's justice to show that everyone must have it. He may be suggesting that argument in his remark that "[w]e might have conjectured beforehand that the knowledge of what everyone is obliged to do and thus also to know would be within the reach of everyone" (4.404; *Foundations*, p. 20). But he may also mean that morality itself would not be fair were such knowledge not within the reach of everyone.

11 For a fuller account see Schneewind 1997b.

promising most perfection. This view of the single function of will is open to Leibniz and Wolff because they hold that desires and pleasures are simply confused and indistinct perceptions of perfection. They are thus not different in kind from cognitions, though they are cognitions focusing on different aspects of reality than those we think of as purely theoretical.

As early as 1764 Kant made remarks suggesting that he did not hold this position, and by 1770 he had worked out many aspects of his general rejection of the Leibniz-Wolff view of sensation.[12] A student in Kant's metaphysics class reported his opinion with admirable concision:

> Wolf wished to derive everything from the faculty of knowledge and defined pleasure and unpleasure [*Lust und unlust*] as action of the faculty of knowledge. He also called the faculty of motivation a play of representations, and so merely a modification of the faculty of knowledge. Here one thinks one has unity of principle . . . but this is here impossible. (28.674)

Kant thus sides with Locke in his understanding of pleasure and desire. Pleasure is an agreeable feeling, caused by external objects but not telling us anything about them (5.206; *Judgment* I.45). Desires are impulses toward things, caused by awareness of the things, but, again, not informing us of anything about what we are moved toward. Since neither pleasures nor desires are cognitions they cannot be either reasonable or unreasonable. Sometimes our feelings rise to such a pitch that they make us fail to compare the various pleasures and pains available to us, and to act without thinking (7.254; *Anthropology*, p. 122). Then our passions are unreasonable, not because they misrepresent the world, as the Leibnizians think, or are caused by false beliefs, as Hume holds, but because they make us fail to use reason to put them in perspective.

Leibniz and Wolff, taking as given a meaningful and harmonious universe, think that the desires and passions are implicitly orderly, and that simply increasing the distinctness of our thoughts will make that order more explicit. Kant holds no such view. Happiness, for him, comes from the gratification of our desires, which we can neither create nor (as Kant eventually came to admit) eradicate.[13] They do not natu-

---

12   See "On Sicknesses of the Head" 2.261, and the "Inaugural Dissertation" 2.394, *TP*, p. 387; 2.405, *TP*, p. 399.

13   Contrast 4.428; *Foundations*, p. 46, with 6.58, 28, 36; *Religion*, pp. 51, 23, 31. Kant does not become quite as enthusiastic about the passions as Descartes was. "[I]n examining the passions," he says, "I have found almost all of them to be good,

rally have any humanly meaningful order, even though they are part of the natural order. The natural disarray of the passions and desires is as much a given in Kant's ethics as the lack of order in sensation is in the theoretical philosophy. In the third *Critique* Kant draws a strong conclusion from this view. We cannot, he says, form any realizable idea of happiness, or of the complete gratification of our desires. Even if nature obeyed our every wish and our powers were unlimited, our idea of happiness is too wavering and fluctuating to allow us to attain what we think we seek. And even if we aimed at no more than satisfying "the true wants of nature in which our species is in complete and fundamental accord," what we mean by happiness would remain unattainable. "For [man's] own nature is not so constituted as to rest or be satisfied in any possession or enjoyment whatever" (6.430; *Judgment* II.92–3).

The first task of the will, for Kant, is to try to bring order into our desires, by accepting some as part of our happiness and rejecting others. For this Lockean task Kant thinks no firm rules can be given.[14] Egoism in morals, as propounded by Helvetius and La Mettrie, is therefore a hopeless enterprise. But there is a negative rule, the rule of morality. It is not, as the egoist's rules would be, an instrumental rule, but one that controls the ends proposed by desire. The will's second task is to see to it that this limiting rule is always followed.

Malebranche, Clarke, and Price held that morality cannot be rightly understood as directing us merely to bring about happiness or good. Believing that we are in fact moved by moral reasons as well as by desire-based reasons, they concluded that we must possess a faculty or power enabling us to choose between them. Kant may well not have known the ethical writings of any of them, but in Crusius he saw a theorist who was making their kind of point. He agreed with Crusius that the requirements of morality are incommensurable with those of prudence, that we can be moved by both, and that we must have a power of choice that enables us to decide which way to act.[15] He thus rejected an important aspect of the Leibniz-Wolff account of will – but not all of it. For Leibniz, the will, as the desire for the greatest available perfection, contains its own rule for making decisions. Leibniz thus differs from Malebranche and Locke, who placed our freedom in our ability to suspend choice and then simply to choose. For neither of them does the power of choice have its own inner directive; and in this their views resemble those of Clarke and Price, according to whom the will

and to be so useful in this life that our soul would have no reason to wish to remain joined to its body for even one minute if it could not feel them" (*Writings* III.300).

14   Cf. 6.215–16; *MM*, pp. 43–4.

15   Kant owned Maupertuis's work (see Warda 1922) and so could have been aware of his strong statement of the strict commensurability of all reasons for acting.

simply says yes or no. The Crusian will, however, has its own innate directives for governing practice. They are indeed drastically different from the single Leibnizian rule, strikingly foreshadowing the kind of complexity Kant attributes to practical rationality. But both Crusius and Kant agree with the Leibnizian view that the will is more than a simple power of accepting or rejecting a proposed motive.

Kant initially followed Crusius in his view of the structure of the power that enables us to be self-governing. He construed the will as the rational demand for consistency in action. Confronted with a clamorous desire, the will would test the moral acceptability of a proposal for satisfying it and provide an alternative motive to resist it if the proposal failed the test. In his later work he came to think he needed to add a power of choice – the *Willkür* – to the will as practical reason, the *Wille*. The power of choice enables us to decide between the call of desire and that of morality. Kant thinks we might have it even without having the kind of practical reason we have. It would function like the Clarkean will, enabling us to choose even where the alternatives are indifferent; in other cases its choices would be determined by the relative strengths of desires and passions. The will itself is neither free nor unfree. As pure practical reason, it provides us permanently with the option of acting solely on the reason which its own legislative activity gives us. The power of choice, which enables us to opt for morality or against it, is a free power. Because we can choose, we never have to accede to desires which, though certainly part of ourselves, are caused in us by our encounters with the world outside us. Kant has combined a Crusian will with the kind of freedom of indifference defended by Malebranche, Locke, and Clarke, in order to allow not only for spontaneity but for autonomy.

iv. *Natural law, obligation, and moral necessity*

Kant's view of the facts of human psychology ally him with the empiricists; and it is thus not surprising that the empiricist natural lawyers should have provided him with what he took to be the central problem concerning human sociability. He did not accept their solution; but he thought they were essentially right in seeing the issue of social conflict as the first problem for which morality had to be suited. The natural law theorists thought only a morality built around a specific concept of law and obligation would be serviceable. They ran into difficulties in explaining their concepts. Kant meant his own theory to clear up the difficulties. His proposed solution to the problems was so radical that it would have horrified the theorists from whose views he started.

One reason for taking Kant to have accepted the natural law prob-

Kant and moral philosophy

519

lematic of conflict is the fact that he makes the concept of moral law basic and defines other moral concepts in terms of it. In taking this view he breaks with Wolff as well as with Hutcheson; but the position is standard among the natural lawyers. Christian Thomasius, for example, in his explicitly Pufendorfian *Institutiones Jurisprudentia Divinae* of 1688,[16] comes very rapidly to a definition of law in terms of the command of a superior (I.I.28). He then goes on to define the concepts of duty (I.I.33), subjective right (I.I.82), obligation (I.I.134), just or right action (I.I.143), permitted and honorable action (I.I.145), and finally just person (I.I.153), all via the concept of law. Leibniz, by contrast, develops ethical definitions in a different order. For him love is prior to law and obligation. He starts with charity or love arising from knowledge and with this concept provides an account of law and obligation as needing no external legislator for their binding power. (See Chapter 12.iii.)

Kant's assertions about the empirical aspects of human nature give further evidence of his acceptance of the natural law problematic.[17] We are naturally prone to discord, Kant says in the *Anthropology*, and only reason enables us to move toward peace with one another. Our inclinations to be free from interference by others and our sexual desires might not lead to endless conflict, but the *"manias for honor, for power, and for possession"* must, since they can be gratified only in society, yet their very nature requires that we compete (7.322, 268; *Anthropology*, pp. 183, 135). In the essays on history Kant portrays humans as desiring and needing one another's company and support while at the same time resisting social control and tending to unlimited self-aggrandizement. Nature brings about the development of human capacities by means of mutual antagonism in society, Kant says, explaining that

[b]y 'antagonism' I mean the unsocial sociability of men, i.e., their propensity to enter into society, bound together with a mutual opposition which constantly threatens to break up the society. Man has an inclination to associate with others. . . . But he also has a strong propensity to isolate himself from others, because he finds in himself . . . the unsocial characteristic of wishing to have everything go according to his own wish. (8.20–2; *History*, p. 15)[18]

16 References are to book, section, and paragraph numbers of Thomasius, *Institutiones Jurisprudentia Divinae*.

17 For an extensive discussion of this aspect of Kant's views, see Wood 1991. I disagree with several points of interpretation in this work, but Wood's discussion of Kant's statements on the empirical data about human nature is excellent. Brender 1997 is a valuable discussion of the social and psychological difficulties that Kant thinks moral agents face in sustaining the world-view that they must hold.

18 See also "Conjectural Beginning of Human History," where the Rousseauian strain in Kant's historical thought is quite evident, 8.109–24, *History*, pp. 53–68. Cf.

The Grotians make law and obligation central to morality because they think humans are prone to conflict and that only obligations arising from laws backed by sanctions can control them. God's commands make certain acts *morally*, and not merely prudentially, necessary. We cannot treat them as showing us goods that we naturally desire and can attain if we obey. To do so would be to treat them as merely advice. How, then, are we to understand our motive to obey God's laws? Motivation, for all the natural lawyers, is tied to desire and that in turn to good. We know that goods and ills are connected to God's commands. The commands are laws; and laws are by their nature backed by sanctions. But if we obey God's laws only in order to avoid punishment, we hardly show that we have morally admirable characters. Morality then seems purely mercenary. A desire to show gratitude to God by obeying his commands might indeed move some people. But it plainly does not move everyone. May those who lack it say that they could not obey and in their inability find an excuse for their transgressions? In Chapter 7.v, I followed Pufendorf's efforts to deal with these problems, showing the difficulty he has in explaining a nonmercenary motive for moral obedience. I noted that although he appeals to a kind of reverence for God's command he has no theory of will adequate to account for it. And I suggested that this is in part because his theory of moral entities forces him to grapple, for the first time, with the problem raised for those who hold that morality requires a motive that takes us out of the natural causal order.

Kant, as I said, probably had not read Pufendorf, but he faces the same problem. He sees law and obligation as needing to be explained in terms of moral necessity, the concept that gave Pufendorf so much difficulty. Kant agrees with Leibniz that there are different kinds of necessity. But Leibniz's moral necessity, the necessity of using means to attain one of my ends, could not, on Kant's Crusian view, explain distinctively moral obligation. As I noted earlier, Kant thinks that all our desires for specific goods are contingent. Hence any such desire can be abandoned if the cost to us of pursuing it is too great. This enables us to escape from any particular means – ends obligation at our own good pleasure.[19] Being prudentially obligated is like being advised, leaving it up to the agent whether or not to pursue the end about which advice is

---

6.471, *MM*, p. 263: "Man is a being meant for society (though he is also an unsociable one)."

19   We have to pursue happiness, but we can always refuse to make gratification of a specific desire part of our happiness, just as we can refuse on moral grounds to accept a desire as a reason to act.

given.[20] With Crusius Kant held that this kind of hypothetical obligation does not capture what is essential to morality. But even Crusius's account does not satisfy Kant. For Crusius, distinctively moral duties arise from laws that God ordains in order to achieve *his* ends. As Kant sees morality, however, it is constituted by a law that binds regardless of *anyone's* ends. The distinction between hypothetical and categorical imperatives is thus Kant's, however close Crusius came to it.

Kant also saw that Leibniz's analytic necessity would be unsuitable for explaining the kind of necessity involved in morality. It was not until he worked out the idea of a priori synthetic necessity that he could think he had what he needed. The moral law, he could then say, constitutes a synthetic necessity in all rational wills, God's as well as ours. To finite agents the necessity appears in terms of the moral ought. Moral necessity is not causal necessity, so we can fail to do what it is morally necessary for us to do. The agent's own rational will thus performs the task for which the natural lawyers and Crusius brought in the will of God. It enacts the law that we have compelling justification to obey, regardless of our own contingent ends.

If the rational will might account for moral necessity and morally justifying reasons, Kant, alerted by Hutcheson, recognized the need to explain the motivating or exciting power of awareness of this necessity. He eventually solved the problem by introducing an a priori motive, respect. To do so, he had to make a fundamental break with the motivational theories of the perfectionists and to go well beyond Pufendorf. Respect is a motive that, unlike all others, is not oriented by or to the good. It arises necessarily from our own legislating of the moral law. If awareness of good provides motivating reasons to act, enacting the moral law does so as well. The point is central to Kant's ethics. For Leibniz and Hume, only desire can make us act. The availability of desire-based motives therefore dictates what morality can require.[21] Kant holds instead that "man's moral capacity must be estimated by the law" (6.404; *MM*, p. 205). He can do so because he thinks of practical reason as itself motivating.

The natural lawyers saw morality as a means of solving the problem posed by our unsocial sociability. Rousseau thought that the difficulties of living together in a purely natural condition, guided only by means – end reasoning, would force us into a new kind of practical rationality.

20   As I noted in Chapter 12.v, Barbeyrac had come close to pointing out exactly this difficulty in Leibniz's view.

21   "There is no passion . . . capable of controlling the interested affection, but the very affection itself, by an alteration of its direction." So Hume, explaining the motivational force behind justice; but the point is general (*Treatise*, p. 492).

We can be transformed into sociable beings by a contract requiring us to pursue happiness only in ways agreeable to everyone who accepts its terms. Kant thinks that what enables us to live together despite our quarrelsomeness is that we are, by our very nature, more than means – ends reasoners. Simply because we possess practical reason we can constrain our desires in the name of a law that requires the universal acceptability of our plans. Doing what the law says one must is as rational as doing what brings about something one wants. A motive not originating from an end is a necessary counterpart to a nonteleological law of human action. Kant thinks it takes both to make law prior to love, or, as we would say, the right prior to the good.

If the appeal to synthetic a priori necessity and to the a priori motive the moral law carries allows Kant to think he can solve the kind of problem about will that Pufendorf faced, it does so at a price the natural lawyers would not have wished to pay. Kant may have shown how to make obligation and moral necessity central to morality while preserving the freedom to disobey the law. But Kantian autonomy does not allow moral law to be constituted by the command of one rational being to another. Kant subverts natural law theory in the course of reworking some of its central tenets.

v. *Methods of ethics*

Butler and the intuitionists who followed him held that everyone just sees or knows what to do, in almost every case; but they offered no systematic method for obtaining moral knowledge. Kant holds that everyone can use the categorical imperative to reason out what they ought to do in particular cases, and to see also why they ought to do it. Bentham made the same claim for his greatest happiness principle, though he did not emphasize its availability to the common understanding as Kant did. They are, to the best of my knowledge, the first philosophers to make such claims.[22]

Those who held that most people are not able to do their own moral thinking had, of course, little incentive to seek such a method. Hobbes offered a formula "by which we may presently know, whether what we are doing be against the law of nature or not." It is summarized by the well-worn maxim, "Do not that to others, you would not have done to yourself," which Hobbes thought could be used by even the simplest

---

22   Paley objects to Grotian natural law theory that it does not serve the purpose of system of ethics, which is "the direction of private consciences in the general conduct of human life" (*Principles* ix). But though holding a principle like Bentham's, he says nothing about its use by individuals. He stresses instead the importance of general rules and habits of following them.

person (*De Cive* III.26). But Hobbes does not try to explain why the method succeeds in picking out acts that are made right by features other than the one the method uses. Hence, even if his method of ethics shows us the right act, it does not show us why the act is right. Consequently its users would have to take it on authority that it is a reliable method. Locke wanted plowmen and dairymaids to take their morals from the pulpit, Wolff from the professor; neither they nor Spinoza, who thought the common folk needed stories in order to grasp moral truth, offered to explain how ordinary people were to make the decisions of daily life in the absence of the authorities. Even Crusius, despite his insistence that we must each be able to see for ourselves what God commands us to do, does not think that there is a method showing everyone both what to do and why it is to be done. Conscience acts through a feeling which directs and motivates us, without showing us the reason for its directives. Scholars may be able to acquire clear knowledge of the essential perfections of God and man and then infer what we are to do, using the principle that God wills us to do what conforms to these essential perfections (*Anweisung*, or *Guide*, pp. 214–15, 226–7). But though the two methods always yield the same results, only one is available to everyone (see Chapter 20.vi).

Kant's method of ethics and the intuitionists' insistence that everyone can just see what morality requires bear on both moral and epistemological concerns. Morally, they are part of the effort to explain and justify the rejection of moralities of obedience. Epistemologically they are directed against moral skepticism. The intuitionists make a straightforward, old-fashioned claim to know first principles in the only way such principles can be known. Kant's own method is antiskeptical in a quite different way, one that links him not with the intuitionists but with the British sentimentalists. Shaftesbury, Hutcheson, and Hume all hold that we give rise to morality when we feel a special kind of approval of a desire or motive that we notice in ourselves or in others. I suggested that their position is a kind of response to Pyrrhonic skepticism, resembling Montaigne's own way of living with that view. Montaigne, I said in Chapter 4.ii, does not find it necessary to get beyond Pyrrhonic "appearances." Instead he responds to them in terms of what is most enduring within himself. His ruling form shows itself in his reaction to the way things seem to him – to the feelings that his desires, his reading, and his own experience arouse in him. Whatever constancy he achieves results from his ruling pattern, which is unlikely to be the pattern for others but which provides him with enough guidance to get him through life. In showing how an assessment arising from oneself of the various incentives one feels within oneself can replace knowledge of externally given principles and values, he was pointing to what I have been calling a method of ethics. If we must live within the appearances, we can find our way through them even without reliable belief about how things really are.

What Montaigne's ruling form enabled him to do was to assent to or reject some of the promptings he felt within himself. Malebranche, who, like everyone else, was a reader of Montaigne, holds that when we will, we consent to be moved by an existing desire or motive. Lockean suspense of willing concludes with a similar consent. So too does choice made by the will as Leibniz and Wolff see it. Crusius holds that we act only when the will connects its force with a desire. For these post-Montaignians, the consent is morally sound only if it is governed by a consideration external to the self. Malebranche's will should be guided by the Order shown in ideas in God's mind, Locke's by the laws of nature, Leibniz's by the objective degree of perfection, Crusius's by God's command. For Shaftesbury, Hutcheson, and Hume, however, moral virtue requires only the felt approval of a felt incitement to action. They offer what we might think of as a skeptic's method of ethics (see Chapters 14.v and vii; 17.ii). The skepticism they have in view is not Cartesian but Pyrrhonian – a form of skepticism that also concerned Kant.[23]

For Hutcheson and Hume, approval by the moral faculty makes certain motives virtuous; and it is quite possible that Kant read Shaftesbury as saying no more than that. Moral goodness, on that view, is not discovered by the moral faculty but constituted by it. The moral sense is then like the Pufendorfian divine will that creates moral entities. Although the world without the moral feelings would contain motives directed toward the benefit of others, it would contain no moral attributes. It is a neutral universe, and only our response to it makes it otherwise. If our approval is what makes some motives good, others bad, then we are not subject to error as we would be if we had to know an objective Order in God's mind, or an objective degree of perfection.[24] And if our own approval makes motives good, then, despite Hobbes, when ordinary people test proposed motives by the law, they are not using some secondhand criterion of morality given them by an authority. We can all determine what is right because our own feelings make it right.

Kant plainly agreed with this voluntarist aspect of sentimentalism although he rejected the sentimentalist account of approval. But the knowledge involved in Kantian morality as autonomy is knowledge of the self's own way of thinking. Like Clarke, Kant grounds his purely

23   Tonelli 1967, pp. 100–2, says that Kant would understand the skeptic as one who sets appearances against appearances.

24   Of course we may be mistaken about our own motives – as Kant thinks we are prone to be.

formal principle on the need to avoid self-contradiction; unlike Clarke –
and unlike any moral philosopher before him – he makes it the sole
principle of morals. What we test in using it is the self's desires. The
world by itself, whether we can know it as it is or whether we live only
in a realm of appearances, is not the source of moral guidance. For Kant
a moral world will result, if at all, from the guidance their inner constitution gives the agents who are its members.

vi. *Virtue, love, and perfection*

Like Butler and his intuitionist followers, Kant is committed to the
belief that commonsense moral beliefs are essentially sound. Unlike
Reid he does not explicitly claim that such beliefs are to be used as tests
of any proposed moral principle. But it is more important for him than it
is for Pufendorf or Spinoza or Bentham to show that most firmly held
commonsense moral convictions would be supported by his basic principle. He may not have been successful in meeting this challenge, but in
his *Metaphysics of Morals* and, with even more detail, in his lectures on
ethics, he certainly tried. After several changes of view he found ways
to incorporate virtue, love, and the quest for perfection into a basic
morality of law.

Like Hume, and unlike the perfectionists, Kant gave a major role to
his own version of the Grotian school's distinction between perfect and
imperfect duties. The distinction occupied him throughout his life, although he did not elaborate it in detail until the late *Metaphysics of
Morals*.[25] He uses it both to give a far fuller account of virtue than the
Grotians gave and to explain where love comes into morality.

In the *Foundations* Kant discusses the distinction between perfect and
imperfect duties only briefly. In a footnote he remarks that a perfect
duty is "one which allows no exception in the interest of inclination"
(4.421n; *Foundations*, p. 39n), thus suggesting that the sole special feature of imperfect duties is that we may carry them out or not, as we
prefer. Then he reformulates the distinction between the two kinds of
duty in terms of the difference between maxims that cannot be coherently thought as universal laws, and maxims that can be thought but

---

25   In what follows I am much indebted to Kersting 1982. For Kant's enduring
interest in the distinction, see the 1763 essay on "Negative Magnitudes," 2.182–4, *TP*,
pp. 221–3; the mention in *Dreams*, noted in Chapter 22.vi; *Reflexionen*, 19.10 (no.
6457), 17 (no. 6469), 30 (no. 6498), 51 (nos. 6517–6519), which are all quite early; 94
(no. 6582), 102 (no. 6597), 105 (no. 6603), 125 (no. 6653), 138 (no. 6709), 152 (no. 6760),
probably from the late 1760s and early 1770s; 261 (no. 7165), 308 (no. 7309), late notes.

not willed as laws (4.424; pp. 41–2).[26] At this point in his thinking, however, Kant does not discuss virtue, and he dismisses love as inclination or feeling, or as tender sympathy, in one sentence. It cannot be commanded. It must be replaced by "beneficence from duty," which is practical love (4.399; pp. 15–16). The love commandment of the New Testament, he thinks, would be conceptually incoherent if understood as requiring a feeling.

In the *Metaphysics of Morals* Kant presents a substantially altered view. In place of the one fundamental practical principle (in several formulations) of the *Foundations*, we now have two principles, one governing duties of law or justice (*Rechtspflichten*), the other duties of virtue or morality (*Tugendpflichten*). Legal duties require us to perform external actions, moral duties to have certain maxims. The principle of legal duties is that we are to act externally only in ways that allow "the freedom of the will of each to coexist together with the freedom of everyone in accordance with a universal law" (6.230; *MM*, p. 56). The principle of virtue is that we are to "act according to a maxim of *ends* which it can be a universal law for everyone to have" (6.395; p. 198). These ends, Kant says, are our own perfection and the happiness of others. The idea of compellability, strikingly absent from the *Foundations*, is given a role. But it is tied, not to the distinction between perfect and imperfect duties, but to the principle of legal duties. Kant thinks he is asserting an analytic proposition when he says that acts to which someone has a right may properly be obtained by compulsion (6.231; p. 57). But the adoption of ends cannot in principle be compelled. Virtue must result from free choice (6.381; p. 186).

The natural lawyers, making law enforceable by definition, distinguished the moral from the legal by taking the former as the domain of laws binding on all human beings, the latter as the domain of laws varying from state to state. They were never able to explain how we can be compelled to have the caring motives required for the performance of imperfect duties. Kant is in accord with Thomasius, whose work, however, he does not cite, in solving the problem by saying that compulsion is at home only for a domain of legality, and that ethics concerns an equally important but wholly different aspect of action. Virtue and the principled concern for character fall within the domain of ethics.

It is significant that Kant does not rely on Pufendorf's thesis that the perfect duties are more important for the existence of society than the imperfect. The perfect duties are prior to the imperfect in that they spell

---

26 In discussing the duty to help others, Kant contrasts duties necessary for the continuation of "mankind" and duties going beyond that to helpfulness – a version of the Pufendorfian explanation of the distinction (4.430; *Foundations*, pp. 48–9).

out the conditions under which we may act to carry out our imperfect duties. But the imperfect duties are the ones we must carry out to acquire merit. For Kant this is no little matter. Without the acquisition of merit, we are not entitled to happiness and can have no reason to suppose we will attain it. Yet we necessarily seek happiness, and our will to make personal sacrifices in order to act justly would be hampered if we could not think our own desires would ultimately be satisfied.

A distinction between perfect and imperfect duty retains a significant place within the Kantian domain of ethics. There are negative duties of virtue that are precise, and positive duties that are not. Thus the moral law forbids us to commit suicide, or to refuse to use our possessions for our own well-being. Because these duties are precise, they are perfect; and we therefore have perfect duties to ourselves as well as to others, though we can only be compelled to carry out those involving the rights of others. Imperfect duties to ourselves, like those to others, require us to have certain ends, but we cannot determine on a priori grounds alone what to do in order to achieve them or what acts would best express our attachment to these ends. Consequently, in these cases, "what is to be done cannot be determined according to rules of morality . . . only judgment can decide this according to rules of prudence (pragmatic rules)" (6.433n; *MM*, pp. 228–9). Kant here abandons the natural law view that the virtues are habits of obedience to laws. But he follows the Grotian rejection of Aristotle's doctrine of the mean and his replacement of the Aristotelian wise man's cognitive insight with prudential skill, itself not a sign or outcome of virtue (6.404; *MM*, p. 205).

In opposition to Hutcheson and Hume, Kant holds that virtue requires us to be moved by our awareness of the basic moral principle, not by simple feeling and not even by habitual feeling. As he said to his students, "One may have kindness of heart without virtue, for the latter is good conduct from principles, not instinct" (27.463; *LE*, p. 215). The virtuous agent for Kant is strong or resolute: not in Descartes's sense of sticking to one's plan of action and thereby demonstrating the power of one's will, but in resisting the pull of desires tempting one to act against morality (6.407–9; *MM*, pp. 207–9). In his final position, however, Kant allows a direct concern for the good of others to have an immediate motivational role in morality. We do not act with the thought that we are doing our duty when we act to carry out the duties of virtue. If we have performed a duty of virtue, we have made (say) the well-being of a friend our own end. In acting to bring it about, therefore, our purpose is not "to do our duty" but "to bring about the well-being of our friend." We adopt the end out of duty, not love; and although acting for it is not the same as acting from love, love can be added.

Helping others to achieve their ends is a duty. If a man practices it often and succeeds in realizing his purpose, he eventually comes to feel love for those he has helped. Hence the saying: you *ought* to *love* your neighbor . . . means . . . *do good* to your fellow-man, and this will give rise to love of man in you. (6.402; *MM*, p. 203)[27]

By distinguishing morality into a domain of right and a domain of virtue Kant tried to resolve the tension between law and love that runs through early modern moral philosophy. The natural lawyers would not have been as dissatisfied with this element of the Kantian morality of autonomy as they would have been with his basic principle. Hume himself would not have found it wholly alien to his views, and Smith would have seen that the *Metaphysics of Morals* at least accommodates his belief that only jurisprudence can give precise and definite rules. The Leibnizian perfectionists, however, would have been quite dissatisfied with Kant's final treatise on morals. Considering morality as a means toward the end of increasing perfection, they had no use, as they had no conceptual room, for sharp distinctions between laws of justice and laws of love, or between perfect and imperfect duties. Kant rejects the ancient idea that there is only one virtue (6.405; *MM*, p. 206). For the Leibnizians all virtues are in the end the one virtue of increasing perfection. That virtue admits neither imprecision nor limit. And because for Leibniz metaphysics provides the theory that enables moral philosophy to guide practice, the first task for each of us is self-perfection. We must have accurate knowledge of the doctrine of substances if we are to exhibit true justice and virtue.

The kind of understanding of Leibniz-Wolff perfectionism that motivated Kant's Rousseauian rejection of it is brought out powerfully by an incident in the life of Salomon Maimon, a destitute rabbi who turned philosopher after leaving Poland and moving to Berlin in 1779. The impoverished Maimon, invited as a worthy scholar to the home of a wealthy merchant for dinner, was taken to the son's room after the meal. The son reports:

> as he told me that the purpose of his trip to Berlin was only to pursue knowledge, I showed him some mathematical books, from which he begged me to read him aloud some sentences. I did so; but never was I so shaken as then, when I saw tears flowing from his eyes, and heard him weep aloud. O, my son, he said to me, weeping, how happy you are, to have and to be able to use, when you are so young, the tools for the perfection of your soul. Lord of all the world! If achievement of perfection

---

27 Kant was saying similar things in his ethics lectures at a much earlier stage. See, e.g., 27.417, 419; *LE*, pp. 180, 181.

is the vocation of man, pardon me the heavy sin if I ask, why until now the means for living true to my vocation were kept from poor me.[28]

After Rousseau's heart-altering impact, Kant had of course to reject Leibnizian perfectionism. In his teaching, if not in his writing, he returned repeatedly to consider it. For most of the thirty courses he gave on moral philosophy, he used two Wolffian textbooks by Alexander Gottlieb Baumgarten.[29] One of them expounds the elements of Wolffian ethical theory, the other goes into great detail about our specific duties to God, ourselves, and others. For the most part Baumgarten fed his students moral commonplaces, and Kant does not reject them. Instead he presents them as required not by the pursuit of perfection but by the categorical imperative.

He does not abandon self-perfection as a part of morality; but he transforms it. He makes it, as the Cambridge Platonists did, a matter of the heart rather than the head, of the will and the feelings rather than the intellect. A marginal note in his copy of one of the textbooks gives Kant's view concisely: "The proposition 'Make yourself perfect' can be seen as the principle of ethics if it is taken to say simply 'Be good, make yourself worthy of happiness, be a good man, not a merely happy one.'"[30] What is required is not endless improvement in the extent and distinctness of our cognitions. For Kant, we all always know the one thing we need to know for moral perfection: the moral law. The task is not to improve our knowledge, but to increase our virtue – our strength in obeying the law in the right spirit. Because moral perfection is a condition of the will, we can strive for it only for ourselves. The moral perfection of others cannot be our business; their happiness can and should be.

Self-perfection is a duty to oneself, for both Wolff and Kant. And Kant agrees with the Wolffians in holding that such duties "take first place, and are the most important of all." He thinks, however, that the Wolffians, and everyone else, fail to understand such duties. They are not, as Wolff has to hold, tied to the pursuit of one's own happiness. They are not instrumental duties at all.[31] They are required by respect

---

28   Maimon pp. 344–5, quoted there from a memoir about Maimon published in 1801.

29   For the number of times Kant taught ethics, see Arnoldt 1909, pp. 173–344, the basic work on Kant's teaching. See also Stark 1993, pp. 326–7, for additional consideration of his textbooks, and the introduction to *LE*.

30   *Reflexionen* 19.298 (no. 7268).

31   This puts Kant at odds with most of his predecessors. Pufendorf, Clarke, Hutcheson, and Crusius all treat duties to self as duties concerning oneself that are owed to God, or to other people – duties to keep oneself able to obey or to help.

for the freedom of which each of us is a bearer. To ignore them is to violate the condition of carrying out one's duties at all. We lose all inner worth, Kant says, if we are servile, or sell our bodies to others, or commit suicide. Unless we perform our duties to ourselves we cannot properly carry out our duties to others (27.340ff.; *LE*, pp. 122ff.). Then we cannot contribute to the perfection of the moral world; but that, Kant tells his students at the end of the course, is the final human vocation. "Every individual must endeavor to order his conduct in accordance with this end, whereby he makes his contribution such, that if everyone does likewise, perfection is attained" (27.470; *LE*, pp. 220–2). For the Leibnizians God sees to it that the world is necessarily the best world there can be. Kant leaves with us the responsibility for perfecting the world as well as ourselves.

Butler thinks that prudential concern for our own well-being deserves moral approval, and Price holds that since we have a duty to bring about happiness in general, we have a duty to concern ourselves with our own happiness too. Kant, by contrast, makes the pursuit of our own happiness part of what we need to do as a means to keeping ourselves virtuous.

Epilogue

24

Pythagoras, Socrates, and Kant: Understanding the history of moral philosophy

"In moral philosophy we have come no further than the ancients." So Kant told his students (9.32 and 28.540). He was not modest about his own achievements in the theory of knowledge. Why did he not claim that the critical understanding of morality was as revolutionary as its epistemological counterpart? He certainly thought about the issue. Unlike Aristotle, who summarized the opinions of his predecessors in metaphysics but not in ethics, Kant regularly taught his students something about the history of moral philosophy, and particularly about the ancients. He seems to have lectured less often on the history of other philosophical subjects, but he drafted an important prize essay assessing the progress recently made in metaphysics.[1] Is it only because no academy had a competition on the subject that Kant wrote no comparable essay about progress in ethics?

To ask these questions is to ask about Kant's understanding of his own historicity as a moral philosopher. The question leads us to ask as well how Kant understood the point of philosophical ethics. In Chapter 22.ii I pointed to some indications that at a formative period Kant felt uneasy about the vocation of a philosopher. I also noted his rejection of the Wolffian belief in the social need for authoritative pronouncements about morality from scholars who spend their lives studying it. Why, then, on Kant's view, did moral philosophy matter – if it did?

To answer these questions we need to find out what versions of the history of moral philosophy were available to Kant. Here the situation is a little more complicated than we might assume.

---

1   Although Baumgarten's textbooks in ethics contain nothing on history, the surviving student notes show that Kant gave lectures on ancient ethics and commented more or less fully on some modern theories each time he taught the course. The lectures on metaphysics suggest that Kant was less regular in including history in them. The early *Reflexionen* on ethics contain a great many historical sketches; once Kant settled on the scheme, in the mid or late seventies, there are fewer.

i. *The Socrates story*

The treatment of moral philosophy as a separate discipline with its own history, and not simply as a part of philosophy to be covered in general histories, began in seventeenth-century histories of theories about the law of nature and of nations. Of these the most notable is one I have referred to several times, the substantial *Historical and Critical Account of the Science of Morality* that Jean Barbeyrac published in 1706 as a preface to his French translation of Pufendorf's *De Jure Naturae et Gentium*. Adam Smith included a partial review of the work of his predecessors in *The Theory of Moral Sentiments;* but the first comprehensive history was Stäudlin's work of 1822. There have been other histories of ethics since then, and the field of history of ethics seems now to have achieved some recognition as a subspecialty within the general history of philosophy. But there has been little discussion of the special problems of historiography that it raises.[2] This is perhaps partly due to the fact that there seems to be no controversy about the outlines of the history of ethics.

The version of the history of moral philosophy that is most commonly accepted today goes back at least as far as Xenophon. He tells us that Socrates broke with his predecessors by attending to a new set of issues. He did not dispute, as they did, about the cosmos and the nature of things in general. He asked instead about human affairs (*Memorabilia* I.11–12). Cicero elaborates on the point. Socrates, he says, "was the first to call philosophy down from the heavens and set her in the cities of men . . . and compel her to ask questions about life and morals and things good and evil" (*Tusculan Disputations* V.iv.10–11). In the opening paragraph of *Utilitarianism* (1861), John Stuart Mill calls upon this tradition. "From the dawn of philosophy," he says,

> the question concerning the *summum bonum* or . . . the foundation of morality, has been accounted the main problem of speculative thought. . . . And, after more than two thousand years, the same discussions continue, philosophers are still ranged under the same contending banners, and neither thinkers nor mankind at large seem nearer to being unanimous on the subject than when the youth Socrates listened to the old

2   Histories of the history of philosophy such as those of Braun 1973, Gueroult 1984–8, and Santinello 1993 concentrate on general histories and do not take note of the rise of histories of disciplines within philosophy. In studies of historiographical issues in philosophy (e.g., Gracia 1992) there has been no discussion of the historiography of ethics comparable with that which has taken place concerning political theory, stimulated in important part by the work of Quentin Skinner and John Pocock. There are of course some exceptions (e.g., Irwin 1993).

Protagoras, and asserted . . . the theory of utilitarianism against the popular morality of the so-called Sophist.

Long before Mill, Hobbes gave notable expression to a variant of the
Socrates story without making any mention of its hero. He allows, as I
pointed out (Chapter 5.iv), that there were reasonably adequate "moral
sentences" among the natives of North America. Just as corn and
grapes grew wild before their uses and the way to cultivate them were
known, "so also there have been divers true, general, and profitable
speculations from the beginning, as being the natural plants of human
reason." To improve them requires philosophy, which in turn requires
leisure. But the Greeks, who had ample time, made no great progress in
moral philosophy; nor did the Jews, despite having a "school of the law
of Moses." He mentions Christ but says no more of him than that the
Jews failed to understand him (*Leviathan* XLVI.6–12). And he leaves us
to gather what we know he elsewhere asserted, that he himself was the
first to replace natural moral belief with a science of morality that transforms such beliefs into moral knowledge (cf. XXX.5).

Mill offers a theory to account for the fact that the question of the first
principle of morality remains open after so many centuries of inquiry. In
all the sciences, he says, much information and many low-level theorems come to light long before the most basic principles are discovered. Mankind learns many more or less general truths from experience; only later does careful analysis enable us to extricate the
fundamental concepts and principles of a science from the mass of
details. Moral beliefs are like others. Hence, it is not surprising that
common sense should possess some sound *beliefs* about moral rules.
But we will not have secure *knowledge* about morality until we discover
its true foundations (*Utilitarianism* I.1–2).

It is still standard to say that moral philosophy began with Socrates
and has been carried on continuously ever since. Thus Bernard Williams
begins a major study of moral philosophy as follows:

> It is not a trivial question, Socrates said: what we are talking about is how
> one should live. Or so Plato reports him, in one of the first books written
> about this subject. . . . The aims of moral philosophy . . . are bound up
> with the fate of Socrates's question.[3]

According to what I shall call the Socrates story of the history of
moral philosophy, the situation we are in is as follows. Although we
have not reached agreement about the basis of morality, we know the
tasks that we moral philosophers should undertake. We are trying to
answer the question Socrates raised: how to live. People have always

3   Williams, 1985, p. 1.

had opinions on the matter, but it is very hard to get an indubitable answer based on an undeniable foundation. It is so hard that skeptics ask us to doubt that there is an answer, or even a real question. Perhaps, as Mill says, the difficulty exists in all disciplines. Or perhaps, as others think, there are special problems about morality that make the task of developing its theory harder than the tasks facing physics. These problems may account for the fact that we seem not even to have made any generally accepted progress toward the answer, much less found it. Still, the issues are there, and we should continue working on them. If we study earlier moral philosophy, it is because we may gain some insights from our predecessors, or at least avoid their errors.

ii. *The Pythagoras story*

Because the Socrates story is simply taken for granted today it is important to be aware that for many centuries an alternative view of the history of moral philosophy was widely held. Like the Socrates story, it carries with it a distinctive view of the tasks of the discipline. The underlying thesis of the alternate history is that the basic truths of morality are not the last to be discovered. They have been known as long as humans have been living with one another. Whatever moral philosophy is, therefore, it is not a search for hitherto unknown scientific knowledge.[4]

The alternative narrative takes several forms. The oldest version gives importance to a question most of us would not naturally ask. We will be inside the story once we see why we might ask it. The question is, Was Pythagoras a Jew?

The background for the question is the assumption that the biblical narrative provides the unquestionable framework within which all human history must be located. Bossuet's *Discourse on Universal History* (1681) is perhaps the greatest modern monument built on this assumption, but not the only one. As Santinello's study of Renaissance histories of philosophies shows, it was long common to assume that all wisdom comes from God. One major task for historians, therefore, was to ex-

---

4   I am grateful to Dr. Jennifer Herdt for her very helpful criticisms of an early version of what follows. For one way of giving a general account of the differences between the two stories about moral philosophy, referring however to epistemology generally rather than to ethics, see Ernest Sosa, *Knowledge in Perspective* (Cambridge, 1991), pp. 158–9. See also James Griffin, *Value Judgement* (Oxford, 1996), p. 131, for sketches of two views of the task of moral philosophy that are rather close to the two I discuss.

plain its presence in cultures not directly descended from the Jews.[5] Those who undertook these enterprises believed that philosophy is an important human activity, which must have a providentially assigned role. They had a special problem about morality and its relation to moral philosophy. The truth about morality was revealed very early in human history, and it has not changed. William Law, arguing against Mandeville, gives us a clear eighteenth-century statement of this point:

> When Noah's Family came out of the Ark, we presume, they were as well educated in the Principles of Virtue and moral Wisdom, as any People were ever since; There was therefore a Time, when all the People in the World were well versed in moral Virtue. . . .
> He therefore that gives a *later* account of the Origin of moral Virtue, gives a *false* account of it.[6]

Belief that the Noachite revelation was the origin of moral knowledge itself would make it natural to ask why we have moral philosophy anyway. It would also lead us to wonder about how the Greeks could have been the ones to start it.

The answer to the first question lies in human sinfulness. Our nature was damaged by the Fall. It not only dimmed our faculties, lessening our ability to understand God's commands and accept them. It also unleashed the passions. Evildoers, driven by their lusts, seek to avoid the pangs of conscience, so they blind themselves to its clear dictates. They also strive to veil and confuse the moral thoughts of those whom they wish to entangle in their wicked schemes. Bad reasoning is one of their basic tools. Now reason is one of God's gifts to humanity. Among other things it enables us to hold on to at least some of the moral knowledge we need, once revelation has ceased. If reason makes moral philosophy possible, pride leads men to try to outdo one another in inventing schemes and systems of morality, and morality itself gets lost in their struggles. Since the causes of the misuse of reason and of bad philosophy are now ingrained in our nature, there will be no final triumph of good philosophy until after the last judgment. But the battle must be kept up. Moral philosophy is to be understood as one more arena for the struggle between sin and virtue.

As to the Greeks, it may be mysterious *why* God chose them to be the first to philosophize. We can, however, find out *how*, lacking the Noachite and the Mosaic revelations and being as corrupt as the rest of man-

---

5 See Santinello 1993, pp. 21, 26, 28, and especially the discussion of Thomas Burnet, pp. 330ff. See also Harrison 1990, ch. 5, for discussion of the "single-source" theory of religion. Walker 1972 is another important study of this kind of view.

6 William Law, *Remarks upon . . . the Fable of the Bees,* p. 7.

kind, they could have done as well as they did with morality (how well
they did being, again, a subject of debate). Here we come to Pythagoras.

In *Magna Moralia* I.1 Aristotle says that Pythagoras was the first who
attempted to treat of virtue. The remark was frequently cited.[7] And
given Aristotle's standing as the first historian of ancient thought, it
seems that one could hardly ask for more impressive testimony. We can
discover the importance of Pythagoras's priority from a parenthetical
remark that Scipion Dupleix adds to his assertion of it. In his *L'ethique ou
philosophie morale* of 1603 he says that, although Socrates is praised for
his discussion of the rules delivered by moral philosophy, he was not
the first in the field: "it is certain that Pythagoras himself, whom the
Greeks took for a philosopher of their nation (although St. Irenaeus
assures us that he was Hebrew and had read the books of Moses) had
worthily treated of morality" before Socrates did.[8] Here as elsewhere
Dupleix was unoriginal. Ficino, for example, thought he recalled that St.
Ambrose "showed that Pythagoras was born of a Jewish father"; and
there were others.[9] Thus the problem of transmission is solved. If
Pythagoras was the one who initiated moral philosophy among the
Greeks, and he was a Jew, it is clear how the Greeks managed to get the
subject going.

Not everyone thought Pythagoras was actually Jewish; but there
were second-best stories. It was a commonplace that the Greeks got
much from the Jews.[10] John Selden, who traced our grasp of natural law

7   Thomas Stanley, the first English historian of philosophy to write in the
vernacular, repeats the claim, citing this source. Stanley, *History*, p. 395. The passage
from *Magna Moralia*, 1182a12–14, is cited in full in section iii.

8   Dupleix 1632, p. 4. I am told that to the best of our knowledge St. Irenaeus
said no such thing.

9   I owe these last references to Heninger 1974, pp. 201–2, a study of
Pythagoreanism which I found very helpful. Heninger (p. 229 n. 5) lists half a dozen
studies from the seventeenth and eighteenth centuries that contain bibliographies on
Pythagoras's debt to Moses.

10   Herodotus and other ancients attested to Greek debts to Eastern thought
generally, and Isocrates held that Pythagoras in particular had brought into Greek
the philosophy he learned from the Egyptians. See Guthrie 1962, pp. 160, 163.
Guthrie devotes nearly two hundred pages to reviewing the difficulties of studying Pythagoras and Pythagoreanism and summarizing the results of modern
scholarship.

Heninger's fifth chapter (1974, pp. 256–84), gives a full and fascinating account of
various views of what specifically the moral philosophy of Pythagoras, or of the
Pythagoreans, was supposed to be, and the many ways in which Pythagorean views
were given Christian legitimacy and propagated widely. But although he has earlier
noted Pythagoras's alleged debts to the Jews for his moral thought, he does not

back to the Noachite commandments, devoted long pages of his *De Jure Naturali et Gentium* of 1640 to analyzing the testimony of Jewish and Christian writers about the Jewish influence on Pythagoras. He preferred the Greek authorities to the Jewish, as having, he thought, less of a vested doctrinal interest in proving such a debt to the Jews. His conclusion is that the weight of the evidence makes it clear that Pythagoras,

> the primary teacher of Greek theology and the first to be called a philosopher, to whom some also attribute the first doctrine in Greece concerning the immortality of the soul . . . and others wish to credit the first disputations about the virtues, that is, the principles of moral philosophy . . . consulted and heard the Hebrews.[11]

Selden thinks it quite possible that Pythagoras was taught by no less a figure than the prophet Ezekiel.

Henry More is also explicit about the importance of Greek philosophy's debt to the Jews:

> Now that Pythagoras drew his knowledge from the Hebrew fountains, is what all writers, sacred and prophane, do testify and aver. That Plato took from him the principal part of that knowledge, touching God, the soul's immortality and the conduct of life and good manners, has been doubted by no man. And that it went from him, into the schools of Aristotle, and so derived and diffused almost into the whole world, is in like manner attested by all.[12]

explore the bearing of claims about the debts on the historiography of moral philosophy.

11   John Selden, *De Jure Naturali et Gentium iuxta disciplinam Ebraeorum*, in *Opera* I.89. The examination of testimonies occurs in cols. 82–5 and elsewhere. I am indebted to Michael Seidler for having put Selden's passages concerning Pythagoras into quotable English. Selden offers an explanation of why "we do not find many vestiges of Hebrew doctrine in the writings of the Greek philosophers – indeed, that nothing at all occurs there which sufficiently retains the pure and unadulterated nature of its Hebrew origin." The various Greek sects themselves commingled so much, and splintered the old teachings so greatly, that the result is everywhere a hodgepodge. But, he adds, no one doubts that in Platonic as well as Pythagorean doctrine there are teachings derived from the Hebrews (col. 91).

12   More, *Encheiridion*, p. 267. For More and the "ancient theology" see Harrison 1990, pp. 133–5. Harrison does not discuss the Pythagoras story about moral philosophy; the ancient theology was concerned less with moral matters than with such doctrinal concerns as trinitarianism.

We have here the germ of a history of moral philosophy. I do not know how old it is.[13] But I think that some version or other of the Pythagoras story, as I shall call it, must have been assumed, however indistinctly, by a great many philosophers.

iii. *Revelation and reason*

There is a large amount of room for maneuver within this kind of historical schema. Most importantly, it leaves a role for reason while not making revelation superfluous.[14] This in turn gives rise to a somewhat less thoroughly religious story about the history of moral philosophy. Locke and Clarke in England, and Crusius in Germany, all concerned to defend the view that morality *at present* is not dependent on revelation, are still determined to keep revelation historically essential. They replace Pythagoras's Noachite revelation with Christ's, as that through which alone we became able to know the full truth about morality. It seems, Locke says, that

> 'tis too hard a task for unassisted reason to establish morality in all its parts upon its true foundation. . . . We see how unsuccessful in this the attempts of philosophers were before our Saviour's time. . . . And if, since that, the Christian philosophers have much outdone them, yet we may observe that the first knowledge of the truths they have added [is] owing to revelation. (*Reasonableness of Christianity*, p. 61)

Now that Christ has revealed the truth, we can see for ourselves the reasonableness of his teaching, and can even turn our knowledge into a demonstrative science.

It is significant for us that Crusius also accepted a rationalized version of the Pythagoras story that omitted the Jews. A truth is reasonable and philosophical, he says in the preface to his treatise on ethics, when it can be proved by valid arguments from rational starting points. It does not matter where we first learned it. "The duties that the Christian religion imposes on us are grounded in reason. Because our knowledge

---

13   Josephus, in *Against Apion*, trans. H. St. J. Thackeray (Cambridge, 1926, 1966), claims that the Greeks learned much of their science and law from the East, and specifically from the Jews; he mentions Pythagoras in this connection but does not explicitly claim that he was the originator of moral philosophy. See I.13–14, I.165, II.168, where the translator suggests that the dependence of Greek on Jewish thought was first suggested by Aristobulus. Eusebius in the *Preparation for the Gospel* gives a famous description of Plato as Moses Atticizing; but he does not tie Pythagoras to the origins of moral philosophy.

14   More himself says that the eternal son as the Logos, or human reason, as well as revelation, can enlighten us about morals.

of them was dimmed by our corruption [*Verderben*] they had to be repeated. . . . we learn the extent of human corruption from the fact that without divine revelation we would not have grasped the most important and most fully-grounded rational truths" (*Anweisung*, or *Guide*, pref., folios b4–b5).

Neither Locke nor Clarke nor Crusius says anything at all about Noah or the idea that Pythagoras had a Jewish connection. Yet in holding that the Greek philosophers were never able to get very far in figuring out what morality requires, they share with the Pythagoras story the belief that reason without revelation could not discover morality.[15] Locke and Clarke would have known what use Hobbes made of a Socrates version of the history of moral philosophy. They would thus have had strong motivation to adopt the alternative view. And the Pythagoras story's explanation of the role of moral philosophy is indeed implicit in their work as well. With this in mind, we can see, for instance, that Clarke's standard description of Hobbes as "the wicked Mr. Hobbes" is not just an incidental expression of personal revulsion. But none of them gives any account of the history that leads up to their own moral theories.

No one seems to have written a detailed history of moral philosophy resting on the strongest religious assumptions of the Pythagoras story. Barbeyrac's history, the most comprehensive of its time, gives an important role to the rational grasp of moral truth. He assumes, as I have noted, that the basic truths of morality are readily accessible to human reason. They must have been available in the earliest ages, and therefore mankind did not need revelation for its first instruction on how to behave. But Barbeyrac also believes, with the religious Pythagoras story, that human sinfulness leads men to try to evade the demands of morality and to use reason in the effort.[16] He seems to think that Pythagoras had something to do with the origins of moral philosophy, although he hesitates to claim him explicitly as its originator. But he plainly thinks original sin is one of the causes of the moral philosophy

---

15   Locke, *Christianity* 241, pp. 60–1. Clarke, *Lectures II*, in *Works* II.666ff. Gassendi, *Discourses* 3, says, without mentioning any Jewish connection, that Pythagoras was the first to study moral philosophy. He gives no source but was probably drawing on Aristotle.

16   "There has ever been an uninterrupted succession of men, who, seduc'd by a secret desire to shake off the troublesome yoke of duty; and to indulge themselves in the gratification, if not of their sensual and gross Desires, yet at least of their more delicate and refined Inclinations, have employed all the Faculties of their Souls, in extinguishing the Evidence of those Truths, which were most clear . . . in order to involve in their Ruin all certainty of the Rules of Virtue" (Barbeyrac, *Historical Account* III, p. 5).

that opposes the truth about morality, and he cannot refrain from thinking of the philosophers he opposes as wicked men.

Although Barbeyrac and others cite Aristotle as an authority for Pythagoras's priority as a student of virtue, what he said – if it was in fact Aristotle who wrote the *Magna Moralia* – does not present a very strong claim about it. He makes just one remark on the matter: "Pythagoras first attempted to speak about virtue, but not successfully; for by reducing the virtues to numbers he submitted the virtues to a treatment which was not proper to them" (1182a12–14). The rest of the evidence for the literal versions of the Pythagoras story is equally flimsy. It was controverted in the seventeenth century by Culverwell, who complained of the absurdity of supposing that Pythagoras could not know anything unless a Jewish soul had transmigrated into his body and sneered at the Jewish arrogance of supposing no one but they could know the law without "some Jewish manuscript, which they translated into Greek" (Culverwell, p. 62; cf. pp. 67, 75–6). But the Pythagoras story was not finally dismissed until Stäudlin's work.[17]

Stäudlin opens with a brief remark suggesting that morality arises from the interaction between the native powers and dispositions of the human mind and our situation in the world. Its origins lie so far back in antiquity that there is no use speculating about them. There was morality everywhere before there was philosophizing about it, and there were unsystematic and poetic articulations before anything rational appeared. We are as naturally moved to reflect on our own powers as on the world in which we act, and that reflection, carried far enough, is philosophy. Moral philosophy begins with the Greeks: preeminently

---

17   Friedrich Glafey, a German historian of natural law writing some thirty years after Barbeyrac, refuses, unlike Brucker, to report on the thought of the Eastern nations because they left no adequate written accounts. But he takes Pythagoras as the first of the Greek thinkers to give serious attention to morality, and after discussing his philosophy remarks that "we can see in general from this short summary of Pythagorean morality that, just as this man borrowed much from the Jews and the Egyptians, so also the succeeding Greek philosophers themselves made use of his doctrine." Glafey 1965, pp. 26–8; on Selden, pp. 23–5.

In 1786 the German scholar Christoph Meiners published a history of the sciences in which he devoted much space to a critical examination of the alleged Pythagorean writings, dismissing almost all of them as unreliable. I have not been able to consult Meiners's work; I rely on Braun 1973, pp. 173–7.

At the end of the eighteenth century another German scholar produced a brief history of ethics in which Pythagoras is mentioned along with Aristotle's claim about him, omitting, as most of those who cite it do, the phrase "but not successfully." But he says nothing about any link between a first revelation of moral truth to the Jews and its elaboration by the Greeks. See Hoffbauer 1798, pp. 295–6.

with Socrates.[18] Stäudlin allows that Pythagoras had some interesting thoughts about morals, but he himself is not willing to concede that there is any live issue about a Jewish connection. Yet he notes several recent writers who do, and the amount of effort he devotes to getting rid of the Pythagoras story suggests that it is still a live option.[19]

Stäudlin's work is modern in a way that Barbeyrac's is not. What makes it so is not the dismissal of the religious Pythagoras story and its kin. That, after all, is a scholarly conclusion that new evidence might alter.[20] It is rather Stäudlin's attitude toward error. He treats error in moral philosophy as like error in any science. It is no more caused by wicked desires or self-aggrandizing tendencies than are blunders in mathematics. Error comes not from original sin, but from the great difficulty of the subject. The function of moral philosophy is not to defend God's revelation from sinful and perverse reasoners. It is, rather, to raise our spontaneous moral insight to the level of fully reflective knowledge.

iv. *Kant and the Pythagoras story*

Stäudlin was a Kantian, but I do not think that Kant himself saw the history of moral philosophy primarily in terms of the Socrates story. He did not think that philosophy is needed to transform the unsystematic moral convictions of ordinary people from mere belief into warranted moral knowledge, and he made a significant place for revelation in the development of moral thought. With Locke, Clarke, and Cruisius, he tried to combine revelation with reason, and he substituted Christ for Noah or Moses as the one who brought moral truth to mankind. If his view of the history of ethics is thus basically Pythagorean, his interpretation of it transformed that story rather drastically. It enabled him to link his revision of it with an understanding of his own place in the history that seems more appropriate to a Socrates story. But his position here is also not quite like the standard view.

18   Stäudlin 1822, p. 22.
19   Stäudlin 1822, pp. 1–3, 19n, 32–59.
20   There is a more recent version of the Pythagoras story – surely not intended as such – according to which Zeno, the founder of Stoicism, was himself the son of a Jew. Giovanni Reale says that both Zeno and Chrysippus were Jewish and hypothesizes that the Stoic notion of *kathekonta* reflects Zeno's effort to bring Jewish moral categories into Greek philosophy. See Reale's *The Systems of the Hellenistic Age*, trans. John Catan (Albany, 1985), pp. 209, 216, 280–1. He refers to Max Pohlenz as his authority for Zeno's Jewishness. See Pohlenz, *Die Stoa* (Göttingen, 1948–9), I.22, 24–5, 28, and the evidence provided, rather scantily and with what may be an anti-Semitic tone, in II.14n. For doubts about the thesis, see Brent Shaw, "The Divine Economy: Stoicism As Ideology," *Latomus* 44 (1985), pp. 16–54, n. 8 on p. 20.

Kant always schematizes the history of ancient ethics by saying that the ancients took moral philosophy to be the rational search for knowledge of the highest good. The Cynics thought the good could be found in the simple life with no artificial wants; and Rousseau, "that subtle Diogenes," is their modern counterpart. Epicurus took the good to be happiness construed as pleasure, like the modern egoists. Zeno and the other Stoics bravely asserted that the highest good is constituted by virtue alone, which gives a self-satisfaction that suffices for happiness (see, e.g., 27.248–50; LE, pp. 44–7). Kant, like Descartes, thought that Epicureanism had to be added to Stoicism to obtain a true view of the highest good. Happiness is not just moral self-satisfaction; it requires the satisfaction of our nonmoral desires. Virtue is the worthiness to be happy, and the highest good therefore is to be happy in proportion to one's moral merit.[21]

Kant does not say that he himself is the first or only philosopher to hold this view. He does say that it is what Christ taught. In a fairly early note he claims that Christian thought is more philosophical than that of Hutcheson and Wolff, and in a note from the late 1770s he links Epicurus, Zeno, and Christ: "Epicurus taught [us] to seek happiness without special worthiness to be so. Zeno the worthiness, without having happiness in mind . . . Christ happiness through worthiness to be so" (19.120–1, no. 6634). Still later he claims that the Christian ideal of holiness is superior to the Stoic ideal of wisdom. It is plainly Christ rather than the philosophers who got matters right: "Epicurus wanted to give a motive for virtue and took from it its inner worth. Zeno wanted to give virtue an inner worth and took from it its motive. Only Christ gives it inner worth and also a motive" (19.309, no. 7312; 176, no. 6838; cf. 197–8, no. 6894, comparing Christ and Plato).

In his lectures Kant was quite free with such statements. In one, he says that "only since the time of the evangelists has the complete purity and holiness of the moral law been perceived, though it lies in our own reason" (27.294; LE, p. 86). In another he remarks that "The moral law must have purity. The Gospel has such purity in its moral law, as did none of the ancient philosophers, who even at the time of the evangelic teacher were merely brilliant pharisees" (27.301; LE, p. 92). A later historical comment makes the basic point explicit: "All the concepts of the ancients concerning humility and all the moral virtues, were impure and inconsistent with the moral law. The gospel was the first to present us with a pure morality, and as history shows, nothing else came near it" (27.350; LE, p. 130). Christ is here presented as a philosopher contemporary with some of "the ancients," correcting them by teaching a truth they failed to see.

---

21 Malebranche has a similar view; see Morale I.III.xiii.

We cannot dismiss these remarks as meant merely for Kant's young students. All three *Critiques* assign important functions to the Christian religion. In the first Kant says that we did not have right ideas of God "until the moral concepts were purified" and that it was the "greater preoccupation with moral ideas, which was rendered necessary by the extraordinarily pure moral law of our religion," that led us to a better idea of the divinity (*Pure Reason* A817 = B845). In the second *Critique* he remarks that it was "the moral teaching of the Gospel that first brought all good conduct of man under the discipline of a duty clearly set before him" (5.86; *Practical Reason*, p. 89). Christianity alone, "even when not regarded as a religious doctrine," gives us the only sufficient grasp of the highest good. The ancients failed to find it themselves.[22] Yet we need it for all of philosophy. In a note in the third *Critique* Kant attributes to Christianity the origin of the thought that we must believe possible what theoretical reason cannot prove: that proper adherence to morality will bring us happiness. The idea is carried by the word "fides"; Kant adds that "this is not the only case in which this wonderful religion has . . . enriched philosophy with far more definite and purer conceptions of morality than morality itself could have previously supplied. But once these conceptions are found, they are *freely* approved by reason" (6.471–2 n; *Judgment* II.146n).[23]

The first *Critique* opens with the famous claim that "in one species of its knowledge" the human mind cannot help asking questions it cannot answer. In theoretical matters it thus suffers from a "perplexity" which, Kant says, "is not due to any fault of its own" (*Pure Reason* Avii). The promulgation of Christianity was, by contrast, "a revelation of the faith which had hitherto remained hidden from men through their own fault" (6.141; *Religion*, p. 132). The fault that hid the truth from us is our propensity to evil. Because of it the morality carrried by Christianity, which we had to have before we could do metaphysics rightly, had to be historically revealed before it could be universally recognized, even though it is always implicit in everyone's heart.[24] In these remarks as

---

22   5.127 and n; *Practical Reason*, pp. 132–3 and n. Kant underlines the general point in his late lectures on metaphysics of morals, after once again reviewing the ancient ideals: "None of the assumed principles is sufficient by itself; they have to be united, and this by a supreme being, as sovereign ruler of the world. . . . Thus the highest philosophical ideal would be a theological one" (27.484–5; *LE*, p. 255).

23   My thanks to Mark Larrimore for this reference. The position is the same as Locke's; see Chapter 8.v.

24   See 6.110–11, 115, 121, 123n; *Religion*, pp. 100, 106, 112, 113n. See also 7.24, *Conflict of Faculties*, p. 37, for the claim that only philosophers can read the Bible in a way that extracts its rational message; and 7.37, 44, 64; pp. 63, 77, 117, for remarks about the need for revelation as a vehicle to bring to consciousness a timeless truth of

well as the explicit statements about Christ as the best of the ancient moral thinkers Kant is making use of a version of the Pythagoras story about the history of moral philosophy.[25]

If this is his perspective, it is clear why he said that in ethics we are no further than the ancients. Christ revealed the truth in antiquity; Kant has restated it but he has not gone beyond it. Who indeed could wish to do so? Kant explicitly says that he has not invented a new moral principle, but only a new formula for one that has always informed morality (5.4n; *Practical Reason*, p. 8n). We can get further light on Kant's understanding of the point or importance of moral philosophy from a look at his view of the corruption that sometimes obscure the principle from us. This in turn illuminates some aspects of his treatment of the history of ethics.[26]

In the Pythagoras story the point of sound moral philosophy is to combat the sinful efforts made by some wicked philosophers to cloud our grasp of morality. Kant departs from the tradition by refusing to denigrate those with whose views he disagrees; he defends Epicurus's way of living, and when discussing the attacks by Hume and Priestley on the rational foundations for religion and morality he goes out of his way to praise their moral character (*Pure Reason* A745–6 = B773–4). And he offers a new interpretation of corruption. Corruption is not shown only by our egoism. There is a general human tendency to one-sidedness, of which excessive attention to one's own happiness is only one symptom. In the *Foundations* Kant does indeed blame our desire for happiness for causing a natural dialectic in which we try to corrupt [*verderben*] the grounds of the laws of duty. From this he derives a need for philosophy, to replace our innocent morality with a more reflective one (4.405–6; pp. 21–2). But this is only one example of the morally dangerous exaggerations to which we are prone.

The early Notes inspired by Kant's study of Rousseau show how varied these are. "If there is any knowledge [*Wissenschaft*] which man needs," Kant remarks,

> it is that which teaches him fittingly to fill the place which is assigned to him in the creation and from which he can learn what one must be to be a man. Suppose he had come to know deceptive enticements above or

which we were unaware, though it is always within us.

25   Against this it must be noted that in the lecture notes on "History of Natural Theology" in his *Lectures on Philosophical Theology* Kant says that by the time of Anaxagoras and Socrates "morality had itself already been founded on secure principles" (28.1125; p. 169).

26   Yovel 1989, chs. 6 and 7, and Gueroult 1977, ch. IV, discuss Kant's views about the history of theoretical philosophy but give no special consideration to his treatment of the history of ethics.

below him which [,] unnoticed [,] had brought him out of his proper place then this instruction will lead him back to the condition of the human and no matter how small or needy he finds himself still he will be just right for his assigned post because he is precisely that which he ought to be. (20.45.17; *Bemerkungen* 36.1)

In another Note Kant adds that a man who pursues "moral qualities" above his capacities withdraws from his post, and the holes he makes in so doing "spread his own corruption" to his neighbors (41.19; 33.1).

The theme is taken up again in the second *Critique,* where Kant stresses that when doing our duty "our position among rational beings" is not that of volunteers, acting at our own pleasure. Rather, "the stage of morality on which man . . . stands is respect for the moral law." To this reminder about our proper place Kant joins some warnings about the "shallow, high-flown fantastic way of thinking" to which those are liable who take themselves to be able to be moral without acting from respect (5.82–5; *Practical Reason,* pp. 85–8).

Again and again in discussing the Stoics, and in his infrequent remarks about Plato, Kant accuses them of forgetting the proper place of human beings in the universe. Plato is a mystic, an enthusiast, a fanatic (see, e.g., 27.305, *LE,* p. 94; 19.95 no. 6584; 108, no. 6611; 196, no. 6894). And for all his admiration of Stoicism, Kant thinks it makes overstrained demands on human nature. "Man fancifully exaggerates his moral capacity," Herder reports Kant as telling his class in the early 1760s,

and sets before himself the most perfect goodness; the outcome is nonsense; but what is required of us? The Stoic's answer: I shall raise myself *above myself,* . . . rise superior to my own afflictions and needs, and with all my might be *good,* be the *image of godhood.* But how so, for godhood has no obligations, yet you certainly do. . . . Now the god departs and we are left with *man,* a poor creature, loaded with obligations. *Seneca* was an impostor, *Epictetus* strange and fanciful. (27.67; *LE,* p. 32)

If the Epicureans succumb to "deceptive enticements" below the human, the Stoics – and Plato to a far greater degree – yield to those above it. Even that subtle Diogenes Rousseau has taken matters too far. Kant is as averse to these distortions of humanity as Montaigne was (Chapter 3.v). He teaches the history of ethics to warn his students about the way in which one-sided visions of mankind subvert morality. In claiming to unite Epicurus and Zeno through his idea of the highest good, he is thus trying to defend the message of the Gospels against the many-sided effects of the corruption to which we are all prone. In this respect, Kant understands the aim of moral philosophy in what I have called Pythagorean terms.

There is, however, an additional, more Socratic, side to Kant's view of the function of moral philosophy. It is to help make the transition from a historical faith to a universal religion whose core is pure rational morality. Historical faith was available only to those who had access to its records; moral religion is universally available. By revealing, for the first time, that religion is basically morality, Christ started us on that "continual approach to pure religious faith," which will one day enable us to "dispense with the historical vehicle" that initially carried the message (6.115; *Religion,* pp. 105–6). The religion of reason, Kant says, "is a continually occurring divine (though not empirical) revelation for all men" (6.122; p. 113). Kant has contributed to the progress of morality by showing that it rests on a purely rational principle, which itself dictates the essentials of religious faith. Moral philosophy thus does more than combat corruption. If it does not transform mere belief into knowledge by giving it foundations, it shows that the moral knowledge we have explicitly possessed since Christ revealed it is a matter of pure practical reason, and explains how such a morality is possible.

v. *Has moral philosophy a single aim?*

Both the Socrates story and the Pythagoras story (in its more rationalistic as well as its more religious versions) illustrate the interconnections among our conceptions of the aim or task of moral philosophy, the proper understanding of its history, and the nature of morality. The two grand narratives are similar in holding that moral philosophy has essentially a single task, though each assigns it a different one. But the assumption that there is one single aim that is essential to moral philosophy gives rise to difficulties for both views.

One difficulty lies in formulating the aim. Perhaps it is plausible to hold that we and Socrates are asking the same question if the central issue is described as Williams describes it. Yet we might wonder whether identifying the question of moral philosophy as "How should one live?" is useful for those interested in the history of the subject. The Socratic question, so stated, is extremely general. To take it as locating "the aims of moral philosophy," we must surround it with a number of unspoken assumptions. For instance, we must not take it to be a question about how one should live with respect to health, or income, or eternal well-being. Are we then to take it as a general question about how we should live in order to be happy? We have only to think of Kant's ethics to see that this will not identify an inquiry central to all moral philosophy.

The single-aim view seems to rest on a theory about the essences of philosophical disciplines, which is itself contestable. If we look historically at what moral philosophers have said they were trying to do, we do not come up with a single aim uniting them all. Compare, for instance, Aristotle's claim that moral philosophy should improve the lives of those who study it with Sidgwick's belief that "a desire to edify has impeded the real progress of ethical science."[27] Recall the Stoic aim of finding the way to personal tranquillity; Hobbes's aim of stabilizing a society put in danger by religious fanaticism; Bentham's aim of locating a principle to show everyone the need for major political, social, and moral reform; Parfit's aim of developing a new, wholly secular, science of morality.[28] Unless we leave the statement of the aim quite vague, it will be difficult to find one on which these thinkers agree. If we are more definite, then it seems that we will be required to say that anyone not sharing the favored aim is not really doing moral philosophy. Whatever the single aim assigned to the enterprise, we would be forced to deny the status of moral philosopher to many thinkers usually included in the category.

Those holding a Pythagoras story version of moral philosophy's single task face some additional difficulties. They must assume that the moral knowledge which is always to be defended can be identified in some way that does not presuppose the truth of any specific theory, and that it is always and everywhere essentially the same. Yet it is implausible to claim that Greek morality, the morality of the Decalog, and the liberal morality of modern Western democracies are in essence identical. The claim can be made out, if at all, only by proposing as "the essence" of these moralities some interpretation of them, probably in philosophical terms, which was not available to some or all of those whose moralities are at issue.

These objections to single-aim views about moral philosophy are themselves both historical. The historian will have a further problem with the outlook. It implies that since we and past moral philosophers share aims and goals, the best way to understand our predecessors is to look at them in the light of our own view of the truth about morality. Even allowing, as some philosophers do, that our own views may not be the last word, it is still tempting, on a single-aim approach, to suppose that we know the best word yet, and that therefore no other standpoint is needed for examining what has gone before.

The historian will complain that insistence on describing the views of past thinkers in our own terminology forces us into anachronism. If we are interested in what our predecessors were doing and thinking, we must try to understand them in terms they themselves had available. It is obvious that Hume could not even have conceived the aim of "anticipating Bentham." But it is just as misleading to describe him as "trying

---

27 Aristotle, *Nicomachean Ethics* 1179a35–b4; Sidgwick 1907, p. vi.
28 *Reasons and Persons* (Oxford, 1984), p. 453.

to develop a rule-utilitarian theory of justice." Although he discovered some of the important differences between the morality of actions within social practices and the morality of independent actions, the idea of utilitarianism as well as the distinction between "act" and "rule" versions of it are much later inventions. We may have good reason for thinking of his theory in terms like these, but we are not, in so doing, giving a historical account of it. Worse, we may be overlooking its historical distinctiveness by forcing it into our own molds.

vi. *Continuity and change in moral philosophy*

We cannot, it seems, write a history of moral philosophy without having some idea of the aims of the discipline; and we cannot have a well-grounded idea of its aims without having some awareness of its origins and history. The difficulties for the historian arising from this conclusion are not wholly avoidable. But they are less acute if we give up thinking of moral philosophy as having some single essential aim and suppose instead that philosophers at different times were trying to solve different problems.

As historians, we can work with a very general concept of morality, taking it vaguely and imprecisely as the norms or values or virtues or principles of behavior that seem to be present in every known society. We will study those who try to reflect philosophically on the matters thus described. No doubt our idea of what counts as "philosophical reflection" will be marked by our present conception. But we will not try to impose much more uniformity on past efforts than is carried by these two reference points. We will not need to decide whether commonsense morality, ancient or modern, is mere opinion or genuine knowledge. We will not, in particular, suppose that everyone who thought about morality in a way we consider philosophical was trying to solve the same problem or answer the same questions. We will think instead that the aims of moral philosophy – the problems that moral philosophers thought required reflection – are at least as likely to have changed as to have remained constant through history.

Why might there be such alterations in the questions or problems that set the differing aims of philosophical reflection about morality? One answer is that there have been times of upheaval when the norms involved in our common life have been called into question by social, religious, and political changes. The need to blend Christian belief with an inherited culture coming from Greece and Rome is one such case. The problems arising from the disintegration of even the appearance of a unified Christendom was another. Perhaps Parfit's concern to work out a wholly secular morality, or the apparent fact that there is no hope for agreement on conceptions of the good, indicate yet further points of change. The history of moral philosophy, we may think, itself provides important clues to the eras at which the stresses on widely accepted norms and values became overwhelming and change was necessary. If philosophers do little to bring about the strains, they sometimes provide means to diagnose or even to cope with them.

If we take this approach we will be led naturally to ask some kinds of question about the history of moral philosophy that we may overlook if we think the discipline centers on only one question. On the single-aim assumption we will suppose that we always know what moral philosophers were trying to do. They were trying to solve the essential problem. Without this assumption, we will need to ask what past philosophers were doing in putting forward the arguments and conclusions and conceptual schemes they favored. We will ask about the point or purpose of using these arguments. The answers will have to be historical. Because we think that the answers to such questions may vary from time to time, we will ask just how the thinkers we study differ from earlier thinkers and from those of their contemporaries whose work they knew. What our subjects refused to ask or assert will matter as much to us as their positive claims. Knowing the former will enable us, as knowing the latter alone will not, to understand what their aims for moral philosophy were. To know what they refused to include we must know what they might have included, and did not. Here only historical information, and not rational reconstruction of arguments in the best modern terms, will tell us what we need to know.[29]

One benefit of this approach is that it gives us a way of checking on our interpretations or readings of past moral philosophy. There is historical evidence about the vocabularies available to our predecessors, and about the issues that mattered to them and to their publics. We may lack documentary evidence about a philosopher's own specific intentions in publishing a given book. But we can assume that he meant to be understood by a living audience, and not just by posterity; and what writers as well as readers could have understood is set to a large extent, although not wholly, by the language they already possessed. Even innovative terms and concepts require some sort of introduction via existing notions. To learn what resources were available to a philosopher, we must look outside his or her writings. We may need to examine theological works, sermons, political pamphlets, old editions of classical authors, contemporary dictionaries, and literary writings, as well as the other philosophers our subject read. If we do not check our accounts of what past philosophers said in this manner, we are in serious danger

29   I am much indebted to work by Quentin Skinner and by John Pocock on these issues; for a helpful review see Tully 1988, and the methodological essays in Pocock 1985.

of mistaking our own fantasies about what they "must have meant" for what they really did mean.

Single-aim theorists may reply that on this view there is no continuing subject of moral philosophy whose history we can try to write. But to say this is to oversimplify. Continuities are quite compatible with the discontinuities that arise from changing problems and aims. It seems highly probable that all societies complex enough to generate philosophical reflection must handle certain problems of social and personal relations. Views about the fair or proper distribution of the necessities of life, or about the relative praise- or blame-worthiness of individuals, seem always to arise in such societies. Study of different ways of structuring such views is a constant theme that gives moral philosophy some of its identity amid its differences.

Some arguments and insights about what makes for coherent views of morality are portable. Since they may be carried over from one situation to another, they provide further elements of continuity in the work of moral philosophers. When, for example, Cudworth said that "good" could not be defined as "whatever God wills," he turned against Descartes and Hobbes the same kind of argument that Plato's Socrates sketched against Euthyphro. G. E. Moore later presented other arguments against the definability of "good." Cudworth was trying to preserve the possibility of a loving relation between God and man that could not have concerned either Socrates or Plato; Moore had quite different aims in view. One could write a useful history concentrating simply on the question of definability.[30] But to do so would be to ignore historically crucial differences in the uses to which claims of indefinability were put. I do not wish to minimize the importance of portable arguments. They provide a major set of linkages between past and present moral philosophies. But they do nothing to support the claims of the single-aim historian. Praxiteles and Brancusi both used chisels, no doubt, but we do not learn much about their art from noticing the fact.

Single-aim philosophers will undoubtedly feel that more significance must be assigned to these portable arguments. They will say that such arguments represent what moral philosophy is all about – the discovery of the truth about morality. Plato and Cudworth and Moore all saw the same thing, even if they described somewhat differently what they saw and put their discovery to different uses. They did not discover a mere tool for carrying out some external aim. They themselves say that they are in search of the truth about morality itself, and it is quite possible that they found an important part of it. Progress in moral philosophy, as in science, involves replacing false and one-sided

30 See Prior 1949, a useful short study.

theories with true and comprehensive ones about the designated subject matter of the discipline. History is useful only when philosophical assessment of the arguments of past philosophers helps us with our present projects.

Histories of moral philosophy can of course be written on such assumptions; and assessment of arguments given in the past is important to the historian. The historian needs to know what led to the alteration or abandonment of various views. Failure to achieve coherence or to produce valid supporting arguments may explain the change in some cases. But the single-aim view leaves unexplained a great deal that the historian will naturally wish to consider. Why do some theories emerge and flourish and then disappear, why do some recur, why is there so little convergence, what does moral philosophy as a practice or discipline do in and for the societies in which it is supported? It is more useful for the historian to turn away from the single-aim view and adopt a variable-aim approach instead.

vii. *Progress in moral philosophy*

If we take the variable-aim view of the subject, we will not be strongly inclined to make much of the question of progress or regress. We will look at the enterprise of rationally examining norms and virtues as one of the tools that various societies have used to cope with different problems they faced in shaping or preserving or extending a common understanding of the terms on which their members could live with one another. We will not think of moral philosophy as standing apart from and above the moral discourse of society. We will take it as being simply one participant in the discussion of moral issues. In moral philosophy we will hear the voice that asks us to stand back from current issues and describe them in the most general terms we can discover – or invent. Its hope is that by so doing we can reformulate the problems in more manageable ways. The very stance seems to make it natural to use an atemporal mode of discourse, but the rhetoric of moral philosophy need not conceal the fact that those who use it are located in their own times as well as in a timeless web of abstractions.

It is not hard to understand how questions that were of great importance at one time may lose their hold at another. The conditions giving the questions urgency may have altered. Or new and more pressing problems may have emerged. The abandonment of one question and the move to consider a new one may itself be a major kind of progress in moral philosophy. I am myself strongly inclined to think that change of this kind is essential from time to time to enable moral philosophy to avoid sterility. If so, it is all the more important for the historian to work on assumptions that bring it to the fore instead of hiding it.

Those of us who hope to see the development of a fully secular understanding of morality need not have any interest in some of the problems that Kant tried to solve. Ignoring them, we of course pay no heed to the conditions they impose on what can count as a satisfactory moral philosophy. If, for instance, we do not think that a prime task for moral philosophy is to show that God and we belong to a single moral community, then we will not have Kant's reason for insisting that our theory show how there can be moral principles necessarily binding on all rational beings. There may be other reasons for holding that there must be such principles, but we will not think the requirement self-evident. Principles for humans may be enough.

Although we may hold that our time presents its own problems to moral philosophy, we may also think that the answers Kant worked out for his problems are useful in coping with ours. And if we share his passionate conviction concerning the equal moral capacity of all normal human beings and their equal dignity, we may well think that something like his basic moral principle is more likely to yield an adequate solution to our problems than any other principle yet invented.

Bibliography

1. Sources

I list here sources I have drawn on that were published prior to 1800, including historical studies.

Individual authors

Allestree, Richard (1619–81; authorship uncertain)
The Whole Duty of Man. London, n.d.

Althusius, Johannes (1557–1638)
The Politics of Johannes Althusius: Politica methodice digesta. Trans. Frederick S. Carney. London, 1964.

Ames, William (1576–1633)
Conscience with the Power and Cases Thereof. 1639. (No translator or publisher given)
The Marrow of Theology. Trans. John D. Eusden. Durham, 1983.
Technometry. Trans. Lee W. Gibbs. Philadelphia, 1979.

Anselm, St., of Canterbury (1033–1109)
Anselm of Canterbury. Ed. and trans. Jasper Hopkins and Herbert Richards. 4 vols. Toronto, 1976.

Aquinas, St. Thomas (1225–74)
On Charity. Trans. Lotte H. Kendzierski. Milwaukee, 1984.
Summa Theologica. Trans. Fathers of the English Dominican Province. New York, 1947.

Aristotle (384–322 B.C.E.)
Magna Moralia. Trans. St. George Stock. Oxford, 1915.
Politics. Trans. Ernest Barker. Oxford, 1946.
Nicomachean Ethics. Trans. Terence Irwin. Indianapolis, 1985.

Augustine, St. (354–430)
The City of God. Trans. Henry Bettenson. London, 1972.
On Christian Doctrine. Trans. D. W. Robertson Jr. Indianapolis, 1958.

Aurelius, Marcus (121–180)
Meditations. Trans. Maxwell Staniforth. London, 1964.

Bacon, Sir Francis (1561–1626)

Works. Ed. James Spedding, R. L. Ellis, and D. D. Heath. New York, 1878.

Balguy, John (1686–1748)

    A Collection of Tracts Moral and Theological. London, 1734.

Barbeyrac, Jean (1674–1744)

    An Historical and Critical Account of the Science of Morality . . . from the earliest times down to . . . Pufendorf. Trans. Carew. 1706. In Pufendorf, *On the Law of Nature of Nations*.

    Jugement d'un anonyme . . . avec des reflexions du traducteur . . . In Pufendorf, *Les devoirs de l'homme*.

Baumgarten, Alexander (1714–62)

    Ethica Philosophica. In Kant, *Gesammelte Schriften* 27.732–869, followed by a reprint of the edition of 1763, pp. 871–1028.

    Initia Philosophiae Practicae. In Kant, *Gesammelte Schriften* 19.7–91.

    Metaphysica (1742). 1757. In Kant, *Gesammelte Schriften* 15.5–54, 17.5–226.

    Metaphysik. Trans. G. F. Meier. Halle, 1766.

Bayle, Pierre (1647–1706)

    Historical and Critical Dictionary, Selections. Trans. Richard Popkin. New York, 1965.

    Oeuvres diverses. Ed. Alain Niderst. Paris, 1971.

    Oeuvres diverses. Introd. Elisabeth Labrousse. Vols. II– III, 1727. Vol. IV, 1731. Reprint, Hildesheim, 1966, 1968.

    Oeuvres diverses. Choix d'articles tires du Dictionnaire historique et critique. Introd. Elisabeth Labrousse. 2 vols. Reprint, Hildesheim, 1982.

    Philosophical Commentary. Trans. Amie Goodman Tannenbaum. Bern, 1987.

Bentham, Jeremy (1748–1832)

    Bentham's Theory of Fictions. Ed. C. K. Ogden. London, 1932.

    Collected Works of Jeremy Bentham. Ed. J. H. Burns, John Dinwiddy, and F. Rosen, Oxford, 1968–.

    A Fragment on Government and *An Introduction to the Principles of Morals and Legislation*. Ed. Wilfrid Harrison. Oxford, 1948.

Berkeley, George (1685–1753)

    Works. Ed. A. A. Luce and T. E. Jessop. 9 vols. London, 1948–57.

Bonnet, Charles (1720–93)

    Essai de psychologie. In *Oeuvres d'histoire naturelle et de philosophie*, vol. 17. Neuchatel, 1783.

Boyle, Robert (1627–91)

    Selected Philosophical Papers of Robert Boyle. Ed. M. A. Stewart. Indianapolis, 1991.

Bramhall, John (1594–1663)

    Works. Vol. 4. London, 1844.

Brown, John (1715–66)

    Essays on the Characteristics of the Earl of Shaftesbury. 1751. Reprint, Hildesheim, 1969.

Brucker, Johann Jakob (1696–1770)

    Erste Anfangsgründe der philosophischen Geschichte. 2nd ed. Ulm, 1751.

    Historia critica philosophiae a mundi incunabilis ad nostram usque aetatem deducta. 2nd ed. 6 vols. Leipzig, 1776–7.

Burlamaqui, Jean-Jacques (1694–1748)

Principes du droit naturel. Geneva, 1748.

Burnet, Thomas (1635?–1715)

Remarks upon an Essay concerning Humane Understanding. London, 1697.

Second Remarks upon an Essay concerning Humane Understanding. London, 1697.

Third Remarks upon an Essay concerning Humane Understanding. London, n.d. [1699].

Butler, Bp. Joseph (1692–1752)

The Analogy of Religion, Natural and Revealed, to the Constitution and Course of Nature. In *Works*, vol. II.

Fifteen Sermons Preached at the Rolls Chapel. In *Works*, vol. I.

Works. Ed. J. H. Bernard. 2 vols. London, 1900.

Calvin, John (1509–1564)

Institutes of the Christian Religion. Ed. John T. McNeill. Trans. Ford Lewis Battles. 2 vols. London, 1941.

Carmichael, Gershom (1672–1729)

Gershom Carmichael on Samuel Pufendorf's de Officio Hominis et Civis. Compiled by John N. Lenhart. Trans. Charles H. Reeves. Cleveland, 1985.

Charron, Pierre (1541–1603)

De la sagesse, trois livres. 2nd ed. 1604. Ed. Amaury Duval. 3 vols. Paris, 1820.

Of Wisdom. Trans. Samson Lennard. London, n.d.

Petite traicté de la sagesse (1606). In *De la sagesse, trois livres*, vol. 3.

Cicero (106–43 B.C.E.)

De Finibus. Trans. H. Rackham. Cambridge, 1971.

De Officiis. Trans. Walter Miller. Cambridge, 1961.

De Re Publica and *De Legibus*. Trans. Clinton Walker Keys. Cambridge, 1977.

Tusculan Disputations. Trans. J. E. King. Cambridge, 1989.

Clarke, Samuel (1675–1729)

A Discourse concerning the Being and Attributes of God. In *Works*, vol. II.

A Discourse concerning the Unchangeable Obligations of Natural Religion, and the Truth and Certainty of the Christian Revelation. In *Works*, vol. II.

Dr. Clarke's Remarks upon a Book, Entitled A Philosophical Inquiry concerning Human Liberty. In *Works*, vol. IV.

Leibniz-Clarke Correspondence. In *Works*, vol. IV.

The Leibniz-Clarke Correspondence. Ed. H. G. Alexander. Manchester, 1984.

Letters concerning Liberty and Necessity. In *Works*, vol. IV.

Sermons I–CXIV. In *Works*, vol. I.

Sermons CXV–CLXXIII. In *Works*, vol. II.

Works. 4 vols. London, 1738. Reprint, New York, 1978.

Collins, Anthony (1676–1729)

A Discourse of Free-Thinking (1713). New York, 1978.

A Philosophical Inquiry concerning Human Liberty (1717). New York, 1978.

Crusius, Christian August (1715–75)

Anweisung, vernünftig zu Leben. Leipzig, 1744. Reprint, ed. G. Tonelli. Hildesheim, 1969.

Entwurf der nothwendigen Vernunft-Wahrheiten. Leipzig, 1745. Reprint, ed. G. Tonelli. Hildesheim, 1964.

Cudworth, Ralph (1617–88)

A Sermon Preached before the House of Commons. March 31, 1647. In Patrides, *The Cambridge Platonists.*

A Treatise concerning Eternal and Immutable Morality. London, 1731. Reprint, Hildesheim, 1979.

A Treatise of Free Will. Ed. John Allen. London, 1838. Reprint, Hildesheim, 1979.

The True Intellectual System of the Universe. London, 1678. Reprint, Hildesheim, 1977.

Culverwell, Nathaniel (1619–51)

An Elegant and Learned Discourse of the Light of Nature (1652). Ed. Robert A. Greene and Hugh MacCallum. Toronto, 1971.

Cumberland, Richard (1631–1718)

Traité philosophique des loix naturelles. Trans. Jean Barbeyrac. Amsterdam, 1744.

A Treatise of the Laws of Nature (1672). Trans. John Maxwell. London, 1727.

d'Alembert, Jean (1717–83)

Essai sur les éléments de philosophie. Paris, 1986.

Darjes, Joachim Georg (1714–91)

Erste Gründe der philosophischen Sitten-Lehre. 4th ed. Jena, 1782.

d'Holbach, Paul Henry Thiry, Baron (1723–89)

La morale universelle, ou les devoirs de l'homme (1776). 2 vols. Paris, 1820.

Système de la nature. London, 1781. Reprint, Paris, 1990.

Système Social. 2 vols. London (?), 1773. Reprint, Hildesheim, 1969.

de la Forge, Louis (1632–66)

Traité de l'esprit de l'homme (1666). Ed. Pierre Clair. Paris, 1974.

de Sade, D. A. F. (1740–1814)

Juliette. Trans. Austryn Wainhouse. New York, 1968.

Justine, Philosophy in the Bedroom, and Other Writings. compiled and trans. Richard Seaver and Austryn Wainhouse. New York, 1965

Oeuvres complètes. Ed. Annie Le Brun and Jean-Jacques Pauvert. Vol. 3, 1986. Vols. 8–9, 1987.

Descartes, René (1596–1650)

Les passions de l'ame. Ed. Geneviève Rodis-Lewis. Paris, 1964.

The Passions of the Soul. Trans. Stephen H. Voss. Indianapolis, 1989.

The Philosophical Writings of Descartes. Vol. I. Trans. John Cottingham, Robert Stoothoff, and Dugald Murdoch. Cambridge, 1985.

The Philosophical Writings of Descartes. Vol. II. Trans. John Cottingham, Robert Stoothoff, and Dugald Murdoch. Cambridge, 1984.

The Philosophical Writings of Descartes. Vol. III: *The Correspondence.* Trans. John Cottingham, Robert Stoothoff, Dugald Murdoch, and Anthony Kenny. Cambridge, 1991.

Deschamps, Jean

Cours abrégé de la philosophie wolffienne en forme de lettres (1741–47). Hildesheim, 1991.

Diderot, Denis (1713–84)

Encyclopédie, ou dictionnaire raisonné . . . Paris, 1751–80.

Oeuvres. Ed. André Billy. Paris, 1951.

Oeuvres. Vol. I: *Philosophie.* Ed. Laurent Versini. Paris, 1994.

Oeuvres complètes. I. Le modèle anglais. Ed. Arthur M. Wilson et al. Paris, 1975.

Oeuvres politiques. Ed. P. Verniere. Paris, 1963.

Political Writings. Ed. John Hope Mason and Robert Wokler. Cambridge, 1992.

Diogenes Laertius (c. 200–250)

Lives of Eminent Philosophers. Trans. R. D. Hicks. 2 vols. Cambridge, 1991.

Domat, Jean (1625–95)

Oeuvres completes. Ed. Joseph Remy. Vol. I: *Traité des lois* (1689). Paris, 1828.

Duns Scotus, John (1266–1308)

Duns Scotus on the Will and Morality. Ed. and trans. Allan B. Wolter, Washington, D.C., 1986.

Dupleix, Scipion (1569–1661)

Ethique ou philosophie morale. Paris, [1610]. 1645. Reprint, Paris, 1994.

du Vair, Guillaume (1556–1621)

The Moral Philosophy of the Stoics (1598). Trans. Thomas James. Ed. Rudolf Kirk. New Brunswick, N.J., 1951.

La philosophie morale des Stoiques. 1585.

Enfield, William

The History of Philosophy . . . drawn up from Brucker's Historia Critica Philosophiae. 2 vols. London, 1791.

Filmer, Sir Robert (1588–1653)

Patriarcha and Other Writings. Ed. Johann P. Sommerville. Cambridge, 1991.

Fletcher, Andrew, of Saltoun (1655–1716)

Selected Political Writings and Speeches. Ed. David Daiches. Edinburgh, 1979.

Fontenelle, Bernard le Bovier de (1657–1757)

Du bonheur (1724). In *Histoire des Oracles,* ed. Willy de Spens, pp. 131–48. Paris, 1966.

Fordyce, David (1711–51)

The Elements of Moral Philosophy. London, 1754.

Formey, J. H. S. (1711–97)

La belle Wolffienne (1741–53). Hildesheim, 1983.

Garve, Christian (1742–98)

Uebersicht der vornehmsten Principien der Sittenlehre. Breslau, 1798.

Gassendi, Pierre (1592–1655)

Abrégé de la philosophie de Gassendi. By François Bernier. 2nd ed., 1684. 7 vols. Paris, 1992.

Opera Omnia. Lyon, 1658. Vol. II. Reprint, Stuttgart, 1964.

Selected Works. Ed. and trans. Craig B. Brush. New York, 1972.

Three Discourses, of Happiness, Virtue, and Liberty. London, 1699. Anonymous translation of Bernier, *Abrégé de la philosophie de Grassendi,* vol. 7.

Gay, John (1699–1745)

"Concerning the Fundamental Principle of Virtue or Morality." London [1731]. Prefixed to King, *An Essay on the Origin of Evil.*

Gellert, Christian Fürchtgott (1715–69)

Moralische Vorlesungen. Ed. Sibylle Späth. In *Gesammelte Schriften,* ed. Bernd Witte, vol. VI. Berlin, 1922.

Geulincx, Arnold (1624–69)

Ethik oder über die Kardinaltugenden. Trans. Georg Schmitz. Hamburg, 1948.

Glafey, Adam Friedrich (1692–1753)

Vollständige Geschichte des Rechts der Vernunft. Leipzig, 1739. Reprint, Aalen,
   1965.
Gottsched, Johann Christoph (1700–66)
   Erste Gründe der gesammten Weltweisheit. In *Ausgewählte Werke,* ed. P. M.
      Mitchell, vol. 5. Berlin, 1983.
Grotius, Hugo (1583–1645)
   Commentary on the Law of Prize and Booty (De Jure Praedae Commentarius)
      (1604). Trans. Gwladys L. Williams and Walter H. Zeydel. Oxford, 1950.
   De Veritate Religionis Christianae. Amsterdam. 1669.
   The Jurisprudence of Holland. Trans. Robert Warden Lee. Oxford, 1953.
   On the Law of War and Peace (De Jure Belli ac Pacis Libri Tres). Trans. Francis W.
      Kelsey. Oxford, 1925.
   The Rights of War and Peace. Trans. anon., from Barbeyrac's French translation.
      London, 1738
   The Truth of the Christian Religion. Trans. John Clarke, London, [1709] 1827.
Haller, Albrecht von (1708–77)
   Gedichte. Ed. Dr. Ludwig Hirzl. Frauenfeld, 1882.
Harrington, James (1611–77)
   Oceana. In *The Political Works of James Harrington,* ed. J. G. A. Pocock. Cam-
      bridge, 1977.
Hartley, David (1705–57)
   Observations on Man, His Frame, His Duty and His Expectations. 5th ed. 2 vols.
      London, [1749] 1810.
Heineccius, Johann Gottlieb (1681–1741)
   A Methodical System of Universal Law. Trans. George Turnbull. 2 vols. London,
      [1737] 1763.
Helvetius, Claude Adrien (1715–71)
   De l'esprit (1758). Verviers, 1973.
   De l'homme (1772). 2 vols. Paris, 1989.
   On the Mind. London, 1759.
   Treatise on Man (1772). Trans. W. Hooper. 2 vols. London, 1810.
Herbert, Edward, Lord, of Cherbury (1582–1648)
   On Truth. Trans. Meyrick H. Carré. Bristol, 1937.
   De Religione Laici (1645). Ed. and trans. Harold R. Hutcheson. Yale Studies in
      English, vol. 198. New Haven, 1944.
   The Life of Edward, First Lord Herbert of Cherbury, written by himself. Ed. J. M.
      Shuttleworth. London, 1976.
Hobbes, Thomas (1588–1679)
   Body, Man, and Citizen. Ed. Richard S. Peters. New York, 1962.
   De Cive. The English Version. Ed. Howard Warrender. Oxford, 1983.
   De Corpore (1656). In *English Works,* vol. I.
   Elements of Law. Ed. Ferdinand Tönnies. Cambridge, 1928.
   English Works. Ed. Sir William Molesworth. 11 vols. London, 1839–45.
   Leviathan. Ed. Edwin Curley. Indianapolis, 1994.
   Leviathan. Ed. Richard Tuck. Cambridge, 1991.
   Man and Citizen. Ed. Bernard Gert. Indianapolis, 1991.
Hoffbauer, Johann Christoph (1766–1827)

Anfangsgründe der Moralphilosophie und insbesondere der Sittenlehre, nebst einer allgemeinen Geschichte derselben. Halle, 1798.

Hooker, Richard (1553–1600)
Of the Laws of Ecclesiastical Polity. Ed. A. S. McGrade. Cambridge, 1989.
Works. Ed. W. Speed Hill. 5 vols. Cambridge, 1977–.

Hume, David (1711–76)
Dialogues concerning Natural Religion (1776). Ed. Norman Kemp Smith. Edinburgh, 1947.
Enquiry concerning the Human Understanding (1748) and *Enquiry concerning the Principles of Morals* (1751). Ed. L. A. Selby-Bigge, rev. Peter Nidditch. Oxford, 1975.
Essays (1777). Ed. Eugene F. Miller. Indianapolis, 1985.
The Letters of David Hume. Ed. J. Y. T. Greig. Oxford, 1932.
The Natural History of Religion (1757). Ed. H. E. Root. London, 1956.
A Treatise of Human Nature (1739–40). Ed. L. A. Selby-Bigge, rev. Peter Nidditch. Oxford, 1978.

Hutcheson, Francis (1694–1746)
An Essay on the Nature and Conduct of the Passions, with Illustrations on the Moral Sense (1728). 3rd ed. 1742. Reprint, ed. Paul McReynolds. Gainesville, 1969.
Illustrations on the Moral Sense. Ed. Bernard Peach. Cambridge, 1971.
An Inquiry into the Original of Our Ideas of Beauty and Virtue in Two Treatises. I. Concerning Beauty, Order, Harmony, Design. II. Concerning Moral Good and Evil (1725). 4th ed. London, 1738.
A Short Introduction to Moral Philosophy. Trans. Anon. Dublin, 1787.
A System of Moral Philosophy. 2 vols. London, 1755.

Johnson, Samuel (1709–84)
Prose and Poetry. Ed. Mona Wilson. Cambridge, 1967.

Justinian (482–565)
The Digest. Trans. Charles Henry Monro. Vol. I. Cambridge, 1904.
The Institutes. Trans. Peter Birks and Grant McCleod. Ithaca, N.Y., 1987.

Kant, Immanuel (1724–1804)
Anthropology from a Pragmatic Point of View. Trans. Mary J. Gregor. The Hague, 1974.
Bemerkungen in den "Beobachtungen über das Gefühl der Schönen und Erhabenen." Ed. Marie Rischmüller. Kant-Forschungen, vol. 3. Hamburg, 1991.
The Conflict of Faculties. Trans. Mary J. Gregor. New York, 1979.
Critique of Judgement. Parts I, II. Trans. James Creed Meredith. Oxford, 1911, 1928.
Critique of Practical Reason. Trans. Lewis White Beck. Indianapolis, 1959.
Critique of Pure Reason. Trans. Norman Kemp Smith. New York, 1950.
Eine Vorlesung Kants über Ethik. Ed. Paul Menzer. Berlin, 1924.
Foundations of the Metaphysics of Morals. Trans. Lewis White Beck. Indianapolis, 1959.
Gesammelte Schriften. Berlin, 1902–.
Kant: Philosophical Correspondence, 1759–99. Ed. and trans. Arnulf Zweig. Chicago, 1967.
Kants Rechtslehre. Ed. Bernd Ludwig. Hamburg, 1988.

Lectures on Ethics. Ed. Peter Heath and J. B. Schneewind. Trans. Peter Heath. Cambridge, 1997.

Lectures on Philosophical Theology. Trans. Allen W. Wood and Gertrude M. Clark. N.Y., Ithaca, 1978.

The Metaphysics of Morals. Trans. Mary Gregor. Cambridge, 1991.

Observations on the Feeling of the Beautiful and the Sublime. Trans. John Goldthwaite. Berkeley, 1960.

On History. Ed. Lewis White Beck. Indianapolis, 1963.

Political Writings. Ed. Hans Reiss. Trans. H. B. Nisbet. 2nd ed. Cambridge, 1991.

Religion within the Limits of Reason Alone. Trans. Theodore M. Greene and Hoyt H. Hudson. New York, 1960.

Theoretical philosophy, 1755–1770. Trans. and ed. David Walford and Ralf Meerbote. Cambridge, 1992.

Universal Natural History and Theory of the Heavens. Trans. W. Hastie. In *Kant's Cosmogony,* ed. Willy Ley. New York, 1968.

What Real Progress Has Metaphysics Made in Germany since the Time of Leibniz and Wolff? Trans. Ted Humphrey. New York, 1983.

King, William (1659–1729)

An Essay on the Origin of Evil (De Origine Mali) (1702). Trans. Edmund Law. London, 1731.

La Mettrie, Julien Offray de (1709–51)

Discours sur le bonheur. Critical edition by John Falvey.

In *Studies on Voltaire and the Eighteenth Century,* ed. Theodore Besterman, vol. CXXXIV. Banbury, 1975.

Man a Machine (1748) and *Man a Plant.* Trans. Richard A. Watson and Maya Rybalka. Indianapolis, 1994.

Oeuvres philosophiques (1751). 2 vols. Paris, 1987.

Law, William (1686–1761)

Remarks upon a late Book, entitled "The Fable of the Bees" (1724). In *The Works of the Reverend William Law,* vol. II. London, 1892.

A Serious Call to a Devout and Holy Life (1769). In *The Works of the Reverend William Law,* vol. IV. London, 1893.

La Rochefoucauld, François (1613–80)

Oeuvres complètes. Ed. L. Martin-Chauffier and Jean Marchand. Paris, 1964.

Lee, Henry

Anti-Scepticism. London, 1702.

LeGrand, Anthony (d. 1699)

An Entire Body of Philosophy According to the Principles of the Famous Renate des Cartes (1672). Trans. Richard Blome. London, 1694.

Leibniz, Gottfried Wilhelm (1646–1716)

Die philosophische Schriften. Ed. C. J. Gerhardt. 7 vols. Berlin, 1875–90.

Discourse on Metaphysics. In *Philosophical Papers and Letters.*

The Leibniz-Clarke Correspondence. Ed. H. G. Alexander. Manchester, 1956.

Lettres et opuscules inédits. Ed. L. A. Foucher de Careil. Paris, 1854.

Monadology. In *Philosophical Papers and Letters.*

New Essays on Human Understanding. Trans. and ed. Peter Remnant and Jonathan Bennett. Cambridge, 1982.

Philosophical Essays. Ed. and trans. Roger Ariew and Daniel Garber. Indianapolis, 1989.

Philosophical Papers and Letters. Trans. and ed. Leroy E. Loemker. 3rd ed. Dordrecht, 1969.

Political Writings. Trans. and ed. Patrick Riley. 2nd ed. Cambridge, 1988.

Principles of Nature and Grace. In *Philosophical Papers and Letters.*

Selections. Ed. P. P. Wiener. New York, 1951.

Specimen Dynamicum. In *Philosophical Papers and Letters.*

Textes inedits. Ed. Gaston Grua. 2 vols. Paris, 1948.

Theodicee, das ist, Versuch von der Güte Gottes . . . vermehrt von Johan Christoph Gottscheden (1744). Ed. Hubert Horstmann. Berlin, 1996.

Theodicy (1710). Ed. Austin Farrer. Trans. E. M. Huggard. LaSalle, 1985.

Lipsius, Justus (1547–1606)

Six Bookes of Politickes. Trans. William Jones. London, 1594.

Two Bookes of Constancy (1584). Trans. John Stradling. 1594. Reprint, ed. and introd. Rudolf Kirk. New Brunswick, N.J., 1939.

Locke, John (1632–1704)

Correspondence. Ed. E. S. de Beer. 8 vols. Oxford, 1978–.

An Early Draft of Locke's Essay. Ed. R. I. Aaron and Jocelyn Gibb. Oxford, 1936.

An Essay concerning Human Understanding (1689). Ed. Peter Nidditch. Oxford, 1979.

Essays on the Law of Nature. Ed. W. von Leyden. Oxford, 1954.

A Letter concerning Toleration (1689). Trans. William Popple. Ed. James Tully. Indianapolis, 1983.

Questions concerning the Law of Nature. Ed. and trans. Robert Horwitz, Jenny Strauss Clay, and Diskin Clay. Ithaca, N.Y., 1990.

The Reasonableness of Christianity (1695). Ed. I. T. Ramsey. Stanford, 1958.

Some Thoughts concerning Education. Ed. John Yolton and Jean Yolton. Oxford, 1989.

Two Tracts on Government. Ed. Philip Abrams. Cambridge, 1967.

Two Treatises of Government. Ed. Peter Laslett. Cambridge, 1988.

Works. 3 vols. London, 1727.

Lucretius (c. 99–c. 55 B.C.E.)

De Rerum Natura. Trans. W. H .D. Rouse and Martin Ferguson Smith. Cambridge, 1982.

Luther, Martin (1483–1546)

Martin Luther: Selections from His Writings. Ed. John Dillenberger. Garden City, N.Y., 1961.

Works. Ed. Jaroslav Pelikan and Helmut T. Lehman. 55 vols. Philadelphia, various dates.

Machiavelli, Niccolo (1469–1527)

The Chief Works and Others. Trans. A. Gilbert. 3 vols. Durham, 1965.

Discourses on the First Decade of Titus Livius. In *The Chief Works and Others,* vol. I.

The Prince. In *The Chief Works and Others,* vol. I.

The Prince. Ed. Quentin Skinner and Russell Price. Cambridge, 1988.

Maimon, Salomon (1753–1800)

Lebensgeschichte. Ed. Zwi Batscha. Frankfurt am Main, 1984.

Malebranche, Nicholas (1638–1715)
Dialogues on Metaphysics. Trans. Willis Doney. New York, 1980.
The Search after Truth (1674–5). 6th ed. 1712. Trans. Thomas M. Lennon and
   Paul J. Olscamp. Columbus, 1980.
Traité de morale (1684). Ed. Michel Adam. 2nd ed. In *Oeuvres complétes,* vol. XI,
   ed. Andre Robinet. Paris, 1975.
Treatise on Ethics. Trans. Craig Walton. Dordrecht, 1993.
Treatise of Morality. Trans. James Shipton, London, 1699.
Treatise on Nature and Grace. Trans. Patrick Riley. Oxford, 1992.
Mandeville, Bernard de (1670–1733)
An Enquiry into the Origin of Honour. Ed. M. M. Goldsmith. London, 1971.
Fable of the Bees. Ed. F. B. Kaye. 2 vols. Oxford, 1924.
A Letter to Dion (1732). Introd. Jacob Viner. Los Angeles, 1953.
Maupertuis, Pierre Louis Moreau de (1698–1759)
Essai de philosophie morale (1749). In *Les oeuvres de Maupertuis,* vol. 2. Berlin,
   1753.
Melanchthon, Philipp (1497–60)
Melanchthon on Christian Doctrine. The Loci Communes of 1555. Trans. and ed.
   Clyde L. Manschreck. New York, 1965.
Mendelssohn, Moses (1729–86)
Abhandlung über die Evidenz (1764). In *Gesammelte Schriften,* ed. Fritz Bam-
   berger and Leo Strauss, vol. II. Stuttgart-Bad Cannstatt, 1931.
Montaigne, Michel de (1533–92)
Complete Essays. Trans. Donald M. Frame. Stanford, 1965.
Oeuvres completes de Michel de Montaigne. Ed. Albert Thibaudet and Maurice
   Rat. Paris, 1962.
More, Henry (1614–87)
An Account of Virtue, or, Dr. Henry More's Abridgement of Morals (1666). Trans.
   Edward Southwell. London, 1690. (English translation of More's *Enchiri-
   dion Ethicum*)
Moyle, Walter (1672–1721)
Essay upon the Constitution of the Roman Government. In *Two English Political
   Tracts,* ed. Caroline Robbins. Cambridge, 1969.
Müller, August Friedrich (1684–1761)
Einleitung in die philosophischen Wissenschaften. Leipzig, 1733.
Neville, Henry (1609–83)
Plato Redivivus (1681). In *Two English Political Tracts,* ed. Caroline Robbins.
   Cambridge, 1969.
Nicole, Pierre (1625–95)
Oeuvres philosophiques et morales. Ed. C. Jourdain. Paris, 1845. Reprint, Hil-
   desheim, 1970.
Ompteda, D. H. L., Freyherr von
Litteratur des gesammten sowohl natürlichen als positiven Völkerrechts. Regens-
   burg, 1785.
Paley, William (1743–1805)
The Principles of Moral and Political Philosophy (1786). New York, 1839.
Pascal, Blaise (1623–62)
Oeuvres complètes. Ed. Louis Lafuma. Paris, 1963.

Pensées. Trans. A. J. Krailsheimer. London, 1966.

The Provincial Letters. Trans. A. J. Krailsheimer. London, 1967.

Perkins, William (1558–1602)

A Discourse of Conscience (1596) and *The Whole Treatise of Cases of Conscience* (1606). Ed. Thomas F. Merrill. Nieuwkoop, 1966.

Plutarch (c. 46–120)

Moralia. Vol. VI. Trans. W. C. Helmbold. Cambridge, 1970.

Moralia. Vol. XIII, part II. Trans. Harold Cherniss. Cambridge, 1976.

Price, Richard (1723–91)

Four Dissertations (1778). Ed. John Stephens. Bristol, 1990.

Political Writings. Ed. D. O. Thomas. Cambridge, 1991.

A Review of the Principal Questions in Morals (1758; 3rd ed. 1787). Ed. D. Daiches Raphael. Oxford, 1948.

Richard Price and the Ethical Foundations of the American Revolution. Ed. Bernard Peach. Durham, 1979.

Priestley, Joseph (1733–1804)

Priestley's Writings on Philosophy, Science and Politics. Ed. John A. Passmore. New York, 1965.

Pufendorf, Samuel (1632–94)

Les devoirs de l'homme et du citoien. Trans. Jean Barbeyrac. 4th ed. Amsterdam, 1718.

Elements of Universal Jurisprudence. Trans. W. H. Oldfather. Oxford, 1931.

On the Duty of Man and Citizen according to the Law of Nature. Ed. James Tully. Trans. Michael Silverthorne. Cambridge, 1991.

Of the Law of Nature and Nations. Trans. Basil Kennett. London, 1729.

On the Law of Nature and Nations (1672). Trans. C. H. Oldfather and W. A. Oldfather. Oxford, 1934.

On the Natural State of Men. Trans. Michael J. Seidler. Lewiston, 1990.

Political Writings. Ed. Craig L. Carr. Trans. Michael J. Seidler. Oxford, 1994.

Rachel, Samuel (1628–91)

On the Law of Nature and of Nations (1676). Trans. John Pawley Bate. Washington, D.C., 1916.

Reid, Thomas (1710–96)

Essays on the Active Powers of Man (1788). In *Works of Thomas Reid.*

Essays on the Intellectual Powers of Man (1785). In *Works of Thomas Reid.*

The Philosophical Orations of Thomas Reid delivered at Graduation Ceremonies in King's College Aberdeen, 1753, 1756, 1759, 1762. Ed. D. D. Todd. Trans. S. M. L. Darcus.

Philosophical Research Archives 3 (1977), pp. 916–90.

Practical Ethics. Ed. Knud Haakonssen. Princeton, 1990.

Works of Thomas Reid. Ed. Sir William Hamilton. 2 vols. Edinburgh, 1863.

Rousseau, Jean-Jacques (1712–78)

Diskurs über die Ungleichheit. Ed. and trans. Heinrich Meier. Paderborn, 1984.

Emile, or Education. Trans. Allan Bloom. New York, 1979.

The First and Second Discourses. Ed. Roger Masters. Trans. Roger Masters and Judith Masters. New York, 1964.

The First and Second Discourses and *Essay on the Origin of Languages.* Trans. Victor Gourevitch. New York, 1986.

Oeuvres complètes. Ed. Bernard Gagnebin and Marcel Reymond. Vol. I, 1959.
   Vol. II–III, 1964. Vol. IV, 1969. Vol. V, 1996. Paris.
On the Social Contract and *Political Economy*. Ed. Roger Masters. Trans. Judith
   Masters. New York, 1978.
Political Writings. Ed. C. E. Vaughan. 2 vols. Cambridge, 1915.
Sanches, Francisco (c. 1550–c. 1623)
   That Nothing Is Known (1581). Trans. Elaine Limbrick and Douglas Thomson.
      Cambridge, 1988.
Sanderson, Robert (1587–1663)
   Lectures on Conscience and Human Law (1647). Ed. and trans. Chr. Wordsworth.
      Lincoln, 1877.
Sarasin, J.-Fr. (1615–54)
   Discours de morale sur Epicure (1645–46). In *Oeuvres*, ed. P. Festugière, 2. 37–74.
      Paris, 1926.
Selden, John (1584–1654)
   Opera Omnia. 3 vols. London, 1726.
Seneca (4 B.C.E.–65 C.E.)
   Moral Essays. Trans. J. W. Basore. 3 Vols. Cambridge, various years.
Sextus Empiricus (131–200)
   Against the Ethicists. Trans. R. G. Bury. Cambridge, 1968.
   Outlines of Pyrrhonism. Trans. R. G. Bury. Cambridge, 1971.
Shaftesbury, Anthony Ashley Cooper, Third Earl (1671–1713)
   Characteristics of Men, Manners, Opinions, Times, etc. (1711). Ed. John M.
      Robertson. 2 vols. London, 1900.
   Inquiry concerning Virtue or Merit. In *Characteristics of Men*, vol. I.
   An Inquiry concerning Virtue, in Two Discourses. A photoreproduction of the
      1699 edition. Ed. Joseph Filonowicz. Delmar, 1991.
   Life, Letters, and Philosophical Regimen. Ed. Benjamin Rand. London, 1900.
   Preface. In Whichcote, *Works*, vol. III.
   Standard Edition of Shaftesbury's Works. Edited by Gerd Hemmerich, Wolfram
      Benda, and Ulrich Schödlbauer. N.p., n.d.
Smith, Adam (1723–90)
   Essays on Philosophical Subjects. Ed. W. P. D. Wightmen and J. C Bryce. Oxford,
      1980.
   An Inquiry into the Nature and Causes of the Wealth of Nations. Ed. R. H. Camp-
      bell and A. S. Skinner. Oxford, 1979.
   Lectures on Jurisprudence. Ed. R. L. Meek, D. D. Raphael, and P. G. Stein.
      Oxford, 1978.
   The Theory of Moral Sentiments. Ed. D. D. Raphael and A. L. Macfie. Oxford,
      1976.
Smith, John (1618–52)
   Select Discourses. London, 1660.
Spinoza, Benedict (1632–77)
   Ethics. In *Collected Works*, ed. and trans. Edwin Curley, vol. I. Princeton, 1985.
   Tractatus Theologico-Politicus. In *The Political Works*, ed. and trans. A. G.
      Wernham. Oxford, 1958.
Stanley, Thomas.(1625–78)
   The History of Philosophy. London, [1655–62] 1721.

Suarez, Francisco (1548–1617)
De Legibus. Ed. Luciano Perena. Madrid, 1971–.
De Legibus (On Law and God the Lawgiver). In *Selections.*
De Triplici Virtute. In *Selections.*
Defensio Fidei Catholicae. In *Selections.*
Selections from Three Works. Trans. Gwladys Williams, Ammi Brown, and John Waldron. Oxford, 1944.
Taylor, Jeremy (1613–67)
Ductor Dubitantium. In *The Whole Works,* ed. Reginald Heber, vols. XI–XII. London, 1822.
Tetens, Johann Nicolaus (1736–1807)
Philosophische Versuche über die menschliche Natur und ihre Entwicklung (1777). 2 vols. Hildesheim, 1979.
Thomasius, Christian (1655–1728)
Drey Bücher der Göttlichen Rechtsgelahrtheit. Halle, 1709. (German translation of Thomasius 1687–8).
Einleitung zur Sittenlehre (1692). Ed. Werner Schneiders. Reprint, Hildesheim, 1968.
Fundamenta juris naturae et gentium (Law of Nature and of Nations). Halle, 1705.
Grundlehren des Natur- und Völcker-Rechts. Trans. Johann Gottlieb Zeidler. Halle, 1705.
Institutiones jurisprudentiae divinae (1687–8). 7th ed. 1730. Reprint, Aalen, 1963.
Toland, John (1670–1722)
Christianity not Mysterious. London, 1696.
Traherne, Thomas (1637–74)
Christian Ethicks (1675). Ed. Carl L. Marks and George Robert Guffey. Ithaca, N.Y. 1968.
Voltaire, F. M. A. (1694–1778)
Candide, Zadig, and Selected Stories. Trans. Donald Frame. New York, 1961.
Mélanges. Ed. Jacques van den Heuvel. Paris, 1961.
Philosophical Dictionary. Trans. Peter Gay. New York, 1962.
Selections. Ed. Paul Edwards. New York, 1989.
Whichcote, Benjamin (1609–83)
Eight Letters of Dr. Antony Tuckney and Dr. Benjamin Whichcote. Ed. Samuel Salter. London, 1751.
Works (1751). 4 vols. Reprint, New York, 1977.
Wolff, Christian (1679–1754)
Preliminary Discourse on Philosophy in General. Trans. Richard J. Blackwell. Indianapolis, 1963.
Psychologia Empirica (1732). Ed. Joannes Ecole. Hildesheim, 1968.
Psychologia Rationalis (1734). Ed Jean Ecole. Hildesheim, 1972.
Rede von der Sittlehre der Sineser. Trans. G. F. Hagen. In *Gesammelte kleine philosophische Schriften* (1740). Reprint, Hildesheim, 1981.
Vernünftige Gedancken von dem gesellschaftlichen Leben der Menschen (1721). Ed. Hans Werner Arndt. Reprint, Hildesheim, 1975.
Vernünftige Gedancken von der Menschen Tun und Lassen zu Beförderung ihrer Glückseligkeit (1720). Ed. Hans Werner Arndt. Reprint, Hildesheim, 1976.

Vernünftige Gedancken von Gott, der Welt und der Seele des Menschen, auch alle Dingen Überhaupt (1719). Ed. Charles A. Corr. Reprint, Hildesheim, 1983.
Wollaston, William (1660–1724)
   The Religion of Nature Delineated. London, [1722] 1726.
Xenophon (c. 430–c. 355 B.C.E.)
   Socratic Memorabilia. Trans. Sarah Fielding. London, 1847.
Zedler, Johann Heinrich (publisher)
   Grosses vollständiges Universal-Lexicon. Leipzig, 1733–.
Zwingli, Huldrych (1484–1531)
   Writings. Vol. 2. Trans. H. Wayne Pipkin. Allison Park, Pa., 1984.

Collections

Adam, Antoine, ed. *Les libertins au XVIIᵉ siècle.* Paris, 1964.
Bahr, Ehrhard, ed. *Was ist Aufklärung?* Stuttgart, 1976.
Bettenson, Henry, ed. *Documents of the Christian Church.* Oxford, 1947.
Cragg, Gerald R., ed. *The Cambridge Platonists.* New York, 1968.
Erb, Peter C., ed. *Pietists: Selected Writings.* New York, 1983.
Idziak, Janine Marie, ed. *Divine Command Morality.* New York, 1979.
Johnson, William Stacy, and John H. Leith, eds. *Reformed Reader A Sourcebook in Christian Theology.* Vol. I: *Classical Beginnings, 1519–1799.* Louisville, 1993.
Long, A. A., and David Sedley, eds. *The Hellenistic Philosophers.* Vol. I: *Translations of Principal Sources.* Cambridge, 1987.
Monro, D. H., ed. *A Guide to the British Moralists.* London, 1972.
Patrides, C. A., ed. *The Cambridge Platonists.* London, 1969.
Raphael, D. D., ed. *British Moralists.* Oxford, 2 vols., 1969.
Schneewind, J. B., ed. *Moral Philosophy from Montaigne to Kant.* 2 vols. Cambridge, 1990.
Selby-Bigge, L. A., ed. *British Moralists.* 2 vols. Oxford, 1897.

2. Commentary

Aaron, Richard, 1971. *John Locke.* 3rd ed. Oxford.
Abercrombie, Nigel, 1936. *Origins of Jansenism.* Oxford.
Adams, Marilyn McCord, 1987. *William Ockham.* 2 vols. Notre Dame.
Adams, Robert M., 1987. *The Virtue of Faith.* Oxford.
   1994. *Leibniz: Determinist, Theist, Idealist.* New York.
Albee, Ernest, 1901. *A History of English Utilitarianism.* London.
Alderman, William, 1923. "The Significance of Shaftesbury." In *Publications of the Modern Language Association* 38, pp. 175–93.
   1931. "Shaftesbury and the Doctrine of Moral Sense in the Eighteenth Century." *Publications of the Modern Language Association* 46, pp. 1081–94.
Allison, Henry E., 1987. *Benedict de Spinoza.* New Haven.
   1990. *Kant's Theory of Freedom.* Cambridge.
Alquié, Ferdinand, 1974. *Le cartesianisme de Malebranche.* Paris.
Anderson, Georg, 1923. "Kants Metaphysik der Sitten – Ihre Idee und ihr Verhältnis zur Ethik der Wolffschen Schule." *Kantstudien* 28, pp. 41–61.

Annas, Julia, 1993. *The Morality of Happiness*. Oxford.

Annas, Julia, and Jonathan Barnes, 1985. *The Modes of Scepticism*. Cambridge.

Aquist, Lennart, 1960. *The Moral Philosophy of Richard Price*. Lund.

Ardal, Pall, 1966. *Passion and Value in Hume's Treatise*. Edinburgh.

   1977. "Another Look at Hume's Account of Moral Evaluation." *Journal of the History of Philosophy* 15, pp. 405–21.

   1984. "Hume and Reid on Promise, Intention, and Obligation." In *Philosophers of the Scottish Enlightenment*, ed. V. Hope. Edinburgh.

Arnoldt, Emil, 1909. *Gesammelte Schriften*. Vol. V: *Kritische Exkurse im Gebiete der Kantforschung*. Ed. Otto Schöndörffer. Part II. Berlin.

Atwell, John E., 1986. *Ends and Principles in Kant's Moral Thought*. The Hague.

Aune, Bruce, 1979. *Kant's Theory of Morals*. Princeton.

Ayer, A. J., 1980. *Hume*. Oxford.

Baier, Annette, 1979. "Good Men's Women: Hume on Chastity and Trust." *Hume Studies* 5, pp. 1–19.

   1980. "Hume on Resentment." *Hume Studies* 6, pp. 133–49.

   1982. "Hume's Account of Our Absurd Passions." *Journal of Philosophy* 79, pp. 643–51.

   1985. "Frankena and Hume on Points of View." In her *Postures of the Mind*, pp. 157–73. Minneapolis.

   1991. *A Progress of Sentiments*. Cambridge, Mass.

Baier, Kurt, 1966. "Moral Obligation." *American Philosophical Quarterly* 3:3 (July), pp. 210–26.

Baird, A. W. S., 1975. *Studies in Pascal's Ethics*. The Hague.

Barber, W. H., 1955. *Leibniz in France*. Oxford.

Barker, Ernest, 1948. "Paley and His Political Philosophy." In his *Traditions of Civility*. Cambridge.

Barker, John, 1975. *Strange Contrarieties: Pascal in England during the Age of Reason*. Montreal.

Barnard, F. M., 1971. "The 'Practical Philosophy' of Christian Thomasius." *Journal of the History of Ideas* 32, pp. 221–46.

Barnouw, Jeffrey, 1992. "Passion as 'Confused' Perception in Descartes, Malebranche, and Hutcheson." *Journal of the History of Ideas*, 53, pp. 397–424.

Baron, Hans, 1955. *The Crisis of the Early Italian Renaissance*. Princeton.

Bärthlein, Karl, 1965. "Zur Lehre von der 'recta ratio' in der Geschichte der Ethik von der Stoa bis Christian Wolff." *Kantstudien* 56, pp. 125–55.

Baumgardt, David, 1952. *Bentham and the Ethics of Today*. Princeton.

Beck, Lewis White, 1960. *Commentary on Kant's Critique of Practical Reason*. Chicago.

   1969. *Early German Philosophy*. Cambridge, Mass.

Bedford, R. D., 1979. *The Defence of Truth*. Manchester.

Beiser, Frederick C., 1987. *The Fate of Reason*. Cambridge, Mass.

   1996. *The Sovereignty of Reason*. Princeton.

Bell, David, 1984. *Spinoza in Germany from 1670 to the Age of Goethe*. London.

Benden, Magdelene, 1972. *Christian August Crusius: Wille und Verstand als Prinzipien des Handelns*. Bonn.

Benichou, Paul, 1971. *Man and Ethics*. Trans. E. Hughes. New York.

Bennett, Jonathan, 1984. *A Study of Spinoza's Ethics*. Indianapolis.

Berlin, Isaiah, 1980. *Against the Current*. New York.
Berman, Harold J., 1983. *Law and Revolution*. Cambridge, Mass.
Bernstein, Andrew, 1980. *Shaftesbury, Rousseau, and Kant*. London.
Bett, Richard, 1990. "Carneades' Distinction between Assent and Approval." *Monist* 73, pp. 3–20.
Bidney, David, 1940. *The Psychology and Ethics of Spinoza*. 2nd ed. New Haven.
Bittner, R., and Konrad Cramer, eds., 1975. *Materialian zu Kants "Kritik der praktischen Vernunft."* Frankfurt am Main.
Blackstone, William T., 1965. *Francis Hutcheson and Contemporary Moral Theory*. Athens, Ga.
Blackwell, Richard J., 1961. "The Structure of Wolffian Philosophy." *Modern Schoolman* 38, pp. 203–18.
Blakey, Robert, 1833. *History of Moral Science*. 2 vols. London.
Bloch, Ernst, 1986. *Natural Law and Human Dignity*. Cambridge, Mass.
Bloch, Olivier René, 1971. *La philosophie de Gassendi*. The Hague.
Blom, John J., ed., 1978. *Descartes: His Moral Philosophy and Psychology*. New York.
Blumenfeld, David, 1995. "Perfection and Happiness in the Best Possible World." In Jolley, pp. 382–410.
Bobbio, Norberto, 1947. "Leibniz e Pufendorf." *Revista di filosofia* 38, pp. 118–29. 1993. *Thomas Hobbes and the Natural Law Tradition*. Trans. Daniela Gobetti. Chicago.
Bock, Gisela, Quentin Skinner, and Maurizio Viroli, eds., 1990. *Machiavelli and Republicanism*. Cambridge.
Boler, John, 1993. "Transcending the Natural: Duns Scotus on the Two Affections of the Will." *American Catholic Philosophical Quarterly* 67:1, pp. 109–26.
Bostrenghi, Daniela, ed., 1992. *Hobbes e Spinoza. Scienza e Politica*. Naples.
Bourke, V. J., 1968. *History of Ethics*. 2 vols. New York.
Bowle, John, 1951. *Hobbes and His Critics*. London.
Bowring, John, 1843. *Memoirs of Bentham*. In *The Works of Jeremy Bentham*, ed. John Bowring, vol. X. London.
Bradley, F. H., 1927. *Ethical Studies* (1876). 2nd ed. Oxford.
Brandt, Reinhard, and Werner Stark, eds., 1987. *Neue Autographen und Dokumente zu Kants Leben, Schriften und Vorlesungen*. Kant-Forschungen I. Hamburg.
Braun, Lucien, 1973. *Histoire de l'histoire de la philosophie*. Paris.
Brender, Natalie, 1997. *Precarious Positions: Aspects of Kantian Moral Agency*. Ph.D. dissertation, Johns Hopkins University. Baltimore.
Bricke, John, 1974. "Emotion and Thought in Hume's 'Treatise.'" *Canadian Journal of Philosophy* (suppl.) 1, pp. 53–71.
Broad, C. D., 1930. *Five Types of Ethical Theory*. London.
Brockliss, L. W. B., 1987. *French Higher Education in the Seventeenth and Eighteenth Centuries*. Oxford.
Brown, Charlotte, 1988. "Is Hume an Internalist?" *Journal of the History of Philosophy* 26:1 (January), pp. 69–87.
Brown, Gregory, 1995. "Leibniz's Moral Philosophy." In Jolley, pp. 411–40.
Brown, Keith, ed., 1965. *Hobbes Studies*. Oxford.

Brown, Peter, 1983. *Augustine of Hippo*. Berkeley.

Brown, Stuart, 1984. *Leibniz*. Minneapolis.

ed., 1979. *Philosophers of the Enlightenment*. Sussex.

ed., 1991. *Nicholas Malebranche*. Assen.

Bruford, W. H., 1962. *Culture and Society in Classical Weimar*. Cambridge.

Brush, Craig B., 1966. *Montaigne and Bayle*. The Hague.

Buckle, Stephen, 1991. *Natural Law and the Theory of Property*. Oxford.

Bull, Hedly, Benedict Kingsbury, and Adam Roberts, eds., 1992. *Hugo Grotius and International Relations*. Oxford.

Burke, Peter, 1987. *Montaigne*. Oxford.

Burkill, T. A., 1971. *The Evolution of Christian Thought*. Ithaca, N.Y.

Burns, J. H., ed., 1991. *Cambridge History of Political Theory, 1450–1700*. Cambridge.

1993. "Nature and Natural Authority in Bentham." *Utilitas* 5:2, pp. 209–20.

Burnyeat, Myles, 1979. "Conflicting Appearances." *Proceedings of the British Academy* 65, pp. 69–111.

1980. "Can the Sceptic Live His Scepticism?" In *Doubt and Dogmatism: Studies in Hellenistic Philosophy*, ed. M. Schofield, M. Burnyeat, and J. Barnes. Berkeley.

ed., 1983. *The Skeptical Tradition*. Berkeley.

1984. "The Sceptic in His Time and Place." In Rorty, Schneewind, and Skinner, pp. 2225– 54.

Burtt, Shelley, 1992. *Virtue Transformed*. Cambridge.

Busch, Werner, 1979. *Die Entstehung der kritischen Rechtsphilosophie Kants 1762–1780*. Berlin.

Campbell, R. H., and Andrew S. Skinner, eds., 1982. *The Origin and Nature of the Scottish Enlightenment*. Edinburgh.

Campbell, T. D., 1971. *Adam Smith's Science of Morals*. London.

Carboncini, Sonia, 1989. "Christian August Crusius und die Leibniz-Wolffsche Philosophie." *Studia Leibnitziana Supplementa* 26, pp. 110–25.

Carnois, Bernard, 1987. *The Coherence of Kant's Doctrine of Freedom*. Trans. David Booth. Chicago.

Cassirer, Ernst, 1945. *Rousseau, Kant, Goethe*. Princeton.

1953. *The Platonic Renaissance in England*. Trans. James P. Pettegrove. Austin, Tex.

Chadwick, Owen, 1957. *From Bossuet to Newman: The Idea of Doctrinal Development*. Cambridge.

Champion, J. A. I., 1992. *The Pillars of Priestcraft Shaken*. Cambridge.

Chandler, John, 1985. "Divine Command Theories and the Appeal to Love." *American Philosophical Quarterly* 22 (July), pp. 231–9.

Chappell, Vere, 1994a. "Locke on the Freedom of the Will." In *Locke's Philosophy*, ed. G. A. J. Rogers, pp. 101–21. Oxford.

1994b. "Locke on the Intellectual Basis of Sin." *Journal of the History of Philosophy* 32:2, pp. 197–207.

ed., 1994c. *The Cambridge Companion to Locke*. Cambridge.

Charron, Jean Daniel, 1960. *The "Wisdom" of Pierre Charron: An Orignal and Orthodox Code of Morality*. Chapel Hill.

Charvet, John, 1968. *The Social Problem in the Philosophy of Rousseau*. Princeton.

Chroust, Anton-Hermann, 1943. "Hugo Grotius and the Scholastic Natural Law Tradition." *New Scholasticism* 17:2, pp. 101–33.

Ciafardone, Raffaele, 1982. "Über das Primat der praktischen Vernunft vor der theoretischen bei Thomasius und Crusius mit Beziehung auf Kant." *Studia Leibnitiana* 14:1, pp. 127–35.

Clark, M. L., 1974. *Paley.* Toronto.

Clarke, Stephen R. L., 1985. "God-Appointed Berkeley and the General Good." In *Essays on Berkeley,* ed. John Foster and Howard Robinson, pp. 233–53. Oxford.

Coleman, Dorothy Gabe, 1987. *Montaigne's "Essays."* London.

Colman, John, 1972. "Bernard Mandeville and the Reality of Virtue." *Philosophy* 47, pp. 125–39.

1983. *John Locke's Moral Philosophy.* Edinburgh.

Cone, Carl B., 1952. *Torchbearer of Freedom: The Influence of Richard Price on the Eighteenth Century.* Lexington, Ky.

Corr, Charles A., 1975. "Christian Wolff and Leibniz." *Journal of the History of Ideas* 36, pp. 241–62.

Costello, William S., 1958. *The Scholastic Curriculum at Early Seventeenth Century Cambridge.* Cambridge, Mass.

Cottingham, John G., 1988. "The Intellect, the Will, and the Passions: Spinoza's Critique of Descartes." *Journal of the History of Philosophy* 26, pp. 239–57.

Cottle, Charles E., 1979. "Justice As an Artificial Virtue in Hume's *Treatise.*" *Journal of the History of Ideas* 40, pp. 457–66.

Cragg, Gordon, R., 1950. *From Puritanism to the Age of Reason: A Study of Religious Thought in the Church of England, 1660–1770.* Cambridge.

Craig, Edward, 1987. *The Mind of God and the Works of Man.* Oxford.

Crane, R. S., 1967. "Anglican Apologetics and the Idea of Progress, 1699–1745." In his *The Idea of the Humanities,* vol. I, pp. 214–87. Chicago.

Cranston, Maurice, 1983. *Jean-Jacques: The Early Life and Work of Jean-Jacques Rousseau, 1712–1754.* Chicago.

1991. *The Noble Savage: Jean-Jacques Rousseau, 1754–1762.* Chicago.

Cranston, Maurice, and Richard Peters, eds., 1972. *Hobbes and Rousseau.* Garden City, N.Y.

Cranz, F. Edward, 1959. *An Essay on the Development of Luther's Thought on Justice, Law, and Society.* Cambridge, Mass.

Crimmins, James E., 1983. "John Brown and the Theological Tradition of Utilitarian Ethics." *History of Political Thought* 4, pp. 523–50.

1990. *Secular Utilitarianism: Social Science and the Critique of Religion in the Thought of Jeremy Bentham.* Oxford.

1994. "Bentham's Political Radicalism." *Journal of the History of Ideas* 55, pp. 259–81.

Crocker, Lester, 1952. *Two Diderot Studies: Ethics and Aesthetics.* Baltimore.

1959. *An Age of Crisis: Man and World in Eighteenth Century French Thought.* Baltimore.

1963. *Nature and Culture: Ethical Thought in the French Enlightenment.* Baltimore.

Crowe, M. B., 1972. *The Changing Profile of Natural Law.* The Hague.

Cua, A. S., 1966. *Reason and Virtue.* Athens, Ohio.

Cumming, Ian, 1955. *Helvetius: His Life and Place in the History of Educational Thought*. London.

Cumming, Robert, 1955. "Descartes' Provisional Morality." *Review of Metaphysics* 9, pp. 208–35.

Curley, Edwin, 1978. *Descartes against the Skeptics*. Cambridge, Mass.

1988. *Behind the Geometrical Method*. Princeton.

1990. "Reflections on Hobbes: Recent Work on His Moral and Political Philosophy." *Journal of Philosophical Research* 15 (May), pp. 169–250.

1992. "I Durst Not Write So Boldly." In Bostrenghi, pp. 497–595.

Dalgarno, Melvin T., 1984. "Reid's Natural Jurisprudence: The Language of Rights and Duties." In Hope.

d'Angers, Julien-Eymard, 1954. *Pascal et ses précurseurs*. Paris.

d'Arcy, Eric, 1961. *Conscience and Its Right to Freedom*. London.

Darnton, Robert, 1995. *The Forbidden Best-Sellers of Pre-Revolutionary France*. New York.

Darwall, Stephen L., 1989. "Obligation and Motive in the British Moralists." In *Foundations of Moral and Political Philosophy*, ed. Ellen F. Paul, Fred D. Miller Jr., and Jeffrey Paul, pp. 133–50. Oxford.

1992. "Conscience As Self-Authorizing in Butler's Ethics." In *Joseph Butler's Moral and Religious Thought*, ed. Christopher Cunliffe, pp. 209–41. Oxford.

1995. *The British Moralists and the Internal 'Ought'*. Cambridge.

Davidson, Donald, 1980. "Hume's Cognitive Theory of Pride." In his *Essays on Action and Events*, pp. 277–90. Oxford.

Davie, George E., 1961. *The Democratic Intellect*. Edinburgh.

1973. *The Social Significance of the Scottish Philosophy of Common Sense*. Dundee.

Davis, J. C., 1981. *Utopia and the Ideal Society*. Cambridge.

Deane, Herbert A., 1963. *The Political and Social Ideas of St. Augustine*. New York.

Dedeyan, Charles., 1987. *Diderot et la penseé anglaise*. Paris.

Delahunty, R. J., 1985. *Spinoza*. London.

Delbos, Victor, 1926. *La philosophie pratique de Kant*. 2nd ed. Paris.

Deleuze, Gilles, 1988. *Spinoza: Practical Philosophy*. Trans. Robert Hurley. San Francisco.

de Muralt, André, 1978. "La structure de la philosophie politique moderne. D'Occam a Rousseau." In *Souveraineté et pouvoir. Cahiers de la Revue de Théologie et de Philosophie* (Geneva) 2, pp. 3–83.

Dent, N. J. H., 1988. *Rousseau*. Oxford.

Denzer, H., 1972. *Moralphilosophie und Naturrecht bei Samuel Pufendorf*. Munich.

Derathé, Robert, 1948. *Le rationalisme de J. J. Rousseau*. Paris.

1950. *J. J. Rousseau et la science politique de son temps*. Paris.

de Vleeschaumwer, Herman-J., 1962. *The Development of Kantian Thought*. Trans. A. R. C. Duncan. London.

Dibon, Paul, ed., 1959. *Pierre Bayle, le Philosophe de Rotterdam*. Amsterdam.

Dihle, Albrecht, 1982. *The Theory of Will in Classical Antiquity*. Berkeley.

Dinwiddy, John, 1975. "Bentham's Transition to Political Radicalism." *Journal of the History of Ideas* 35, pp. 683–700.

1989. *Bentham*. Oxford.

Domenech, Jacques, 1989. *L'ethique des lumières*. Paris.

Donagan, Alan, 1989. *Spinoza*. Chicago.

Döring, Detlef, 1992. *Pufendorf-Studien*. Berlin.
Douglas, A. E., 1965. "Cicero the Philosopher." In *Cicero,* ed. T. A. Dorsey. London.
Ducharme, Howard M., 1986. "Personal Identity in Samuel Clarke." *Journal of the History of Philosophy* 24, pp. 359–83.
Dufour, Alfred, 1991. "Pufendorf." In Burns, pp. 563–88.
Duggan, Thomas, 1976. "Active Power and the Liberty of Moral Agents." In *Thomas Reid: Critical Interpretations,* ed. Stephen F. Barker and Tom L. Beauchamp. Philadelphia.
Dumont, Louis, 1977. *From Mandeville to Marx*. Chicago.
Duncan, A. R. C., 1957. *Practical Reason and Morality*. London.
Duncan-Jones, Austin, 1952. *Butler's Moral Philosophy*. London.
Dunn, John, 1969. *The Political Thought of John Locke*. Cambridge.
Dussinger, John A., 1981. "'The Lovely System of Lord Shaftesbury': An Answer to Locke . . . ?" *Journal of the History of Ideas* 42, pp. 151–8.
Ebeling, Gerhard, 1970. *Luther: An Introduction to His Thought*. Trans. R. A. Wilson. Philadelphia.
Ecole, Jean, 1990. *La métaphysique de Christian Wolff*. 2 vols. Hildesheim.
Edwards, Charles, 1970. "The Law of Nature in the Thought of Hugo Grotius." *Journal of Politics* 32:4, pp. 784–807.
    1981. *Hugo Grotius*. Chicago.
England, F. E., 1929. *Kant's Conception of God*. London.
Erdmann, Benno, 1876. *Martin Knutzen und seine Zeit*. Leipzig.
Falk, W. D., 1976. "Hume on Is and Ought." *Canadian Journal of Philosophy* 11, pp. 359–78.
Faulkner, Robert K., 1981. *Richard Hooker and the Politics of a Christian England*. Berkeley.
Fay, C. R., 1956. *Adam Smith and the Scotland of His Day*. Cambridge, Mass.
Febvre, Lucien, 1982. *The Problem of Unbelief in the Sixteenth Century* (1942). Trans. Beatrice Gottlieb. Cambridge, Mass.
Ferguson, James P., 1974. *The Philosophy of Dr. Samuel Clarke and Its Critics*. New York.
    1976. *Dr. Samuel Clarke: An Eighteenth Century Heretic*. Kineton, England.
Ferrarri, Jean, 1979. *Les sources française de la philosophie de Kant*. Paris.
Feuerlein, Emil, 1859. *Die philosophische Sittenlehre in ihren geschichtlichen Hauptformen*. 2 vols. Tübingen.
Fichter, J. H., 1940. *Man of Spain: Francisco Suarez*. New York.
Fiering, Norman, 1981. *Jonathan Edward's Moral Thought and Its British Context*. Chapel Hill.
Finnis, John, 1980. *Natural Law and Natural Rights*. Oxford.
Fitzgibbons, Athol, 1995. *Adam Smith's System of Liberty, Wealth and Virtue*. Oxford.
Flathman, Richard, 1992. *Willful Liberalism*. Ithaca, N.Y.
    1993. *Thomas Hobbes: Skepticism, Individuality and Chastened Politics*. Newbury Park, Calif.
Fogelin, Robert J., 1985. *Hume's Skepticism in the Treatise of Human Nature*. London.
Forbes, Duncan, 1975. *Hume's Philosophical Politics*. Cambridge.

Forster, Eckhart, ed. 1988. *Kant's Transcendental Deductions*. Stanford.

Forsyth, Murray, 1982. "The Place of Richard Cumberland in the History of Natural Law." *Journal of the History of Philosophy* 20, pp. 23–42.

Foster, M. B., 1935–6. "Christian Theology and Modern Science of Nature." Parts I and II. *Mind* 44 (1935), pp. 439–65; 45, pp. 1–27.

Frame, Donald, 1965. *Montaigne, a Biography*. New York.

France, Peter, 1983. *Diderot*. Oxford.

Franck, Ad., 1881. *Réformateurs et publicistes de l'Europe, dix-septième siècle*. Paris.

Frankena, William, 1955. "Hutcheson's Moral Sense Theory." *Journal of the History of Ideas* 16, pp. 356–75.

    1983a. "Concepts of Rational Action in the History of Ethics." *Social Theory and Practice* 9:2–3, pp. 165–79.

    1983b. "The Ethics of Right Reason." *Monist* 66:1, pp. 3–25.

Freeman, Eugene, and Maurice Mandelbaum, eds., 1975. *Spinoza, Essays in Interpretation*. LaSalle, Ill.

Friedrich, Hugo, 1991. *Montaigne* (1949). Trans. Dawn Eng. Berkeley.

Fruchtman, Jack, Jr., 1983. "The Apocalyptic Politics of Richard Price and Joseph Priestley: A Study in Late Eighteenth-Century English Republican Millenarianism." *Transactions of the American Philosophical Society* (Philadelphia) 73:4, pp. 1–125.

Garrett, Don, ed., 1996. *The Cambridge Companion to Spinoza*. Cambridge.

Gascoigne, John, 1989. *Cambridge in the Age of Enlightenment*. Cambridge.

Gaskin, J. C. A., 1988. *Hume's Philosophy of Religion*. 2nd ed. New York.

Gause, Fritz, 1974. *Kant und Königsberg*. Ostfriesland.

Gauthier, David, 1969. *The Logic of Leviathan*. Oxford.

    1990. *Moral Dealing: Contract, Ethics, and Reason*. Ithaca, N.Y.

Gauthier, René Antoine, 1970. *L'éthique à Nicomaque*. 2nd ed. Vol. I. Louvain.

Gay, John H., 1963. "Matter and Freedom in the Thought of Samuel Clarke." *Journal of the History of Ideas* 24, pp. 85–105.

Gerrish, B. A., 1962. *Grace and Reason*. Oxford.

Gibson, A. Boyce, 1932. *The Philosophy of Descartes*. London.

Gierke, Otto, 1934. *Natural Law and the Theory of Society, 1500 to 1800*. 2 vols. Trans. Ernest Barker. Cambridge.

Glathe, Alfred B., 1950. *Hume's Theory of the Passions and of Morals*. Berkeley.

Goldmann, Lucien, 1964. *The Hidden God*. Trans. Philip Thody. London.

    1971. *Immanuel Kant*. London.

Goldsmith, M. M., 1985. *Private Vices, Public Benefits: Bernard Mandeville's Social and Political Thought*. Cambridge.

    1988. "Regulating Anew the Moral and Political Sentiments of Mankind: Bernard Mandeville and the Scottish Enlightenment." *Journal of the History of Ideas* 49, pp. 587–606.

Gouhier, Henri, 1983. *Rousseau et Voltaire*. Paris.

Gourevitch, Victor, 1988. "Rousseau's Pure State of Nature." *Interpretation* 16:1, pp. 23–59.

Gracia, Jorge J. E., 1992. *Philosophy and Its History*. Albany, N.Y.

Grave, S. A., 1960. *The Scottish Philosophy of Common Sense*. Oxford.

Grean, Stanley, 1967. *Shaftesbury's Philosophy of Religion and Ethics*. Athens, Ohio.

Green, F. C., 1955. *J. J. Rousseau*. Cambridge.

Greene, Robert A., 1991. "Synderesis, the Spark of Conscience, in the English Renaissance." *Journal of the History of Ideas* 52:2, pp. 195–219.

Gregor, Mary, 1963. *The Laws of Freedom.* Oxford.

1993. "Kant on Obligation, Rights and Virtue." *Jahrbuch für Recht und Ethik* 1, pp. 69–102.

Grendler, Paul F., 1963. "Pierre Charron: Precursor to Hobbes." *Review of Politics* 25, pp. 212–24.

Grimsley, Ronald, 1973. *The Philosophy of Rousseau.* Oxford.

Grisez, Germaine, Joseph Boyle, and John Finnis, 1987. "Practical Principles, Moral Truth, and Ultimate Ends." *American Journal of Jurisprudence* 32, pp. 99–151.

Griswold, Charles, 1991. "Rhetoric and Ethics: Adam Smith on Theorizing about the Moral Sentiments." *Philosophy and Rhetoric* 24:3, pp. 213–37.

Grua, Gaston, 1953. *Jurisprudence universelle et théodicée selon Leibniz.* Paris.

1956. *La justice humaine selon Leibniz.* Paris.

Grunwald, Max, 1986. *Spinoza in Deutschland* (1897). Aalen.

Gueroult, Martial, 1977. *Etudes de philosophie Allemande.* Hildesheim.

1984. *Descartes' Philosophy Interpreted According to the Order of Reasons.* 2 vols. Trans. Roger Ariew. Minneapolis.

1984–8. *Dianoématique: Histoire de la histoire de la philosophie.* Paris.

Gulyga, Arsenij, 1981. *Kant.* Frankfurt am Main.

Guthrie, W. K. C., 1962. *A History of Greek Philosophy.* Vol. I. Cambridge.

Gysi, Lydia, 1962. *Platonism and Cartesianism in the Philosophy of Ralph Cudworth.* Bern.

Haakonssen, Knud, 1981. *The Science of a Legislator.* Cambridge.

1985a. "Hugo Grotius and the History of Political Thought." *Political Theory* 13:2, pp. 239–65.

1985b. "Natural Law and the Scottish Enlightenment." *Man and Nature* (Edmonton) 4, pp. 47–80.

1988. "Moral Philosophy and Natural Law: From the Cambridge Platonists to the Scottish Enlightenment." *Political Science* 40, pp. 97–110.

1990. "Natural Law and Moral Realism: The Scottish Synthesis." In M. A. Stewart, pp. 61–85.

1996. *Natural Law and Moral Philosophy: From Grotius to the Scottish Enlightenment.* Cambridge.

1997a. "The Character and Obligation of Natural Law according to Richard Cumberland." In *English Philosophy in the Age of Locke,* ed. M. A. Stewart. Oxford.

1997b. "Divine/Natural Law Theories in Ethics." In *The Cambridge History of Seventeenth Century Philosophy,* ed. Michael Ayers and Daniel Garber. Cambridge.

Haakonssen, Knud, and Udo Thiel, eds., 1993. *History of Philosophy Yearbook.* Vol. 1. Australasian Society for the History of Philosophy. Canberra.

Haggenmacher, Peter, 1983. *Grotius et la doctrine de la guerre juste.* Paris.

Halevy, Elie, 1928. *The Growth of Philosophical Radicalism.* Trans. Mary Morris. London.

Hall, A. Rupert, 1980. *Philosophers at War: The Quarrel between Newton and Leibniz.* Cambridge.

Hamilton, Bernice, 1963. *Political Thought in Sixteenth Century Spain*. Oxford.

Hampshire, Stuart, 1951. *Spinoza*. London.

1977. *Two Theories of Morality*. Oxford. Reprinted in his *Morality and Conflict*. Cambridge, Mass.

Hampton, Jean, 1986. *Hobbes and the Social Contract Tradition*. Cambridge.

Hardie, W. F. R., 1968. *Aristotle's Ethical Theory*. Oxford.

Harrison, Jonathan, 1976. *Hume's Moral Epistemology*. Oxford.

1981. *Hume's Theory of Justice*. Oxford.

Harrison, Peter, 1990. *"Religion" and the Religions in the English Enlightenment*. Cambridge.

Harrison, Ross, 1983. *Bentham*. London.

Hart, H. L. A., 1982. *Essays on Bentham*. Oxford.

Haydn, Hiram, 1950. *The Counter-Renaissance*. New York.

Hayek, F. A., 1967. "Dr. Bernard Mandeville." *Proceedings of the British Academy* 52, pp. 125–41.

Hazard, Paul, 1963a. *European Thought in the Eighteenth Century* (1946). Trans. J. Lewis May. New York.

1963b. *The European Mind, 1680–1715* (1935). Trans. J. Lewis May. New York.

Heimsoeth, H., D. Henrich, and G. Tonelli, eds., 1967. *Studien zur Kants philosophischer Entwicklung*. Hildesheim.

Heinekamp, Albert, 1969. *Das Problem des Guten bei Leibniz. Kantstudien* Ergänzungsheft 98. Bonn.

1989. "Das Glück als höchstes Gut in Leibniz' Philosophie." In *The Leibniz Renaissance*, pp. 99–125. Florence.

Hendel, C. W., 1962. *Jean-Jacques Rousseau: Moralist*. 2nd ed. Indianapolis.

Heninger, S. K., 1974. *Touches of Sweet Harmony*. San Marino, Calif.

Henrich, Dieter, 1957. "Hutcheson und Kant." *Kantstudien* 49, pp. 49–69.

1960. "Der Begriff der sittlichen Einsicht und Kant's Lehre vom Faktum der Vernunft." In *Die Gegenwart der Griechen im neuern Denken*, ed. Dieter Henrich, Walter Schulz, and Karl-Heinz Volkmann-Schluck, pp. 77–115. Tübingen.

1963. "Über Kant's früheste Ethik." *Kantstudien* 54, pp. 404–31.

1992. *Aesthetic Judgment and the Moral Image of the World*. Stanford.

1994. *The Unity of Reason*. Ed. Richard L. Velkley. Cambridge, Mass.

Heppe, Heinrich, 1984. *Reformed Dogmatics*. Trans. G. T. Thomson. Grand Rapids, Mich.

Herman, Barbara, 1993. *The Practice of Moral Judgment*. Cambridge, Mass.

Hermand, Pierre, 1972. *Les idées morales de Diderot* (1923). Hildesheim.

Heyd, David, 1982. *Supererogation*. Cambridge.

Hill, Thomas E., Jr., 1992. *Dignity and Practical Reason in Kant's Ethical Theory*. Ithaca, N.Y.

Hinrichs, Carl, 1971. *Preussentum und Pietismus*. Göttingen.

Hirschman, Albert O., 1977. *The Passions and the Interests: Political Arguments for Capitalism before Its Triumph*. Princeton.

Hobart, Michael E., 1982. *Science and Religion in the Thought of Nicholas Malebranche*. Chapel Hill.

Hochstrasser, Tim, 1993. "Conscience and Reason: The Natural Law Theory of Jean Barbeyrac Revisited." *Historical Journal* 36:2, pp. 289–308.

1995. "The Claims of Conscience: Natural Law Theory, Obligation, and Resistance in the Hugenot Diaspora." In *New Essays on the Political Thought of the Huguenots of the Refuge*, ed. John Christian Laursen, pp. 15–51. Leiden.

Höffe, Ottfried, ed., 1989. *Grundlegung zur Metaphysik der Sitten, ein kooperativer Kommentar.* Frankfurt am Main.

Hoffman, Paul, 1986. "The Unity of Descartes's Man." *Philosophical Review* 95:3 (July), pp. 339–70.

1990. "Cartesian Passions and Cartesian Dualism." *Pacific Philosophical Quarterly* 71, pp. 310–33.

1991. "Three Dualist Theories of the Passions." *Philosophical Topics* 19:1, pp. 153–200.

Hoffmann, Alfons, ed., 1902. *Immanuel Kant. Ein Lebensbild nach Darstellungen der Zeitgenossen.* Halle am Saar.

Hont, Istvan, 1987. "The Language of Sociability and Commerce: Samuel Pufendorf and the Theoretical Foundation of the 'Four States Theory.'" In Pagden, pp. 253–76.

Hont, Istvan, and Michael Ignatieff, eds., 1983. *Wealth and Virtue.* Cambridge.

Hope, Vincent, ed., 1984. *Philosophers of the Scottish Enlightenment.* Edinburgh.

1989. *Virtue by Consensus.* Oxford.

Horkheimer, Max, 1988. "Montaigne und die Funktion der Skepsis." In *Gesammelte Schriften*, ed. Alfred Schmidt, vol. 4, pp. 236–94. Frankfurt am Main.

Horowitz, Irving L., 1954. *Claude Helvetius: Philosopher of Democracy and Enlightenment.* New York.

Horowitz, Maryanne Cline, 1971. "Pierre Charron's View of the Source of Wisdom." *Journal of the History of Philosophy* 9, pp. 443–57.

1974. "Natural Law As the Foundation for an Autonomous Ethic: Pierre Charron's *De la sagesse.*" *Studies in the Renaissance* 21, pp. 204–27.

Hostler, John, 1975. *Leibniz's Moral Philosophy.* London.

Howald, Ernst, Alois Dempf, and Theodor Litt, 1981. *Geschichte der Ethik vom Altertum bis zum Beginn des 20. Jahrhunderts.* Munich.

Hruschka, Joachim, 1990. "Die Person als ein Zweck an sich selbst." *Juristen Zeitung* 45, pp. 1–15.

1992. "Universalization and Related Principles." *Archives for Philosophy of Law and Social Philosophy* 78:3, pp. 289–300.

Hudson, W. D., 1970. *Reason and Right.* San Francisco.

Hulliung, Mark, 1983. *Citizen Machiavelli.* Princeton.

Humberstone, L., 1992. "Direction of Fit." *Mind* 101:401 (Jan.), pp. 59–84.

Hundert, E. J., 1994. *The Enlightenment's Fable: Bernard Mandeville and the Discovery of Society.* Cambridge.

1995. "Bernard Mandeville and the Enlightenment's Maxims of Modernity." *Journal of the History of Ideas* 56:4, pp. 577–94.

Ilting, Karl-Heinz, 1983. *Naturrecht und Sittlichkeit.* Stuttgart.

Inwood, Brad, 1985. *Ethics and Human Action in Early Stoicism.* Oxford.

Irwin, T. H., 1992. "Who Discovered the Will?" *Philosophical Perspectives* 6, pp. 453–73.

1993. "Tradition and Reason in the History of Ethics." In *Foundations of Moral and Political Philosophy*, ed. Ellen Frankel Paul, Fred D. Miller Jr., and Jeffrey Paul, pp. 45–68. Oxford.

Jack, Malcolm R., 1975. "Religion and Ethics in Mandeville." In Primer 1975b, pp. 34–42.

1989. *Corruption and Progress: The Eighteenth Century Debate.* New York.

Jackson, R., 1943. "Bishop Butler's Refutation of Psychological Egoism." *Philosophy* 18, pp. 114–39.

Jacob, Jane, 1976. *The Newtonians and the English Revolution, 1689–1720.* Ithaca, N.Y.

James, E. D., 1972. *Pierre Nicole: Jansenist and Humanist.* The Hague.

James, Susan, 1994. "Internal and External in the Work of Descartes." In *Philosophy in an Age of Pluralism*, ed. James Tully, pp. 7–19. Cambridge.

Jensen, Henning, 1978. "Common Sense and Common Language in Thomas Reid's Ethical Theory." *Monist* 61, pp. 299–310.

Jodl, Friedrich, 1906. *Geschichte der Ethik.* 2 vols. 2nd ed. Stuttgart.

Jolley, Nicholas, ed., 1995. *Cambridge Companion to Leibniz.* Cambridge.

Jones, Howard, 1981. *Pierre Gassendi, 1592–1655.* Nieuwkoop, Netherlands.

1989. *The Epicurean Tradition.* London.

Jones, Peter, 1982. *Hume's Sentiments: Their Ciceronian and French Context.* Edinburgh.

Jonsen, Albert R., and Stephen Toulmin, 1988. *The Abuse of Casuistry.* Berkeley.

Joseph, H. W. B., 1947. *Lectures on the Philosophy of Leibniz.* Ed. J. L. Austin. Oxford.

Joy, Lynn Sumida, 1987. *Gassendi the Atomist.* Cambridge.

Kahn, Charles H., 1988. "Discovering the Will: From Aristotle to Augustine." In *The Question of "Eclecticism,"* ed. John M. Dillon and A. A. Long. Berkeley.

Kalinowski, Georges, and Jean-Louis Gardes, 1974. "Un logicien déontique avant la lettre: Gottfried Wilhelm Leibniz." *Archiv für Rechts- und Socialphilosophie* 60:1, pp. 79–112.

Kavka, Gregory S., 1986. *Hobbesian Moral and Political Theory.* Princeton.

Kelley, Donald R., 1990. *The Human Measure: Social Thought in the Western Legal Tradition.* Cambridge.

Kemp, John, 1968. *The Philosophy of Kant.* Oxford.

Kenny, Anthony, ed., 1969. *Aquinas.* New York.

Kent, Bonnie, 1995. *Virtues of the Will.* Washington, D.C.

Keohane, Nannerl O., 1980. *Philosophy and the State in France.* Princeton.

Kersting, Wolfgang, 1982. "Das starke Gesetz der Schuldigkeit und das schwächere des Gütigkeit." *Studia Leibnitiana* 14, pp. 184–220.

1983. "Der kategorische Imperativ, die vollkommenen und die unvollkommenen Pflichten." *Zeitschrift für Philosophische Forschung*, pp. 404–21.

1984. *Wohlgeordnete Freiheit.* Berlin.

King, Peter, 1830. *The Life of John Locke.* London.

King, Preston, ed., 1993. *Thomas Hobbes: Critical Assessments.* 4 vols. London.

Kirk, Kenneth E., 1927. *Conscience and Its Problems.* London.

1932. *The Vision of God.* London.

Kirk, Linda, 1987. *Richard Cumberland and Natural Law.* Cambridge.

Klein, Lawrence, 1984. "The Third Earl of Shaftesbury and the Progress of Politeness." *Eighteenth-Century Studies* 18:2, pp. 186–214.

1993. "Shaftesbury, Politeness and the Politics of Religion." In *Political*

Discourse in Early Modern Britain, ed. Nicholas Phillipson and Quentin Skinner. Cambridge.

1994. *Shaftesbury and the Culture of Politeness*. Cambridge.

Klibansky, Raymond, and Ernest C. Mossner, eds., 1954. *New Letters of David Hume*. Oxford.

Knox, Ronald, 1950. *Enthusiasm*. Oxford.

Kobusch, Theo, 1993. *Die Entdeckung der Person. Metaphysik der Freiheit und modernes Menschenbild*. Freiburg.

Köhl, Harald, 1990. *Kants Gesinnungsethik*. Berlin.

Kopper, Joachim, 1983. *Ethik der Aufklärung*. Darmstadt.

Körner, Stefan, 1955, *Kant*. London.

Kors, Alan C., 1976. *D'Holbach's Coterie*. Princeton.

Kors, Alan C., and Paul J. Korshin, eds., 1987. *Anticipations of the Enlightenment in England, France, and Germany*. Philadelphia.

Korsgaard, Christine M., 1986a. "Skepticism about Practical Reason." *Journal of Philosophy* 83:1, pp. 5–25.

1986b. "Kant's Formula of Humanity." *Kantstudien* 77:2, pp. 183–202.

1986c. "Aristotle and Kant on the Source of Value." *Ethics* 96, pp. 486–505.

1989. "Personal Identity and the Unity of Agency." *Philosophy and Public Affairs* 18:2, pp. 101–32.

1996. *Creating the Kingdom of Ends*. Cambridge.

Krailsheimer, A. J., 1962. *Studies in Self-Interest from Descartes to LaBruyere*. Oxford.

Krause, Otto Wilhelm, 1982. *Naturrechtler des sechzehnten Jahrhunderts*. Frankfurt am Main.

Kraye, Jill, 1988. "Moral Philosophy." In Schmitt et al., pp. 303–86.

Krieger, Leonard, 1965. *The Politics of Discretion: Pufendorf and the Acceptance of Natural Law*. Chicago.

Kuehn, Manfred, 1987. *Scottish Common Sense in Germany, 1768–1800*. Kingston.

Küenburg, Max, 1925. *Ethische Grundfragen in der jüngst veröffentlichten Ethikvorlesung Kants*. In *Philosophie und Grenzwissenschaften*, vol. I, no. 4. Innsbruck.

Kupperman, Joel J., 1985. "Francis Hutcheson: Morality and Nature." *History of Philosophy Quarterly* 2, pp. 195–202.

Laboucheix, Henri, 1982. *Richard Price As Moral Philosopher and Political Theorist* (1970). Trans. Sylvia Raphael and David Raphael. Oxford.

Labrousse, Elizabeth, 1983. *Bayle*. Oxford.

Lacey, Michael J., and Knud Haakonssen, eds., 1991. *A Culture of Rights*. Cambridge.

Landsberg, Ernst, 1898. *Geschichte der deutschen Rechtswissenschaft*. Part III. Munich.

Larmore, Charles, 1993. *Modernité et morale*. Paris.

Larthomas, Jean-Paul, 1985. *De Shaftesbury à Kant*. Paris.

Latzer, Michael, 1994. "Leibniz's Conception of Metaphysical Evil." *Journal of the History of Ideas* 55:1, pp. 1–15.

Laude, Patrick, 1994. "Les leçons de l'amour-proper chez Pierre Nicole." *Revue des Sciences Philosophiques et Théologiques* 78:2, pp. 241–70.

Laurent, Pierre, 1982. *Pufendorf et la loi naturel*. Paris.

Laursen, John Christian, 1993. "Michel de Montaigne and the Politics of Skepticism." *Historical Reflections/Reflexions Historiques* 16:1, pp. 99–133.

Lefêvre, Roger, 1966. *Condillac.* Paris.

Lehmann, Gerhard, 1969. *Beiträge zur Geschichte und Interpretation der Philosophie Kants.* Berlin.

1980. *Kants Tugenden.* Berlin.

Lehrer, Keith, 1989. *Thomas Reid.* London.

Leidhold, Wolfgang, 1985. *Ethik und Politik bei Francis Hutcheson.* Munich.

Leites, Edmund, ed., 1988. *Conscience and Causistry in Early Modern Europe.* Cambridge.

LeMahieu, D. L., 1976. *The Mind of William Paley.* Lincoln, Neb.

Levi, Anthony, 1964. *French Moralists: The Theory of the Passions, 1585–1659.* Oxford.

Lieberman, David, 1989. *The Province of Legislation Determined.* Cambridge.

Lindgren, J. Ralph, 1973. *The Social Philosophy of Adam Smith.* The Hague.

Loemker, Leroy E., 1972. *Struggles for Synthesis: The Seventeenth Century Background of Leibniz's Synthesis of Order and Freedom.* Cambridge, Mass.

Long, A. A., ed., 1971. *Problems in Stoicism.* London.

1986. *Hellenistic Philosophy.* 2nd ed. Berkeley.

Louden, Robert B., 1986. "Kant's Virtue Ethics." In *Philosophy* 61, pp. 473–89.

Lovejoy, Arthur O., 1908. "Kant and the English Platonists." In *Essays Philosophical and Psychological in Honor of William James,* by his colleagues at Columbia University, pp. 265–302. New York.

1961. *Reflections on Human Nature.* Baltimore.

Lyons, David, 1973. *In the Interest of the Governed.* Oxford.

MacDonald, Scott, ed., 1991. *Being and Goodness.* Ithaca, N.Y.

MacIntyre, Alasdair, 1959. "Hume on Is and Ought." *Philosophical Review* 68, pp. 451–68.

1966. *A Short History of Ethics.* New York.

1988. *Whose Justice? Which Rationality?* Notre Dame.

Mack, Mary P., 1962. *Jeremy Bentham: An Odyssey of Ideas, 1748–1792.* London.

Mackie, J. L., 1980. *Hume's Moral Theory.* London.

Mackintosh, James, 1872. *On the Progress of Ethical Philosophy* (1835). 2nd ed. Ed. William Whewell. Edinburgh.

Macklem, Michael, 1958. *The Anatomy of the World.* Minneapolis.

Mahoney, John, 1987. *The Making of Moral Theology: A Study of the Roman Catholic Tradition.* Oxford.

Marshall, David, 1986. *The Figure of Theater.* New York.

Marshall, John, 1994. *John Locke: Resistance, Religion and Responsibility.* Cambridge.

Martens, John W., 1994. "Romans 2.14–16: A Stoic Reading." *New Testament Studies* 40, pp. 55–67.

Martens, Wolfgang, 1968. *Die Botschaft der Tugend.* Stuttgart.

Martineau, James, 1891. *Types of Ethical Theories.* 3rd ed. Oxford.

Martinich, A. P., 1992. *The Two Gods of Leviathan.* Cambridge.

Masters, Roger, 1968. *The Political Philosophy of Jean-Jacques Rousseau.* Princeton.

Mattern, Ruth, 1978. "Spinoza and Ethical Subjectivism." *Canadian Journal of Philosophy* (suppl.) 4, pp. 59–82.

Mautner, Thomas, 1989. "Pufendorf and the Correlativity Theory of Rights." In *In So Many Words*, ed. Sten Lindström and Wlodzimierz Rabinowicz, pp. 37–57. Uppsala.

Mauzi, Robert, 1960. *L'idée du bonheur dans la littérature et la pensée françaises au XVIIIᵉ siècle*. Paris.

Mayr, Otto, 1986. *Authority, Liberty and Automatic Machinery in Early Modern Europe*. Baltimore.

McAdoo, H. R., 1949. *The Structure of Caroline Moral Theology*. London.

McClelland, Charles E., 1980. *State, Society and University in Germany, 1700–1914*. Cambridge.

McCosh, James, 1875. *The Scottish Philosophy*. London.

McCracken, Charles, 1983. *Malebranche and British Philosophy*. Oxford.

McFarland, J. D., 1979. *Kant's Concept of Teleology*. Edinburgh.

Medick, Hans, 1973. *Naturzustand und Naturgeschichte der bürgerlichen Gesellschaft*. Göttingen.

Meek, Ronald L., 1976. *Social Science and the Ignoble Savage*. Cambridge.

Menzer, Paul, 1897. *Der Entwicklungsgang der Kantischen Ethik bis zum Erscheinen der Grundlegung der Metaphysik der Sitten*. Berlin.

1898. "Der Entwicklungsgang der kantischen Ethik in den Jahren 1760 bis 1785." *Kantstudien* 2, pp. 290–322; 3, pp. 41–104.

Mesnard, Jean, 1965. *Pascal*. Paris.

Meyer, R. W., 1952. *Leibniz and the Seventeenth Century Revolution*. Trans. J. P. Stern. Cambridge.

Meylan, Phillipe, 1937. *Jean Barbeyrac*. Lausanne.

Miller, David, 1981. *Philosophy and Ideology in Hume's Political Thought*. Oxford.

Miller, James, 1984. *Rousseau, Dreamer of Democracy*. New Haven.

Mintz, Samuel I., 1969. *The Hunting of Leviathan*. Cambridge.

Modeer, Kjell A., ed., 1986. *Samuel Pufendorf, 1632–1982*. Stockholm.

Mondadori, Fabrizio, 1989. "Necessity ex Hypothesi." In *The Leibniz Renaissance*, pp. 191–222. Florence.

Monro, D. H., 1975. *The Ambivalence of Mandeville*. Oxford.

Moore, James, 1976. "Hume's Theory of Justice and Property." *Political Studies* 24:2, pp. 103–19.

1977. "Hume's Political Science and the Classical Republican Tradition." *Canadian Journal of Political Science* 10:4, pp. 809–39.

1988. "Natural Law and the Pyrrhonian Controversy." In *Philosophy and Science in the Scottish Enlightenment*, ed. Peter Jones, pp. 20–38. Edinburgh.

Moore, James, and Michael Silverthorne. 1983. "Gershom Carmichael and the Natural Jurisprudence Tradition in Eighteenth Century Scotland." In Hont and Ignatieff, pp. 73–87.

Moore, W. G., 1969. *La Rochefoucauld*. Oxford.

Morgan, Vance G., 1994. *Foundations of Cartesian Ethics*. Atlantic Highlands, N.J.

Mossner, E. C., 1954. *The Life of David Hume*. Oxford.

1971. *Bishop Butler and the Age of Reason*. New York.

Moyal, Georges J. D., ed., 1991. *René Descartes. Critical Assessments*. Vol. IV. London.

Muirhead, J. H., 1931. *The Platonic Tradition in Anglo-Saxon Philosophy*. London.

Mulholland, Leslie A., 1989. *Kant's System of Rights*. New York.

Mulvaney, Robert J., 1968. "The Early Development of Leibniz's Concept of Justice." *Journal of the History of Ideas* 39, pp. 53–72.

1975. "Divine Justice in Leibniz's Discourse on Metaphysics." *Studia Leibnitiana* (suppl.) 14, pp. 61–82.

Myers, Milton L., 1983. *The Soul of Modern Economic Man.* Chicago.

Naville, Pierre, 1967. *D'Holbach et la philosophie scientifique au XVIIIᵉ siècle.* 2nd ed. Paris.

Nell, Onora (O'Neill), 1975. *Acting on Principle.* New York.

Noonan, John T., Jr., 1993. "Development in Moral Doctrine." *Theological Studies* 54, pp. 662–77.

Normore, Calvin, 1994. "Ockham, Self-Motion, and the Will." In *Self-Motion from Aristotle to Newton,* ed. Mary Louise Gill and James G. Lennox, pp. 291–303. Princeton.

Norton, David Fate, 1974. "Hutcheson's Moral Sense Theory Reconsidered." *Dialogue* 13, pp. 3–23.

1977. "Hutcheson on Perception and Moral Perception." *Archiv fur Geschichte der Philosophie* 59, pp. 181–97.

1982. *David Hume: Common-Sense Moralist, Sceptical Metaphysician.* Princeton.

1985a. "Hume's Moral Ontology." *Hume Studies* (suppl.), 85, pp. 189–214.

1985b. "Hutcheson's Moral Realism." *Journal of the History of Philosophy* 23, pp. 397–418.

ed., 1993. *The Cambridge Companion to Hume.* Cambridge.

Noxon, James, 1973. *Hume's Philosophical Development.* Oxford.

Nutkiewicz, Michael, 1983. "Samuel Pufendorf: Obligation As the Basis of the State." *Journal of the History of Philosophy* 21, pp. 15–29.

O'Brien, Wendell, 1991. "Butler and the Authority of Conscience." *History of Philosophy Quarterly* 8:1, pp. 43–57.

O'Connor, D. J., 1952. *John Locke.* London.

O'Higgins, J., 1976. *Determinism and Freewill.* The Hague.

O'Neill, Onora, 1989. *Constructions of Reason.* Cambridge.

Oakley, Francis, 1961. "Christian Theology and the Newtonian Science: The Rise of the Concept of the Laws of Nature." *Church History* 30, pp. 433–57.

1984. *Omnipotence, Covenant, and Order.* Ithaca, N.Y.

Oberman, Heiko, 1963. *The Harvest of Mediaeval Theology.* Cambridge, Mass.

Oestreich, Gerhard, 1982. *Neostoicism and the Early Modern State.* Cambridge.

Olscamp, Paul J., 1970. *The Moral Philosophy of George Berkeley.* The Hague.

Osler, Margaret J., ed., 1991. *Atoms, Pneuma, and Tranquillity: Epicurean and Stoic Themes in European Thought.* Cambridge.

1994. *Divine Will and the Mechanical Philosophy.* Cambridge.

Othmer, Sieglinde, 1970. *Berlin und die Verbreitung des Naturrechts in Europa.* Berlin.

Outram, Dorinda, 1995. *The Enlightenment.* Cambridge.

Pagden, Anthony, ed., 1987. *The Languages of Political Theory in Early-Modern Europe.* Cambridge.

Palladini, Fiammetta, 1990. "Di una critica di Leibniz a Pufendorf." In *Percorsi della ricerca filosofica,* pp. 19–27. Rome.

Palladini, Fiammetta, and Gerald Hartung, eds., 1996. *Samuel Pufendorf und die europäische Frühaufklärung.* Berlin.

Parfit, Derek, 1984. *Reasons and Persons*. Oxford.

Parkinson, G. H. R., 1970. *Leibniz on Human Freedom. Studia Leibnitiana,* suppl. 2. Weisbaden.

Passerin d'Entreves, A., 1951. *Natural Law.* London.

Passmore, J. A., 1951. *Ralph Cudworth: An Interpretation.* Cambridge.

Paton, H. J., 1946. *The Categorical Imperative.* London.

Paulsen, Friedrich, 1919. *Geschichte des gelehrten Unterrichts.* Vol. I. Leipzig.

Peach, Bernard, 1958. "Shaftesbury's Moral *Arithmeticks.*" *Personalist* 39, pp. 19–27.

Penelhum, Terence, 1975. *Hume.* New York.

  1985. *Butler.* London.

Perelman, Chaim, 1980. *Introduction historique à la philosophie morale.* Brussels.

Peters, Richard, 1956. *Hobbes.* London.

  1972. *Hobbes and Rousseau.* New York.

Peterson, Susan Rae, 1984. "The Compatibility of Richard Price's Politics and Ethics." *Journal of the History of Ideas* 45, pp. 537–47.

Phillipson, Nicholas, 1981. "The Scottish Enlightenment." In Porter and Teich, pp. 19–40.

  1989. *Hume.* London.

Pintard, René, 1943. *Le libertinage érudite dans le premiére moitié du XVIIᵉ siécle.* Paris.

Platts, Mark, 1988. "Hume and Morality As Matter of Fact." *Mind* 97:386, pp. 189–204.

Pocock, J. G. A., 1975. *The Machiavellian Moment.* Princeton.

  1985. *Virtue, Commerce, and History.* Cambridge.

Pohlmann, R., 1971. "Autonomie." In Ritter, pp. 701–19.

Pomeau, René, 1969. *La religion de Voltaire.* 2nd ed. Paris.

Popkin, Richard, 1979. *The History of Scepticism from Erasmus to Spinoza.* Berkeley.

  1980. *The High Road to Pyrrhonism.* San Diego.

Porter, Roy, and Mikulas Teich, eds., 1981. *The Enlightenment in National Context.* Cambridge.

Poser, Hans, 1980. "Die Bedeutung der Ethik Christian Wolffs für die deutsche Aufklärung." *Studia Leibnitziana* (suppl.) 19, pp. 206–17.

Postema, Gerald J., 1986. *Bentham and the Common Law Tradition.* Oxford.

Primer, Irwin, 1975a. "Mandeville and Shaftesbury: Some Facts and Problems." In Primer 1975b, pp. 126–41.

  ed., 1975b. *Mandeville Studies.* The Hague.

Prior, Arthur N., 1949. *Logic and the Basis of Ethics.* Oxford.

Probst, Peter, 1994. *Kant: Bestirnter Himmel und moralisches Gesetz.* Würzburg.

Randall, John Herman, 1965. *The Career of Philosophy.* Vol. 2. New York.

Raphael, D. D., 1947. *The Moral Sense.* Oxford.

  1949. "Bp. Butler's View of Conscience." *Philosophy* 24, pp. 218–38.

  1972. "The Impartial Spectator." *Proceedings of the British Academy* 59, pp. 335–54.

Rapp, Hans, 1982. "Grotius and Hume on Natural Religion and Natural Law." *Archiv für Rechts- und Sozialphilosophie* 68, pp. 372–87.

Rawls, John, n.d. "Lectures on Kant's Ethics." Unpublished typescript.

Raymond, Marcel, 1957. "Du jansénisme à la morale de l'intérêt." *Mercure de France* (June), pp. 238–55.

Ree, Jonathan, 1974. *Descartes*. London.

Reibstein, Ernst, 1953. "Deutsche Grotius-Kommentatoren bis zu Christian Wolff." *Zeitschrift für ausländisches öffentliches Recht*, 15:1–2 (Oct.), pp. 76–102.

Reich, Klaus, 1939. "Kant and Greek Ethics." *Mind* 48, pp. 338–54, 447–63.

Reiner, Hans, 1983. *Duty and Inclination*. The Hague.

Rendall, Janet, 1978. *The Origins of Scottish Enlightenment*. New York.

Rescher, Nicholas, 1979. *Leibniz: An Introduction to His Philosophy*. Oxford.

Rex, Walter, 1965. *Essays on Pierre Bayle and Religious Controversy*. The Hague.

Riley, Lawrence Joseph, 1948. *The History, Nature, and Use of EPIKEIA in Moral Theology*. Washington, D.C.

Riley, Patrick, 1982. *Will and Political Legitimacy*. Cambridge.

1983. *Kant's Political Philosophy*. Totowa, N.J.

1986. *The General Will before Rousseau*. Princeton.

1996. *Leibniz' Universal Jurisprudence*. Cambridge, Mass.

Rist, John M., 1969. *Stoic Philosophy*. Cambridge.

ed., 1978. *The Stoics*. Berkeley.

Ritter, Christian, 1971. *Der Rechtsgedanke Kants nach den frühen Quellen*. Frankfurt am Main.

Ritter, Joachim, ed., 1971. *Historisches Wörterbuch der Philosophie*. Vol. I. Darmstadt.

Ritzel, Wolfgang, 1985. *Immanuel Kant. Eine Biographie*. Berlin.

Rivers, Isabel, 1991. *Reason, Grace, and Sentiment*. Vol. I. Cambridge.

Robbins, Caroline, 1959. *The Eighteenth Century Commonwealthman*. Cambridge, Mass.

1969. *Two English Political Tracts*. Cambridge.

Roberts, James Deotis, Sr., 1968. *From Puritanism to Platonism in Seventeenth Century England*. The Hague.

Roberts, T. A., 1973. *The Concept of Benevolence*. London.

Robinet, André, 1955. *Malebranche et Leibniz*. Paris.

Rochot, Bernard, 1944. *Les travaux de Gassendi sur Epicure et sur l'atomisme, 1619–1658*. Paris.

1955. "Le philosophe." In *Pierre Gassendi, sa vie et son oeuvre*, pp. 71–107. Paris.

Röd, Wolfgang, 1969. "Erhard Weigl's Lehre von den entia moralia." *Archive für Geschichte der Philosophie* 51, pp. 58–84.

1970. *Geometrischer Geist und Naturrecht*. Munich.

Rodis-Lewis, Geneviève, 1970. *La moral de Descartes*. Paris.

Rogers, G. A. J., and Alan Ryan, eds., 1988. *Perspectives on Thomas Hobbes*. Oxford.

Rohls, Jan, 1991. *Geschichte der Ethik*. Tübingen.

Rommen, H. A., 1947. *The Natural Law*. Trans. Thomas R. Hanley. St. Louis.

Rorty, Amelie, 1978. "Butler on Benevolence and Conscience." *Philosophy* 53, pp. 171–84.

Rorty, Richard, J. B. Schneewind, and Quentin Skinner, eds., 1984. *Philosophy in History*. Cambridge.

Rosen, Frederick, 1983. *Jeremy Bentham and Representative Democracy*. Oxford.

Ross, G. MacDonald, 1984. *Leibniz*. Oxford.

Ross, Ian Simpson, 1972. *Lord Kames and the Scotland of His Day*. Oxford.

Rossi, Philip J., and Micheal Wreen, eds., 1991. *Kant's Philosophy of Religion Reconsidered*. Bloomington.

Rossvaer, Viggo, 1979. *Kant's Moral Philosophy*. Oslo.

Rowe, William L., 1991. *Thomas Reid on Freedom and Morality*. Ithaca, N.Y.

Rüping, Hinrich, 1968. *Die Naturrechtslehre des Christian Thomasius und ihre Fort-bildung*. Bonn.

Rupp, Gordon, 1953. *The Righteousness of God: Luther Studies*. London.

Russell, Paul, 1993. "Epigram, Pantheists, and Freethought in Hume's *Treatise*: A Study in Esoteric Communication." *Journal of the History of Ideas* 54:4, pp. 659–73.

Sabrié, J. B., 1913. *De l'humanisme au rationalisme: Pierre Charron*. Paris.

Sacksteder, William, 1982. *Hobbes Studies (1879–1979): A Bibliography*. Bowling Green.

Sandberg, Karl C., 1966. *At the Crossroads of Faith and Reason*. Tucson.

Santilli, Paul C., 1992. "What Did Descartes Do to Virtue?" *Journal of Value Inquiry* 26:3, pp. 353–65.

Santinello, Giovanni, ed., 1993. *Models of the History of Philosophy: From Its Origins in the Renaissance to the "Historia Philosophica" (1981, 1988)*. Trans. C. W. T. Blackwell and Philip Weller. Dordrecht.

Sarasohn, Lisa T., 1982. "The Ethical and Political Thought of Pierre Gassendi." *Journal of the History of Philosophy* 20, pp. 239–60.

    1985. "Motion and Morality: Pierre Gassendi, Thomas Hobbes, and the Mechanical World-View." *Journal of the History of Ideas* 46, pp. 363–70.

    1991. "Epicureanism and the Creation of a Privatist Ethic in Early Seventeenth Century France." In Osler, pp. 175–95.

    1996. *Gassendi's Ethics*. Ithaca, N.Y.

Sayce, R. M., 1972. *The Essays of Montaigne: A Critical Exploration*. London.

Schilpp, P. A., 1938. *Kant's Pre-Critical Ethics*. Evanston, Ill.

Schmitt, Charles, Quentin Skinner, Ekhard Kessler, and Jill Kraye, ed., 1988. *The Cambridge History of Renaissance Philosophy*. Cambridge.

Schmucker, Josef, 1961. *Die Ursprünge der Ethik Kants*. Meisenheim.

Schneewind, J. B., 1977. *Sidgwick's Ethics and Victorian Moral Philosophy*. Oxford.

    1983. "Moral Crisis and the History of Ethics." *Midwest Studies in Philosophy* 8, pp. 525–42.

    1984. "The Divine Corporation and the History of Ethics." In *Philosophy and History*, ed. Rorty, Schneewind, and Skinner, pp. 173–92.

    1986. "The Use of Autonomy in Ethical Theory." In *Reconstructing Individualism*, ed. Thomas C. Heller, Morton Sosna, and David E. Wellbery. Stanford.

    1987. "Pufendorf's Place in the History of Ethics." *Synthese* 72:1, pp. 123–55.

    1990. "The Misfortunes of Virtue." *Ethics* 101:1, pp. 42–63.

    1991. "Natural Law, Skepticism, and Methods of Ethics." *Journal of the History of Ideas* 52:2, pp 289–314.

    1992a. "Autonomy, Obligation and Virtue: An Overview of Kant's Ethics." In *The Cambridge Companion to Kant*, ed. Paul Guyer, pp. 309–41. Cambridge.

    1992b. "History of Ethics: Seventeenth and Eighteenth Century." In *Encyclope-

dia of Ethics, ed. Lawrence Becker and Charlotte Becker, vol. I, pp. 500–9. New York.

1993a. "Classical Republicanism and the History of Ethics." *Utilitas* 5:2, pp. 185–208.

1993b. "Kant and Natural Law Ethics." *Ethics* 104, pp. 53–74.

1994. "Locke's Moral Philosophy." In *The Cambridge Companion to Locke,* ed. Vere Chappell, pp. 199–225. Cambridge.

1995. "Voluntarism and the Origins of Utilitarianism." *Utilitas* 7, pp. 87–96.

1996a. "Barbeyrac and Leibniz on Pufendorf." In Palladini and Hartung, pp. 181–9.

1996b. "Voluntarism and the Foundations of Ethics." In *Proceedings and Addresses of the American Philosophical Association* 70.2, pp. 25–42.

1996c. "Histoire de la philosophie morale." In *Dictionaire d'ethique et de la philosophie morale,* ed. Monique Canto-Sperber, pp. 651–7. Paris.

1997a. "No Discipline, No History: The Case of Moral Philosophy." In *History and the Disciplines: The Reclamation of Knowledge in Early Modern Europe,* ed. Donald Kelley. Rochester.

1997b. "Active Powers." In *Cambridge History of Eighteenth Century Philosophy,* ed. Knud Haakonssen. Cambridge.

Schneider, Hans-Peter, 1967. *Justitia Universalis.* Frankfurt am Main.

Schneiders, Werner, 1971. *Naturrecht und Liebesethik.* Hildesheim.

ed., 1983. *Christian Wolff, 1679–1754.* Hamburg.

Schnoor, Christian, 1989. *Kants Kategorischer Imperative als Kriterium der Richtigkeit des Handelns.* Tübingen.

Schobinger, Jean-Pierre, ed., 1988. *Die Philosophie des 17. Jahrhunderts.* Vol. 3: *England.* Basel.

Schofield, Malcolm, and Gisela Striker, eds., 1986. *The Norms of Nature.* Cambridge.

Schrader, Wolfgang, 1984. *Ethik und Anthropologie in der englischen Aufklärung.* Hamburg.

Schröer, Christian, 1988. *Naturbegriff und Moralbegründung: Die Grundlegung der Ethik bei Christian Wolff und deren Kritik durch Immanuel Kant.* Stuttgart.

Scott, W. R., 1900. *Francis Hutcheson.* Cambridge.

Scott-Taggart, M. J., 1966. "Mandeville: Cynic or Fool?" *Philosophical Quarterly* 16:64, pp. 221–32.

1968. "Butler on Disinterested Actions." *Philosophical Quarterly* 18, pp. 16–28.

Screech, M. A., 1983. *Montaigne and Melancholy.* London.

Sève, René, 1989. *Leibniz et l'école moderne du droit naturel.* Paris.

Shackleton, Robert, 1988. "The Greatest Happiness of the Greatest Number: The History of Bentham's Phrase." In his *Essays on Montesquieu and the Enlightenment.* Oxford.

Shahan, Robert W., and J. I. Biro, eds., 1978. *Spinoza: New Perspectives.* Norman, Okla.

Sharp, Frank Chapman, 1912. "The Ethical System of Richard Cumberland and Its Place in the History of British Ethics." *Mind,* n.s., 21, pp. 371–98.

Shaver, Robert, 1995. "Hume's Moral Theory?" *History of Philosophy Quarterly* 12.

Shearer, Edna, 1915. *Hume's Place in Ethics.* Bryn Mawr, Pa.
Shklar, Judith, 1969. *Men and Citizens: A Study of Rousseau's Social Theory.*
   Cambridge.
   1987. *Montesquieu.* Oxford.
Sidgwick, Henry, 1889. *Outlines of the History of Ethics.* (1886) 4th ed. London.
   1907. *The Methods of Ethics* (1874). 7th ed. London.
Skinner, Quentin, 1966. "Thomas Hobbes and His Disciples in France and England." *Comparative Studies in Society and History* 8, pp. 153–67.
   1972. "Conquest and Consent: Thomas Hobbes and the Engagement Controversy." In *The Interregnum,* ed. G. E. Aylmer, pp. 79–88. London.
   1978. *The Foundations of Modern Political Thought.* 2 vols. Cambridge.
   1981. *Machiavelli.* Oxford.
   1990. "Thomas Hobbes: Rhetoric and the Construction of Morality." *Proceedings of the British Academy* 76:26, pp. 1–61.
Smith, D. W., 1965. *Helvétius, a Study in Persecution.* Oxford.
   1993. "Helvétius and the Problems of Utilitarianism." *Utilitas* 5:2, pp. 275–90.
Smith, Michael, 1987. "The Humean Theory of Motivation." *Mind* 96:381, pp.
   36–61.
Smith, Norman Kemp, 1941. *The Philosophy of David Hume.* London.
Smyth, Damian, ed., n.d. *Frances Hutcheson.* A Special Symposium. Supplement
   to *Fortnight.*
Snare, Frank, 1975. "The Argument from Motivation." *Mind* 84, pp. 1–9.
Sommerville, J. P., 1982. "From Suarez to Filmer: A Reappraisal." *Historical
   Journal* 25:3, pp. 525–40.
Sorell, Tom, 1986. *Hobbes.* London.
   1987. *Descartes.* New York.
   1993a. "Morals and Modernity in Descartes." In Sorell 1993b, pp. 273–88.
   ed., 1993b. *The Rise of Modern Philosophy.* Oxford.
   ed., 1996. *Cambridge Companion to Hobbes.* Cambridge.
Sorley, W. R., 1894. "The Philosophy of Herbert of Cherbury." *Mind* 3, pp. 491–
   540.
Speck, W. A., 1975. "Mandeville and the Eutopia Seated in the Brain." In Primer
   1975b, pp. 66–79.
Spellman, W. M., 1988. *John Locke and the Problem of Depravity.* Oxford.
Spink, J. S., 1960. *French Free Thought from Gassendi to Voltaire.* London.
Stalley, R. F., 1986. "The Will in Hume's *Treatise.*" *Journal of the History of Philoso-
   phy* 24, pp. 41–53.
Stark, Werner, 1993. *Nachforschungen zu Briefen und Handschriften Immanuel
   Kants.* Berlin.
Starobinski, Jean, 1985. *Montaigne in Motion.* Trans. Arthur Goldhammer.
   Chicago.
State, S. A., 1991. *Thomas Hobbes and the Debate over Natural Law and Religion.*
   New York.
Stäudlin, Carl Friedrich, 1822. *Geschichte der Moralphilosophie.* Hannover.
Stein, Peter, 1980. *Legal Evolution: The Story of an Idea.* Cambridge.
Steinmetz, David. C., 1988. "Calvin and the Absolute Power of God." *Journal of
   Medieval and Renaissance Studies* 18:1, pp. 65–79.

Steintrager, James, 1971. "Morality and Belief: The Origin and Purpose of Bentham's Writings on Religion." *Mill Newsletter* 6:2, pp. 3–15.

1977. *Bentham.* Ithaca, N.Y.

Stephen, Leslie, 1876. *History of English Thought in the Eighteenth Century.* 2 vols. London.

Stephens, John, 1986. "The Epistemological Strategy of Price's *Review of Morals*." *Enlightenment and Dissent* 5, pp. 39–50.

1987. "Price, Providence and the *Principia*." *Enlightenment and Dissent* 6, pp. 77–93.

Stewart, Dugald, 1854. *Dissertation exhibiting the Progress of Metaphysical, Ethical, and Political Philosophy since the Revival of Letters in Europe* (1815, 1821). In *Collected Works,* ed. William Hamilton, vol. I. Edinburgh.

Stewart, John B., 1992. *Opinion and Reform in Hume's Political Philosophy.* Princeton.

Stewart, M. A., ed., 1990. *Studies in the Philosophy of the Scottish Enlightenment.* Oxford.

1991. "The Stoic Legacy in the Early Scottish Enlightenment." In Osler, pp. 273–96.

Stewart, M. A., and John P. Wright, eds., 1994. *Hume and Hume's Connexions.* University Park, Pa.

Stoeffler, F. Ernest, 1973. *German Pietism during the Eighteenth Century.* Leiden.

Stolleis, M., ed., 1977. *Staatsdenker im 17. und 18. Jahrhundert.* Frankfurt am Main.

Striker, Gisela, 1986. "Antipater, or the Art of Living." In *The Norms of Nature,* eds. Malcolm Schofield and Gisela Striker, pp. 185–204. Cambridge.

1987. "Origins of the Concept of Natural Law." *Proceedings of the Boston Area Colloquium in Ancient Philosophy,* vol. II, ed. John J. Cleary, pp. 79–94. Lanham.

1990. "Ataraxia: Happiness As Tranquillity." *Monist* 73:1, pp. 97–110.

1991. "Following Nature: A Study in Stoic Ethics." In *Oxford Studies in Ancient Philosophy,* vol. 9, ed. Julia Annas, pp. 1–74. Oxford.

1996. *Essays on Hellenistic Epistemology and Ethics.* Cambridge.

Stroud, Barry, 1977. *Hume.* London.

Sturgeon, Nicholas, 1976. "Nature and Conscience in Butler's Ethics." *Philosophical Review* 85, pp. 316–56.

Sullivan, Robert E., 1982. *John Toland and the Deist Controversy.* Cambridge, Mass.

Sullivan, Roger J., 1989. *Immanuel Kant's Moral Theory.* Cambridge.

Tack, Reiner, 1974. *Untersuchungen zum Philosophie- und Wissenschaftsbegriff bei Pierre Gassendi (1592–1655).* Meisenheim am Glan.

Taylor, Charles, 1989. *Sources of the Self.* Cambridge, Mass.

Teichgraber, Richard F., III, 1986. *"Free Trade" and Moral Philosophy.* Durham, N.C.

Thomas, D. O., 1977. *The Honest Mind: The Thought and Work of Richard Price.* Oxford.

Thomas, D. O., John Stephens, and P. A. L. Jones, 1993. *A Bibliography of the Works of Richard Price.* Aldershot.

Thompson, W. D. J. Cargill, 1984. *The Political Thought of Martin Luther.* Ed. Philip Broadhead. Sussex.

Thomson, Ann, 1981, *Materialism and Society in the Mid-Eighteenth Century: La Mettrie's "Discours preliminaire."* Geneva.

Tierney, Brian, 1982. *Religion, Law, and the Growth of Constitutional Thought.* Cambridge.

    1983. "Tuck on Rights: Some Medieval Problems." *History of Political Thought* 4:3, pp. 429–41.

    1988. "Villey, Ockham and the Origin of Individual Rights." In *The Weightier Matters of the Law,* ed. John Witte Jr. and Frank S. Alexander, pp. 1–31. Atlanta.

    1989. "The Origins of Natural Rights Language." *History of Political Thought* 10:4, pp. 615–46.

    1991. "Marsilius on Rights." *Journal of the History of Ideas* 52:1, pp. 3–17.

Todd, Margo, 1987. *Christian Humanism and the Puritan Social Order.* Cambridge.

Tonelli, Giorgio, 1967. *Studien zu Kants philosophischer Entwickelung.* Hildesheim.

Topazio, Virgil W., 1956. *D'Holbach's Moral Philosophy.* Geneva.

Trianosky, Gregory, 1978. "On the Obligation to Be Virtuous: Shaftesbury and the Question, Why Be Moral?" *Journal of the History of Philosophy* 16, pp. 289–300.

Tuck, Richard, 1979. *Natural Rights Theories.* Cambridge.

    1983. "Grotius, Carneades, and Hobbes." *Grotiana,* n.s., 4, pp. 43–62.

    1987. "The 'Modern' Theory of Natural Law." In Pagden, pp. 99–119.

    1988. "Optics and Sceptics: The Philosophical Foundations of Hobbes' Political Thought." In Leites, pp. 235–63.

    1989. *Hobbes.* Oxford.

    1993. *Philosophy and Government, 1572–1651.* Cambridge.

Tulloch, John, 1874. *Rational Theology and Christian Philosophy in England in the Seventeenth Century.* 2nd ed. 2 vols. Edinburgh.

Tully, James, 1980. *A Discourse on Property.* Cambridge.

    1988. *Meaning and Context: Quentin Skinner and His Critics.* Princeton.

    1993. *An Approach to Political Philosophy: Locke in Contexts.* Cambridge.

Turner, R. Steven, 1974. "University Reformers and Professorial Scholarship in Germany, 1760–1806." In *The University in Society,* ed. Lawrence Stone, vol. 2. Princeton.

Tuveson, Ernest, 1947–8. "The Origin of the Moral Sense." *Huntington Library Quarterly* 11, pp. 241–59.

    1953. "The Importance of Shaftesbury." *Journal of English Literary History* 20, pp. 267–79.

    1960. *Imagination As a Means of Grace.* Berkeley.

Tweyman, Stanley, 1974. *Reason and Conduct in Hume and His Predecessors.* The Hague.

    1976. "Truth, Happiness and Obligation: The Moral Philosophy of William Wollaston." *Philosophy* 51, pp. 35–46.

Vartanian, Aram, 1960. *La Mettrie's "L'homme machine."* Princeton.

Velkley, Richard L., 1989. *Freedom and the End of Reason.* Chicago.

Venturi, Franco, 1971. *Utopia and Reform in the Enlightenment.* Cambridge.

Vienne, Jean Michel, 1991. "Malebranche and Locke: The Theory of Moral Choice, a Neglected Theme." In Brown 1991, pp. 94–108.

1995. "La morale au risque de l'interpretation: L'*Encheiridion Ethicum* d'Henry More." *Archives de Philosophie*, 58:3, pp. 385–404.

Villey, Michel, 1957. *Leçons d'histoire de la philosophie du droit*. Paris.

1968. *La formation de la pensée juridique moderne*. Paris.

Viner, Jacob, 1972. *The Role of Providence in the Social Order*. Princeton.

Viroli, Maurizio, 1988. *Jean-Jacques Rousseau and the "Well-Ordered Society."* Cambridge.

Voitle, Robert, 1961. *Samuel Johnson the Moralist*. Cambridge, Mass.

1984. *The Third Earl of Shaftesbury, 1671–1713*. Baton Rouge, La.

von Eckhardt, Bettina, 1980. *Ethik der Selbstliebe*. Heidelberg.

von Selle, Götz, 1956. *Geschichte der Albertus-Universität zu Königsberg in Preussen*. Wurzburgh.

Vorländer, Franz, 1855. *Geschichte der philosophischen Moral, Rechts- und Staats-Lehre der Engländer und Franzosen*. Marburg.

Vorländer, Karl, 1977. *Immanuel Kant: Der Mann und das Werk*. (1924). Hamburg.

Wade, Ira O., 1971. *Intellectual Origins of the French Enlightenment*. Princeton.

1977. *The Structure and Form of the French Enlightenment*. 2 vols. Princeton.

Walker, D. P., 1972. *The Ancient Theology*. Ithaca, N.Y.

Walker, Ralph C. S., 1978. *Kant*. London.

Walton, Craig, 1972. *De la recherche du bien, A Study of Malebranche's Science of Ethics*. The Hague.

Wand, Bernard, 1971. "Religious Concepts and Moral Theory: Luther and Kant." *Journal of the History of Philosophy* 9, pp. 329–48.

Ward, Keith, 1972. *The Development of Kant's View of Ethics*. Oxford.

Warda, Arthur, 1922. *Immanuel Kants Bücher*. Berlin.

Warrender, Howard, 1957. *The Political Philosophy of Hobbes*. Oxford.

Watkins, J. W. N., 1965. *Hobbes' System of Ideas*. London.

Watson, Gerard, 1971. "The Natural Law and Stoicism." In Long, pp. 216–38.

Weinstock, Jerome, 1976. "Reid's Definition of Freedom." In *Thomas Reid: Critical Interpretations*, ed. Stephen F. Barker and Tom L. Beauchamp. Philadelphia.

Wellman, Kathleen, 1992. *La Mettrie: Medicine, Philosophy, and Enlightenment*. Durham, N.C.

Welzel, Hans, 1962. *Naturrecht und materiale Gerechtiget* (1950). 3rd ed. Göttingen.

1986. *Die Naturrechtslehre Samuel Pufendorfs* (1958). Berlin.

Wendel, François, 1963. *Calvin*. Trans. Philip Mairet. London.

Werner, Karl, 1859. *Grundriss einer Geschichte der Moralphilosophie*. Vienna.

Whelan, Frederick G., 1985. *Order and Artifice in Hume's Political Philosophy*. Princeton.

Whewell, William, 1852. *Lectures on the History of Moral Philosophy in England*. London.

Wieacker, Franz, 1967. *Privatrechtsgeschichte der Neuzeit*. 2nd ed. Göttingen.

Wilenius, Reijo, 1963. *The Social and Political Theory of Francisco Suarez*. In Acta Philosophica Fennica 15. Helsinki.

Williams, Bernard, 1985. *Ethics and the Limits of Philosophy*. Cambridge, Mass.

Williams, Howard, 1983. *Kant's Political Philosophy*. Oxford.

Williams, T. C., 1968. *The Concept of the Categorical Imperative.* Oxford.

Wilson, Catherine, 1989. "Critical and Constructive Aspects of Leibniz's Monadology." In *The Leibniz Renaissance,* pp. 291–303. Florence.

1990. "Nostalgia and Counterrevolution: The Case of Cudworth and Leibniz." In *Leibniz' Auseinandersetzung mit Vorgängern und Zeitgenossen,* ed. Ingrid Marchlewitz and Albert Heinekamp, pp. 138–46. *Studia Leibnitiana Supplementa* 27. Stuttgart.

Wilson, Margaret, 1978. *Descartes.* London.

Winch, Donald, 1978. *Adam Smith's Politics.* Cambridge.

Winkler, Kenneth P., 1985. "Hutcheson's Alleged Realism." *Journal of the History of Philosophy* 23, pp. 179–94.

Wokler, Robert, 1975. "The Influence of Diderot on the Political Theory of Rousseau: Two Aspects of a Relationship." In *Studies on Voltaire and the Eighteenth Century,* ed. Theodore Besterman, vol. 132, pp. 55–112. Banbury.

1994. "Rousseau's Pufendorf: Natural Law and the Foundations of Commercial Society." *History of Political Thought,* 15.

1995. *Rousseau.* Oxford.

Wood, Allen W., 1970. *Kant's Moral Religion.* Ithaca, N.Y.

1978. *Kant's Rational Theology.* Ithaca, N.Y.

ed., 1984. *Self and Nature in Kant's Philosophy.* Ithaca, N.Y.

1991. "Unsocial Sociability: the Anthropological Basis of Kantian Ethics." *Philosophical Topics,* 19:1, pp. 325–51.

Wood, Neal, 1988. *Cicero's Social and Political Thought.* Berkeley.

Woolhouse, R. S., 1983. *Locke.* Minneapolis.

Worden, A. B., ed., 1978. *Edmund Ludlow, a Voice from the Watch Tower.* Camden Society, 4th Ser. London.

Wundt, Max, 1964. *Die Deutsche Schulphilosophie im Zeitalter der Aufklärung* (1945). Hildesheim.

Wundt, Wilhelm, 1917. *Ethics.* Trans. M. F. Washburn. Vol. II. London.

Yolton, John W., 1970. *Locke and the Compass of Human Understanding.* Cambridge.

1985. *Locke, an Introduction.* Oxford.

1986. "Schoolmen, Logic, and Philosophy." In *The History of the University of Oxford,* ed. L. S. Sutherland and L. G. Mitchell, vol. V. Oxford.

Yovel, Y., 1980. *Kant and the Philosophy of History.* Princeton.

ed., 1989. *Kant's Practical Philosophy Reconsidered.* Dordrecht.

Zarka, Yves Charles, 1995. "Ralph Cudworth et le fondement de la moral: L'action, le sujet et la norme." *Archives de Philosophie* 58:3, pp. 405–20.

Zebrowski, Martha K., 1994. "Richard Price: British Platonist of the Eighteenth Century." *Journal of the History of Ideas* 55:1, pp. 17–35.

Zurbuchen, Simone, 1991. *Naturrecht und Natürliche Religion.* Würzburg.

Index of names

Aaron, R. I., 145 n12, 147 n15
Abercrombie, N., 272 n21, 275 n29, 314
  n9
Abraham, 8, 25
Adam, 21, 31, 32, 88, 197, 211, 219, 231–2,
  263 n2, 272, 354, 356 n5, 471
Adams, M., 25 n13
Adams, R., 136 n27, 243 n14
Addison, J., 390 n19
Albee, E., 101 n3
Alexander the Great, 47, 49, 50
Allestree, R., 354 n1
Alphonsus, 491 and n22
Alquié, F., 232 n17
Althusius, J., 27 n20
Ambrose, St., 538
Ames, W., 63 n8
  conscience, 93 and n21, 99
  suspension of will, 146 n14, 348 n40
Anaxagoras, 546 n25
Annas, J., 42 n5, 57 n30
Anselm of Canterbury
  on the devil's responsibility, 21–2 and
  22 n8, 65, 228, 500
Aquinas, St. Thomas
  knowledge of law, 20–1
  on natural law, 19–21
  Pelagianism, against, 30
  and responsibility, 21
  and virtues, 19–20, 77, 287
  will and intellect, 20
  and Calvin, 33; and Charron, 57; and
    Cumberland, 102–3, 107; and Duns
    Scotus, 23, 25; and Grotius, 77 and
    n35; and Hobbes, 84–5; and Leibniz,
    237; and Suarez, 59, 61, 63, 64, 65
  also 11, 17, 23 n10, 26, 27 n17, 75 n30,
    77 n35, 78 and n39, 124 and n16, 128
    n22, 156 n29, 239 n6, 270, 343 n25
Aristobulus, 540 n13
Aristotle
  alleged modern neglect, 286

influence, 17
  on Pythagoras, 538, 542
  and Barbeyrac, 542; and Charron,
    56; and Clarke, 317; and Cumber-
    land, 104, 117; and Grotius, 76–8,
    82, 104, 204; and Hobbes, 86 and n7;
    and Kant, 527; and Luther, 32; and
    Montaigne, 48; and More, 204;
    and Adam Smith, 394; and Suarez,
    65
  also 26, 31 n29, 44 n11, 47 n15, 50, 72
    n24, 77 n36, 236, 257 n37, 265, 266,
    269, 271 n18, 288, 533, 541 n15, 542
    n17, 549 and n27
Arnauld, A., 275, 277 n31
Arnoldt, E., 529 n29
Athanasius, 194
Augustine, St.
  on evil, 244
  on free will, 212, 241
  and Leibniz, 237, 241, 244; and Pascal,
    272 and n20; and Suarez, 61
  also 26, 30, 22 n9, 45 n14, 87 and n10,
    212 n20, 282, 364 n12, 417 n11, 500
Aurelius, Marcus, 68 n17

Bacon, Sir F.
  his voluntarism, 141, 158
  and Grotius, 66
  also 10, 66 n10, 306 n38
Bahr, E., 432 n5
Baier, A., 374 n28
Bailyn, B., 289 n9
Baird, A., 273 n22, 274 n26
Balaam, 348
Balguy, J., 384 n10
Barber, W., 433 n6, 461 n9, 498 n29
Barbeyrac, J.
  Aristotle, cites, 542
  on Grotius, 66, 67, 73–5, 97, 141
  his history, 534
  Leibniz, reply to, 12, 250–9

593

Index of subjects

absolute power, *see* power
active, 187, 221, 244, 311, 320
  power, God alone possesses, 226; human, 176, 312 and n4, 313–14, 318, 401, 402, 450; will as, 446
  reason as, 381, 414
acts
  inherent obligatoriness or rightness of, 74, 305, 321; denied, 121, 305
advice, *see* counsel
agency, 182, 242, 311–4, 400
  agent and spectator, 390
  agent as cause, 401
  central to morality, 380–1, 385–6
  as free choice, 313
  no privileged position, 361
  rational, 318, 320
  requires moral intuition, 396
appearances
  discussed by Herbert, 177
  and skepticism, 43, 51–2, 305, 360, 523–5
approval
  capricious without external guide, 421
  constitutes motives virtuous, 334, 359–61, 524
  as feeling revealing order, 302, 310, 503
  as function, 385
  how it operates, 360
  as love, 338, 363
  as mere sensation, 381
  not unique feeling, 389
  origins of, 405–6, 410
  from others, 278, 390, 405
  requires special sense, 337, 338–9
  and sympathy, 363–4, 389–90
  toward standing motives, 362
association of ideas, 405–6, 407, 415
atheism, 8, 9, 11, 12, 37, 256, 263, 458, 462
  discussed by Bayle, 254, 279–81; Butler, 546; Charron, 54–5; Clarke, 311; Crusius 454; Cudworth, 206–7, 208; de Sade, 424; Descartes, 296; Diderot,

466, 468, 480; Hobbes, 83, 97; La Mettrie, 462, 465; Pufendorf, 139; Rousseau, 480; Shaftesbury, 308 Spinoza, 225; Wolff, 444
  and morality, 281, 308, 465
  and taste for doing good, 419, 464, 468
authority
  of beliefs, 46, 51, 91, 116, 126, 131, 185, 491
  of conscience, 346–7
  external, 7, 39, 45, 81, 94, 134, 136, 181–2, 193, 196, 303, 309, 473, 478
  needed for common morals, 322–3, 386
  public moral, lost, 45
  and strength, 135–6, 154–5, 253, 345–6, 386
autonomy, 3 and n2, 6, 13, 483, 500, 507, 509, 518, 522, 528
  and self-governance contrasted, 6, 513–15
  in God, 497, 500
  voluntarism, against, 512–13

babies, 81 n44, 86 n7, 108
being and good, identity of, 123, 139, 237, 238, 246, 495
benevolence, 86, 103, 105, 106–8, 112 n14, 150, 192, 253, 315, 321, 410, 513
  as general principle, 344, 349–52
  giving others heavenly, not earthly, goods, 234
  as motive, sole virtue, 334, 336, 352
  origin, 406–7
  quantifiable, 341–2, 342 n20
  relation to love, 334, 363
  whether whole of virtue, 351–2, 369, 380, 383–4, 391, 402, 404, 408
best possible world, 113, 227, 239–40, 241, 244–5, 255, 257, 321, 436, 438, 461, 495, 530
  rejection of concept, 320, 455
boniform faculty, 204–5

requires self-denial, 327–8
and teleology, 286
unity of self, 307–8
alleged neglect in modern moral phi-
    losophy, 286–7
See also Christianity, and virtue
voluntarism
    argument for, 25, 121–2, 139
    and empiricism, 10
    function of, 99–100
    importance of, 250, 509
    in Bacon, 141; Calvin, 32–3; Crusius,
        445, 453–6; Descartes 184–5; Duns
        Scotus, 22–5; Gassendi, 270–1;
        Hobbes, 95–6, 98–100; Hume, 375–7;
        Kant, 495, 496–7, 510–13; Locke,
        141–2, 149–52, 154, 157–9; Luther,
        29–31; Montaigne, 46; Ockham, 25;
        Pufendorf, 121–2, 128, 133, 135–6,
        138–40; Suarez, 58, 60, 61;
        Thomasius, 160–2
    origins, 21–5
    overview, 250–1, 509–10
    and toleration, 462
    what, 8–9, 48, 251
    See also intellectualism

war, 6–7, 54, 56–7, 66–7, 83, 84, 89, 142
will
    compares amounts of perfection, 437,
        515–16
    and conscientiousness, 447–8
    as consent to motive or desire, 233,
        446, 449, 524
    constitutes standards, 23–5, 30–1, 32,
        60–1, 65, 122, 141–2, 447, 487, 494–
        7, 501, 512, 524; mediating view,
        61

corrupt, 35
duality in, 21–3, 65, 210, 352–3, 383–4,
    452–3, 475
follows belief about good, 20–1, 22,
    108, 182, 188–9, 212, 232, 243 and
    n15, 269, 299, 318; sometimes, 34,
    137; does not, 146, 299, 500; can fol-
    low belief about justice, 22; and
    about order, 232; or duty, 401; or law,
    500; problem, 213–14, 500; no for-
    mula for, 299, 359
has inherent direction, 23, 232–3, 243–
    4, 448, 450–1, 517–18
has innate ideas, 448, 450
includes desire, moral motive, 446
as last appetite in deliberation, 90
as noumenal, 515
and Order, 227–8
person determines, 401
and repentance, 51
and suspension, 146 and n14, 172, 191,
    213–4, 232 and n19, 233, 269, 332,
    517
that minds must have, 446
weakness of, 319
whether a separate faculty, 137, 187,
    213, 243, 437, 446, 515
Wille and Willkür, 518
within our power, 191
See also freedom of will; indifference of
    will; voluntarism
wisdom, 53–4
    contentment, 240, 255
    as intuitive knowledge of God, 220,
        223, 224–5
    and morality, 56, 187, 223

zetetic, 179 and n17

Index of biblical citations